NICHOLAS TIMMINS is Public Policy Editor of the *Independent*, having previously been its Political Correspondent, and its Health and Social Services Correspondent from its foundation; before that he held similar posts on *The Times*. He has also worked for the Press Association and *Nature*. This is his first book.

from the reviews:

'Timmins's book is remarkably fair... the first comprehensive biography of the welfare state from 1945 to the present day [and] a pleasure to read.' MALCOLM RUTHERFORD, *Financial Times*

'Nicholas Timmins worked on this detailed and readable book for six years – and it shows. Few books deserve being described as "definitive" or "magisterial" as richly as this one does. Its scope is enormous, dealing with the welfare state from its early inspirations to the present day. It would hardly be possible to read this book – whatever one's political convictions – and not find much food for thought. It ranks as an extremely stimulating book which will be read for years to come.' CONOR MCGRATH, *Parliamentary Monitor*

'This history of the welfare state... is not only a social history, but above all a history of policy in the making and of the ideas, politicians and thinkers that have shaped it. *The Five Giants* is a book which no one who speaks, writes or thinks about social policy will want to miss, still less to admit to having not read. Particularly when read over a short period (and it is an easy read for all its length, avoiding effortlessly the jargon to which its individual subjects frequently give rise) it offers a unique sense of the sweep of events.' TESSA JOWELL, *Health Service Journal*

'A well-researched book: it is useful to have all basic information on the subject (both the dry and the juicy) in one place. This is not the only recent work on the subject, but if anyone is able to read only one book, this should be it.'

JAD ADAMS, *Times Educational Supplement*

continued overleaf

'Ambitious – and successful... In these 600 pages Timmins dissects and organizes the 50-year period with skill and clarity. His book inhabits that territory between good journalism and academic research, which has so often produced the best contemporary history in Britain.'   MALCOLM WICKS, *New Statesman*

'Eminently readable... for those who have a neat interpretation of history devoid of people and accidents, Timmins' book is a healthy but enjoyable antidote.'   HOWARD GLENNESTER, *Guardian*

'Timmins writes with authority, and much inside information, on recent history. He has written the best account so far of Tory social policy since 1979. But the larger achievement of the book is to place the era of Thatcher and Major in the longer term perspective of World War Two. Timmins is no academic historian, but he has made good use of the work of academics, blending their findings with flair and enthusiasm. The result is a first-class history in which a detailed exposition of social policy is combined with narrative pace and lively portraits of the people involved.'

PAUL ADDISON, *Independent on Sunday*

'Positively moving... Timmins takes trouble to chart the improvements in education, health and housing which the majority of people in Britain have enjoyed in the time covered by his book.'

ROBERT WRIGHT, *Scotsman*

'Exceptional... a work of prodigious scope and illuminating analysis, a text of true scholarship.'   IAN MUNRO, *Lancet*

'Outstandingly acute... a highly readable book that adds to our knowledge of the evolving history of the welfare state and provides an indispensable source for coming to a sensible view about its successes and failures. Timmins brings alive both the process of making policy and its impact.'

RUDOLF KLEIN, *British Medical Journal*

'The best account of British social policy since the war.'

DAVID WILLETTS, *Times Literary Supplement*

NICHOLAS TIMMINS

The Five Giants

A Biography of the Welfare State

FontanaPress
An Imprint of HarperCollins*Publishers*

Fontana Press
An Imprint of HarperCollins*Publishers*
77–85 Fulham Palace Road,
Hammersmith, London W6 8JB

Published by Fontana Press 1996
1 3 5 7 9 8 6 4 2

First published in Great Britain by
HarperCollins*Publishers* 1995

ISBN 0 00 686318 3

Set in Linotron Aldus

Printed in Great Britain by
HarperCollinsManufacturing Glasgow

For Zoe, Jonathan and Robert
In the hope that as and when they need it, it will still be
there. And to all those people, users and providers, politicians,
civil servants, academics, doctors, managers, teachers and
others who attempt to explain the workings of the welfare state
to ignorant hacks. Without them the reporting of the subject
would be even worse than it is.

Social reform is a process, not an event: a kind of drama.
David Donnison, *The Politics of Poverty* (1981), p.viii

I do not agree with those who say that every man must look after himself, and that intervention by the state . . . will be fatal to his self-reliance, his foresight and his thrift . . . It is a mistake to suppose that thrift is caused only by fear; it springs from hope as well as fear. Where there is no hope, be sure there will be no thrift.
Winston Churchill, *Liberalism and the Social Problems* (1909), p. 209

'Two nations: between whom there is no intercourse and no sympathy; who are as ignorant of each other's habits, thoughts, and feelings, as if they were dwellers in different zones, or inhabitants of different planets; who are formed by a different breeding, are fed by a different food, are ordered by different manners, and are not governed by the same laws.'
'You speak of —' said Egremont hesitatingly, 'the rich and the poor?'
Benjamin Disraeli, *Sybil* (1845), Book II, chapter 5.

Contents

Illustrations

Plates

'From cradle to grave . . .' The *Daily Mirror*'s front page, December 2, 1942 (reproduced by permission of Mirror Syndication International)

Sir William Beveridge (Hulton Deutsch)

Health made Bevan's name, but he was proud of his housing (Hulton Deutsch)

Rab Butler as President of the Board of Education (Hulton Deutsch)

Tony Crosland, Secretary of State for Education and Science (Hulton Deutsch)

Dr Guy Dain and Dr Charles Hill (Hulton Deutsch)

Jim Griffiths talks in 1955 to Richard Crossman (Hulton Deutsch)

The young Barbara Castle at the 1944 Labour party conference

Dr Derek Stevenson (© The Telegraph plc, London 1975)

David Ennals in hospital on the 30th anniversary of the NHS in 1978 (Press Association)

Sir Keith Joseph at the Conservative Party Conference in 1985 (Richard Open/Camera Press)

Norman Fowler in 1986 (The Independent/Brian Harris)

Roy Griffiths (Universal Pictorial Press & Agency Ltd)

Kenneth Clarke and Michael Portillo (The Independent/Edward Sykes)

Bevan's council housing in Hainault and newly modernised bathroom and unmodernised washing facilities in flats on the LCC's Millbank Estate (Greater London Record Office Photograph Library)

Ronan Point in 1968 (Mirror Syndication International)

Houses in St Paul's Cray (Peter Van Arden)

Child in hospital in 1930s (Hulton Deutsch)

'Babies under glass' in 1944 (Hulton Deutsch)

Modern intensive care of the 1990s (Mirror Syndication International)

First family allowance day in Stratford, East London, 1946 (Hulton Deutsch)

Social Security Offices of the 1980s and 1990s (Benefits Agency) **TBC**

Classes at Snowsfield Primary School in 1944 and 1954 (Greater London Record Office Photograph Library)

Class at Snowsfield Primary School in 1994 (Snowsfield Primary School)

Integrated Illustrations

Preface

There are undeniable structural difficulties in writing a narrative account of five or six not always closely related subjects across fifty years. The approach here has broadly been to break the story up by government and divide it again by subject – education, health, social security, for example. But a word of warning is necessary. Narrative thrust has been given precedence over organisational tidiness. Bits of subjects therefore crop up in places other than under their specific headings, particularly in Chapters 9, 10, 13, 16, 19 and 20 where themes as well as the story are pulled together. They also appear out of their strict chronology. The development of second pensions, for example, is dealt with in the late 1950s but not mentioned again in detail until the mid-1970s when what happened to failed schemes from the sixties and early seventies is discussed. Anyone, therefore, attempting to follow a particular subject rather than read the whole book would need to combine section headings with both a reading of the top and tail of each chapter, and judicious use of the index.

A note about titles is needed. I have used what felt right, which means inconsistency. Later knighthoods and peerages are therefore frequently ignored (I know who Ted Short is, but struggle to place Lord Glenamara). Conversely, where someone has long been 'Sir' or 'Lady' somebody I have tended to use the title even ahead of their elevation to it. I hope no individual feels insulted. Scotland, Wales and Northern Ireland will, alas, because like so many British histories this is effectively England's story with both the wrinkles and the larger differences elsewhere largely avoided. I offer as a poor excuse lack of space and the way the British government assembles its statistics.

Any book like this is the work of many hands and even more brains. Aside from the primary debts listed in the introduction I have incurred many more. Well over fifty people, from current and former politicians and civil servants to ministerial advisers and actors in the welfare state's drama, have given me time for interviews. Most are acknowledged in the end notes. Some, because they are serving civil servants, cannot be named.

A few provided help knowing they might not emerge too happily from the process. To all of them I am grateful. There were others to whom I should have talked, but I simply ran out of time. To these I apologise.

Then there are debts to journalistic colleagues, particularly a string of past education editors of the *Independent*, Peter Wilby, Ngaio Crequer and Colin Hughes. Along with David Walker of the BBC, Malcolm Dean of the *Guardian*, and Tony Bevins of the *Observer*, they lent me their brains, their time and their books, while many others have lent me their copy, conversation and company over the years. Sue Johnson at the Policy Studies Institute library rapidly met requests for the oddest books and articles without raising an eyebrow.

At crucial moments three professorial Peters, Peter Scott of Leeds University, Peter Kemp of York University, and Peter Hennessy of Queen Mary and Westfield College, London University, rescued me by providing references, as did Tony Lynes, Ronnie Bedford and Charles Webster, the official historian of the National Health Service.

As a journalist rather than a historian, I have chiefly relied on others' gutting of the Public Record Office for the period for which such records are available. Alistair Cooke at Conservative Central Office was, however, generous enough to let me loose in the party's records in the Bodleian Library up to and including the crucial period of policy formation ahead of the 1979 general election. I am grateful to him for both the access and the permission to refer to documents, and to Dr Sarah Street and Dr Martin Moore for helping me find my way around them.

A dozen or so authors deserve special mention as well as being listed in the bibliography. Nobody can write about Beveridge without owing a huge debt to José Harris's wonderful, multi-faceted biography of him. David Donnison's works, but particularly his *Politics of Poverty*, are inspirational: object lessons in how to write about social policy. I doubt I could have managed to cover education without Brian Simon's mighty and passionate *Education and the Social Order*, or Harry Judge's illuminating *A Generation of Schooling*, or the sharp analysis and easy writing of Stuart Maclure and Maurice Kogan. Brian Ellis's official history of pensions from 1955 to 1975 is a starred first example of how to make a horrendously complex subject seem simple and interesting. Nobody should write about the NHS without reading Enoch Powell, Rudolf Klein, and Charles Webster. And anything written by Nicholas Deakin is always stimulating, particularly his 1987 version of *The Politics of Welfare*. On a broader front, the 1940s are brilliantly served by Peter Hennessy's *Never Again*, Paul Addison's *The Road to 1945* and *Now the War is Over*, and

Angus Calder's *The People's War*, while Kenneth O. Morgan's works, and particularly *The People's Peace*, his history of Britain 1945–90, are indispensable – as is Hugo Young's study of Margaret Thatcher, *One of Us*.

When I started work on this book in 1993, there was really no substantial modern post-war history available to match Derek Fraser's fine work *The Evolution of the British Welfare State*, which takes the story up to Beveridge. Shortly after I started, Rodney Lowe's *The Welfare State in Britain since 1945* appeared. It is completely different in character from this work, much more academic and analytical, concentrating on what he dubs the 'classic' welfare state up to 1976 and then moving on to 1990 in less depth. It is an excellent book. But it is not this one. I hope in some small way this will complement that.

Finally there are more personal cheques to sign. Three people – Tony Bevins, David Walker and Julian Le Grand, the Richard Titmuss Professor of Health Policy at the London School of Economics – suffered the whole book in draft. David Willetts read chapters sixteen to nineteen. David Donnison read the housing sections, Dr Gordon Macpherson those on health, Sir George Godber the NHS material up to 1974, and Stuart Maclure the education sections. Frank Field, Sir Patrick Nairne, Sir Geoffrey Otton, Norman Warner, Robin Wendt and (as a prelude to an interview) Shirley Williams all read chapters, or parts of chapters, within their competence, as did two, by convention anonymous, civil servants. All saved me from errors of both fact and judgement, large, small and downright embarrassing. All made it a better book. Some provided criticisms I have not been able to answer. If there is credit, they deserve much of it. The undoubted remaining errors of fact, judgement and tone remain all mine.

Much is due also to John Pawsey, my agent, to Betty Palmer, my copy editor, and to Philip Gwyn Jones, Caroline Hotblack and Kate Harris at HarperCollins for various forms of faith and aid, some beyond the call of duty.

The most personal cheques of all go to Tony for his energising encouragement and superbly pedantic reading of texts and to Jerry, both of whom at times had more faith in this project than I did; to Audrey Maxwell for organisation and memories; to Zoe, Jonathan and Robert for their wonderful forbearance; but most of all and for all of those to Elaine, *sans qui . . .*

Introduction

Theory is so much clearer than history.
E. P. Thompson, The Poverty of Theory (1978), p. 237

Freedom from Want cannot be forced on a democracy or given to
a democracy. It must be won by them.
Sir William Beveridge, 20 November 1942

This book started life one September Sunday six years ago when Peter
Hennessy, in one of his more Tigger-ish moods, bounced into the *Independent* to deliver his 'Whitehall Watch' column. He had been working on
Never Again, his history of Britain from 1945 to 1951, and had been
re-reading the Beveridge report. 'Someone,' he said, 'needs to write a
good modern history of the welfare state, and you ought to do it. You
can call it *The Five Giants*. You just start with Beveridge with tears in his
eyes and work forwards.'

The idea seemed frankly farcical. I was covering the government's NHS
review and John Moore's attempt to recast the language of welfare. I had
just acquired two more small children. There seemed not enough hours
in the day. I was a journalist, not a historian. And there were large parts
of the welfare state about which I knew nothing. The idea, however, would
not go away. If there was much about which I was ignorant, there were
bits of the subject about which I did know something. On and off, I'd
spent more than fifteen years reporting them. For some of the more
exciting events related here from the mid-1970s on, as Max Boyce would
put it, 'I was there.' Other motivations piled in. When, in Keith Joseph's
final days as Secretary of State for Social Services, I first started reporting
what the academics would call social policy, I had wished for a single
volume which simply told the story of how we had got there – the events,
ideas, personalities, issues and pressures which had taken the post-1945
welfare state to that point. One that had the best quotes and some of the

best jokes all in one place and referenced, and which provided at least a background from which some of the more technical issues could be tackled. Something between Gibbon's *Decline and Fall of the Roman Empire* and *1066 and All That* – only for the welfare state and all in one volume. There were single-subject accounts, but none which covered the waterfront or provided quite that mix.

Other motives included bemusement at how the Portillos, Redwoods and the other younger Thatcherites of this world – all of them broadly my age, the generation of whom Ian Kennedy, Professor of Medical Law and Ethics at King's College, London, once said, 'if you say *soixante-huit* to them, they don't think you've got a digit wrong' – could have such heartfelt hostility to an idea for which I had an instinctive sympathy. To me, and for all its myriad faults, some form of collective provision had always seemed, to put it at its lowest, the least bad way of organising education, health care and social security – things we all need, and which not all of us can guarantee to provide for ourselves either all the time or at the time they are needed. The challenge had always seemed how to improve the workings of the welfare state, not how to dismantle it.

Furthermore, as someone who had grown up with the swings and round-abouts of alternating Labour and Conservative governments, I became increasingly aware that most people under forty have only limited adult memories of life before Thatcher. The period before that, despite the way Kenneth Clarke would have it, is now history, not current affairs. Yet a little history can improve understanding of the current debates about the welfare state, and limit the chances of getting carried away by them.

It is quite important to know that virtually every day since 1948 the NHS has been said to be in crisis, and that for the last forty-five years morale within it has invariably never been lower. It is worth understanding that every time unemployment rises significantly, there is, like a bad dog that has its day, a spell when the unemployed are blamed as work-shy scroungers before unemployment settles at a new plateau. It is worth knowing that in education, yesterday has almost always been better than today, despite rising numbers passing ever more advanced levels of exam-inations and reaching higher education in ever greater numbers in every year (with two exceptions) since 1945. It can help to put the Conservatives' stewardship of the NHS into perspective to know that the first Secretary of State to be sued by a patient for failing to provide an operation was a Labour minister, not a Conservative. Such knowledge matters because it can ward off false despair – the sort which in 1987 afflicted the Tories over the NHS, when they felt they would never gain any credit for it and came the closest they ever have to dismantling it.

Then again, there is the need to attack a few myths. For example that before Margaret Thatcher's arrival in 1979 all was sweetness and light, and that all was well with the welfare state. It wasn't. Or that there have been no advances to go alongside the reverses in the past fifteen years. There have.

But if the view that there was a Golden Age in which a lavishly funded welfare system operated in a rosy glow of consensus needs challenging, so does the obverse view which has begun to gain currency – that there never was any real agreement about ends and means, and that the Conservatives always did have a blueprint for breaking the thing up. It is an interpretation advanced in triumph by some on the right who believe their schema for the world is about to come to fruition. It is subscribed to on the left by those who want to believe in a conspiracy theory, and by some who now want to blame themselves for not seeing it coming. It is constructed by trawling through past pamphlets, essays and speeches for the source of ideas now in play such as grant maintained schools, or vouchers for training. Such a view misrepresents history. It is the equivalent of arguing that because in today's Labour Party there are still people who believe in nationalising the top 200 companies, then if a future Labour government did nationalise them, it would prove that always to have been the Labour Party's secret aim. Such a view is plainly tosh. Its equivalent is to argue that because there were Conservatives in the 1950s and 1960s who pressed for cash-limited vouchers, for privatisation of both supply and demand, and for a drastic rolling back of the welfare state, then that was always the secret Tory agenda. The ideas did exist, but they were not then in the plans of any political party, any more than nationalising the top 200 companies is in Labour's in 1995.

Equally, attempts to portray repeated Treasury proposals for new NHS charges or the raising of the school starting age as part of the Conservatives' desire to undermine the welfare state misunderstands the Treasury's function. It propounds such ideas to governments of all colours because part of the Treasury's job is to stop governments spending money. The proposals Gaitskell backed in 1951 to scrap the NHS dental service and introduce 'hotel' charges for NHS beds were almost as draconian as anything proposed by his Conservative successors. But they were not introduced, any more than a Cabinet majority was ever assembled for the more extreme pieces of surgery proposed for health and education by the Treasury, by Chancellors and even at times by Prime Ministers under the Conservatives between 1951 and 1964. Equally, the Treasury and Treasury ministers proposed loans in place of student grants, and significant benefit cuts, to Labour as well as Conservative governments.[1] In judging how far there was a consensus about the welfare state, one must look at what actually happened, not just at the naughty thoughts each side harboured.

The counter-myth to the conspiracy of the right is that before 1979 satanic socialists set out to control the nation by placing it in some universalist cradle-to-grave feather bed aimed at sapping its moral fibre and taking the Great out of Britain. This doesn't wash. For a start, from 1945 up to 1979 the Conservatives controlled the welfare state for almost exactly the same period as Labour, and were responsible for some of its most expansionary phases. If the Conservatives at times moved to make services more universal – launching the first great explosion in higher education, for example – Labour, equally, joined Conservative governments in extending means-testing. The welfare state (the phrase has its own problems which we'll come to in a moment) is after all a living, moving, breathing being, bits of whose boundaries have moved back and forth under both parties in the past fifty years. It is not some fixed nirvana which we either draw nearer to or retreat from.

A further motivation to write this book was anger – anger that it is impossible now to travel on the London underground or walk the streets of our big cities without finding beggars, or, more often, without beggars finding us. That, in my lifetime, did not happen before the late 1980s. There were the down-and-outs on the Embankment. There were the spikes, the left-over remnants of the Poor Law workhouses, which housed the alcoholics and schizophrenics who avoided all the ropes in the safety net. But there were no young people, their lives blighted, sleeping in doorways in the Strand.

Then – and despite that anger – there was the perverse need to declare that, even after well over a decade of ideological assault, the welfare state still exists. Almost everyone to whom the idea of the book was mentioned instantly cracked a joke about the need to be quick about it before the thing disappeared. Most publishers wanted to call it From Cradle to Grave. Yet when welfare state services still take two-thirds of an annual government expenditure totalling £262 billion, the animal, whatever strains it may be under, can hardly be said to be dead. Create a strong enough perception that the welfare state is dying, however, and you make it easier to lop off further chunks without anyone asking where they went.

And then it just seemed fun. The story of the welfare state is a great adventure – a story worth telling, particularly when all its fiftieth anniversaries were looming.

And so in the end the book got written. It did so only because Andreas Whittam-Smith was generous enough to provide in 1993 a six-month sabbatical from the *Independent*. In turn I was lucky enough to be able to spend that time at the Policy Studies Institute as a Distinguished Visiting Fellow, funded by money from the Joseph Rowntree Foundation. The PSI's monastic cells, learned but practical inmates and good library made it an ideal place to be. These, along with what is owed to Peter Hennessy for donating the idea, are my primary debts. There are many other listed in the Preface.

The finished book may not be what any of those who helped so much envisaged. Nor does it answer all the challenges given as motives for writing it. What it does represent is a perhaps over-ambitious stab at twisting the kaleidoscope of the post-war history of Britain. In most versions, the welfare state, certainly after 1945–51, plays only a walk-on part. This one attempts to put the welfare state centre stage while allowing economic, political and even cultural events to play the walk-on roles. They are, however, there and they are crucial to the story, because they do so much to define and limit what can be done. The welfare state, after all, is itself a key cog in the economy. Too much discussion of social policy, too much measurement of its success and failure, appears at times to take place in a vacuum, untainted by the realities of the world at the time.

One theme which repeatedly emerges is the law of unintended consequences: that decisions taken for the best of motives will often go awry. This applies to governments seeking expansion, for example by providing larger subsidies to high-rise flats to produce more housing. But it applies equally to governments trying to draw back: for example, by withholding benefits from sixteen- and seventeen-year-olds because they should be in education, work or training, not on the dole. It is a lesson the right would do as well to remember as the left.

One issue should perhaps be dealt with here because it stands outside the narrative. In the mid-1980s, Correlli Barnett's brilliant and detailed polemic *The Audit of War* helped influence Tory hostility to the welfare state. Barnett saw the 'New Jerusalem' of the welfare state itself, along with the historic and continuing failure to organise high-grade technical education, as the twin causes of Britain's relative economic decline. His thesis has been widely debated elsewhere and by others far better informed than I. But while the second half of his argument has force, the first seems overstated. Other Western countries also developed modern and much more extensive welfare states after the Second World War, most ended up spending appreciably higher shares of their income on them than Britain did – and almost all achieved higher growth rates.[2]

Britain, physically less scarred by war, had laid the foundations of its welfare state earlier. But to argue that it crippled the economy seems, in Sir Alec Cairncross's phrase, 'badly out of focus'. Cairncross calculates that spending on education, health, housing, pensions and unemployment benefit reached about £1.5 billion in 1950 – half as much again in real terms as before the war. But defence expenditure never ran below £750 million after 1945, roughly twice as much in real terms as in 1938, and reached more than £1400 million again in 1952. Food subsidies, which are arguably a part of the welfare state but are also an economic regulator put in place to keep prices down, cost approaching £500 million in 1949 – more than any single social service.[3] Almost £2.5 billion in cash compensation or commitments to interest-bearing stock went through the national accounts after 1945 to pay for nationalisation.[4] To argue that any one of those caused Britain's relative post-war decline would be as logical or illogical as to argue that the welfare state did. The causes are complex, not singular or bipolar. They involve such measurables as the loss of markets and capital base during the war, and Britain's post-Imperial role after 1945 as the world's third largest military power and international policeman. They equally involve such immeasurables as to how far the country felt it needed to strive, having just won the war, and why labour relations, and hence productivity, were so bad. Indeed, to argue that the welfare state should not have been established, or should not have been established yet, is to ignore political reality. A country which had covered large tracts of East Anglia in concrete to launch bomber fleets, and the south coast in Nissen huts to launch the largest invasion the world had ever seen, could hardly turn round to its citizenry and say it was unable to organise a national health service; that it couldn't house its people; or that it would not invest in education. Furthermore, compared to pre-war levels, the big surge in welfare state spending started in the late 1950s, not in the immediate post-war period which Barnett rightly identifies as one of the critical periods when Britain failed to invest in its industrial base. But that begins to jump ahead in the story.

Before we start, a word about definitions is needed. There is no agreement about what constitutes 'the welfare state'. Even the origin of the phrase is the subject of learned dispute.[5] It was popularised in Britain in 1941 by an Archbishop of York and only adopted by Clem Attlee in time for the 1950 election. The *Oxford English Dictionary* can be a little slow, but the phrase only reached the dictionary's addenda in 1955 and with a definition we would now use in 1964.[6] At times its boundaries have been drawn so tightly as to exclude most of the social security budget, limiting it to what the Americans call 'welfare': payments to the poor plus what we, in the national accounts, still call 'welfare foods'. At others, as in Pauline Gregg's 1967 book *The Welfare State*, it has been drawn to embrace virtually the whole of the economic and social history of Britain from 1945, including nationalisation, the neo-corporatism of NEDO, and beer and sandwiches at Number Ten – the aspects of Britain as a welfare state that Baroness Thatcher plainly did want to roll back in 1979, and over which she was largely successful.

The phrase also suffers the drawback of being static, as though 'the welfare state' were a perfect work, handed down in tablets of stone in 1945, never to be tampered with. Even to use the phrase is to set artificial frames. As an entity it does not exist – it is a collection of services and policies and ideas and taxes, including tax reliefs, whose boundaries expand and contract over time. It can never, at any one moment, be said to have been assembled or dismantled. Beveridge hated the phrase and refused to use it, disliking its 'Santa Claus' and 'brave new world' connotations.[7] I would rather not have had to.

For this book it is defined in the strictly limited sense of representing the antonyms to the 'five giants on the road of reconstruction' which Beveridge identified, the policies and services created to combat Want, Disease, Ignorance, Squalor and Idleness. Even here, boundary problems proliferate. Is legal aid part of the welfare state or not? Is planning, given that the New Towns clearly were? Is training, given that much of it has always been employer-funded, and yet it is a subject closely linked to education and one in which governments inevitably get involved?

The imperfect solution to these quandaries has been to be deliberately eclectic and to write about what most interests me. This decision extends to the book's coverage of the mainstream services of health, education, social security, housing, social services, and, in lesser detail, employment policy. Thus it is possible to read *The Five Giants* and scarcely know that nurses exist or that Commonwealth immigration, which greatly affected the welfare state and was greatly affected by it, took place. The development of family planning – a profoundly controversial subject at the time – rates only a sentence or two. Social work is covered, but sketchily, it being one of those subjects where if you scratch too far below the surface you fall into an extremely large hole. The book distorts by omission.

Welfare foods and food subsidies which at times consumed large sums of taxpayers' money are barely mentioned; nor is the tobacco concession of two shillings and fourpence a week that, up to 1957, went to those pensioners who were prepared to swear that they smoked, in order to compensate them for a hike in tobacco tax in the 1940s. School examinations are only touched on. By no means all changes to benefits or housing subsidies have been charted, and training receives the lightest of looks. The list could go on. The excuse is twofold. First, even in a book this size, not everything can go in. As one former permanent secretary put it: 'You have to remember that every minister who went through here wanted to leave his or her mark on the system and very few of them failed entirely.'[8] He was speaking of social security; but his remark could apply to any of the government departments or subjects covered. And second, I had a tale to tell. There is a lot of detail here. But too much detail, too many by-ways and sub-plots, can spoil a story worth telling. *The Five Giants*, then, is not a book of accounting, or even of analysis, though there is a little of each within it. It is primarily a biography of a subject still very much alive. I hope it proves worth reading.

NICHOLAS TIMMINS
January 1995

PART I

THE PIPERS AT THE GATE OF DAWN

CHAPTER 1

'Thank you, Sir William'

> In every country it is unfortunate not to be rich; in England it is
> a horrible misfortune to be poor.
>
> *Alexis de Tocqueville, Voyages en Angleterre et en Irlande en 1835*

> 'They used to tell me I was building a dream . . .'
>
> *E. Y. Harburg, 'Brother can you spare a dime', American song of the Great
> Depression, opening line*

> At this stage of the war, the main ideas of reconstruction were in
> their first bloom, but largely, also in a state of suspended animation.
> Like the sleeping beauty, they awaited the prince's kiss. In almost
> every field of reconstruction, Beveridge's report of December 1942
> was to be the decisive breath of life.
>
> *Paul Addison, The Road to 1945, p. 171*

IN JUNE 1941, Sir William Beveridge was called in by Arthur Greenwood to be offered a job. Greenwood was the Labour Minister for
Reconstruction in Britain's wartime coalition government. Beveridge was
an egotistical sixty-two-year-old civil servant who believed his destiny
was to organise key parts of Britain's war effort. He was asked instead
to chair an interdepartmental committee on the co-ordination of social
insurance. The task hardly sounded inspiring. With tears, not of joy but
of bitter disappointment, in his eyes, he accepted.[1] It was the strangest of
starts to one of the greatest of adventures – the founding of Britain's
modern welfare state.

Beveridge's reaction was perhaps not surprising, for he was no ordinary
civil servant. He was already well known as a radio broadcaster, academic,
public servant and newspaper columnist; a man with more careers behind
him than most ever enjoy. He was also by any standard, despite his
detractors (of whom there were plenty), a member of the Great and the

Good, at a time when such a class was perhaps more easily defined than in the 1990s.

Born the son of a British judge in India in 1879 into a house staffed by twenty-six servants, he was schooled at Charterhouse. At Oxford he read mathematics and classics before, in 1903 at the age of twenty-four, he became in effect an Edwardian social worker and researcher at Toynbee Hall, the university foundation for the poor in the East End. It was there that 'he learned the meaning of poverty and saw the consequences of unemployment.'[2] The impoverishment of this part of London was to affect others in the tale of Britain's welfare state, including Clement Attlee and Sir Keith Joseph, even if the conclusions each was to draw from the experience were to be rather different.

At Balliol, Beveridge recalled, the Master, Edward Caird, used to urge his charges 'to go and discover why, with so much wealth in Britain, there continues to be so much poverty and how poverty can be cured'.[3]

Oxford and Toynbee Hall triggered in Beveridge a lifelong interest in unemployment and broader social questions, turning the young man into a social reformer, but one whose academic training convinced him that policy should be based on exhaustive research and detailed analysis. In his autobiography, Beveridge characterised his own progress at the time as being from 'Oxford to Whitechapel, Whitechapel to Fleet Street, Fleet Street to Whitehall'.[4] On the way, however, there had been a visit early in 1907 to Germany, where he had studied the systems of compulsory social insurance for pensions and sickness, though not yet for unemployment, which Bismarck had introduced in the 1890s. It was an important and fitting lesson, for Bismarck's is the only name to rank above Beveridge's as a welfare state designer, although of a rather different model.

Late in 1905 the twenty-six-year-old Beveridge, on a recommendation from Caird, was installed as a leader writer at the Tory *Morning Post*, a newspaper which eventually merged with the *Daily Telegraph*. There he was given licence to write on social policy and advocate labour exchanges and unemployment insurance, drawing on the forms of social insurance he saw in Germany. That work brought him to the attention of the thirty-three-year-old Winston Churchill, who four years earlier had crossed the floor of the Commons from the Conservative to the Liberal benches. In July 1908, Churchill brought Beveridge into the Board of Trade as a full-time civil servant. Over the next three years, Beveridge played a crucial role in the creation of a national network of labour exchanges of which he became the first director; and then in the formation of the world's first, if initially highly limited, statutory insurance scheme against unemployment. The measure was introduced in 1911 by David Lloyd George and by Churchill, who by 1906 had become so imbued with the cause of social reform that he declared Liberalism to be 'the cause of the left-out millions'.[5]

In government service, Beveridge had seen Lloyd George as Chancellor introduce the first state pensions, dubbed by their grateful recipients 'the Lord George' (because only a Lord could afford to be so generous), and had seen the spectacular row over the 1909 'People's Budget' which raised the money to pay for them. The pensions, Lloyd George declared, lifted 'the shadow of the workhouse from the homes of the poor'. Churchill, more temperately, declared of the first relatively meagre means-tested payments: 'We have not pretended to carry the toiler on to dry land. What we have done is to strap a lifebelt about him.'

The first unemployment insurance in 1911 covered only about 2.75 million men, or roughly one in six of the workforce, in industries at high risk of cyclical unemployment such as iron and steel and shipbuilding. It ran out after fifteen weeks. But with it came the first state-backed insurance scheme for health. Lloyd George's famous 'Ninepence for Fourpence' was more comprehensive, covering all male workers earning less than £160 a year. For the worker's compulsory fourpence (just under 2p) a week, the employer had to add threepence and the state twopence. The scheme was administered by 'approved societies' and provided the services of a 'panel' family doctor, but no right to hospital care or medicine; with that came sick pay of ten shillings (50p) a week, but no cover for wives and children other than a maternity grant. What marked out the health and unemployment measures of the 1911 National Insurance Act from anything that went before was that both were contributory, compulsory and state organised, with employers, employees and the taxpayer, through the state, each contributing: the so-called tripartite system. What they were not was comprehensive.

The same Liberal Government had also introduced the first tentative legislation on free school meals (for large families only), school medical inspections, and the first overtly redistributive budget – the 'People's Budget' – to pay for it all. The House of Lords, then still the power-base of the landed aristocracy, was faced by a new supertax and what were, in effect, wealth taxes. They threw out what Lloyd George had declared to be 'a war budget' – one 'for raising money to wage implacable warfare on poverty and squalidness'. He added the hope, which he almost lived to see realised, that 'before this generation has passed away we shall have advanced a great step towards that good time when poverty and wretchedness and human degradation which always follow in its camp will be as remote to the people of this country as the wolves which once infested its forests.'[6] The result, after a long battle, was the 1911 Parliament Act which removed for ever the right of the Lords to delay financial legislation.

Beveridge was thus not only a close Whitehall observer but a key player in the formation of what has been dubbed the 'ambulance state' – the lifebelt precursor to the modern welfare state which thirty years on he was to do so much to help create.

With the arrival of the First World War, Beveridge moved in to the Ministry of Munitions, where he was involved in deeply controversial moves to mobilise manpower and where he worked directly with Lloyd George. In 1916 he went to the Ministry of Food, becoming one of the chief architects of rationing and price control. He finished his first Whitehall career in 1919 at the age of thirty-nine as the ministry's Permanent Secretary.

Peace saw him leave the civil service to become director of the London School of Economics, transforming it into a great base for the social sciences. During a spell as Vice Chancellor of London University he commissioned its massive and Teutonic Senate House (the building Hitler earmarked to be his London headquarters). In 1937 he went back to Oxford as Master of University College. His academic appointments did not, however, to use the title of his autobiography, remove him entirely from power and influence. In 1934 he was appointed chairman of the Unemployment Insurance Statutory Committee, whose job it was to keep the insurance fund solvent, and in 1936 he was brought back to Whitehall to help devise the rationing that operated from 1940. In 1941, when Greenwood called him in, Beveridge had a knowledge of the origins and scope of social services in Britain that was probably unequalled.

He was connected everywhere. R. H. Tawney, the great Christian socialist thinker, was his brother-in-law and friend. He knew well Sidney and Beatrice Webb, founders of the Fabian Society, who in fact had introduced him to Churchill. (Churchill's aside,'I refuse to be shut up in a soup kitchen with Mrs Beatrice Webb',[7] appears to have been no barrier to the appointment.) It was in fact Mrs Webb who had first proposed a free health service for all in her minority report of the Poor Law inquiry of 1909. Clement Attlee and Hugh Dalton, two men to whom would fall the job of finding the cash for Beveridge's plan, had been lecturers on his staff at the LSE. Dalton was to be Attlee's first Chancellor of the Exchequer in 1945. As well as having worked with Churchill, Beveridge was a friend of John Maynard Keynes, whose new economics were to make the welfare state possible, and he knew Seebohm Rowntree, whose landmark studies of poverty in York in 1899 had first helped drive the 1906 Liberal Government into its reforming zeal and whose follow-up study in 1936 was to influence Beveridge's own report. In a line to the future, his research assistant at Oxford was a bright young economist called Harold Wilson.

But Beveridge was not an easy man. José Harris, in her biography, is reduced to summing him up as 'rather baffling'. To some, she says:

> he seemed wise and loveable, to others overbearing and vain. To some he was a man of dazzling intellect, to others a tedious bore. To some he was endlessly generous and sympathetic, to others harsh and self-centred to the point of complete insensitivity. By some he was seen as a humane, radical and visionary reformer, by some as a dangerous bureaucrat, by some as a sentimental idealist with his 'head in the clouds and his feet in the pond'. He has been described to me personally as 'a man who wouldn't give a penny to a blind beggar' and as 'one of the kindest men who ever walked the earth'.[8]

Others have been terser and harsher. Angus Calder in *The People's War* describes him as 'the outstanding combination of public servant and social scientist', but adds: 'He was also vain, humourless and tactless.'[9]

He tried to run the LSE as an autocracy, inducing a mutiny by the staff in favour of a constitution. Lionel Robbins, a young lecturer at the school who would later produce the Robbins report of 1963 which initiated the great post-war expansion of British universities, once said: 'I doubt if it ever occurred to him to regard the great men of those days as his equals, let alone, what some of them certainly were from the academic point of view, his superiors.'[10]

Arrogance, brilliance and a belief in statistical evidence did not prevent him from espousing unlikely ideas. Harold Wilson, when Prime Minister, would recall having to talk him out of a firm belief that fluctuations in unemployment were linked to the price of wheat which was in turn affected by a sun-spot cycle.[11] The weather, it seemed for a time, was all that there was to blame. He drove himself and others hard. Wilson, staying with him in his pre-war days at Oxford, recalls him rising at six to take an icy bath, following it with a couple of hours' work before breakfast. If he was far from easy either to know or to work with, he was also no more consistent than the rest of us. Over his lifetime his views varied from strong support for the free market to a *dirigiste* view of the advantages of central control and planning during the First and Second World Wars, via a distinct if intermittent sympathy with Fabian socialism. At times he favoured generous social welfare, at others he believed 'the whip of starvation' was a necessary precondition for economic advance.[12] After his report was published he was to become briefly a Liberal MP, and it is as a liberal and indeed Liberal document that his great work is best read: an attempt to bridge the desire for security and an end to poverty on one bank with encouragement for individuals to stand on their own two feet on the other.

A mere four years before his clarion call for full employment, social security from cradle to grave, a national health service, and a war against ignorance and squalor, he had been for two long walks with Beatrice Webb, then in her eighties, over the downs near her Hampshire home. Her diary records:

> His conclusion is that the major if not the only remedy for unemployment is lower wages . . . if this does not happen the capitalist will take his money and his brains to other countries where labour is cheap . . . he admitted almost defiantly that he was not personally concerned with the condition of the common people.[13]

If his desire for reform appeared to have waned, the war was to change that. But its arrival in 1939 left him bitter and frustrated. His talent and past experience, he felt, demanded a role in government. He bombarded government departments with offers of assistance, stringent criticism and unsolicited advice. He complained bitterly that 'the present crew have no conception at all of how to plan for war.' Along with other veterans of First World War administration, he gravitated to Keynes's Bloomsbury house during the autumn and winter of 1939. The 'ancient warhorses', to use José Harris's phrase, denounced Chamberlain's incompetence to each other and devised alternative strategies.[14]

When Churchill became Prime Minister in May 1940, Beveridge wrote to remind the old bulldog of their 'old association' and to offer his talents. He followed up with letters to Attlee, Ernest Bevin and Herbert Morrison, the key Labour ministers in the newly formed coalition government. None wanted the awkward and arrogant ex-Permanent Secretary around. Bevin, whom Beveridge was later to feel had betrayed him, did offer him charge of a new welfare department in the Ministry of Labour. 'I didn't feel that welfare was up my street,' Beveridge said. '. . . organisation of manpower was my goal.'

One by one, Keynes and the others were absorbed into Whitehall as part of the flood of academics whose presence was to do so much to help win the war against Nazi Germany. But Beveridge, who hardly helped his case by the style in which he proffered advice and sought work, remained outside. Finally, in July 1940, Bevin asked him to carry out a brief survey – in a firmly non-executive capacity – of wartime manpower requirements. At last Beveridge was doing the work he wanted to do. The survey done, in December he again became a full-time civil servant as under-secretary for the military service department at the Ministry of Labour. There he drew up the list of reserved occupations exempt from call-up; but he continued to demand from Bevin an ever larger role in running manpower.

The two, however, did not get on. Beveridge, condemned by so many as autocratic, in turn applied the same adjective to Bevin's mountainous personality. The bull-necked 'tsar' of the Transport and General Workers Union, in Kenneth Morgan's memorable epithet,[15] had been brought in from the general secretaryship of the union to provide the sound base for labour relations in wartime that the First World War had so notably lacked. Bevin saw his remit coming firmly from 'my people'. And while he used a range of Beveridge's ideas during the months they worked together, it seems plain he did not trust with any executive responsibility a man he almost certainly associated with the coercive and at times damaging manpower policies that Beveridge had helped draw up in 1914–18.[16]

At the beginning of June 1941 someone else got the job Beveridge wanted: Godfrey Ince, who went on to become the department's permanent secretary, was made Director General of Manpower. Beveridge was taken off administrative work and put in charge of a study on the way skilled manpower was being deployed into the forces. Four months before, however, in February, the Trades Union Congress had been to government to lobby about the hopelessly untidy mess of sickness and disability schemes by which workers were then covered. An inter-departmental committee was proposed to Cabinet in April. Bevin, having initially opposed the idea, suddenly saw it as a way of getting rid of someone whom he had clearly come to see as a pain in the neck.[17] It was Greenwood who formally made the job offer, but Beveridge recorded twenty years later that it was Bevin who 'pushed me as chairman of the Social Insurance Committee by way of parting with me . . . my removal from the Ministry of Labour . . . was "a kicking upstairs" '[18] away from the work he believed he was cut out to do. Hence the tears that started to his eyes.

Indeed, so disillusioned was Beveridge that he appears for some months to have done little or nothing about his new task. His appointment, announced on 10 June 1941, attracted much parliamentary and press comment. But Beveridge spent the next months touring military bases and finishing his study on how the army was wasting skilled engineers. His reaction is perhaps understandable. The terms of reference – 'to undertake, with special reference to the inter-relation of the schemes, a survey of the existing national schemes of social insurance and allied services, including workmen's compensation, and to make recommendations' – scarcely sounded like the dawn of a revolution or the making of a place in history.

While Home Office and Ministry of Health officials had higher hopes, the Treasury saw the committee merely as 'a tidying up operation', one of its senior officials declaring that the terms of reference had been made 'as harmless as they can be made'.[19] Bevin's parting shot, according to Beveridge, was that the inquiry 'should essentially be official in character, dealing with administrative issues rather than with issues of policy'.[20] Arthur Greenwood, however, saw it as something a lot bigger and gave briefings to that effect, inspiring Fleet Street so to write it up.[21] The day after the committee was formally announced several newspapers reported in remarkably similar terms that it would be 'the widest and most comprehensive investigation into social conditions . . . with the object of establishing economic and social security for every one on an equitable basis'.[22]

Certainly something, if only at a tidying-up level, needed to be done. If, forty years on in 1984, Norman Fowler concurred in his civil servants' judgement that the social security ship needed to be hauled in 'to have the barnacles scraped off it',[23] in 1941 the social security system – if it could even be called that – was a vessel full of holes and rotten planks through which it was only too easy to fall. It was showing all the strains and anomalies that piecemeal growth of voluntary and state provision over the previous forty-five years had produced since the Workmen's Compensation Act of 1897.

Seven different government departments were directly or indirectly involved in providing cash benefits of one kind or another. To modern eyes, some of these seem mighty strange: Customs and Excise, for example, administered 'the Lord George', the first state pension. But by 1941 there were three different types of pension, and three different types of unemployment benefit, all operating under different rules. War victims and their dependants were helped by the Ministry of Pensions, but the civilian disabled, widows and orphans were the responsibility of the Ministry of Health. The Home Office had its finger in the pie through running workmen's compensation in some industries. For many, however, cover for industrial injuries was provided by for-profit insurers who scandalously tried to buy off claimants with inadequate lump sums when disaster struck. 'Indoor servants' in private houses were excluded from the state unemployment insurance scheme; those in 'establishments and institutions' were included. Health insurance now provided panel doctors for those in work who earned less than £420 a year, but that still covered less than half the population. Wives and children remained excluded. Sickness benefit was provided through non-profit-making 'approved societies' whose benefits varied as widely as their performance. A good one might provide a nursing home, dental treatment and spectacles, a poor one only the minimum sickness benefit guaranteed by the state. And beneath and alongside all this, local authority committees, the inheritors of the Elizabethan Poor Law, paid means-tested benefits to those in need.

The result was 'different rates of benefit involving different contribution conditions and with meaningless distinctions between persons of different ages' as Beveridge was to say in his report.[24] There he picked out just one example of the many he said could be found. A married man with two children, he recorded, received 38s. od. (£1.90) a week if unemployed. If he then became sick and unavailable for work, his benefit more than halved to 18s. od. An unemployed youth of seventeen, by contrast, received 9s. od.; but 12s. od. if he was sick. It was this considerable mess that Beveridge was set to sort out. He did so in the grandest of styles, and on a scale that no one who appointed him could possibly have envisaged.

The first hint of what he was planning, and that he had no intention of just tidying a few things up, came in July when he produced a paper for the committee headed 'Social Insurance – General Considerations'. 'The time has now come,' he declared, 'to consider social insurance as a whole, as a contribution to a better new world after the war. How would one plan social insurance now if one had a clear field . . . without being hampered by vested interests of any kind? The first step is to outline the ideal scheme, the next step is to consider the practical possibilities of realising the ideal, and then the changes of existing machinery that would be required.'

Beveridge aside, the committee was staffed entirely by officials. There was a civil servant apiece from each of the seven departments involved in social insurance. In addition, there was the inevitable official from the Treasury, one from the Ministry of Reconstruction, the Government Actuary, and a representative each from the Assistance Board and the Friendly Societies. They spent the summer drawing up background papers and inviting evidence, while Beveridge's attention was elsewhere.

In all, 127 pieces of written evidence were to be received, and more than 50 private evidence sessions held with witnesses. But only one piece of written evidence had arrived by December 1941 when Beveridge circulated a paper entitled 'Heads of a Scheme' which contained the essence of the final report a year later. The paper proposed unifying the existing schemes, paying flat rate benefits at a rate high enough to provide 'subsistence' – that is, sufficient to live on, free of poverty – while the whole should be financed by contributions divided between the insured, employers and the state. As Point One, the paper opened with the key statement which was to stretch his terms of reference up to and beyond their limit and which was to underpin the whole report.

1 No satisfactory scheme for social security can be devised [without the] following assumptions.

A A national health service for prevention and comprehensive treatment available to all members of the community.

B Universal children's allowances for all children up to 14 or if in full-time education up to 16.

C Full use of powers of the state to maintain employment and to reduce unemployment to seasonal, cyclical and interval unemployment, that is to say to unemployment suitable for treatment by cash allowances.[25]

So there it was. The nation needed a national health service; tax-funded allowances for children; and full employment to make social security work.

The reliance on insurance – though insurance backed by the state, so-called 'social', as opposed to private, insurance – reflected what already existed even if less than half the population was covered in 1941. It also reflected what Beveridge had helped design for the unemployed in the years after 1908 and his own long-held beliefs. In 1924 he had written a tract for the Liberals advocating 'insurance for all and for everything'. Always opposed to means-tests, he had like many of his compatriots become affronted by both their enormous expansion and the harshness of the particular tests used during the Great Depression of the 1930s. He wanted to see benefits paid as of right. One consequence of the insurance principle, the paper states, is that 'no means test of any kind can be applied to the benefits of the Scheme'.

But while Beveridge believed that everything that could be insured for should be, he had also come to see that benefits for children could not be run that way. To combat poverty and at the same time provide work incentives, it was essential that children's benefits be paid at the same rate whether the parent was in or out of work. For if only means-tested help was given for children, then the low-paid with large families would be better off out of work than working, unless benefit rates were to be set dangerously low; and family allowances would also help to prevent poverty among the low-paid. Rowntree's work had shown that low wages in large families were the primary cause of poverty in 1899 and even his 1936 study showed they still played a significant role. Thus, Beveridge concluded, children's allowances had to be tax funded, not insurance based. He had additional motives for backing family allowances. The war had seen the cancellation of the 1941 census, and on the information available Beveridge believed erroneously that the birth-rate was still declining, as it had been in the 1930s. It was a trend he believed required to be reversed in the national interest.

'Once this memorandum had been circulated,' Beveridge declared blithely in his autobiography, 'the committee had their objectives settled for them and discussion was reduced to consideration of the means of attaining that objective.'[26]

They had indeed, and there was to be no little annoyance among the committee members at Beveridge's general unwillingness thereafter to listen to their views, other than on technical matters. But point one of the memo had another instant effect: it alerted the government to the scale of what he had in mind. Alarm bells started to ring. Beveridge was asked to withdraw his three assumptions, and refused. On 17 January 1942, Greenwood wrote to him after talking to the Chancellor, Sir Kingsley

Wood, declaring that 'in view of the issues of high policy which will arise' the departmental representatives should in future be regarded merely as 'advisers and assessors'. The report would be signed by Beveridge alone and 'be your own report'. The civil servants 'will not be associated in any way with the views and recommendations on questions of policy which it contains'.[27] In other words, the government was damned if it was going to let itself be committed.

Work on the committee speeded up through 1942 as witnesses were called and evidence taken. But the credit (or reproach: some see the report and its aftermath as a key cause of Britain's post-war decline) for the report's popular impact may need to go as much to Janet Mair as to Beveridge himself.

Jessy, as Janet Mair was known, was the wife of David Mair, a somewhat austere mathematician and civil servant who was Beveridge's cousin. She and Sir William had become close before the First World War, Mrs Mair sharing, in José Harris's words, Beveridge's 'dreams and ambitions'. A powerful personality in her own right, she and Beveridge were to marry a fortnight after the report was published. They had, however, already scandalised the 'lady censors of the University world' when Mrs Mair moved into the Master's lodgings at University College at the outbreak of war.[28] Jessy also had, in Peter Baldwin's words, 'a knack of putting in the baldest terms the ideas that lay more implicitly in her husband's writings'.[29]

During the crucial stages of the report's compilation in the spring and summer of 1942, Jessy was staying with relatives in Scotland. But it was she, according to José Harris, who 'greatly encouraged' Beveridge not just to rationalise the existing insurance system but to lay down long-term goals in many areas of social policy.

There is no evidence to suggest that Mrs Mair was responsible for any of Beveridge's substantive proposals. But much of his report was drafted after weekends with her in Edinburgh, and it was she who urged him to imbue his proposals with a 'Cromwellian spirit' and messianic tone. 'How I hope you are going to be able to preach against all *gangsters*,' she wrote, 'who for their mutual gain support one another in upholding all the rest. For that is really what is happening in England . . . the whole object of their spider web of interlocked big banks and big businessmen [is] a frantic effort to maintain their own caste'. And she urged Beveridge to concentrate on three main policy objectives – 'prevention rather than cure', 'education of those not yet accustomed to clean careful ways of life', and 'plotting the future as a gradual millennium taking step after step, but not flinching on ultimate goals.'[30]

Beveridge of course had a track record as journalist and broadcaster, not just as an academic and administrator, and could express ideas clearly. He was fond of lists: 'ten lions on the path', 'six principles', 'three assumptions', as well as his 'five giants'. But nothing else he wrote – certainly not his *Full Employment in a Free Society* whose preparation two years later was to worry both Churchill and his Chancellor – has the same rich blend of Cromwellian and Bunyanesque prose to be found in the drably titled *Social Insurance and Allied Services.*

When the report was published on 1 December 1942 its reception was ecstatic. On the night before there were queues to buy it outside HMSO's London headquarters in Kingsway. The first 60,000 copies of the full report at 2s. od. (10p) a time were rapidly sold out. Sales topped 100,000 within a month and more than 200,000 by the end of 1944.[31] It is hard to believe that most of those who bought it made it through to the end. Much of this 200,000-word excursion through technical exposition and complex appendices is heavy going. Even Beveridge's own section is hard work, and the report may well rank alongside Stephen Hawking's *A Brief History of Time* as one of the most bought but least read books ever published in Britain. What made its reputation and provided its impact was the twenty-page introduction and the concluding twenty-page summary, separately published in a cut-down version at 3d. Combined with the full report this took sales above 600,000:[32] in HMSO folklore, nothing is said to have outsold it until the Denning report on the Profumo scandal twenty years later.

And that introduction and summary were couched in terms unlike those of any government report before or since. Beveridge declared that he had used three guiding principles. First that 'a revolutionary moment in the world's history is a time for revolutions, not patching'. When the war was 'abolishing landmarks of every kind', he declared, now was the time to use 'experience in a clear field'.[33] Second, his plan for security of income – social security – was principally an attack upon Want. 'But,' he went on, hammering the point home with mighty capital letters, 'Want is only one of five giants on the road of reconstruction, and in some ways the easiest to attack. The others are Disease, Ignorance, Squalor and Idleness.' Third, he stressed that social security must be achieved by co-operation between the state and the individual. 'The State should offer security for service and contribution. The State in organising security should not stifle incentive, opportunity, responsibility; in establishing a national minimum, it should leave room and encouragement for voluntary action by each individual to provide more than the mimimum for himself and his family.' But that minimum should be given 'as of right and without means test, so that individuals may build freely upon it'.

Taking social insurance as the base, he wrote in boldly the three assumptions needed to make it work: family allowances, a national health service, and 'maintenance of employment'. In the conclusion of the main report, he expanded the themes in Bunyanesque terms. The plan, he said, 'is not one for giving to everybody something for nothing and without trouble'. It involved 'contributions in return for benefits'. War offered the chance of real change, for 'the purpose of victory is to live in a better world than the old world'. And, most importantly, he stated that in itself social security was 'a wholly inadequate aim'; it could only be part of a general programme.

> It is one part only of an attack upon five giant evils: upon the physical Want with which it is directly concerned, upon Disease which often causes that Want and brings many other troubles in its train, upon Ignorance which no democracy can afford among its citizens, upon Squalor . . . and upon the Idleness which destroys wealth and corrupts men.[34]

In that one ringing paragraph Beveridge encapsulated much of post-war aspiration. By seeking not only freedom from want, but a national health service, improved education, full employment and an attack upon Squalor (which Beveridge saw as being as much about town and industrial planning as about housing), he gave the vital kick to the five giant programmes that formed the core of the post-war welfare state: social security, health, education, housing, and a policy of full employment, the giants constructed to combat Beveridge's five giant evils.

The report in practice does not mention education apart from its trumpet call for the attack on Ignorance. Nor does it deal in any detail with housing save for his struggle over how to handle rents within social security. Even a Beveridge could not stretch his terms of reference that far. The sections on how the health service would work are undisguisedly tentative. Beveridge himself stressed the need for further study. But the necessity of comprehensive health care 'without a charge on treatment at any point'[35] is repeatedly driven home – not just to prevent poverty, but on economic grounds, to help keep people working, and quite simply on moral ones:

'restoration of a sick person to health,' he states, 'is a duty of the State and the sick person, prior to any other consideration'.

If the report's impact at home was spectacular, it was also pushed heavily overseas by an initially enthusiastic Ministry of Information. Details of 'The Beveridge Plan' were broadcast by the BBC from dawn on 1 December in twenty-two languages. Copies were circulated to the troops, and sent to the United States where the Treasury made a $5000 profit on sales.[36] More copies were dropped into France and other parts of Nazi-occupied Europe where they caused concern at the highest level. After the war, two papers marked 'secret' and providing detailed commentary on Beveridge's plan were found in Hitler's bunker. One ordered that publicity should be avoided, but if mentioned the report should be used as 'obvious proof that our enemies are taking over national-socialist ideas'. The other provided an official assessment of the plans as 'no "botch-up" . . . a consistent system . . . of remarkable simplicity . . . superior to the current German social insurance in almost all points'.[37]

Overnight Beveridge became a national hero – in Paul Addison's phrase, 'The People's William'.[38] It was 'like riding an elephant through a cheering mob', Beveridge said.[39] Halls were packed to hear him expound his proposals in the rather prissy Edwardian tones that marked his speech. He broadcast and wrote about it endlessly, batting down critics who said his proposals would lead to feather-bedding and moral ruin. When an American declared that if Beveridge had had his way in the days of Good Queen Bess there would have been no Drake, Hawkins or Raleigh, he replied with a touch of the wit that his critics would deny him: 'Adventure came not from the half starved, but from those who were well fed enough to feel ambition.'[40]

A little seventeenth-century evangelical language, however, in a boringly titled and dense government document, even when propounded by a well-known Oxford don, is not enough to explain the report's impact. To understand that we must go back, through the influence of the Second World War, to the Great Depression of the 1930s, the outcome of the Great War, and even beyond.

The Boer War (1899–1902) had provided one part of the stimulus for the great reforming programme of the Liberal Government of 1906 when it was discovered that almost half those volunteering to fight in South Africa were medically unfit. The First World War exposed the same problems even more brutally and on a much larger scale. One survey showed that one conscript in three was not fit enough to join the forces.[41] Only a third were judged Grade One. By the time of the Second World War, seven out of ten were put in the top grade.[42]

The mud and carnage of Flanders and the Somme, the days of 'lions led by donkeys', also changed British society for good. The Victorian era and the gilded summers of its Edwardian afterglow, in which hideous poverty had come to exist alongside abundant wealth, were to be swept away for ever. Lloyd George, in language Beveridge would have recognised, declared in 1917:

> The present war . . . presents an opportunity for reconstruction of industrial and economic conditions of this country such as has never been presented in the life of, probably, the world. The whole state of society is more or less molten and you can stamp upon that molten mass almost anything so long as you do it with firmness and determination . . . the country will be prepared for bigger things immediately after the war . . . and unless the opportunity is seized immediately after the war I believe it will pass away.[43]

The Welsh wizard found poverty abhorrent and the agenda from which he was working bore striking similarities to Beveridge's almost thirty years later: unemployment insurance, health, housing and education, and a desire to end the 1834 Poor Law which had established the workhouses and the principle of 'less eligibility'. In order to provide a vigorous incentive for self-help, the 1834 Act required that Poor Relief be set at a standard *below* the earnings that an industrious labourer 'of the lowest class' could achieve, regardless of the impact that policy had. The view then was strong, and its echoes can still be heard today, that poverty was the fault of the individual and should be punished. As the Royal Commission whose report produced the Act put it: 'Every penny bestowed, that tends to render the condition of the pauper more eligible than that of the independent labourer, is a bounty on indolence and vice . . . nothing is necessary to arrest the progress of pauperism, except that all who receive relief from the parish should work for the parish exclusively, as hard and for less wages than independent labourers work for individual employers.'[44] Individuals would thus be forced, as far as possible, to stand on their own two feet. There was no intent here to prevent poverty, only to avert starvation.

Despite Lloyd George's words, in 1917 too little was done too late. But before the grand vision collapsed, there was a brief illusion that all was well. The rapid removal of wartime controls brought a short but spectacular boom, producing the certain assumption, in the phrase of the day, that it was 'business as usual'. Significant strides were made in education and the expansion of council housing. Unemployment insurance, limited to a few high-risk industries in 1911, was further extended in 1920 to cover around twelve million workers, roughly three-quarters of the workforce.

But Britain's share of world trade proved to have contracted sharply during the war. The economy swung rapidly into recession. In 1922 the 'Geddes axe', named after Sir Eric Geddes who chaired the economic committee, introduced swingeing public spending cuts. These curtailed plans for educational expansion and left Lloyd George's euphoric promise of 'Homes Fit for Heroes' with a desperately hollow ring. As the new unemployment insurance came in, the total number of unemployed increased in the summer of 1920 to more than a million. Between then and the summer of 1940 it never fell below that mark and at times rose above three million.[45] The new experience of mass unemployment dominated social policy for the next twenty years, for it rapidly destroyed the insurance basis of the 1911 and 1920 Acts. Large numbers either exhausted their right to benefit, or were thrown out of work without having earned it in the first place. Fearing large-scale unrest and the Bolshevism which had just produced the Russian revolution, the government responded with a series of *ad hoc* measures starting in 1919 with Christopher Addison's 'out-of-work-donation' for the unemployed: the words 'the dole' entered the vocabulary. The payment was not means-tested, and semi-inadvertently it established the principle that the state had a commitment to maintain all the unemployed, not just those whose insurance payments were up to date. But at the same time it undermined the insurance principle.

Worse was to come. In 1929 the American stock market collapsed, bringing in its wake the deepest recession the modern world has known. Its length was not matched in Britain until the early 1990s when the very welfare state created in reaction to the 1930s helped mitigate the effects. In the early 1930s, Keynes had yet to ride to the rescue on the white charger of his new economics. He was still developing his theories: indeed, the jibe at the time (which with the name changed can still be used today) was that 'where five economists are gathered together there will be six opinions and two of them will be held by Keynes'. Cutting the soaring expenditure on the unemployed to defend the gold standard became the sole touchstone of British economic policy. It smashed the Labour Government in 1931. Ramsay MacDonald was left as Prime Minister of a new National Government, but effectively a prisoner of the Tories, to carry out the blood-letting of 'severe surgical operations' on Britain's economy.[46]

Insurance benefits were cut, and those who had exhausted their benefit or lacked sufficient contributions to qualify were transferred to the Public Assistance Committees of local authorities, who in 1929 had replaced the Poor Law guardians. The committees were empowered to enforce a stringent household means-test. As Derek Fraser put it:

> The means test, like the workhouse before it, was destined to leave an indelible mark on popular culture. The means test of the early 1930s was a family one which involved a household assessment of need, taking into account the income of all its members, be it the few shillings pension of the aged parent, or the coppers earned on the son's paper round. Its inquisitorial tone produced resentment and frustration among applicants and heightened family tension, already aggravated by the loss of patriarchal dignity and discipline consequent upon unemployment itself.

In effect it put the unemployed 'right back on the Poor Law (though not in name) which, locally administered, exhibited wide regional variations in scale and conditions of benefit. Injustice only added to the demoralisation.'[47] A father whose son or daughter found work could see his benefit ended. George Orwell recorded it as 'an encouragement to tittle-tattle and the informer'. A word from a jealous neighbour spotting a new coat or pair of shoes could bring the means-test men round demanding to know where the money had come from. Its effects became seared into the national soul.

In 1934 responsibility for the means-test and its attendant benefits was removed from local authorities and placed in the hands of a national Unemployment Assistance Board which at least applied rather more consistent rules. Freed of their direct financial responsibility for the unemployed, local authorities found in the late 1930s that their Poor Law responsibilities for children, the sick, the elderly, widows and deserted wives began, in Fraser's words, 'to mellow'. A 1937 report from Political and Economic Planning, an early independent research organisation and think-tank, records them slowly evolving into something faintly recognisable as the social services departments to come: 'Instead of the grim Poor Law of the nineteenth century with its rigorous insistence on the principle of "less eligibility" and the workhouse test we have a liberal and constructive service supplementing the other social services, filling in gaps and dealing with human need in the round in a way which no specialist service could ever be expected to do.'[48] Such a picture, according to Sir George Godber, then a medical officer with the Ministry of Health, remained very

much that of the best. 'Some of the services, particularly the accommodation for "wayfarers", could be grim indeed when I was inspecting them
in 1939.'[49]

Unemployment, as Fraser says, had become 'the central issue of the
inter-war years. Its malignant canker had poisoned millions of homes; it
had blighted whole industrial regions; it had disinherited a generation;
and it had laid low an elected Government.' The Pathé News images of
the Jarrow Crusade of 1936 are the most potent symbol of the times. Two
hundred men, selected from hundreds of volunteers among the 8000 made
redundant after the Tyne shipyard and its linked industries closed, marched
to London and on Parliament led by their MP 'Red Ellen' Wilkinson
(whom we will meet again). Their cheerful discipline washed through with
despair still comes through the flickering black and white film. In the short
term they received and achieved nothing – indeed, on their return they
learned their dole had been cut; as the Unemployment Assistance Board
explained, while on the march they would not have been available for
work had any turned up.[50]

Yet unemployment was far from touching everybody equally. While it
reached 67 per cent in Jarrow, it was a mere 3 per cent in High Wycombe,
and 7 per cent in London's Deptford.[51] Britain's first great twentieth-
century experience of mass unemployment was as regional as its return
was to be in the recession of the early to mid-1980s. As in the eighties –
though not the nineties – it was heavy engineering, coal, steel, and ship-
building that were razed by foreign competition. The twenties and thirties
added to that the dramatic decline of King Cotton in Lancashire and the
slower decline of Yorkshire wool: the world was discovering that it wanted
fewer of the 'millions of yards of calico and thousands of steam engines'[52]
that Britain had previously provided. So it was chiefly the north of England, Scotland and Wales that suffered.

None the less, other parts of the country and the middle classes were
not entirely immune. In 1934 it was estimated that 300,000 clerks, office
managers, engineers, chemists and the like were out of work, white-collar
workers whose earnings were too high to qualify for the state insurance
schemes and who thus did not appear in the general statistics.[53] In 1936,
when the worst was over, Fowey in Cornwall, Ross on Wye, and Keswick
in the Lake District featured alongside Wigan, Hartlepool and Glasgow as
priority places for official contracts because their adult unemployment had
run at above 25 per cent in the previous year. But it remains true that
even at the absolute nadir of the slump, more than three-quarters of the
workforce was still working. And overall – again a pre-echo of the eighties

– those in work enjoyed real, rising standards of living over the two decades before World War II. In fact the thirties was to be the last decade for half a century when it could fairly be said that the rich got richer while the poor got poorer.

The 1930s not only saw George Orwell chronicle the plight of lower England in *The Road to Wigan Pier*, it also saw J. B. Priestley's *English Journey*. The novelist and critic travelled from Southampton to Newcastle by way of most points in between and back to London. He found three Englands. There was 'Old England' of the cathedrals, the colleges and the Cotswolds, 'a luxury country' that 'has long since ceased to earn its own living'. Then there was the nineteenth-century England: 'the industrial England of coal, iron, steel, cotton, wool, railways' with 'thousands of rows of little houses all alike', 'detached villas with monkey trees', 'mill chimneys, slums, fried-fish shops' and 'good-class draper's and confec-tioner's' – all existing in 'a cynically devastated countryside' itself dotted with 'sooty dismal little towns and still sootier grim fortress-like cities'. It was an area he described as 'the larger part of the Midlands and the North' but 'existing everywhere'. This England, Priestley judged, 'is not being added to and has no new life poured into it. To the more fortunate people it was not a bad England at all, very solid and comfortable.'[54] But this England also contained the England of the dole, one that looked as if it had 'devoted a hundred years of its life to keeping gigantic sooty pigs. And the people who were choked by the reek of sties did not get the bacon.'

It was this England that also contained Hebburn and Jarrow, its iron-works derelict and its shipyards nearly so when Priestley visited in 1933, three years before the march. He pronounced the town quite simply 'dead'.

> Wherever we went there were men hanging about, not scores of them but hundreds and thousands of them. The whole town looked as if it had entered a perpetual, penniless bleak Sabbath. The men wore the drawn masks of prisoners of war. A stranger from a distant civilization . . . would have arrived at once at the conclusion that Jarrow had deeply offended some celestial emperor of the island and was now being punished. He would never believe us if we told him that in theory this town was as good as any other and that its inhabitants were not criminals but citizens with votes.[55]

Writing nine years before Beveridge, in an unconscious premonition of things to come and using the same capital letters, Priestley railed: 'If

Germans had been threatening these towns instead of Want, Diseases, Hopelessness, Misery, something would have been done, and done quickly.'[56]

Priestley also found a third England – and not one which appealed much to his fastidious taste. That was 'the new post [First World] war England . . . the England of arterial and by-pass roads, of filling stations and factories that look like exhibition buildings, of giant cinemas and dance halls and cafés, bungalows with tiny garages, cocktail bars, Woolworths, motor-coaches, wireless, hiking, factory girls looking like actresses, greyhound racing and dirt tracks, swimming pools, and everything given away for cigarettes and coupons.'[57]

It was also, he might have added, the England of the middle-class estates of twenties semis that were just starting to explode into the thirties suburban private house building boom, the England of Beckenham and Bromley and of Metroland, the rise of the clerk and the demise of the servant, the heyday of ribbon development, of the Great West Road, the Art Deco of the Firestone and Hoover factories, the days of 'glass and white tiles and chromium plate'.[58] This England was a country of which a large section had prospered despite the celestial emperor's view of Jarrow.

But all three of these Englands, along with the rest of the United Kingdom, went again to war in 1939. And it was war which merged them closer into one.

As if to underline that not all social progress halted in the 1930s, the school leaving age had been due to rise to from fourteen to fifteen on 1 September 1939. But in the early hours of that morning German tanks rolled into Poland and the mass evacuation of schoolchildren and mothers from Britain's cities, planned since the time of Munich, began.

In three days – war was finally declared on Sunday the third – an incredible one and a half million people were decanted into the countryside, including 827,000 schoolchildren, 524,000 mothers and their children under school age, and 103,000 teachers and helpers.[59] It was the start of the massive movements of population that were to stretch and bend the old class system as never before, one of the effects of a war which impinged on the civilian population in a way that 1914–18, for all its carnage on foreign fields, never did. While it slew the flower of a generation, from whole families of yeomen recorded on village war memorials to the gilded contemporaries of Robert Graves, the First World War did not throw people together as the Second did. It did not force one half of England to see how the other half lived. The Second World War, Paul Addison says, in *The Road to 1945*:

> hurled together people of different social backgrounds in a series of massive upheavals caused by bombing, conscription, and the migration of workers to new centres of war industry. Over the war as a whole there were 60 million changes of address in a civilian population of about 38 million, while more than five million men and women were drawn into the three armed services. There were one and a half millions in the Home Guard, and about the same number in the various Civil Defence services, by the end of 1940. More than one and a quarter million evacuees, over half of them children, were billeted on families in the reception areas in February 1941. The number of women working in industry increased by 1,800,000 between 1939 and 1943. In air-raid shelters, air raid warden's posts, Home Guard units, and overcrowded trains where soldiers barged into first class compartments, class barriers could no longer be sustained. 'It is quite common now,' Lord Marley was reported as saying in 1941, 'to see Englishmen speaking to each other in public, although they have never been formally introduced.'[60]

Many of the first evacuees soon returned home. But the impact of incomers who were mostly (though not entirely) from poorer inner city areas on the more comfortable countryside was remarkable. Ben Wicks in *No Time to Wave Goodbye*, his remarkable compilation of evacuees' experiences (he was one himself), records children brought up in the days before mass television who, having watched cows being milked, were convinced they were being offered urine to drink; some who had never slept in a bed and preferred the floor; while Richard Titmuss told of the child who said to his visiting mother: 'They call this spring, Mum, and they have one down here every year.'[61]

Mabel Louvain Manning took in two boys.

> The first morning I was awoken about 6 am by such a noise, it was the boys fighting in bed! One had a bloody nose which had splattered all over the wall. I cleaned them up and got them ready for breakfast. They had no idea how to use a knife and fork and picked up a fried egg by their fingers. They didn't like stew or pies, only beans in tomato, which they wanted to eat out of a tin, and chips.
>
> When they came to me, one was wearing wellingtons, the other plimsolls, and no coats or extra shirts or underclothes. I cadged what I could

from friends, and then decided to write to the parents for more. The mother wrote back saying she would have to get their suits and shoes out of pawn, which she did, and sent them down.[62]

There were horrified tales of nits, lice and scabies, taken up by a press amazed by stories of children sewn into their only clothes. In Dorset a couple took in a mother and three children.

It was very hot weather when war broke out, but those older children went all round my house urinating against the walls.

Although we had two toilets, one being outside with very easy access for them, they never used them. Although my husband and I told the children and the mother off about this filthy habit they took absolutely no notice and our house stank to high heaven.[63]

A more revealing tale of life in the under-toileted Glasgow slums came from the Scottish mother who told her six-year-old: 'You dirty thing, messing up the lady's carpet. Go and do it in the corner.' The evacuation produced happier humour, too. Jean Chartrand recorded two boys billeted on a cousin's farm asking to help with the milking. 'One boy had put the pail under the cow's udders and was holding it there while the other boy was the using the cow's tail like a pump-handle. They were both very disgusted when there was no milk forthcoming.'[64]

Some made lifelong friends from the experience, other children found themselves abused and exploited, emotionally, physically and even sexually, and never recovered. The lesser shocks were not all one way. Eileen Stoddart recalled coming from a 'very respectable home. Some of the girls ended up in tiny cottages, three to a single bed, with bedbugs which they had never seen before in their lives. I wasn't allowed to wash my hair for four months since we had to bring the water up the hill from the village pump.'[65] The overall impact of the whole experience, however, is summed up by one child's memory of her family taking in three sisters. 'We had never seen the like before and seriously learned how the other half lived.'[66] Or as Rab Butler, the creator of the 1944 Education Act, was to put it: 'It was realized with deepening awareness that the "two nations" still existed in England a century after Disraeli had used the phrase.'[67]

By the time Beveridge was appointed, the war had progressed through Dunkirk and the Battle of Britain to the Battle of the Atlantic as the convoys from America worked to save Britain from potential starvation and defeat. Food was rationed, with the Board of Trade, not the Labour

Government of 1945, coining the phrase 'fair shares for all' as clothes rationing came in. And there had been the Blitz. By June 1941, the month Beveridge took on his task, more than two million homes had been damaged or destroyed by bombing, 60 per cent of them in London.[68] Bombs respected neither class nor income. The Luftwaffe may have effected a slum clearance programme around Britain's docks that it would take years of post-war housing programmes to equal, but they also took out homes in Mayfair and Belgravia and the comfortable suburbs of towns when targets were missed or bombs jettisoned on the way home. Not just cities and big towns up and down the land were hit, but eastern and southern coastal areas in 'tip and run' raids. Some 100,000 people had been killed or seriously injured and the Emergency Medical Service was already running an embryo national health service by providing free treatment to 'casualties' – a definition which included evacuees.

Civil defence brought social classes together as much as the armed forces. My mother, a slip of an eighteen-year-old who worked as an ambulance attendant when the bombs began to fall on Bristol, recalls giggling with her middle-class friends at the shy approaches of dustmen too old and too young for call-up when they first sat at opposite ends of the canteen waiting for the siren's call. 'We just didn't know people like them, or they people like us,' she recalls. 'We had never heard such language. But when you saw the risks they'd take to pull people out of bombed buildings, there couldn't any longer be any sense of them and us.'

Claims of social cohesion can be overdone. The prison population almost doubled to more than 21,000, much of the increase owing to sentences for looting. An élite still lived better than the rest and black markets flourished. Nicholas Davenport, the highly successful and socialist City journalist wrote in the spring of 1941: 'Not a week passes without the Ministry of Food prosecuting hundreds of food offenders and the Board of Trade dozens of offenders against clothes rationing and quota laws.'[69] But that same rationing was to change dramatically the nutritional status of the British people during the course of the war. Richard Titmuss, who told the official tale of the war's social effects, recorded that 'the families in that third of the population of Britain who in 1938 were chronically undernourished had their first adequate diet in 1940 and 1941 . . . [after which] the incidence of deficiency diseases, and notably infant mortality, dropped dramatically.'[70] It became known early on that the Royal Family too had ration books and ate Spam, while the King posed for a publicity photograph as he joined a 'Pig Club' – just about anything that was left over could be used for pig swill and converted into pork and bacon.[71]

Eleanor Roosevelt, visiting King George VI and Queen Elizabeth, found windows blown out in Buckingham Palace and a black line painted round the inside of the bath, above which it was not to be filled. The Queen's remark after Buckingham Palace was hit: 'It makes me feel I can look the East End in the face',[72] may sound sentimental, even patronising. It contained, however, a truth.

The switch to a war economy had also virtually eliminated unemployment. By the summer of 1941 it was down to 200,000 and falling. In 1943, soon after Beveridge reported, it had fallen to a mere 62,000, most of whom were in transit from one job to another.[73] Not only that, wages were rising. And Keynes, the uncertain prophet in the wilderness of the early 1930s, had now become the fount of Keynesianism. He had published his *General Theory of Employment, Interest and Money* in 1936 and had been in the United States where he had seen in Roosevelt's New Deal the effects of ideas similar to those he advanced. Since June 1940 he had been inside the British Treasury, his influence plain on the 1941 Budget. While there were battles still to be fought before Keynesian economics ruled, the results of the government's ever-growing economic intervention appeared to be demonstrating that his theories worked on this side of the Atlantic, too.

Things plainly were changing. *The Times* had gone pink, or so it seemed to right-wing Tories. In October 1941, Geoffrey Dawson, who had done so much to scar the paper's reputation by his support for appeasement, was replaced by Robin Barrington-Ward, a Balliol contemporary of Beveridge. The paper's official chronicler records Barrington-Ward as a radical Tory who was 'inclined by temperament to welcome social change in advance, prepare for it, and so control it.'[74] He took the paper to the left. Earlier that year E. H. Carr, the leftish historian, had been appointed assistant editor, from which position he argued consistently for the need to espouse social justice as the aim after the war. In a sense, the then small group of Tory reformers, whose views had first been clearly articulated in 1938 when a rather obscure back-bench rebel called Harold Macmillan had defined the politics he was to follow in a book called *The Middle Way*, had found a voice in the leader columns of *The Times*. Even before Dawson left, however, a new tone had begun to emerge. An editorial on 1 July 1940 declared:

> Over the greater part of Western Europe the common values for which we stand are known and prized. We must indeed beware of defining these values in purely 19th Century terms. If we speak of democracy we do not mean a democracy which maintains the right to vote but forgets the right to work and the right to live. If we speak of freedom we do not mean

a rugged individualism which excludes social organisation and economic planning. If we speak of equality we do not mean a political equality nullified by social and economic privilege. If we speak of economic reconstruction we think less of maximum (though this job too will be required) than of equitable distribution.

Labour's right-wing egalitarians, Tony Crosland in the 1950s or Roy Hattersley in the 1990s, could have said amen to that. One Tory MP was later to growl (though not in the context of the welfare state) that *The Times* had become merely 'the threepenny edition of the *Daily Worker*', the Communist Party paper which was suppressed for a time during the war.[75] If the voices on *The Times* were a-changing, they were not alone. The *Economist*, long the guardian of financial orthodoxy, could pronounce that the 'old controversy' over 'the question of whether the state should make itself responsible for the economic environment' was 'as dead as a doorknocker – that is, useful for making a noise but nothing else.'

Newspapers may shape the world around them, but they also reflect it. The churches had found a new vigour in siding with the underdogs, running meetings demanding social justice after the war. In this William Temple, appointed on Churchill's recommendation as Archbishop of Canterbury in early 1942, played a key role. He was to bless Beveridge's marriage later that year and still later was to be contemptuously described as Beveridge's 'warm-up man' by Correlli Barnett, the Cambridge historian whose influential reinterpretation of the Second World War puts Beveridge high on the list of Great Satans responsible for Britain's postwar decline.[76] In 1941, while still Archbishop of York, Temple had written *Citizen and Churchman* in which he defined the 'Welfare-State' in contrast to the Power-State of the continental tyrannies.[77] A meeting of the Industrial Christian Fellowship in the Albert Hall in October 1942, at which Temple spoke, drew *ten thousand* participants. 'The general demands included . . . a central planning for employment, housing and social security,' *Picture Post* reported.[78] It was thus fertile ground into which Beveridge was to plant his dragon's teeth, seeking to raise up giants to respond to the 'five giant evils' he had identified.

Moreover, during 1942 the Conservatives found themselves losing by-elections to some of the oddest characters ever to sit in Parliament. Labour, the Liberals and the Tories did not stand against each other because of the coalition – indeed, Labour actively backed some of the Conservative coalition nominees. The awkward independents, standing on the vaguest and most confused of platforms, still won. Screaming Lord Sutch should have been born earlier. Soon Labour was to find its own candidates losing by-elections in similar circumstances.

Mass Observation, the pioneering opinion poll organisation, found in December 1941 that one person in six said the war had changed their political views. 'Eight months later, in August 1942 [four months before the Beveridge report], the proportion was one in three,' Angus Calder records. 'At this time it was also found that only one-third of the voters expected any of the existing parties to get things done as they personally wanted them after the war. This minority was mostly Labour or Communist.'[79] The old Conservative front was collapsing. What might be dubbed the new progressive centre of Tory politics which was to receive Labour's inheritance in 1951 was yet to have its day.

The sense that something more than victory over Nazi Germany had to be planned was also present in government itself, even if the terms were not yet very clearly defined. Churchill had, after all, appointed Arthur Greenwood Minister for Reconstruction – the same Greenwood who as Labour deputy leader, standing in for an ill Attlee in the Commons debate on the eve of war, had been urged by Leo Amery from the government benches to 'Speak for England, Arthur.'

Churchill, back on the Conservative benches, had his days as a Liberal social reformer the better part of thirty years behind him, but he still retained Liberal or even Whiggish sentiments. His interest in home affairs had dissipated in the 1930s in the face of his concern for Empire and the threat of Fascism. But addressing the boys of his old school, Harrow, in 1940, he said: 'When this war is won, as it surely will be, it must be one of our aims to establish a state of society where the advantages and privileges which have hitherto been enjoyed only by the few shall be far more widely shared by the many, and by the youth of the nation as a whole.'[80] He had sent R. A. ('Rab') Butler to the Board of Education and appointed him chairman of a new Conservative Post-War Problems Committee. In August 1941 he met Roosevelt for the first time off Newfoundland where they agreed on the Atlantic Charter – a joint statement of war aims, even though the United States was not yet formally in the war. The pair called on all nations to collaborate 'with the object of securing for all improved labour standards, economic advancement, and social security'. Peace should bring 'freedom from fear and want'.[81] Beveridge was to exploit that statement in his report, citing it as backing for his plan.

And against this background, as Sir William prepared his report, the war raged outside Britain itself. On 22 June 1941, less than a fortnight after Beveridge's appointment, Hitler had attacked the Soviet Union. Britain at last was not alone. For those with an abiding loathing of Communism, and who had seen the perfidious Nazi–Soviet pact of August 1939 allow the Soviet Union to swallow Finland and the German tanks to roll into Poland barely a week later, this was as hard a moment as any in the war. Not least for Churchill. In a broadcast that showed both courage and statesmanship, he declared that Nazism was indistinguishable from the worst features of Communism. 'No-one has been a more consistent opponent of Communism than I have been for the last 25 years. I will unsay no word that I have spoken about it.' But he went on to declare that with the tanks rolling, 'the [Soviet] past with its crimes, its follies and its tragedies flashes away . . . I see the ten thousand villages of Russia . . . where maidens laugh and children play . . .' and '. . . the cause of any Russian fighting for his hearth and home is the cause of free men and free peoples in every quarter of the globe.'[82] Most people believed initially that the Soviet Union would be smashed. But in July, Stalin announced his horrific but awe-inspiring 'scorched earth' policy. By September British ships were on the nightmarish Arctic convoys to Archangel carrying aircraft and other supplies. At the end of that month 'Tanks for Russia' week was launched in British factories: they came out with the legends 'Stalin', 'Marx', 'Lenin' and 'Another for Joe' chalked on the sides. And as Hitler became bogged down in the Russian winter snows and Moscow held, admiration for Soviet sacrifices grew. A conviction became widespread well outside the ranks of the Communists and Labour's left that the Soviet system could not be all bad. There can be few more symbolic exemplars of this particular time than the Christian and Conservative T. S. Eliot, then based at Faber & Faber, turning down the manuscript of *Animal Farm*, the savage and prophetic satire of the Russian revolution and Soviet system written by the atheist and socialist George Orwell. Eliot did so on the grounds that it did not offer 'the right point of view from which to criticise the political situation at the present time'.[83]

The success of Beveridge's report with its universalist and collectivist themes has to be seen against this complex backdrop. There were three more factors which were to give it the greatest impact of any British social document of the twentieth century.

The first is that Beveridge argued along the grain of current thinking. He may have drafted his report before he saw the evidence, but he already knew what much of its substance would be. José Harris writes:

One of the most striking features of the evidence submitted to the Beveridge Committee was the very widespread expectation among witnesses that the inquiry was going to lead to radical, even 'Utopian' social change. Quite where this expectation came from is not entirely clear, but it may well have derived from Beveridge himself and from his frequent references in articles and broadcasts to the abolition of poverty and to post-war social reform. A second striking feature was the very wide degree of support among witnesses for the kind of reform that Beveridge already had in mind – a measure of the extent to which Beveridge himself was interpreting rather than creating the spirit of the times. Again and again witnesses pressed spontaneously and independently for measures which afterwards became the main policy proposals of the Beveridge Report – namely, family allowances, full employment, a universal health service, a uniform system of contributory insurance, subsistence-level benefits and the reduction or abolition of public assistance.[84]

Not everyone believed in planning for a New Jerusalem, let alone a Utopia. Sir John Forbes Watson, Director of the Confederation of British Employers, virtually urged Beveridge to abandon the report:

I want to say here – it will go on the shorthand note, but I do not know that I want to say it publicly – we did not start this war with Germany in order to improve our social services; the war was forced upon us by Germany and we entered it to preserve our freedom and to keep the Gestapo outside our houses, and that is what this war means.[85]

Others shared that view and believed improvements could not be afforded. J. S. Boyd, vice-president of the Shipbuilding Employers' Federation told the committee:

I am saying something I would not like printed – there may have been excellent reasons in the last war for talking about homes fit for heroes and there may be excellent reasons today for talking about improving the social services, but at the same time any of us who are trying to think at all do realize and do appreciate that the problems after the war are not problems that the man in the street concerns himself about, and you may be causing a much greater degree of danger by telling him something which in fact even the most optimistic of us may fear will be impossible after the war.[86]

The industrialists' desire not to go on the record may be significant; and the employers were not united. In November 1942, when Beveridge's report was complete but not yet published, 120 senior industrialists including the head of ICI produced 'A National Policy for Industry' which called for companies to be responsible for proper housing for their employees, for supplementing the state pension and for subsidies to prevent unemployment. They also sought family allowances and the raising of the school leaving age to sixteen. The report had as much of corporate paternalism as state action about it. But in suggesting that big companies should almost become miniature welfare states the industrialists, if not in the same regiment as Beveridge, were marching to a similar beat.

The route Beveridge took, however, was not preordained. Evidence to the committee threw up alternatives of which he was already aware and which were to be recurring themes in the post-war years. Several witnesses argued for the abolition of contributions. Benefit should be funded either from taxation or from an identifiable surcharge on income tax. That Beveridge opposed, first because of its implied extension of means-testing, and second because of the Treasury's longstanding opposition to earmarked taxes. Equally, there were arguments for flat-rate benefits paid for by graduated contributions: those who earned more would pay more. Both Political and Economic Planning and the Association of Approved Societies, who ran health insurance, pressed for that measure, which Beveridge dismissed, José Harris records, as the epitome of the 'Santa Claus state'. 'I believe there is a psychological desire to get something for which you have paid . . . the tradition of the fixed price is very strong in this country. You do not like having to pay more than your neighbours.' Others including the International Labour Office praised the kind of 'earnings-related system commonly found on the Continent', where benefits were not flat but graduated according to previous earnings.[87]

All these Beveridge rejected, objecting that earnings-related benefits would damage savings. In so doing he took the British social security system down a road that was both recognisable – the insurance basis already used for both employment and health – and very different from the earnings-related systems adopted over most of the rest of Europe after the war. For all the rhetoric in the early part of the report that 'a revolutionary moment in the world's history is a time for revolutions', Beveridge in many ways was far from revolutionary. He produced something people would recognise. And he recognised himself what he had done. In paragraph 31 he stated that his proposals 'spring out of what has been accomplished in building up security piece by piece'. In important ways, he added, the plan was 'a natural development from the past. It is a British revolution.' Both in its incrementalism – the way in which in large measure it stuck to the old system of flat-rate benefits paid for by flat-rate contributions split three ways between employee, employer and state – and in its choice of a path other countries did not follow, Beveridge's report was indeed a *very* British revolution.

The second additional factor in the report's reception was that Beveridge through broadcasts, articles and half-leaks – he was an occasional member of the massively popular radio 'Brains Trust' – had made very certain that the world knew it was coming. He had repeatedly referred publicly to 'equality of sacrifice' and the possibility of abolishing poverty. In March 1942, more than six months before the report, *Picture Post* could write: 'Everybody has heard of Sir William Beveridge.'[88] As early as April 1942, a Home Intelligence report noted: 'Sir William Beveridge's proposals for an "all-in" social security scheme are said to be popular', and by the autumn Home Intelligence was recording that: 'Three years ago, the term social security was almost unknown to the public as a whole. It now appears to be generally accepted as an urgent post-war need. It is commonly defined as "a decent minimum standard of living for all".'[89]

Harold Wilson had turned down the secretaryship of the committee. But Frank Pakenham (the future Lord Longford) was a friend and assistant of Beveridge, sympathetic to his work, and well connected in Fleet Street. He acted as an unofficial public relations officer.[90] Brendan Bracken, the Minister of Information, wrote to Churchill in October: 'I have good reason to believe that some of Beveridge's friends are playing politics and that when the report appears there will be an immense amount of ballyhoo about the importance of implementing the recommendations without delay.'[91] There was indeed. In mid-November the ever-tactful Beveridge unwisely told a *Daily Telegraph* reporter that his proposals would take the country 'half-way to Moscow', a statement he promptly disowned but which only lowered by a few more degrees the icy reception the report was to receive from right-wing Tories and parts of government.[92]

A frantic debate in fact was already under way over what facilities Beveridge should be given to publicise his recommendations. It was finally resolved on 25 November by Churchill minuting Bracken: 'Once it is out he can bark to his heart's content.'[93] Bracken changed tack. He apparently saw the report as a great morale-booster at home and for the troops, and a useful propaganda weapon overseas. His ministry recognised the force of Beveridge's own declaration in the report that 'the purpose of victory is to live in a better world than the old world'. Beveridge added that 'each individual citizen is more likely to concentrate upon his war effort if he feels that his Government will be ready in time with plans for that better world.' Where ministers were to part company with Beveridge was over the third clause of that sentence: 'that, if these plans are to be ready in time, they must be made ready now'.[94]

The final piece of luck and timing which ensured the report's ecstatic reception lay with Montgomery and the British Eighth Army. The Japanese attack on Pearl Harbor a year earlier had seen the United States finally enter the war, but apart from survival, and the heroism of the Soviet Union, there had been little else to celebrate since 1939. Monty had gone into action at El Alamein at the end of October. The battle started badly. But on 4 November a BBC announcer, his voice shaking with excitement, delivered General Alexander's Cairo communiqué stating that Rommel was in full retreat in Egypt. The news from North Africa only got better. Churchill in one of the war's best remembered aphorisms pronounced on the 10th: 'Now is not the end. It is not even the beginning of the end. But it is, perhaps, the end of the beginning.'[95]

Suddenly, after three years, there was a future to look forward to – and one that the times demanded should be very different from the past. On 15 November, for the first time since war was declared, Churchill ordered that the church bells ring out, not to announce invasion but to celebrate Monty's victory.[96] A fortnight later the Beveridge report was published, its own words ringing out like a great bell. In his final paragraph Beveridge became more Churchillian than Bunyanesque:

> Freedom from want cannot be forced on a democracy or given to a democracy. It must be won by them. Winning it needs courage and faith and a sense of national unity: courage to face facts and difficulties and overcome them; faith in our culture and in the ideals of fair-play and freedom for which century after century our forefathers were prepared to die; a sense of national unity overriding the interests of any class or section. The Plan for Social Security in this report is submitted by one who believes that in this supreme crisis the British people will not be found wanting.[97]

There were – and still are – many battles to be fought against Beveridge's five giants. His report's popular impact was a matter, in José Harris's judgement, 'partly of luck and partly of careful calculation' but partly also simply of the times in which it was made.[98]

Beatrice Webb commented rather acidly how odd it was that Beveridge of all people had become a national hero. But if one sentence had to sum up popular reaction, it is the breathless enthusiasm of the Pathé News interviewer on the night the report was published. The white-haired, waistcoated, oh-so-Edwardian figure of Beveridge intoned to the massed cinema audiences of the great British public: 'I hope that when you've been able to study the report in detail, you'll like it. That it will get adopted, and, if it's so, we shall have taken the first step to security with freedom and responsibility. *That* is what we all desire.'

The interviewer replies, all italics and capital letters and deference: '*Thank You – Sir William*'.

CHAPTER 2

From cradle to grave

> This is the greatest advance in our history. There can be no turning back. From now on Beveridge is not the name of a man; it is the name of a way of life, and not only for Britain, but for the whole civilized world.
>
> *Beveridge to Harold Wilson shortly after his report came out, recounted in Wilson, The Making of a Prime Minister, 1986, p. 64*

THE PUBLIC RECEPTION of the Beveridge report was indeed ecstatic. The leader writers of all the newspapers, the *Daily Telegraph* excepted, blessed it.[1] *The Times* called it 'a momentous document' whose 'central proposals must surely be accepted as the basis of Government action. The main social standards on which the report insists are moderate enough to disarm any charge of indulgence.'[2] A survey of public opinion shortly after publication showed 86 per cent in favour and a mere 6 per cent against. Most notably, the better off favoured it almost as enthusiastically as those who stood to gain most. Among employers only 16 per cent felt they would gain directly, but 73 per cent favoured its adoption. For those defined as upper-income groups, 29 per cent felt they would gain, but 76 per cent supported the plan. Among the professions the figures were 48 and 92 per cent.[3] Home Office intelligence reports monitored, in Paul Addison's words, 'an extraordinary anxiety that somehow the report would be watered down or shelved'.[4]

Such anxiety was not without justification. Some instantly said it could not be afforded, even as others argued that the benefits Beveridge was proposing were too low. The journalist J. L. Hodson recorded in his diary the evening he heard Beveridge broadcast the details of his plan:

> Some of the Big Business gentlemen are already calling it a scheme that will put us all on the Poor Law. Unless prices are to fall a good deal after the war, the scheme errs on the side of modesty of benefits paid. £2 a week [the sum Beveridge recommended for the pension and an unemployed

married man] won't go very far. T. Thompson writes me from Lancashire: 'Beveridge has put the ball in the scrum all right. I wonder what shape it will be when it comes out.'[5]

It proved to be a rather different shape. But the first question was whether it would come out at all.

Sir Kingsley Wood, the Chancellor of the Exchequer, struck first, even before the report's publication. On 17 November he minuted Churchill that the plan involved 'an impracticable financial commitment'. Wood in his youth had led the battle by the Friendly Societies against Lloyd George's 1911 health insurance package. He now told Churchill that Beveridge's plan would increase taxation by 30 per cent. It would not abolish want, but it would give money to those who did not need it. 'The weekly progress of the millionaire to the post office for his old age pension would have an element of farce but for the fact that it is to be provided in large measure by the general tax payer,' Kingsley Wood declared, launching a theme that would be echoed time and again down the years. He added: 'Many in this country have persuaded themselves that the cessation of hostilities will mark the opening of the Golden Age (many were so persuaded last time also). However this may be, the time for declaring a dividend on the profits of the Golden Age is the time when those profits have been realized in fact, not merely in imagination.'[6]

By contrast Keynes, whom Beveridge had repeatedly consulted over dinners in West End clubs, believed the plan broadly workable and affordable.[7] He was later to argue that 'the suggestion that is being put about in some quarters that there are financial difficulties is quite unfounded.'[8] After listening to Keynes, Beveridge had in fact trimmed his original ideas considerably in an attempt to keep costs down. The biggest single factor here was his proposal that old age pensions should be phased in over twenty years as people's contribution records grew. But he had also agreed that family allowances be paid only for the second and subsequent children, and he had dropped plans to have full insurance for housewives, and benefits for those unable to work because they were caring for sick or aged relatives.[9]

Some of Churchill's closest advisers also disputed Wood's view. Lord Cherwell, his economic adviser and close personal confidant, thought it 'altruistic but worth its cost', and likely to 'improve rather than worsen our economic position'. But he worried that the expenditure would alienate opinion in the United States on whom Britain's economy was now heavily dependent. Americans would think they were being asked to pay for

British social services. But he observed perspicaciously: 'On the other hand there has been so much carefully engineered advanced publicity that the Government's hand may have been forced.'[10]

While Churchill's advisers argued, the government began desperately playing for time. The report was promptly referred to a committee of officials chaired by Sir Thomas Phillips, an old adversary of Beveridge who had originally worked for him in the Board of Trade. The committee accepted the principles of universality and a comprehensive health service, but still challenged key aspects of the social security side of Beveridge's scheme.[11] It fell to Sir William Jowitt, who had replaced Greenwood as the Minister for Reconstruction, to tell the Commons on publication day that the government would merely 'formulate its conclusions'.[12] The government, however, had a real problem. As a coalition it was almost bound to be divided between its Labour and Tory parts on such issues; moreover, the Labour and Tory parts were themselves divided internally. Some Conservative ministers supported the plan: Leo Amery, for instance, described it as 'essentially Conservative';[13] others like Kingsley Wood damned it; yet others believed simply that no commitment could yet be made. Labour ministers, unsurprisingly, were in favour. But Bevin, his old distrust of Beveridge surfacing, took strongly against it, declaring – inaccurately – that many parts were unacceptable to the unions. Attlee and Dalton were in favour but remained lukewarm in pressing for implementation. Dalton in particular had noted a minute from Churchill in which the Prime Minister said he could not commit himself without a general election to test popular support.[14] Dalton feared Churchill would win such an election by a landslide, taking Labour off the map.

It was left to Herbert Morrison, newly in the War Cabinet, to argue vigorously and in some financial detail the case for a firm immediate commitment.[15] To accept the Treasury's pessimism, 'would be a surrender to idiocy in advance,' he declared. The social benefits of the plan were 'very great' and it represented 'a financial burden which we should be able to bear, except on a number of very gloomy assumptions'.[16] He lost, but Churchill shifted his ground. The government would undertake to prepare the necessary legislation, but it would require a new House of Commons to commit the expenditure.[17]

Two months after the report's publication, parliamentary pressure finally forced a debate. Sir John Anderson, Lord President of the Council, 'a dry old civil servant-turned-minister',[18] led for the government with so little enthusiasm for Beveridge's plan that he inflamed not only the Labour benches but a significant minority on his own side. MPs heard him declare 'there can at present be no binding commitment. Subject only to that . . . I have made it clear that the Government adopt the scheme in principle.'[19] The following day Kingsley Wood, the Chancellor, 'lingered with apparent satisfaction over the financial perils of the plan'.[20]

Since the start of the war, however, the Conservative Party had ceased to be a coherent body of opinion. The thirty-five-year-old Quintin Hogg (the future Lord Hailsham), neatly characterised by Angus Calder as 'a frothing, bubbling, mockable but curiously clever young man',[21] had returned from the front to join a dining group of other youngish Tory MPs which met at 'a little restaurant in the Charing Cross Road'[22] (Conservatives having always had a penchant for plotting in supper clubs). The MPs were much attracted by Macmillan's *Middle Way* view of a mixed economy steering a course between socialism and old-style *laissez-faire* capitalism, and were busy forming themselves into the Tory Reform Committee which was to receive tacit encouragement from Conservative ministers such as Butler, Eden and Macmillan himself. 'What brought us together,' Lord Hailsham recalled almost fifty years later, 'was our feeling that the attitude of our leaders in the corridors of power as exemplified by their pussy-footing over the Beveridge Report was unduly unconstructive and unimaginative.'[23] Taking as his formula 'publicly organized social services, privately owned industry',[24] Hogg saw Beveridge as 'a relatively Conservative document' and tabled a motion seeking the immediate creation of a Ministry of Social Security. More than forty other Conservative MPs signed it.

Jim Griffiths, to whom would finally fall the implementation of Beveridge, capped that from the Labour benches with an even stronger call for immediate implementation. In the cruel but clever way of politics Herbert Morrison – possibly as a punishment precisely because he had been the most overt supporter of Beveridge in the War Cabinet – had been given the task of winding up for the government at the end of the third day. Faced with defending a negative policy that he had tried to make more positive, he produced what Jim Griffiths was to call 'the best debating speech Morrison ever made', underlining those parts (sixteen of the twenty-three recommendations) that the government did accept even if it did not yet intend to act.[25] The speech did enough to stop the Conservatives from rebelling. But 121 MPs from the Labour, Liberal and Communist parties together with 11 independents voted with Jim Griffiths. Among them was David Lloyd George casting his last ever Commons vote. It proved one of the biggest revolts of the war against the government. More than one historian has seen it as a defining moment in Labour's 1945 election victory.[26]

The debate finished on 18 February and in the course of that month six by-elections, 'a general election in miniature',[27] were held. The Beveridge report featured strongly in each campaign. In four of the six seats the Conservative vote dropped by 8 per cent even though Labour and the Liberals did not stand. The Home Intelligence department of the Ministry of Information was reporting 'a disappointed majority', adding 'the Government is thought to be trying to kill or shelve the report.'[28]

Churchill reacted. On 21 March 1943, in a broadcast entitled 'After the War' – his first wartime broadcast to concentrate on the home front – he continued to warn against imposing 'great new expenditures on the State without any relation to the circumstances which might prevail at the time'.[29] But recognising 'a duty to peer through the mists of the future to the end of the war' he promised a four-year plan 'to cover five or six large measures of a practical character'. These would be put to the electorate after the war and implemented by an incoming government.

He did not mention the Beveridge report by name, an omission that can only have been deliberate. But he promised 'national compulsory insurance for all classes for all purposes from the cradle to the grave'. It was, he said, 'a real opportunity for what I once called "bringing the magic of averages to the rescue of the millions".' To that he added the abolition of unemployment. 'We cannot have a band of drones in our midst, whether they come from the ancient aristocracy or the modern plutocracy or the ordinary type of pub-crawler', and the voice of Keynes could be heard in Churchill stating that government action could be 'turned on or off as circumstances require' to control unemployment. There was, he accepted, 'a broadening field for State ownership and enterprise' and his vision included a housing drive, educational reform, and much expanded health and welfare services. 'Here let me say there is no finer investment for any community than putting milk into babies.'[30]

Thus it was Churchill, rather than Beveridge, who defined social security as running 'from the cradle to the grave' – a phrase used by both the *Daily Mirror* and the *Daily Telegraph* on publication day – as he signed the wartime coalition up to it. What Lord Woolton, the future Tory party chairman, was to call 'the shandy gaff' of Conservatism and Socialism, which was to dominate post-war politics for thirty years, was beginning to emerge.[31]

Churchill's initial opposition to Beveridge needs explaining. First and foremost his attention was fixed firmly on winning the war, without worrying much about what was to come afterwards beyond hazy notions of some continuation of the coalition with himself at the head. This was, after all, still only 'the end of the beginning'. D-day remained eighteen months away. Second, he had to hold together a coalition which contained Labour but also a Tory party that was itself divided on the plan. Third, his doubts over the affordability of the proposals can be seen as genuine. And fourth, despite the fact that Beveridge had constructed something that Churchill would recognise and had himself implemented thirty years earlier – social insurance – the new plan was very different in character.

The social insurance Churchill had helped introduce had been designed, broadly, for the working classes, with the Poor Law in reserve as the ultimate safety net. The better off had been excluded from the state-organised unemployment and health schemes. Beveridge's plan was thus not 'the cause of the left out millions' which Churchill had espoused as young man, but the cause of all the millions.

And finally Churchill had been infuriated by Beveridge's determination to get the government to act immediately, as revealed both in the repeated pleas in the text of the report and in the pre- and post-publication publicity that he had sought. The Prime Minister was reported 'to have taken strong exception to the report, to have refused to see the author and forbidden any government department to allow him inside its doors'.[32] Churchill proved, however, on one level as good as his broadcast word, while on another getting his way. A month after the broadcast a Whitehall committee chaired by Thomas Sheepshanks was set up to consider implementation of Beveridge's report, eventually producing a White Paper on Social Security in 1944.[33] The same year the government published White Papers on a National Health Service and on Employment Policy, set up a Ministry of National Insurance, and delivered the 1944 Education Act. A housing White Paper followed in March 1945 and on 11 June, as virtually the final act of the coalition government, the Family Allowances Act became law. It provided five shillings (25p) a week for the second and all subsequent children to every family in the land – real money at a time when the average male manual wage was £6. The first universalist benefit of the modern welfare state had been created, even if its actual payment fell due under a Labour government. Yet only to that, and to the Education Act whose financial impact in mid-1945 was yet to be fully felt, did Churchill commit significant sums of the taxpayers' money ahead of a general election.

Beveridge himself – who in March had spoken from a Liberal Party platform on the theme of 'a people's war for a people's peace'[34] – set to work on a follow-up report on how to achieve full employment. But he found himself frozen out of Whitehall, the Treasury officials whom he had invited to join his study withdrawn. The government refused to commission his report: indeed, it worked frantically to get out its own White Paper, which proposed a 'high and stable level of employment' ahead of Beveridge's *Full Employment in a Free Society*. José Harris judges that the way he had courted massive advance publicity for the 1942 report 'was seen by many people inside Government as a flagrant breach of Whitehall conventions and as an attempt to usurp the powers and functions of the regular policy making machine'.[35] He was not to work in Whitehall again until 1949, when the Labour Government appointed him to head an inquiry into the BBC monopoly.

CHAPTER 3

A very British revolution

> It was the totalizing ambition of his [Beveridge's] report that made
> its proposals so striking; the complete coverage against risks for all
> people. All for one and one for all. The Three Musketeers meet the
> Government Actuary.
>
> Peter Baldwin, 'Beveridge in the longue dureé', York Papers, Vol. A, p. 30

A LAYMAN READING the Beveridge report today is likely to be
impressed not just by the way it provides the blueprint – if one that
was far from entirely followed – for the modern social security system;
nor only by its trumpet calls for the creation of the other giants of the
modern welfare state. Even more striking, it contains almost all the key
arguments that have raged about the welfare state since its publication.

You could almost believe, listening to the debate about its future in the
mid-1990s, that despite very changed circumstances there is nothing new
under the sun. Indeed, from one of the many faces of the prism through
which the report can be viewed, its proposals for social security may best
be seen not as a great innovation but as an attempt at a knife-edge balance
between competing and quite possibly irreconcilable goals. Beveridge also
confronted a series of issues that neither he nor anyone in the succeeding
fifty years has managed satisfactorily to settle. Chief among this group
were: the seemingly easy question of what is meant by poverty; how to
cope with housing subsidy; and the treatment of women within the social
security system. Chief among the competing goals were the desire to
provide security as of right, set against incentives for work and saving;
and the balance between individual freedom and compulsion – compulsion
for the good of all and for the good of the individual.

It may be a truism, but before you can abolish poverty you have first
at some level to decide what you mean by it. Poverty was not a word
Beveridge used. Throughout the report he settled for the then common
synonym 'Want'. It was his bold claim that Want could be 'abolished'
which gave the report much of its popular appeal. As Tom Wilson put it,

'the general public understood what was intended, and that was enough to win their enthusiastic support.'[1] But poverty has to be defined, and a minimum income quantified, if it is to be avoided.

Beveridge's answer was a 'subsistence' income, a term he defined as meaning 'benefit adequate to all normal needs, in duration and in amount'.[2] He instantly conceded that there were 'unavoidable difficulties' in putting cash figures on such a concept. He had, none the less, to do so; and to set his benefit rates Beveridge drew extensively on the work of Seebohm Rowntree, the British Medical Association, a League of Nations study, and figures from the government-run Family Budget Survey which covered food, clothing, fuel, light, household sundries and rent. In several places the report suggests that the benefit levels he recommends are scientifically based,[3] and he specifically criticises the levels of benefit set before the war precisely because 'none of them were designed with reference to the standards of the social surveys.'[4] But his report is also full of the uncomfortable recognition that any definition of poverty is subjective. The science behind his benefit levels gave them some justification, but it remained an imprecise and subjective science.

Plainly a homeless, shoeless, starving figure in the December snows is poor. Victorian England had plenty of those, and many more people living at standards not much better. Rowntree and Booth in the 1890s did much to categorise and quantify what was only too plainly to be seen. Move much above that level, however, and poverty becomes subjective and relative. Even the precise amount of food needed to avoid poverty is open to argument, and it would be hard to contest that the poorest Edwardian slum dweller was not better off than the starving victims of Somalia's or Rwanda's wars in the 1990s. It was the rediscovery of this blindingly simple concept that was to put one of the final nails in the coffin of John Moore's career as Secretary of State for Social Services forty-seven years after Beveridge wrote his report.

Beveridge was well aware of the problem. 'Determination of what is required for reasonable human subsistence is to some extent a matter of judgement,' he conceded early in the report. 'Estimates on this point change with time, and generally, in a progressive community, change upwards'[5] – the very point with which John Moore was to have such difficulty. Equally, Beveridge conceded that neither could 'any single estimate, such as is necessary for the determination of a rate of insurance benefit, fit exactly the differing conditions of differing households'.[6] For all the evidence he cites for arriving at his cash benefits, there is no real attempt to hide the essential arbitrariness of the exercise. Time and again he uses phrases such as: 'It is reasonable to put the allowance for clothing as . . .'[7] or 'It is suggested that [a particular sum for other items] . . . should be adequate.'[8] The argument about whether his benefit scales, or those introduced by the Labour Government, actually provided a subsistence income, and whether mere subsistence – freedom from physical want – was in itself a sufficient goal, was to rage on long after his report was published.

There were other difficulties. People on his subsistence income might not necessarily spend their money with 'complete efficiency'. The basic calculations, he said, assumed that the recipient 'buys exactly the right food and cooks and uses it without waste. Some margin must be allowed for inefficiency in purchasing, and also for the certainty that people in receipt of the minimum income required for subsistence will in fact spend some of it on things not absolutely necessary.' He thus threw in a margin of 2s. od. for a couple and 1s. 6d. for a single adult.[9] In addition he touched on an issue which would grow in importance as even the full employment enjoyed in the post-war years failed completely to wipe out long-term unemployment.

> Strictly the figures for clothing and one or two minor items relate only to short periods of unemployment and disability, during which expenditure on renewals can be postponed; more will be needed in prolonged interruption of earnings. On the other hand, there should be room for readjustment in such matters as rent or retrenchment in the margin [the margin referred to above which allowed for inefficient or inessential spending]. On the whole, it seems fair to balance these considerations against one another and make no change in the benefit as between short and long interruption of earnings during working years.[10]

Beveridge, to be fair, stated quite openly that he was designing his system to cope with 'normal cases', a phrase he repeatedly used. He was bringing Churchill's 'magic of averages' to the average person. Insurance could not in fact cope with everything, and beneath the insurance plan there had still to be a safety net – National Assistance, or what has now become income support. That would still be needed 'to meet *abnormal* [my italics] subsistence needs'.[11] Under Beveridge's assumption of full employment, long-term joblessness would be abnormal.

Then there was rent, an issue which resolutely refused to be normal. In 1947 owner-occupiers made up just 26 per cent of households. A mere 13 per cent of households were council tenants, the remainder renting

privately in one form or another.[12] Then as now there were wide variations
in rent for the same quality and size of housing – more than a tenfold
difference. Beveridge struggled with whether to pay an average allowance
for rent. The effect of that would be to leave those in more costly homes
below subsistence level once they had paid it, and those in cheaper homes
than the average better off financially. The alternative was to pay rent in
full for pensioners and the insured unemployed as already happened for
those on means-tested national assistance. That, however, raised problems
of incentives, about which Beveridge was particularly hard-nosed when it
came to the elderly. If rent was met in full for pensioners, 'it will appear
indefensible that those who just before retiring have been able to secure
good accommodation at a relatively high rent should thereby retain this
advantage for the rest of their lives, in kind if not in cash, as compared
with those who have been less fortunate or less foreseeing. On the other
hand, if those who are already drawing pension on the basis of one rent
are free to move to more expensive accommodation and have their pension
increased accordingly, pensions will come to look like subsidies to landlords.' Had Mrs Thatcher's government in the 1980s taken a similarly
tough view, it would not have designed the poll tax specifically to take
account of little old Tory ladies rattling around on their own in large
houses from which their children had fled; and history might have been
different.

Rent was one of three 'special problems' Beveridge identified, and after
many hours of work and nine pages of discussion in the report, he recognised that he had failed to solve it – that it involved bigger questions such
as housing policy and the distribution of industry. Beveridge went for a
flat rate allowance within unemployment benefit,[13] admitting he was having 'to make the best of a difficult situation'. The Labour Government in
1948 dropped that idea and instead met actual housing costs, subject to a
means-test. How housing costs should be handled was to remain a permanent thorn in the flesh of the welfare state.

Women also posed problems, given the scheme Beveridge had devised.
Indeed in his original 'heads of a scheme' he acknowledged: 'The treatment
of married women is one of the most troublesome problems in social
security.'[14] Feminist writers (and not only feminist writers) have bitterly
attacked Beveridge for his views and recommendations. There is some
justice in that, but only some. The assaults tend to ignore that Beveridge
was of his time and that if he failed to foresee radical changes to come,
then that foresight was also denied to many others. In fact his recommendations did much to improve women's position. Before his report single

women enjoyed virtually the same right as men to unemployment benefits if in work, but only means-tested assistance if they had never worked or had not paid enough contributions. On marriage, women became 'adult dependants' on their husbands and, apart from the maternity grant, they had no rights under the health insurance scheme. 'None of these attitudes is defensible,' Beveridge declared.[15]

By the time he was writing, women were pouring into the workforce: an extra 1.8 million were recruited into industry alone between 1939 and 1943, in addition to those who joined the armed forces and took other work. In 1940, the qualifying age for their pension had been dropped to 60, to encourage them to undertake war work. It was the start of a dramatic change in women's role and status. But Beveridge shared the widespread assumption that after the war, as after the First World War, women would simply go home to be housewives. The 1931 Census (the most up-to-date figures Beveridge had available) showed that more than seven out of eight married women did not work. As he told the committee, 'provision for married women should be framed with reference to the seven rather than the one';[16] so he assumed in the report that 'during marriage most women will not be gainfully employed'.

Beveridge also shared another common concern. Britain was seen to have 'a population problem' – not as in the 1970s of potentially too many people, but of potentially too few. During the 1930s the birth-rate had fallen. In fact by 1942 it was rising, a product of a record number of marriages on the eve of war and a sharp rise in illegitimacy,[17] but Beveridge was not to know that. 'In the next thirty years,' he said in the report, 'housewives as mothers have vital work to do in ensuring the adequate continuance of the British race,'[18] adding later: 'with its present rate of reproduction, the British race cannot continue; means of reversing the recent course of the birth rate must be found.'[19] He not only expected married women to be housewives, he also wanted incentives for marriage and child-bearing. He therefore recommended a marriage grant (that was never implemented), maternity grant, maternity benefit for thirteen weeks for those in work, family allowances and widow's benefits; and in addition women and children were to fall within the ambit of the new, free, national health service. The package as a whole 'puts a premium on marriage, in place of penalising it', he declared.[20]

In addition to the cash that was to be paid as family allowances to ensure 'subsistence' both in and out of work, Beveridge also wanted to keep tax allowances for children. In that decision lay the seeds of the great Child Benefit battle. He in part wanted them retained because he held mildly eugenicist views. Although he did not say so in the report, he believed the tax allowance, which is worth more to the better off, would encourage the middle and professional classes – 'the more successful' in society, as he put it – to have more children.[21] (Similar reflections about the desirability of who should do the breeding were to sink Sir Keith Joseph's chances of leading the Tory party thirty-three years later.) He thus clothed his recommendations for women in pro-marital and pro-women rhetoric. Marriage gave women a 'new economic status' and they should thus begin 'a new life in relation to social insurance'.[22] Recognition that housewives performed 'necessary service not for pay' even led Beveridge, after much agonising about whether it would encourage family break-up, to recommend a rather unsatisfactory separation benefit to be paid when marriages broke down – unless, of course, the woman was the guilty party. This, too, was never implemented.

Beveridge did not formally oppose married women working. Indeed, he proposed benefits for those who did through a special lower rate of national insurance contribution which they had the choice of paying – although it produced lower unemployment and disability benefits as it was assumed that the husband would already be providing a home to live in. But work by married women was likely to be 'intermittent', Beveridge believed, and he did not see the income from it as a crucial part of the household's financial survival. All this stemmed from his view that benefits should provide only a basic income and that man and wife were 'a team'. Thus the woman's pension, and her entitlement to benefit during her husband's unemployment and disability, came from her share in that partnership. This even stretched to the old age pension being notionally cast as a pension for a couple that was reduced for single people, rather than being seen as a single person's pension to which extra was added for a dependant. Beveridge disliked the concept of wives as dependants, and he argued that his proposals ended that. The description 'adult dependant', he said, should be reserved 'for one who is dependent on an insured person but is not the wife of that person'.[23]

His concept of the married woman's role – and crucially his rhetorical recognition that she derived rights from her 'vital unpaid service'[24] – proved in tune with the times. Mass Observation recorded 70 per cent of women giving the report, with its recognition of the value of unpaid women's work, unqualified support.[25] Some did see through the rhetoric, recognising that the improvements Beveridge's proposals undoubtedly brought did not fundamentally change the married woman's position. Elizabeth Abbott and Katherine Bombas, for example, in a 1943 pamphlet for the Women's Freedom League, argued that 'the actual proposals . . . leave her as before, a dependant and not a partner'.[26]

In fact the framework Beveridge had chosen – a work-based scheme, founded on employee contributions – inevitably left women who did not work dependent on their husbands' contributions. The other failures of the scheme included its inability to deal adequately with the large post-war rise in single parenthood, divorce and separation, but to blame Beveridge for that is a little like blaming medieval armourers for not foreseeing the effects of gunpowder. In 1938 there were just 10,000 divorce petitions. By 1945 the number had increased two and a half times, but still only to 25,000[27] – a tiny fraction of the 160,000 divorces a year achieved in the mid-1980s.

Disability, too, presented difficulties. For those injured at work a separate industrial injuries scheme could be created. And for those not injured at work who simply became disabled, unemployment benefit was available if they had paid sufficient contributions. Others, however, would have to fall back on means-tested national assistance and local authority services. Carers do not feature in the report, in part because if married women are not expected in the main to work, they are there for other 'vital duties'. And Beveridge could not have foreseen the extent to which medical science would preserve life among many more people who acquired their disability at birth or in childhood and so never had the chance of qualifying for non-means-tested benefits through insurance contributions.

If these were the chief issues Beveridge failed to resolve – issues that are with us still – his report also reflects vividly the conflicting goals that ran through the debates about social security both before and after its publication. Throughout, he attempted to balance rights with duties, incentives against security, and individualism against collectivism. Thus he wanted as far as possible to have benefits paid as of right, without the means-tests which he said made help available 'only on terms which make men unwilling to have recourse to it'.[28] But he balanced that with the duty of having to contribute.

Benefit in return for contributions, rather than free allowances from the State, is what the people of Britain desire. This desire is shown both by the established popularity of compulsory insurance and by the phenomenal growth of voluntary insurance against sickness, against death and for endowment, and most recently for hospital treatment. It is shown in another way by the strength of popular objection to any kind of means test. This objection springs not so much from a desire to get something for nothing, as from resentment at a provision which appears to penalise what people have come to regard as the duty and pleasure of thrift, of putting pennies away for a rainy day. Management of one's income is an essential element of a citizen's freedom. Payment of a substantial part of the cost of benefit as a contribution irrespective of the means of the contributor is the firm basis of a claim to benefit irrespective of means.[29]

There was another reason why Beveridge went for an insurance system rather than a tax-based one. In the 1940s liability for income tax started much higher up the income scale than it does now. Many in the working class did not pay. As late as 1949 a single man did not start paying income tax until he was earning 40 per cent of average manual wages, while a married man with two children under eleven had to earn fractionally above average manual earnings to pay any income tax at all. Over the years, under governments of all colours, the income tax threshold fell as government spending – not just on the welfare state – expanded. By 1992, the equivalent percentages were down to below 25 per cent and 29 per cent respectively.[30] It is one factor that led lower earners progressively to question the value of the welfare state.

Beveridge was clear that he did not want a 'Santa Claus' state which appeared to give something for nothing, and in the 1940s a tax-based social security system would have been chiefly paid for by business, the then much smaller middle class, and those above them. What the less well paid did already have to find, however, were the existing national insurance contributions for the health and unemployment schemes. Unlike income tax, they were used to paying these. Indeed, Beveridge went to some lengths to suggest, with questionable accuracy, that the contributions he proposed amounted to 'materially' less in aggregate than the sums already paid out for national insurance contributions, for voluntary policies covering sickness, death and endowment, for hospital treatment policies and for medical fees.[31] It was another reason why he wanted 'Benefit in return for contributions, rather than free contributions from the State'. In suitably Thatcherite terms, he also argued that citizens 'should have a motive to support measures for economic administration' and 'should not be taught to regard the State as the dispenser of gifts for which no one needs pay'.[32]

Furthermore, Beveridge worried about incentives to work and to save and to encourage people to take responsibility for their own lives. 'The State in organising security should not stifle incentive, opportunity, responsibility; in establishing a national minimum, it should leave room and encouragement for voluntary action by each individual to provide more than the minimum for himself and his family.'[33] Indeed, in harsher words later in the report, he said that 'to give by compulsory insurance more than is needed for subsistence is an unnecessary interference with individual responsibilities'.[34]

Thus his whole scheme was built on a *minimum* income to provide subsistence, not on the model followed in most of Europe of providing earnings-related benefits. What Beveridge built was a platform on which everyone could stand, with a safety net below it in the form of means-tested national assistance for those who lacked the contributions to qualify. It was, however, a platform down to which anybody who was slightly better off fell if they became unemployed or disabled. He did not, as the continental countries did, attempt to build a system which maintained the individual's economic place in society, if only for a time. It was to be a minimalist, not a maximalist provision, one that left in Beveridge's word 'room' – in practice incentives – for those who could afford it to provide for themselves over and above the state scheme.

In addition, this minimum provision was to be based on flat-rate contributions in return for flat-rate benefits. Critics have since divined in this the basic flaw in Beveridge's grand design. He wanted to provide something that took people off means-tested benefits. But because he pitched his insurance benefits at subsistence level – a level that would only meet 'reasonable human needs' and even then only for 'normal' cases – the amount paid was little different from the sums provided by the safety net of means-tested national assistance. That had to be the case, unless those on national assistance were to be given less than enough to live on – too little to prevent Want. As a result, there was little in financial terms to make national insurance benefits more attractive. Their attraction lay in their being paid by right, without a means-test.

On top of that, however, Beveridge wanted not just flat-rate benefits, but flat-rate contributions in which everyone paid the same for the same cover. That meant the contributions had to be pitched low enough to be affordable by the low-paid. Such contributions, however, were simply not able to generate enough cash to pay benefits at well above the national assistance rates without either a large Exchequer subsidy, which did not appear politically achievable, or much heavier contributions from employers, which would simply be passed on in either lower wages or higher prices. In this way, the very solidarity Beveridge sought – everyone paying the same in return for the same benefit – helped undermine his aim of abolishing Want.

Beveridge's insistence on a minimum also came about because the man who once believed the unemployed needed the 'whip of starvation' to ensure economic advance,[35] still worried about work incentives. He in fact favoured, without listing it in his recommendations, a minimum wage. But at the same time he believed that 'the gap between income during earning and during interruption of earning should be as large as possible for every man.'[36] Again, this reinforced the argument for a minimum standard of benefit.

In line with his attempt to balance rights with duties, but also to keep people in touch with work, he recommended both a training benefit and arrangements that would be recognised by those who in the 1980s and 1990s called for American-style Workfare for the unemployed. He did so, however, in a context which was not implemented. For Beveridge recommended that unemployment benefit should be paid without time limit, not just for the first six months as was the case before he reported, nor for the twelve months that was actually implemented in 1948. To reduce someone's income just because they had been out of work for a certain period was 'wrong in principle', Beveridge said.[37] Most men would rather work than be idle. But the danger of providing adequate benefits indefinitely was that men 'may settle down to them'. Thus he said men and women should be 'required as a condition of benefit to attend a work or training centre' after six months, the requirement arriving earlier in times of good employment and later in times of high unemployment. The aim would be twofold: to prevent 'habituation to idleness' but also 'as a means of improving capacity for earning'. There was a clear precursor here for the gradual tightening of entitlement to benefit and the requirement for training and Re-start programmes that Lord Young, Patrick Jenkin and their successors were to introduce in the 1980s. Attaching such conditions to benefit, Beveridge also noted, would unmask malingerers, and those claiming benefit while working.

For young persons, Beveridge said, 'who have not yet the habit of continuous work the period [before training] should be shorter; for boys and girls there should ideally be no unconditional benefit at all; their enforced abstention from work should be made an occasion for further training.'[38] Neither of these work and training requirements was implemented: the full employment (indeed, labour shortages) of the 1940s and 1950s made them seem unnecessary. The recommendation that the young should be denied unconditional benefit would have to wait until the days of John Moore and Lord Young forty-five years later, with disastrous results for some.

*   *   *

In his report Beveridge attempted to reconcile a new universalism that did indeed stretch from the cradle to the grave – from maternity grant to funeral grant by way of all-in insurance – with incentives to work, to save and to take individual responsibility, while at the same time checking abuse. In so doing he redefined the social security debate, but also defined the battleground as it has been fought over ever since. The left would ever after be able to stress the universalism of Beveridge and his desire to end poverty through all standing together to help each other. The right would look at his insistence on leaving room for private initiative; that the state should not provide all, but only a basic minimum, and then in return for clear-cut duties. Each, over time, would issue calls to go 'Back to Beveridge': to which bit of Beveridge would depend on who was doing the calling.

The plan was indeed unconsciously eclectic in many of its underlying ideas. It contained bits of Socialism and bits of Conservatism in its liberal mix. The way in which its vision yoked together competing ideas into what appeared to be a coherent whole helps explain why it proved in the end acceptable to all political parties: it contained something for everyone. The flaws in its design, however, ensured there can never, in any pure sense, be a return to Beveridge. That is not just because he failed to design that unattainable goal, an ideal system. The rest of Europe, while taking in the main a different road from Beveridge's very British revolution, equally failed to design fault-free systems. Their route (generally earnings-related benefits linked to earnings-related contributions, often run locally or independently of central government and often through bodies more like friendly societies than the state) also ran into difficulties. Any social security system must generate conflicts between individual and collective responsibilities, between rights and duties, between incentives and security of income. It may never be got right once and for all; the balance will endlessly shift. And it was on to such shifting sands that Beveridge's report was launched. Before it came into effect, however, a general election had to be held.

Precisely how and why Labour won its unexpected landslide in 1945, producing the first ever majority Labour Government is outside the scope of this book,[39] but three quotations can explain it for present purposes. The first is from Lord Hailsham, recalling a conversation he had with a French officer in the Lebanon as early in the war as 1942, before he even returned for the Beveridge debate. The Frenchman

> remarked that it would be difficult after the war to avoid socialism. 'Au contraire,' said I, 'il sera impossible.'

'Pourquoi?'

'Parce qu'il est déjà arrivé.' In this I was not far wrong.[40]

The second source is Churchill to Lord Moran: 'I am worried about this damn election. I have no message for them now.'[41] At Walthamstow, near the end of the campaign, his worries were confirmed as for once he was booed into silence by a 25,000-strong crowd demanding 'What about jobs?' and 'What about houses?'[42]

The third quotation is also from Hailsham: 'Again and again during the 1945 elections I was greeted with voters who exclaimed to me absurdly: "We want Winston as Prime Minister, but a Labour government." When I explained patiently that that was the one thing they could not have, they were wont to reply: "But this is a free country, isn't it? I thought we could vote for who we want."'[43]

While the electorate might have trusted Winston, they chose, with memories of the 1930s still fresh, not to trust the Tories with the reconstruction of Britain, a project that involved much more than just Beveridge and his five giants. Before Labour took power, however, the foundations of post-war education – that most political of all the arms of the welfare state – had been laid.

PART II

THE AGE OF OPTIMISM

1942–51

CHAPTER 4

Butler – Education

> Upon the education of the people of this country the fate of this country depends.
>
> *Disraeli, quoted by R. A. Butler in frontispiece of the 1943 White Paper*
> *Educational Reconstruction*
>
> We are not likely to see another dissolution of the monasteries.
>
> *Professor H. C. Barnard, writing in 1947 on the public schools*

EDUCATION IS the most political of all subjects, for it is firmly about the future. It defines the sort of society people want to see. At one extreme, for those who believe that the next generation should be more equal than the present one, the demand is for equal access to equally good education for all – although furious arguments can then follow about what is meant at which stage of a child's life by 'equal access' and 'good', given wide variations in home background, income, aspirations and ability. At the other is a belief that there will always be inequalities and that it is better to organise for that reality, selecting out the high fliers to ensure that they do fly high and are thus able to support the mass for whom it might be safer all round if expectations were not too greatly raised. Education locks into a host of other issues. Should society be culturally or industrially equipped? Should important cultural, religious and economic differences between particular groups be sustained or suppressed? Should extra resources go into helping the least able, boosting the average or ensuring that the brightest are fully stretched? Should the ultimate aim of education be wealth creation, or should it simply be provided in its own right and for its own sake, to free people for the richer enjoyment of life through the knowledge, skills and concepts instilled?

Not all these conflicting objectives are necessarily incompatible all the time, but they do ensure that education is deeply political in the broadest, and far from purely party, sense. How it should be organised, what should be taught, how it should be taught, to whom and for what purpose, were to become some of the most closely fought issues of the modern welfare state. There is a certain irony, therefore, in the fact that education was the first of the five giants to be reformed, and reformed by a Conservative. In July 1941, R. A. ('Rab') Butler went to Downing Street to be appointed President of the Board of Education. His own account sets the scene:

The PM saw me after his afternoon nap and was audibly purring like a great tiger. He said, 'You have been in the House [of Commons] for 15 years and it is time you were promoted.' I said I had only been there for 12 years but he waved this aside. He said, 'You have been in the Government for the best part of that time [Butler was currently in the Foreign Office] and I want you to go to the Board of Education. I think you can leave your mark there. You will be independent. Besides,' he said with rising fervour, 'you will be in the war. You will move poor children from here to here,' and he lifted up and evacuated imaginary children from one side of his blotting pad to the other; 'this will be very difficult.' He went on: 'I am too old now to think you can improve people's natures.' He looked at me pityingly and said: 'Everyone has to learn to defend himself. I should not object if you could introduce a note of patriotism into the schools. Tell the children that Wolfe won Quebec.' I said that I should like to influence what was taught in schools but that this was always frowned upon. Here he looked very earnest and commented, 'Of course not by instruction or order but by suggestion.' I then said that I had always looked forward to going to the Board of Education if I were given the chance. He appeared ever so slightly surprised at this, showing that he felt that in wartime a central job, such as the one I was leaving, is the most important. But he looked genuinely pleased that I had shown so much satisfaction and seemed to think the appointment entirely suitable. He concluded the interview by saying 'Come and see me to discuss things – not details, but the broad lines.'[1]

Two days after taking over, Butler met the Archbishop of Canterbury. Three weeks later that was followed up by a session with a deputation of thirty-three Free Church and Anglican leaders with the Archbishop again at their head. They had come to discuss their 'five points', almost all of which related to religious education. Butler judged the meeting 'successful', finished it by asking a slightly startled Archbishop to close with a prayer,[2] and promptly went on holiday.

After more than forty years during which religion has ceased to be a central issue in British schools, an explanation is needed for Butler's holding his first substantive meetings with the churches. Until the 1830s schooling had been entirely voluntary with no state funding. A country that had produced Shakespeare, Milton, Newton and Smeaton and in the early nineteenth century had Faraday, Stephenson, Telford and Keats in its ranks had just four universities in Scotland and two in England – Oxford and Cambridge. Fewer than ten public (that is, private, fee-paying, boarding) schools were in existence, although there was a spread of endowed and often ancient grammar schools, private tuition, and small 'dame' schools taught by women in private houses. In addition, a little very rudimentary teaching for the young was provided in Sunday Schools or in elementary schools which were run by church-sponsored voluntary societies. In 1818 just 7 per cent of children attended day school. The beginnings of an educational movement were, however, under way, although there were still strong fears that 'too much education might lead to disaffection' in a society where the labour and service of the many supported the wealth and leisure of the few. Lord Melbourne, the Whig Prime Minister, famously told Queen Victoria in the late 1830s: 'I do not know why there is all this fuss about education. None of the Pagets [the Marquis of Anglesey's family] can read or write and they do very well.'

The industrial revolution, however, produced a demand for better educated workers to which the state was finally to respond. In 1833 a half-empty House of Commons approved a £20,000 grant for school building to help the two church-based school societies, one Anglican and one Free Church, which had been founded in 1811 and 1810 respectively.[3] The Anglican society's full title, The National Society for Promoting the Education of the Poor in the Principles of the Established Church, in a sense says all that needs to be said about education before 1830.

Parliament as a whole was barely interested. Although this was the moment when the state first became involved in any way in education, the government was still spending more in a year on the Queen's stables than on educating its children.[4] The church schools were helped because they were about the only people standing on the barren field; the Catholic schools were later also to receive funds. But by opting to subsidise church schools rather than create secular state ones, Parliament invested in a problem that Butler would still be grappling with more than a century later, for religious feeling ran high. Nonconformists bitterly opposed Anglican instruction in schools, as did Roman Catholics, and vice versa. Sir James Graham, the Home Secretary in 1841, was to complain bitterly: 'Religion, the Keystone of education, is in this country the bar to its progress.'[5] For the various church societies – Church of England, Roman Catholic and the Nonconformists embracing various brands of Methodists,

Quakers, Baptists, Congregationalists, Unitarians and others – went to war.

What was taught and how it was taught was not yet remotely the business of the government. What was taught was heavily biased towards the Bible. How it was taught was in many schools the 'monitorial' system: one teacher taught the older pupils who in turn taught the younger ones. Andrew Bell, the driving force behind the National Society, a bitter rival to the Quaker Joseph Lancaster who was patron of the British and Foreign, said: 'Give me twenty-four pupils today and I will give you twenty-four teachers tomorrow.' In this way a hundred children could be 'taught' by one master.[6]

Slowly, amid passionate rows between the various churches about who should be aided, and between all of the churches and those few who favoured state education about whether the godless state even 'had a right to educate', government aid spread to books, equipment and teachers' salaries. In 1839 the very first inspections carried out by Her Majesty's Inspectorate of Schools began. Scotland still had more universities than England (and proved better endowed in schooling also), but in 1825, in part because Nonconformists remained barred from Oxbridge (they were not admitted until the 1850s), London University was founded and 1833 saw the creation of the University of Durham.

Parliament's interest grew and Royal Commissions on Oxbridge, the elementary schools, endowed schools and the nine public schools followed in the 1850s and 1860s. In 1867 working-class men in urban areas, where schooling was least good, gained the vote, and in 1870, W. E. Forster produced his Elementary Education Act – introducing the first state schooling at a time when an estimated 700,000 children aged between six and ten were in school but an estimated one million were not.[7] Up to this point, as Derek Fraser nicely puts it, the only way to receive a state education was to be 'a cadet, a felon or a pauper' since the army, prison and workhouse did provide at least some schooling.[8]

Forster's Act, landmark though it was, merely tried in his own words to 'fill up the gaps'. 'We must take care . . . not to destroy the existing system in introducing a new one.'[9] It allowed school boards to be established in areas of clear need to provide elementary schools. The boards were financed by a mix of government grant and local rates and they were directly elected – the view having grown that a direct local interest in education was vital if progress was to be achieved. In this way, education became an interest of local government, although central government grants to the voluntary church schools continued. Schooling was still neither free (as it was already in the New England states of America) nor compulsory. The school boards could award free places, in Forster's words, 'to parents who they think really cannot afford to pay' and with government approval could even establish free schools 'under special circumstances' – in effect, chiefly in the poorest areas of large towns. While hinting that he personally favoured free schooling, Forster argued the Treasury's case that providing it for all would be 'not only unnecessary but mischievous. Why should we relieve the parent from all payments for the education of his child . . . the enormous majority of them are able, and will continue to be able to pay these fees.'[10] Parents were expected to find around a third of the cost of education. Subject in each case to parliamentary approval, the boards were also allowed to frame by-laws making education for five- to twelve-year-olds compulsory. Gradually they began to exercise this power. By 1876 half the population was under compulsion, and in 1880 school was made compulsory for all five- to ten-year-olds. For ten- to fourteen-year-olds the picture still varied widely around the country.

In theory, the new, non-denominational state schools were to complement the church ones, which in return for their grant now had to allow parents to withdraw their children from religious instruction. This was an attempt to settle the religous issue. In practice, as Harry Judge put it, 'in many places the parson and the school board glowered at one another, and fought for pupils and resources'.[11] A dual educational system, which duelled, had been created.

Meanwhile the public schools were expanding rapidly, catering for a growing middle class at a time of rapid economic expansion. Their ethos was stamped on them by Dr Thomas Arnold, headmaster of Rugby from 1827 to 1841. Correlli Barnett in *The Audit of War*, his assault on the causes of Britain's post-war decline, writes that Arnold:

> through the medium of disciples who went on from Rugby to become leading figures in other public schools . . . was more responsible than any other single person for the nature of later Victorian élite education and the character both of the revamped ancient public schools and all the numerous new ones that opened between 1840 and 1900 to cater for the swelling middle classes.[12]

That character was hierarchical, games-playing, privileged, classics-based, robust Christianity. The Clarendon Royal Commission on the public schools in 1864 complained that natural science was 'practically excluded' and that their education was thus 'narrower than it was three centuries ago'; this exclusion was 'a plain defect and great practical evil'.[13] Barnett argues that these public school attitudes transferred into the 'liberal' education of Oxford and Cambridge, based on 'Greats': mathematics, classics and philosophy. Not for them science, technology, the creation of wealth. The universities, John Stuart Mill said in 1867, 'are not intended to teach the knowledge required to fit men for some special mode of gaining their livelihood. Their object is not to make skilful lawyers, or physicians, or engineers, but capable and cultivated human beings.'[14]

Thus, Barnett argues, the combined impact in the mid-nineteenth century of the public schools and Oxbridge was that:

> Henceforward the British governing élite was to be composed of essay-writers rather than problem-solvers – minds judicious, balanced and cautious rather than operational and engaged; the temperament of the academic rather than the man of action. Moreover this was to be an élite aloof from the ferocious struggle for survival going on in the world's market place; more at home in a club or senior common room than a factory.[15]

Or, as Peter Hennessy has put it, the public schools' 'mid-nineteenth-century role has been depicted as doubly malign by continuing to misshape an old aristocracy based on blood and land while absorbing and equally deforming a new aristocracy sired by the sweat and money of the men who made Britain's and the world's first industrial revolution.'[16]

If that was what was happening to the élite, life was infinitely worse at the other end of the social scale. Another Royal Commission, this time on technical instruction, toured Europe to report in 1884 that schooling in Germany was 'over-whelmingly superior . . . the dense ignorance so common among workmen in England is unknown.' They added: 'Your commissioners cannot repeat too often that they have been impressed with the general intelligence and technical knowledge of the masters and managers of industrial establishments on the Continent.'[17]

As education was being studied, local government was being reformed and to answer these concerns in 1889 the newly created counties and county boroughs were empowered to provide technical education. By coincidence in 1890 a new tax on spirits was introduced. In one of the rare examples of the Treasury agreeing to an earmarked tax, it was persuaded to hand the proceeds over to the county schools. 'Whisky money' started to help finance secondary education. Meanwhile, in part as a result of the great burst of Victorian philanthropy, colleges that would become the redbrick universities of the great cities were being founded in Birmingham, Liverpool, Manchester, Bristol and Leeds, and in 1889 they received their first government grant, totalling £15,000.[18]

By the 1890s, however, the voluntary church-based schools were once again in financial difficulties. Because the board schools had access both to the rates and to government grants, the quality as well as the quantity of the education they provided was outstripping that of the church schools. Approaching half of the under-elevens were now in board rather than church schools and the boards had started to invest in post-eleven-year-old education.

Robert Morant, a young civil servant of the type it is doubtful that the service could tolerate today, believed Britain faced 'an educational emergency' and determined to sort out the ragged patchwork of provision. He was another friend of the Webbs and another product of Toynbee Hall. A former tutor to the royal princes of Siam, he became known in Whitehall as a 'magnificent hustler'. The difficulty was how to get his political masters to act. On Boxing Day 1898 he quietly slipped into his office for a clandestine meeting to persuade a London County Council official to bring a test case over whether school boards could legally fund secondary education under the 1870 Act.[19] The auditor ruled they could not: it was unlawful for a school board to fund anything other than elementary education. Politically, however, the demand for secondary education was such that it could not be halted. So by this conspiratorial sleight of hand Morant, of whom it was said, 'he was not unprincipled but he was unscrupulous',[20] got what he wanted – reform.

Arthur Balfour's 1902 Education Act created a Board of Education to replace the sub-committee of the Privy Council through which since 1833 money had been channelled to education, and a government minister was appointed as its President. The 2500 elected school boards were amalgamated into local education authorities which in turn became a full part of local government. They were given powers to fund education 'other than elementary'. Secondary and technical education could thus be provided, along with teacher training colleges. But the Act also ended central government grants to both the state and voluntary schools. The church schools would now receive their grants for current spending (they were to be entirely responsible for their own capital spending) from local government in return for one-third of the seats on their governing bodies.

The result was another explosion of sectarian religious feeling. There were bitter and opposing protests about 'Rome' and 'Canterbury' 'on the Rates', while some Nonconformists went wild. In Wales they threatened passive resistance and withheld their rates.[21] The Liberals exploited these divisions with 'splenetic fury' as a means of uniting their own supporters and the issue contributed to the Liberal landslide victory over the Tories in 1906. It was the election that first made Winston Churchill a minister and was a lesson he would never forget. The Act, however, produced 'a surge forward in secondary education comparable with that in elementary education after 1870'. External examinations were developed. County and county borough secondary schools grew apace along with the independent grammar schools, many of which became direct grant schools after 1907 when grants from the Board of Education were offered in return for a quota of 25 per cent free places.

In 1916, Lloyd George sent the European historian H. A. L. Fisher to Education and the 1918 Education Act finally abolished fees in elementary schools, raised the school leaving age to fourteen, and ensured that not less than half the cost of education was met from central government funds. Legislation allowing twelve- to fourteen-year-olds to work part-time in factories was repealed. Much of the education up to fourteen, however, was still in elementary schools, not in the secondaries or grammars. And Fisher's grander vision – allowing, but not compelling, local authorities to develop nursery schools and 'day-continuation schools' in which fourteen- to sixteen-year-olds would spend eight hours a week for forty weeks of the year – largely fell to the Geddes axe of 1922 which cut educational spending by about one-third. The mid-1930s economic crisis saw free scholarships to the selective secondary schools replaced by means-tested 'special places', although popularly these remained known as scholarships. While provision over the two decades did indeed grow, and various brave attempts to alter the shape of education were made, the effect of the economic blizzards was 'to freeze the educational pattern for much of the inter-war years'.[22]

Education, as Butler inherited it, looked broadly like this. Schooling up to fourteen was compulsory and free, with the great bulk of pupils staying in elementary or 'all age' schools until they left at fourteen (although many of the schools had developed junior and senior sections). Some stayed in the 'all age' schools until eighteen. In 1938, the last year for which there are pre-war statistics, 88 per cent of all pupils were in such schools.[23] A small group of brighter children, selected by examination at eleven, went on 'special place' scholarships to local authority secondary schools, many of which had been modelled on the independent grammars. Overall, just under half of their places (45 per cent) were free, the remainder being taken up by fee-payers arriving at ages between eleven and fourteen. The proportions in individual secondary schools varied enormously, however.

Independent of the local authority maintained sector were the public schools and the old endowed grammar schools; many of the latter now being direct grant schools, receiving financial help from the Board of Education in return for a proportion of free places. A variety of other types of assisted school also existed including commercial, trade, nautical and junior technical schools, and the 'central' schools, a mix of selective and non-selective municipal schools for eleven- to fifteen-year-olds. Private tutoring still flourished.

Very broadly – and it can only be very broadly – elementary schools catered for the working class up to the age of fourteen, a small proportion of these children escaping on scholarships into secondary education. Fees tended to exclude the working class who did not win scholarships. The secondaries mainly absorbed the lower middle-class children who stayed on either through scholarships or because their parents could pay, while the middle class and above could afford the independent grammars and public schools if their children did not win free places. Schooling reflected the gradations of society. The view of the Schools Inquiry Commission of 1868 that '. . . the different classes of society, the different occupations of life, require different teaching'[24] could still be seen in practice.

What all this meant has been chronicled by Corelli Barnett – 'that tireless enumerator of Establishment failings', in Peter Hennessy's phrase[25] – and by Brian Simon, the equally tireless educational historian. The vast majority of children left school at fourteen with no formal qualifications, exam passes or failures, of any kind. They 'were pushed off the plank straight into the job market'.[26] Of roughly 3.5 million children aged between thirteen and eighteen, only 470,000 or one in seven were in maintained schools, the great bulk of these leaving at sixteen. In 1938 a mere 19,000 stayed on until they were eighteen. Of these 'only 8000 emerged with the Higher School Certificate, the potential passport to university or other higher education' and just over half those actually got to university.[27] This 'half-cock' education system, in Barnett's phrase, most neglected the talent of working-class children, for all too few of them hurdled the obstacles into secondary education and then on to university.[28]

Of the 50,000 students in universities, just over half had started life in elementary schools. But overall it was calculated that one in 150 of the children in elementary schools reached university, against one in twenty for secondary schools and one in eight for the public schools.[29] Not only was class structure vividly reflected in British education, the nation's overall educational record had slipped against its competitors. In the mid-1930s, even if Scotland and Wales did much better, England had only one student at university for every 1000 of the population. In Germany the figure was 1:604, in France 1:480 and in the United States 1:125.[30] In addition, British university education remained heavily arts-dominated. Imperial in London was the only science and technology based college, and science and technology courses accounted for only 25 per cent of university students.[31] There were 149 technical colleges, but their full-time as opposed to part-time tally was only 9000 students. Of nearly three million fourteen- to eighteen-year-olds who had left school only one in twenty-five was on even a part-time course.[32]

This was the unimpressive educational record which Butler confronted in 1941, the war having only compounded the situation. School building had halted, while the evacuation programme had left 500,000 children in January 1940 getting no schooling at all.[33] Butler inherited, however (and Beveridge exploited), powerful movements for reform. In the Labour movement, R. H. Tawney's role was critical. Peter Hennessy describes him operating as 'a kind of tweedy one man pressure group, producing ideas through a haze of herbal tobacco smoke pushing them gently in one forum after another until they caught on'.[34] As early as 1922, under his influence, Labour published *Secondary Education for All*. In 1926 he was a member of the Board of Education's consultative committee which in the Hadow report produced the same target – secondary education for all from the age of eleven and the raising of the school leaving age to fifteen (legislated for in 1936, but defeated by the outbreak of war); in other words the creation of something much closer to modern primary and secondary education.[35] Secondary schools should be divided into selective grammars, promoting a 'literary or scientific curriculum', and non-selective secondary modern schools which would provide a more 'realistic or practical trend in the last two years'. Hadow was followed in 1938 by Spens, another Board of Education report, which recommended an end to fees in all state schools and a tripartite division of secondary education into grammar, secondary modern and technical schools.

So while little happened to change the pattern of education in the 1930s, the pressure for growth in provision, and for a change in its nature, was on. And as Butler took over there was one other factor. The public schools were in crisis both conceptually and financially. They had been under attack since the First World War. In 1929, Robert Graves in his autobiography *Goodbye to All That* excoriated Charterhouse and the 'fundamental evil' of 'what passed as the public school spirit'. By his account that included bullying, violence, adolescent homosexuality and a profound philistinism, despite a classics-based education, that left him with 'an oppression of the spirit I hesitate to recall in its full intensity'.[36] Graham Greene's symposium *The Old School* joined the assault in 1934 and demand for the type of education offered by public schools began to decline. In the summer of 1939, Harrow decided to close a boarding house, cutting its size from 600 to 500 pupils, and the *Journal of Education* predicted that some newer public schools would find it difficult to survive. They were being challenged by the 'improvement in the quality of instruction at ordinary secondary schools', and were in trouble. Their claim to 'a special fitness to rule' was attacked by Charles Douie, a former assistant prinicipal of University College London and old boy of Rugby, who said: 'I cannot believe that the England of tomorrow will tolerate privilege in education'.[37]

Faced by a mounting financial crisis, the public school heads turned for help to Sir Cyril Norwood, a former headmaster of Marlborough and Harrow, now chairman of the Secondary Schools Examination Council. He identified Harrow, Marlborough, Lancing, Tonbridge and Repton as public schools whose future was either under threat or in serious doubt[38] and began to explore with the Board of Education the possibility of public funding in return for access. In the *Spectator* in late 1939 and early 1940 he acknowledged the 'growing hostility' to public schools. 'It is hard to resist the argument that a State which draws its leaders in overwhelming proportions from a class so limited as this is not a democracy, but a pluto-democracy,' he said, 'and it is impossible to hope that the classes of this country will ever be united in spirit unless their members cease to be educated in two separate systems of schools, one of which is counted as definitely superior to the other.'[39] The defeat of the British Expeditionary Force in France brought forth powerful internal as well as external criticism. T. C. Worsley, a master at Wellington, railed: 'We are where we are, and shall be where we shall be, owing, largely, if not wholly, to the privileged education which the ruling classes have received in the last forty years.' He added: 'If the public schools are national assets because of their leadership training qualities, what are we to think of those qualities when we survey the mess into which their leadership has brought us?'[40] To achieve a 'common elementary education for all' would be a great advance. David Low's *Evening Standard* cartoons of Colonel Blimp, the epitome of the old school tie that had brought Britain through Munich to a war in which the early days saw nothing but defeat or the grimmest of survival, also helped damage the public schools' standing.

Churchill at times felt that change was not only inevitable but necessary.

He told the boys at Harrow in December 1940 that 'after the war the advantages of the public schools must be extended on a far broader basis.' Early in 1941 the *Sunday Dispatch* reported him as arguing that they should return to their long-forgotten original purpose of providing education for poor scholars, and David Chuter Ede, the Labour minister and education specialist who was Butler's number two, recorded in his diary in February 1942:

> The PM was glad to know that public schools were receiving our attention. He wanted 60 to 70 per cent of the places to be filled by bursaries – not by examination alone but on the recommendation of the counties and the great cities. We must reinforce the ruling class – though he disliked the word 'class'. We must not choose by the mere accident of birth and wealth but by the accident – for it was equally an accident – of ability. The great cities would be proud to search for able youths to send to Haileybury, to Harrow and to Eton.[41]

Butler's own attitude to public schools is defined by his biographer, Anthony Howard, as 'agnostic'. In early 1942 he told Chuter Ede both that 'he would not exclude a child because his parents could afford to pay but he would not admit a child who had fallen on his head while out hunting with the Quorn [the prestigious Leicestershire hunt]'. But he equally noted that the Conservative Party would be 'up in arms unless a boy could get into a public school on payment'. In April 1943 in a letter to his own son's housemaster at Eton, he said: 'I do not personally think that the whole of the public school system is necessarily the best form of education, particularly when there is too much worship of games and the herd spirit.'[42]

Perhaps unsurprisingly, Labour and every educational body on the left firmly wanted the public schools either brought into the national system[43] or simply abolished. So too did the local government officials who ran education. The Association of Directors and Secretaries of Education produced *A Plan for the Future* in 1942 that gave considerable prominence to the need to merge public and private education into one system. They sought 'a common system of education national in scope . . . free, compulsory and universal'.

Other forces were also at work. If *The Times* had gone pink, the *Times Educational Supplement* had gone almost revolutionary. Harold Dent, a former Leicester schoolmaster, had just become editor. During 'those war-torn years', the *TES* recorded in its 75th anniversary supplement,

'. . . H. C. Dent drove himself on all cylinders to take a lead in policy-making using a reinvigorated educational supplement as his vehicle . . . the *TES* became not just a forum for discussion of the nascent 1944 Act but a new kind of educational journal campaigning for a reform thorough enough to last beyond post-war euphoria.'[44]

Dent enunciated the principle of equality of opportunity in a series of powerful leading articles that coincided with both Butler's and Beveridge's appointments. What was needed was 'total reform based on a new conception of the place, status and function of education in a democratic State, not a patching and padding of the present system'. An opportunity was present 'which may not recur for centuries – if ever'. The present system, he said, 'has been a most effective safeguard of the social stratification we all in our heart of hearts bow down to and worship'. There would be 'the strongest and bitterest opposition' to change and those seeking it would need to be resolute – 'ruthless if need be'. He was to argue elsewhere, 'we can look for no permanent new order in society unless we have a new order in education.'[45] And in the final leader of the series, he declared, 'the full working out of the principle of equality of opportunity will involve changes in the social order extending far outside the field of education.'[46]

These changes were being born in the war, and Dent was far from unrepresentative. On 21 December 1940, the Archbishop of Canterbury, the Roman Catholic Archbishop of Westminster and the Moderator of the Free Church Federal Council wrote to *The Times* stating that the churches jointly sought, among other aims as 'the Foundations for Peace', the abolition of extreme inequalities of wealth and possessions, but also that every child, regardless of race or class, should have equal opportunities of education suitable for development of their particular capacities.

Meanwhile, the Board of Education's officials had not been idle. In November 1940, the board's permanent secretary Sir Maurice Holmes set up a planning group of senior officials, minuting that: 'It is clear from references in the press that other persons and bodies have ideas on post-war educational reconstruction and I think this is a matter in which the Board should lead rather than follow.'[47] With the approval of Herwald Ramsbotham, Butler's predecessor, who was eager to introduce reform, the officials (many of them evacuated to the Durley Dean Hotel in Bournemouth for the duration of war) drew up what became known from its cover as the 'Green Book'. It was meant to form the basis of preliminary talks with interested parties on a possible post-war educational settlement and was compiled under the direction of R. S. Wood, the board's deputy secretary. In January 1941 he minuted: 'we may assume that responsibility for the direction of the nation's effort in the immediate post-war years will remain in the hands of a National Government prepared to face radical changes in our social and economic system and contemplating not merely restoration or a return to normality, but reconstruction in a very real sense . . . while policies will have to command the support of the main elements in all parties, it is clear that the war is moving us more and more in the direction of Labour's ideas and ideals.'[48]

By June 1941 the Green Book was being distributed. It had the rubric 'highly confidential' stamped on its cover, but as one academic later observed, it was put about 'in such a blaze of secrecy that it achieved an unusual degree of publicity'.[49] One of Butler's early acts was to publish a summary of its contents and to disclose that an inquiry into a secondary school curriculum suitable for education up to fifteen was under way under Sir Cyril Norwood.

The man who at this point took over education was to become not only one of the dominant figures in post-war Conservative politics, but one of those who in the 1940s steered the Tories into the post-war Middle Way consensus. Already chairman of the Conservative Committee on Post-War Problems, R. A. Butler was thirty-nine at the time of his appointment. A man of urbane charm mixed with fierce intelligence and a certain telling asperity, he was the product of Marlborough and Cambridge. His father was Sir Monty Butler, an Indian civil servant from a long line of scholar-administrators who became Master of Pembroke College, Cambridge (Rab himself later becoming Master of Trinity). The family included a string of Cambridge dons, two headmasters of Harrow, a tradition of high-minded reformism and links across the breadth of British life. Butler's father-in-law, for example, was Samuel Courtauld, the reforming industrialist who had signed the National Policy for Industry produced just before the Beveridge report. Paul Addison judges that Butler 'understood the domestic consequences of the war better than any other Conservative minister'.[50]

His early meetings with the churches took place because they remained the great stumbling block to reform. Since the turn of the century the Church of England's role in education had declined, largely because of its need to match support from the rates with voluntary efforts. The number of schools it ran was down by a quarter to 9000, and the proportion of pupils it was educating had fallen by half to 20 per cent as local authorities built up the state schools. These, however, were concentrated in the more populous urban areas; many of the C of E schools were in villages where the local parson provided religious instruction and the local Tory squirearchy raised much of the funding. Often they were the only schools in such areas, causing resentment among Nonconformists and Catholics who were forced to subject their children to the firmly Anglican bent of much of the education.

The proportion of Nonconformist schools had also declined, but the Roman Catholic influence, by contrast, had strengthened. Their school total had risen by 200 to 1200 over the same period and they were educating, at primary or elementary level, 8 per cent of the children. Between them in 1939 the churches still ran more than half the schools in England and Wales, though catering for well under half the pupils. In almost every way, however, the 1,250,000 children in these voluntary schools were getting a worse deal than the 3,000,000 in state schools. 'Their buildings were older, their classrooms more antiquated, their amenities in every way inferior.'[51]

There were further complications. The 1926 Hadow report had been implemented to the extent that elementary 'all age' schools were in theory being reorganised into proper primary and secondary schools. That meant new buildings. But the churches had difficulty finding the necessary capital, so many of their schools remained small, inefficient and largely unreorganised, taking children up to fourteen and even older.[52] Any attempt to raise the school leaving age to fifteen or even – the ultimate aim – to sixteen was bedevilled by the churches' inability to find the capital to make that a reality. Any serious attempt at secondary education for all meant either providing much greater direct support for church schools, risking raising again the barely dormant cries of 'Rome and Canterbury on the rates', or asking the churches largely to withdraw from education after the age of eleven. They would not contemplate the other possibility – handing over their schools wholesale to the state. As Butler put it, 'educational progress would not be possible unless the problem of the Church schools could be solved.'[53]

Furthermore, denominationalism put restrictions on teachers. Chuter Ede, for example, a man nearing sixty who had lived through the school religious strife of the first decade of the twentieth century, had been born a Unitarian, but had been taught in a Church of England school. He went on to become a teacher, and both managed a C of E school and had been chairman of the county council which helped finance it. But short of changing his religion he could never hope to teach in it. The Free Churches and the increasingly influential and organised National Union of Teachers, whose roots lay in the elementary schools, wanted all schools transferred to direct local education authority control, with the Free Churches favouring Christian instruction but insisting it must be firmly non-denominational.[54]

Well though Chuter Ede understood it, Butler may not have appreciated at first quite how viciously this hornets' nest could sting.[55] On 12 September 1941, shortly after his return from holiday, Butler sent Churchill a note, reminding him of his offer of advice, and proposing a major education Bill. He listed the main issues to be solved:

> There is, first, the need for industrial and technical training and the linking up of schools closely with employment. Secondly, a settlement with the Churches about Church schools and religious instruction in schools. Both these questions are nationwide. Thirdly, there is the question of the public schools, which may easily raise widespread controversy.[56]

Had Butler achieved this agenda, Correlli Barnett would have been a happier man and Britain perhaps a more prosperous place. Churchill, however, who had in part been made a minister by the religious controversies in education in the first decade of the century, reacted as though he had been himself been stung. The next day (a Saturday) he promptly minuted Butler:

> It would be the greatest mistake to raise the 1902 controversy during the war, and I certainly cannot contemplate a new Education Bill. I think it would also be a great mistake to stir up the public schools question at this present time. No one can possibly tell what the financial and economic state of the country will be when the war is over. Your main task at present is to get the schools working as well as possible under all the difficulties of air attack, evacuation, etc. If you can add to this industrial and technical training, enabling men not required for the Army to take their places promptly in munitions industry or radio work, this would be most useful. We cannot have any party politics in wartime, and both your second and third points raise these in a most acute and dangerous form. Meanwhile you have good scope as an administrator.[57]

Butler records: 'Sir Maurice Holmes took the Prime Minister's minute as a veto on education reform and wrote me a philosophic letter,' one Butler later described as 'disappointingly compliant'.[58] It is a masterpiece of Mandarinese.

> R. S. Wood and I have discussed the PM's minute to you. I do not think we need be unduly cast down. It seems to me axiomatic that a major measure of educational reform will be demanded in quarters which make

the demand irresistible, and the question then is not whether but when such reform will be brought about.

And there are, I feel, some advantages in having more time than ever your revised programme contemplated for reaching the greatest common measure of agreement on the more contentious issues, so that from this point of view the PM's frigid reception of your proposals has its brighter side.

However, if educational legislation is to be shelved till the war is over, we shall then be able to think more clearly in terms of bricks and mortar than is possible while the war is in progress, and so form reasonably sound estimates of the dates when this and that measure of reform can become operative. The delay is of course disappointing, particularly to those of us who, like myself [Holmes was 57], cannot hope to accompany you into the Promised Land, but that you will lead the Children of Israel there, I do not doubt.[59]

Butler, fortunately for the nation's children and the Conservative Party's future, was made of sterner stuff. In his memoirs he records: 'Basing myself on long experience with Churchill over the India Bill [the great man had initially refused to contemplate Indian independence, only finally to embrace its inevitability], I decided to disregard what he said and go straight ahead. I knew that if I spared him the religious controversies and party political struggles of 1902 and side-tracked the public schools issue, I could win him over. I intended to have an Education Bill.'[60] He spent the next eighteen months attempting to do just that. 'It was the religious issue that took the time,' Butler later wrote.[61] The one weapon he had to hand was the state of the church schools. The one solution available for the religious teaching controversy was something called the 'agreed syllabus' originally drawn up in Cambridgeshire in 1924 by a committee of Anglicans, Free Churchmen and teachers to provide religious instruction in the county's schools. By 1942 more than 100 of the 400 local education authorities were using it. The syllabus was sufficiently non-denominational to keep the Nonconformists happy, while sufficiently C of E to allow some Anglican school managers to hand their schools over to the local authority in return for a promise that the agreed syllabus would be used.[62] Churchill became intrigued by it, dubbing it 'the County Council Creed'. But while some Anglicans were happy to live with it, others were not and the Roman Catholics disliked it, Cardinal Hinsley, the head of the Catholic Church in Britain, dubbing it 'disembodied Christianity'.[63]

Early talks with the churches did not go well. The Roman Catholics were adamant about retaining their own schools, arguing they paid rates and taxes for the upkeep of local authority schools 'which their consciences would not let them use' while having spent millions over the decades to provide their own. 'They were determined they would not be lost now,' Butler records.[64] On the Anglican side, the Archbishop of Canterbury was Cosmo Gordon Lang, seventy-seven years old and chairman of the governors of Charterhouse. In November 1941 he made Butler apprehensive by insisting that the future of the public schools was of 'paramount importance'. It was therefore a considerable relief to Butler that Lang retired within six months. Churchill replaced him with William Temple, despite the new archbishop's leftish leanings (apart from popularising the term 'welfare state' he had once, for seven years, been a Labour Party member). In Conservative circles 'his political tendencies were suspect,' Butler said in his memoirs, recording Temple as being 'physically obese, but intellectually and spiritually a first-class athlete . . . we have few bishops today who could hold a candle to him.'[65]

Temple, at sixty-one, 'looked exactly like one of Dickens's true philanthropists; a portly, chubby-faced, twinkling-eyed, bespectacled figure with a gusty laugh, exuding goodwill from every pore,' according to Angus Calder. 'Buoyantly self-confident, utterly serene in his acceptance of his mission of leadership, Temple himself had never known doubt or want.' The son of a former Archbishop of Canterbury, he had 'easy brilliance' and 'far from being an impassioned extremist' he was the 'quintessence of compromise'.[66] At the age of twenty-eight he had become headmaster of Repton, but from twenty-seven for sixteen years he had been president of the Workers Educational Association, the 'working class university' which ran part-time, weekend and factory-based lectures and courses. Sir Maurice Holmes's prescient judgement was that his appointment to Canterbury offered 'a chance of getting the Church of England into play'.[67] Without him, the religious settlement in the 1944 Act may well not have happened. Temple and Butler's rapport was one of those occasions when personalities, whether they gel or clash, matter in politics.

What tipped Temple to his side, according to Butler, was a meeting at the Board of Education's Kingsway headquarters in the summer of 1942, not long after the Archbishop's appointment, 'one hot morning in the conference room, its windows blitzed out and covered with cardboard, no air in the room'.[68] Butler described to Temple the Board of Education's 'Black List', the list of physically seriously substandard schools to which Chuter Ede had drawn his attention.[69] Of the 731 on the list, 543 of them were church schools – perhaps not surprising when more than 90 per cent of the church schools were over forty years old and the churches alone were responsible for capital spending. Butler records that Temple was moved by the figures and 'said he had not realized what a bad state the church schools were in'.[70]

In essence, Butler put it to him that the Church of England could continue to maintain its schools only at the expense of the children within them.[71] The Archbishop agreed to back Butler's subtle but effective scheme for solving the issue, which appeared to offer the church schools a choice. They could become either 'controlled' or 'aided'. If controlled, the local education authority would take over all the schools' costs, appoint almost all teachers and have a majority of managers or governors, while undertaking to use the 'agreed' religious syllabus. If aided, the LEA would provide running costs, but the church managers would be responsible (with a 50 per cent government grant) for bringing buildings up to standard. The managers would then retain the right to appoint teachers, control religious instruction and have a majority on the managing or governing body. Controlled status met the objections of the Free Churches over denominational teaching while reassuring Anglicans – or at least low church Anglicans – about the continuing Christian nature of the teaching. Butler's own judgement was that 'for the plan to succeed Anglican schools would have to opt for controlled status in large numbers.'[72]

Temple argued publicly for the plan, using the scale of the financial challenge facing the church to help win round the Church Assembly. The church school societies and the Catholics had yet to be brought into line, however, the Catholics arguing that the 50 per cent grant was not enough. Butler put his considerable personality to work in a series of formal and informal meetings to settle the issue; at one point he went to stay at Leicester with Sir Robert Martin, a key figure in the National Society, where he 'sat with him at The Brand [a public house] until a late hour' persuading him of the viability of his proposals. The Roman Catholics proved a tougher nut to crack, despite what Butler called his 'wanderings' – repeated private visits to their homes and cathedrals. He complained in his autobiography that one of the chief problems was that they had 'no special leader; those at the summit were very old and it was difficult to establish any personal contact.' He later blamed himself for his failure to find 'one man of dignity and reliability with whom one can perpetually be in touch on a personal basis'.[73]

This was not all Butler's fault. While the other churches would meet him jointly, the Catholics would not. Butler recalled meeting Archbishop Amigo of Southwark in November 1942:

After much sounding of the bell, a sad looking, rather blue faced Chaplain let me in and we climbed a massive palace stair to the first floor where the Archbishop was sitting, fully robed, in a small room overlooking the ruins of Southwark Cathedral. His window was wide open on his left hand so that he could at once take in the tragic picture of the ruins and inhale the chilly morning air.

The Archbishop asked immediately we had sat down what I had come to see him for. I obliged by informing him; but it was not an auspicious beginning. He said that a 50 per cent grant was not sufficient and that he saw no chance of agreement with politicians . . .

This interview indicated the nature of the head-on collision with the Roman Catholic Church.[74]

From time to time, according to Butler, various Catholic bishops would back his plan in private. 'But in the event none of them attempted to control their own supporters, believing that their anxieties justified them in encouraging a fuss.'[75] Indeed, they went to public war in letters to The Times and elsewhere. Churchill eyed the row with a mixture of delight and real concern. When Cardinal Hinsley wrote to The Times on 2 November 1942 insisting on the independence of Catholic education, and declaring that 'no political party will seek to be able to, or be able to set at naught the respect of the British people for minorities', Churchill cut it out and sent it round to Butler pasted to a piece of cardboard with the message, 'There you are, fixed, old cock.'[76] Butler also described Churchill ringing him up to complain that 'you are landing me in the biggest political row of the generation'.[77] He was to record acidly in his memoirs that Churchill's interest in education was 'slight, intermittent and decidedly idiosyncratic'.[78]

Butler continued preparing his Bill regardless, but the Cardinal's letter scotched any hope of a commitment to legislation in that autumn's King's Speech.[79] Butler's dedication to education, however, was demonstrated at this point when he turned down the post of Viceroy of India, just as Chuter Ede, who is something of an unsung hero of the Education Act both as an able and immensely knowledgeable deputy to Butler and as the key conduit to Labour MPs, had turned down a move from Education in the February of the same year. In part what saved Butler was the Beveridge report, published exactly a month after the Cardinal's letter. Beveridge in his grandiloquent aside had sought the destruction of the giant Ignorance. The report may have had enemies in high places, but the sense that some measures must be taken grew. Education proved to be the card the

Conservatives could play, if not to divert the pro-Beveridge forces, at least to appease them. Butler had already found encouragement from Sir Kingsley Wood, the Chancellor, who had told him in September that he 'would rather give money for education than throw it down the sink with Sir William Beveridge'.[80]

If the churches had to be tackled, the public school issue too had to be settled. Butler started off talking to their Governing Bodies Association, undertaking direct negotiations with them as he did with the churches. Quite how far he was prepared to go remains unclear even now, and in his autobiography he is surprisingly coy on the subject. Whatever happened, in Anthony Howard's judgement, 'politically at some point his nerve failed him' and in June 1942 he kicked for touch, setting up an independent inquiry under the Scottish judge Lord Fleming, a move that Butler said 'temporarily removed the fuse' from the issue.[81] Quite why he did so has to be the subject of speculation. But Churchill's original note forbidding an education Bill in September 1941 had expressed alarm that stirring up a public school issue which Butler himself had said would cause controversy would be 'a great mistake'. Butler knew the religious issue, though not central to education *per se*, had to be settled to get secondary education for all; and some in the Church of England whom Butler desperately needed as allies were themselves strong proponents of the public schools, including Dr Geoffrey Fisher, Bishop of London, like Temple a former head of Repton and the man who was to succeed him as Archbishop of Canterbury. In early 1942, in Anthony Howard's phrase, he had produced 'ominous rumblings' on the preservation of the public schools. For Butler, settling the churches was plainly more central than settling the public schools.

At any rate, Fleming was appointed in June along with twenty members and three Board of Education assessors, with relatively lily-livered terms of reference 'to consider means whereby the association between the public schools and the general educational system of the country could be developed and extended'. In the Commons, Butler was even vaguer, saying the inquiry would investigate 'how the facilities of a boarding school education *might* [my italics] be extended to those who desired to profit by them, irrespective of their means'. Press reaction was mixed, the *Manchester Guardian* declaring it would be 'disastrous if it confined itself to schemes for providing free places in boarding school', adding that 'the nation is ready for daring and imaginative treatment of its problems.'[82] The *Daily Express*, however, plainly believed real action was planned, announcing that a 'public school revolution' was under way.[83]

The committee's membership was a distinctly mixed bag including Robert Birley, headmaster of Charterhouse and a future head of Eton, who had already suggested to the Board of Education that his pupils in future might be 50 per cent state aided and 50 per cent fee-paying. There were three more public school heads and the headmistress of Roedean; Dr Geoffrey Fisher; two local government specialists, the chairman of Lancashire Education Committee and the chief education officer of the West Riding; G. D. H. Cole; and two trade unionists.

Butler in his memoirs says he had been told that 'Fleming was a distinguished Scottish judge who could be relied upon to provide impartiality; I had not been prepared for the limitations of his views or for the humourlessness with which he gave them rein.' After two years' work Fleming produced what Butler judged to be a 'sensationally ingenuous' report.[84] Its recommendation was that LEAs could, if they wished, offer a 25 per cent share of places, to be paid for out of the rates, at public schools willing to allocate such places. It thus, in Anthony Howard's phrase, depended on 'two-way traffic: a local authority ready to make a heavy investment in individual pupils rather than in a collective facility like a school swimming bath, and a headmaster or a governing body prepared to accept such "guinea pigs" as part of the school's regular entry.'[85] Moreover, Fleming's report was not handed over until two months after the education Bill's third reading and a mere week before Royal Assent. As Butler put it, 'the first-class carriage had been shunted on to an immense siding'.[86]

A version of Fleming was later enacted, but the public schools' financial crisis had eased, and as Howard records the scheme soon foundered, 'with public school headmasters making only a token obeisance in its direction and local education authorities, in the period immediately after the war, becoming increasingly reluctant to favour a particularly bright child as against the general mass of run-of-the-mill pupils in their care'.[87] By 1948 a mere 155 places had been taken up by local authorities under the Fleming scheme.[88]

Fleming has been judged by many as a great lost opportunity. The combination of financial crisis in the public schools themselves and widespread criticism of their role and performance in the early 1940s provided the only time in the twentieth century when the political will and political votes to integrate them into the national education system just might have been assembled. Instead the public schools and private schooling were to remain a running sore in the education debate, poisoning arguments about the class-bound nature of Britain and equality of opportunity for ever and a day. Anthony Howard believes it was Butler's 'one real failure in his general strategy for educational reconstruction'. Butler, he says, was enough of a meritocrat not to approve of birth alone providing the winning educational ticket, and 'he was quite enough of a central planner to realise just what the eventual impact of the withdrawal of the top 5 per cent of parents from a national structure of secondary education would be. He needed them to be involved, as he confessed in old age, if only to make sure, through their influence and articulacy, that standards in the State sector were kept high . . . The time was ripe, the public mood was propitious, the opportunity was there. And yet he contrived to throw it all away.'[89]

While Butler was manoeuvring his way through the church and public school problem, Sir Cyril Norwood had been at work on the secondary school curriculum. His report in 1943 followed Hadow, Spens and the Green Book in confirming the expected divide of secondary education for all into three different types of school: selective grammars, selective technical schools, and secondary moderns. It did so in language that in later years was to have an uncomfortably patronising ring.

Like Gaul, the committee believed that children were divided into three parts. Those 'interested in learning for its own sake' who could 'grasp an argument' and care 'to know how things came to be as well as how they are'. A pupil who 'will have some capacity to enjoy, from an aesthetic point of view, the aptness of a phrase or the neatness of a proof' who can take 'a long view and hold his mind in suspense'. Those were the grammar school children who would 'enter the learned professions', or take up 'higher administrative or business posts'.[90] The technical schools would be for children whose abilities 'lie markedly in the field of applied science or applied art . . . to prepare boys and girls for taking up certain crafts — engineering, agriculture and the like.' The secondary modern was for the pupil who 'deals more easily with concrete things than with ideas. He may have much ability but it will be in the realm of facts . . . He may see clearly along one line of study or interest and outstrip his generally abler fellows in that line; but he often fails to relate his knowledge or skill to other branches of activity. Because he is interested only in the moment he may be incapable of a long series of interconnected steps; relevance to present concerns is the only way of awakening his interest, abstractions mean little to him . . . he may or may not be good with his hands or sensitive to music or art.'

Much of this argument was based on the IQ work of the 1920s and 1930s, which was not uncontroversial even at the time. Its leading exponent was Sir Cyril Burt, the educational psychologist, some of whose work was later to be discredited as fabricated. He had been an adviser and witness to the Hadow and Spens inquiries and was Professor of Psychology at University College London. Sir Toby Weaver, a future deputy secretary at the Ministry of Education when the official mind on these issues had changed in favour of comprehensive schools, characterised this as 'a general belief, I believe totally false, that children were divided into three kinds. It was sort of Platonic. There were golden children, silver children and iron children.'[91]

The Norwood report was anxious not to make this division at eleven-plus rigid. The schools should have 'such parity as amenities and conditions can bestow', and from 'one type of education to another there should be ease of transfer, particularly, though not exclusively, in the early stages, for the transition from primary to secondary education is not a break but a process.' Particularly at thirteen-plus the peformance of children should be 'sympathetically and skilfully reviewed'.

But while the Board's official mind was on a tripartite system, the stream which would in time become the comprehensive river was already running. At this point the term usually used was 'multilateral' and its definition was not always clear. To some it meant three types of school on one site, not one comprehensive school. The Spens committee in 1938 (Sir Will Spens was a former tutor of Butler's at Corpus Christi College, Cambridge) had considered multilaterals but had 'reluctantly' come down against them. They would need to be big – 'say 800 [pupils] or possibly larger' – which would mean much new and expensive school building. 'We cannot therefore recommend the general creation of multilateral schools, even as the goal of a long range policy.' Spens was firm, however, that 'parity between all types of secondary school is a fundamental require-ment': the same teachers' pay, class sizes, and building requirements until the sixth form, that is, post-sixteen education, was reached. 'The multi-lateral idea, though it may not be expressed by means of the multilateral school, should in effect permeate the system of secondary education as we conceive it.'[92]

Some of the left had latched firmly on to the multilateral idea. The Labour-controlled London County Council declared against segregated sec-ondary schooling as early as 1935 and by 1944 was including comprehen-sives in its post-war development plan. Harold Dent of the *Times Educational Supplement* declared in his 1942 book *A New Order in English Education*: 'I am utterly opposed to the idea of segregating adolescents in different types of school.' He recorded 'at least a strong minority opinion (latterly growing increasingly in strength) among educationists in favour of the "multi-lateral school", ie the single school with a wide enough range of activities to meet the needs of all pupils.'[93] And in the same year the National Association of Labour Teachers persuaded the Labour Party Conference to call on the Board of Education 'to encourage as a general policy, the development of a new type of multilateral school'.[94] But the idea, as yet, was still being formed. It did not command mass support. For many Labour MPs and councillors, equality of opportunity lay in ending fee-paying in grammar schools, thus opening them up to bright working-class children.

As these arguments proceeded, Beveridge finally gave Butler the chance to get his Bill. Called down to Chequers in March 1943 by Churchill to help prepare his 'After the War' broadcast – the one which committed Churchill in principle to 'cradle to grave' social security and much else beside – Butler seized Winston's new willingness to talk about post-war reconstruction and told him that he was drafting legislation. 'To this he paid no attention at all. I repeated in a louder voice, "I am drafting an Education Bill." Without raising his head from the papers before him on the counterpane, he said simply that I must show him my plans when they are ready and that he was sure they would be very interesting. I gladly left it at that.' Butler promptly went to see the Treasury ministers and assured Sir Kingsley Wood and later his replacement Sir John Anderson that, despite the enormous capital and current spending involved in his plan, 'full implementation would take at least a generation.' They therefore became 'reasonable and helpful' over finance, agreeing with Churchill that education was 'the lesser evil than the Beveridge scheme'.[95] In addition, no other minister on the home front had plans ready to launch – the advantage of Butler's two-year run-in.

In June 1943 a White Paper was published,[96] a few days later the Norwood report unsurprisingly supported its proposals, and in January 1944 the Bill, unaltered in substance from the White Paper, was given its second reading. James Stuart, the chief whip, saw the beauty of its 122 clauses and eight schedules being that 'it would keep the parliamentary troops thoroughly occupied; providing endless opportunities for debate, without any fear of breaking up the Government.'[97] Controversy remained over the church schools, particularly from the Roman Catholics. But Butler records that 'despite the anxiety raised by this opposition, indeed largely because of it, there was a desire on the part of both government and back-benchers to get this matter out of the way before an election.'[98]

The second reading proved placid and the Bill went into a committee of the whole house, to keep those MPs occupied. It took eight days to get through the first twenty-seven clauses, the closest call being when a Conservative, Mrs Thelma Cazalet Keir, tried to write in a date for the school leaving age to rise to sixteen. It was to be 1972 before that was finally achieved.

When trouble came, it proved to be not over the churches but over equal pay for women teachers. Butler opposed this measure, mindful of Churchill's and the Treasury's insistence on minimising cost. He attempted to justify his opposition by arguing that there would be widespread knock-on effects on civil service pay. Mrs Cazalet Keir, however, who managed the not inconsiderable feat of being both a Christian Scientist and teetotaller, and a member of the Tory Reform Group dining club, persuaded the group to back her amendment on equal pay which also gained much Labour support. The government, with some of the 'less sprightly ministers' failing to get out of Whitehall and into the division lobbies in time, went down by one vote – 117 to 116 – the coalition's only significant defeat of the war years. Churchill, who felt that too much was being taken for granted about winning the war and who was irked at the continuing loss of by-elections, resolved to 'rub the rebels' noses in their mess'. With Labour ministers such as Bevin and Ede threatening their own side with resignation if the government lost, a confidence motion reversing the defeat was tabled. Churchill, needless to say, got a thumping majority.

But the government's stance had two effects. Butler calculated that Churchill's use of the brute club of a confidence vote paid 'a handsome dividend': 'thereafter no member proved so bold as to press an amendment which was unacceptable to the Government if there was any prospect of its being carried.' That gave the remaining more controversial parts of the Bill an easier passage.[99] Historians believe its other effect, however, was that, like the Beveridge vote, it contributed to Labour's landslide the next year. Even the *Economist* at the time said it would reinforce the number of electors who 'suspected that the Government was ruthlessly obstructing reform'.[100]

In his memoirs Butler accused Quintin Hogg and the Tory reformers of an 'overweening attitude', describing the vote as 'that fateful night',[101] while twenty years on again Quintin Hogg replied in his that the issue was about equal pay for women teachers' equal work. 'Even now I feel it difficult to see how any sane man or woman with an eye to the future, let alone the politically sensitive R. A. Butler, could have disagreed with Thelma or with us.' It seemed 'an elementary piece of social justice' which needed to be agreed 'if only as an example of the line which was expected to be taken in social policy after the war, and which was in fact so taken . . . the episode was bad for Churchill, bad for Rab, bad for the Conservative party and bad for Britain.'[102]

That alarm over, the Bill proceeded smoothly, the third reading turning 'almost into an embarrassing *festschrift*'. Sir Edward Campbell, the rather obscure Tory MP for Bromley said: 'We called the old Act, the Fisher Act. How are we going to remember this Bill? Shall we not call it the Butler Act?'[103] So indeed it became. Churchill telegraphed his congratulations to Butler as it became law in August, telling him he had won 'a lasting place in the history of British education'.[104] The first of the five giants designed to combat Beveridge's giant evils was in place. Implementation had barely started a year later, however, when this large step towards post-war reconstruction proved insufficient to persuade the electorate to trust the Tories with the rest of the task.

CHAPTER 5

Butler's legacy

It shall be lawful for His Majesty to appoint a Minister whose duty it shall be to promote the education of the people of England and Wales and the progressive development of institutions devoted to that purpose . . .

Education Act 1944, first sentence

The effect as I see it will be as much social as educational. I think it will have the effect of welding us all into one nation, when it's got thoroughly worked out, instead of two nations as Disraeli talked about.

R. A. Butler, speaking about the Education Act in a Central Office of Information film, 1944

B UTLER'S ACT was indeed a mighty creation. 'To make a précis of it would take at least as long as to play a football match,' Butler observed.[1] It was, however, to prove as important for its omissions as its achievements, although those were numerous. First it settled, apparently once and for all, the religious question – though not quite in the way Butler and the Board of Education expected. Their original calculation was that only 500 of the 9000 Anglican schools would opt for what was from their own point of view the more costly independence of 'aided' rather than 'controlled' status. In fact 3000 chose the aided route.[2] But the settlement, of which the Catholics soon took advantage without ever formally accepting it, did effectively remove religion as a central educational issue. Not until Kenneth Baker's 1988 Education Act introduced opted-out grant maintained schools and Muslims began seeking their own state-funded schools did religious instruction again reach the centre of the debate.

The Bill made secondary education to fifteen a reality for all, and made it free. Tuition fees in all maintained schools were abolished. The sole exceptions were the 'direct grant' independent grammars which were still able to charge fees for the non-state-aided places. The words 'elementary schooling' were consigned to the historical dustbin, although achieving the end of these 'all-age' schools would take a distressing twenty years finally to complete. Formal distinctions linking teachers' salaries to the funding of different types of secondary school were in theory abolished, in practice made less stark. Free school milk, meals, transport and medical inspections, plus improved inspection procedures were all legislated for, and the obligations and powers of local education authorities to provide scholarships for higher education (student grants) were extended. Independent schools for the first time had to register and face inspection. In general, pupils were 'to be educated in accordance with the wishes of their parents' – a vaguely delineated and heavily circumscribed right for parents to choose their child's school which would grow into a major battleground.

Local authority control of education was rationalised, the number of authorities involved falling from 400 to 146 in England. The smaller boroughs, known as 'Part III' authorities, which controlled only elementary schools lost the right to do so. Primary, secondary and further education, 'a continuous process conducted in three successive stages', became the responsibility solely of counties and county boroughs. A new set of central powers was created for a new Minister of Education 'to secure the effective execution by local authorities, under his control and direction, of the national policy for providing a varied and comprehensive service in every area'.[3] The minister was given powers to 'prevent the unreasonable exercise of functions' by local education authorities or governors, and reserve powers to act if they were in default.

Therein, in a sense, lay the rub. For while the Act placed a number of duties on local authorities and strengthened central control, many of the minister's powers were reserve powers. Butler was living with history; and the history which even in 1939 had left the churches with large-scale and burdensome responsibilities for education had also left local authorities running the rest of the school system. It was primarily a local, not a central, government function, and it was proudly defended terrain: Butler had to battle with significant parts of local government just to get rid of the 'Part III' authorities. And the resistance to central control – partly because of the long history of strife over religious education – was deeply inbred. Butler's first remark to Churchill on taking the job reflected that sensitivity: 'I said that I should like to influence what was taught in schools, but that this was always frowned on.'[4]

Thus, while the Act gave the minister powers to require local education authorities to draw up plans, and powers then to approve them, only in exceptional circumstances could the ministry dictate solutions. The powers were more of guidance, of influence and then of veto, rather than direction. In addition, they applied chiefly to organisation. There was no direct power to dictate what should be taught. The curriculum could indeed be influenced by advice and circular, it could and would be affected by the requirements of national examinations, but the minister could not lay it down. It is arguable that through financial regulations, ministers in fact had much more power and leverage than they used: but if they did, the culture remained against their using it.

Even guidance and advice was not entirely a ministerial matter. It was to be assembled in part by drawing on the newly created Central Advisory Councils. Their duty was to advise ministers 'upon such matters connected with educational theory and practice *as they think fit* [my italics], and upon any questions referred to them by him'. Equally, the examination councils, while having ministry officials on them, were staffed by teachers and the education professionals. The councils talked to government and listened to it, but remained firmly and constitutionally independent. In a sense, education was to be run by two forms of bipartisan deal: the local authorities in partnership with the minister; and the minister and local authorities in partnership with the education professionals. No one was to be really in control.

All this provided a potentially healthy diversity, in contrast to monolithic state-dictated education systems. But such pluralism also produced a system which proved remarkably difficult to modify from the centre when problems were encountered. Given, to use Beveridge's phrase, 'a clear field', something very different, more *dirigiste* or just simply more controllable, might have been devised. Had that happened, Kenneth Baker would not have been complaining just before he stunned the educational world with GERBIL, his Great Education Reform Bill of 1987 which produced the biggest single change since Butler, that 'our education system is not the product of a single directing mind – a Napoleon or a Bismarck – let alone the expression of a single guiding principle. It has grown up by a process of addition and adaption. It reflects a good many historical compromises. In short, it is a bit of a muddle, one of those institutionalised muddles that the English have made peculiarly their own.'[5]

Butler, however, did not have a clear field. Like Beveridge, he had to adapt history in a coalition government whose main partners wished to avoid domestic conflict when there was still a war to be won. That made compromise easier, but the imposition of grand visions harder. For a start, educational reform had to be sold to Conservative back-benchers. And they, taken as a whole, and despite the emerging Tory Reform Group, were less keen on reform than Labour. Butler once complained his own side were 'a stupid lot' and on another occasion said: 'I find in education that much of the drive towards a vaguely progressive future comes from Labour.'[6] As a result fees in direct grant schools were retained, despite Butler's appearing to favour their abolition.[7] When Labour MPs divided the Commons on the issue, they lost. And at one point Butler, despite his agnostic view of public schools, felt the need to provide the Conservative back-bench 1922 Committee with a vague assurance that their position would be safeguarded after the war[8] – as indeed it was. On top of that, the Treasury and Churchill were endlessly worried about what money would be available. Whenever it came to reconstruction, Butler records, 'the crippling qualities of expense were much in the minds of my coalition colleagues.'[9]

All this helps to explain the loss of the opportunity to integrate public schools into the state education system. There would never again be a moment when that would be at all feasible, and given the damage done by the public/private divide to education since, it is tempting to argue that Butler solved the wrong issue. Plenty of private education exists elsewhere in Europe, but it is often chosen for religious and cultural reasons, not for the class and opportunity-based divisions that have so marked Britain's particular version of the public/private split.

Butler's political motto, however, was always Bismarck's 'the art of the possible' and settling the religious issue was the *sine qua non* for educational advance. Moreover, agreement had to be reached with churches who counted among their leading figures strong proponents of the public schools. In the end resolving the religious issues was more important than the problem of public schools. In addition, it was far from clear how their integration could be achieved.[10] Nationalisation was an unlikely course for a coalition government. Drawing their teeth through central government's compulsorily buying up large numbers of places would have been costly when Butler was not only under instruction not to spend but had bigger things to spend his money on, notably raising the school leaving age for all rather than buying a public school education for a few. The right would have opposed any such move; the left saw the initial effect of buying up places as propping up the public schools when they wanted abolition. But abolition – banning private education – was not on. Furthermore, there were obvious difficulties, which the Fleming report failed to answer, about how state-funded children were to be selected for this private, boarding education at prestigious schools. If they were chosen for intelligence and ability the better state schools would see their brighter pupils creamed off. If these were not to be the sole criteria, then what basis should be used for selection? Fleming had no clear answer to that, and by the end of the war the public schools' financial crisis was over and whatever chance there had been of a solution was gone.

Some of the more radical measures which were in the Act fell through the mesh of its permissive powers – those that allowed, but did not oblige local authorities to do things, or which laid a duty to do them but only after the minister had set a starting date. Thus the Act provided not just for secondary education for all up to fifteen, but for a later rise to sixteen 'as soon as it has become practicable'.[11] It was to take nearly thirty years for that to happen. Equally, the Act allowed local authorities to provide both nursery education and part-time attendance at county colleges up to eighteen, both to become compulsory on a day to be decided. That day never came, so that high-grade technical education, a concern of countless official reports from the mid-nineteenth century onwards, fell by the way-side. This occurred despite Butler having made it item number one on the list of three issues to be resolved that he had sent Churchill just weeks after his appointment. His officials' Green Book, too, had stressed the 'urgent need, in the interests of the industrial and commercial prosperity of this country, to secure an improved system of technical and commercial training'.[12] The Green Book had even toyed with centralising higher tech-nical education, questioning whether it can 'properly continue to be left to local initiative'. Butler himself minuted R. S. Wood asking how it could be fitted into the Bill. 'Politics is said to be "l'art du possible". The question is – what is possible; and what is our order of priority?'[13]

The issue was discussed at length with the Ministry of Labour. Bevin, remarkably, favoured school-leavers being sent at fourteen to state board-ing schools in redundant service camps for two years to be given a blend of academic and practical skills, before receiving further education and training until they were twenty. As Minister of Labour, no one knew better than Bevin the shortage of skilled manpower. But when a remark-ably similar programme, which included a state takeover of the public schools, was put to the Conservative Central Council in September 1942 it was thrown out root and branch by the party's rank and file as a form of fascism, leaving Butler looking for less dramatic solutions.[14]

One of the key difficulties may well have been, as Barnett argues, that no industrial or commercial body brought pressure on the Board of Education 'of that relentless and effective kind exerted by the churches'. As a result 'the crucial question of providing the nation with an education for capability from primary school up to technical university equal to that of her competitors was squeezed away to the sidelines.'[15] A committee was set up with the blessing of the TUC and the British Employers' Federation to examine day-continuation education. It reported in September 1943, after the White Paper but before the Bill. But another committee which examined higher technical education under Lord Eustace Percy was not even appointed until April 1944, when the Bill was well into its parliamentary run. It finally reported, after the Act took effect, in 1945.

The outcome was that the Act did place a duty on local authorities to provide 'adequate facilities for further education'. It also provided powers for the minister, as soon as it was considered 'practicable to do so', to require LEAs to draw up plans for more day-continuation colleges, just forty of which had been established by 1938 and only one of which, in Rugby, was compulsory.[16] In the event, no minister ever found it practical so to do. Barnett argues that the Act 'offered not so much an executive operational framework as an opened gate to an empty construction site on which local authorities might or might not (depending on their zeal and the effectiveness of the ministry's nagging) build the technical and further education system that Britain so desperately needed.'[17]

The problem, however, was that the local authorities were not the only players in this game. As Butler's talks with Bevin illustrate, responsibilities for education and training were divided within government. Training had always always been seen as a matter for employers, while even education had taken time to become a full-blown responsibility for the state. Technical education and vocational training thus fell between the stools of employers, the Ministry of Labour and the Ministry of Education. The county colleges were to depend on a reform of apprenticeships (then five years long) and industrial training which the employers never undertook. In the full employment after the war, many were only too happy to take on unskilled and poorly educated teenagers and still make profits without the need to invest in the training and day release that the county colleges required. As for the unions, training was never more than a minor bargaining chip in industrial relations. The drive from industry for better training existed far more in industrialists' rhetoric than in reality. In the schools themselves, technical education fell between the grammars, whose highest aim was to produce entrants for universities that remained heavily arts-based, and secondary moderns, providing the low-grade practical education that was designed for their 'iron' children.

The universities remained largely outside the Act, save for strengthened powers for local authorities to provide student grants. They were after all independent, responsible neither to central nor to local government, though part-funded through the University Grants Committee. Nursery schooling suffered the same fate as technical education – provided for in the Act, but to be compulsory only when a date was set. Butler had rated both as priorities. 'Equality of opportunity would remain something of an empty phrase if children entered the period of compulsory schooling from conditions of family deprivation, or left it to pursue what Churchill called blind-alley occupations,' he said in 1971, explaining his Act's nursery and technical education provisions. But nearly thirty years on from 1944, he judged pre-schooling to be still 'patently inadequate', while fewer than half of under-eighteens were released from industry for voluntary, not mandatory, part-time education. A price was paid in all this in terms of Britain's fitness to fight its way in a competitive world.

If one concept, one 'guiding principle' to use Kenneth Baker's phrase, underpinned the 1944 Act it was equality of opportunity – the aim Butler referred to in his memoirs and which was spelt out in the White Paper's introduction. The battle to define precisely what equality of opportunity meant, however, was to dominate much of the history of post-war education.

For some, for whom comprehensive schooling was to become the keystone definition, Butler's White Paper and Act with their tripartite (or tri-partheid as some put it with acid wit) system of grammars, technical and secondary moderns came to be seen as a thoroughly 'Tory' measure[18] – the word here being firmly used as a term of abuse. In fact the Act was far subtler than that. In itself it did not set out the tripartite system, even though the White Paper made clear that was what was expected. The Act merely required education according to pupils' 'ages, abilities and aptitudes', opening the door to multilateral or comprehensive schools. It did so because in fact there was no absolute consensus, even in official circles, about the ideal organisation of secondary education – or even the precise purpose of education.

The White Paper reveals the struggle in the official mind to balance four aims: equality of opportunity with diversity of provision; and parity of esteem between the different schools which would provide that diversity with social unity. For education, in this coalition White Paper, was not just about developing people's talents. It included, as Butler's assertion quoted at the beginning of this chapter shows, an element of what was to become the hotly disputed issue of 'social engineering' in education. The White Paper[19] stated – providing a talismanic slogan for ever after for those who favoured comprehensives – that: 'There is nothing to be said in favour of a system which subjects children at the age of eleven to the strain of competitive examination on which not only their future schooling but their future careers may depend.' Instead, children should 'be classified, not on the results of a competitive test, but on an assessment of their individual aptitudes largely by such means as school records, supplemented, if necessary, by intelligence tests.'

Even so, it added, the choice should not be finally determined at eleven. At thirteen or even later there should be facilities for transfer, and 'if the choice is to be a real one, it is manifest that conditions in different types of school must be broadly equivalent.' Grammar schools, the paper acknowledged, enjoyed at the time a prestige which 'completely overshadows all other types of school'. Equal treatment was needed: though it has to be added that quite how the schools were meant to become equally valued when the Spens report of 1938 had estimated that a mere 15 per cent of secondary school pupils would go to grammars was not explained.

The White Paper went on to say that while grammars, secondary moderns and technical schools would indeed be the main types, 'it would be wrong to suppose that they will necessarily remain separate and apart. Different types may be combined in one building or on one site . . . in any case free interchange of pupils from one type of education to another must be facilitated.' Diversity, it also stated, 'must not impair the social unity within the educational system which will open the way to a more closely knit society and give us the strength to face the tasks ahead'. So even in the coalition White Paper, education was also seen as a means of social engineering. Butler himself had some sympathy for the idea of multilateral schools. He once told Ede he was 'more in favour of it than any of us'.[20] But he saw them as an addition to the variety. His real aim, never to be achieved, was 'social equality in the secondary schools of various types',[21] a view many Labour MPs and councillors shared at the time.[22]

In practice, despite the White Paper, the eleven-plus became a competitive exam and transfer between schools after eleven a rarity. Technical schools, left in the hands of local authorities to organise, never took off; at most they educated 2 per cent of the school population. This third leg of Butler's tripod, as Barnett puts it 'the one that might have fostered a technological national culture in place of a literary one . . . was simply never built'. The secondary modern school, 'though greatly expanded in numbers in the postwar era, was to remain in the eyes of parents and children alike a mere educational settling-tank for academic failures'. How could it be otherwise 'with staff of inferior quality to that in the grammar school, with resources per child barely a third of those enjoyed by the grammar school, and with no examination specifically designed for its pupils but instead only the highly academic General Certificate of Education formulated by university examining boards for the benefit of the bookish?'[23]

Any assessment of Butler's Act, however, must concur with Harold Dent's judgement: for all that it did not provide everything it was 'the greatest measure of educational advance since 1870, and probably the greatest ever known'. That is not incompatible with one of Butler's drier judgements on his own handiwork, that it essentially codified best existing practice.[24] In resolving some issues, his Act ducked others, leaving open ground that in years to come was to be fought over with all the vehemence of the religious issue that the Act finally settled.

CHAPTER 6

Bevan – Health

The health of the people is really the foundation upon which all their happiness and their powers as a state depend.
Benjamin Disraeli, 1877

This is the biggest single experiment in social service that the world has ever seen undertaken.
Aneurin Bevan, 7 October 1948

In the case of nutrition and health, just as in the case of education, the gentlemen in Whitehall really do know better what is good for the people than the people know themselves.
Douglas Jay, 1937

The Emergency Hospital Scheme was in the short run the financial salvation of the voluntary hospitals, but in the longer term proved a major factor in their post-war nationalization. The scheme illuminated the enormous financial deficiencies of the voluntary hospitals and gave to the public hospitals a more prominent place in the hospital system. For the first time, many of the wealthier and more highly educated members of society became patients in public hospitals and were distressed and eager to reform what they had seen and experienced. Likewise, doctors serving under the EHS had to serve in all kinds of hospitals and were often shocked at what they saw.
Dr Gordon Macpherson in BMA, Health Services Financing, p. 32.

It was the first health system in any Western society to offer free medical care to the entire population. It was, furthermore, the first comprehensive system to be based not on the insurance principle, with entitlement following contributions, but on the national provision of services available to everyone. It thus offered free and universal entitlement to State-provided medical care. At the time of its creation it was a unique example of the collectivist provision of health care in a market society.

Rudolf Klein, *The Politics of the NHS*, 1983, p. 1

Medical provision before the war depended upon a primitively unstable mixture of class prejudice, commercial self-interest, professional altruism, vested interest, and demarcation disputes.

Arthur Marwick, *British Society Since 1945*, p. 49

IMPLEMENTATION OF Butler's Act was to fall to Labour. But the issue which was to cause the biggest welfare state row immediately after 1945 was not to be education, Beveridge's social security plan, or even housing, though that too was to see its fair share of controversy. It was the National Health Service that took the lion's share of the headlines, despite proving the most enduring of the 1945 Labour Government's achievements.

Labour's 146 majority was the biggest ever known, outstripping by two even Margaret Thatcher's 1983 victory. Labour MPs horrified the Tories by singing 'The Red Flag' in the Commons chamber, and into government came Aneurin Bevan: one of Labour's great saints or sinners, depending on which part of his career is in view at the time and which section of the Labour Party is making the judgement. He was Attlee's biggest gamble as a ministerial appointment, one of only two Cabinet ministers who had not served in the wartime coalition. 'A stormy petrel' with 'a magic all of his own' in the words of Kenneth Morgan, who judged him to be 'the most hated – if also the most idolized – politician of his time'. The forty-five-year-old ex-miner, however, proved himself at the Ministry of Health to be 'an artist in the uses of power'.[1]

In the 1930s he had been expelled from the party for advocating a popular front. During the war he was a running rebel on the back-benches and was almost expelled again, Churchill once condemning him as 'a squalid nuisance'.[2] Macmillan fondly remembered him as an 'uncontrollable star – perhaps almost a comet', a man who 'could not forget and never wanted to forget the sufferings he had seen in the mining valleys of South Wales'. He judged him 'in many ways the most brilliant and the most memorable of them all' – the 'all' being the 1945–51 Cabinet to which Macmillan gave the accolade of 'one of the most able Governments of modern times'.[3] Just as Butler is remembered for his Education Act, Bevan's name will always be associated with the NHS.

On 26 July, the day the election result was announced, the British Medical Association was meeting in the Great Hall of BMA House in Tavistock Square, a massive, neo-classical, red-brick building originally designed by Sir Edwin Lutyens for the Theosophical Society with the Great Hall as its temple. The Society had been unable to afford the mighty edifice which came to symbolise all the self-important solidity the medical profession felt was its right – a building where as late as the 1930s the clerical staff were under instruction not to share the lift with the great London consultants who arrived to do their business in top hats and frock coats.[4]

The BMA debate was interrupted by the news that in Labour's landslide Sir William Beveridge, the man who had demanded a National Health Service three years earlier, had lost the Berwick seat he had taken for the Liberals in 1944. Some delegates broke into a cheer. 'I have spent a lot of time,' one eminent Harley Street surgeon said, 'seeing doctors with bleeding duodenal ulcers caused by worry about being under the State.'[5] Well before Bevan arrived, the doctors were deeply suspicious about the form any proposed National Health Service would take. That very worry, however, reflected a remarkable consensus which the doctors shared and Bevan inherited: that there was going to be a National Health Service. The question was what form it would take.

Included in Bevan's inheritance was the Emergency Medical Service, plans for which were drawn up by Chamberlain's government in the wake of Munich and in fear of what the Blitz would – and did – mean. The creation of the EMS followed surveys conducted in 1937 and 1938 which showed just how deficient hospital services were. By October 1939 the government had provided nearly 1000 new operating theatres, millions of bandages and dressings, and tens of thousands of extra beds in 'hutted annexes' some of which remained in use for more than two decades after the war. A national blood transfusion service had been created. As the war progressed, free treatment under the emergency scheme had gradually to be extended from direct war casualties to war workers, child evacuees, firemen and so on, until a sixty-two-page booklet was needed to define who was eligible. Although the elderly and others remained excluded, between 1939 and 1945 'a growing section of the population enjoyed the benefits of the first truly "national" hospital service'.[6] Wartime proved that a national health service could be run.

The Emergency Medical Service had itself heavily extended what existed

before. On the hospital side just before the war there were 1334 voluntary
hospitals and 1771 municipal hospitals. The former ranged from the
twenty great English teaching hospitals each with around 500 beds, of
which no fewer than thirteen were in London along with nine post-
graduate hospitals such as the Great Ormond Street Hospital for Sick
Children, to tiny cottage hospitals of ten beds or less. The average was a
mere sixty-eight beds. The number of voluntary hospitals, and particularly
the number of small ones, had grown sharply after the First World War.
Among the older foundations St Bartholomew's could claim almost 800
years of history, but many such as the Royal Free, whose name encapsulated its aim, had been founded during the great burst of Victorian philanthropy aimed at improving the health care of the poor. This, initially,
they did successfully, in as far as medical knowledge then allowed success.
In 1891, 88 per cent of the voluntary hospitals' income came from gifts
and investments. By 1938, however, only 33 per cent of their revenue
came this way, and less in some cases. Payments from patients had risen
from 11 per cent to 59 per cent of their income,[7] financed either out
of patients' own pockets, by health insurance through, for example, the
middle-class British Provident Association, or from factory savings
schemes and Saturday Hospital Funds. These last, into which people paid
against future treatment, were run by the hospitals themselves. For the
less well-off such schemes often bought out-patient but not in-patient
treatment. Lady Almoners controlled means-tested access to beds, and
substantial donors were often allocated free beds to distribute to the
deserving, so a letter of reference from a JP or a councillor or from the
local gentry might have to be begged to ensure admission.[8] Increasingly
the voluntary hospitals came to rely on charges and on private patients.
The price of survival, as Ruldolf Klein has put it, became 'to an extent
the repudiation of the inspiration which had led to their creation in the
first place'.[9]

Despite all these stratagems, flag days, and 'a begging bowl [always] at
the end of the ward; you would not dare to pass that bowl if you visited
on those days',[10] by the late 1930s many of the voluntary hospitals, which
accounted for about one-third of the beds, were in deep financial trouble.
Even the great teaching hospitals endlessly teetered on the edge of bank-
ruptcy. As early as 1930, the House Governor of the Charing Cross Hospital declared that the hospitals could not rely on sweepstakes and
competitions for survival and predicted that within ten years they would
be nationalised – state-supported and state-controlled.[11] In 1932 out of
145 voluntary hospitals in London, 60 failed to balance their books,[12] and

by 1938 the hospitals were pleading with the Ministry of Health for state grants.[13]

Geoffrey Rivett, a senior health department civil servant who was a driving force behind the controversial new family doctor's contract in the 1980s, records in his history of the London hospital system:

> It was said that a hospital need never despair so long as it was bankrupt, but the plaintive cry of 'funds urgently needed and beds closed' led in the end to the belief that the voluntary system was not only insolvent, but might not be worth saving.[14]

The Second World War and the Emergency Medical Service did save it, but only for a time. In these hospitals, consultants had honorary, unpaid appointments; they made their income from private patients while treating the less well off free. As a result specialist care was only available in parts of the country wealthy enough to provide sufficient private practice to attract specialists. These more prosperous areas were, needless to say, not necessarily those with the greatest need. Elsewhere, surgery and anaesthetics were carried out by GPs (family doctors) working in the hospitals. What this could mean, even after the founding of the NHS, has been illustrated by Dr Julian Tudor Hart, who recalled that just before specialists replaced GPs at Kettering General Hospital where he worked in 1952, a young woman with acute intestinal obstruction was admitted. At Kettering GPs did the surgery,

> helped once a week by a part-time consultant who travelled 100 miles by rail from London.

The family doctor opened the abdomen to find multiple obstructions caused by Crohn's disease. He excised four or five segments along the seven metres of small intestine, leaving the loose ends to be reconnected. Then his troubles began; which end belonged to which? Never having met this unusual condition before, he had waded into the macaroni without planning his return. In those days emergency surgery was still regarded by patients as a gamble with death. If he had confidently reconnected the tubes as best he could, praying he hadn't created any collisions, dead ends or inner circles, he would probably have been acclaimed whatever the outcome. Being a man of integrity, he persuaded his GP-anaesthetist colleague to keep the patient unconscious for what turned out to be four hours, with a small coppice of metal clamps splayed out from the incision, telephoned the London consultant, and waited for him to come up by the next train to sort it all out. Remarkably, the patient survived. It was the last anecdote of a closing era of GP surgery; the professionals put an end to all that, and not before time.[15]

Alongside the voluntaries were the municipal hospitals, many of which had grown up as appendages to the 1834 workhouses: some were still called the 'Workhouse Infirmary'. Run by local authorities, these were regarded in the main by doctors, nurses and patients alike as grossly inferior to the voluntary hospitals – certainly outside the big cities – and real stigma attached to many. They comprised a mix of old Poor Law institutions, the great mental illness 'bins', and the 'fever' and 'TB' (tuberculosis) hospitals. Most depended on general practitioners to service them. They ranged in quality from the occasionally excellent to the awful. But they had in the decade before the war been supplemented in some cities by a determined expansion of purpose built hospitals. Before 1930 only three local authorities had exercised a right under the 1875 Public Health Act to establish general hospitals. But by 1938, councils in England and Wales provided 75,000 general beds (as opposed to the mental or fever beds they ran) and the London County Council was arguably the biggest hospital authority in the world, rivalling in size the entire voluntary sector. Middlesex developed a hospital service of the highest class, while City hospitals in Birmingham, Bristol, Newcastle, Sheffield and Nottingham set new standards for local authority provision, attracting academics as well as employing specialists and staff doctors. Access to their general hospital beds was means-tested, although on one estimate only about 10 per cent of costs were recovered from patients.[16] None the less, the stigma of the old Poor Law hospitals which made up the bulk of local authority provision still left many reluctant to resort to them: 'There was a certain sense of shame in being taken there,' patients recorded.[17] Patients from just over the border in the next authority would often be refused admission to empty beds, and voluntary hospitals dumped patients who failed to respond to treatment on to the Poor Law infirmary for the chronic sick.[18]

The two systems thus fought among themselves and against each other. Sir George Godber, who was to become the greatest of the Chief Medical Officers the NHS has seen, helped run the 1937 survey which revealed the appalling physical state of many hospitals and the acute shortage of beds. Run down though they were, he recalled, 'the physical difficulties imposed by unsatisfactory buildings were less important than the defects in district services resulting from competition, if not overt hostility, between the several hospitals providing them'.[19]

The local authorities, who numbered several hundred, also ran a range of other health services. These included the school medical service, some home nursing, a small number of health centres, and ante- and post-natal care: most births were midwife-delivered home births, with a doctor only called if complications arose. One mother in 350 died in childbirth.

Family doctor or GP services remained based on Lloyd George's 'Ninepence for Fourpence' National Health Insurance, and 43 per cent of the adult population was covered for a 'panel' doctor by 1938.[20] Ninety per cent of GPs took at least some part in the scheme. Non-working wives and children, the self-employed, higher income earners and many of the elderly, however, remained excluded. Hospital treatment was not covered, and the Approved Societies which ran the scheme offered wide variations in 'extra' cover for dentistry, spectacles (which many people bought for 6d. [2.5p] at Woolworths) and sometimes some hospital care. Schoolchildren and the poor could get free treatment, subject until 1942 to the humiliating 'family means-test' in front of the Relieving Officer, and some queued at the 'casualty' or 'dispensing' departments of the voluntary hospitals seeking treatment for illnesses that ranged from the minor, which really needed only a GP's attention, to the horrifyingly major.

An Aberdeen woman quoted in Margaret Whitehead's compilation of pre-NHS memories, recalls getting rheumatic fever on top of scarlet fever when her mother took her to the dispensary because they could not afford a doctor. 'I took scarlet fever . . . and I was ill for a few days and my mother took me to the dispensary. We had to walk to the dispensary because it was free there, we couldn't afford to pull in a doctor. 'Cos my mother would have had the doctor in the house maybe . . . well, at least twice a week, 'cos she had eight of us. And you know what it is, there's always something wrong with one. And it had to be serious before she took in a doctor because she couldn't afford to pay for it.'[21]

Some GPs only saw their panel patients at lock-up surgeries, receiving private patients in their homes; others took the private patients through the front door, the panel being relegated to a side 'surgery' door. As with the voluntary hospitals, the need to supplement panel income with private practice concentrated family doctors' services more heavily in wealthier areas. But even for the middle classes and for those who were not poor, doctors' fees with the cost of medicine on top could be crippling, not to mention the possibility of hospital bills. Muriel Smith of Chelmsford recalled:

We were married in October 1937 and if we ever needed to see the doctor, the fee was one guinea . . . we had to be really ill to consider facing up to this. The men did if they were not well enough to go to work, but the women very rarely bothered. My weekly household money was one pound and my husband's total salary was three pounds. When my son was born in 1946, the bill for the nursing home was £22 and the ambulance came to £1 5s. It is quite remarkable the difference between those long ago days and the ease with which we were able to cope with my husband's illnesses after the war – a hernia operation, piles operation, three weeks in hospital after a slight heart attack and constant free care from then until his second heart attack three years later, when he died in Guy's.[22]

Of course, many GPs played Robin Hood, waiving fees when they could, for the poor and for the middle class. My mother remembers her rather austere family doctor in Hull in 1947 refusing to send a bill for treating a recurrent bout of the malaria my father (by then a Methodist minister) had acquired as an infantryman in Burma. 'I don't charge the cloth,' he said, explaining that in return GPs referred to the church those who needed pastoral not medical care. But there were limits to such charity and inter-profession trading. Many GPs outside the more prosperous private patient areas were far from well off. Nationally only about one-third of GPs' income came from panel patients.[23] They supplemented panel income with work in municipal hospitals, or for factory owners, or occupational health work under the eagle eye of the local authority medical officer whose punitive attitude to payment and control helps explain the doctors' deep distrust of either a local authority-run service or any suggestion that they should be forced to become 'civil servants' employed by the state.

Against this background, it is hardly surprising there was a powerful movement for reform. Beatrice Webb is usually credited, in her minority report of 1909 to the Royal Commission on the Poor Law, with the first call for a 'public medical service' or 'state medical service', but much else had happened before Bevan took office. To highlight just some of the many streams which combined into the flood that made a national health service inevitable, 1920 saw a committee established by the Ministry of Health under Lord Dawson which argued that 'the best means of maintaining health and curing disease should be made available to all citizens.' In 1926 a Royal Commission foreshadowed a tax-funded NHS by observing that 'the ultimate solution will lie, we think, in the direction of divorcing the medical service entirely from the insurance system and recognising it along with all other public health activities as a service to be supported from the general public funds.'[24]

By 1930 the British Medical Association was backing 'a general medical service for the nation' though on the basis of extending national insurance to include hospital care. Rather surprisingly, the BMA foresaw the whole being managed by the larger local authorities.[25] In 1933 the Socialist Medical Association was seeking a comprehensive, free and salaried medical service run by local government and in 1934 this became the official policy of a Labour Party crippled by the split over Ramsay Macdonald's National Government.

The growing importance of local government services reinforced the perception that insurance no longer provided the answer, and by 1938 the planning of the Emergency Medical Service was turning Ministry of Health minds to how a permanent national health service might be created. Less than three weeks after the outbreak of war, Sir Arthur MacNalty, the Ministry of Health's Chief Medical Officer, offered a counter to a paper by Sir John Maude, the Ministry's deputy secretary. Sir John had foreseen either 'the gradual extension of National Health Insurance to further classes of the community and by new statutory benefits, or the gradual development of local authority services'. MacNalty provided a third option – that the hospitals should be administered 'as a National Hospital Service by the Ministry'. Such a system was already practically established through the Emergency Medical Service, he argued. It would be 'difficult and in many cases impossible for voluntary hospitals to carry on, owing to the high costs of modern hospital treatment and the falling off of voluntary subscriptions after the war'. He judged that the voluntary hospitals and local authorities would resist, as might the medical profession, 'but I am certain they [the doctors] would, for the most part, welcome national control in preference to being controlled by local authorities.' It was, he suggested, 'a revolutionary change, but it is one that must inevitably come.'[26]

Such an approach – the one Bevan eventually adopted – would mean 'a radical change in the policy of the ministry. Hitherto, we have always worked on the assumption that the Ministry of Health was an advisory, supervisory and subsidising department, but had no direct executive functions.' And that remarkably prescient sentence foresaw many of the battles to come in the 1980s as the issue of how to manage as opposed to administer the NHS finally reached centre stage.

MacNalty's was far from the only model being kicked around in the Ministry of Health at the time. Sir Arthur Rucker, who was to become the deputy secretary, argued for yet another option – more of a mixed economy. Joint hospital boards should plan both municipal and voluntary hospital services, he argued, financial support for the voluntary hospitals being dependent on their co-operating and providing agreed services under contract.

As the Ministry of Health pondered, the British Medical Association came back into the game. In August 1940 it set up a Medical Planning Commission of no fewer than seventy-three members drawn from the BMA, the medical Royal Colleges, and the Society of Medical Officers of Health (the local authority chief doctors), along with observers from the health ministries. The Commission's 'draft interim report' emerged in June 1942 as Beveridge was working on his report. Among much else, it again foresaw large regional councils, though loaded with medical representation, running hospitals in which consultants would be salaried. They would choose between being 'whole-timers', or part-timers who would retain the right to private practice. For GPs, the commission proposed a mix of basic salary, capitation fees (a fee for each patient on the doctor's list), and payment for services not covered by capitation. The sale of practices – nominally for 'goodwill' – would cease. This report in large measure was drafted by Dr Charles Hill, then the BMA's deputy secretary but already known to the public as 'the radio doctor'. The BMA report was remarkable in foreshadowing the way both GPs and consultants would operate in future, although not before a full-blown war had been fought between Bevan and the Association which until the eleventh hour appeared to threaten the very establishment of the NHS.

At the BMA's annual representative meeting in July, the report received a muted reception. It was, however, not only passed, but the meeting also agreed by ninety-four to ninety-two votes that, while still insurance-based, the scheme should cover the whole community, not just 90 per cent of the population with the remainder forced to continue under private practice.[27] The implication of this decision, which the BMA was to restate (though with a qualification) in May 1945 before Bevan's appointment, were huge, although it appears not to have been entirely recognised at the time. For if 100 per cent of the population could join, family doctors were bound to become dependent on public funds. If the service proved popular with the public, private general practice was bound to wither.

In December, Beveridge delivered his Assumption B: that a comprehensive health service would underpin his social security recommendations. His report caused unease at BMA House, according to Dr Elston Grey-Turner, then a young assistant secretary who went on to become the BMA's secretary and its official historian. The storm signal, he says, was an aside suggesting that under a national health service, 'the possible scope of private general practice will be so restricted that it may not appear worthwhile to preserve it'.[28] If private practice went, family doctors would become dependent for all their income on the state, whether through local or national government. The spectre of state control, of doctors being civil servants, was raised. As yet, no one was saying when anything would actually happen. But as pressure to implement Beveridge mounted irresistibly, Churchill's March 1943 broadcast finally allowed plans for a national health service to be drawn up, even if no expenditure could be committed before an election.

Ernest Brown, the leader of the National Liberals and Minister of Health in the coalition government, opened discussions with a tentative suggestion that doctors might be salaried local authority employees. Hill exploded. He warned a mass meeting of doctors to be ready 'for a fight . . . [against] the translation of a free profession into a branch of the local government services'.[29] In November, Brown was replaced by Henry Willink, and after the best part of a year of consultations, chiefly with the medical profession, the voluntary hospitals and the local authorities, the White Paper *A National Health Service* emerged in February 1944.[30]

Its opening statements were both noble and crystal clear: that everybody 'irrespective of means, age, sex, or occupation shall have equal opportunity to benefit from the best and most up-to-date medical and allied services available'; that the service should be 'comprehensive' for all who wanted it; that it should be 'free of charge', and that it should promote good health 'rather than only the treatment of bad'. It was now certain that a National Health Service, largely tax-financed, free at the point of use, and comprehensive, covering family doctors, dentists, hospital services and more, would arrive. Its precise form, however, remained far from clear. For Willink's document was a compromise. It proposed some thirty joint boards of grouped local authorities who would take over the municipal hospitals, while Rucker's suggestion resurfaced that voluntary hospitals should be free to make a contractual relationship with the boards 'for the performance of agreed services set out in the plan'. Here in the most embryonic of forms was an outline of the internal market that the Conservatives finally introduced into the NHS in 1990.

Family doctors, the White Paper proposed, should be employed by a Central Medical Board, which would have the power to prohibit new doctors practising in over-doctored areas. GPs, who overwhelmingly worked single-handed, would be encouraged to group themselves in health centres provided by local authorities. While the precise methods of payment remained unclear, the White Paper said there was 'a strong case for salary' in health centres.

'Like all compromise proposals designed to reconcile multiple and conflicting objectives, the White Paper left most of the actors involved feeling dissatisfied,' Rudolf Klein has recorded.[31] Local government hospitals had escaped nationalisation, but many local authorities would lose control of their hospitals, while the voluntary hospitals believed they would suffer 'a mortal blow through the cessation of income from patients'. The GPs had escaped council control and retained the right to private practice (despite strong objections from Clement Attlee during the White Paper's drafting); but they had no clear form of payment offered save the hint of salaries.[32]

The BMA's council saw in the proposals 'the thin end of the wedge of a form of service to which it is overwhelmingly opposed – a State-salaried service under local authorities'.[33] The British Medical Journal, under its fierce, and fiercely independent, editor Dr Hugh Clegg, warned that if the ideas went through it was hard to see 'how private practice as we know it today can survive as much more than a shadow of itself'.[34] Willink's White Paper went out to consultation. Well over a year later in June 1945, after Labour had left the coalition government but with the general election still to be held, he proffered a string of further compromises. These were approved by Cabinet and conveyed to the BMA in private, but not made public. The Central Medical Board and its powers disappeared. Health centres were to be experimental. Doctors both in them and outside were to be paid by capitation fees, not salary. Concessions were also offered to the voluntary hospitals. The new joint authorities were to be planning, not executive bodies, and the existing multiplicity of local authorities would retain control over their existing hospitals – a recipe for a dog's breakfast if ever there was one. John Pater, a Ministry of Health civil servant at the time and future NHS historian, judged it a system 'of almost unworkable complexity', one which it was 'just as well' did not survive.[35]

This was the state of play when Bevan arrived. What Rudolf Klein has termed a 'sedimentary consensus' existed, built up over many years, that a National Health Service would be introduced. It was a consensus, however, marred by a profoundly suspicious body of doctors fearful of state control, plus a collection of other interests none of which were satisfied by what was proposed. 'By the end of the war,' Charles Webster, the official historian of the NHS has judged, 'all the government schemes lay in ruins, while the powerful interest groups were more divided than ever they had been.'[36]

Bevan's first act was to sink into the well-upholstered chair in his new ministry – and then banish it. 'This won't do,' he declared, 'it drains all the blood from the head and explains a lot about my predecessors.' His second was to charm all around him. 'He sold himself to the Ministry within a fortnight,' Sir Wilson Jameson, the Chief Medical Officer, told Bevan's biographer, Michael Foot. Sir William Douglas, according to Foot a natural Conservative who was nearing retirement, was transferred in as Permanent Secretary only to tell a friend a few days after Bevan's appointment that he thought him 'a terrible fellow. I'll never forgive him for all those attacks on Churchill during the war. I made it clear that I would carry on only for three months until they'd got someone else.' A few months later the same friend asked again what he thought of Bevan. 'What are you driving at?' replied Douglas. 'He's the best Minister I ever worked for. I've made it clear that while Bevan's there, I'll stay.' The same charisma worked initially on the BMA council. 'We expected to see a vulgar agitator,' Dr Roland Cockshut, who was to become one of Bevan's most fierce opponents, said. '. . . However, the first thing I noticed was that the fiend was beautifully dressed. We were quite surprised to discover he spoke English.' He proved, Cockshut concluded, to have 'the finest intellect I ever met'. He told the doctors he intended to do the job for five years when no previous health minister had lasted longer than three.[37] The meeting ended with an ovation, and only the next day did council members start pinching themselves and asking 'what the hell were we doing, cheering him yesterday?' The British Medical Journal warned its readers that the Welsh Aneurin from whom he took his name was 'both a bard and a warrior'.[38]

Bevan's third act was to draw up the proposals that in March 1946 were to form the National Health Service Bill. Within his first month he reached the fundamental conclusion that Willink's revised plans for the hospitals would not work. In his own words, he judged that Willink had 'run away from so many vested interests that in the end he had no scheme at all'.[39] His answer to the hospital problem was to take the lot, municipal and voluntary, into public ownership – the idea floated by the house governor of Charing Cross in 1930 and revived in 1939 by MacNalty as 'revolutionary' but 'inevitable', though it had never formed part of any government or party proposal. Sir John Hawton, the deputy secretary in charge of hospitals who in the 1950s became Permanent Secretary and who was for ever a Bevan fan, told Michael Foot:

At our very first full discussion, Bevan put his finger on the hospital arrangements devised by Willink as the greatest weakness. And, of course, he was right. They would never have worked. I came away that night with instructions to work out a new plan on the new basis he proposed.[40]

In this, Bevan made his biggest break with all that had gone before.

Bevan's other key piece of business in the autumn and winter of 1945 was to strike up a close and, it was to prove, life-saving relationship with the Presidents of the three main Royal Colleges – the surgeons, physicians and obstetricians. Of the three, Sir Alfred (later Lord) Webb-Johnson of the surgeons and Lord Moran of the physicians were to be the pivotal figures. Webb-Johnson came to address Bevan in correspondence as 'My dear Aneurin'.[41] Moran, the former Sir Charles Wilson, was already an almost mythical figure. Distrusted in BMA circles as 'Corkscrew Charlie', he was Churchill's personal doctor and was president of the physicians for a near-record nine years. Politically sinuous, vain, immensely able and determined to spread specialist care across the country, Moran told Michael Foot that he initiated the approach to Bevan because 'the service was inevitable, so it at once became important, if the doctors were to have any say in things, that Bevan, as Minister for Health, should look upon them as allies and seek their advice.'[42]

In practice and theory the Royal Colleges were members of the thirty-strong committee that the BMA had set up to negotiate with Willink. The Royal Colleges' presidents, however, were careful to keep their own channels of communication with Bevan open, while Bevan, in line with the constitutional position he had long held as a back-bencher, refused to negotiate with the BMA until the Bill was published. That did not prevent him talking to people, and dinners at Prunier's with Moran along with other meetings shaped crucial parts of the deal that made the NHS. Moran related to Michael Foot a conversation with Bevan:

BEVAN: I find the efficiency of the hospitals varies enormously. How can that be put right?

MORAN: You will only get one standard of excellence when every hospital has a first-rate consultant staff. At present the consultants are all crowded together in the large centres of population. You've got to decentralize them.

BEVAN: That's all very well, but how are you going to get a man to leave his teaching hospital and go into the periphery? [He grinned] You wouldn't like it if I began to direct labour.

MORAN: Oh, they'll go if they get an interesting job and if their financial future is secured by a proper salary.

BEVAN (AFTER A LONG PAUSE): Only the State could pay those salaries. This would mean the nationalization of the hospitals.[43]

The college presidents also convinced Bevan that he would have to allow part-time consultants to continue private practice in NHS 'pay beds'. Without that concession there was a real risk that specialists would refuse to join the health service, and would, in Bevan's words, set up 'a rash of private nursing homes all over the country'[44] which would undermine the very comprehensiveness of the service Bevan was seeking to establish. In addition, Lord Moran talked Bevan into merit awards, on top of basic salary, for those doctors whom their peers judged worthy. A decade later, Bevan at a private House of Commons dinner was to boast wryly in one of his most famous asides, 'I stuffed their mouths with gold.' The remark was not given currency until 1964 by Brian Abel-Smith, when it provided one small element of the growing resentment over private practice that exploded in Barbara Castle's great pay beds row.[45] At Prunier's, as Professor Abel-Smith has put it:

> The top doctors obtained *à la suite* terms in the Health Service: part-time payment for loosely defined sessions, the secret disposal of Treasury funds to those of their number whom Lord Moran and his two colleagues thought more meritorious, the lion's share of the endowments of the teaching hospitals to pay the costs of their researches, and the right to private practice – much as before. The consultants had gained regular remuneration without any loss of freedom and were being trusted to use this freedom responsibly.[46]

Labour's left wing, whence Bevan came, proved far from happy with this deal. But, as Michael Foot has put it, 'to get the specialists into the hospitals and to keep them there as regularly as possible was crucial to the whole enterprise.'[47] In the long run, the concessions split the medical profession and put the Royal Colleges, with the powerful voices of Webb-Johnson and Moran, on Bevan's side. Without that, it is doubtful if the NHS would have been born at all; and the steady spread of consultants across the country, which did so much after 1948 progressively to improve standards of care outside London and the big cities, would not have occurred. The mighty battle which was still to be fought with the BMA, despite some of the ballot results to come, was to be between Bevan and the GPs rather than Bevan and all the doctors.

Before the Bill could be published, however, Bevan had to sell it to the Cabinet and in October he sought a decision on 'one big question of principle' – whether to nationalize the hospitals. His argument was simple: the voluntary hospitals were dead. In this he had the backing of the magnificently named Sir Edward Farquhar Buzzard, a former President of the BMA and Regius Professor of Medicine at Oxford, who had publicly delivered the same diagnosis to the press a year earlier.[48] To keep them going, Bevan told the Cabinet, around 80 or 90 per cent of their revenue under any national health service would have to come from public funds and 'I believe strongly that we must insist on the principle of public control accompanying public financing.' In this the teaching hospitals and postgraduates would be given special status on three grounds: their quality and standing; because 'it is a good thing in itself to keep separate a field for independent experiment in method and organisation'; and because the state should not dictate the medical curriculum. The local authority hospitals too should be nationalised, he said. The great bulk of local authority areas were too small to run good ones, the rates could not bear the full cost of the service, and complex cross-financing arrangements would be needed if rich areas were not to have better services than poor ones. The 'voice of the expert' (chiefly the doctors) had to be brought into the planning and running of the services. There was thus a powerful case for 'starting again with a clean slate'.[49] Bevan acknowledged the proposal would mean 'extinction' for most voluntary hospitals and would 'provoke an outcry' both from them and from local authorities. The attitude of the doctors, he conceded, was uncertain. But again, probably unconsciously, he echoed MacNalty: 'if the choice were before them between a primarily local government service and primarily nationalised service, the overwhelming majority would prefer the latter.'

In a tantalising aside, he acknowledged that if local government were reorganised into regions (a Labour policy) then the hospitals might revert to regional government. Given that Labour has repeatedly toyed with that idea and is considering it again at the time of writing, it is worth exploring the reaction. His memo brought Herbert Morrison, Lord President of the Council, leaping to the local authorities' defence. Morrison had made his name as leader of the London County Council in the 1930s, when local government, at least in terms of breadth of function, was in its heyday.

'We should be cautious about any step which will weaken local government,' Morrison argued. The government's nationalisation plans were already likely to remove gas, electricity, probably passenger transport and possibly water from them. And Bevan, he complained, was 'on the horns of a dilemma'. If the proposed appointed regional hospital boards were 'subject to the Minister's directions on all questions of policy, finance, establishments and so on, then they will be mere creatures of the Ministry of Health, with little vitality of their own.' Yet under a nationalised state system 'it is difficult . . . to envisage the alternative situation in which, in order to give them vitality, they are left free to spend Exchequer money without the Minister's approval and to pursue policies which at any rate in detail may not be the Minister's, but for which he presumably would be answerable.'[50]

Local government ran a better hospital service than Bevan gave it credit for, he said – adding in a touch of raw politics that the health minister would be launching a war with local authorities ahead of council elections in November and the spring. He offered, however, no solution to the voluntary hospital problem, admitted he had no 'conclusive argument against nationalising the hospitals', conceded that a nationalised system might be inherently more efficient, and opened with the courtesy of describing Bevan's paper as 'brilliant and imaginative'.

Four days later, desperate for a decision to get ahead with his plan, Bevan hit back, arguing that putting the voluntary hospitals under local government would 'rouse a tornado compared with any passing thunderstorm my scheme may provoke'. He added: 'any scheme which leaves responsibility for the hospital service with local authorities must be unequal in its operation. This would be unjust to the public who will pay equal contributions.' The regional boards 'would be the agents (though not, I hope, in any derogatory sense the creatures) of my department' with 'substantial executive powers, subject to a broad financial control'. If the scheme was sound, the political consequences need not be feared, and if Morrison described it as imaginative: 'is not that exactly what we were returned to be?' Neither of the present systems – municipal or voluntary – would do. Such a chance to make the health services 'the admiration of the world . . . comes but once, perhaps, in a generation . . . if it is not done now it will not be done in our time.'[51]

The row went to Cabinet two days later, where Morrison reiterated objections that hospital nationalisation was not in the party manifesto: indeed, municipalisation had been Labour's policy. Local pride and voluntary enthusiasm mattered, Morrison argued, and there would be 'a very large transfer of liability from the ratepayer to the taxpayer' under Bevan's plan. He was backed by Chuter Ede, now Home Secretary, and some others. But Arthur Greenwood, chairman of the Cabinet's social services committee, Ellen Wilkinson the education minister, and Emmanuel Shinwell, Minister of Fuel, backed Bevan as did George Buchanan, the Scottish health minister. Lord Addison, once Lloyd George's Minister of Health, an anatomist who was 'easily the most distinguished doctor ever to enter politics' and who had effectively founded the Medical Research Council, did the same. The seventy-six-year-old Addison, now leader of the Lords, argued that nationalisation would greatly assist medical education. Attlee summed up strongly in Bevan's favour.[52]

What Morrison half hinted at, but which never in the 1940s became quite the core of the argument, is that in practice there are profound difficulties in having an elected body, which will almost inevitably come under party political control, disposing of purely central government funds – an argument that was to become even stronger in the 1980s when cash limits were introduced. Without their own funds the local politicians will blame all failures on lack of central government cash. They may even refuse to implement government policy, as was to happen with health authorities in the 1980s when local government had influence on them (though not control). Given the tendency of political control of local authorities to move against the government of the day, such a recipe is one for conflict rather than creative tension between the centre and the periphery. Only if elected bodies raise at least some of their own funds can the responsibility for running the service – and raising more from their electors if more is judged to be needed – be safely entrusted to them. It is a case, if conflict is to be avoided, of 'no representation without taxation'.

Morrison lost the argument in October, but continued the fight, leaving Bevan to 'damn and blast' him to his wife Jennie Lee when he returned home at night. In December, however, the issue was finally settled in Bevan's favour.[53] For years afterwards Morrison would refer sourly to 'Nye's precious health service', particularly after its launch when Bevan succeeded in extracting ever-growing sums for it despite the extreme financial difficulties Labour then faced.[54]

When the Bill and accompanying White Paper[55] were published in March 1946, however, it was not the idea of nationalising the hospitals but Bevan's proposals for GPs which nearly sank the whole scheme. Ironically, these differed in substance not at all from the ideas the BMA's own Medical Planning Commission had put forward three years earlier. But Dr Charles Hill, the scribe of that report and now the BMA's Secretary, appeared to have forgotten everything.

Bevan proposed that family doctors should be paid a basic salary, and capitation fees on top. The sale of practices would be abolished and £66m was offered in compensation – a sum that even the BMA admitted was fair.[56] On this Bevan was adamant. He was to tell the Commons: 'I have always regarded the sale and purchase of medical practice as an evil in itself.'[57] It was 'inconsistent with a civilized community . . . for patients to be bought and sold over their heads. When I am told that all they desire is that patients should have the best medical treatment, how can that be argued when a doctor succeeds to another doctor's panel not on account of personal qualifications but on the size of his purse?'[58] In addition, he proposed that GPs should be encouraged to work in partnerships in health centres provided by local authorities. Bevan's only substantive departure from the BMA's own 1942 proposals was that he revived the controls, which Willink had dropped, to prevent new GPs entering over-doctored areas.

The BMA exploded. Doctors argued that the plans would lead to a full-time salaried service under either the state or local government. Doctors would be reduced to civil servants, clinical independence and freedom of speech would be threatened, and Bevan himself as Minister of Health would have enormous powers to direct them. Some of the language used now seems incredible. Dr Alfred Cox, a former secretary of the BMA, wrote to the British Medical Journal declaring: 'I have examined the Bill and it looks to me uncommonly like the first step, and a big one, towards National Socialism as practised in Germany. The medical service there was early put under the dictatorship of a "medical Fuehrer". This Bill will establish the Minister of Health in that capacity.' Dr Cox was far from alone. At a meeting of 1000 doctors in Wimbledon Town Hall shortly after the Bill was published, Bevan was called 'a dictator' and 'an autocrat'. 'This Bill,' declared one doctor, 'is strongly suggestive of the Hitlerite regime now being destroyed in Germany.' Another denounced the hospital proposals as 'the greatest seizure of property since Henry VIII confiscated the monasteries'.[59]

What Bevan proposed for the GPs was in the end what happened. And given both that the BMA had itself outlined remarkably similar proposals and that the doctors' fears simply failed to materialise, an explanation of their apparently paranoiac reaction and the lengths to which they took the argument is needed. It falls in three parts. The first lies in the structure, history and some of the personalities of the BMA – particularly in the structure, which was to cause the association similar problems once a decade between the 1960s and the 1980s over various virulent disputes about doctors' contracts. Second, the doctors' fears were genuine and they had evidence to support their view that a full-time salaried service was the final goal. And third, the dispute about their contract was played out against the background of the hospitals being nationalised – a revolutionary departure which left plenty of room for argument about its implications.

The BMA was in some ways the very model of democracy, but it was an unwieldy democracy. Its nominal governing body was and is the representative body, normally called together at the annual representative meeting. It could take binding 'decisions of the association' by two-thirds majority. Below that was the council, a large body of some seventy members. The day to day work, however, was undertaken by the chairman, the secretary and his staff (at this time the BMA had no executive) and through the *ad hoc* negotiating committee. The chairman was one Dr Guy Dain, a pocket battleship of bristling energy, a strong believer in individualism whose motto was that 'responsibility is the salt of life'. (He had it translated into Latin when he was knighted.) He had become convinced ever since Ernest Brown's suggestion of a salaried service in 1943 and since the report of 'that old blighter Beveridge' that the ministry wanted to turn doctors into civil servants. John Pater, a civil servant at the time, judges he became 'increasingly emotional' in his belief that he was defending the freedom of the profession.[60] Dain and Hill, however, while they could negotiate as spokesmen, could not agree terms without reference back to the representative body.

Anything the BMA's negotiators came back with had to be manoeuvred through these conferences and meetings. And the plain fact for the BMA was and is that it is always easier to make an impassioned speech against any proposal than a reasoned, and possibly complex one, for it. Dr Charles Hill, thirty years after the event, conceded:

It is undeniable that emotional outbursts in public at critical times, inevitable in a large body at times of crisis, did sometimes embarrass the profession's spokesmen by the headlines they stimulated and the somersaults of policy they encouraged . . . Furthermore, the Representative Body did declare itself – in advance of any Government plans – in favour of many features of a health service which it subsequently rejected. It did tend sometimes to ignore such gains as its representatives had secured and immediately to switch its attention to the points on which it had not won, however important or unimportant they were. Balance sheets of gains and losses are not always judged dispassionately in large assemblies, where oratory and emotion prevail. Tactics are better devised in private by the few than publicly by the many.[61]

Thus, not to be overthrown, BMA negotiators have often on platforms to sound at least as militant as the most militant of the voting doctors before them – people who were no mere cannon fodder but articulate and almost by definition individualistic men and women. More than once in the next fifty years, the association was to paint itself into corners in this way.

Furthermore, then more than now, those doctors who attended the representative body and the council were not necessarily representative of the profession as a whole. In the 1940s, the BMA was much more GP-dominated than it was to become. The Royal Colleges, whose role strictly is to supervise education and standards, not pay and rations, also played more part in medical politics than they did in later years. Harry Eckstein, an early chronicler of the founding of the NHS who also produced a detailed study of the BMA as a pressure group, observed that to partake in medical politics doctors needed money and time. At a time when many GPs in poorer areas were low earners, the representative body meetings were 'inevitably weighted in favour of age, affluence, private practice and the suburb'. In other words, those who had least to gain as doctors from a National Health Service were more likely to be those who voted at the BMA's very public and well reported meetings, and the decisions of those meetings were strongly reflected in the interpretation of events and advice that BMA leaders then put to doctors in the rash of plebiscites between 1946 and 1948. Bevan found, as Lloyd George had put it in 1911, that 'a deputation of doctors was a deputation of swell doctors'.[62]

Dain, Hill and the members also remembered history. Lloyd George had, to an even greater extent than Bevan, refused to negotiate with the medical profession over the National Insurance Act. In 1913 the BMA had assembled 27,400 signed pledges from family doctors refusing to participate until its terms were met. Ironically, in a position that was reversed in the 1940s, it had then been the consultants, who were unaffected by the measures, who largely orchestrated the opposition.[63] When the 1911 Act came into force, however, GPs fearing they would lose potential patients to rivals, suddenly signed on in droves, leaving the association routed, divided and humiliated. This time, Dain and Hill, desperate to maintain the doctors' unity and preserve the BMA, repeatedly consulted the troops, calling special representative meetings and holding plebiscites which only helped give publicity to the more furious opponents of the proposals.

The doctors also had good grounds for their suspicion that a full-time salaried service was the ultimate goal. Ernest Brown, a National Liberal, had proposed it; it had been Labour policy since 1934; and as recently as April 1943 the party had reiterated the proposal for all doctors, not just GPs, in *A National Service for Health*. That document had included a bar on private practice for those employed by the state.[64] Bevan had formally rejected this part of party policy. Michael Foot records that he 'desperately wanted the patient to have free choice of doctor. He saw it as the best safeguard against poor service from the general practitioner.'[65] He was to tell the Commons that to make doctors salaried would mean allocating patients to doctors and vice versa. Capitation, on the other hand, encouraged the doctor to provide a good service in order to attract and keep the patient who could move if dissatisfied, but he also wanted a small basic salary to allow young doctors to keep body and soul together while they built up a practice.

If Bevan rejected a salaried service, that still left him with his own back-benchers to placate for dropping party policy. Twice in the second reading debate in April 1946 he remarked that the profession was not ripe for a salaried service, adding: 'There is all the difference in the world between plucking fruit when it is ripe and plucking it when it is green.' Arthur Greenwood only compounded their suspicions by declaring in the wind-up to the debate: 'What was published by my party in 1943 . . . we of course stand by.'[66] The BMA and its leaders heard only those sentences, not Bevan's repeated assurances that there would be no full-time salaried service. In addition Grey-Turner, the BMA's official historian, concedes there was 'an emotional, even political,' undercurrent to the dispute. 'When [in 1945] Churchill in his own words was "immediately dismissed by the British electorate from all further conduct of their affairs", many in the middle classes were uneasy.' Statements by Labour ministers such as 'we are the masters now' and Shinwell's declaration that he did not care 'a tinker's cuss' for the middle classes only compounded that feeling. In the middle of the dispute Willesden Borough Council attempted to force all its employees, its medical officers included, to join a trade union. (The BMA at this stage was, jealously and proudly, not one.) Doctors did not have to be paranoid to see that as another straw in the wind.[67] Such attitudes and actions 'provoked resentment and belligerence in professional people,'[68] and doctors, if anyone did, considered themselves professionals.

Thus throughout the dispute-wracked months between April 1946 and 5 July 1948 – vesting day for the National Health Service – the argument was repeatedly heard that Bevan's plans for GPs were 'the thin end of the wedge' and 'could lead, sooner rather than later' to a full-time salaried service with 'doctors becoming a branch of the civil service'. The consultants were told that would be their fate too, once they took salaries in the nationalised hospitals, despite the distinctly favourable terms Bevan had contrived for them. Given that no one quite knew what a nationalised hospital meant, even though the Emergency Hospital Service had provided a national system for seven years, the fears may have been groundless. That did not at the time make them as ludicrous as they later appeared to be.

The BMA, let alone the profession, was in practice of course never united. Webb-Johnson for the surgeons described the Bill as 'bold and statesmanlike'.[69] Moran repeatedly defended it, accusing opponents of distorting the arguments and resorting to slogans. The surgeon Henry Souttar, the immediate past president of the BMA who had chaired the Medical Planning Commission, pronounced it 'exceedingly good'.[70] Professor Johnstone Jervis, President of the Society of Medical Officers of Health, declared it 'incontestably the greatest thing that has ever been done in social medicine in any age and country'.[71] And while the British Medical Journal bitterly attacked Bevan, The Lancet argued for the plan. Many newspapers sided with the doctors and the Tories in their objections. But the then more numerous Labour-supporting papers backed Bevan, and The Times and the Economist both gave the plan a consistently favourable press.

The detailed and tortuous course of the battle between Bevan and the doctors has been well told elsewhere[72] and a number of issues other than the central one of whether doctors would become full-time salaried civil servants and thus denied clinical freedom and free speech, wove in and out of the dispute. But the Bill achieved its Royal Assent in November 1946, at which point a BMA plebiscite showed 54 per cent of doctors opposed to entering detailed discussions on NHS regulations (including pay) with Bevan.

The three Royal College presidents intervened. In January 1947 they wrote to Bevan seeking assurances and clarification on key issues including the basic salary. Bevan was proposing this should be £300 pa – enough to get a young doctor started, hardly enough to make him a state employee. The presidents' action, the equivocal ballot result, and Bevan's conciliatory reply cornered a special BMA representative meeting into starting talks.[73] These dragged on through 1947 to break down at a meeting in December when Bevan, who had been all milk and honey throughout the year, exploded. According to Dr Solly Wand, 'he threatened us and raved at us. He waved his finger in the air and said that if, as a result of anything the profession did, the number of patients who signed on was much less than 95 per cent, he would make serious reductions in capitation fees.'[74] The breakdown came because the BMA was still demanding such extensive changes that fresh legislation to construct a new and very different Act would have been needed. Bevan declared that Parliament decided the law, not doctors, and refused to let them dictate to the government.

In January 1948, with Hill insisting that the months of negotiation had made it 'absolutely clear that these proposals mean and are intended to mean a whole-time salaried service under the state', another plebiscite was held.[75] The doctors were told that the independence of medicine was at stake. The *British Medical Journal* declared that Bevan's refusal to amend the Act, 'strengthens this belief'.[76] The BMA council's message to the membership stated that the issue was not money or compensation, but 'the intellectual freedom and integrity of the profession'. If a majority voted against the service, including 13,000 of the 20,000 GPs, the BMA would advise the profession not to join the NHS.

The result was overwhelming, and stunning for the government: 84 per cent of doctors voted, and 86 per cent of those (including 17,000 general practitioners) were against accepting service under the Act.[77] Bevan, who had been under growing pressure for months from Morrison and others who had seen the whole enterprise as likely to end in tears unless the doctors were placated, refused to waver. He issued a terse statement. 'The Act will come into operation on 5 July in accordance with Parliament's decision.'[78]

Some newspapers, the *Observer* and the *Glasgow Herald* included, called for his resignation. Between the February ballot result and the end of March there was complete deadlock. It was the Royal College presidents, led by 'Corkscrew Charlie', who rode once again to the rescue. In late March after private consultations with Wilson Jameson, the Chief Medical Officer,[79] Lord Moran wrote to Bevan suggesting that he introduce amending legislation. It would stipulate that a whole-time salaried service could not be introduced by regulation, but only by a full Act of Parliament. Webb-Johnson and Mr William Gilliatt, now the obstetricians' president, backed him. On 7 April, Bevan told Parliament he would do just that – pointing out for good measure that if doctors really believed they would be turned into civil servants by the basic salary which would now apply only for the first three years, they could hand it back. It was the decisive intervention. If the NHS Act was Bevan's baby, the Royal College presidents were its midwife. Moran's intervention, Bevan told him in a private letter, was 'the most helpful thing said by any doctor in the whole of this business'.[80]

In substance, given his repeated assurances that he did not intend a full-time salaried service and the clear reasons he had outlined as to why he opposed one, Bevan had given away little. But his offer to embody those assurances in legislation received an enthusiastic reaction in both Parliament and the media.[81] The battle in fact was over. The BMA, however, did not yet realise that, any more than did the British Dental Association which as late as June 1948 was still trying to organise a boycott of the service.[82] Furious doctors who had already been condemning the Royal College presidents as 'Quislings'[83] for their earlier interventions renewed the charge and relations between the BMA and the Royal Colleges were never to be quite the same again. The effect of the intervention echoed down the succeeding years: the heinous 'betrayal' by the Royal Colleges was one of the first stories told me by a BMA doctor when I became a health correspondent in 1974. These strained relations were to have further ramifications in the NHS's history.

The association's leaders put fourteen questions to Bevan, including continued worries about free speech, rights of appeal to the courts over dismissal, and objections to the ban on selling practices. Bevan replied, promising a right to speak out in patients' interests which he enshrined in doctors' terms and conditions of service. That right was only to be undermined not by a 'National Socialist' Labour minister as the doctors feared, but by Kenneth Clarke, a Conservative health minister, and the nearest the Tories have produced to a Bevan of their own in his intransigent determination not to be dictated to by the doctors.

At a deeply divided council meeting, the BMA decided once again to go to a plebiscite telling the members that, despite gains, not all fourteen of their queries had been answered satisfactorily and that on balance 'the freedoms of the profession are not sufficiently safeguarded'. Seventy-four per cent of the doctors voted. They split 52 per cent against joining the NHS to 48 per cent in favour. But the number of GPs refusing to join was now only 9588 out of the 20,000 – far short of the 13,000, or two-thirds, that the BMA had said was necessary to make the Act unworkable. Doctors on the ground were finally beginning to believe the great Welshman's word. In addition, 'the great and natural fear of many general practitioners was that enough of their colleagues might join the service on the appointed day to make it workable, and so would take away the bulk of the patients,' Grey-Turner records.[84] The events of 1913 were repeating themselves.

There had been warning signals. A mere 6000 doctors had contributed to an independence fund the BMA set up in April to finance continued opposition, and in March it had become apparent, according to Grey-Turner, that there was 'no clear cut plan as to how doctors were to carry on their practices, and earn their incomes, if they refused to join the National Health Service'.[85] Dr Alfred Cox, who had originally condemned Bevan as a Fuehrer and the Bill as 'National Socialism', and who had been the association's secretary during the 1911–13 dispute, now wrote to the *BMJ* warning that then the leaders had fought on when doctors, satisfied by Lloyd George's concessions, had flocked to join the panel scheme. 'Is history to repeat itself?' he asked.[86]

The BMA's council opened talks with Bevan on the final details of remuneration for doctors, and on the package of amending legislation. By the end of May at the final special representative meeting, Dain had to announce that 26 per cent of GPs in England and more than 36 per cent in Scotland and Wales had already signed up. Solly Wand told the meeting that whether the representatives liked it or not, their army 'had started to go home'.[87] A frantic last-ditch manouevre to get the BMA to fight on was defeated,[88] and a mere five weeks from the launch of the NHS the doctors formally agreed to take part. Like Waterloo, however, it had been a damn close-run thing. On 18 June, seventeen days before the Appointed Day, Dain finally promised that 'the profession will do its utmost to make the service a resounding success'.[89]

CHAPTER 7

'With a song in my heart' – Health and Social Security

On Monday morning you will wake up in a new Britain, in a state which 'takes over' its citizens six months before they are born, providing care and free services for their birth, for their early years, their schooling, sickness, workless days, widowhood and retirement. All this with free doctoring, dentistry and medicine – free bath-chairs, too, if needed – for 4/11d out of your weekly pay packet. You begin paying next Friday.

Daily Mail, 3 July 1948

I can remember this particular day. Everything was in a radius of a few minutes walk, and she [mother] went to the opticians. Obviously she'd got the prescription from the doctor. She went in and she got tested for new glasses. Then she went further down the road . . . for the chiropodist. She had her feet done. Then she went back to the doctor's because she'd been having trouble with her ear and the doctor said he would fix her up with a hearing aid. I remember her saying to the doctor on the way out, 'Well the undertaker's is on the way home. Everything is going on, I might as well call in there on the way!'

Alice Law, recalling 5 July 1948; Peter Hennessy, Never Again, p. 174

I remember a Medical Officer of Health in Birmingham, now dead, telling me they were so terrified that there would be a stampede for everything free on the day that the staff arrived early and literally barricaded themselves into their offices, peering out. Needless to say, this being Britain, soon after 9 o'clock a neat, orderly and not very long queue of mothers and babies formed up outside.

Celia Hall, Medical Editor, Independent, 1989

On July 5, the brass band from Yorkshire Main Colliery trooped up to the doctor's surgery in Edlington, South Yorkshire, and began to play. The doctor hung a Union flag out of the window and gave them all a drink. The NHS had arrived.

Dr Michael O'Donnell, the GP's son, speaking on the 40th anniversary of the NHS; Independent, 5 July 1988

'I used to be a miner,' he told the girl on the counter, 'but I had to give it up through a strained back. Will there be anything for me in the new benefit scheme?' The counter clerk, imbued with the new spirit of helpfulness, replied 'We're all new here and we're not too sure about the industrial injuries scheme. But if you come back and see us on the fifth of July, I'm sure we'll be able to fix you up with something.'

Ministry of National Insurance official; Peter Hennessy, Never Again, p. 175

On 4 June 1944, two days before the D-Day landings, Churchill invited Bevin to accompany him to Portsmouth to say farewell to some of the troops. 'They were going off to face this terrific battle,' Bevin recounted, 'with great hearts and great courage. The one question they put to me as I went through their ranks was: "Ernie, when we have done this job for you are we going back on the dole?" . . . Both the Prime Minister and I answered: "No, you are not."'

Angus Calder, The People's War, p. 570

THE WAR over the NHS was to leave the Labour Party deeply suspicious of the BMA for the next thirty-five years. But it also damaged the standing of the Conservative Party as the future guardians of the welfare state. For on both second and third readings the Tories voted against the Bill. Timothy Raison, who founded the journal *New Society* before becoming a Conservative Home Office and Education Minister, acknowledged in his history *Tories and the Welfare State* that the votes 'provided the Labour party with a stick with which they sought to beat the Conservatives for years to come'.[1]

In both cases, the Conservatives had put down reasoned amendments, and in the second reading debate fiercely attacked Bevan. The force of their attack was not entirely to do with health. Bevan was also responsible for housing, over which Labour in the earlier part of its term was in deep trouble. Four months before, in December 1945, Bevan had been the chief target in the first Tory censure motion of the new Parliament as Churchill, whose relations with Bevan were always fraught, attempted to paint him as a dogmatic, ideological, administrative incompetent in his public housing programme.[2] The same charge, the Conservatives hoped, might be made to stick over the National Health Service.

Their amendment at second reading stated, truthfully enough, that the Tories too wished to establish 'a comprehensive health service'. But it attacked Bevan's plan for destroying local ownership of hospitals; for wrecking the voluntary hospitals; and for preparing the way for a full-time salaried service which would threaten the doctor–patient relationship. Willink, now the Conservative health spokesman, and his deputy Richard Law also accused him of 'weakening the responsibility of local authorities without planning the health service as a whole'. This last had some truth. In part to placate Morrison and the local government lobby, Bevan had left maternity and child welfare, district nursing, health centres and other services with local government while arguing that logically they too should be transferred. Morrison had protested that if they went it would mean 'the loss by British local government of all or most of its responsibilities in this important field [health] – in which it has done some of its best work and in which, so to speak, it won its spurs'.[3] It was equally true, however, that the new regional hospital boards and management commit-tees had their work cut out simply taking over the existing voluntary and municipal hospitals. 'If they had been given the whole NHS to run they would have been overwhelmed,' Sir George Godber, the future Chief Medical Officer later judged. 'Primary care and community services would have been the losers.'[4]

Bevan's plan also had the effect of divorcing GPs from the hospitals. How plainly that was perceived at the time is not clear. But the spread of consultants across the country progressively made the GPs who had treated their own patients as surgeons, anaesthetists and physicians into suppli-cants to the salaried specialists for treatment of their patients in hospitals. Far less did consultants 'need' GPs for private patient referrals. As a result, the GP's status within the medical profession declined. There were dramatic improvements in the quality of care as specialists replaced ill-trained journeymen, but the result was a tripartite service, not a unified one. Hospital, local authority, and family doctor services were each run by different authorities, the last also embracing pharmacy, dental and ophthalmic services. The problems caused by piecemeal management were to be a recurring theme of the next fifty years of the NHS. But the doctors' profound hostility to local government made handing over control of the whole service to local authorities impossible, and it was equally impracticable to create a unified service by transferring the remaining council services to the state-run NHS.[5]

If Bevan had to defend himself against the Tories, he had to do the same in committee against those of his own back-benchers who were angry at the abandonment of party policy on a salaried family doctor service; at the consultants' preservation of private practice within the NHS; and at the downgrading of local government. Bevan handled both sides with 'scintillating and dialectical brilliance' according to Sir Frederick Messer, the Labour MP for Tottenham who became chairman of the North West Metropolitan Regional Hospital Board. 'As one who disagreed with him at the beginning on some things and at the finish agreed with him on most, I think his outstanding success was the way he applied the anaesthetic to supporters on his own side, making them believe in things they had opposed almost all their lives.'[6]

But at third reading the Conservatives again voted against the Bill, tabling if anything a stronger amendment.[7] By parliamentary tradition, an Opposition only votes against third reading if it opposes the principle of a measure. The Conservatives did not oppose the principle of a comprehensive health service, but such was the furore outside Parliament over Bevan's proposals that the Tories allowed themselves to be tempted into opposition. Future Tory apologists could point to back-bench speeches strongly in favour of the principle. Derrick Heathcoat-Amory, a future Chancellor of the Exchequer, declared that 'by any test, this is a tremendous measure: there can be no question about that . . . those of us who feel bound to vote for the amendment do so with a sense of very real regret.'[8] But a vote is a vote. And the Labour message that the Tories could not be trusted with the NHS went deep into the British psyche.

The Appointed Day, 5 July 1948, was by any standards one of the great days of British history. Bevan, who had slightly soured it by calling the Tories 'lower than vermin' in a speech in Manchester the night before, formally handed over symbolic keys to the NHS at Park Hospital in Trafford – where exactly forty years on a lottery to try to keep the hospital going was launched.[9] The NHS, he had declared, would 'lift the shadow from millions of homes' and in the weeks that followed people did indeed rush to use the service. 'One would think the people saved up their illnesses for the first free day,' one GP complained. Dentists, of whom there was anyway a shortage and only half of whom had joined by vesting day, were soon booked solid for months ahead while a five-month wait for spectacles rapidly developed.[10] John Marks, who will figure later in this

Daily Mirror

DEC 2

No. 12,159
Registered at the G.P.O. as a Newspaper.

ONE PENNY

Beveridge tells how to

BANISH WANT

Cradle to grave plan | All pay— all benefit

SIR WILLIAM BEVERIDGE'S Report, aimed at abolishing Want in Britain, is published today.

He calls his Plan for Social Security a revolution under which "every citizen willing to serve according to his powers has at all times an income sufficient to meet his responsibilities."

Here are his chief proposals:

All social insurance—unemployment, health, pensions—lumped into one weekly contribution for all citizens without income limit—from duke to dustman.

These payments, in the case of employees, would be:

Men 4s. 3d.	Employer 3s. 3d.
Women 3s. 6d.	Employer 2s. 6d.

Cradle to the grave benefits for all, including:

Free medical, dental, eyesight and hospital treatment;

Children's allowances of 8s. a week each, after the first child.

Increases in unemployment benefit (40s. for a couple) and abolition of the means test; industrial pension in place of workmen's compensation.

A charter for housewives, including marriage grant up to £10; maternity grant of £4 (and 36s. for 13 weeks for a paid worker); widow's benefit; separation and divorce provision; free domestic help in time of sickness.

Old age pensions rising to 40s. for a married couple on retirement.

Funeral grants up to £20.

To work the scheme a new Ministry of Social Security would open Security Offices within reach of every Citizen.

The 1d.-a-week-collected-at-the-door insurance schemes of the big companies would be taken over by the State.

Sir William says the Plan depends on a prosperous Britain, but claims that it can begin by July 1, 1944, if planning begins at once.

[See pages 4, 5 and 7]

Allies separate Axis armies in Africa

AMERICAN and French forces were reported last night to have driven a wedge between the two Axis armies in North Africa—between Nehring, fighting to hold Bizerta and Tunis, and Rommel, at bay at El Aghelia.

Messages from North Africa and New York stated that the Allies have reached the Tunisian coast between Gabes and Sfax.

Nehring's land communications with Tripolitania—where the Africa Korps is preparing for the next big attack by General Montgomery's Eighth Army—have thus been cut off.

The Americans and French are believed to have pushed to the coast through desert-like country from Gafsa, in Central Tunisia.

In the Bizerta-Tunis triangle Morocco radio reported that the British First Army has crossed the Axis minefields to come to grips with the main defences.

The French are reported to have captured Pont du Fahs, a railway town 35 miles south of Tunis.

Quit Bizerta 'Drome'

The air battle over Tunisia is being fought with an intensity believed in the unequalled since the Battle of Britain.

As the struggle grows fiercer the Germans throw in planes rushed to North Africa from Western Europe and Russia.

One Nazi pilot shot down in Tunisia was flying over Stalingrad less than a fortnight ago.

Bizerta airfield has been so devastated that it was believed at Allied H.Q. last night that most of the Luftwaffe bombers and fighters have been driven back to Sicily.

Flying Fortresses have also pounded Tunis, Sfax and Gabes.

RAF bombers rained explosives on Bizerta without a pause during Monday night, and daylight had scarcely appeared yesterday when other Allied aircraft took up the attack.

El Agheila spearhead

Patrol activity by the advanced spearhead of the Eighth Army on the El Agheila front yesterday means that the battle for this vital position may be opening.

Indications of our growing strength in this advanced area are our constant air attacks on enemy communications on the road between El Agheila and Tripoli, and on the two enemy bases at Misurata and Tripoli.

German radio last night admitted that the spearhead of the Eighth Army had pushed over to Ras Sam, and yesterday's Italian communiqué also reported activity between advanced units.

FDR AND DE GAULLE

President Roosevelt said yesterday that he would be glad to receive General de Gaulle, but he had not invited him to visit him.

Darlan is 'Chief of State'

ADMIRAL DARLAN has created an Imperial Council at Algiers and has assumed the powers of Chief of State in French Africa, Morocco radio announced last night.

The radio said Darlan has assumed the power as Chief of State as representative of Marshal Pétain, who is at present a prisoner.

"French Africa has resumed an official status which will enable it, pending the liberation of Metropolitan France, to defend the general interests of the Empire, to remain effectively the fight at the side of her Allies and to represent France in the world."

The Imperial Council has already held its two first meetings.

Admiral Darlan presided over the sittings, which were attended by General Nogues, Governor - General Boisson, Governor - General Chatel, General Giraud, and General Bergeret.

STATEMENT ON DARLAN IN SECRET

The position of Admiral Darlan and the military developments in North Africa are to be subjects of a statement in secret session in the Commons.

When Mr. Eden announced this yesterday he added that an opportunity would be provided for a debate if desired.

NO COMMONS DEBATE BEFORE NEW YEAR

FIRST Commons comments on Sir William Beveridge's plan will be made at the next sitting, as the I.L.P. amendment to the Address is so broadly phrased that it will embrace any reconstruction proposals of this kind.

Labour Front Bench may indicate some of his party's reactions, but, as Sir William Jowitt indicated yesterday, the report will not be fully debated until the New Year.

The people of Occupied Europe are being told by radio of the report and its implications.

From down in twenty-two languages, they will be shown how Britain, even in the midst of war, has grappled with social problems. Just as in the past she took a lead on questions of social security.

Sir William will explain his report on the radio at 9.25 tonight.

Govt. give hint of post-war planning

CHOOSING the eve of the publication of Sir William Beveridge's long-awaited report on Social Security, the Government yesterday gave the country its first indication of their own plans for post-war Britain.

These include the continuance of rationing for some time and control of industry (some industries being taken over as public corporations); the development of agriculture, forestry and public utilities like electricity.

The Government also announced the immediate setting up of a new Ministry of Town and Country Planning; and the rejection of the Uthwatt Committee proposals for placing main responsibility for planning in the hands of a permanent commission.

Victory First

Sir William Jowitt, Paymaster-General, answering a debate on reconstruction in the House of Commons, said:

"We must not allow ourselves to be distracted by talk of reconstruction from the stern task of securing victory.

"Talk of reconstruction is a mockery if the world is to remain hereafter under the constant fear of aggression."

Sir William referred to the Beveridge Report and said:

"The ideal of Social Security is one to which all thinking men and women can subscribe. We must harness this work as part of our reconstruction work as a whole.

"I hope that early in the New Year members will be in a position to discuss the main questions raised in the Report."

Sir William said it seemed obvious that the immediate

Continued on Back Page

'From cradle to grave…' The *Daily Mirror*'s front page, 2 December 1942.

Above: Sir William Beveridge – slaying giants.

Below: Health made Bevan's name, but he was proud of his housing. 'We shall be judged for a year or two by the number of houses we build. We shall be judged in ten years' time by the type of house we build.'

Above: Rab Butler as President of the Board of Education: 'The effect [of the 1944 Education Act]... will be as much social as educational. I think it will have the effect of welding us all into one nation.'

Right: Tony Crosland, Secretary of State for Education and Science, opening an open-plan primary school in 1967. In 1956 he had written: 'The school system in Britain remains the most divisive, unjust and wasteful of all the aspects of social inequality.'

Above: 'Do we want a state medical service?' Dr Guy Dain, the BMA's chairman of council, and Dr Charles Hill, its secretary and a future Conservative housing minister, deliberate.

Below: Across the years: Jim Griffiths (*left*), the man who implemented the Beveridge Report, talks in 1955 to Richard Crossman, who was shortly to attempt to redesign it.

story, qualified as a doctor on the day the NHS started, and worked at Wembley Hospital.

We were inundated with people wanting wigs. I had a misery of a consultant called King who was bald as a coot himself and people would come in demanding wigs from him. I used to do the odd locum in general practice, and people would ask for cotton wool to use as padding, and for free surgical spirit, or come in asking for aspirin. There was abuse – because suddenly it was all free. But the other side was the colossal amount of very real unmet need that just poured in needing treatment. There were women with prolapsed uteruses literally wobbling down between their legs that had been held in place with cup and stem pessaries – like a big penis with a cup on it. It was the same with hernias. You would have men walking round with trusses holding these colossal hernias in. And they were all like that because they couldn't afford to have it done. They couldn't afford to consult a doctor, let alone have an operation. And at the same time as the NHS arrived medicine was starting to be able to do more. I saw penicillin come in as a medical student, and as a houseman I was one of the first people to treat TB meningitis with streptomycin. The child survived. Admittedly it was a gibbering idiot, but it survived. Before that it was a 100 per cent death rate.[11]

Dr Alastair Clarke, a Clydeside GP two years before the NHS, remembers thirty to forty previously uninsured women coming to his surgery with similar long-standing gynaecological problems in the first six months. But he also recalled how the arrival of the NHS transformed life for many doctors as well as patients:

I used to charge 1/6d for a consultation. They laid the money on the desk as they came in. It was all rather embarrassing. I used to charge 2/6d to 7/6d for a visit, the highest rate for foremen and under-managers. We'd send out the bills, but about a quarter would be bad debts and some you simply didn't bill because you knew they couldn't pay. The NHS thankfully got rid of all that.[12]

The result of vast unmet need and recent medical advance was an almost instant example of one of the NHS's recurring preoccupations – an expenditure crisis. Bevan himself within eighteen months was admitting: 'I shudder to think of the ceaseless cascade of medicine which is pouring down British throats at the present time.'[13]

He had been aware of the unpredictability of the costs in advance, telling

Dalton it would take a full year's experience to know them – although he did suggest, falsely as it turned out, that the high early costs would fall as the backlog of disease was treated. He had also foreseen – and taken pride in – something which all health ministers should take to heart, but by which many have been beaten down. 'We never shall have all we need,' he had declared. 'Expectation will always exceed capacity.'[14] In addition, 'the service must always be changing, growing and improving; it must always appear inadequate.' And he recognised the impact to come of the nationalised structure, with appointed boards for whom he, as the Minister of Health, was answerable to Parliament. The House of Commons order paper would be covered with questions. 'Every mistake which you make, I shall bleed for,' he told the Royal College of Nursing a month before the service was launched. 'I shall be going about like Saint Sebastian, bleeding from a thousand javelins . . . all I shall be is a central receiver of complaints.'[15]

But the appointed day was not just for the NHS. It was also the start of modern social security. Beveridge's report finally came into effect.

Its very first fruits had ripened before Labour came to power. In May 1944 the government won its 'White Paper race' with Beveridge to produce Command 6527, the coalition White Paper on *Employment Policy*. Beveridge was miffed at the government's refusal to commission it from him, and at the refusal to let civil servants help with his own 'private enterprise' effort, *Full Employment in a Free Society*. He nevertheless described the Government White Paper as 'epoch-making' and 'a milestone in economic and political history', though he remained critical of some of the tools it proposed to use to maintain full employment.[16]

The White Paper dripped with the influence of Keynes. In Beveridge's words, it dismissed the Treasury's great 'economic fallacy' of the 1920s and 1930s which had been succinctly defined by Churchill in his 1929 Budget speech as the world crashed into the Great Depression. 'It is the orthodox Treasury dogma steadfastly held,' Churchill told the Commons then, 'that, whatever might be the political and social advantages, very little additional employment can, in fact, and as a general rule, be created by State borrowing and State expenditure.' Beveridge commented: 'By the renewed experience of full employment [that dogma] has been consumed in the fires of war, and the White Paper may be regarded as a ceremonial scattering of the ashes.' It was to be another thirty years before, phoenix-like, it rose again, reincarnated as monetarism.

The White Paper's crucial sentences were that the government accepted 'as one of their primary aims and responsibilities, the maintenance of a high and stable level of employment after the war . . . Total expenditure on goods and services must be prevented from falling to a level where general unemployment appears.' No precise definition of 'high and stable' was given. Indeed the only time full employment has been defined by a British government was in 1951 when Hugh Gaitskell, the Labour Chancellor, told the United Nations that Labour's definition was 'a level of unemployment of 3 per cent *at the seasonal peak*'.[17] This was slightly lower than Beveridge's 1944 figure of 3 per cent jobless *on average*. (Unemployment has natural fluctuations, for example when school leavers reach the job market or winter weather hits the construction industry.) But the difference proved academic. The bad winter of 1963 aside, it was to be the 1970s before unemployment rose above 3 per cent at all and between 1945 and 1970 it averaged little more than half that – 1.8 per cent. The one great exception was in the awesome winter of 1947. Then, during the Great Freeze, with bread rationed (something that had been necessary in neither World War), the meat ration cut, and stockpiled coal frozen so solid it could not be moved, unemployment briefly hit 2,000,000. 'Shiver with Shinwell and Starve with Strachey' the newspapers proclaimed, pillorying the ministers of fuel and agriculture.[18]

The vital Keynesian tool for achieving full employment was demand management: 'a policy for maintaining total expenditure'. During recessions the government would spend on 'the permanent equipment of society'; in essence it would invest in public works and publicly funded projects while attempting to influence private capital investment and expenditure by raising and lowering interest rates.

Full employment was already a reality in 1948 and would remain so for a quarter of a century. Family allowances, another part of the Beveridge plan, had also been enacted under the Conservative Minister Leslie Hore-Belisha (who as Minister of Transport had given his name to the Belisha beacons which adorn zebra crossings). With Labour's victory, Jim Griffiths, the MP who had divided the Commons over the coalition government's weak-kneed commitment to the Beveridge report in 1943, took over the recently created Ministry of National Insurance's small but palatial accommodation at 6 Carlton House Terrace. Griffiths, a man with 'all the Welsh eloquence of Bevan without the egotism' according to Douglas Jay,[19] had become a social security expert,[20] recording that for Labour the Beveridge report had fallen 'like manna from heaven'. He felt it entirely suitable and 'symbolic' that social security for all was to be run from a building 'once the citadel of aristocratic power'. He arrived to find Hore-Belisha in tears at the loss of the chance to implement the plan more fully. 'This is the end of my career,' he told Griffiths.[21]

It was to take three Acts of Parliament on top of the existing Family Allowances Act to implement the social security side of the Beveridge plan. Griffiths's first job was to find the money to start paying out family allowances. 'I made the first of many visits to the Treasury. The Chancellor, Hugh Dalton, gave me the money "with a song in his heart", as he told our [party] conference to the delight of our supporters and the fury of his critics.'[22] The mercurial Dalton rapidly proved one of the welfare state's firmest backers. It was he who at about the same time was agreeing with Bevan that the NHS should ideally be both overwhelmingly tax-funded and comprehensive from the start, not introduced piecemeal. 'After Bevan, Dalton was the chief architect of the NHS,' Michael Foot, no friend of Dalton politically, judged.[23] His support, together with big increases in subsidy for Bevan's council house programme, came despite the appalling financial situation Labour inherited. President Truman, overnight, had cancelled the Lend-Lease which had sustained Britain through the war. Only the United States' agreement, after months of difficult negotiation in late 1945, to a deferred $3.5 billion loan repayable over fifty years from 1951 made the welfare state possible. Without it, services would almost certainly have been cut, not developed.[24]

The first 5s. od. (25p) family allowances were paid on August Bank Holiday 1946 and by 5 July 1948 three million families were in receipt of them at a cost of £59 million a year: 'surely one of the best investments the state ever made,' Griffiths judged.[25] He had his own bitter memories from the Welsh valleys of 'the tragedy of the "compo" man' – the compensation negotiators from the private insurers who would often persuade the victims of mining and industrial accidents to settle for inadequate lump sums rather than try to take the companies to court under the tortuous law which surrounded workmen's compensation. Griffiths's first legislation was the Industrial Injuries Act 1946 which effectively nationalised routine compensation, taking it away from the employers and private insurance companies. Weekly benefits and disablement pensions were paid, and tribunals rather than costly litigation used to settle cases.[26]

The National Insurance Act followed shortly. When news of his appointment had reached his native village, the minister recalled, one old neighbour asked another, 'What is this job Jim Griffiths has got?' The prompt reply was: 'Why man, boss of the Prudential.' Griffiths related:

I came near to agreeing with him when I read the first clause of the National Insurance Bill: 'Every person who, on and after the appointed day, being over school-leaving age and under pensionable age, is in Great

Britain and fulfils such conditions as may be prescribed as to residence in Great Britain, shall become insured under this Act and thereafter continue to be insured throughout his life under this Act'. In plain English it was to be all in: women from sixteen to sixty and men to sixty-five . . . [it] brought in everybody from the barrow boy to the field marshal.[27]

This Act was the core of the Beveridge report: state-run insurance, paid for by employers, employees and the general taxpayer, from cradle to grave. Flat-rate contributions in return for flat-rate benefits, but twice as many of them as the schemes they replaced: unemployment and sickness benefits, maternity grants and allowances, allowances for dependants, retirement pensions and the £20 death grant which was enough, just, to pay for a minimal funeral.

The basic benefit rates were set at 26s. od. (£1.30) for a single person and 42s. od. (£2.10) for a married couple. And in one of the two key breaks Griffiths made with the Beveridge plan, old age pensions were to be paid in full from the Appointed Day. As an economy measure, Beveridge had recommended they should be phased in, starting (in 1942 prices) at 10s. od. (50p) a week and rising by two-year instalments over twenty years to the full rate. 'I found this unacceptable,' Griffiths said. The proportion of pensionable age population had risen from 6 per cent at the turn of the century to 13 per cent by 1946. But 'the men and women who had already retired had experienced a tough life. In their youth they had been caught by the 1914 war, in middle age they had experienced the indignities of the depression, and in 1940 had stood firm as a rock in the nation's hour of trial. They deserved well of the nation and should not wait for twenty years.'[28] The new pensions started within three months of the 1946 Act becoming law and although it was a mighty expensive decision, almost certainly nothing else would have been politically tenable. Even the wartime coalition, with Churchill at its head insistent that expenditure could not be committed until the war was over, had in 1943 rejected phasing in.[29]

The final plank in the new vessel, the National Assistance Act, followed, piloted jointly through Parliament by Griffiths and Bevan. It redesigned the means-tested safety net to be stretched beneath the minimum platform of insurance benefits that Beveridge had devised. The most hated part of the old system, the household means-test, had already been abolished in 1942 and replaced by individual means-testing. The Bill's self-declared and bold aim was 'to terminate the existing poor law'. It nationalised the responsibilty for cash payments, removing them from the old local government-based Public Assistance Committees, and renamed them National Assistance. The local authorities, however, did retain welfare services for those who by 'age, infirmity or any other circumstances' were in need.[30] These included old people's homes, which were already steadily replacing the old workhouses, meals on wheels, and other services – the precursors of the social services departments.

Apart from paying pensions in full, the other key change from Beveridge was the level at which benefits were pitched. Beveridge had insisted they must provide 'subsistence' – enough to live on – despite the difficulties of defining that sum. Thomas Sheepshanks's civil service committee, set up in 1943 in the wake of Sir William's report, had abandoned subsistence, using different arguments to reject the principle for different benefits, while the Treasury had argued that subsistence simply could not be afforded.[31] The benefits Griffiths paid were higher than those the coalition had subsequently proposed in its 1944 White Paper, and he told the Commons: 'I believe we have in this way endeavoured to give a broad subsistence basis to the leading rates.'[32] In his 1969 autobiography, he still appeared to believe that was the case.[33]

But as Brian Abel-Smith has recorded: 'The index measuring the cost of living had been fiddled by both governments. The prices of sub-items which figured in the index were held down while comparable items were allowed to increase in price. By the time the full scheme was introduced in 1948 . . . benefit rates were nearly a third below what Beveridge had recommended as necessary for subsistence.'[34] More important, he adds, they were only just above the means-tested National Assistance payments, and those applying for assistance usually had their rent paid in full. Those on the non-means-tested insurance benefits did not. As a result, many more people than had ever been intended were to fall back on to the safety-net of means-tested benefits, because retirement, unemployment and the other insurance benefits were pitched too low and did not provide separately for housing costs (one of the problems Beveridge had wrestled with and failed to crack).

In addition, the benefits were not indexed to increase with inflation. Griffiths did consider linking benefits to prices, but officials took a narrow, compartmentalised view of the national insurance fund and persuaded him that contributions would have to change each time benefits were increased. 'In the end I provided in the Act that the minister should review the scale of benefits every five years.'[35]

All this attracted little attention at the time. But the impact of the decisions was profound and forms part of the next fifty years' history of the welfare state. Their effect by the early 1990s, as summed up by Professor Abel-Smith, was that 'in so far as freedom from want is attained in Britain, it is by undergoing a means test, not through national insurance. Beveridge's residual safety-net has grown to become the key agency, providing ultimate protection to more than eight million persons.'[36] But on 5 July 1948 such considerations were not even a cloud in the sky. The safety net was a safety net. In 1938 there had been 1,600,000 claimants of means-tested benefits. By July 1948 the figure was virtually half that, and many of the 842,000 affected were claiming only small supplements to insurance benefits.[37]

If the great day was a spectacular political and social achievement, it was also a magnificent administrative one. Organising the new National Health Service had been a large undertaking. It was nothing to setting up family allowances and insurance cover for the entire adult population. Work had started in 1944 after the Ministry of National Insurance was created with just ninety-seven staff. At its most mammoth, in the 1970s, its successor department was to employ well over 100,000. Even in 1948 a vast central office had to be created to handle the 25 million contribution records there would be, plus the records for 6 million married women eligible under their husband's contributions, and the expected 300,000 references to them each day. Former prisoners of war were roped in to help build Newcastle Central Office on the massive sixty-acre site that was to become the nerve centre for Britain's social security system. H. V Rhodes, the ministry's Director of Organisation, has told the tale of how the operation was put together amid austerity, desperate materials shortages and hopelessly scattered manpower. Looking back in 1949, he said, was 'rather like reviving a nightmare'.[38]

The still privately-run local railway company was persuaded to build a halt purely to service the central office site, on which fourteen acres of 'temporary' buildings were erected. They would 'no doubt last for a while', Rhodes predicted drily in 1949 of buildings that were still in use in the 1990s. By 1948, the ministry had combined the work of six government departments and the 6128 approved societies which ran the existing health insurance scheme. But before the national insurance benefits started, the 'small operation' of providing family allowances to 2.75 million families by August 1946 had to be achieved. A disused airscrew factory in Gateshead was commandeered and 6500 staff were transferred in April 1945 from the Home, Health and Labour departments to the new ministry.

Of these new staff, 3500 were scattered around Blackpool, working in the bedrooms of 413 different hotels and boarding houses. They had been evacuated from London for the war, and had no desire to go to Newcastle. The new Family Allowance, with a baby printed on the cover of every order book, nearly did not make it. The special security paper needed proved almost unobtainable, and the ministry found it could neither beg, borrow nor steal the 150 addressing machines needed. 'Almost at the last moment, a considerable number of the machines were flown in from Germany,' Rhodes recalled.

As national insurance day was contemplated, Griffiths insisted on having 1000 local offices, even if some were part-time, so that every member of the population would be within five miles of one. The Ministry of Works pronounced in July 1946 that that was 'probably impossible'. Griffiths just went ahead, ordering the 800 National Insurance Inspectors to 'keep a sharp lookout' for any likely property, while appealing to MPs and local councillors to join the hunt. Meanwhile the ministry turned its mind to finding 1000 safes for the local offices when lack of steel was holding up factory building. On the Appointed Day, 912 offices opened, after 350 million forms, 45 different leaflets and 25 codes of instruction for the staff had somehow been prepared and printed. Sixteen thousand of what by early 1949 was a 39,000 strong staff had been sent on training courses. Griffiths, determined to break from the atmosphere of the Poor Law, had also insisted on plain English, courteous and friendly service, and 'as good a standard of decoration as the austerity of the times would permit'. Both these achievements faded as the system became more complex and overburdened, and as breaking from the physical atmosphere of the old poor law took a lower priority in government spending.

Like the creation of the National Health Service, it had been a massive act of faith. 'Only with an immense effort [were] the lines cleared and the great new vessel of social insurance slid down the slips [on time],' Rhodes recorded. Those undertaking such an exercise, he added, had to be 'brave optimists who never take no for an answer' – displaying a blithe faith in an uncertain future that was not to be seen again until the two Kenneths, Clarke and Baker, revamped health and education in the 1980s. 'In the earlier stages of a large-scale organisation,' Rhodes said, in words their critics would happily have applied to the Kens, 'detail is the deadly nightshade.'

But if social security and health were to prove the biggest of the giant services of the welfare state, they had not been at the top of the public's list of concerns in 1945. Top priority in the opinion polls during the election had been housing.

CHAPTER 8

'The Tremendous Tory' – Housing

> Housing . . . differs from other fields of social administration
> because the aspect of it which attracts the keenest attention – the
> building of new houses – is exposed to all the winds that blow in a
> draughty economic climate.
>
> *David Donnison, Housing Policy since the War, 1960, p. 9*

> If nothing else, I will go down in history as a barrier between the
> beauty of Britain and the speculative builder who has done so much
> to destroy it.
>
> *Aneurin Bevan, answering a censure debate on housing in 1950*

'BRITAIN EMERGED from the war with 200,000 houses destroyed, another 250,000 so badly knocked about that they could not be lived in and a similar number severely damaged. Millions of men and women were about to come home, and the marriage and birth rates were rising fast. The pre-war building labour force of a million men had fallen to a third of this number, mainly concentrated in south-east England in the path of the flying bomb and rocket attacks. The rents of privately owned houses had been frozen at their 1939 levels, and in England and Wales 71,000 houses had been requisitioned [for office use] by local authorities.'[1]

Thus David Donnison on the housing position Labour inherited. Over the course of war something like a quarter of Britain's 12.5 million houses had been damaged.[2] There had been much make do and mend when two-thirds of those with building skills were in the armed forces and the remainder were reserved for war work: the building of runways for bombers or camps for the armed forces took priority. The scale of devastation at times has to be reduced to smaller numbers to make it comprehensible. As late as June to September 1944, the V1 flying bombs and then the V2s completely wrote off 25,000 houses and at their peak were damaging 20,000 *a day* in London alone.[3] Late in the year 45,000 building workers were drafted in from the provinces, but many had to sleep in

Wembley Stadium precisely because there was no accommodation. The armed forces released some building workers early and by March 1945 nearly 800,000 homes had been repaired after a fashion. Even so 'many bombed out families were living in huts erected with the help of American troops and former Italian prisoners of war'.[4]

It was hardly surprising that housing dominated both the election and the mailbags of the new Parliament's MPs. Michael Foot, newly elected for Plymouth Devonport, recalled: 'The housing shortage caused more anguish and frustration than any other of the nation's manifold problems . . . every MP and every councillor was being besieged by the endless queue of the homeless.'[5] Amidst the confusion, however, Donnison records, 'there was determination and high confidence, fortified by an underestimate of long term needs, a war-won capacity for bold decisions, and a strong sense of social priorities.'[6]

In March 1945, the coalition government had broken new ground with a White Paper which for the first time accepted the principle of affording 'a separate dwelling for every family desiring to have one'.[7] To achieve this the White Paper suggested that between 3 and 4 million houses would need to be built in the first 10 to 12 years after the war. The lower end of that target was achieved. But it would take six years to build the first million, three more to build the second and three more to complete the third[8] – and the White Paper's estimate of demand proved to be far from accurate. Against the last three years of peace, marriages were 11 per cent up in the first three post-war years, and births up by no less than 33 per cent.[9] The post-war baby boom, which was to strain education, the health services and the social security budget as well as housing, was under way. In addition, under the strain of war, divorces in 1945 were 250 per cent up on 1938, splitting households and again increasing housing needs.[10]

During the election Labour had appeared to promise the earth. Bevin offered 'Five million houses in quick time' while being careful not to specify what 'quick time' meant.[11] Stafford Cripps allegedly claimed that 'housing can be dealt with within a fortnight'. Arthur Greenwood dismissed the coalition figures as 'chicken feed'.[12] It was a chicken that came home to roost.

Housing was then part of the Ministry of Health, so the task of providing the houses fell to Bevan, on top of the massive task of founding the NHS. Given the impact poor housing can have on health, there was an intellectual logic to this. After it was removed by Attlee and put in with local government in 1951, repeated arguments would be heard down the decades for reuniting the two. But, given the scale of the health and housing challenges in 1945, Attlee's failure to split the department earlier, or at least co-ordinate the housing programme more effectively, is widely seen as his greatest administrative error.[13] Bevan had to work not only with Dalton, who as Chancellor had to find the cash, but with the Ministry of Works which directed the building industry, licensed private builders (who were subject to controls) and controlled building materials. The Ministry of Supply, however, also had its fingers in the materials pie, of which there were far too few slices to go round. Steel, wood and almost everything else ran desperately short, while Britain had few currency reserves with which to pay for imports after the war. The Board of Trade was thus at times involved, while the Ministry of Labour, in 1945, still had powers to control and direct manpower. In addition, the Ministry of Town and Country Planning could refuse sites for housing or anything else. Scotland was run separately. *Picture Post* at one point calculated that there were ten ministerial cooks attempting to make the broth.[14]

Bevan's chief agents for house building were the local authorities – all 1700 of them, ranging from the London County Council, with a long and fine tradition of public housing, to tiny authorities that had hardly ever built a thing.

None of this was a recipe for rapid progress. Bevan did himself less than justice by jibing years later that while at health he spent only five minutes a week on housing,[15] when at times the doctors complained that he spent too much time on housing and not enough on them.[16] He inherited plenty of figures from the coalition government, but little by way of a plan. Lord Portal, the Minister of Works, had promised half a million of the pre-fabs, compact pre-fabricated bungalows, which from 1944 had started appearing on bomb sites. Steel for their frames could not be spared, however. Aluminium and concrete alternatives were designed, aircraft factories were turned over to their production, and although 125,000 were erected by 1948 they cost two-thirds more than the original estimate. Bevan hated them, describing them as 'rabbit hutches', although they proved in practice cosy and surprisingly popular. Isolated examples still existed in the 1990s, despite their ten-year life expectancy,[17] with some even being proposed for preservation orders.

Housing was to prove much less of a policy departure from pre-war days than health, education or social security. It was chiefly the emphasis that Bevan changed. The degree to which he did so, however, and the failure to build large numbers of new homes quickly was to cause controversy.

The two decades before the Second World War, despite the bitter disappointment over 'homes fit for heroes' had in fact seen the biggest output of new houses in Britain's history.[18] Local authority house building, whose origins stretched back to Victorian times, had become well established. Slum clearance had begun. Even so, council houses in 1939 accounted for only about one in eight of the stock. Three-quarters of the new homes between the wars had been privately built, the bulk of these for purchase rather than rent. In addition, growing numbers of tenants had bought their homes from their landlords. As a result the slow beginnings of the decline in the private rented sector, and what was to become a dramatic shift to owner-occupation, were already under way. The number of owner-occupiers had more than quadrupled between 1918 and 1938, even if that increase still left only just over a quarter of housing in owner-occupation, against 60 per cent privately rented and 13 per cent in council ownership.[19]

Bevan spectacularly reversed the balance between private and public in house building, while resisting the creation of some sort of nationalised National Housing Corporation to build the homes – a course urged by Morrison, Douglas Jay, who was Attlee's economic adviser, and by Lord Addison, who had had his own troubles with local authorities as Lloyd George's health and housing minister.[20] Bevan's policy was to restrict severely private house-building, allowing only one private house for every four built by local authorities, to order local authorities to requisition empty houses and derequisition those it had taken over as offices, to toughen rent controls, put first priority on repairs to unoccupied war-damaged dwellings, and charge local authorities with the task of building, either through direct labour organisations or on contract with private builders. He persuaded Dalton not only to treble the subsidy for council housing and extend it from forty to sixty years, but to shift the balance so that three-quarters of the cost rather than two-thirds came from the Exchequer, and only a quarter from the rates.

This last provided the cash. Sir John Wrigley, the senior civil servant who was sceptical such a case could be won, recalled receiving a 'sharp, almost supercilious refusal' when he first put it to the Treasury. 'Bevan thereafter must have had private talks with Dalton,' Foot records. 'Sir John was advised to reopen the question with all the blandness he could muster. "My minister," he said at the next meeting of the committee, "still thinks that the figure of three to one would be appropriate." "And my minister agrees," the Treasury official replied.'[21]

The continued restrictions on private house-building, Bevan's strictures on the unreliability of the 'speculative private builder', and the big expan-

sion planned for council housing outraged the Tories, who took advantage
of the pitifully slow progress in the early months to pillory Bevan. Churchill accused him of 'chilling and checking free-enterprise house building
which had always provided the bulk of the nation's houses'. Bevan, he
charged, was guilty of 'partisan spite' in refusing to enlist 'all house building agencies of every kind'.[22] In fact private builders got the bulk of the
work. But they were building homes for rent for local authorities, not
homes for sale to those who could afford to buy in the private sector.

Outside Parliament, the situation briefly looked frightening. 'In the
summer of 1946 it was possible for a family to find itself 4,000th on the
local council's waiting list. Some were ex-servicemen with young children
who could not even find lodgings, because the landlord had a no children rule,'
Alan Jenkins relates.

Agitators took over, organizing mass meetings in Leicester Square, and
'vigilantes' went about cities looking for apparently vacant buildings, even
if they had 'sold' [or 'requisitioned'] notices outside . . . An empty Nissen
hut at an airport could house two families, so if there was no one looking,
you moved in. Landlords might cut off the water, gas, electricity; but in
desperation you could use candles and spirit stoves. The climax was reached
in the 'Great Sunday Squat' of September 1946 at Duchess of Bedford
House, an empty block of flats in Kensington. Like so much Communist
organisation, it was orderly, efficient and quiet. Elsewhere in the country,
squatters occupied abandoned Army camps [more than 46,000 ended up in
them]. They were not evicted because the Government suddenly realized
that this was really rather a good idea which they ought to have thought
of themselves.[23]

The real problem was less the tool Bevan used to do the job – the local
authorities – than the lack of the most crucial tools of all: manpower and
materials. At one Cabinet meeting, Bevan exploded: 'Where are all the
people I need for my programme?' Attlee drily replied: 'Looking for
houses, Nye!'[24]

Housing was not the government's only building priority. Scarce men
and materials were equally desperately needed to get Britain's factories
out of wartime and into peacetime products and to build schools, hospitals
and the long-promised health centres. It was the last two categories that
suffered, and suffered heavily. Slowly the situation improved as Bevan's
ministry showered local authorities with circulars – five a week in 1946.[25]
The figures rose from just 1000 houses and 10,000 pre-fabs completed

by December 1945, together with 60,000 unoccupiably damaged homes repaired, to 55,400 house completions in 1946, 139,000 in 1947, and 227,000 in 1948.[26] The 125,000 pre-fabs (which continued to be put up until 1951) added to these totals.

If the game, from the point of view of the politicians, the press and the homeless, was about numbers, Bevan had two equally important ends in view: standards and mix. Had his successors had the political courage to hold to those principles, Britain's post-war housing problem might have been massively diminished. His stance did involve a painful trade-off between quality and quantity, but he held rigidly to the view that: 'We shall be judged for a year or two by the *number* of houses we build. We shall be judged in ten years' time by the *type* of houses we build.'[27] And he held this line at the most difficult of times, when much real homelessness existed, not the 1970s redefinition of it as having nowhere suitable to live.

Bevan pushed up the old minimum standard for council housing from 750 square feet of room space to 900, with lavatories upstairs as well as down. He insisted that the Cotswold authorities be allowed to use the local stone, and that Bath be allowed to build stone terraces, despite the greater expense. And he wanted his new housing mixed. In 1948 he removed the requirement in pre-war legislation that housing should be provided only for 'the working classes'. He had something close to a romantic William Morris aesthetic about housing, one of the few things he shared with Churchill. 'We should try to introduce into our modern villages and towns what was always the lovely feature of English and Welsh villages, where the doctor, the grocer, the butcher and the farm labourer all lived in the same street. I believe that is essential for the full life of a citizen . . . to see the living tapestry of a mixed community.'[28]

He railed against ghettos, whether for the working class or the aged. 'We don't want a country of East Ends and West Ends, with all the petty snobberies this involves. That was one of the evil legacies of the Victorian era,' he said. And 'I hope that the old people will not be asked [by the local authorities] to live in colonies of their own – they do not want to look out of their windows on an endless procession of the funerals of their friends; they also want to look at processions of perambulators.'[29] As he was repeatedly urged to cut standards in order to boost numbers, he equally repeatedly refused, declaring it to be 'the coward's way out . . . if we wait a little longer, that will be far better than doing ugly things now and regretting them for the rest of our lives.'[30] The results of Bevan's policy can still be seen in the quality and size of housing constructed in the 1940s despite the formidable odds. Dalton was to cut the standards in 1951, dubbing the fiery Bevan 'a tremendous Tory' for his views on the need for three-bedroom houses and extra lavatories. Macmillan was to cut them further, Bevan's successors increasingly indulging in the numbers game at the expense of standards, diversity and social mix. The consequence proved not great new housing for the people, but too many great new slums.

Standards and housing layout were strictly as much the business of Lewis Silkin at the Ministry of Town and Country Planning, but the two men fortunately got on. Silkin had been influenced by the Garden City movement, whose pioneer was Ebenezer Howard at the turn of the nineteenth century.[31] Howard's vision of 'slumless, smokeless cities' was realised in the greenfield private development sites of Letchworth and Welwyn Garden City, which began building in 1903 and 1919 respectively. Letchworth was designed by Raymond Unwin, the architect also of New Earswick, the model village commissioned by Joseph Rowntree near his cocoa works in York. Unwin's work heavily influenced the more human-scale and village-like developments of local authorities both before and after the Second World War. It was this legacy which the Town and Country Planning movement took over, bitterly resisting the ribbon development of the thirties, and combining it with a more right-wing plea for green belt legislation in order to protect the countryside from the repulsive encroachment of the lower middle classes and from the unplanned loss of good agricultural land.[32]

In 1946, despite 'no whisper of the new towns in the Labour manifesto',[33] the New Towns Act appeared. There were eventually to be twenty-five of them, housing two million people. Of the first fourteen, eight were built around London, surrounded by green belt to keep them free of the city: an extension to Welwyn, plus the new Crawley, Bracknell, Hemel Hempstead, Hatfield, Stevenage, Harlow, and Basildon (later to become the home of Essex man). Six more went to regional development areas: Corby in Northamptonshire, Cwmbran in what is now Gwent, East Kilbride and Glenrothes in central Scotland and Newton Aycliffe and Peterlee in Durham. Beveridge was appointed chairman of the last two and threw himself into the job with characteristic vigour; but he found their limited social mix of chiefly young skilled working class wearing. 'The people are nice and the troops of children are lovely, but there's no conversation,' he was to complain. Macmillan eventually fired him in 1952 for being 'too old', earning Beveridge's opinion that he was 'a pompous ass' with 'no manners'.[34]

Although the New Towns were mostly built on greenfield sites, in those that had village centres Silkin found himself pilloried by Home Counties residents with no more desire than the people of Hampshire in the 1980s and 1990s to allow even the skilled working-class decanted from the great city on to their patch. At Stevenage, Silkin was greeted with howls of 'Gestapo' and 'Dictator' and had sand put into the petrol tank of his car. Protesters later changed the signs at the railway station to 'Silkingrad'.[35]

The New Towns were to be one of the greater successes of post-war planning, but by the time Labour left office in 1951 most were still largely building sites, in part because just as the housing situation started to improve Labour faced its darkest hour. For the catastrophic winter of 1947 was followed by the convertibility crisis which shook the triumphant Labour Government to its core. As a condition of the $3.5 billion post-war loan, the United States had insisted that sterling held around the world should become convertible to dollars. That day was due on 15 July 1947. The big freeze had already crippled exports, the balance of payments deficit was soaring, and as convertibility bit millions of dollars from the loan drained away as investors swapped their pounds for dollars, rushing the country towards bankruptcy. In one month $700 million went, until in August the Americans agreed to convertibility being suspended – as it turned out, for eleven years.[36] The final £25 million of the loan was drawn down in March 1948. Only the simultaneous promise of help from the Marshall Aid plan, conceived in the early summer of 1947 by the former United States general and finally agreed in April 1948, bailed Britain out, in part by funding European economic revival and thus stimulating a better market for British exports. The price of the crisis at home was spending cuts, implemented first by Dalton and then by the austere Stafford Cripps.

Bevan had to agree to plans that were calculated to slash housing completions in 1949 to 140,000.[37] The lead-time in reducing capital spending meant that 1948 still saw 227,000 permanent houses completed – almost 90,000 up on the previous year – and the easing of economic conditions that year in fact led to 197,000 completions in 1949, not the cut to 140,000 originally planned. But under Labour the figures were not again to climb above 200,000, sticking at 198,000 and 194,000 in 1950 and 1951.[38] Housing was forced to take its place in the economic priorities, something Bevan found himself cornered into accepting in part because he did such a brilliant job of defending the burgeoning NHS budget. Sir John Wrigley gloomily told Bevan in 1947: 'If we build more than 200,000 houses, I'll be sacked by the Chancellor, and if I build less I will be sacked by you.'[39]

Although the criticism of Bevan's record on housing became less ferocious with the big rise in completions in 1948, Labour remained on the defensive. Even at the Labour Party conference, of which he was a darling, Bevan faced criticism. In 1949, in Blackpool, he argued that despite the huge waiting lists, swollen by demographic pressures, he had not only made good all the wartime destruction but had, by then, provided Britain with more houses per head of population than ever before. There remained, he pleaded defensively, great timber shortages. Had the timber been there 'what would you take the building workers from to build more houses – schools . . . hospitals . . . mental homes . . . nurses' hostels . . . the factory programme?' Yet again, he rehearsed his refusal to cut the standard or size of homes. 'We will not build houses today which in a few years' time will be slums.'[40]

Traditionally, housing has been branded the welfare state failure of Bevan and the 1945 Labour Government, chiefly on the grounds that too few houses were built. Certainly disillusion with the housing shortage contributed to Labour's defeat. Between them, however, Bevan and Dalton provided more than a million good quality homes between 1945 and 1951, homes that were to be popular when the tenants gained the right to buy them in the 1980s. They also set the pattern of local authority building for rent that was to be followed for a generation by both Tories and Labour until, at its peak in 1979, a third of the stock was council housing. Given the way that preference for public over private turned out, it may be that rather than numbers which is the more questionable part of the record. Bevan and Dalton, however, cannot be blamed for the quality and style of housing that their successors adopted.

CHAPTER 9

The Final Foundations

By the time Labour left office in 1951 it had succeeded in presiding over a massive expansion of secondary schooling which in practice confirmed the distinctions in an already divided educational system.
Roy Lowe, Education in the Post-War Years, 1988, p. 53

[In the late 1940s] The award of a grammar school place at the age of eleven was equivalent to more than doubling the resources devoted to that child if it had gone to a modern school.
John Vaizey, The Costs of Education, 1958, p. 102

I wondered why I felt deep down angry having read the draft. Then I realised that Mr Squeers had given me a quizzical look across the years.
Ellen Wilkinson, on reading the proposed secondary modern school curriculum, 1946 in Vernon, Ellen Wilkinson, 1982, p. 222

There was a terrible shortage of teachers. The first ten years was all hands on deck to get schools built and more teachers in them.
Sir Toby Weaver, Deputy Secretary, Department of Education and Science, 1946–73

In its final form, as it emerged in 1948, the NHS represented the victory of the values of rationality, efficiency and equity . . . But there are other values . . . a view which stressed responsiveness rather than efficiency, differentiation rather than uniformity, self-government rather than national equity.
Rudolf Klein, The Politics of the NHS, 1983, p. 28

BEFORE BEVAN'S health and housing programmes took off, before Griffiths's social security Acts, but with the reality of full employment, it fell to Ellen Wilkinson, the fiery flame-haired heroine of Jarrow, 'five foot of dynamite' (she was actually 4ft 10in) and 'the pocket pasionaria',[1] to start implementing Butler's Education Act.

By the time Labour took power in July there had been a year of 'massive, even frenetic' planning among the 146 education authorities.[2] It had been a time of high optimism, what one county chief education officer was to call, with considerable prescience, perhaps 'the last grand flourish and fanfare of local government'.[3]

However, not only was the school leaving age to be raised to fifteen on 1 April 1947, but the birth-rate (one of Bevan's banes in housing and health) had been rising since 1942. That year it was up 73,000 to 652,000. In addition, the infant mortality rate was falling sharply under the influence of improved treatment and better wartime diets for the poor. Between 1942 and the end of 1947, no fewer than a million more children were born in England and Wales than in the previous five years. These all had to be found school places at the age of five, on top of the extra 200,000 places and 13,000 teachers needed to raise the school leaving age.[4] The victims of this demographic shift in the school population proved to be the plans for nursery education and the major restructuring of secondary education that had been envisaged in the more enlightened parts of Butler's White Paper and Act.

To get the show on the road, wonderful Nordic-sounding acronyms were enlisted. To achieve ROSLA (Raising of the School Leaving Age), HORSA and SFORSA (Hutting Operation for the Raising of the School Leaving Age and School Furniture Operation for the same purpose) came into being. In addition an emergency scheme, drawn up by the coalition, put 35,000 ex-servicemen and recruits from business and commerce through a crash twelve-month teacher-training course. Although it took over-long to get up to speed, it leavened the traditional teacher intake with people who had healthy experience of the outside world.[5] Most, however, went to the primaries and the secondary moderns, where the birth-rate and the new school leaving age were chiefly increasing the numbers. The effect, unwittingly, was to reinforce the status distinction between grammars, with their better educated and better trained staff, and the secondary moderns.[6]

Such was the pressure and the competition elsewhere in the economy for raw materials and manpower (it was manpower shortage, not unemployment, which was Labour's recurrent problem), that the Cabinet twice debated postponing ROSLA. In August and September 1945, Ellen Wilkinson achieved agreement easily enough that the date should stick. It was seen, in her words, as 'a political necessity' and in Herbert

Morrison's as a 'test of the Government's sincerity'. The date held even though it was realised that for a time it would mean makeshift accommodation and over-large classes. But in late 1946, Dalton, in all else the welfare state's generous, even over-generous, friend, panicked. It would mean 'a direct loss to the national labour force which will reach 370,000 by September 1948 . . . at a time when the whole economy is badly overstrained,' he argued. A five-month postponement would also allow preparations to be much more complete.[7]

This was a battle that Ellen Wilkinson's Permanent Secretary, Sir John Maud (later Lord Redcliffe-Maud), judged she had to win, or the already limited resources for education would go elsewhere.[8] She arrived at Cabinet issuing barely veiled threats of resignation. Postponement would deprive 150,000 children of a whole year's education, and 'the children to suffer most would be precisely those working-class children whose education has already been so seriously interrupted by the war. They would all be children of working-class parents; and parents in better circumstances would remain free to keep their children at school,' she told the Cabinet. If it was put off, the same intensity of effort to hit a date would never again be achieved. The country needed higher levels of skills, not less skilled workers immediately. Whenever governments hit trouble, she said, education was the first casualty.[9]

In a sense, the same argument that had kept children out of school in the nineteenth century, the need for their work, was being heard again. Ellen Wilkinson won, Dalton recording in his diary that he did not mind. 'I had never been keen on this.'[10] Barely a week later she ventured in the great freeze to an icy meeting to open the Old Vic Theatre School, its roof blitzed open to the sky, the room without heating. She caught pneumonia and on 6 February, at the age of 55, she died.[11] ROSLA was her memorial, George Tomlinson, a Lancashire weaver who had left school at ten, her successor.

Red Ellen's and George Tomlinson's reputations have suffered heavily in the hands of Labour critics for their failure to bend the permissive nature of Butler's Act to Labour goals, particularly over secondary education and comprehensive schools. The new Ministry of Education officials were still firmly in the grip of the idea that there were gold, silver and iron children. Neither minister, it is argued, did enough to challenge that assumption.[12] Ellen Wilkinson, like so many other players in the welfare state's story, was the product of a strong Methodist background. She was schooled at Ardwick Higher Elementary Grade in Manchester and fought her way to that city's university in 1910, when women undergraduates were a rarity.

She used to claim she had been born into the 'proletarian purple'.[13] Her memories of her own schooldays were that 'the top few pupils were intelligent and could mop up facts like blotting paper . . . but we were made to wait for the rest of the huge classes . . . we wanted to stretch our minds but were merely a nuisance.'[14] This was hardly the background likely to produce an automatic champion of mixed ability or multilateral schools, and her biographer Betty Vernon, while firmly defending her reputation, concedes she was 'in no way . . . an educational expert'. Like many Labour MPs, she respected the grammar schools and had no intention of destroying them. She believed that Butler's 'parity of esteem' in the tripartite system could be achieved, and reflected the same confusion that even her fiercest Labour critics sometimes displayed over the need to preserve grammar-school standards while seeing comprehensives as an ideal.[15] In addition, for twelve of the last eighteen months of her life – her period at education – she was 'desperately ill' with chronic bronchitis and asthma.

Wilkinson had inherited *The Nation's Schools*, Butler and Ede's May 1945 circular advising local authorities on how plans for the new secondary system should be drawn up. It argued strongly for the tripartite system of grammar, technical and secondary modern schools, and discouraged multilaterals. 'It would be a mistake to plunge too hastily on a large scale into a revolutionary change . . . innovation is not necessarily reform.'[16] A circular Ellen Wilkinson approved six months after Labour took office opened the comprehensive door fractionally wider, but *The New Secondary Education*, issued in June 1947 after her death, again heavily reflected the ministry's view that a tripartite system should be maintained. She had read the pamphlet, which indeed eventually carried her foreword, in March 1946 and had exploded in anger. 'This pamphlet', she had declared, 'is fundamentally phoney because it subconsciously disguises the real question that has to be answered, namely, "What shall we do to get miners and agricultural workers if a hundred per cent of the children able to profit from it are offered real secondary education?" Answer . . . give the real stuff to a selected 25 per cent, steer the 75 per cent away from the humanities, pure science even history.'

Her anger came in part because, however astonishingly in hindsight, the intention was actually to reduce the intake of grammar and technical schools combined to 25 to 30 per cent of the school population to avoid diluting standards,[17] while the secondary modern curriculum, responsibility for which was left heavily with the schools themselves, was assumed to be essentially concrete and practical.

'Can't Shakespeare mean more than a scrubbing brush?' Red Ellen raged. 'Can't enough of a foreign language be taught to open windows on the world a bit wider – I learnt French verbs saying them as I scrubbed floors at home.' It was suggested merely that 'something of the sciences, maths and arts might be taught' while history was 'banished as too difficult . . . or was it possibly too dangerous if an intelligent child asked awkward questions? (Don't worry how we got India, let's go and do some nice work at the forge!)'[18]

Whatever her personal stance, as Margaret Thatcher was to find fifteen years later, tough-minded ministers with strong personal views cannot always shift the education department's official mind. Ellen Wilkinson's criticisms seem to have changed the pamphlet little. Two months after her outburst a circular which she approved confirmed in even starker terms what she was railing against.

With the school leaving age due to rise to fifteen, some secondary moderns, many of which were converted higher elementary schools, were proposing to enter suitable children for the School Certificate, then the main grammar-school qualification, instead of following tradition and decanting their children into the world of work largely qualification-free, save for attainment tests in the 'three Rs' of reading, writing and arithmetic. Almost unbelievably, the new circular debarred any school other than a grammar from entering any pupils for any external examination under the age of seventeen. In effect, secondary modern children would have to stay on two years beyond the planned school leaving age to gain a public qualification.[19] There could be no clearer indication of how some saw education as being defined – an élite in grammars and cannon-fodder elsewhere. So much for Butler's 'parity of esteem'.

The worst of this situation was rescued a year later, in September 1947. With George Tomlinson now in charge, the newly reconstituted Secondary Schools Examination Council proposed a new examination, the General Certificate of Education (GCE). That would be taken at a minimum age of sixteen – one year rather than two beyond the minimum school leaving age. The standard of a pass, however, was to be the 'credit' level of the old School Certificate, which was well above the simple pass mark. GCEs did not start until 1951, but this decision was to set for years the mould of public examinations, which in turn heavily influenced the character of schools, both secondary modern and grammar. The only justification in the report for the high benchmark was that it would be 'beneficial and stimulating' and would give a pass 'real significance'. Its aim, however, was plain enough. In the words not of Labour critics but a later government report produced under the Conservatives in 1960, the hope had been to ensure that the examination was 'beyond the reach of any but those in selective courses' – those in grammar schools and, if they ever developed in any numbers, the selective technical schools.

It was against these arguments, and the massive shortage of building materials and skills to provide almost any new schools other than those to service Bevan's new housing estates and to replace bombed-out ones, that the new secondary organisation was conducted. What extra building there was had to concentrated on new primary places to meet the baby-boom and on the (often hutted) extensions to existing schools to accommodate the raised school leaving age. In October 1945, Ellen Wilkinson wrote that 'the question of building permanent schools must wait until the housing situation has eased . . . it has taken all the weight I could bring to bear in Cabinet to get the extra provision for [HORSA] classrooms, but I should not myself find it within my conscience to take away labour from housing where we could manage with prefabricated huts.'[20]

These conditions hardly left room for much in the way of new multilateral schools. To have big enough sixth forms, the ministry was calculating that comprehensives would need to be huge – 1500 to 1700 places. It still saw multilaterals (which could be different types of school on the same site, or different types of school linked as one, or what would now be recognised as a comprehensive) as experimental. So they were: in effect there were none. So when some authorities planned to move quickly to comprehensives, as Labour-controlled Middlesex did, George Tomlinson approved the plans for only three schools, not the six the county wanted.

The London County Council drew up plans to go entirely comprehensive, its sweeping proposals to put 91 per cent of its children into them drawing fire even from supporters of the idea. Harold Dent wrote in 1954: 'The idea of the comprehensive school has never quite recovered from the blow dealt it when England's largest municipality decided to adopt it. Even some people not entirely averse from the idea of trying out the comprehensive, or multi-lateral school, criticised the London County Council for embarking upon a total policy of comprehensive schools instead of beginning by setting up one or two as an experiment.'[21] Indeed, one of the fairest criticisms that can be made of proponents of both systems is that neither over the next forty years organised any really robust research to show which system, comprehensives or grammar/secondaries, produced the best results overall.

Comprehensives did, however, begin to emerge. Windermere in

Westmorland won the distinction of being the first in 1945, and that with only 220 pupils, and the Welsh island of Anglesey became the first all-comprehensive county in 1950. But by the time Labour left office in 1951, there were fewer than twenty genuine comprehensive schools in England and Wales[22] along with some bilaterals – usually a mix of grammar and technical school. Comprehensive activists persuaded the Labour Party conference in 1946 and 1947 to call for a policy of 'common schools', and by 1951 the idea was in the manifesto. But it was there only in the weasel words of 'greater equality of opportunity', for the Labour Party as a whole was not won over to comprehensives and was not so to be until the mid-1960s.[23] Many Labour authorities were proud of their grammar schools and teachers held as wide a spread of opinion on the issue as any other grouping, the National Union of Teachers only adopting comprehensives as union policy when the government finally did so in the 1960s. Between 1945 and 1951 the grammars themselves mounted a vigorous defence of their role, led intellectually by heads of the still independent direct grant schools, 164 out of 232 of which had survived a pruning of their numbers by Labour.[24] Dr Eric James, headmaster of Manchester Grammar School, argued that comprehensives would involve 'a retardation in the progress of the most gifted children'. That would be a denial of equal opportunity, he maintained, neatly turning the argument used by the supporters of comprehensives on its head. It would also be 'a national disaster', denying the best education to those best suited to solve the country's problems.[25] That argument was to be heard many times in succeeding years, and many Labour politicians both nationally and locally had sympathy with it. They may have wanted equality of opportunity, but many were themselves the products of grammar schools. They knew from personal experience how grammars gave the chance to bright, working-class children to break free. Labour, Kenneth Morgan has said, retained 'an instinctive faith in the grammar schools, the bright working-class child's alternative to Eton and Winchester'.[26] And the *Times Educational Supplement* commented in 1951 when Labour left office that 'it is extremely doubtful whether Mr Tomlinson ever once lifted a hand' to encourage more comprehensives.[27]

Educational development was not eased by the convertibility crisis of 1947 which, after a spell of considerable economic growth, was followed by the sterling crisis of 1949 and the spectacular devaluation of the pound from \$4 to \$2.80. Both crises produced spending cuts. The emergence of the Cold War followed by rearmament for Korea in 1950 put further pressure on social spending. The increase in education spending slowed from a £24.5 million rise in 1948–9 on a budget of £138 million the previous year, to an increase of only £7.5 million for 1951–2 taking it to just £200 million, the slow-down in growth coming against rising numbers of pupils as the baby-boom generation reached school age.

As a result nursery education went by the board. The promised county colleges for post-fifteen education failed to emerge. Technical schools remained a rarity. Competition for grammar school places if anything increased. Classes of fifty and sixty (Butler's Education Act had aimed at thirty) were common as late as 1949, some in schools that had been blacklisted since long before the war. As late as 1951 a Commons debate showed around 250,000 children were still being taught in classes of more than forty, with 83,000 of them in classes of fifty or more.[28]

There were plenty of silver linings. The quality of provision did slowly improve. School fees had gone, outside the public schools and a proportion of direct grant school places – a boon to the middle classes, who had mainly paid them in the past, but also opening up education to working-class children who had frequently faced family pressure to start work so as to earn money rather than cost it. Compulsory education now lasted a year longer, even if some teachers initially struggled to know what to do with the extra time in crowded classrooms with no examination goals to convince non-grammar school children of its value. New schools were being built: 150 new secondaries were under way in 1951, mainly in the suburbs, and some were of award-winning design and quality.[29]

There had also been gains in higher education. Several thousand men and women discharged from the armed forces were put through university without the normal pre-entry qualifications. Many came at an age older than the usual student, glad to be alive and with an immense enthusiasm, producing what some dons in the days of student revolt in the late 1960s were to remember as a brief golden age. Too late for the schools-based Butler Act, the Percy report in 1945 called for a rapid increase in the number of engineering graduates in a limited number of local technical colleges. The report, however, drew a damaging distinction between universities and technical colleges, arguing that universities were for scientists, the colleges for technologists. An arcane and very British dispute over whether the awards should be a degree (BTech) or a diploma (Dip. Tech.) held up into the 1950s even the real progress Percy did offer, the universities jealously guarding their right to award degrees while the professional institutions, the mechanicals, electricals and others, fought to protect their position as the awarders of professional qualifications.[30] As the *Times Educational Supplement* was later to put it, the outcome was 'the universities taking the high road and the technical colleges the low'.[31]

The case for expanding higher education was strengthened a year later, however, when the Barlow committee on scientific manpower, set up by Labour, recommended a doubling of science graduates. The invention of radar for the Battle of Britain had helped save the country at the beginning of the war. Penicillin had saved lives in the middle and was coming into civilian use. Hiroshima and Nagasaki had produced a cataclysmic conclusion, and the scientists were now promising unlimited cheap power from 'atoms for peace'. A faith in science had been triggered that was not to peak until after Wilson had turned its promise into the election-winning 'white heat of the technological revolution' in 1963. 'Never before has the importance of science been so widely recognised,' the Barlow committee stated, 'or so many hopes of future progress and welfare founded upon the scientist.'[32]

Intelligence tests that had been used to argue for restrictions in the number of grammar school places were now used to argue for more scientists. Only 1 per cent of the age group went to university, Barlow argued, but 5 per cent were bright enough. Numbers could be doubled *and* standards raised.[33]

The committee reported the universities split over expansion – Oxford and Cambridge resisting, the others in favour – and recommended the creation of 'at least one new university'.[34] Given that Morrison had cleverly chosen Sir Alan Barlow, the second secretary to the Treasury, to chair the committee, the normal Treasury defences were breached and the report rapidly accepted. In what John Carswell, slightly tongue in cheek, has called 'a quiet measure of nationalisation', the University Grants Committee was enlarged, given a full-time chairman and told by Dalton to become a positive agent for change. Since 1919 the UGC had been an almost independent and 'highly respectable backwater' of the Treasury, dishing out small sums to the universities. Now it was told to 'assist . . . in such plans for the development of the universities as may from time to time be required to ensure that they are fully adequate to national needs'. Its staff rose rapidly from five to twenty-two, and government's relationship with the universities began to change fundamentally. Carswell records that from 1946 on, government grant became 'not only indispensable to the universities, it constituted the greater part of their income.'[35] State scholarships for students expanded, and the University College of North Staffordshire opened at Keele in 1950. University student numbers jumped from 52,000 in 1945 to 84,000 in 1951, finally reaching 100,000 in

1958. Much of this expansion, however, proved to be in the universities' traditional world of the arts, less of it in the sciences which Barlow had been set up to promote, although even Barlow had said expansion in the humanities should not be 'sacrificed' to the need for more scientists and technologists.[36] By 1950 the proportion on pure science courses had risen from 15 to 20 per cent, but applied science students numbered only 1 in 100.[37]

Despite the expansion, Labour's educational achievements in 1945–51 are judged harshly by historians. Kenneth Morgan, in his great assessment of that government, concludes: 'It is hard to avoid the view that education was an area where the Labour government failed to provide any new ideas or inspiration', although the new investment, the new impetus at elementary level, and the large increase in the school population did 'pave the way for the educational boom of the fifties and sixties'.[38]

Brian Simon, key champion of comprehensives, has been harsher. 'No serious challenge, indeed, no challenge of any kind, had been launched at the citadels of power in the world of education.'[39] By 1951 the numbers still in the old 'all-age' elementary schools had been cut from well over a million of the 6.5 million schoolchildren – but only to 800,000. In a few areas of population growth, such as Essex, children were excluded from school for lack of facilities.[40] The grammar, direct grant and public schools went on largely untouched. The secondary moderns failed to achieve parity of esteem. And overcrowding in primary schools saw a rapid growth of private, often poorly staffed, preparatory schools for younger pupils in converted houses and mansions.[41] Yet most of this apparent failure merely reflected the scale of what was needed to get the baby-boom generation into school and to keep the fourteen- to fifteen-year-olds there. And set against shortages of buildings, teachers, materials and money which dominated the early post-war agenda it seems harsh to complain that Labour failed to launch a comprehensive reorganisation for which there was no consensus even within Labour's own ranks.

If education had suffered from the two great economic crises Labour faced in 1947 and 1949, each of which brought cuts in planned spending, the 1949 sterling crisis also hit the health service in its first year.

The NHS proved spectacularly more expensive than expected. The original estimate for the first nine months had been £132 million. Actual spending, at £208 million, proved two-thirds higher. The first full year, 1949–50, required another 70 per cent rise to £358 million, although the following year the rate of increase fell to a mere 10 per cent.[42] Bevan did a far better job than Tomlinson of defending his corner, but in 1949 even he had to agree with Cripps on legislation which allowed a prescription charge to be included in the amending Act he had promised the doctors. He nevertheless staved off its actual introduction. Morrison could be heard muttering that 'Nye is getting away with murder' when other programmes including housing were being cut.[43]

In February 1950, Labour was returned to power but with its mighty majority slashed to six. The hunt for economy in the NHS resumed, Bevan having to agree to a Cabinet committee to monitor expenditure. Then in June came the Korean War. Over the next six months what became a £4.7 billion three-year rearmament programme was devised. It was to cripple the increasingly successful export drive, slash non-military industrial investment, and again squeeze social spending. In January 1951, Bevan was moved to the Ministry of Labour, resentful at having been passed over both as Chancellor on Cripps's resignation and as Foreign Secretary when Morrison replaced the ailing Bevin.[44]

By April, Hugh Gaitskell, the new Chancellor, was adamant that charges for dental treatment (chiefly dentures) and spectacles would be introduced. Bevan had fought and fought against the proposal, and on 21 April he resigned. He damned the rearmament programme as 'physically unattainable without grave extravagance in its spending'[45] (a view which proved right, Churchill's government rapidly scaling it down).[46] When rearmament was costing billions, the charges would raise a mere £13 million, and £30 million in a full year.[47] It was, Bevan told the Commons, 'the arithmetic of bedlam'.[48] Harold Wilson and John Freeman went with him, and Labour was plunged into almost a decade of internecine warfare between the Bevanite left and Gaitskellite right that was to play no small part in sustaining the Conservatives in power for thirteen years, and in erecting shibboleths about the definitions of socialism which scarred Labour for many years thereafter.

Within three years of its birth, the completely comprehensive and free health service had ceased to be. Peter Hennessy has summed up the clash: 'Bevan regarded charging for teeth and spectacles as a betrayal of the fundamental principle of a free NHS. Gaitskell saw it as both common sense and an aid to good housekeeping.'[49] That battle was to be fought both within Labour ranks and between Labour and the Conservatives for years to come. In October 1951 the exhausted Labour Government, with Bevin dead, Cripps out of office and dying, Dalton largely a spent force, and Bevan back in his old role of back-bench rebel, went to the polls. The Conservatives were returned with a majority of seventeen. Churchill was again prime minister. A 1s. od. (5p) prescription charge, made possible by Labour's legislation, was introduced in 1952 with a flat-rate charge for all dental treatment added to Labour's charge for dentures. The welfare state had completed its founding period.

CHAPTER 10

Conservatives, Consensus and the New Jerusalem

I am proud of our achievement. There is an immense amount more to do. Let us go forward in this fight in the spirit of William Blake:

> *I will not cease from mental strife,*
> *Nor shall my sword sleep in my hand*
> *Till we have built Jerusalem*
> *In England's green and pleasant land.*

Clement Attlee's final words to the 1951 Labour Party conference, three weeks before the Conservatives were returned to power

And so it was that, by the time they took the bunting down from the streets after VE-Day and turned from the war to the future, the British in their dreams and illusions and in their flinching from reality had already written the broad scenario for Britain's postwar descent . . . As that descent took its course, the illusions and the dreams of 1945 would fade one by one – the imperial and Commonwealth role, the world-power role, British industrial genius, and, at the last, New Jerusalem itself, a dream turned to a dank reality of a segregated, subliterate, unskilled, unhealthy and institutionalised proletariat hanging on the nipple of state maternalism.

Correlli Barnett, The Audit of War, p. 340

By 1951, a plausible updated version of a land fit for heroes had been built on the scarred foundations of an ancient, war-ravaged community. From 1945–51 onwards, Labour's central political faith, its prime claim to be the unique custodian of the progressive idea, lay with its inextricable identification with the rise and decline of the welfare state.

Kenneth O. Morgan, Labour in Power, p. 187

It was decency socialism, very Clem Attlee – fair play, fair chances, fair shares and co-operative conduct.

Neil Kinnock, interview, 1993

The Labour government which was swept to power in the summer of that year [1945] had, in the fields of social reform and reconstruction, only to complete the work which the Coalition had begun and in some cases bring forward Bills already drafted.

R. A. Butler, The Art of the Possible, p. 125

To the question, 'Would there have been a welfare state if the Conservatives had won in 1945?', the answer is plainly yes. There was by then a consensus that there would, even if the phrase itself, popularised by Archbishop Temple,[1] was only slowly entering common parlance. At the simplest level, it is tempting to point merely to the three 'Bs' – Beveridge, soon to become a Liberal MP, devising social security, the Conservative Butler producing the Education Act, and the Labour Bevan founding the NHS – as answer enough.

The reality, of course, is more complex. It was none the less the coalition's Education Act, drawn up by the Conservative Butler, which Labour implemented. Equally, despite alarm about the cost, there would have been Conservative social security provisions along the Beveridge lines. The Family Allowances Act had already been passed. The wartime coalition had agreed that phasing in pensions over twenty years was not politically tenable. Jim Griffiths's Bills went through the Commons with Conservative assent and barely a dissenting voice. He had found drafts of them on taking office, which he modified but did not alter fundamentally. It is entirely possible that a Conservative government would have backed away from some of the social security compromises it had made with its Labour and Liberal partners in coalition, just as Willink, in the interregnum between the coalition and Labour's victory, further modified the NHS proposals.[2] Benefit rates might well have been less generous. But the broad structure is unlikely to have been radically different. The insurance base was acceptable to the Conservatives in coalition and there is little or nothing to suggest the system would have been much more selective, or less universal.

There would, too, have been a National Health Service, free at the point of use. That was coalition policy and remained Willink's stance. Guy Dain, the chairman of the BMA's council, told a secret session of its representative body in May 1945 that an 'all-in' NHS appeared to be the unanimous policy not just of the then government, but of Parliament.[3] The NHS would have looked very different. Even though Willink in a 1962 health service debate was generous enough to declare that 'this is an opportunity for me to admit that in my view the Labour government was right when it undertook the daunting step of taking over 1334 voluntary and 1771 municipal hospitals',[4] it remains difficult to see a Conservative Government nationalising the hospitals in the way Bevan engineered. The alternative creation might not have worked as well as the NHS, the range of services might have been less comprehensive and it is impossible to see what different compromises a Conservative government would have forged with the doctors. But even Bevan (in his more emollient moods when he was not calling the Tories 'vermin') was prepared to admit that 'every party made its contribution' to the NHS,[5] while Attlee went out of his way to stress the cross-party nature of the measure on vesting day in 1948.

The White Paper *Employment Policy* had been a coalition effort and had defined a government commitment to 'high and stable' employment, even if the tools it adumbrated required further development. Even in housing, the coalition was already heavily involved and a Conservative administration would have had to be even more so, given the immense legacy of wartime damage and the demographic and electoral pressures. Local authorities would not have been chosen as almost the sole source of supply, as they were in the early years of the 1945 government: controls on private house building were gradually eased in the years to 1951. But in the past Conservative governments had put money into council houses and Macmillan was to use them as a major tool in his housing drive.

Butler, in arguing that Labour had only to complete the work of coalition, greatly overstates the case. But it is plain that the welfare state was in the making well ahead of 1945. Some of this is just the force of history. Modern welfare states of widely differing design in their details emerged at varying rates, but in general rapidly, across the rest of the industrialised world after 1945. Modern industrial societies have to have them. They all, like the UK, had been developing them before the Second World War.

At the most naïve level, once rural economies break up and money rather than barter or labour, in return for shelter, protection and care, becomes the dominant means of exchange, societies have to make some collective provision in cash and kind unless they are prepared to let the weakest literally go to the wall. The rural economy with extensive family networks can cope up to a point even with the village idiot, exchanging food and shelter for whatever limited work can be done. The modern cash economy is largely denied that option. It has to provide benefits, in cash or kind, paid for collectively by those who do not know the recipients, unless it is prepared to see people starve or die unnecessarily.

Of course Britain's welfare state, like those in the rest of Europe, was created as much more than just a rescue system for the weak. They all dramatically brought the middle classes and above into the net – indeed, that is one of the defining shifts of the 1940s. In Britain it meant that the middle class no longer had to pay the market cost of private health care or take out private insurance. No longer did they have to pay school fees. Their children came to receive maintenance grants at university, and it was disproportionately their children who reached university. Indeed it is the huge middle-class stake in 'free' education and health care that have made those the most enduring and popular features of the welfare state. The middle class, like everyone else, also received maternity benefits and family allowances, along with the prospect of a state pension and a death grant of a size that at the time would buy a basic funeral. These cash benefits, however, were flat-rate and so were relatively less important to them than to the less well off. Although they had a stake in social security, it was a lesser stake than in education and health – one factor which may help to explain the slowly growing scepticism over social security in a society which progressively became more middle class with a shrinking labouring class. But if the welfare state gave the middle class a major shareholding, it also produced a significant transfer of resources from the better off to the less well off. As importantly, and arguably even more importantly, it shifted resources between the generations at key moments in life. People paid taxes in middle life when in work, and in return were helped with their children's upbringing and education, were guaranteed help when sick, and were assisted in old age when earning ceased. There was therefore, and remained, a widespread vested interest – or, to put it more kindly, a mutual interest – in the welfare state, on top of the 'never again' revulsion felt over the effects of the 1930s depression.

That revulsion was far from confined to the Labour Party and those who voted for it. Harold Macmillan had written *The Middle Way* in 1938, with its advocacy of a mixed economy and far greater state intervention than was believed in by the Tory party of the 1930s. He would never forget the poverty and unemployment he had seen in his Stockton-on-Tees constituency. During the war *The Middle Way* became the creed for the burgeoning Tory Reform Group and once in opposition Churchill gave

Butler, Macmillan, Eden and other increasingly senior figures in the party the position and influence to develop those ideas into a radical rethink of the Conservative position.

Needless to say, furious inter-party conflict remained. One of the ironies of politics can be that the closer Government and Opposition are to each other's position, the louder any distinctions between them may have to be proclaimed. Thus it was over health and housing. The nationalisation of iron and steel, too, caused splenetic divisions, the industry over the years being nationalised, de-nationalised, re-nationalised and finally privatised. Yet even Sir John Anderson, the Treasury 'dry', to use modern parlance, who had helped enrage the Tory Reform Group back-benchers over Beveridge, acknowledged that: 'In the case of the Bank of England, Transport, Cable and Wireless, Electricity and Coal the onus of proving the need for socialisation may not unreasonably be held to have been discharged.'[6] It was in the main ailing but essential industries, and the public utilities which clearly played a social as well as commercial role, which Labour nationalised, not flourishing industries which would make large profits for the state to spend.

'The overwhelming electoral defeat of 1945 shook the Conservative Party out of its lethargy and impelled it to re-think its philosophy and re-form its ranks with a thoroughness unmatched for a century,' Butler has recorded.[7] Indeed, for a time the party was so seared by its past that its Young Turks, including Macmillan, argued it should change its name.[8] So large was Labour's majority that the Tories even toyed with the idea of proportional representation as a road back to at least a share of power. Socialism, Butler says, had provided the electorate 'with a vision and a doctrine to which we had no authoritative answer or articulated alternative'.[9] And the Conservatives were faced, Butler was to judge in the mellowness of hindsight, not just with a new intake of the horny-handed sons of toil but with a significant body of new middle-class Labour MPs who 'had little desire to subvert existing institutions: a moderate affluence was, in their view, respectable and their main (and legitimate) targets were the remaining extremes.'[10] The Conservatives' predicament was one of 'magnitude and difficulty'. It was 'our need to convince a broad spectrum of the electorate, whose minds were scarred by inter-war memories and myths, that we had an alternative policy to socialism which was viable, efficient and humane, which would release and reward enterprise and initiative but without abandoning social justice or reverting to mass unemployment.'[11] By the time of the next election the Conservatives had to show that they had 'accommodated themselves to a social revolution'.[12]

It was Butler who was to lead what became a Tory revolution as, in Anthony Howard's words, the Conservatives' 'philosopher-in-chief'. Churchill appointed him chairman of both the moribund Conservative Research Department and the cumbersomely named Advisory Committee on Policy and Political Education to which the Conservative Political Centre was answerable. Together they formed what Butler dubbed 'a thinking machine' – a precursor of the modern think-tanks. Into the research department came a galaxy of future stars: Reginald Maudling concentrating on economics, Iain Macleod on social policy, and Enoch Powell. Then in 1946, after a dispirited party conference had called for a new approach, Churchill appointed Butler chairman of what proved to be the most important body of them all, an industrial committee whose members included rising stars such as Macmillan, David Eccles, Peter Thorneycroft and Derrick Heathcoat-Amory, as well as more established names such as the two Olivers, Lyttelton and Stanley.

The outcome was the *Industrial Charter*, described by Anthony Howard as probably 'the most memorable concession a free enterprise party ever made to the spirit of Keynesian economics'.[13] It is not, as Butler himself was to confess, the most riveting of reads. He still had the powerful, free-market, *laissez-faire* right wing to deal with in the person of such wonderfully named back-benchers as Sir Waldron Smithers and Sir Herbert Williams, the latter convinced that the Conservatives in the war had been led to accept 'pink Socialism'.[14] There were other Tory MPs for whom, as Macmillan put it in 1947, 'time does not merely stand still, it runs backwards.'[15] They had on their side the might of the Beaverbrook press, notably the *Daily Express*, *Sunday Express* and *Evening Standard*, then in its heyday. Butler attempted to outflank his opponents by boring them. 'Rarely in the field of political pamphleteering,' he observed, 'can a document so radical in effect have been written with such flatness of language and blandness of tone.' The aim was to give the party 'a painless but permanent face-lift; the more unflamboyant the changes, the less likely were the features to sag again. Our first purpose was to counter the charge and the fear that we were the party of industrial go-as-you-please and devil-take-the-hindmost, that full employment and the Welfare State were not safe in our hands.'[16]

So while the charter did have much on industry (accepting the nationalisation of the Bank of England, coal and the railways on a case by case basis) and on co-operation within industry (much of which now reads as rather idealistic and quaint), its core was the Keynesian duty of the government to regulate the economy. It was a remarkable revision of the

party's 1930s position. 'Perhaps its [the government's] greatest duty,' the
document said, 'is to ensure that such main priorities as the maintenance
of employment and our well-developed social services are fulfilled before
subsidiary objectives are sought and that the tasks set are not beyond the
capacity of the resources available.'[17]

There was a healthy Conservative qualification at the end of that sentence – in effect, 'we have to be able to afford it'. But equally, the first
duties of government were clearly spelt out. The charter was thus, in
Butler's words, 'first and foremost an assurance that, in the interests of
efficiency, full employment and social security, modern Conservatism
would maintain strong central guidance over the operation of the economy.' The charter contained plenty to mark Conservatism out from Socialism. Indeed, its objective was to state a clear alternative. There were
themes which were to recur endlessly over the years: the improvement
of incentives via lower taxation, the removal of controls, the shrinking of
the civil service, the sharpening of competition.[18] But it finally defined
what Lord Woolton was to call the 'shandy gaff' of Labour/Tory central-
ism which was to be the core of British politics for the next thirty years.

For all the charter's bland language it was far from certain the right
would acquiesce, and the admittedly partisan *Tribune* predicted it would
'split the Tory party as it has not been divided for a half a century'.
The prediction proved no better than the grammar and at a carefully
stage-managed Conservative Party conference in Brighton in 1947 the
right was routed by this renewal of 'One Nation' Conservatism. The
charter went through despite a hiccup recorded by Maudling, who was
asked by Churchill to provide a five-line summary for his winding-up
speech. Churchill read it slowly, only to declare: 'But I don't agree with
a word of this.' 'But, sir,' Maudling was forced to protest, 'this is what
the conference adopted.'[19]

Anthony Howard's judgement is that the charter 'ended up virtually
sealing the party off from its pre-war past'. Butler, more grandiloquently,
echoed the *Spectator*'s view that it destroyed 'the last excuse for labelling
the Conservative party as reactionary'.[20] That may have been true internally in 1947. But *The Right Road for Britain*, a document produced two
years later which formed the basis for the 1950 and 1951 manifestos,
shows how far the party knew it had still to go to convince the public.

In 1949 it was still felt necessary to produce an immensely detailed
three-page appendix, packed with small print and headed 'Our contribution
to the social services 1918–1945', listing all such measures passed 'by
Parliaments with Conservative majorities'. With a rather desperate air, it

presented the Tories as the real founders of the welfare state. The body of the document stated: 'The Conservative party has welcomed the new social services which it has done so much to create. We regard them as mainly our own handiwork. We shall endeavour faithfully to maintain the range and scope of these services, and the rate of benefits.' Indeed, it even went so far as to argue that the 'vast experiment in social organisation' in which Britain now 'led the world' had been 'the work of the Conservative and Liberal Parties' and that Labour in the past four years had merely 'carried out in partisan spirit the plans prepared by the National Coalition Government with its large Conservative majority. They have no claim to any achievement of their own.'

None of this made *The Right Road* a cosily bipartisan effort. Other strains of thought remained extant. In 1945, Friedrich von Hayek, the Austrian free market economist, had written *The Road to Serfdom*, asserting that all forms of socialism and economic planning end inescapably in tyranny. It sold widely; Sir Waldron Smithers, for one, was a Hayek fan and its influence may even have inspired Churchill's disastrous claim in the 1945 election that Labour would introduce a Gestapo. Hayek himself was installed at the London School of Economics, where he provided a powerful counterpoint to the arguments of the social policy wizards who became known as 'Titmuss and the Titmice': first T. H. Marshall, who provided a theoretical construct which legitimized the welfare state as a historical force, then Titmuss himself, and later Brian Abel-Smith, Peter Townsend and their successors, all of whom heavily influenced the thinking not just of Labour but of more moderate Conservatives by providing both a critique and a renewal of the vision of the welfare state as well as of its detailed implementation.

By 1949, Hayek's influence had waned, with his star not set to rise again politically until the mid-1970s. His influence, none the less, can be seen in the opening sentence of *The Right Road for Britain* which stated baldly: 'Britain today has the choice of two – and only two – roads. One leads downwards to the Socialist state and inevitably into communism.' The other, of course, was the Conservative way, including a commitment to 'the property-owning democracy'. (That was the only memorable phrase ever attributed to Anthony Eden, who had popularised it at the 1946 Tory party conference, using it to embrace employee share ownership and profit sharing as well as home ownership.)[21] A review of rent controls was promised and it was noted acidly that it now took three men to build what two had built before the war. Seamlessly, however, the document also pledged more four- and five-bedroom council houses for larger families, and more smaller ones for elderly couples and single people.

The preservation of grammar schools was beginning to emerge as a Tory theme, but *The Right Road for Britain* also conceded that 'Under certain circumstances, variations of the multi-lateral idea may well be adopted', and while the party wanted to get rid of price controls and rationing it underlined that for necessities 'we shall *not* until there is enough to go round'.[22] So long did the image of the 'bad old Tory days' linger that a popular question-and-answer version of the pamphlet even referred directly to them and asked: 'Q: Is it true that the Conservatives want to cut the social services? A: This is a deliberate lie.'[23]

The fact that not just the party's leaders but its activists had changed was shown at the 1950 party conference, held after the general election. With the Conservatives having made much of Labour's failure to achieve the 300,000 houses a year built before the war, the conference became restive during a housing policy debate with representatives clamouring for a concrete Tory target. They started to chant: 'Three hundred thousand.' When the chair ruled such a move out of order the normally compliant ranks of Conservatives were for once reduced to uproar. Lord Woolton, the Tory party chairman, was sitting beside Butler and whispered, '*Could* we build 300,000?' to which Butler replied 'The question is *should* we?' – a distinction that Anthony Howard judges went straight over 'that populist politician's head'. Butler added, however, that if the question was whether such a target was technically feasible, then the back-room staff should be consulted. David Clarke, the director of the Conservative Research Department, off the platform, said it could be done, and Lord Woolton stepped forward to declare: 'This is magnificent. You want a figure of 300,000 put in? Madam chairman, I am sure that those of us on the platform here will be very glad indeed to have such a figure put in!'[24] Butler was to comment thirty years later on Lord Woolton's 'This is magnificent': 'So, in a sense, it was. Both the promise and the achievement were magnificent politically; economically, however, they placed a severe strain upon our resources which contributed to the difficulties of 1954–5.'[25]

In this way the Tory party went into the 1951 election committed to building 300,000 houses a year and to the maintenance of the rest of Britain's welfare state. The question then arises, did this amount to a consensus? And if so, how long did it last? If the definition is taken to mean unanimity, then plainly there was no consensus, not even within parties let alone between them. The left of the Labour Party – and at times not just the left – remained implacably opposed to private provision in education and health, for example, and fought to have their extinction included in the party programme. Within the Conservative Party the acceptance of a far greater degree of collectivism by Butler, Eden, Macmillan and Heath had still to contend with the remaining free market adherents of Hayek. Between the parties there remained fierce practical disputes about, for example, the role of the private and public sectors in housing – arguments which reflected key underlying distinctions in philosophy: the value of personal freedom and ownership against collective provision, of universality against selectivity, of choice against equality. It remained true that in an ideal world, untrammelled by realities and electoral considerations, Labour would happily have spent more and the Conservatives less. On the broadest of fronts – the handling of the economy, nationalisation, fiscal redistribution – profound differences between the parties remained.

But on the narrower issue of the welfare state and the services provided under it, the areas of agreement for a long time proved more important than areas of dispute, despite genuine battles over particular policies and a fierce picking of differences. The maintenance of full employment, for example, remained a shared goal right up to the late 1970s. It might not have done. In early 1952 the Treasury put to Butler, then Chancellor, a programme called ROBOT after the initials of the Treasury civil servants – ROwan, BOlton and OTto Clarke – who constructed it. It proposed floating the pound, producing steep rises in prices of imported food and raw materials and a consequent surge in unemployment. Butler believed in the scheme, stating in his memoirs that the decision not to go ahead was 'a fundamental [economic] mistake'. But Lord Cherwell, one of Churchill's key advisers, saw Butler's proposal as 'a reckless leap in the dark' which would have 'appalling political and economic consequences at home and abroad',[26] and with Eden, Woolton and others against opposition built to the point where, as Butler later recorded, 'among ministerial colleagues I could count Oliver Lyttelton alone as a consistent supporter.' The scheme was rejected in the face of a range of objections among which the fear of unemployment loomed large. Had it gone ahead history would have been different and, as Butler noted wryly and regretfully, 'the term Butskellism might never have been invented.'[27]

But it was rejected and the consensus on full employment held. Other parts of the welfare state faced similar challenges in the early Conservative years. Education and health were subjected to repeated assaults by the Treasury under Chancellors ranging from Butler through Macmillan and on to Peter Thorneycroft with proposals ranging from excluding dental and ophthalmic services from the NHS to cutting a year from either end of compulsory schooling. Hard and long battles were fought in Cabinet and Cabinet committees on these issues, to the point where it is arguable that the Conservatives once in government were less plainly committed to the welfare state up to 1958 than they were afterwards – 1958 being the year Macmillan allowed his Chancellor, Thorneycroft, to resign rather than accept cuts which included a hospital boarding fee, removal of the family allowance from the second child and a string of other options for retrenchment of the welfare state.

Yet despite these alarms, the fact is that no effective challenge to universal, free secondary schooling was mounted and tax-funded higher education was to expand dramatically. The same applied in health, where again a universal service free at the point of use survived essentially unscathed, despite the introduction of some charges. On social security the Conservatives accepted and broadly maintained the universalism of Beveridge. The levels of benefit that were set came, over time, to see more people relying on means-tested benefits. But no universal benefits became means-tested and the biggest battles up to the 1970s were over how and how far to extend second pensions, not how to cut back existing provision.

None of this amounts to a true consensus – absolute agreement on what should be done about every area at every time. What it does demonstrate is a large degree of consensus in action – though not in thought – with its degree varying by time and by subject. Labour did not, for example, abolish private education, any more than the Conservatives introduced charges for hospital admissions. And while the construction of a second pension was a bitterly contested subject for twenty years, the final introduction of SERPS, the State Earnings Related Pension Scheme, was to prove in 1976 a bipartisan measure despite, by then, a decade of Conservative rhetoric about greater selectivity. Up to the 1980s the differences between the parties produced for the welfare state services an oscillation around a mean, rather than any great swing in one direction or the another. The trend was in favour of the social democratic ideas embodied by the institutions and services of the welfare state. In these circumstances, and held within pragmatic bounds, the differences between the parties need make no difference to the broad shape of welfare. Given full rein, however, the views of the Conservative right or the Labour left would lead to very different societies.[28]

Michael Fraser joined the Conservative Research Department in 1946 and was only to lose his role in it, by then as chairman, when Mrs Thatcher became leader thirty years later. In 1987, as Lord Fraser of Kilmorack, he summed it up thus:

> In a fundamental sense there must always be a good deal of common ground between the main parties alternating in government in a free society. When in power, after all, they are governing the same country, with the same history, people, problems and elbow-room, or lack of it, within the same world. Because the two main parties coming out of the coalition government in 1945 had already hammered out, not without some hard bargaining and horse-trading, the broad policies for dealing after the war with those social problems that had been identified and prepared for during the war on the basis of the Beveridge Report, the Employment Policy White Paper and the Butler Education Act of 1944, there was for a time an unusual degree of apparent unity of aim. To say, however, that the situation after 1945 amounted to a 'consensus' is a myth of more recent origin. No one thought that at the time. The real position was like that of two trains, starting off from parallel platforms at some great London terminus and running for a time on broadly parallel lines but always heading for very different destinations.[29]

There were to be plenty of bouts of rhetoric – and occasional policy gestures – about what those different destinations were over the years. As early as 1950 the brightest of the new intake of Tory MPs, including Macleod, Angus Maude, Powell and, in a strictly limited role, Edward Heath, produced the *One Nation* pamphlet whose endorsement of the welfare state was tempered by important qualifications. In both parties there would be individuals and groupings who would argue for more extreme positions. But in terms of what was put to the electorate it would be the late 1970s and early 1980s before the differences of the destinations were spelled out in stark terms.

In 1945, in A. H. Halsey's phrase, Labour inherited a Britain that was 'by today's standards . . . a poverty stricken country exhausted by war'.[30] And yet by 1951, despite austerity, Cripps, rationing (which for a time after the war became even more stringent and did not finally end until 1954); despite utility furniture (which was virtually all that was available until 1949), the absence of bananas for five and a half years up to 1946, and the fact that the street lights did not go back on in Piccadilly until 1949 (four years after the war ended and a decade after they had gone out); despite all this, Britain was slowly becoming more prosperous. While the convertibility crisis, devaluation and the impact of the Korean War each shook the Labour Government's confidence and set back planned spending, the overall record of the six years was of growth, rapidly rising production and an export-led boom. The 1945–51 era was also the period of long, hot, almost Edwardian summers, of Bradman, Compton and Edrich, of record football league and cinema attendances (a third of the population went to the pictures once a week, one in eight twice a week).[31] It was the Britain of young Richard Attenborough playing the delinquent Pinky in the film of Graham Greene's *Brighton Rock* and Dirk Bogarde murdering, in *The Blue Lamp*, the same Jack Warner who was to rise seemingly eternal on television as the avuncular *Dixon of Dock Green*. The 1940s and early 1950s was the Britain of those now grainy classics *Brief Encounter* and *The Third Man*, Ealing comedies like *Passport to Pimlico* -- a cheerful revolt against rationing and bureaucracy – and *The Lavender Hill Mob*, and the boom in Butlin holiday camps. There was the 'New Look', 'spivs' – the first self-confident denial of the collective spirit the war was meant to have established – and endless 'fiddling' of coupons. Dockers discovered the strike weapon and turned themselves into the shock troops of the working class, producing the first manifestations of the 'I'm All Right Jack' philosophy. Britain had moved from the government-sponsored 'Britain Can Make It' exhibition in 1946 (dubbed by the wags 'Britain Can't Have It', as almost all the goods displayed were for export only) to the muddy excitement (and controversy) of the Festival of Britain in 1951, built on a rubble-strewn bomb site with the Festival Hall symbolising a musical revival which included the reintroduction of the Proms and the rise of 'Flash Harry' (Sir Malcolm Sargent). Publishing boomed as paper controls ended, *Animal Farm* finally saw the light of day, *Brideshead Revisited* presented an elegy for a lost age and Graham Greene produced *The Heart of the Matter* and *The End of the Affair*. C. P. Snow started his 'Strangers and Brothers' sequence. Lumps of sculpture by Henry Moore and Barbara Hepworth started to be scattered approvingly across the landscape and Francis Bacon, Graham Sutherland and Stanley Spencer begin to gain a wider audience. The first national parks were established; the Pennine Way was planned. Legal aid emerged as a small and unobtrusive part of the welfare state, but one which when it started in 1950 covered almost 80 per cent of the population.

It remained, however, a Britain where many newly-wed couples still lived with their parents for lack of any other home; where tenement slums still existed, terraced houses could still shelter several families sharing a gas ring and a single lavatory, and where families would still find they would have to wait nine or ten years for a council house. More than 40 per cent of households did not have a fixed bath and 15 per cent had to share a lavatory,[32] television sets were a treasured rarity, pianos were still valued, and virtually every home had a Bakelite or wood cabinet mains radio.

In the Britain of 1951, Neil Kinnock, an eight-year-old in the Welsh valleys, was about to benefit not just from attending a grammar school but from the further education that in the 1980s would allow him to declare, in one of the few moments in that decade which caught the resonance of the post-war achievement, that he was 'the first Kinnock in a thousand generations' to go to university. John Major was a nine-year-old in Worcester Park, about to follow the same path to grammar school, though not to university. Tony Blair, whose education would take in the Scottish public school Fettes and Oxford University, was not even born. Hilda Margaret Roberts was of an earlier generation, the one before the welfare state. A scholarship girl at the grant-aided grammar school in Kesteven in 1936, her alderman and grocer father had been able to find the funds that let her take up a place at Oxford in 1943. As the Conservatives took office in 1951, she was already twenty-five, a losing candidate at Dartford in both 1950 and 1951. But she was on her way.

PART III

CONSOLIDATION

1951–74

CHAPTER 11

'You've never had it so good': Conservatives 1951–64

> Wealth and welfare are partners. They both rose under Attlee's socialism, Macmillan's opportunity society and Butskell's consensus.
> *A. H. Halsey, 'A Sociologist's View of Thatcherism' in Skidelsky, ed., Thatcherism, p. 186*

> The memory of massive unemployment began to haunt me then and for many years to come.
> *Harold Macmillan, recalling Stockton in the 1920s, quoted in Horne, p. 71*

> Let's be frank about it, most of our people have never had it so good.
> *Macmillan at party rally in Bedford, 1957*

FROM 1948 TO 1973 Britain enjoyed a sustained period of economic growth, averaging around 2.8 per cent a year. With growth the welfare state expanded, and at times expanded rapidly. More could be afforded, more could be and was done.

There were of course economic ups and downs, some much sharper than others. The two and a half decades saw the arrival of 'stop-go' – or perhaps more accurately 'go-stop', in which economic stimulus led to overheating in the form of inflation or big balance of payments deficits, to be followed by contraction and then expansion again. But it was not until the early 1970s that the bedrock of the welfare state, full employment, first cracked. Even then the fissure was relatively small: in 1971–2, when for the first time unemployment averaged more than 3 per cent over the year, it did so by only the finest of margins. Such figures are low by the standards of the 1980s and 1990s, but what now seem minor shifts in the jobless total stimulated intense controversy; and there was continuing concern at levels of structural unemployment in some parts of Britain that were often double the national average.

None the less, after the initial, painful hiccup over rearmament during the Korean War, the late fifties and early sixties became dubbed the age of affluence. In the mid-1950s, Conservative economic policy was dubbed by the *Economist* 'Butskellism',[1] combining the names of the present and previous Chancellors, Butler and Gaitskell. Neither liked the label. Butler was to cavil in his autobiography that 'both of us spoke the language of Keynesianism. But we spoke it with different accents and with a differing emphasis.'[2] After 1955 the cross-party conflict over the handling of the economy sharpened noticeably. None the less, the phrase did capture what in retrospect looks like a broad economic consensus.

This did not mean that there was a consensus on spending on the welfare state. Housing was put top of the Conservatives' list of priorities and everything else – hospitals, health centres, schools, books – languished for some years a long way behind, a fact made much of by Labour. But there was still perpetual alarm within the government at the apparently inexorable growth in social spending. Repeated attempts at retrenchment in health, social security and education were made by successive Chancellors and the Treasury, but these met with only the most limited of success and were to culminate with the resignation of Peter Thorneycroft as Chancellor of the Exchequer in January 1958. A proto-monetarist faced with inflation and a sterling crisis, Thorneycroft had proposed curbing the money supply and freezing public spending through a package of measures with options including ending the family allowance for the second child, reducing the NHS ophthalmic service, increasing the NHS element in the national insurance contribution, introducing a 'boarding fee' or hotel charge in hospitals, and raising the price of school milk. After three Cabinet meetings Macmillan summed up strongly against him, arguing that the family allowance proposal was 'contrary to the traditions of the Conservative Party' and that the other measures would create disaffection and fresh wage claims. Only the increase in NHS contributions was allowed through. When Thorneycroft resigned, taking his junior ministers Enoch Powell and Nigel Birch with him, Macmillan, soon to be ironically characterised by the left-wing cartoonist Vicky as 'Supermac', insouciantly dismissed the loss of his Treasury team as 'a little local difficulty'. Social priorities, which included the impact on employment and the housing programme, and the fear of higher wage demands, had taken priority over the fear of inflation. This was, in a small way, a turning point for the welfare state. As Kenneth Morgan has put it: 'The battle fought out over

ROBOT in 1952 was again won by the consensus, one-nation party, with the significant difference that Butler was now chief among the doves.'[3]

The economy continued to expand and Macmillan's retort to a heckler in Bedford, in fact delivered at one of the rockier moments for the economy, came to dominate the 1959 general election; helped along by the first recognisably 'give-away' pre-election Budget, it turned into the slogan 'You've never had it so good'.

That Budget was to lead to another dose of 'stop' and a mild recession in 1962. But it remains true that over the whole of the Conservatives' tenure up to 1964 there were unmistakable indicators of growing personal wealth and comfort. Production of television sets exceeded a million a year in 1953. The number of cars on the roads rose from 2.5 million in 1951 to more than 6 million by 1964. The proportion of households owning a refrigerator rose from 5 to 37 per cent, those owning washing machines from 11 to 52 per cent. As the 1950s moved into the 1960s the baby-boom generation of the war produced a new word, 'teenagers', bringing skiffle and Teddy Boys in Edwardian drapes. Max Bygraves charted the changing times with 'Fings ain't what they used to be' ('They've changed our local palais into a bowling alley' and '. . . Paris is where we spend our outings'). Coffee bars and rock and roll gave way to the twist and Dansette record players which played LPs made of plastic rather than black acetates which smashed when dropped. As the Macmillan era closed four lads in Liverpool were sending small but heaving audiences mad in a place called the Cavern.

It was only from the middle 1950s onward that it become apparent that although the economy was expanding and Britain was becoming more affluent, its industries were making do with obsolete equipment while the rest of Europe re-equipped. Europe's prosperity was increasing at roughly twice the rate of Britain's as the post-war version of relative decline set in. Each period of 'stop' and 'go' affected the welfare state. Equally, some of the welfare state policies were affecting the economy. Chief of these was housing. And it was housing which first and most clearly showed the party divide over the boundaries of the public and private sectors in welfare.

Housing

The Ministry of Housing was like cricket, you could see the runs, the houses were being built.

Harold Macmillan, quoted in Hennessy, Whitehall, p. 438

This is my moment and I intend to ram it home.
Ben Parkin, speaking in the Commons at the height of the Rachman scandal,
Hansard, 22 July 1963, col 1119

A drama of optimism turning into arrogance and ending in disaster
. . . if lifts and security [had] worked, the story would be very
different.
Patrick Nuttgens on high-rise housing, The Home Front, 1989, p. 95

Politically, we had to remember that raising the rents of nearly
two-thirds of the total houses, affecting anything between 16 and 20
million people, was not exactly an easy operation.
Harold Macmillan, Tides of Fortune, p. 444

Labour's departure in 1951 saw the end of a six-year period (twelve, if
the war is taken into account) when the building of new homes had come
close to being a state service. Three-quarters of all new building had been
council houses, publicly financed through central government grant and
rates; and all of it had been state controlled: private houses, and even
repairs above the most minor, had required licences. Bevan had, however,
turned down the idea of nationalising housing, and first he and then Dalton
had gradually eased restrictions on private house building, allowed councils
to lend for house purchase, and introduced improvement grants for private
housing. But when Macmillan, the new housing minister, started to shift
more sharply the boundaries between public and private provision the
issue acquired a new ideological and political edge.

When Bevan departed, housing had been split from its fifty-year association with health. Macmillan, in evidence of intent over the 300,000
houses target set by the Tory party conference, promptly renamed Dalton's
Ministry of Local Government and Planning the Ministry of Housing and
Local Government and set out to make his and the Tories' reputation as
guardians of the welfare state.[4] He had not wanted the job, telling Churchill: 'I know nothing whatever about the housing problem.' To that the
Prime Minister replied with considerable foresight: 'It is a gamble – [it
will] make or mar your political career.'[5] For the next three years, with
Churchill's backing, Macmillan put housing at the head of the welfare
state queue, beating other areas for resources and launching in earnest
the numbers game that was to dominate housing policy for much of the
next twenty years.

With the showmanship that was increasingly to mark him out, within three months of taking office Macmillan announced 'The Great Housing Crusade'.[6] He needed a crusade to protect him from the Treasury. For the first year of Conservative rule was a period of economic crisis, as officials warned the new Chancellor, Butler, that the blood was 'draining from the system' and that Britain was once again staring ruin in the face.[7] The pledge to build 300,000 houses became Macmillan's 'sheet-anchor' allowing him to ride out the economic gale[8] and resist cuts through a mixture of elegant bullying, the odd hint at resignation and a reorganisation of his department on wartime-like lines of control. The net result, he noted, was 'more than my fair share'[9] of resources.

To reorganise a department 'concerned with guidance, advice, supervision, sometimes even warning and reproof, but never with positive action',[10] Macmillan brought in as Director-General Sir Percy Mills, an industrialist who had been controller of machine tools during the war. The appointment caused no little friction in Whitehall, not least with Beveridge's old adversary Sir Thomas Sheepshanks who was now Macmillan's permanent secretary.[11] Macmillan once brutally dismissed him as 'useless'.[12] The resentment of Mills was one of the early signs that a civil service leavened and enlightened during the war with outside expertise now once again regarded itself as the sole guardian of policy development and administration.

Almost everything except labour still remained in short supply – bricks, steel, timber, cement; Macmillan at one point complained that surely the last of these could be produced more quickly when all it amounted to was 'Thames mud and chalk'.[13] To hit 300,000 a year, Macmillan cut further the minimum size for council housing which Dalton had already eroded, encouraged the building of smaller two-bedroom houses by councils, and relaxed and then removed licences for private house building. His aim, he declared, was 'to set the builders free'. He also allowed the first post-war council house sales, the aim being to cut Treasury subsidies for rents and to generate more capital.[14] Some 3000 were sold by the 1955 election.[15] Macmillan thus initiated a policy which in a different form would eventually become Mrs Thatcher's icon. As he told the Commons in December 1951, in what was to become a recurring Conservative theme: 'We wish to see the widest distribution of property. We think that, of all forms of property suitable for such distribution, house property is one of the best.'[16]

But as Macmillan himself made clear, crucial to the numbers game was the cut in the size of council houses. The smaller ones were now popularised as 'The People's House' and promoted to the public on the grounds that while they might be smaller, their rent was lower. There were repeated exhortations to reduce the number of bricks and other materials used. 'Unless we get the economies, we shan't get the houses,' he declared. Timber and steel shortages also saw the introduction of much more reinforced concrete and of steel-reinforced lintels, a permanent change in housing construction.[17]

'The fierce and almost frantic pursuit of the housing target filled my mind,' Macmillan remembered. The monthly figures provided 'a scorecard on which the eyes of all the critics, friendly and hostile' were riveted. Bets were laid between political colleagues on whether completion figures would be attained.[18] It was not quite a case of 'never mind the quality feel the width'; but it was heading that way as quality and quantity came into conflict. Macmillan's resolution of the problem differed from Bevan's, and problems for the future were created.

Quantity, however, was needed. By 1952, early returns from the first population census in twenty years indicated one million more households than dwellings, and more than two million dwellings which were shared by two or more families.[19] This grim picture, despite a million houses having been built since 1945, was the result of demographic change. Since 1931, the population of England and Wales had risen by only 10 per cent, but the number of households had increased by 28 per cent, or nearly three times as fast: the result of more single elderly, survivors of the First World War, and the growing popularity of both marriage and smaller families. Thus over twenty years, the number of one and two person households had risen from 29 to 39 per cent of the total, while the number of big households (six members or more) had halved from 16 to 8 per cent.[20] Macmillan achieved his numbers, helped in part by the 'valuable inheritance' of the New Towns, a development he regarded as showing 'real imagination' on Labour's part.[21] He was aided by Sir Percy Mills and the regional housing boards they set up, the drive of Dame Evelyn Sharp, an under-secretary who was shortly to become one of Whitehall's few female Permanent Secretaries, and the ministerial expertise of the self-made engineer Ernest Marples, who shocked colleagues when he arrived in Parliament in 1945 sporting orange-brown shoes beneath his blue suits.[22] Macmillan once acknowledged simply: 'Marples made me PM: I was never heard of before housing.'[23]

The target was reached in 1953 when 318,000 houses were built and was comfortably exceeded in 1954 when another 357,000 were added. Moreover, more than a quarter of these new homes, against 15 per cent in 1952, were in the private sector.[24] What had been a trickle of private homes was becoming a stream 'to augment or even to some extent replace the rising river of subsidised housing,' Macmillan noted.[25] New housing, however, was only part of the problem. With the numbers rolling in, he turned his attention to the slums and the linked problem of rent which he described as 'the most intricate and politically dangerous' of the housing issues.[26]

In July 1952 a report from the Sanitary Inspectors' Association had pointed out that houses were falling out of use as fast as they were being built, or faster.[27] A key reason was rent levels. In 1951 in England, 53 per cent of houses remained privately rented and less than 30 per cent were owner-occupied.[28] Many rents, however, had been controlled since 1939, some of them at levels set in the 1920s. The mesh of controls meant that rents could vary two-and-a-half-fold for identical houses in the same street with the same amenities.[29] Frequently rent income was too small for landlords to finance repairs. Homes that had once been good were becoming slums, and slum clearance, the Luftwaffe's contribution aside, had been halted by the war. Anything between 280,000 and 500,000 homes were calculated to need clearance, against the 140,000 slum dwellings whose demolition had been halted in 1939.

Macmillan therefore prepared to switch the programme's emphasis to include repair, conversion and slum clearance. In 1953 he proposed that councils would be able to take over slums for their site value only, turning local authorities into slum landlords but ones charged with clearing them and able to set realistic rent levels for the replacement housing. Aside from the New Towns, which were taking overspill from the cities, councils were given bigger subsidies for slum clearance than for other forms of new building. And as part of this 'Operation Rescue' a limited rent increase, a 'repairs increase', was allowed in the private sector where landlords could demonstrate by certification that they had put homes into good repair in the past three years – this last to protect tenants who in despair had undertaken repairs themselves. In addition, all new private houses and flats would be free of rent control. 'The opposition to this [the easing of rent restrictions] was considerable,' Macmillan recorded. 'But I felt it was another move to freedom.'[30]

Macmillan faced Bevan at his stormiest. Labour was into the leftward shift that, from the end of the war at least up to 1983, it took each time it went into opposition – at least in terms of its policy as passed by annual conferences. The Tories equally were to move right when not in power, whatever finally happened when they returned to government. Bevan argued that all rent-controlled private property should be taken over by the councils, municipalising, though not nationalising, some five to six million homes. Landlords could not be trusted to spend rent increases on repairs, he argued. Only local authorities could find the cash and therefore they should take over the homes.

Morrison, among others, wanted nothing to do with that, but in 1956 the Labour Party conference endorsed the policy. Arthur Greenwood, in recommending this 'full-blooded Socialism' to the conference, commented accurately that it was 'probably the biggest socialization project that has yet been attempted in the democratic world'.[31] Its object was to 'take the profit out of private landlordism' and 'make housing a social service'. Had such a policy ever been implemented, housing would indeed have become just that, with well over 60 per cent of homes council controlled. This policy of mass municipalisation was balanced by the promise of more generous local authority mortgages for home owners. But even Green-wood could see that 'entirely new problems' would be created if the local authority was 'virtually the only landlord in the area'.[32] Needless to say this never happened, although the idea survived into the 1959 manifesto, hedged with let-out qualifications about timing. Nothing, however, could better illustrate the real differences that would remain over the public sector/private sector divide in the welfare state. Where Bevan was right, as Macmillan much later conceded, was that the 'repairs increase' he allowed in rent was too small to have much effect. (Bevan, having his cake and eating it, had dismissed the increase as 'a mouldy turnip'.)

If Macmillan hit his targets by relaxing controls on the private sector and by cutting standards in the face of overwhelming demand, his immediate successors Duncan Sandys, Henry Brooke, Charles Hill, Sir Keith Joseph and then Labour's Dick Crossman all helped grow the bitter harvest that became the real disaster of post-war housing – system build, the high-rise towers and the great slab blocks of deck-access flats. It started almost by accident. Up to the mid-1950s traditional houses dominated. In 1953 just 23 per cent of public sector housing approvals were for flats, and only 3 per cent of those were for high-rise: blocks of six storeys and above. But from 1956, Sandys started paying higher subsidies for high-rise blocks. Up to then, he told the House of Commons, all flats had received the same subsidy.

Since construction, in practice, costs more as you go higher, the result has been that flats in low blocks have been more heavily subsidised in relation to costs than flats in high blocks. Apart from being inequitable, this has unintentionally influenced local authorities to concentrate on building blocks of three, four and five storeys, which, I believe, many honourable members will agree are most monotonous.[33]

No one dissented. From then on, the taller the block the bigger the subsidy in order to eliminate the financial advantages of erecting low-rise buildings. On such wonderfully egalitarian and aesthetic grounds, the explosion in high-rise was, almost unintentionally, launched. Within four years, the proportion of high-rise had risen five-fold to 15 per cent of the construction programme, and by 1966 it accounted for 26 per cent of all homes started.[34]

The guilty men – they were almost all men – were not just those in government. An unintended conspiracy of town planners, builders, engineers and architects, together with local councillors who believed they were doing their best but frequently failed to consult those they were rehousing, produced what became a costly and alienating fiasco. 'Tower blocks were part of architectural and municipal prestige,' the architectural historian Patrick Nuttgens has recorded, '– a desire to make a mark on the landscape, to display technical proficiency and to announce the arrival of a new age.'[35] In Birmingham, Harry Watton, the Labour leader known as 'little Caesar', was taken to see one of Bryant's new system-build blocks at Kidderminster. Sheppard Fidler, the city architect recalled:

> To get to the block we passed through a marquee which was rolling in whisky, brandy and so on, so by the time they got to the block they thought it was marvellous – they wanted to change over the whole [housing] programme [to these]. As we were leaving, Harry Watton suddenly said: 'Right! We'll take five blocks' – just as if he was buying bags of sweets. 'We'll have five of them and stick them on X' – some site he'd remembered we were just starting on.[36]

Rod Hackney, an architecture student in Manchester in the early 1960s, has caught the flavour of the time as well as anyone in *The Good, the Bad and the Ugly*, his autobiographical account of the road to community architecture. The road ran from the 1930s and Walter Gropius, the founder of the Bauhaus, via the Modern movement to Le Corbusier's 'cities in the sky'. In 1946, Corbusier's *Towards a New Architecture* was published in Britain with its ringing declaration that 'we must create the mass-production spirit. The spirit of constructing mass-production houses. The spirit of living in mass-production houses. The spirit of conceiving mass-production houses.' In well under a decade, the spirit had turned into a flood of buildings. 'By the mid-fifties traditional building methods were considered slow, cumbersome and a hindrance,' Hackney records. 'The only way to build new homes on a massive scale was unrestrained use of the standardized mass-produced materials advocated by the Modernists. A vast proportion of these systems had to be imported from France, Denmark and – ironically – West Germany. Entire rooms were shipped over and were then slotted together like Lego on site.' There was 'blind faith in "hip" modern building materials – off-the-peg panels, concrete, glass, metal, plastics and aluminium . . . if one dared question the long-term performance of the new, the reply was swift: in the same way that technology had developed the materials, it would also develop solutions to problems as and when they were required.'[37]

The modern movement and its sub-section the new Brutalism, which believed in the 'honesty' of bare concrete, seemed to meet the demands of cheapness, speed and what rapidly became the lack of space as the Town and Country Planning Act preserved green belt and put pressure on inner city land. The only answer seemed to be a version of the approach adopted by the first Tesco supermarkets: pile 'em high and sell 'em quick, or in this case build 'em quick, for in theory high rise gave savings on drains, roads, services and other infrastructure. This suggestion proved to be an illusion; high rise was eventually found to cost more than traditional ways of building. Politically, however, the numbers game was all there was. In later years, Keith Joseph's hand would go over an anguished face and he would mutter 'disaster, disaster' when he contemplated what he had built when housing minister in the early 1960s. 'I was genuinely convinced I had a new answer. It was prefabrication and, Heaven help me, high blocks . . . the best of intentions and the worst of results.'[38] He was to recall sadly: 'I didn't have a philosophy. I was just a "more" man. I used to go to bed at night counting the number of houses I'd destroyed and the number of planning approvals that had been given . . . Just *more*.'[39] Almost no one asked the families from the massively expanding slum clearance programme what they thought of all this. Nicholas Taylor, an assistant editor at the *Architectural Review*, recalled the massive arrogance still present as late as 1967 when he proposed that some evidence should be sought on what people actually wanted, to go with an issue on 'the best of current housing'. He was scornfully dismissed by the proprietor with the words: 'But we KNOW what should be done!'[40]

Initially, many of these housing schemes attracted awards and inter-national recognition. But, as Rod Hackney has put it, 'Utopia showed early signs of cracking up.'[41] Flat roofs that were fine in sunnier climes soon succumbed to British rain. Concrete became stained, crumbled, and spalled – partly the result of additives slung in to speed setting. Key joints leaked, sometimes because they had been packed with newspaper and concrete bags by builders on piece rates who were too impatient to wait for the right fittings. The result too often was 'sodden walls and squelching floors',[42] and high fuel bills even when residents could control their own heating rather than having to rely on whole block systems which were often inefficient. Maintenance costs proved awesome. Lifts and rubbish chutes failed. As the physical environment deteriorated it was found that whole buildings and even estates could spiral down to decay and fear at alarming speed. By 1960, within two years of being built, the twin ten-storey blocks of Oak and Eldon Gardens in Birkenhead were subject to blackouts and flooding as the electrical and fire-fighting equipment was sabotaged and as children swung from balcony to balcony on the hose-reels. Two toddlers fell to their deaths and acts of arson led to repeated evacuations.[43] Even when vandalism did not reach that pitch, the long corridors and dark corners of deck access flats proved terrifying. Soon, Rod Hackney noted, 'the only people giving awards and plaudits to archi-tects were the muggers and burglars.'[44]

This perception took time to grow, and for some tower blocks and the massive slab flats proved a success: single people, the childless and even better-off families can value them when they are built to a high standard and well maintained. The mighty towers of the Barbican development in the City of London remain popular. But for too many families the public developments proved a disaster. Mothers could not see children playing many floors below amid both poorly maintained concrete and a social mix that the very planning process had set askew. Long lost by the late 1950s and early 1960s was Bevan's romantic vision of a socially mixed village. The slum terraces that were cleared often included privately rented, council and owner-occupied housing. However, once the intention to 'improve' an area by demolition and replacement was announced, blight descended, sales became impossible and prices slumped. For the council, this could conveniently cut the cost of compulsory purchase which might not be finally enacted for years. But as tower and slab blocks slowly gained their awesome reputation many of the most able fled the prospect of rehousing, leaving a mix of community that was far from balanced, and which was often rehoused with scant regard for placing people near neighbours and families. Housing ghettos in the sky began to be created.

Over time these conditions were to have a deeply corrosive effect on the public perception of council housing, both for those who lived in it and those who did not. At its peak, high-rise only accounted for well under 10 per cent of local authorities' housing stock[45] – a figure which none the less meant homes for more than 1.5 million people.[46] But tower blocks, and the at times even more massive slab blocks, came to dominate city skylines. Jack Straw, Peter Shore's political adviser at the Department of the Environment in the late 1970s and twice Labour's housing spokesman, says that these developments 'did for public sector housing. It was an alien form of housing which became intrusive to the rest of the population. Up to the mid-1950s council blocks in the main were four or five storeys, no different in style and scale from the private blocks in north Westminster, for example. Suddenly the skyline of every large town and city was disfigured by these "welfare blocks". The middle classes didn't mind paying for council housing. What they did mind was being literally overshadowed by welfare housing that was destroying their skylines.'[47]

High-rise became an all-party disaster at both national and local level, but it was rent that was the chief source of party conflict over housing in the late 1950s and early 1960s. Compounding the problem of repairs was the fact that, while swathes of privately rented housing were appalling – well over a third of its households lacked hot water and one-fifth exclusive use of a lavatory[48] – people had got used to low rents. Real earnings had outstripped rent rises three-fold since 1938. By 1955 official figures suggested that on average less was being spent on rent than on either drink or tobacco.[49] Macmillan had lamented, 'it is hard to get back the idea that the first thing on which the family income should be spent is living accommodation.'[50] A further complication was that council house rents, despite subsidies, were often more realistic than private ones. As a result, particularly in the more attractive housing, it was foremen and skilled workers who made up the largest section of council tenants, while the least well off often had to fall back on the worst of the private rented sector. In addition, amid full employment, the shrinking share of private renting was hampering labour mobility.

With well over a third of the houses and much more of the population renting privately, an instant free-for-all in rents was impossible when housing shortages still existed. The 1957 Rent Act, introduced by Powell and Sandys, carried through by Brooke and Reginald Bevins, produced staged decontrol. Rents at the top end of the market were deregulated over three years, affecting in the main, but not exclusively, the middle classes. Rents below that were raised, but remained controlled. As tenants moved out, however, rents could be re-set free of controls. With Labour's official policy now municipalisation the parliamentary battle was furious, despite the Bill's second reading in 1956 being overshadowed by the Suez crisis. Labour MPs denounced it as 'vicious class legislation' warning that tenants would be 'thrown to the wolves', left starving, or put on the streets by exploitative landlords who would do no repairs.[51] Labour promised the Act's repeal, the pledge becoming, in Keith Banting's words, 'a symbol of historic differences between the two parties'.[52]

In practice creeping decontrol took time to take effect. Initially evictions were few, rent increases limited. At the end of 1958, the *Manchester Guardian* judged the Act to be working: 'The general expectation seems to be that the Act will, as promised, make rather more accommodation available.'[53] Particularly in London, however, the demographic pressures continued to mount. The service industries, growing rapidly in the age of affluence, were pulling low-paid workers into the capital, among them West Indian immigrants encouraged to Britain to boost the labour supply. At the same time, slum clearance ahead of rebuilding was diminishing the stock. Housing shortages were growing. By 1960 and 1961, rents were rocketing on renewal, homelessness was rising, bishops started to march, and the ministry found it had no decent figures on the private rented sector with which to fight back against the numbers that social scientists at the LSE headed by David Donnison were collecting. These showed that the private rented sector was still shrinking, while the rate of repair was not improving.[54]

Slowly and increasingly explosively, housing became a media story. What made it detonate in 1963 was Perec Rachman. A Polish immigrant after the war, he had started in 1954 buying up the ends of leases in big multiply-occupied houses in Notting Hill and other parts of west London. His methods of shifting tenants out of unfurnished rooms so that he could re-let them, nominally furnished and at uncontrolled rents, were never too gentle. Faced with a house full of statutory tenants paying protected pre-war rents, Rachman would combine racial prejudice with business, according to the *Sunday Times* account which eventually revealed his methods. He would let one room to eight West Indians, 'all accomplished musicians', and tell them he liked parties. Within three months the 'stats' – statutory tenants – would have left, replaced by ranks of West Indian immigrants or poor whites, desperate for housing and paying uncontrolled furnished rents amid appalling overcrowding. Alternatively, the house would be sold vacant for five times the sum Rachman had paid for it.[55] If tenants refused to move, the heavies – ex-wrestlers and boxers – would be sent in. On one occasion, Rachman simply took the roof off a house when some tenants refused to leave. Others were intimidated, physically assaulted, had their furniture destroyed, or found that all-night 'clubs' had been established in their basements. In St Stephen's Gardens, Paddington, residents and tenants famously fought back, once flooding one of the clubs to close it and on another occasion sawing up a staircase and electrifying it with metal fittings to prevent Rachman's roadies evicting a couple.[56] Attempts by the police and local and public health authorities to deal with him were defeated by a web of holding companies so complex that it was never finally established how many properties he owned, although the minimum estimate at his peak in 1959 was 150 involving at least 1000 tenancies.[57]

Rachman had been at work since the mid-1950s and indeed had died in 1962. The fuse that was to explode his name into a permanent place in the English language was the knowledge held by one of his firmest opponents, Ben Parkin, the Labour MP for Paddington, that Mandy Rice-Davies had been his mistress. When Rachman's name came up in one of the court cases around the Profumo affair in 1963, Parkin pounced – injecting Rachman, housing and intimidation into the already fetid tale of Mandy Rice-Davies, Christine Keeler, and the Secretary of State for War who had shared his mistress with a Russian spy. With Rachman dead, the libel laws which had held back his full exposure no longer applied and the link to Profumo provided scintillating topicality and a fresh breath of life to a fading story. A month's worth of media exposure resulted, running on into the summer 'silly season' when newspapers are short of news. Rachman, his methods, and the state of London housing were suddenly *the* issue.

Even *The Times* went graphic. It described:

A young girl, near to tears . . . [in] the pitifully small room in which she and her husband had to live. There was no water, except for a cold tap in the backyard down three flights of dark rickety stairs. The one lavatory for the 11 people in the building was too filthy to use. Cooking facilities had to be shared. The house was rat-infested and the walls so ridden with bugs and beetles that the girl was afraid to replace the ancient wall-paper which helped to some extent to keep them from crawling into the room.[58]

Labour went to war. Harold Wilson, recently elected leader of the party, launched into the Tories over Rachman and the rent increases the Act had caused. The government's response, that Rachman had been at work before the 1957 Rent Act and that housing shortages, not the Act, were the root cause, cut no ice. All ministers could promise was an inquiry, the Milner

Holland report which did not emerge until 1965. 'Rachmanism' became such an integral part of the language that twenty-five years later, when Nigel Lawson announced that tax breaks in the Business Expansion Scheme could be used to provide new rented housing, Gordon Brown, Labour's Treasury spokesman, felt only the need to label it 'state-subsidised Rachmanism' in order to condemn it.[59] It mattered not that Milner Holland finally estimated that only 1 per cent of London tenants were facing abuse and intimidation, or that its surveys showed that well over 80 per cent of tenants and in some cases more than 90 per cent were satisfied with their landlords. As Keith Banting put it, 'the balance in the housing debate had shifted decisively.'[60] Landlords were bad, tenants were exploited. It was one of the messages which helped Labour to its 1964 election victory.

Richard Crossman promptly replaced the Conservative legislation with Labour's own Rent Act. It restored security of tenure, created 'fair rents' with rent tribunals to hold the ring between landlords and tenants, and allowed three-yearly rent rises. After all the *Sturm und Drang* over the 1957 Act, it was to prove a remarkably bipartisan piece of legislation. Crossman, despite in the 1950s being seen as a firebrand of the left, had in 1960 himself been instrumental in quietly killing off Labour's policy for the mass municipalisation of rented housing. His Rent Act in the end attempted to strike a real balance between landlord and tenant, rather than deliberately driving the private landlord out of business. As a result housing finally emerged in the mid-1960s as defiantly not a mass social service. Rather it was a firmly mixed economy, with Crossman's measures including encouragement for home ownership as well as a renewed council housing drive. It remained, however, a mixed economy in which the returns from owning housing for rent remained too small to be attractive. The private rented sector continued remorselessly to shrink.

Meanwhile the Rent Act experience had caused the Ministry of Housing itself to lose faith in the private rented sector. Its civil servants were now headed by the formidable Dame Evelyn Sharp, described by Macmillan as 'without exception the ablest woman I have ever known'[61] and by Crossman as 'like Beatrice Webb . . . in the sense of wanting improvement and social justice quite passionately and yet a tremendous patrician and utterly contemptuous and arrogant, regarding local authorities as children which she has to examine and rebuke for their failures.'[62] She had wanted no more truck with Labour's 1959 policy of municipalisation than Crossman. Equally, however, she believed it 'very doubtful' whether 'the growing division of society into council tenants and owner-occupiers can be satisfactory.'[63] By the early 1960s her department's officials were casting around for another private supplier of housing. Their answer after visits to Scandinavia was the non-profit-making housing association. Sir Keith Joseph, ever willing to experiment, invested £25 million in a pilot project in 1961 and in July 1963 a dozen two-bedroom flats in Birmingham became the first housing association homes to take in tenants.[64] Publicly funded, but independently provided, housing associations became the very first of a new type of body, neither traditionally state-owned nor strictly in the private sector, but used by the state as its agent: a very early version of a model that by the early 1990s and much adapted would include grant-maintained schools and NHS Trusts. In the dying weeks of the Conservative Government, Sir Keith, battered and bruised by Rachman, announced the first £100 million loan to the newly formed Housing Corporation to expand the idea.

Social Security

> Already it is possible to see two nations in old age; greater inequalities in living standards after work than in work.
> Richard Titmuss, on the impact of occupational pensions, 1955, in Essays on the Welfare State, p. 74

> Too small and far too timid a step forward . . . a little mouse of a scheme.
> Iain Macleod speaking on the new Tory pension scheme in the Commons, Hansard, 27 January 1959, col 1013

If housing generated the most controversy between 1951 and 1964, social security, other than pensions, probably provided the least. Particularly in the earlier years, there was a real sense that the problem of 'want' had been cracked. True, the failure to pitch insurance benefits high enough meant that many more people than anticipated ended up supplementing them with national assistance. From 842,000 clients in July 1948, the National Assistance Board found itself with a million on its books by 1949 and 1,800,000 by 1954, a figure which then fluctuated by 200,000 either way until the mid-1960s.[65]

But many of the claimants were old: full employment saw to that. The stigma and pain of the loathed household means-test had gone. Home visits by local officers armed with discretion to pay extra for special needs formed the core of the service. There was an intellectual understanding by left-inclined social scientists and the more rigorous Tories such as Powell and Macleod that something had gone really rather wrong with Beveridge's plan for an insurance-based scheme supported by only the smallest of means-tested safety nets; and there was one real attempt in 1955 by the long-forgotten Oliver Peake to float large numbers off the means-test by a 22 per cent rise in insurance benefits. But the Board by the mid-1950s had sunk into a 'quiet obscurity'. It was believed by its supporters to be delivering a humane and effective service.[66]

Benefits in those days of low though increasingly worrying inflation were not uprated annually. Between 1948 and 1964 the insurance benefits were raised six times, while the means-tested ones saw ten increases.[67] The two thus marched out of step. As a result confusion over objectives was revealed on both sides of the political fence, although a confusion which paradoxically illustrated the practical consensus over social security whatever the remaining differences in political philosophy. As Deacon and Bradshaw describe in their definitive record of the British means-test: 'Sometimes insurance was increased by more than assistance – at which point the Government claimed that it was reducing the role of the means-test and the opposition complained that help was not going to those who needed it most. On other occasions, assistance was increased more and then exactly the same debate was held in reverse, with the Government extolling the virtues of selectivity and the opposition complaining about the means test.'[68]

Where consistency was achieved in the mid-1950s was over the joint realisation that the chicken of paying pensions in full from 1948 was about to come home to roost. A large number of the growing army of pensioners who had made only ten years' contributions were about to retire. The national insurance fund was heading for a horrible deficit. In addition, Richard Titmuss at the London School of Economics, along with others, was drawing attention to a growing gulf in old age between those with occupational pensions and those who had only Beveridge's subsistence-level state pension which had increasingly to be topped up with national assistance to cover rent. 'The outlines of a dangerous social schism are clear,' Titmuss warned in 1955, 'and they are enlarging.'[69] Labour, as part of its increasing attacks on the government over its failure to fund health and education at the levels needed to match demand, focused on pensions to argue that Conservative policies were failing to achieve sufficient redistribution towards the least well-off, among whom pensioners were the largest group.

Later that year, Gaitskell succeeded Attlee as Labour leader. 'In his hatchet-burying mood,' Douglas Jay, the economist and former President of the Board of Trade, who was then a senior Labour figure, recalled, 'Gaitskell laboured very hard to get everyone, particularly Bevan, Wilson and Crossman, working harmoniously together. Rightly he saw that what Crossman needed was a real hard practical job to do which would divert him from playing politics. So Gaitskell asked him to head a formal and expert Labour party committee to re-think the whole pensions and national insurance system in the light of . . . ten years experience. I was to join the committee. We also had the exceedingly valuable help of Richard Titmuss, Brian Abel-Smith and Peter Townsend. This was the best job Crossman ever did.' Jay went on:

> The two central principles which in the course of the argument became increasingly clear to us, and in the end won unanimous agreement were these; first that since the ordinary man or woman would rather pay £1 a week as an insurance contribution than as income tax, and so feel that he or she had earned their own pension, the contributory principle was right [a married man with two young children in 1956 still had to earn 97 per cent of average manual earnings to pay any income tax]; and secondly since a single fixed contribution and pension for all must mean either too high a contribution for the lowest paid, or too low a pension for the well paid, it was inevitable that the contribution and pension must be earnings-related in the future if pensions were eventually to ensure a decent living standard in old age.[70]

The chief snag, Jay records, was the rapid growth since 1948 of schemes run by employers – occupational pensions. In 1936 a mere 1.8 million people were members of such schemes. By 1956 that had risen to 8 million, around a third of the workforce, chiefly covering white collar staff including the civil service. The employers would resist higher contributions, arguing that they were already paying into their own schemes. A typically 'English compromise' was proposed: they would be able to contract out of higher contributions in return for the pensions they paid. Much of the credit for designing the scheme, which aimed eventually at half-pay on retirement against the fifth of average earnings that the existing pension provided, goes to Titmuss and his colleagues. The plan was published in May 1957, enthusiastically endorsed despite Crossman's confession to his diary that its details remained 'three-quarters baked',[71] and was thrown down as a challenge to the Tories. It was to take twenty years to come to fruition.

Crossman's plan was remarkable for abandoning 'fair shares for all', the wartime slogan Labour had adopted as a sound socialist tenet. Earnings-related pensions would mean more for the better off – a stark departure from Beveridge's subsistence principle and a move towards more continental 'citizenship' models of social security. But it won union support. A TGWU-backed Fabian pamphlet was already arguing that: 'The only test by which a pension can be judged is by its relation to the wage packet earned at work. This is the way the boss looks at his pension and that is the way we should look at ours.'[72] The unions also backed a state-run scheme as occupational pensions were commonly not transferable: workers saw them as a form of golden handcuffs, tying people to particular firms and even enforcing discipline within them. The more perceptive Conservative critics, while vigorously in favour of private provision, also saw that lack of transferability meant that existing occupational schemes reduced labour mobility, an issue that was finally to lead to sweeping changes in pension provision in the 1980s. There was therefore the beginning of a cross-party alliance available.

That was not evident in 1957–9. None the less John Boyd-Carpenter, the Minister for Pensions and National Insurance, was forced to respond in the face of these challenges and the escalating crisis over how to pay for pensions. Initially he dismissed Titmuss and his colleagues as 'a skiffle-group of professors' who had got their sums wrong.[73] When the sums broadly held up, he and others attacked the scheme as extravagant and inflationary, arguing that higher contributions by employers would mean higher prices – a point Beveridge drove home from his seat in the Lords as he spelt out his anathema to this departure from his principles.[74] Boyd-Carpenter's final response was a vastly more limited scheme to introduce 'graduated' pensions. Above a low threshold, employees were to pay a percentage contribution on their earnings up to a £15 a week ceiling. This earned them 'bricks' of extra pension: 6d. (2.5p) a week for every £7.50 paid by a man and £9 by a woman. This was not strictly earnings-related, and no formal provision was made for up-rating the graduated pension alongside inflation. Younger workers were thus faced with the prospect that the 'sixpenny bricks' they had paid for early in life would be worth next to nothing when they retired. The scheme was presented firmly as an alternative for those who lacked occupational cover, and the benefits were deliberately limited to avoid competition with occupational schemes. For good measure employers were allowed to contract out on certain conditions. Finally, no secret was made of the fact that the higher contributions were intended at least as much to put the national insurance fund back into balance as they were to produce any sort of pensions revolution. The 1958 White Paper stated bluntly as its first objective: 'to place the National Insurance scheme on a sound financial basis'.[75] The White Paper also formally abandoned Beveridge's plan of relating contributions to the final cost of providing pensions. Instead, Boyd-Carpenter said, contributions would be set no higher than needed to balance income with expenditure as the scheme developed.

The limitations of Boyd-Carpenter's scheme brought fierce cross-party argument at the 1959 election. Labour branded it 'a swindle' and the minister 'a good bargain'. He in turn charged that Labour's plan was 'financially unsound'. The issues were far too complex, however, to make much impact on the electorate and in 1961 the minister's 1959 legislation came into force.

For all that it was 'a mouse' of a scheme which in terms of improving pensions was an almost complete failure, Boyd-Carpenter's pension plan did increase the scope of occupational pensions through the introduction of a new principle into British social security: the right to opt out. It applied only to the graduated, not the basic pension, and Labour had accepted the need for that in relation to its own earnings-related scheme. Crossman and his colleagues had done so on pragmatic rather than ideological grounds, believing the move necessary to win over the public sector unions whose white collar members already enjoyed generous pensions. For Boyd-Carpenter it was much more a matter of ideology, according to Sir Alex Atkinson, then his Whitehall private secretary. 'It was not, I would have said, politically necessary at the time. The National Association of Pension Funds, who were the main people in the field, were only lukewarm about it. They would have been quite happy to go on selling their pensions on top of a state graduated scheme. But Boyd-Carpenter was very keen to have private provision rather than public provision where one could, and for that reason was very keen that occupational pensions should survive. He was worried that if they could not contract out, employers would cut back on them – and in that I think he was probably more farsighted than the people actually running the schemes, who were not too worried.'[76]

For the Tory right, however, the 1961 pensions scheme established a principle which was to be harked back to. By the late 1980s not only were individuals as well as employers being allowed to opt out of the state earnings-related pension scheme, but proposals to allow people to opt out of the national health service, education, and the basic state pension were both being canvassed by think-tanks and considered within government.

Education

> Many of them will finish up as bank clerks . . . and why not graduate bank clerks?
> *Richard 'Otto' Clarke, Treasury official, discussing the Robbins Report, see John Carswell, Government and the Universities in Britain, p. 51*

> The delusion that there are thousands of young people about who are capable of benefiting from university, but have somehow failed to find their way there, is . . . a necessary component of the expansionary case . . . more will mean worse.
> *Kingsley Amis, Encounter, July 1960*

> The lasting achievement of Robbins and his statisticians was to demonstrate that the so-called pool of ability was in fact a vast lake.
> *Gareth Williams, 'The End of the Robbins Era', Yearbook of Social Policy 1972, p. 63*

Macmillan's victory in the housing numbers game had a price. It was paid by education and health. The economic gale which blew around the Korean War not only heavily restricted expansion in both fields, it also brought the first challenges within government to the new consensus regarding the welfare state. If all that is examined is what finally happened, which policies were in the end pursued, then at least up to 1970, and almost as convincingly up to 1979, the whole period can fairly be painted as a broad, if loose, consensus. Final policy, however, is the outcome of discussion within Whitehall and Westminster by the government in power. And here, under the Conservatives, the consensus concerning the welfare state was at various times over the fifty years from Beveridge much less robust than it proved to be in practice in the outside world.

This is in part because the Treasury, as the guardian of the nation's finances, has an inbuilt hostility to public spending; and that strand in Conservative thinking which is hostile to collective provision, and which believes in individual freedom and incentives, has at times linked with the Treasury's desire to save cash. A further factor is the gladiatorial nature of the way public spending is decided. Just as spending ministers often overbid with the aim of getting at least something, so the Treasury and its key ministers, the Chancellor and the Chief Secretary who is responsible for public spending, frequently have to canvass far greater cuts than they can hope to achieve merely to keep expenditure under control. The result can produce fundamental challenges to the welfare state. As Rodney Lowe has recorded in his account of the Treasury's failed efforts to clamp down on spending between 1955 and 1957: 'welfare policy was not, as conventionally assumed, consistently and sympathetically embraced within Whitehall. It came under frequent attack.'[77]

Thus the NHS saw in 1951–2 the first of many assaults on its basis as a comprehensive service, free at the point of use. And that was just one of the ways in which Rab Butler started behaving far less in his role of creator of the 1944 Education Act and engineer of the post-war consensus, and far more in the traditional role of Chancellor – the man proposing unthinkable measures and likely to implement them if they are approved. Florence Horsburgh was the new education minister. Churchill, as Butler had found, was not greatly interested in education. He was, however, interested in housing and it was Macmillan's houses which were built in preference to Horsburgh's schools. Virtually Butler's first act as Chancellor was to declare a moratorium on school building, and Horsburgh spent much of her three years repeatedly fighting off a series of Treasury proposals to raise the school entry age to six, to drop the school leaving age back to fourteen, and to reintroduce school fees in all state schools or, failing that, to charge those staying on beyond school leaving age.[78] As late as 1953, when Korea was no longer the immediate cause, Butler was demanding: 'We must think in terms of major changes in policy as well as constant pruning', and he returned to the assault again in 1954.[79]

None of these more drastic proposals was put into effect, but the squeeze on education was evident to the point where George Tomlinson, shortly before his death, accused Butler of the 'murder of his own child' (the 1944 Education Act)[80] while even the *Economist* said that no part of the government's economy drive 'has incurred so much criticism as the cuts in educational expenditure'.[81] Up to 1954 spending did not even rise fast enough to match the extra pupils produced by the post-war baby-boom. Pupil/teacher ratios in primary schools actually deteriorated in 1953 and 1954,[82] and not only schools were affected. The number of university students fell from 85,000 in 1950 to 82,000 in 1954.[83]

It was not until late 1954, just ahead of the 1955 general election, that the picture changed with the replacement of Horsburgh by Sir David

Eccles. Eccles's first paper to Cabinet warned: 'We have only a little space in which to give a new enthusiasm for education. Something like shock tactics are required to transform the atmosphere of depression.'[84]

Eccles, who was to serve for more than five years at education in two spells between October 1954 and 1957 and then between 1959 and 1962, was a tough nut. He was the first minister to assume that educational expenditure was an economic investment, indeed a consumer good which should none the less be supplied by the public sector as part of the 'opportunity state' that the Tories were developing as their counterweight idea to Labour's egalitarianism.[85] He told Eden, who succeeded Churchill as Prime Minister shortly after Eccles was appointed, that he was intent on 'bringing the Butler Act to life'. And indeed it was the combination of Eccles's arrival, the over-achievement on Macmillan's 300,000 houses target, and easier economic times which saw the very beginnings of what Brian Simon has called the 'educational break-out' of the late 1950s and the 1960s.[86] Spending rose to provide the new schools that were so desperately needed both to meet demographic pressures and to phase out the 'all-age' schools which the 1944 Act, a decade before, had in theory destroyed. Between 1954 and 1963 more than 2000 new schools were built while 'rural reorganisation' saw the proportion of thirteen-year-olds trapped in 'all age' schools fall from 18 per cent in 1950 to 3.8 per cent by 1961 – although this still represented nearly 26,000 pupils in England.[87]

Attitudes to education were changing. Growing affluence in the 1950s was combining with a sharp contraction in manual employment and a rapid growth in white collar jobs, not only in commerce and the service sectors but within industry itself where technical and scientific skills were increasingly in demand. Education was coming to be seen as the route to individual and collective prosperity, leading children to careers beyond their parents' wildest dreams. In 1956, Tony Crosland in *The Future of Socialism* seized on education as one of the key routes to a more just, efficient and egalitarian society. On the other side of the political divide, Eden took a far greater interest in the subject than Churchill and warned in 1956 that: 'The prizes will not go to the countries with the largest population. Those with the best systems of education will win.' Britain needed many more scientists, engineers and technicians, he said, and 'I am determined that this shortage shall be made good.'[88]

A year later, C. P. Snow produced *The Two Cultures*, a profoundly influential attack on the 'rigid crystallisation' of education into the humanities and the sciences, with science seen as the unfavoured underdog. The same year, Snow's lecture was driven home by the launch of the Soviet

Union's Sputnik, an event which shook the West's belief in its innate technological superiority. Full employment and rising prosperity, meanwhile, had steadily reduced the pressure on children to leave school and start earning, while by the late fifties those born in the 1940s baby-boom were becoming teenagers. The numbers staying beyond the statutory leaving age doubled between 1950 and 1960, and by 1964 had risen close to three-fold.[89] Those achieving two or more A-levels rose from 25,000 in the mid-1950s to 64,000 by 1964.[90] As a result it was actually becoming harder to get into university: only 65 per cent of those with two A-levels were accepted in 1961 against 80 per cent in 1956.[91]

Macmillan's government came under irresistible pressure to match the capacity of higher education to the increasing output from sixth forms. More than twenty towns and cities across the country joined a clamour to become university bases.[92] They had a powerful advocate in Sir Keith Murray, who in 1953 started what proved to be a ten-year spell as chairman of the University Grants Committee. John Carswell, the Treasury civil servant who worked with him, sat on the Robbins committee as an assessor, and went on to be secretary of the UGC, writes in his history of the universities that Murray in manner was 'large, benevolent, persuasive' and in action was 'almost inexhaustible. He was a convinced and consistent expansionist.'[93]

While Robbins is the name for ever linked to the great university expansion, it was under Murray that the target was first raised from the 90,000 students in place in 1956, to 135,000, and then in 1959 to a target of 175,000 by the late sixties or early seventies. It was also under Murray that the colleges at Exeter, Nottingham and Southampton were upgraded to full universities, with the government, by July 1961, persuaded to sanction no fewer than seven completely new universities: Sussex, East Anglia, York, Essex, Lancaster, Kent and Warwick. The university lobby had turned into a power in the land well ahead of Lionel Robbins's appointment. Sir Richard 'Otto' Clarke, the Treasury mandarin in charge of public spending, once remarked after meeting with the determinedly expansionist Vice-Chancellors that they were 'now what the Admirals had been before the war of 1914'.[94] Not only that, higher education had a head start over other spending areas through a historical quirk which made the UGC an arms-length part of the Treasury. As Carswell has put it, 'the UGC was not *under* the Treasury; it was part of it',[95] turning the Treasury into a mini-education department in its own right and therefore an advocate for its expansion at the same time as being the guardian of the public purse.

Meanwhile the great lost opportunity of the Percy report of 1945 had meandered through half a dozen government, parliamentary and other inquiries[96] via the 1956 White Paper on technical education to the designation in 1957 of ten Colleges of Advanced Technology[97] to be backed up by twenty-five regional technical colleges. The CATs, following the post-Percy row over their status, awarded not degrees but degree-equivalent Diplomas in Technology. Because they were directly grant-aided by the Ministry of Education and remained firmly separate from the universities, for which the ministry was not responsible, they soon became the ministry's 'pride and joy' at a time when its relations with schools relied on diplomacy rather than on direct control of the huge sums of money being spent by local education authorities.[98] The CATs began to grow apace. These educational worries linked across into training, producing in December 1962 a White Paper, *Industrial Training*. Without a division, Parliament approved the Act which led in 1964 to the creation of twenty-seven tripartite Industrial Training Boards, raising a levy on employers from which they were given grants for training.[99]

It was amid this existing expansion that Robbins was appointed in February 1961. Beveridge's former lecturer at the LSE, Robbins had become an economics professor at the school, was a friend of Macmillan's and had been tutor to Sir David Eccles, now once again Minister for Education. The fifty-nine-year-old Robbins struck Carswell as 'a bland silver lion'. The huge frame and silver mane contained a gentle manner beneath which 'one sensed a giant paw from which a claw or two would sometimes make a carefully modulated appearance . . . he intended from the first that his report should mark a great advance.'[100]

His terms of reference were not notably expansionary. They were to review 'the pattern' of higher education given the development of the CATs, the growth in regional and local authority technical colleges, the surge in university places already under way, and the expansion in teacher training now needed to meet a second prolonged rise in the post-war birth-rate which started in 1956. Having reviewed 'the pattern of full-time higher education in Great Britain in the light of national needs and resources', Robbins was to advise on 'principles' for its long-term development. As he prepared his report, however, every element in the environment was in favour of yet further expansion. Not only were there strong social and demographic pressures, there was also a growing perception that under Macmillan in his later days Britain had slipped into an Edwardian decline and needed modernising. It was the mood captured at Labour's 1963 conference by Wilson's annexing the 'white heat of the technological revolution' to his party's cause. The Tories too wanted to be part of that. The Robbins report, published in haste in October 1963 just after the party conferences and with an election plainly looming, was one way to demonstrate the Conservatives' commitment at a time when Labour was proposing no fewer than forty new universities on top of the existing thirty-one and arguing that expansion of higher education was a matter of 'national survival'.[101] On the day of publication, the brand new prime minister, Sir Alec Douglas-Home, took the unprecedented step of going on television to accept it.

Robbins's key recommendation – the report dubs it an axiom – was that 'courses in higher education should be available for all those who are qualified by ability and attainment to pursue them and who wish to do so'.[102] If the slogan of the early 1940s had been secondary education for all, that for the early 1960s was in effect tertiary education for all, or at least all who could qualify. Not only would there be many more students, but they would universally be entitled to grants. Robbins was able to take that as given because the Anderson committee, set up in 1958, had seen its recommendations for mandatory student grants implemented while Robbins was at work.[103] Anderson, who had based his recommendations on the very much smaller student population of 1958, had found that 90 per cent of students were then receiving some sort of help – widely though it varied – through state, local authority or university scholarships plus a dose of charity. The committee therefore simply universalised and standardised the grant. Almost overnight the National Union of Students, which negotiated over it, became a body to reckon with, and Robbins, in John Carswell's words, had been handed 'a virtual blank cheque'.[104] Anderson did consider student loans rather than grants, and so did Robbins. Both rejected them, even though Robbins recorded the arguments for and against as being 'very evenly balanced' and noted that in time 'some experiment' with loans might be justified.[105]

The implications of these two key decisions for numbers and costs were huge. Robbins set a target of 50 per cent more higher education students by 1967 and a 250 per cent rise by 1980. That translated into an extra 112,000 students a mere four academic years down the road, and a 340,000 rise to 558,000 by 1980. The bulk of these were to be in universities. In keeping with the widely perceived need for more science and technology graduates, the CATs were to be turned into full universities, and Robbins assumed that two-thirds of the new places due by 1967 would be in science and technology.

In accepting the great bulk of the report, the government committed itself to a ten-year programme costing £3.5 billion at a time when total public spending was only £11 billion a year. Money flowed as if from fountains. Great tracts of green fields disappeared under expanding universities and halls of residence. What John Carswell has dubbed the 'great plastic period' in higher education, and what Robbins had called 'a new dawn', had arrived. It was to prove not quite as glorious as it seemed.

Health

> The unnerving discovery every Minister of Health makes at or near the outset of his term of office is that the only subject he is ever destined to discuss with the medical profession is money.
> *Enoch Powell, Minister of Health 1960–3, Medicine and Politics, p. 14*

> The National Health Service, with the exception of recurring spasms about charges, is out of party politics.
> *Iain Macleod, in Future of the Welfare State, CPC, 1958*

> As an institution, the NHS ranked next to the monarchy as an unchallenged landmark in the political landscape of Britain.
> *Rudolf Klein, The Politics of the NHS, p. 32*

With Bevan's departure the Ministry of Health, in Harry Eckstein's phrase, 'lost caste'.[106] It was shorn of responsibilities for housing and local government and deprived of the seat at the Cabinet table that, with two brief exceptions, it was not to regain until 1968. It became very much a second-tier department; one with a revolving door through which no fewer than six ministers passed between 1951 and 1960. None made any great impact on the service and only one has a name that is now remembered – Iain Macleod. Even he, emerging from Downing Street after being given the job in 1952, had to ask his wife to drive him to a telephone box to consult the directories with which phone boxes were then equipped. 'I have to take over the department and I've no idea where it is,' he told her.[107]

In a sense, the ministry's very anonymity was a sign of the consensus which now existed around the NHS. All parties were content to claim it as their own. By the tenth anniversary debate in the Commons in 1958, MPs on both sides felt able to indulge in a positive orgy of mutual self-congratulation. But such a cosy view hides real battles under the Conservatives in the early 1950s that could have left the NHS looking very different; and it ignores the fact that the first years of the service were dominated, as so much of its history has been, by money.

The NHS was vulnerable on two counts. One, it was still costing far more than expected; and two, the Korean War rearmament made it a target for Butler's general search for economies in which he concentrated on health and education. Within weeks of his arrival as Chancellor no fewer than sixteen different cuts in the service or new charges were being considered by the Treasury and by Harry Crookshank, the new Tory health minister.[108] These ranged from prescription and further dental charges (on top of the charges for dentures which Labour had introduced), through 'hotel' charges for hospital stays, ambulance charges, restrictions on the types of drugs available, to extending pay beds or even to abolishing NHS dental and opticians' services entirely.

Each of these, save for the 1s. 0d. prescription charge and new dental charges, foundered. Lopping complete pieces off the service was seen as politically unpopular by ministers outside the Ministry of Health and as counter-productive by officials within it. And all the other ideas for raising money by new charges failed – as they were to fail time and again over the years – on a twin difficulty: a significant hotel charge for hospital stays, for example, would upset Tory voters while requiring such massive exemptions for the less well off that it would raise relatively little income; a small charge, on the other hand, would still require unavoidable exemptions, leaving little extra revenue once the administrative cost of applying the means-test and collecting the cash had been met. However much the Tories might ideologically favour charges, to remind people what the service cost and to limit demand, administrative practicalities won out over ideology.

Much more clearly than prescription or dental charges, hotel charges would also have represented a fundamental breach of the principle of the NHS – that the service was comprehensive, tax-funded and free at the point of use. Once a charge was made for a hospital bed, whether it was called a hotel bill or a treatment fee, the way would have been open gradually to raise charges and start privatising once again the finance of the NHS. The political price would have been high. As it was, even the relatively limited charges for prescriptions and dental treatment which Crookshank put forward received a considerable battering at the hands of his own back-benchers. Some exemptions had to be introduced for both and the delay in legislating produced a last-minute rush for treatment.

Dr John Marks, then working in general practice, remembered it as 'the busiest night of my life as people tried to get in under the wire.'[109] The new charges raised little; even at their absolute peak they never amounted to more than 5.6 per cent of health service spending.[110]

The bill for the NHS, however, kept on rising. Hilary Marquand, Bevan's successor, had agreed in the dying days of the Labour Government to put a pay dispute with the GPs to arbitration under Mr Justice Danckwerts, a High Court judge. GPs' pay had been fixed on the basis of their pre-war tax returns; and, given that family doctors were no more honest with the taxman than anyone else, it had been fixed rather low. To Butler and Churchill's consternation, Danckwerts accepted in its entirety the BMA's argument for a large increase, producing a £40 million bill in back pay for GPs at a time when total NHS spending in England and Wales was only £400 million. In addition, the award added £10 million a year to the pay bill, against the £2 million that both the Labour and Tory governments had argued was justified.[111] The settlement made the reputation in BMA circles of a forty-year-old deputy secretary, one Dr Derek Stevenson, who combined the dashing good looks of a young Rex Harrison with the staff-officer's qualities he had learnt as a lieutenant-colonel in the Army Medical Service. To him had fallen the task of presenting the BMA's case, and of all the wars on behalf of doctors that Derek Stevenson was later to be involved in he rated the Danckwerts award his major achievement.[112]

Churchill and Butler muttered and moaned and looked for ways out. Churchill demanded: 'Are we bound hand and foot to pay?'[113] But they were, and they did, and the massive pay award did much to reconcile family doctors to the four-year-old NHS. The award had one other significant consequence. As Elston Grey-Turner has recorded: 'Never again would the Government agree to submit a claim from the doctors to arbitration by a High Court judge.'[114] Some other way would have to be found to settle doctors' pay.

Needless to say, the GPs' award sparked off parallel claims from hospital consultants and other staff. In late 1952, with the Treasury alarmed at the ever rising bill, Butler, under pressure from Cabinet hawks including the future Chancellor Peter Thorneycroft, insisted that a committee be established to inquire into the cost of the NHS. It was to prove one of the service's great early landmarks. Attempts to rig the terms of reference to ensure the committee recommended measures to reduce costs were defeated – and defeated by, of all people, Butler who most wanted the inquiry but who realised that restrictive terms of reference would see the government accused of 'embarking on a destructive onslaught on the welfare state'.[115] Its chairman, after some debate and the intervention of Macleod, the new Minister of Health, was Claude Guillebaud, an economist who had been Macleod's tutor at Cambridge and who had a reputation for a left-wing past and independence.[116] In the end the terms of reference asked Guillebaud to do no more than advise on how 'a rising charge' on the Exchequer could be avoided while maintaining an adequate service.[117] It was a shrewd civil servant in the Ministry of Health who noted that such an inquiry might reveal not that too much was being spent, but too little. 'The Treasury,' he minuted, 'are here playing with fire and are liable to get very badly burned.'

What Guillebaud did in effect was look at the workings of the NHS over its first seven years and in all essential respects, to use Charles Webster's biblical phrase, pronounce 'that it was good'.[118] The key finding was based on the work of Brian Abel-Smith, then a young Cambridge economist, working with that man Titmuss again. Their calculations showed that the cost of the NHS, far from being out of control, was in fact falling as a share of Gross National Product. Inflation and extra services, not inefficiency and extravagance, had accounted for the rising bill. And if the same share of national resources had been devoted to the NHS in 1953 as in its first full year of 1949, spending would have been £67 million, or around a sixth, higher.[119] In the light of these findings, the committee found itself unable to support any new charges and instead rather favoured getting rid of the existing ones. It was firmly in favour of more capital spending, which Abel-Smith and Titmuss had shown to have collapsed to a third of its pre-war level. Particularly on capital, where the committee recommended trebling the then spending of around £10 million a year, it was concluded that far from providing measures to cut spending, 'we have found it necessary to make recommendations . . . which will tend to increase the future cost.'[120]

Charles Webster has recorded: 'The Treasury was infuriated by the perceived waywardness of its brainchild,' while the health departments 'outwardly expressed dissatisfaction, but enjoyed inner contentment'.[121] In the judgement of Sir George Godber, the deputy chief medical officer, Guillebaud, 'a first rate man, but a quiet performer, probably saved the NHS.'[122] His report saw off the first of the bouts of panic about the service that governments and the public have enjoyed repeatedly over the past fifty years – the belief that NHS spending is out of control, and that the service is a bottomless pit into which any amount of money can be thrown. It also, however, destroyed a then common belief that the cost of the NHS would fall as the nation was made healthier. 'It is still sometimes assumed that the health service can and should be self-limiting, in the sense that its own contribution to national health will limit the demands upon it to a volume which can be fully met. This, at least for the present, is an illusion.'[123]

In large measure, Guillebaud spiked the Treasury guns. Although the argument thrashed on for some months, the report's publication in January 1956 in practice put an end to various ideas still being tossed around in a secret Social Services Committee of the Cabinet. These included yet again a hospital boarding charge, possibly covered by an insurance contribution; a 'limited list' of drugs available to NHS patients; abolishing the dental and ophthalmic services or switching them to an insurance-based system; or even at one point establishing the NHS on 'a compulsory contributory basis' – using national insurance rather than general taxation. That last scheme, Webster records, at one point commanded 'general agreement'[124] in Cabinet. It foundered, however, in 1957 because no way could be found of increasing national insurance contributions without triggering demands for improved pensions which the government did not then want to tackle. A sharp increase in national insurance contributions did however come in the following year as the sole surviving measure from the package of savings which led to Thorneycroft's resignation.

Thus the NHS, carrying the battle scars of limited charges for prescriptions, dental treatment and spectacles, but otherwise largely tax-funded and free at the point of use, appeared by its tenth anniversary to have slipped into the safe haven of a genuine cross-party consensus. This did not, however, guarantee it a quiet life; in July 1960, Enoch Powell became Minister of Health. His arrival put the ministry back in the political front-line. Powell was a heavyweight, still eight years away from the inflammatory 'Rivers of Blood' speech on immigration ('Like the Roman, I think I see the Tiber foaming with much blood . . .') which was to finish him as a contender for the highest political office. Not yet in Cabinet, he was in 1960 a rising star, talked of as a potential prime minister. Brilliant, iconoclastic, and purveyor of a lethal mix of steely logic and lost empire emotionalism that was to lead him to his moments of both genius and political madness, he had resigned as a Treasury minister along with Peter Thorneycroft over Macmillan's refusal to cut public spending in 1958. His arrival in Savile Row, where the Ministry of Health was now located, coincided with Sir Bruce Fraser becoming the department's permanent secretary and Sir George Godber its chief medical officer.

Fraser and Godber, too, were big guns. Fraser 'tall, slender and dynamic'[125] was the first civil service head of the ministry not linked with the founding of the NHS. He looked forward at what needed to be done, not back on what had been achieved. He came, like Powell, from the Treasury, although the appointment of the one soon after the other was a coincidence.[126] The two had worked together there, and Fraser had been closely involved in the debate on public spending and how to manage it which culminated in the 1961 Plowden report.[127] That had attempted to reconcile the Treasury's requirement for an annual budget in order to control spending with the need in welfare policy for long-term expenditure plans if services were to be effectively developed. The outcome was the five-year rolling programme which was approved each year by the Expenditure Survey Committee but was then subject to revision in each annual bid – the so-called PESC round. It was this work which was to help ease the NHS's problems over capital spending.

Godber, by contrast, was an NHS founder, but one who would never, even into his eighties, be afraid of new ideas. 'A radical egalitarian', in Rudolf Klein's words, he had arrived in the ministry in 1939, just as action was being taken ahead of the war to improve the awful state of the hospital stock. He had himself devised the 1948 plan to spread medical specialists across the country. A barrel-chested, monocled, gimlet-eyed buccaneer of a man, who bestrode the Chief Medical Officer's complex world of doctors, politicians and civil servants like a colossus, he 'had never lost sight of Bevan's hope of universalising the best'.[128] It was thus a triumvirate of some note who took the NHS into the 1960s.

Powell is remembered as one of the few great Ministers of Health, ranking after Bevan, but alongside Castle, Robinson and Clarke as a politician who found the NHS one thing and left it another. This reputation rests on three counts: *The Hospital Plan for England and Wales*,[129] the introduction of community care, and his book *Medicine and Politics* written in 1966 and updated in 1975; it remains the best single slim volume on the NHS despite the changes seen since.

At the time, however, Powell was far from seen as a great minister: rather, he was viewed as a deeply controversial one. His resignation from the Treasury in 1958 had by the 1980s ensured him an honoured place in the Thatcherite pantheon of early monetarists. In early 1961, however, it had merely given him a reputation as a hard-faced, hair-shirted zealot who wanted to cut public spending. When one of his earlier acts was to raise NHS charges, including a doubling of the prescription charge from 1s. 0d. to 2s. 0d. (10p) an item, Labour erupted. The party had just emerged reeling and divided from its 1960 conference vote for unilateral nuclear disarmament with Gaitskell promising to 'fight, fight and fight again' for the party he loved. Powell's raising of charges, his flat Midland tones, past reputation and marble-like defence of his policy, provided both something and someone against whom Labour could unite. The result in early 1961 was one of those occasions in politics when an issue can suddenly acquire a significance far beyond the immediate scale of the proposition itself.

When the first rumours that the Treasury was seeking higher charges circulated, Vicky, the *Evening Standard*'s brilliant left-wing cartoonist, promptly depicted Powell carrying an axe and being only too willing to comply. When Powell announced the increases there was parliamentary uproar that ran on for days. A real issue was at stake. The higher charges made up a record 5.6 per cent of all NHS spending, against 4.5 per cent the year before. As importantly, however, Powell took further the switch which Thorneycroft had started in 1957 of paying for the NHS more from national insurance contributions and less from general taxation. This was making the NHS less egalitarian. National insurance contributions were flat rate, costing the lower paid more of their income; whereas general taxation, based on percentages of earnings and other taxes, financed the NHS with maximum redistributive effect. It was a point well noted by Boyd-Carpenter, who in Cabinet attacked the NHS contribution as a 'hypothecated, regressive poll tax'.[130] As a result of Powell's move, in the early 1960s more than 22 per cent of NHS spending came from contributions and charges combined – both measures which hit the less well-off hardest – against half that figure in the early years of the NHS and around two-thirds of it for most of the rest of its life.[131] Richard Titmuss attacked the package as a 'final charge of dynamite under the welfare state'.[132] Labour launched a censure debate and when, later in 1961, Powell became embroiled in a fierce year-long dispute with nurses who had become enmeshed in Selwyn Lloyd's 'pay pause', his reputation as a hatchet man was sealed. A 'set-and-hold' obituary of him, written in 1963 for the Press Association and which in 1994 still lurked in the *Independent*'s cuttings library, outspokenly paints him almost entirely as a butcher of health and welfare services.

Yet Powell's period at the Ministry of Health was one of considerable renewal. The higher charges were in part to finance the great Hospital Plan which was finally launched in January 1962. It aimed at a £500 million programme over a decade to build 90 new hospitals, drastically remodel 134 more and provide 356 further improvement schemes each costing over £100,000. It was very badly needed. In the first decade of the

NHS not a single new hospital had been built. None had been even been approved until 1956,[133] and while there had been hospital extensions, new theatres, out-patient departments and other refurbishments, in the thirteen years from 1948 only £157 million had been spent, well under a third of the figure that Powell now proposed to spend in a decade. NHS hospitals had, quite simply, lost out to new schools and housing. In the fourteen New Towns, for example, new schools had to be provided for children; patients, however, could still be told to travel for treatment and in 1955 they had boasted 'not a hospital between them'.[134] Kenneth Robinson, Powell's Labour successor as Minister of Health, reckons the hospital programme Powell's 'great achievement', and one that possibly only he as an ex-Treasury minister with a 'dry' reputation could have achieved.[135] Although they failed to get agreement to a full five-year plan for hospital building, Powell and Fraser at least persuaded the Treasury to provide sufficient forward capital undertakings to make sensible planning possible. 'Previously,' Sir Kenneth recalls, 'you never knew whether you were going to get any capital money the year after next.'[136]

Powell's second great memorial is the 'water-towers' speech which heralded the massive run-down in mental illness beds in the large Victorian asylums. From the moment the NHS was founded in 1948, there had been standing concern about the old lunatic asylums and the conditions within them. Bevan himself had warned the Cabinet there could be a scandal at any time, and in the tenth anniversary debate on the NHS he warned again that some were in 'a disgraceful condition'. Kenneth Robinson, the future health minister, was chairman of the mental health committee for the North West Metropolitan Regional Hospital Board and repeatedly raised the issue. In 1954, he pointed to the 'four shortages' of 'beds, buildings, staff and money',[137] which saw patients sleeping nine inches apart or head to toe in corridors. Iain Macleod fretted over the issue, with even Treasury officials admitting privately in his time that conditions were 'little short of a public scandal'.[138] At Banstead hospital in Surrey in the 1950s, Dr A. A. Baker, its deputy superintendent, recalled: 'I was the only consultant on the female side which had 1,500 beds – seven wards of over 100 apiece, almost all of them locked.' One of these was reserved for disturbed patients rejected by other wards.

There was no occupational therapy and patients just sat or stood around the outer edge of the ward in a state of apathy or tense frustration. The smell of paraldehyde [a heavy sedative] filled the air and some patients, in strong clothes which in theory they couldn't tear, were persistently drunk and disorderly on it . . . [some] had been secluded for months even years at a stretch. Time did not permit going round and assessing everyone.[139]

Against this background of a scandal waiting to explode, a Paris drug house in 1953 announced the development of the first phenothiazines,[140] with chlorpromazine (Largactil) launching a pharmacological revolution that made treatment, suppression of symptoms and out-patient procedures for mental illness possible. Attitudes to mental illness were also changing. The Royal Commission on Mental Illness and Mental Deficiency[141] appointed by Macleod produced in 1957 a unanimous report whose recommendations led directly to the liberalising 1959 Mental Health Act. In future, the vast majority of patients would be admitted for treatment voluntarily, without detention, with the Act formally marking the beginnings of community care. 'One of the main principles we are seeking to pursue,' Derek Walker-Smith, as Minister for Health, told the Commons, 'is the re-orientation of the mental health services away from institutional care towards care in the community.'[142] Local authorities supported the move, but while the health department exhorted them to provide more community facilities, they were given little practical help to do so.[143]

The therapeutic revolution saw the population of the massive old lunatic asylums begin to fall from 1954 as some psychiatrists began to take advantage of the new drugs to discharge patients quickly. The decline in numbers was picked up by psychiatrists and statisticians at the Ministry of Health in the late 1950s. Projecting it forward, they predicted that the numbers in long-stay mental hospitals would halve to 75,000 by 1975. In a climate where the institutions were under fire, in which Powell himself had been to see the overcrowding[144] and in which it appeared for a time that mental illness could be simply 'cured' by drugs, Powell struck. He sprang the scheme without warning in a speech to the National Association of Mental Health in March 1961, announcing as a plan the closure which his medical advisers' calculations projected. He did so, however, in the language of apocalypse, telling his stunned audience:

> There they stand, isolated, majestic, imperious, brooded over by the gigantic water-tower and chimney combined, rising unmistakeable and daunting out of the countryside – the asylums which our forefathers built with such immense solidity.

These, he said, were 'the defences we have to storm' and he talked of setting 'the torch to the funeral pyre' of the mental hospitals. With a profligacy which would have horrified the Treasury of the 1980s and 1990s, he said he wanted to see these monuments 'derelict or demolished' rather than put to new use. In closing the hospitals: 'if we err, it is our duty to err on the side of ruthlessness.' The ranks of psychiatrists, administrators, volunteers and social scientists who made up his audience were split down the middle. There was a mix of enthusiastic backing and of horror at what he proposed.[145]

Powell did acknowledge that the programme 'makes no sense' unless there was community care, which implied 'a whole new development of local authority services' for the mentally ill. It fell to Richard Titmuss on the second day of the conference to point out that community care as it then stood was largely a fiction. It was, he said, an idealistic term of uncertain origin which allowed 'in the public mind, the aspirations of reformers [to be] transmuted, by the touch of a phrase, into a hard won reality. What some hope will one day exist is suddenly thought by many to exist already.' The brute fact, he pointed out, was that less per head was being spent on the mentally ill in the community in 1959 than in 1951. What was being proposed implied 'a quite remarkable degree' of optimism and faith.[146]

It was not to be justified. In 1963, Powell did produce a ten-year plan for the Health and Welfare Services along the lines of the famous hospital plan, which in theory set out the developments that local authorities would provide; but it was left to local authorities to provide the funds and many proved reluctant. There were votes in caring for the elderly and for children; fewer votes in taking a new responsibility for the mentally ill. As the economy faltered under first Labour and then the Conservatives, the hospital plan fell behind and the health and welfare plan into disuse; but the long-stay NHS beds still closed, and closed almost at the rate predicted. What did not close, however, was whole hospitals. The result, given their fixed overheads, was that progressively fewer residents were treated at a higher cost per head. Only when asylums were finally shut down completely and their sites sold, could large sums of capital and revenue become available for care in the community, and the first asylum was not finally to close until 1986. As a result, even where health authorities were willing to see their cash move into local authority-funded community care, precious little money leaked over the health/local government boundary to support former residents and the new cases who now received the short-term treatment becoming available in the new psychiatric departments of general hospitals. With too little support available in the community, and too much still tied up in the big institutions, a different sort of scandal was in the making. None the less, Powell had provided the vision, one which exemplified the new and more confident note to which the NHS, like education, was marching in the early 1960s.

CHAPTER 12

Hope springs eternal:
Labour
1964–70

When all the qualifications and exceptions have been totted up, it is not unfair to speak of there being an optimism abroad in British society during the sixties . . . the Welfare State, despite the usual windy posturing of politicians, was now scarcely a matter of debate.
Arthur Marwick, British Society since 1945, pp. 174–5

Great Britain has lost an Empire and has not yet found a role.
Dean Acheson, US Secretary of State, at West Point, 5 December 1962

We have put in hand a dramatic deployment of resources in favour of those in greatest need, in favour of the under-privileged, on all fronts of social action – social security, health and welfare, the housing of our people, the education of our children and our young people – the most massive ever carried through . . . the figures I have given you [a 45 per cent rise in social spending in four years] represent our social priorities, against an economic background that would have driven a Tory government into social retreat and panic demolition.
Harold Wilson to Labour Party Conference, 1967

We were soon to learn that decisions on pensions and taxation were no longer to be regarded, as in the past, as decisions for Parliament alone. The combination of tax increases with increased social security benefits [in 1964] provoked the first of a series of attacks on sterling, by speculators and others, which beset almost every action of the government for the next five years.
Harold Wilson, The Labour Government 1964–70, p. 57

I T IS HARD NOW to recapture the sense of new dawn that Harold Wilson's government, with its bare majority of four, brought to Downing Street in 1964. Wilson's speech to the Labour Party conference at Scarborough the year before, trailing the phrases that were to become the 'white heat of the technological revolution', appeared to offer the promise of a fuller, more equal, more productive society in place of the stagnation and decay that had characterised Macmillan's final phase. In the manifesto's words, a 'fresh and virile leadership' was offered in place of the ineffective if well-meaning amateurism of 'the fourteenth earl', as Wilson had somewhat cruelly dubbed Home. The manifesto poured enthusiasm from every pore, promising to reverse the decline of the 'thirteen wasted years' while bringing new life to the 'vital social services'.[1]

It was the start of high noon for the high priests of planning – the apogee of a two-decade stretch in which both economic and welfare state problems were seen to be susceptible to the answers of planning and agreement. This had started under the Tories in the late 1950s, reaching its high point with the creation of the National Economic Development Council in 1961 and with Powell's hospital and health and welfare plans. It was to stretch on by way of the Robbins report, through Labour's doomed National Plan, via the creation of the polytechnics and a fresh clutch of New Towns, the Seebohm reorganisation of social services, the 1972 education White Paper, and the 1974 reorganisations of the NHS and local government, its effects still being felt late into the seventies. It was a heyday for Royal Commissions and government inquiries, for faith in the views of experts, the whole enterprise undertaken with the certainty that solutions were there if only one could think of them.

From the welfare state's point of view, Wilson's Cabinet appeared star-studded, not just with the largest number of first-class degrees on record, but with big figures who had big ideas about the social services. Chief among these were Dick Crossman and Anthony Crosland. In practice they were as contrasting a pair as Bevan and Bevin (and with names as easily confused by A-level students). Both were the very antithesis of working-class heroes – donnish philosopher-kings, the products of public school (Highgate and Winchester) and Oxford (Trinity and New), but marked by a decade's difference in age and experience.

Crosland, the younger, was a cheroot-smoking, slightly hedonist, centre-right economist with a sardonic wit who had rejected a Plymouth Brethren upbringing and had produced in 1956 The Future of Socialism, 'the most important work of Labour re-thinking since the thirties'.[2] It placed egalitarianism centre-stage in Labour's thinking. Capitalism,

Crosland argued, had been so transformed that socialism should no longer be essentially concerned with nationalisation and public ownership. Instead, its core business should be social equality. That aim was to be pursued in large measure through an education system which offered genuine equality of opportunity, linked to extensions of personal liberty with many of which Roy Jenkins was to make his name as Home Secretary, either enacting or enabling reform of the divorce and censorship laws, the legalisation of abortion and homosexuality, and the abolition of hanging. Crosland, when he went to education, was at the height of his powers, 'perhaps better fitted for his post than any of his successors,' in the judgement of John Carswell, one of the civil servants who worked for him. He was 'adventurous, enthusiastic, confident like a man who feels a strong horse between his knees'.[3]

Crossman, the older man, by contrast was a domineering, often bullying, rumbustious and patrician left-winger ('they're afraid of my brutal brain power' he once proudly declared.)[4] Having devised Labour's national superannuation plan, he had then held the education portfolio in opposition only to find himself switched to housing when Labour reached government. 'I don't know what I've been put here for,' he reportedly told Dame Evelyn Sharp at their first meeting.[5] It was not until 1968 that Crossman moved to health and social security, the departments being amalgamated as he became the first Secretary of State for Social Services. The appointment gave the departments a seat at the Cabinet table again for virtually the first time since Bevan's day – a measure of Crossman's stature but also of the voracious appetite for money the two had developed, making their presence at the top table required. The quirks and timing of politics were to ensure that Crossman's legislative legacy, outside the Rent Act, was minimal. But he fairly fizzed with ideas. Sir Alec Atkinson, who was to become the social security permanent secretary at the DHSS, judged that Crossman's great achievement was 'to change the climate. He brought social security to the forefront of politics, and made it possible for people to do more. Before Crossman it was seen as something too boring for the intellectuals, and too difficult for everyone else. He made it a live subject for discussion. A subject where things could and would happen.'[6]

Thus, under Labour, welfare state issues moved closer to the centre stage of politics. And yet the underlying consensus around these major services was such that they barely rate a mention in Anthony Sampson's panoramic and masterly *Anatomy of Britain*, detailing the 'workings of Britain' in 1962. Education receives a chapter – and a much expanded one in the *New Anatomy of Britain* written to coincide with Labour's victory two years later. But housing, social security, unemployment, the very concept of the welfare state itself, crawl neither into the index nor into more than the most passing of discussion. The welfare state was simply there, part of the background, taken for granted. By the fifth version of Sampson's book, in 1992, that is no longer the case; in *The Essential Anatomy of Britain* the workers and more importantly the workless get their own anguished chapter.

Health

> The old [pre-1948] partnership between the family doctors and the consultants was to some extent a financial partnership: the one needed the other; certainly the consultant needed the goodwill and the recommendation of the general practitioner. There was a cash nexus which the semi-nationalization of private practice and the nationalization of the hospitals destroyed . . . [it is this] resentment against the hospital service which gives passion and intensity to the medical profession's defence of even the most indefensible 'cottage hospitals' . . . the general practitioner regards them as his last toehold in the hospital world, which is being destroyed in a malign conspiracy to get him out altogether. There, at least, he 'has some beds'.
>
> *Enoch Powell, Medicine and Politics, pp. 35–6*

It was on a note of some confidence and renewal that Kenneth Robinson – the son of a GP, protégé of Bevan[7] and a hospital board member since 1950 – became Minister of Health. Virtually his first act was to fulfil the manifesto pledge to abolish prescription charges – a prelude, Labour hoped, to abolishing all NHS charges. The result was a 16 per cent increase in prescribing in the first year which then tailed off, provoking a predictable argument over whether this represented real need among patients who had been put off by the previous charge or an increase in unnecessary trips to the doctor in order to fill up the medicine cabinet.

But while the abolition of charges provided instant good news, the great cloud that greeted Robinson was general practice. Since 1948, Bevan's generous settlement with the consultants – giving them salaries that provided an acceptable standard of living without the need, though with the option, to resort to private practice – had seen their numbers rise and their spread across the country become more even. This, indeed, was one of the NHS's great achievements: putting good specialists in unfashionable places like Barrow or Oldham. The consultants, in a sense, had been further rewarded by Powell's hospital plan. General practice, however, was in crisis. Always the poor relation, medical development had made it more so. By the 1960s, new drugs, new technology and new techniques were making the hospital king. As spending on the hospital service expanded the share for general practice declined. Consultants increasingly looked down on GPs on whom since 1948 they had become much less reliant for income from private practice referrals. The relationship was most bluntly defined by Lord Moran, who in 1958 was giving evidence to a Royal Commission which was to recommend that doctors be given a standing review body to settle their pay. Sir Harry Pilkington, the chairman, had asked 'Corkscrew Charlie' whether GPs and consultants were not on a par:

> I say emphatically no. Could anything be more absurd? I was dean of St Mary's Hospital for 25 years . . . all the people of outstanding merit, with few exceptions, aimed to get on the staff. There was no other aim, and it was a ladder off which some of them fell. How can you say that the people who get to the top of the ladder are the same as the people who fall off it? It seems to me so ludicrous.[8]

'Lord Moran's ladder' rapidly became notorious among family doctors. He spoke, however, a part of the truth, reflecting the attitude of many London teaching hospital consultants and many GPs' view of their own worth. By 1964 a detailed study of general practice found some in despair. One family doctor recorded:

> We're swamped with trivialities. This isn't the sort of work one spent years at university preparing oneself for. There's the utter futility and humiliation of a professional man who feels his training is wasted. The GP has no status because he doesn't do medicine.[9]

Another complained: 'At the moment the GP is more of the waste product of the medical schools than the end product. As a GP one cannot help but feel that the NHS is a consultants' charter, and there is no incentive for the GP to practice good medicine.'[10] There had been moves to tackle this problem. In 1953, for example, the fledgling Royal College of General Practice had been founded (in the teeth of opposition from Moran) to raise standards. Improvements there had been. But by the early to mid-1960s parts of general practice still reflected what J. S. Collings, a New Zealand doctor, had found a decade earlier in less affluent areas:

> As a rule two adjacent rooms serve as waiting and consulting rooms . . .
> In most cases the waiting rooms are too small, cold and generally inhospi-
> table. In peak hours in big practices it is usual to see patients standing,
> waiting their turn . . . and it is not uncommon to see them standing in
> the garden . . . or queuing in the street . . . in several of the surgeries I
> visited there were not examination couches; in many there were no filing
> cabinets, and such records as were kept lay around the room either loose
> or in boxes; in one there was a chair for the doctor only (the patient
> remained standing throughout consultation and examination) . . . Few
> skilled craftsmen, be they plumbers, butchers or motor mechanics, would
> be prepared to work under such conditions or with equipment as bad.[11]

The root of the problem was money, both the amount GPs were paid and the way they were paid it. Not only were their rewards less than those of consultants – a cause of mounting anger which the BMA, representing both groups, found difficult to handle – but the money they did receive came from 'the pool'. A part of its effect was to average out what individual GPs spent on expenses. This system of stifling complexity had the unintended effect of ensuring that a GP who provided good quality staff, premises and services ended up out of pocket, receiving broadly the same sum for expenses however much or little was spent. The incentive, therefore, was to have large lists of patients and spend nothing on them. 'People like us,' Dr John Marks, then a GP in Barnet, recalls, 'who had good premises and nurses were actually subsidising the people who had lock-up shops.'[12]

GPs were beginning to quit in despair. Dr Gordon Macpherson left a six-man practice in Bexhill to join the staff of the British Medical Association. 'Ours was probably in the top 10 per cent of practices for quality and organisation in those days. But general practice was going downhill. Because of the pool system we were hopelessly squeezed. I had got to the stage where my overdraft was two and a half times my income. I was paid £1000 a year. My overdraft was £2500 and my bank manager was saying: "Look, this just can't go on".'[13]

The head of steam built to the point where talks had started and the Conservatives had promised action in their manifesto, but it was under Robinson that the issue erupted. In February 1965, four months after

Labour took office, the doctors' pay review body recommended such a tiny pay award that GPs exploded, demanding 'an entirely new contract of service'. To drive the point home they started collecting signed, undated resignations from the NHS.

Robinson had already decided that the GP crisis was 'the first thing that needed to be tackled'.[14] Official figures as he took office showed family doctor numbers tumbling. Six hundred more a year were quitting than joining as they either simply gave up or emigrated, only adding to a more generalised panic about 'the brain drain'. Timely evidence was also becoming available from the United States showing how health care costs spiralled if general practice collapsed and patients started to shop around for their own specialist care.[15] Robinson (now canonised by the BMA as 'without doubt the most caring health minister we ever had')[16] believed that when it came to general practice 'any reasonable price was worth paying to save it'.[17] That phrase, however, included the word 'reasonable'.

Robinson's father had been a general practitioner surgeon in Warrington in the early part of the century, remembered by Dr Solly Wand, a GP who became chairman of the BMA's council and who performed his first anaesthetic for Robinson's father, as 'one of the best natural surgeons he'd ever come across'.[18] Although his father died when he was twelve, Robinson none the less 'drank in a knowledge of general practice with my mother's milk',[19] watching his father run a large panel practice and a modest private one 'most of whom did not pay their bills when he died!'[20] But despite his sympathy for their cause and 'a ministerial bedside manner',[21] Robinson had a streak of arrogance. He nearly refused to negotiate with the GP leaders under the duress of their threatened resignations. 'I was talked out of that, fortunately, by my civil servants'.

Among the BMA negotiators Robinson faced, the key man was Jim Cameron, the newly elected chairman of the family doctors' committee, a dead straight but artful Scot who needed his iron constitution to handle a phenomenal capacity to absorb his native country's firewater. A Scot who had come south to show the English how to do it, he worked in a well-off practice in Wallington and rates as one of the few great men the BMA has produced. He was flanked by a fluent Welsh wizard, Ivor Jones, a GP from Sunderland, something of a wide boy and remembered by Macpherson as 'the best platform speaker I have heard'. He played the role of 'the hard man with the figures'. Robinson soon dubbed him 'a pirate'[22] – an epithet that caused something of a ruction when it made the front page of the London *Evening News*. Negotiations with him, Robinson later recalled, 'were like cattle-trading'.[23]

Cameron was under considerable pressure. GPs had become so demoralised that a breakaway General Practitioners Association had been founded to ginger the BMA into acting. Overnight it recruited 7000 members before presenting a petition to Parliament and fading as fast as it had flowered. More damagingly for the BMA, the Medical Practitioners Union, a more serious and longer-standing rival, saw its tiny membership rocket as it drew up a 'Family Doctors Charter', significant parts of which Cameron and Jones lifted wholesale during a frantic weekend of preparation as GP leaders put together proposals to save general practice. This competition between medical organisations, however, fanned militancy, only compounding the pressures BMA leaders had previously faced in dealing with Bevan. Throughout, Cameron and his colleagues had to look over their shoulders not only at their own troops, but at rival groups.

In addition, the GPs were far from united over what they wanted. Some favoured continuing with capitation fees – an annual payment per patient registered – as the basis of remuneration. A small minority was prepared to back the salaried service over which the BMA had fought Bevan so bitterly. Others wanted to be paid not so much per patient but, like dentists, a fee for each item of service they delivered. This payment system, essentially modelled on private practice, was used in the United States and Canada and was seen by critics as an incentive for doctors to provide unnecessary treatments. Among its proponents were those GPs (chiefly but not entirely the older ones) who remained unreconciled to the NHS. Seventeen years on from 1948, they still existed. John Marks, the publican's son who qualified the day the NHS started, and whose childhood memories include hospital pound days ('you contributed a pound of sugar, or a pound of tea, or, if you were very wealthy, a pound of money'), was a fervent NHS supporter. 'But for that,' he recalls, 'I was, as late as the mid-1960s, regarded as a Communist by one of my local colleagues. There were people still around then who had a hankering for the good old days – which were actually the bloody awful old days – who would have been quite happy to see the NHS disappear.'

Among the backers of fee-per-item-of-service was Ivor Jones who argued its cause passionately in the negotiations and was much the most solid of the BMA's negotiators on the idea of reviving private practice.[24] He had support to the point where the BMA's annual representative meeting in Swansea in the middle of the negotiations nearly overturned the apple cart by demanding that fee-for-item-of-service be accepted as one method of payment. Robinson refused throughout to have anything to do with it. 'I saw it as the break-up of the concept of the family doctor service. It took a long time to get it off the agenda. But I was absolutely determined not to concede it.'[25] His own agenda included the long-standing Labour Party objective of a salaried service for GPs, coupled with a determination to provide incentives for group practices. This last had been a declared aim of the NHS since 1948, but had foundered on the twin rocks of central and local government's failure to provide health centres and GPs' refusal to work under local government.

As the negotiations started, the undated resignations poured in – 18,000 of them within three weeks, from a total of 22,000 GPs – but the talks continued, often two or three times a week, exhaustive and exhausting and literally in smoke-filled rooms. Four years had already passed since the first Royal College of Physicians' report on the dangers of smoking and the first Cabinet consideration of a ban on tobacco advertising (Enoch Powell had been in favour). But Norman Warner, a principal on the civil service side, recalls the endless meetings at which a string of non-smoking civil servants 'tried to peer through this wall of cigarette smoke to see these rather solid and not very healthy looking figures on the other side'.[26]

Throughout the talks, the mood among GPs remained febrile. A dozen in Birmingham actually resigned from the NHS in mid-negotiation, while at an acrimonious special representative meeting in June, a determined attempt was made to get the mass resignations submitted from July.[27] With ambivalent backing from the BMA, Ivor Jones launched Independent Medical Services, a rudimentary scheme meant to provide an alternative insurance service to the NHS if the GPs did quit. Years later Cameron recalled: 'The militants wanted direct confrontation with the Government. But I knew in my heart of hearts that it could bring down the GP service. Medicine would never have been the same again . . . [it] would have taken us a generation to recover . . . the idea that you could quickly put together a scheme that would replace the NHS was a nonsense.'[28] The possibility that the talks would break down, however, still horrified the consultants. Sir Hector MacLennan, a senior gynaecologist, flew down in fog from Scotland and demanded to see Cameron late at night to tell him that 'women in Glasgow would be having their babies in the gutter'.[29] Fortunately the Ministry of Health still had Godber as chief medical officer and the BMA still had Stevenson as secretary. Many a late night and early morning phone call smoothed the path of the formal negotiations.

The final outcome proved the saving of general practice. Robinson dropped his insistence on a salaried service (though it remained as a largely unexercised option within the package). The GPs dropped their demands for fees for item of service (though they remained in the form of limited incentive payments for immunisations, cervical smears and one or two other items). 'You might say,' Kenneth Robinson recalled of their two opposing positions, 'that we traded the one for the other.' What did emerge was the basic practice allowance the BMA had so bitterly resisted in Bevan's day, extremely generous loans to allow GPs to set themselves up in group practice premises, improvement grants for substandard surgeries, reimbursement for support staff, the attachment of nurses and other staff from the local health authority, post-graduate education, incentives for GPs to practise in under-doctored areas, and a training scheme for new GPs with payments for the trainers. It also produced a thumping pay rise when the pay review body, whose niggardly award in 1965 had triggered the crisis, went the other way and priced the new contract to provide a 33 per cent increase. 'They got far more than I expected,' Robinson recalled. 'And of course it completely bust pay policy.' The award was eventually paid in two halves, a decision the GPs accepted.

The deal not only stopped the rot. It produced a renaissance in general practice, transforming its effectiveness, status and rewards. The long-hoped-for health centres slowly but surely became a growing reality. General practice moved from being a job that half of all GPs in 1963 wished they were not doing, to one that by the 1980s more than half of all medical students deliberately chose.[30]

The dispute marked a watershed in the history of the NHS. It was the first time that doctors (the dozen in Birmingham) had publicly resigned en bloc from the service; more importantly, it was the last time that GPs could credibly threaten to do so. The charter for which they had fought so hard effectively bound them, lock, stock, barrel and mortgage, to the NHS. The cost-rent scheme and other reimbursements made family doctors so dependent for premises, staff and income on the health service that any possibility of quitting en masse and practising privately outside it vanished. Although signed, undated resignations would again be collected, the threat that GPs might actually leave the NHS would never again carry quite the same sting.

In 1965, Marks says, 'I have no doubt whatsoever we would have resigned. I was deeply committed to the NHS. But I'd have been out like a shot because we had been treated appallingly by governments of all colours and because the NHS just wasn't providing a decent service. We felt we were being exploited. Those of us in good practices were more angry than those in the racking practices. I actually have private health insurance because PPP at that time offered it to all doctors without a check on your medical history, and I took it because all of us believed then that the NHS wasn't going to survive. It was that bad. But since then resignation has not really been a credible threat because doctors are in hock to the health service up to here.'[31] Marks's judgement is shared by Robinson. 'Resignation was certainly a real threat at the time. It would have been very difficult for them to survive, but it would not have been inconceivable. After the charter, I don't believe they could have done.'[32]

The charter may have tied GPs into the health service, but it did not end ambivalence over the NHS within the BMA's ranks. So strong did this remain that in 1967, the negotiations over, the association commissioned a study under Ivor Jones's chairmanship of alternative means of financing the service. The committee members included a bright young Tory lawyer by the name of Geoffrey Howe, and Arthur Seldon, guru of the free-market monetarist think-tank the Institute of Economic Affairs. The committee's recommendations, which might politely be called confused, in large measure reflected tensions within the committee itself. They included switching to an insurance-based system for acute hospital care, linked to the right to opt out into private insurance – a recipe which the committee somehow thought could be squared with the conclusion that 'we believe it is neither desirable nor practicable to think in terms of dismantling the NHS.'[33]

If the GP charter was Robinson's great achievement, his 'terrible moment'[34] came in 1968 in the wake of sterling's devaluation. Harold Wilson assured the electorate that the 'pound in your pocket' had not been devalued, Callaghan resigned as Chancellor, Roy Jenkins took over and from every spending department sacrifices were demanded. 'I was on a Morton's fork,' Kenneth Robinson said. 'Every department was. It had to be something very visible and I had the choice of reintroducing prescription charges, which was pretty humiliating, or suspending the hospital building programme. We had already had to trim it back a bit, but in 1968 the issue was suspending it. That would have been a disaster. It would have been years before we got it back on course. So I chose prescription charges, and I have never regretted the decision. And anyway we made so many exceptions – children, old age pensioners, the chronic sick, those on supplementary benefit – that the revenue from the charges when it came in was only about half what the Treasury had hoped for!'[35]

The pattern of exemptions Robinson set still stands, as does the charge. It is unlikely again ever to be abolished. It remained, however, a bitter pill for Labour to swallow, particularly as accompanying it came an increase in dental charges to half of the cost of treatment. The party was roused to fury, twenty-six Labour MPs abstaining and Robinson's own constituency party demanding his resignation, sweetening an unpleasant evening only by stating that it was 'really a way of expressing our dissatisfaction with Mr Wilson and the way he is handling things'.[36]

Social Security and Social Services

> [By 1970] Labour was still identified in the public mind as the party that cared about social policy; but popular triumphs in social policy eluded the government.
>
> Brian Lapping, The Labour Government 1964–70, p. 145

Later than housing, education and health, social security had to wait until the mid-1960s and a second Labour Government for the start of what proved a decade's dramatic expansion in the range and type of benefits offered.

In social security, Wilson's opening shot to match the abolition of prescription charges was the largest ever real terms increase in pensions and other benefits. With that went the righting of some old injustices, including tripling to 30s. (£1.50) a week the income of the 'ten bob widows' – a group whose benefit had been frozen since 1948 – ending in Wilson's words 'a long standing and bitter grievance'.[37] The package, however, was costly, requiring sharp rises in income and other taxes and the introduction of capital gains tax to pay for it all. The result, as Wilson ruefully recorded, was 'the first of a series of attacks on sterling' which led, after a debilitating and arguably pointless three-year battle, to devaluation in 1967.

But with better benefits had come also new ideas. The 'quiet obscurity' which national assistance enjoyed in the 1950s had faded by the early 1960s as evidence mounted from the voluntary societies and others that old people were reluctant to claim and that the stigma of means-tested assistance remained. The dislike may well have been growing: by the early 1960s at least a third of pensioners who were entitled to national assistance were failing to claim.[38] At the time, national assistance still relied heavily on home visits. Officers had considerable discretion to adjust benefit to individual circumstances – to pay extra for laundry, fuel, special diet or other requirements. To its advocates this was seen as the assistance board's great strength, providing a service both personal and humane. To its critics it looked increasingly like an intrusive and inconsistent form of state charity. As Deacon and Bradshaw have put it, in the early days after

1948 it was 'one thing for a claimant to have to tell the Board that he or she needed extra money for clothes or bedding when friends and neighbours were in a similar position and when the cause of need was so obviously beyond the control of any one person. It was quite another to have to show worn clothing to a visiting officer when everyone else had "never had it so good".'[39]

To overcome this reluctance to claim, in the run-up to the 1964 general election Labour not only promised an 'income guarantee' for pensioners – a minimum benefit to be paid free of means-test – but had made it the centrepiece of its social security programme. While all other benefit improvements depended on the rate of economic advance, the manifesto declared, this one was unconditional. The guarantee was the first of what have so far proved largely doomed attempts to bring together tax and social security. While the schemes vary enormously in both detail and impact, the essential aim of Labour's income guarantee, Heath's tax-credit scheme, and a stack of parallel ideas such as Citizen's Income and negative income tax is to integrate the tax and social security systems so that everyone faces just one assessment of their means. The government would then take from those who should pay tax and pay out to those whose income needs to be brought up to a defined level. In theory, such a system can end traditional means-tests. It can reduce or remove the 'churn' between the tax and benefit systems which increasingly has seen people receive benefits with one hand and pay tax out with the other. And, depending on how it is constructed, its advocates variously argue that it could produce a fairer outcome or lower overall income tax levels.

Initially, Labour promised the income guarantee only to pensioners and widows, but hoped over time to extend it to include all claimants and even those in low-paid work.[40] Conceived, in the words of Douglas Houghton, the Cabinet minister who co-ordinated social services policy during Wilson's early years, as 'the answer to all means tests', it was 'one of the firmest of all pledges given by the manifesto of 1964'. He described it as 'simply income tax in reverse – Receive as You Need instead of Pay As You Earn (PAYE)'.[41]

This beguilingly simple idea foundered on the harsh realities that were later to frustrate the Conservatives' tax-credit scheme and, at least to date, all other attempts to rationalise what at first sight seems a needlessly complex system. It was soon found that pensioners' needs for housing and other help proved more complex than could be met by a single, affordable, unmeans-tested sum. In addition, tax returns are filled in annually. But if a pensioner becomes disabled, or someone younger moves in and out of work, cash has to be paid out now and weekly, not next year. Even for pensioners – one of the simpler groups to tackle – there were mounting doubts about whether the scheme could be afforded unless the income guarantee was set so low that there would be large numbers of losers. There was predictable opposition from the Inland Revenue, which not only failed to work out how it could get income tax forms to people who did not pay income tax, but wanted nothing to do with paying cash out, only bringing it in. The scheme 'went on the rocks' in Houghton's words, 'in the economic gales of July 1965' (a moment of trade deficit and sterling pressure during which the *Economist* cheerfully observed that it looked as though the Labour ship 'really is going down'). What was 'salvaged from the wreck'[42] was the Supplementary Benefits scheme.

The National Assistance Board was transformed into a Supplementary Benefits Commission which in turn was partially merged into the Ministry of Pensions and National Insurance to become a new Ministry of Social Security. The commission took over the board's caseload, but operated with appreciably less discretion, while a new and higher rate of benefit was introduced for pensioner claimants. The intention was partly to provide a more guaranteed income, but also to reduce the so-called 'exceptional circumstances additions' – extra weekly payments for special needs such as fuel, laundry and the like which, far from being exceptional, had come to be awarded to six out of ten claimants. Research had also started to show that the use of discretion to make these awards had produced markedly inconsistent and unfair results, not just between one type of claimant and another and one local office and another, but even between different cases dealt with by the same officer. Peggy Herbison, the Social Security Minister, also felt that detailed and intrusive inquiries, in which people were asked to produce their worn-out clothing or household goods, were damaging the reputation of national assistance.

The net effect was to set the means-tested benefits off down a more rights-based road, one it would pursue for twenty years up to Norman Fowler's social security review in 1986. Although large elements of discretion remained in single payments, for cookers or bedding for example, and some extra weekly allowances were retained, the basic benefit, once the means-test had been passed, became an entitlement. The old National Assistance Board rules were codified and turned into rights, the theory being that supplementary benefit would no longer appear to be discretionary state charity for the poorest, but a right for any citizen who got into severe difficulties. In a further attempt to remove stigma, pensioners no longer needed separate books for the insurance-based old age pension and any means-tested assistance required to top it up: what Wilson called the 'humiliation of the two-book system', under which 'proud old people' could not help letting their neighbours see that they were 'on assistance' was ended. When the election came, 'I found [this] one of the most popular of all our reforms.'[43]

If this largely symbolic measure proved to be one of the most popular elements of the new system, that was only fitting, for the change indeed proved larger in symbolism than substance. Crossman, who had yet to take over the DHSS, dubbed it 'brilliantly worked out' but a 'cheap substitute' for the income guarantee.[44] And some of the differences amounted to little more than language. The 'test of need' that the assistance board had applied, with its ring of charity, was renamed a 'test of requirements'. The whole reform, Houghton recalled, was 'lavishly advertised' and sold 'with all the presentational subtleties one could think of'. For once, however, this was not just the usual politicians' desire to be seen to be doing more than was in fact the case. The problem of low take-up by pensioners (who were the main claimants in those days of full employment) was firmly perceived as a presentational one, caused by stigma. If largely presentational changes helped to solve it, such as renaming the benefits 'supplementary' as they supplemented pensioners' income, then merging the old national assistance offices with those paying out national insurance benefits, and then telling people about it all, all that should be done. Within a year the number of claimants rose by 365,000 and Wilson could boast that 'hundreds of thousands of the least well-off members of the community now claimed their rights.'[45]

Much of the gain soon proved illusory. National insurance and supplementary benefit offices did indeed merge, but in name only when it was found that the same staff could not cope with the details of the two very different systems. And while the mainspring of the reform had been the 700,000 pensioners who failed to claim, signs were starting to emerge of the economic and demographic pressures which over the next decade were to change dramatically the population with which the Supplementary Benefits Commission dealt. The number of single parents was increasing slowly but steadily. Medical advance was raising the numbers of disabled living into adulthood – the so-called 'civilian disabled' who had no claim on the insurance-based industrial injuries pensions. Unemployment was still low by the standards of the 1980s and 1990s: for all but the unemployable it remained usually a transient experience. It was none the less beginning to rise. By the end of the 1960s, the Supplementary Benefits Commission felt constrained to explain that many of its local offices lacked lavatories because 'its clients had been inclined to break them' while chairs were screwed to the floor 'because portable chairs had often been thrown at officials'.[46]

With the switch to supplementary benefit came more generous unemployment, sickness and widows' benefits as an earnings-related addition was introduced. Like the Conservatives' 1961 scheme for earnings-related pensions, this was a move away from Beveridge's flat-rate insurance benefits towards a more European social security model. But just as the Tory move over pensions had been driven by the need to get more cash into the national insurance fund – in other words by economics rather than any theoretical construct of social security – so Labour's more dramatic extension of earnings-related benefits had economic rather than social or theoretical motives.

It reflected the mood that had brought Labour to power: the perception that Britain was falling behind, and that part of the answer lay in a 'shake-out' of labour from declining industries into expanding ones.[47] Skilled workers were felt to need greater protection from the short spells of unemployment that would result from such a realignment, so higher benefits were provided for the better paid while the Redundancy Payments Act provided statutory redundancy pay for the first time. 'In a period of rapid industrial change,' Labour argued, 'it is only elementary justice to compensate employees who, through no fault of their own, find that their job has disappeared. Directors and senior executives have long received a "golden handshake"; the same principle of compensation for job loss will now be applied to the whole workforce.'[48]

In all, therefore, the first Wilson government saw a marked expansion in social security benefits and plans laid for much more in Crossman's grand national superannuation scheme, which ultimately fell victim to the 1970 general election. Yet much of this expansion proved to be remarkably bipartisan. Just as Keith Joseph, in the 1970–4 Heath government, was to take on and implement new benefits for the disabled which had been devised under Labour, so Labour in 1964–70 legislated and took the credit for items that were also in the Conservative programme. The Conservative 1964 manifesto had recognised the need for a competitive economy to redeploy its resources, and they too had promised severance pay and a form of earnings-related benefit, so that 'those unable to find a new job right away will be protected against a sharp fall in income'.[49]

Into this mix of new benefits for, so to speak, both the richer and the poorer beneficiaries of the welfare state came a third element – an extension of means-testing by a Labour Government. Like many such extensions, it was done not with the aim of reducing outgoings but of providing new help. In Labour's case it came in two forms. One was the introduction in 1967 of rate rebates, a product of rising local government spending which had made rates too harsh a burden for those on low income. The other was the encouragement of discretionary local authority rent rebates. These offset higher council rents caused by the restrictions on central government subsidy brought in during what had, economically, been roller-coaster years. Thus the electorate not only saw a Labour Government introduce new means-tested rather than universal benefits, but do so with some pride. As with supplementary benefit, Labour was keen people should claim its new rate rebates and a 'strenuous' advertising campaign ensured they did, almost a million claimants joining the books within a year of their introduction.[50]

In contrast to this expansionary but means-tested approach, Labour's final act in 1970 was to gain Royal Assent on the day Parliament was dissolved for a bold attempt to take a much more universalist approach to what had come to be dubbed the sixth arm of the welfare state – the social services. This local authority-run provision consisted in the main of what had been left out or left behind in 1948, after Bevan had stolen many health functions from local authorities and Jim Griffiths had made national assistance a national not a local responsibility. Slowly but surely, and with central government encouragement, the remaining services had developed and grown, fuelled by the late 1950s concept of community care. On the way, the quality and quantity of training provided for fledgling social workers had been transformed by the Younghusband report of 1959 which in turn led to the creation of the National Institute for Social Work.

The range of child care, health and housing, psychiatric and probation, educational and elderly, maternity and disability workers who made up the social services still presented, to the public and providers alike, a confusingly fragmented and overlapping group of services. While local authorities ran all these services, they operated in separate departments and were overseen by different parts of central government, the Home Office looking after the children's service, for example, the Department of Health much but not all of the rest. As Brian Watkin has recorded, by the late 1960s:

> a good many jokes and cautionary tales were being told about families who were being visited by half a dozen or more social workers . . . a family might have dealings with representatives of the children's department, the health department, the welfare department, and with social workers

attached to the housing and education departments, all under the same local authority . . . the family which found itself so unable to cope with the complexity and stresses of modern life that it required all these services was the very family upon which the additional burden of coordinating them and of sorting out the possibly conflicting advice should not have been thrust.[51]

Social work was plainly a service in need of reorganisation in the days when reorganisation for everything and anything – health, local government, education, social security – was in the air. The result in 1968 was the Seebohm report[52] with its recommendations to create unified social services departments with complete responsibility for the needs of their areas, covering not just statutory requirements but any needs which might arise. Thus social services were to become, if not a universal service (not everyone would need social work), at least a universalist service; in the words of the report 'a door on which anyone could knock'. Departments would be there not only to help individuals and families, but to work with groups and communities, stimulating voluntary activity but in turn using voluntary activity to stimulate councils into action.

It was a grand and comprehensive vision and one Labour promptly adopted. It was to prove both too grand and too comprehensive, having within it inherent tensions which Seebohm recognised but could not resolve: how could social workers act in the potentially conflicting interests of the individual and the family and of the community at the same time? And how were social workers to reconcile support for the arguments of community and voluntary groups for more resources with their status as employees of the very body which granted resources? The report none the less marked a great leap forward for the personal social services. It was very much a child of its times – times when it was still felt that if there were problems to be solved, they were, almost by definition, soluble; and that the key difficulty was the way services were organised. The poor, the deprived and the distressed did not always have to be with us.

Housing

> For a few years [from 1964] the British seemed to regain confidence in their capacity to transform their country by purposeful collective action.
>
> *David Donnison and Claire Ungerson, Housing Policy, p. 154*

From 1951 when the Conservatives came to power with a public commitment to build 300,000 houses a year, until 1968 when the Labour government at last abandoned its commitment to build 500,000 houses a year, grand, rounded, national figures, dreamed up on somebody's doodling pad were the main deciding factors in national housing policy.

Brian Lapping, The Labour Government 1964–70, p. 10

We have had too much of the bulldozer.

Anthony Crosland, Towards a Labour Housing Policy, Fabian Tract 41, 1971

Crossman's arrival at housing produced one of the ministry's stormier periods. He came to his first Cabinet post armed with the ingrained belief in open goverment that was to lead to the ground-breaking publication of his *Diaries*, a profound mistrust of the civil service, a determination to do things and a fairly minimal knowledge of housing. The result was some spectacular clashes with Dame Evelyn Sharp, his permanent secretary. His style, she later complained, was 'like a bull in a china shop. I think he *wanted* to be a bull in a china shop, he wanted to hear the china smashing.'[53] Crossman confessed to being 'flabbergasted' at being given the job and at having at speed to read up the party policy 'because it was almost new to me'. Dame Evelyn's caustic verdict in later years was that it was a policy on which Labour 'hadn't done its homework'.[54] The early result was war with the department as Crossman insisted on using outsiders, including Lord Goodman and two members of the Milner Holland committee, David Donnison, the housing specialist from the LSE, and Dennis Pilcher, of the Royal Institution of Chartered Surveyors, to help him devise a replacement for the Conservatives' Rent Act. Donnison, perhaps modestly, says the chief credit should go to Sir Dennis, 'a snuff-taking, silk-handkerchief-wearing high Tory who was more influential than any of us. The ideas about "fair rents" were essentially his.'

Goodman at one of our meetings was asked by Crossman to listen to both of us and then tell him whether we were making sense. So Pilcher and I breakfasted with Goodman at his flat next morning, explained the ideas to him and Goodman dictated a summary, with his endorsement, over the phone to his secretary, in crisp, clear legal language, then turned to us and asked 'Is that all right?' It was.[55]

The outcome was an honest attempt through 'fair rents' and rent tribunals to strike a genuine balance between tenants and private landlords.
The Act did successfully lower the party political temperature over private
rents, surviving the return of the Tories five years later. It did increase
the protection for poor tenants. But in the end it did nothing to improve
the housing in which they lived, nor did it achieve what Crossman suspected was needed: a halt in the progressive decline in the private rented
sector.

In large measure, this was because for many Labour back-benchers a
simple equation remained, drawn from the days of Bevan but reinforced
by Rachman, which read 'council house – good/private landlord – bad'.
Hissing the landlord, in Brian Lapping's phrase, had become a party pas-
time and anything that appeared to subsidise landlords stood little chance
of getting through the Commons when Labour's majority was only three.
It mattered not that among the most needy were, in fact, private tenants;
helping them would also have helped landlords who were depicted as
Rachmanite devils rather than the mix of a few Rachmans, some large
property companies, some ancient trusts and a collection of well-off and
not-so-well-off individuals who owned a house or houses to let. Anything
that either increased private landlords' profits or allowed them to improve
their properties would have helped perpetuate a private rented sector that
too many Labour back-benchers simply believed should be made extinct.

The net result was that the government was to pour large sums of
subsidy into owner-occupation through mortgage interest tax relief,
further large sums into supporting council tenants, first through council
house subsidies and then through rent and rate rebates schemes, while
providing the group that overall was the least well-off – tenants of private
landlords – with no help at all unless they were poor enough to be on
supplementary benefit. The antipathy towards private landlords ran so
deep, however, that at the 1966 general election Wilson could still raise
big cheers at rallies by damning 'the Rent Act' even though Crossman's
Act had by then replaced the Conservative version. It showed that housing
remained a central political issue and explained why Wilson in 1964,
knowing a second general election could not be far away, had cajoled
Crossman into the job with the statement: 'On housing we win or lose.'[56]

Thus Crossman, too, came to play his part in the numbers game, having
moaned on arrival that there was 'no housing programme . . . no information and no plan, there were just a lot of meaningless figures'.[57] He
persuaded Wilson to accept a private target of 150,000 council houses and
250,000 private homes for 1965 – a total of 400,000 which had been hinted

at, but not pledged, in the manifesto. Crossman, like his predecessors, was soon to find that it was the Chancellor not the housing minister who controlled the bank in this particular game of Monopoly. Despite a tripling of council house subsidies and a requirement on local authorities increasingly to favour system build (which often meant high rise) the target was missed in 1965.[58] It was met in 1966, but unfortunately for Labour, Crossman's 1965 housing White Paper had by then turned the 400,000 target into one of 500,000 a year by 1970 – a commitment which Anthony Howard records was 'even more recklessly characterised by Wilson during the 1966 [election] campaign as "not a lightly given pledge – it is a promise".'[59] In practice, Wilson had little choice. So important was housing to the electorate that even that monster promise had been outbid by the Tories. Their manifesto not only pledged 500,000 new homes a year, but promised to reach the target by the end of 1968.[60]

Devaluation in 1967 ensured that Labour got nowhere near half a million. Completions barely reached 350,000 a year in 1968 and fell thereafter, though by 1970 Labour's housebuilding record over six years was better than the Tories' over their last six in office.

The 1965 White Paper may have landed Labour with an impossible dream numerically. It none the less set the seal, if any were needed, on Labour's acceptance of a mixed economy in housing, and one in which the public sector would concentrate on special needs rather than generalised subsidy of housing. 'Once the country has overcome its huge social problem of slumdom and obsolescence and met the need of the great cities for more houses to let at moderate rents,' the White Paper stated, 'the programme of subsidised council housing should decrease. The expansion of the public programme now proposed is to meet exceptional needs . . . the expansion of building for owner-occupation on the other hand is normal; it reflects a long term social advance which should gradually pervade every region.'[61]. That Labour's conversion to the concept of increased owner-occupation was genuine was shown by the exemption of owner-occupied houses from the new capital gains tax, and in Crossman's introducing both the option mortgage scheme, a low interest loan for those whose income was too low to benefit from tax relief on mortgages, and 100 per cent mortgages. One aim in this was to encourage better-off council tenants to become owner-occupiers, releasing council houses 'for the more needy cases'. It was in 1970 as Labour left office that half the households in England and Wales became owner-occupied for the first time.

The climate was shifting in other ways, too. It did so most dramatically when an old lady got up early on the morning of 16 May 1968 to light

the gas in her flat on the 18th floor of the 23-storey, 200-foot-high Ronan
Point block in east London. An eyewitness described what followed:

> The whole place shook. Suddenly our bedroom wall fell away with a
> terrible ripping sound. We found ourselves staring out over London. Our
> heads were only a matter of two feet from the eighty-foot drop. The room
> filled with dust and showers of debris and furniture were plunging past us.
> Suddenly we heard screams. I think it must have been someone falling
> with the debris.[62]

The explosion had blown out the load-bearing walls, producing a progess-
ive collapse of bedrooms and living rooms down one corner of the block
that left five dead and seventeen injured. The blast also killed tower blocks
as a mainspring of local authority building.

A whole range of studies was rapidly assembled showing that the
claimed advantages of high rise – that it was quicker and cheaper – were
a myth, while surveys by councils of their stock in the wake of Ronan
Point painted an alarming picture of buildings which may not have been
in danger of collapse but were still downright dangerous. Most of Birmingham's 429 tower blocks, for example, were found to be shedding brick or
concrete cladding.[63] A mighty repair bill was discovered. Ronan Point
itself, after a grand spell of notoriety and long-fought battles over its
future, was finally demolished to end up as hardcore under the runway of
the Docklands City Airport.[64] The worst tower blocks became increasingly
untenable. In 1979, Wirral District Council claimed the dubious record of
being the first to demolish unlettable flats when it blew up the notorious
Oak and Eldon Gardens in Birkenhead a mere twenty years after they
were built, and a few months after Margaret Thatcher became prime
minister.[65] To some it seemed a fitting symbol of both the state and
future of the welfare state. Television crews were charged for filming,
refreshments were laid on, and soon the crump of tower slums being
demolished became a regular if infrequent spectator sport for both journalists and the public alike.

Extra government subsidy for buildings above five storeys had in fact
been abandoned in 1967 before the Ronan Point explosion[66] as a new
emphasis on renovation had begun to replace the old policies of new
building and slum clearance. That change stemmed partly from a disillusion with high rise which Ronan Point merely epitomised in the most
dramatic form possible: Nicholas Taylor had written in the *Architectural
Review* in 1967: 'More slums are likely to be built within the next five

years than in the past twenty.'[67] But it came also from a realisation that while there remained severe housing shortages in some parts of the country (notably in London and the South-East, where the national media were based) overall the huge building programme since the war was beginning to produce a crude surplus of housing. In 1969, Kenneth Robinson, now Minister of Land, was telling the Commons that by 1973 there would be one million more dwellings than households.[68] Putting those already built into good repair became the new priority.

The shift to renovation became government policy with *Old Houses into New Homes*, the 1968 housing White Paper, and by 1970 the subsidy and other elements of the housing programme were such as effectively to rule out high-rise and high-density schemes. Alas, none of this in itself provided a guarantee of better quality public housing. Following Macmillan's cut in housing standards, the Conservatives in 1959 had set up a committee to review them, the outcome being the eponymous Parker Morris standards of 1961. Its report reflected the growing affluence of the Macmillan era in which two out of three households now had a television and one in three a car. In slightly quaint language the committee concluded: 'Homes are being built at the present time which not only are too small to provide adequately for family life, but also are too small to hold the possessions in which so much of the new affluence is expressed.'[69]

It recommended bigger, better planned, better built and warmer housing. The new standards, however, while intended as minimums for both the public and private sectors, soon tended in the public sector to become maximum requirements. In addition they began life merely as advisory standards. While some local authorities adopted or even exceeded them, others only took them up in 1969, when their use became a condition of subsidy. In terms of floor space, Parker Morris standards never returned the council house to the generous proportions on which Bevan had insisted. Even so the many other improvements in quality soon came into conflict with the demands of quantity as both Labour and Tory governments attempted to get a quart of housing out of a pint pot of spending. Designers found themselves trapped in a 'pincer' of exacting minimum standards set against rigorous cost limits. This squeeze from both above and below produced, in Peter Malpass and Alan Murie's words, 'some most unsatisfactory design solutions',[70] or, as Maxwell Hutchison more bluntly put it, 'more and more "battery housing" estates'.[71]

Against that, the sixties, and Labour's period in particular, saw a new faith in town planning. Alongside the arrival of renovation came conservation areas, the Civic Amenities Act, and, starting in 1961 and finishing in 1970, a new clutch of New Towns[72] the most dramatic of which was to be Milton Keynes, home of the Open University. But housing by the 1960s had become a much more complex, more politicised issue than in the late 1940s and 1950s when only numbers seemed to matter. As David Donnison has recorded:

> Previously most of the new building had been done in green fields or on blitzed urban sites for people whose identity was unknown when decisions to develop were taken. These decisions could therefore be made privately in the back rooms of town halls in consultation between developers, planners, politicians and their advisers. But as the bulldozers bit into densely built areas, it became increasingly obvious who gained from the process, who lost, and who was taking the decisions. People in run-down neighbourhoods learnt that a slum-clearance scheme would mainly benefit the long-established working class, who would be rehoused by the council in new flats. A scheme for rehabilitating houses and improving the environment would probably benefit the invading gentry, buying their way in with the help of improvement grants and tax reliefs. Leaving things alone would benefit poorer immigrants from Ireland, the New Commonwealth and Mediterranean countries, who fended for themselves at the bottom of the housing market. Building new offices, shopping centres and urban motorways would benefit commuters, motorists and others coming from further afield. In rural areas similar choices had to be made between the interests of local people, commuters and passing motorists. Arguments about housing, planning, transport and community became increasingly heated and inextricably entangled with each other.[73]

Education

The Sixties – the decade of the degree.
Anthony Sampson, The New Anatomy of Britain, p. 155

If it's the last thing I do, I'm going to destroy every fucking grammar school in England. And Wales. And Northern Ireland.
Anthony Crosland, in Susan Crosland's Tony Crosland, p. 148

The grammar school still had many powerful and eloquent friends; by 1960 the secondary modern had none.
Harry Judge, A Generation of Schooling, p. 48

Run away to sea rather than go to a secondary modern.
A. J. P. Taylor in 1957, see Harry Judge, A Generation of Schooling, p. 216

Britain, in common with other European countries, is making a
troubled and puzzling journey – the journey from a system of
secondary and higher education designed to educate a small elite,
to a system in which these kinds of education are to be made available
to vastly greater numbers of boys and girls.
Second Newsom report, 1968

People are very rude about the sixties now and not without reason;
but there was in that period a genuine idealism that you could make
children happier and society more agreeable and harmonious, more
at ease with itself, if everyone went to the same sort of school. They
wouldn't stream ahead of other children, they would minimise
competition. 'Love is all you need' sang the Beatles, but the same
thing went on in school.
John Rae in From Butler to Baker, BBC TV, 1994

Crosland arrived at education soon after the general election as the
Cabinet's youngest member and with a following wind that he himself
had done much to create. Education was central to Labour's modernising
platform and it was Crosland's ideology that had done much to put it
there. In *The Future of Socialism*, which had been reissued the previous
year, he had argued that 'as an investment, education yields a generous
return: we badly need more of it.' It would also contribute to the more
egalitarian society that Crosland sought. He arrived as Robbins was being
implemented and armed with a manifesto commitment to end the gram-
mar/secondary divide. It was a radical agenda in the hands of the most
radical Secretary of State for Education since the war. The result, six
months after he took up office, was the most famous circular in the department's history: number 10/65 which firmly 'requested' local authorities
to go comprehensive.

The tide was already flowing. As early as 1952, the idea on which the
tripartite schools system was founded had come under fire when Philip
Vernon published research showing that scores in the supposedly objective
IQ tests which formed the central plank of the eleven-plus examination
could be raised *on average* by fourteen points with only a limited amount
of coaching. This evidence blew a serious hole in the concept of a fixed

pool of intelligence which meant that only a set proportion of children could benefit from grammar school education.[74] It was the starting gun for the biggest and most prolonged educational controversy since the nineteenth-century clashes over whether the state had a right to educate its children. For more than a quarter of a century the battle over selection and comprehensives was to rage on, waxing and waning but never fading entirely away, until in the 1990s, after almost a decade's lull, selection would once again become a central educational issue.

Vernon's study proved the first in a great peal of bells which tolled the end of the tripartite system. Work by educationalists, psychologists and sociologists was fed into a string of official reports – Early Leaving, Crowther, Newsom and Robbins – that had by 1963 left the justifications for the system in tatters.[75] Early Leaving showed that more than half the children of working class parents who made it to grammar school failed to pass three O-levels, and that a third left before they even sat them.[76] Around the same time some secondary moderns started entering the brighter of their eleven-plus failures for the new GCE, and getting good results. Neither side of that equation, which saw eleven-plus successes failing and eleven-plus failures succeeding, said much for quality of selection.

Equally, studies began to show that the number of prized grammar school places which local authorities chose to provide varied wildly around the country. In Gateshead in the early 1950s, 8 per cent of children went to grammar school, while in Merionethshire 64 per cent did so.[77] A study later in the decade showed more typically that nationally 20 per cent of children went to grammar school, but that the proportion of such places locally ranged from 10 per cent to 45 per cent. This fitted neither with the egalitarianism that was becoming more pronounced in Labour's thinking, nor with the more limited equality of opportunity that the Tories argued they were offering through their 'opportunity state'. The argument was further strengthened when one key study showed that however the eleven-plus test was refined, 10 per cent of children – or 60,000 children a year – would end up in the 'wrong' type of school.[78] The eleven-plus, in Robin Pedley's phrase, was becoming 'the most celebrated, most unpopular, yet most potent feature of English education'.[79]

Under David Eccles, for all his expansionism, formal Conservative policy remained to cling to the grammar schools while allowing some comprehensives. Soon after becoming minister in 1954 he declared there would be no 'assassination' of the grammars, while comprehensives were dubbed 'untried and very costly' experiments. In private, however, he recognised the pressures for change. As early as 1955 in a Cabinet memorandum he acknowledged that 'parity of esteem' between schools had not been achieved. He noted 'the disappointment and jealousy felt by parents when their children failed to qualify for grammar school'. Such resentment, he added, 'appears to be growing'.[80] He attempted to square this increasingly angry circle by encouraging secondary modern schools to enter their brighter children for O-levels and by encouraging transfer to grammars to correct 'glaring mistakes' – a policy that was itself an admission that the eleven-plus was far from perfect and that 'parity of esteem' did not exist.

The forces arguing the comprehensive case were not drawn only from Labour's egalitarians who saw the new schools as a solvent for class barriers and inequality – a group whose aims were as much social as educational. They also included educationalists, who saw a massive waste of talent in the divided system, and, perhaps surprisingly, a growing section of the expanding middle class. Unable any longer to buy their less bright child a grammar school place, and unwilling or unable to afford a public school one, they came increasingly to resent the eleven-plus, failure in which could not only damn the individual child but divide families when one sibling passed and another failed. Much of the resulting support for comprehensives, however, as David Donnison observed, was less a vote in favour of comprehensives than a massive rejection of the secondary modern school.[81]

It was to these pressures that local authorities slowly began to respond, putting up comprehensive schemes which Eccles tended to reject unless they could be shown to 'do no damage' to an existing school – a criterion which in practice meant the local grammar should not suffer from a genuine comprehensive opening nearby. It took a Friday the 13th, Macmillan's 'night of the long knives' in 1962 (when a third of the Cabinet including Eccles was sacked), for government policy really to change. For Macmillan's massacre brought in Edward Boyle as the new minister.

Boyle, agnostic, eclectic, brilliant, humane and well to the left of his party – almost 'a reluctant Conservative' according to Maurice Kogan, his private secretary at education[82] – was a very different animal from Eccles. As a junior minister between 1957 and 1959 he had, almost uniquely, visited most if not all of the 146 local education authorities.[83] Like Crosland who was to succeed him, he was at thirty-nine the Cabinet's youngest member. His standing was such that comparisons had even been made with the young Churchill, 'articulate, imaginative and unafraid to dissent'.[84] It was during his tenure that the great xpansion of both education spending and ideas, including the commitment to raise the school leaving age to sixteen in 1970, got fully under way.

What struck Boyle when he arrived was how far the comprehensive idea had progressed. No fewer than 90 of the 146 education authorities had either gone comprehensive or had plans to do so, in whole or in part. Since many of these were not Labour controlled, their plans, he concluded, 'could not simply be written off as politically motivated'.[85] Indeed in places the opposite could be demonstrated. Tory Leicestershire was busy organising middle schools for children aged eleven to thirteen, to allow it go non-selective, at the same time as the Labour-controlled Leicester city was cleaving firmly to its grammars. As Boyle later put it, the notion that comprehensive reorganisation started with circular 10/65 is 'one of the historical myths . . . It didn't. It started a number of years before.'[86]

In Boyle's judgement 1963 was 'the watershed' – a climactic year which he himself kicked off by rebutting the Eccles doctrine that comprehensives were experimental. 'We no longer regard any pattern of organisation as "the norm" compared to which all others must be stigmatized,' he told one of the annual education conferences.[87] Shortly afterwards the Robbins report was published, backing its call for a massive expansion in university places with hard-hitting evidence that working-class children faced far greater hurdles than the middle class in getting to university. Then came Newsom, whose report *Half our Future* examined the education of the less able teenagers: those in secondary modern schools. To ensure unanimity among its members, Newsom ducked tackling the issue of organisation head-on. He did, however, challenge the idea that intelligence was entirely inherited. Social factors, the report argued, were at least as important, if not more so, in educational attainment. At the same time the report's statistics plainly demonstrated that the less able were getting decidedly less than their fair share of resources.[88] Thus in a divided schooling system the idea of 'secondary education for all' was looking increasingly threadbare from both ends of the spectrum. Politically, Boyle set the seal on the argument in his foreword to the report. 'The essential point is that all children should have an equal opportunity of acquiring intelligence, and developing their talents and abilities to the full,' he declared, a statement described by Kogan as 'a milestone in Conservative thinking'.[89] It is one of the measures of how close Boyle and Crosland were on the essentials of the issue that he later acknowledged that the phrase 'acquiring intelligence' came from Crosland's book of a year earlier – *The Conservative Enemy*.[90]

Newsom and Robbins between them 'cemented the work of the

educational sociologists,' Boyle said. 'After 1963 it was hardly contro-versial to say that you had massive evidence of the numbers of boys and girls who were being allowed to write themselves off below their true level of ability.'[91]

It was from this firm base that Crosland could move. He was, in the words of Toby Weaver, then deputy secretary at the newly created Depart-ment of Education and Science, 'the first person to stop talking about comprehensive reorganisation and take a decisive step towards it'.[92] The first decision was whether to 'require' or 'request' local authorities to submit plans for comprehensives. Labour's left was later strongly to criti-cise the decision merely to 'request' action. Crosland acknowledged there was 'a lot of argument inside the department' on the best tactic. Ironically, it was his number two, Reg Prentice, who wanted compulsion – the same Reg Prentice who in later years was to desert to the Tories and as a minister under Mrs Thatcher was to criticise Labour for its *dirigisme*. It was Crosland the 'confirmed egalitarian' who favoured requesting local authorities to act, despite the wonderful explosion at his wife over his determination to close down the grammar schools 'if it's the last thing I do'.

Crosland dismissed Prentice's position as 'an empty toughness',[93] argu-ing that the ministry could not cope with any faster pace of change than that produced by a request. 'For the whole time I was at Curzon Street the thing was going as fast as it could possibly go,' he said,[94] and his judgement that the change would stick better if it was voluntary was borne out by events. There were big passions involved, reflected in the widely different interpretations put on Crosland's circular when it emerged. Peter Preston in the *Guardian* saw it as an 'amiably toothless tiger' while the *Daily Telegraph* declared it 'regrettably dictatorial in tone'.[95]

The grammars did not go down without a fight. There were petitions, marches, and telegrams to the Prime Minister. Tory Central Office exploited a *Daily Express* report in 1963 that Wilson had declared that the grammar schools would be closed 'over my dead body'[96] and at various times both Crosland and Crossman doubted their leader's commitment to such radical educational change.[97] The arrival of genuine comprehensives inevitably meant the closure of grammar schools taking only the brightest 20 to 30 per cent. But the wish to preserve the grammar school ethos produced, in the words of Harry Judge, then head of Banbury Grammar and later Director of Education Studies at Oxford, a desire for 'omelettes without breaking eggs'.[98] Thus Wilson, while being mocked by the edu-cationalists for the phrase, was expressing a widely felt wish and an implied concern about standards when he declared that comprehensives would mean 'a grammar school education for all'. Faced in 1968 with opinion polls showing majorities both against the eleven-plus and in favour of grammar schools, Ted Short, the former headmaster who became Secretary of State for Education, repeated the line.

If there was ambivalence in Labour ranks, there were divisions in Conservative ones. Boyle in 1967 persuaded Ted Heath as opposition leader formally to back the switch to comprehensives. A year later, however, the backlash against the closure of grammar schools was felt at the Tory party conference and a year after that Boyle departed as the Conservatives' education spokesman.

The change was not an easy one to make. The idea of comprehensives may have been essentially simple – Susan, Crosland's American-born wife, summed it up nicely if with a poor sense of the length of American history, by asking if all this fuss was really about 'nothing more nor less than high schools that have existed for a thousand years in America'.[99] But creating them out of the mass of existing school buildings when cash to build new ones was not available was no easy task; in addition, furious arguments would rage on for years about how far selection should remain within comprehensives – whether streaming, setting, banding or mixed ability teaching should be adopted.

The difficulties led Crosland to offer six options (two of which were not fully comprehensive) through which local authorities could end selection. These ranged from the 'orthodox' all-through eleven-to-eighteen comprehensives to various combinations of middle schools and sixth form colleges.[100] In 1966 government cash for new buildings became conditional on local authorities agreeing to go comprehensive, and even the huge reverses in local elections that Labour suffered in 1967 and 1968 did not slow progress, as the new Conservative authorities mainly stuck by the existing plans. Tying cash to new building did ensure that it was comprehensives which were built to provide 'roofs over heads' to match first the rising number of secondary school pupils resulting from the 1956–64 baby-boom, and later the increase from raising the school leaving age. But that equally meant they were more easily provided in areas of expanding population than in declining inner cities, where schools on several sites had often to be yoked together to form comprehensives. By 1970 the proportion of pupils in schools that at least in name were comprehensive had risen from 10 to 32 per cent, and by the time Labour left office only eight authorities were actively refusing to submit plans. Their rearguard action, however, was to ensure that the battle over the grammars would linger on, leaving a bridgehead from which the grammar schools would attempt to break out in the 1990s.

If tertiary and secondary education made all the headlines in the first part of the decade, primary education returned to the fore in the second, through the massive 550 pages of the Plowden report on *Children and their Primary Schools*.[101] Like Newsom, Plowden picked up the theme of educational disadvantage, arguing that it started at the earliest possible age and in the home. It proposed part-time nursery education and 'educational priority areas' as an answer. The latter were to receive extra resources to offset deprivation and disadvantage. It was from Plowden, too, that key phrases such as 'child-centred teaching', 'finding out rather than being told', and 'topic work' all spread from the educational world into common parlance. How far Plowden merely reflected what was already happening in classrooms and how far the report caused it to happen, and to what degree schools did shift away from traditional teaching methods and with what results, have been matters of intense controversy ever since. What is certain is that, whatever the merits of the change, the switch to mixed-ability teaching in primary schools that was being made possible by the steady decline of the eleven-plus, along with the move to more play and projects exemplified by the replacement of rows of desks by grouped tables, in time led to a feeling among parents that this was not schooling as they knew it.

Meanwhile, if taking the nation comprehensive was not controversial enough for Crosland, he walked into a row of his own making within three months of taking office: he turned his attention to the future of more than 150 regional, area and other colleges, mainly technical, which had in a sense been left behind by the Robbins report. The Colleges of Advanced Technology were being developed into universities. But Robbins, in what Carswell has dubbed one of the 'rough edges' of his report, had barely discussed the role of the remaining local authority colleges other than to assume they would award degrees and that some of them, in time, would aspire to university status. This 'ladder from the technical college to paradise which Robbins had left leaning against the wall,' as Carswell put it, 'still disturbed the educational world'.[102] Crosland's response was to pull it away. In a speech at Woolwich whose tone and timing (though not its content) he was later to describe as 'an appalling blunder',[103] he pronounced that the technical colleges would remain separate, in 'the public sector' as opposed to 'the autonomous sector' of the universities. Thus was born Britain's binary system of higher education, a division that was to last for twenty years into the late 1980s when the thirty polytechnics eventually acquired university status, at least in name, and by which time universities had become appreciably less autonomous.

Crosland's reasoning was that vocational, professional and industrially-based courses required a separate sector with a separate tradition and outlook from the universities. If the best colleges were continually to aspire to move up into what he dubbed the 'university club', the residue would remain poor relations locked in an 'unhealthy rat race' to escape their openly inferior status. It was, anyway, 'desirable in itself that a substantial part of the higher education system should be under social control, directly responsible to social needs,' he declared; and, in a turn of phrase that he was later particularly to regret, the former Oxford economics don urged: 'let us move away from our snobbish, caste-ridden, hierarchical obsession with university status.'

Here was yet another attempt to establish a different set of values from the traditional liberal university ones – values more related to the needs of industry in institutions that would mix full-time degrees with part-time and lower-level courses. Given who its author was, however, and what he was doing to schools, there was easy irony to be had in this attempt to run two systems with 'parity of esteem'.

The speech came out, in Crosland's own words, 'in a manner calculated to infuriate almost everybody you can think of'.[104] He was attacked from the left by those who valued the sacred academic autonomy of the universities above the democratic control which Crosland implied that the local authority-run sector would allow. He was attacked by the universities, who smarted at his implication that because the technical colleges were 'responsive' and 'relevant' they were not. And he was attacked by others who simply suspected the policy was an attempt to get degrees on the cheap. In the Lords, Robbins rose to protest that Crosland had turned down his report's vision of a flexible, evolutionary and unitary system of higher education for one consisting of barriers and obstacles. He pointedly highlighted the 'supreme paradox' of a government 'pledged to abolish artificial hierarchy and invidious distinctions in the schools' becoming 'actively engaged in preventing the elimination of artificial hierarchies and invidious distinction in higher education'.[105] He was later to add 'I just can't understand what has happened . . . they are making the system more hierarchical than ever before.'[106]

Crosland never backed away from the policy, genuinely believing in the need for an education rooted in the tradition of the technical college rather than the universities. His critics argued that including technical and part-time training amid the university science and technology would have forced a change of character. Time was soon to reveal a distinct desire by the polytechnics to mimic the universities: charged with keeping their part-time and lower-level courses, they indulged in what critics dubbed 'academic drift', progressively favouring full-time degrees over the part-time and less academic qualifications that parts of industry felt were adequate to their purposes.

Politics as well as principle, however, had played their part in Crosland's decision. Most local authorities in 1965 were Labour controlled. Having in the nineteenth century helped create and sustain the redbrick universities only to see them evolve into autonomous institutions, they were now watching the same thing happen to the colleges of advanced technology. They were in no mood to lose their remaining grip on further and higher education. Thus the technical colleges, in John Carswell's phrase, were 'brigaded into polytechnics and sent over the top, rather like a last line of reserves, into the terrain into which the colleges of advanced technology had marched and disappeared into the mist'.[107]

Toby Weaver, the DES civil servant who was the policy's architect, believed it 'took courage, was revolutionary, and was right', but Susan Crosland concedes that her husband 'had to struggle for the intellectual cohesion' with which to defend it.[108] The thirty polytechnics that finally emerged from the Woolwich speech were often awkward amalgams: the South Bank in London, for example, merged the City of Westminster College of Commerce, the Borough Polytechnic, the Brixton School of Building, and the National College for Heating, Ventilation, Refrigeration and Fan Engineering. And while their students formed part of the numbers explosion of the 1960s and 1970s, parity of esteem for technical and technological education remained as elusive as ever.

In part this was due to a miscalculation by Robbins. Part of his massive university expansion had been predicated on a large growth in numbers of science and technology students who were seen as essential to economic growth. But neither Robbins nor anyone else had looked down into the schools to see what type of students they were producing. The answer came soon enough in a lack of suitably qualified applicants to fill what were often brand new university science complexes. Indeed, there was such a plethora of arts applicants that, almost unbelievably given what had been spent, it was actually proportionately harder to get a university arts place in 1969 than it had been in 1963: only 55 out of every 100 with the minimum two A-levels got through against 63 per 100 six years earlier.[109] All too willingly the emerging polytechnics – for whose costs the Treasury, in a remarkable oversight, had failed to provide an overall limit – took up the strain. They filled up with arts undergraduates, but struggled harder in turn than the universities to fill their technical places.

Despite such difficulties, at the end of the sixties and a quarter-century on from the Beveridge report, the welfare state's condition can only be described as one of mature flowering. The services it provided were bigger, better and more comprehensive than anything that had gone before. Despite high-rise, more people were better housed than ever before. Despite conflicts over individual policies, education had expanded enormously. Despite endless rows about money and a waiting list which remained stubbornly around 500,000 whatever attempts were made to blitz it, the health service remained as popular as ever with the public. It was treating more patients with better techniques in slowly improving hospitals surrounded by GPs who now felt they had a future. Social security had been both reorganised and expanded. Social services had come of age. Jobs were in general easy to get. If ever there was a golden age of the welfare state, this should have felt like it. There ought to have been a sweeping sense of confidence in, and within, the institutions that made it up. In practice, there was not.

CHAPTER 13

The Dawn of Doubt: Labour and Conservatives 1949–70

It must be recognised that a political party, especially in a two-party state, is immensely embracing and can include within its limits diametrically opposite opinion on almost all subjects except the one or two which happen to be the immediate ground of party conflict at the particular time.

Enoch Powell, 'Conservatives and the Social Services', Political Quarterly, 1953, vol.24, p. 157

The voters, now convinced that full employment, generous services and social stability can quite well be preserved, will certainly not relinquish them. Any Government which tampered seriously with the basic structure of the full-employment Welfare State would meet with a sharp reverse at the polls . . . It is this which explains the otherwise curious phenomenon that the Conservatives now fight elections largely on policies which twenty years ago were associated with the Left and repudiated by the Right.

Anthony Crosland, The Future of Socialism, 1956, p. 61

The pressures are such that they will always together be sufficient to make the standard of social services regarded as essential to a civilised community far more expensive than that community can afford . . . there is no foreseeable limit on the social services which the nation can reasonably require except the limit that the Government imposes.

Richard Crossman, Paying for the Social Services, 1969, pp. 9–10

F ROM 1945 TO 1970, despite the odd eddy, the tide of events in the welfare state flowed broadly all one way. The tide of ideas, however, contained many more counter-currents. Conflicting cultures still existed. They had been there all along. As early as 1949, when the Conservatives were struggling to establish a legitimacy as the guardians of the welfare state, *The Right Road for Britain* summarised the party's stance thus:

> The Social Services are no longer even in theory a form of poor relief. They are a co-operative system of mutual aid and self-help provided by the whole nation and designed to give all the basic minimum of security, of housing, of opportunity, of employment and of living standards below which our duty to one another forbids us to permit anyone to fall.[1]

That was a definition of which Beveridge would have approved. Many Labour politicians, however, wanted something that provided more than just a basic minimum. Labour, after all, had a much stronger egalitarian streak: the party saw health, council housing, education and perhaps most particularly the new benefits system as not merely providing minimum services for all but as contributing to a redistribution of income and wealth. The means to achieving that lay in much more than just the social services. The biggest engine for redistribution was full employment, and the ability of those in employment to negotiate themselves a larger share of the cake as a reward for their efforts.

Over the years practical politics was to limit the ambitions of both sides to carry their differences of emphasis to the point where they would have significant differences of outcome. Labour governments, however ambitious, could only afford to do so much, and felt they could only raise taxes so far if they were to be re-elected. Conservative politicians equally found there were votes in promising and delivering more than a basic minimum; and they were well aware that cuts could cost office. Despite this, in the realm of ideas the left developed arguments for a more egalitarian approach, while on the right the case for greater selectivism, in part to allow lower taxation, was maintained. The strains of such tunes are detectable even in the famous *One Nation* pamphlet of 1950. In time this text came to be a form of credo on the welfare state for the Conservative left. By the mid-1980s 'a *One Nation* Tory' had become code for a 'wet'. But at the time, despite in reality providing an overwhelming endorsement of much of then current practice, the pamphlet still insisted on 'fundamental' differences with Labour. 'Socialists would give the same benefits to everyone, whether or not the help is needed, and indeed whether or not the country's resources are adequate,' stated the authors, who ranged across the party from Edward Heath and Robert Carr through Iain Mcleod and on to Angus Maude and Enoch Powell. 'We believe that we must first help those in need. Socialists believe that the State should provide an average standard. We believe that it should provide a minimum standard above which people should be free to rise as far as their industry, their thrift, their ability or their genius will take them.'[2]

Despite its self-consciously Disraelian title, the pamphlet's tone, as Timothy Raison has noted, was 'less obviously One Nation-like than the tone of the older generation like Eden and Macmillan'. The strictures on the need only for a minimum were followed by a tirade against the social consequences of redistribution which the authors argued had already gone too far. Such aggressive rhetoric, however, disguised the fact that precious little was suggested by way of retrenchment, and the pamphlet displays sufficiently Janus-like qualities for both the new right of the 1980s and the traditional left of the Tory party to be able to claim it as part of their inheritance.

Indeed, its intended theme was perhaps spelt out more clearly in summary by Enoch Powell three years later than it had been in the pamphlet itself. One Nation, Powell said in 1953,

> argued that because the Labour government had sought in health, in insurance, in education, in housing to supply through the social services the average standard for all, it had thereby in practice failed to meet the requirements of those in greatest need. The health service, by attempting everything at once, had starved some of the most essential branches like dental health and mental treatment; by building council houses only, the nation had obtained fewer houses altogether; by endeavouring to eliminate differences of educational opportunity, the state was threatening the standards of the ablest; the changing age structure of the population had been too little regarded in the planning of national insurance. The machinery of the welfare state was not helping the weak by its repression of the opportunities and independence of the strong.[3]

In 1952, Macleod and Powell published Social Services: Needs and Means which bluntly stated that the question to be asked was not 'should a means test be applied to a social service' but 'why should any social service be provided without a means test?' The text, however, came to much less brutal conclusions than the question implied, even arguing that the means-test Labour had applied to existing NHS charges was too low.[4]

If One Nation defined a clear philosophical difference between the parties while producing little in the way of policy to express it, others did start to look for alternatives to Macmillan's middle way. In 1957 the Institute of Economic Affairs was founded, a body technically free of political affiliation but dedicated to promoting the free market. Starting off with one employee and a part-time director, Ralph Harris and Arthur Seldon launched what proved to be a twenty-year battle against the odds before anyone who really mattered started to listen. Keynesian economics was in full flood, 1958 being the year Macmillan preferred to lose his entire Treasury team rather than cut public spending and embrace the early monetarism of Peter Thorneycroft, his Chancellor. In such a climate the IEA's attachment to classical economics left it a voice in the wilderness, but in the fifties and sixties it was from the IEA as much as anywhere that proposals for radically different social policies emerged. Initially the institute concentrated on pensions and rents, the burning issues of the day; but by the early to mid-1960s it was promoting what were to be seminal ideas for the right for breaking up state provision through tax reliefs, a return to the market, and the introduction of vouchers. Through the sixties, the IEA's influence slowly began to grow.

Education vouchers had been given currency in 1955 by a then largely unknown Professor of Economics at Chicago called Milton Friedman.[5] The idea was picked up by the British economist Jack Wiseman, who told the 1958 meeting of the British Association for the Advancement of Science that rather than supply free schooling directly, the state should provide parents with vouchers to spend in competing schools. It was taken a step closer to the political mainstream a year later when Brendon Sewill, a leading member of the Conservative research department, advocated it in *Crossbow*, the journal of the Conservative Bow Group. Sewill also tentatively suggested that those who took out private health cover should be able to 'contract out' of the NHS.

By 1961 the IEA had published *Health Through Choice* by D. S. Lees, an economics lecturer at what was to become the University of Keele. He argued that medical care was a consumer good 'not markedly different' from others. Spending on the NHS had probably been lower than consumers themselves would have chosen precisely because politicians rather than the market made the decisions, he argued. His solution was for government to 'move away from taxation and free services to private insurance and fees'. Tax concessions would be allowed to those who could provide for themselves, means-tested assistance would be given to the 'dwindling minority' who could not.[6] By the mid-1960s the IEA was canvassing vouchers for both health and education.[7]

Such proposals remained, however, well away from the centre of the political millrace. When in 1958 the Conservative Political Centre sponsored a set of lectures on *The Future of the Welfare State*, Peter Goldman, the centre's director, opened with as fine a diatribe as any against the system's alleged universalism, linking that to the now well rehearsed argument that more could be done if there were greater selectivity. 'We squander public money on providing indiscriminate benefits and subsidies for citizens, many of whom do not need them and some of whom do not want them.' Meanwhile, he argued, 'slum homes . . . slum schools, slum hospitals and slum prisons reproach a modern community.'[8] What Goldman's paper lacked was any detailed proposal, let alone a worked-out plan, for making the system more selective. If this was true of the backroom boys, it was even truer of the politicians. In the same series of lectures neither Macleod, then Minister of Labour, nor Powell, recently resigned with Thorneycroft from the Treasury, had any radical prescription to offer. Neither did the One Nation Group in *The Responsible Society*, published by the Conservative Political Centre in 1959, despite its rhetorical approval of programmes to 'give most help where it is needed' in preference to 'a flat service'.

Instead, Macmillan, Butler and Macleod were offering the electorate the rhetoric of an 'opportunity state' to match and sustain the welfare state. As with many a political slogan, precisely what the 'opportunity state' meant in policy terms proved remarkably hard to define beyond tax cuts to improve incentives. In part it was no more than a political counter to the egalitarian stream that Tony Crosland had unleashed within the Labour Party with his book *The Future of Socialism*. Macleod rejected 'crass egalitarianism' in favour of opportunities, and defined the opportunity state as 'an equal opportunity for men to make themselves unequal'.[9]

All this was hardly revolutionary. In 1961, however, well away from the reaches of power, many of these ideas were brought together in a remarkable essay by Geoffrey Howe, a rising thirty-four-year-old barrister who was then the editor of *Crossbow*. In a pamphlet which foreshadowed much of the rhetoric of the Thatcher years and canvassed a batch of ideas that thirty years on remain staples of right-wing thinking, Margaret Thatcher's future Chancellor argued that 'Conservatives surely must strive for a large reduction, in the long run, of the public social services . . . Over the whole field of social policy our firm aim should be a reduction in the role of the State.'[10] Howe, who twenty years later would institute the biggest single cut in welfare spending of the post-1979 Tory years, was careful to argue the case that 'Conservatives are, of course –

or should be – quickly roused to anger or compassion by poverty or hardship which strikes them as intolerable in a civilised society. They should be as readily moved as any Socialist to look for reserves of wealth which can legitimately be tapped to abate the evil. But their approach should be pragmatic rather than emotional.' No Tory should be tempted by the idea of income equality, he argued; and given that redistribution can be pushed to the point where it produces economic evils, Conservatives should seek as non-progressive a tax structure as possible.

He went on to attack Enoch Powell for having appeared to accept the growing inevitability of universalism in *The Future of the Welfare State*. He also rebuked Sir Keith Joseph, a One Nation contributor to *The Responsible Society*. 'Few Conservatives,' Howe stated, 'would doubt that the social services for the most part are here to stay. But we should hesitate to agree with Sir Keith Joseph who, while seeking "scope for sensible men to provide additional protection or amenity for their families *on top of* the State provision", plainly expects the State to go on making the basic provision for all of us for ever.'

Conservatives, he said, believing in private property, 'surely must strive for a large reduction in the long run of the public social services. The State must, of course, accept the permanent responsibility of caring for those who cannot provide for themselves.' It must also take on new pioneering tasks as they arise. But 'even in a prosperous society necessary claims on public expenditure can only be met if the social services, as we have come to know them, are drastically refashioned, so that their claims are diminished. Over the whole field of social policy our firm aim should therefore be a reduction in the role of the State.' The problem, he argued, was essentially one of selection. 'Public opinion is instinctively affronted, for example, by the fact that family allowances – obviously too small for the lowest paid worker with a really large family – can find their way into the most prosperous professional home. Equally disturbing is the fact that retirement pensions . . . may be drawn by people with substantial private means.'

Howe went on to advocate an early and not very clearly worked out version of the tax credit or negative income tax which Labour was to attempt after 1964 and on which the Tories themselves were to work hard after 1970. While Labour was attracted to the idea because its promise of a minimum income appeared to get rid of the means-test by using PAYE codes, it appealed to Howe because, looked at the other way round, it made the means-test a 'central' and 'essential' instrument of policy: everyone would face the same test of means. The use of tax codes, he argued, would remove the stigma traditionally attached to means-testing while at the same time making possible more generous payments, because those who no longer needed them would no longer get them. 'The principal objection to the means test has always sprung from the fact that it has been so ruthlessly mean,' Howe argued.

To tie in with this scheme – and showing a fine disregard for the political consequences – Howe proposed cutting existing state pensions back to the level for which people had actuarially contributed. ('Seldon,' he noted, 'does not regard the political difficulties of doing this is as insuperable: Powell takes the opposite view', a judgement which clearly shows which of Seldon and Powell was the politician and just how far Howe still had to travel to become one.) Even more radically, Howe advocated vouchers for both health and education. Parents could then 'surrender the voucher in "payment" for the child's right to attend a State school; or use it in part payment of the fees at a private school'. On top of that the better off, judged by their tax codes, should make a part-payment towards state education (thus effectively means-testing it), while Howe even went on to argue that fees should again be charged for some grammar school places in order to assuage the anger of parents whose children of moderate ability failed the eleven-plus.

He went on to challenge the cost of school meals and milk (free school milk was removed from secondary schools by the 1964–70 Wilson government and then, memorably, from most primary schools by Mrs Thatcher when education minister) while arguing that housing subsidies 'should be directed at families rather than houses', a policy which was implemented tentatively from 1970 and with much more vigour in the 1980s. For health, Howe proposed that 'in essence people should be allowed to "contract out" of the Health Service.' Once 'effectively insured . . . against all the possible risks and costs of ill-health, they should . . . be entitled to receive from the state a reduction of their tax liability equivalent to the average cost per head of the service. This would give individuals more responsibility, make it easier for them to supplement the basic minimum standard of the health service, and substantially diminish the massive authority of the State.'

Overall, Howe concluded, 'A deliberate move must be made towards the creation of a "self-help" State in which the individual is more and more encouraged to provide for himself and his family. Conservatives who have proclaimed their objectives in this way have too often been busy sliding, if not marching, in the opposite direction.' Radical reform of the social services to provide lower tax levels and the resources to 'remodel our cities' was 'long overdue'.

Thus in fifteen pages in 1961, Howe summed up much of what was to become the radical right's agenda during the 1980s. At the time, however, what was most notable about the essay was how much it was the exception to the rule. Howe was not even an MP. The pamphlet failed to ignite any political storm or crusade. Outside his strictures over free school milk and housing subsidies, and apart from the failed attempts to merge tax and benefits in which both sides indulged, not one of his more radical prescriptions crept into any of the four Conservative manifestos between 1964 and 1974. Instead, in the area of the welfare state, and despite some rhetoric about concentrating help where it was most needed, those manifestos can fairly be characterised as an 'anything you can do I can do better' competition with Labour.

Howe's essay, none the less, reflected the growing sense of disillusion among some on the right just at a time when the welfare state also began to come under attack from the left. This did mark a real shift from the 1950s. In 1956, in *The Future of Socialism*, Tony Crosland argued that while more remained to be done a great deal had been achieved, and that Labour in 1945–51 had effectively dealt with primary poverty. This was not the isolated complacent view of a Gaitskellite on the party's centre-right. In 1959, in the wake of the Conservatives' third election victory, Barbara Castle, that year's conference chairman, admittedly in an aside, could tell the Labour Party that 'the poverty and unemployment which we came into existence to fight have been largely conquered.'[11]

By the mid-1960s such comfortable assumptions were being blown apart by the 'rediscovery' of poverty. As Keith Banting has recorded:

> The central figures [in this event] were Richard Titmuss, the Professor of Social Administration at the LSE and his protégés, Brian Abel-Smith and Peter Townsend. While a number of academics were working on poverty, it was these men who effectively forced the issue into political debate. They were convinced that the myths about the generosity of the welfare state had blinkered discussion of social policy, and in the late 1950s they set out to gather the evidence with which to challenge the comfortable assumptions of the day. Their research was explicitly political. They were setting out to reshape policy-makers' interpretation of their environment.[12]

The assumption that people were no longer poor (except for some of the elderly and disabled) was based in part on Seebohm Rowntree's 1950 study in York which, using his subsistence ('enough to live on') measure, concluded that poverty had been largely eliminated by the post-Beveridge reforms. Titmuss and his colleagues, however, believed that the definitions of subsistence were inevitably arbitrary and would in any case be overtaken by rising living standards. 'With rising standards of life, a belief in a subsistence minimum is a belief in ever increasing inequality and class distinction,' Abel-Smith argued in 1958.[13] Maintaining that the least well-off should at least share in rising living standards set the social scientists off in search of a relative measure of poverty. They found it in the benefits paid out in national assistance and supplementary benefit. Arguing that this was what governments gave to those judged to be in need, Abel-Smith and Townsend re-presented the supplementary benefit level as an 'official' poverty line. They further defined an income of supplementary benefit plus 40 per cent (140 per cent of supplementary benefit) as being 'on the margins of poverty', as that sum took in the additional payments made for special needs along with small amounts of income which claimants could receive without their benefit being cut. They then re-analysed family expenditure figures for 1954 and 1960.

The results when national assistance or supplementary benefit was taken as the poverty line were tolerably impressive.[14] The figures showed that almost one in twenty households were living at or below it. When the higher standard of 140 per cent of supplementary benefit was taken, the numbers ballooned. Fourteen per cent of the population or 7.5 million Britons were found to be living 'in poverty' or on its margins. Included among these, to no one's surprise, was a significant number of the elderly. The dynamite was that the figures included nearly 2.5 million children, and that half a million of these were in households where the man was in work, but was earning less than the family would have received if he had stayed out of work and on benefit. The poor family, and the poor working family, were about to be born as a political issue.

As Keith Banting has pointed out, this rediscovery of the poor was 'essentially a statistical concept'. It was certainly not the result of any uprising by those affected, nor the work of MPs or of any political party. 'The poor did not make themselves visible; they were discovered at the bottom of income tables by social scientists.'[15] And generating the figures was not enough: for anything to happen they had to be injected into the political arena. The vehicle proved to be the Child Poverty Action Group (CPAG). Abel-Smith and Townsend, of course, had not been alone in believing poverty still existed or in attempting to define and study it. Harriett Wilson, a criminologist and Quaker who had worked with low income families in Cardiff, had published one of a number of studies in the late 1950s and early 1960s which had begun to highlight financial hardship among unmarried mothers, large families and the elderly.[16] By 1962, at the annual conference of the British Sociological Association where Townsend presented early findings from his work, there was, she says, 'a mood of conspiratorial excitement' developing. 'We were producing empirical evidence of poverty, definitions of poverty and the links of poverty with health.'[17] When Harold Wilson's first Queen's Speech contained no increase in family allowances, Harriett Wilson and other members of the Quakers' social affairs committee called a meeting of social workers and others at Toynbee Hall in East London in March 1965 and asked Abel-Smith to address them and spell out his research findings which were just becoming available in full. The impact was such that the meeting promptly turned itself from a talking shop into an action group.

According to Frank Field, CPAG's second director, the group was so naïve that initially it believed that with a Labour Government 'all they had to do was tell Wilson what the problem was and it would all be solved by Christmas'.[18] It was to be almost a year before the group even bothered to open a bank account, and another year before it took covenanted donations.[19] In the best Fabian tradition, it initially attempted a little élite persuasion, sending to Douglas Houghton, the social services overlord in the Cabinet, a memo drafted by Tony Lynes, a former LSE academic who was to become the group's first secretary. No action materialised. So in December 1965, nine months after the Toynbee Hall meeting, CPAG went public. It fired off another memorandum, this time to the Prime Minister, bearing the signatures of an impressive list of academics, professionals and ex-civil servants. The memorandum was linked to the publication of Abel-Smith's and Townsend's research, under the title *The Poor and the Poorest*, and both were launched at a press conference timed for 23 December – a moment when, as Banting puts it, 'its emotional impact would be highest and competing news lowest'.[20] The resulting headlines – 'Poverty Plea to Wilson', the *Daily Express* declared – backed by graphic tales of verminous children and families unable even to afford soap, marked not only the start of the campaign for what became child benefit, but also the arrival of the modern single-issue pressure group in British politics.

A year later, on 1 December 1966, Shelter was born, five national bodies in the housing association movement combining to demand 'a rescue operation for homeless families in the "blackspot" cities of London, Birmingham, Liverpool and Glasgow'.[21] Days before Shelter's launch *Cathy Come Home*, Jeremy Sandford's and Ken Loach's Wednesday Play on BBC Television, charted the lurch down into homelessness of an ordinary family, one that in the *Daily Telegraph*'s summary at the time 'began married life full of hope . . . and ended it separated from their children as casualties of the welfare state'. The screening was, according to Des Wilson, Shelter's first director, 'coincidental. We didn't know it was coming. Indeed I was working late that night and didn't see the film until long after Shelter was launched.'[22] The impact, however, was devastating. It gave Shelter a start it could not have dreamt of as the organisation picked up the government's own White Paper of 1965 to throw back into the government's face the fact that 'three million families in Britain today still live either in slums, near slums, or in grossly overcrowded conditions.' Shelter rode on the back of CPAG's continuing campaign on family poverty by concentrating its appeal on children. Posters featuring them told the public, 'It's not their fault that a generation of children grow up in misery.'

Suddenly a generation of social campaigners who would soon litter the pages of newspapers with acronyms and names such as CHAR, Gingerbread, SHAC and the Low Pay Unit woke up to the fact that access to the media, contacts with Parliament and a single issue to fight for could lead to change. By July 1967 the Disablement Income Group was holding its first national rally seeking a 'pension' for the 'civilian' disabled – those disabled neither by war nor by industrial injury but by accident or from birth, with more of the latter surviving into childhood and adult life as medicine advanced. To give the rally impact, DIG's formidable founder and secretary Megan Du Boisson, a forty-four-year-old Godalming housewife, wheelchair-bound from multiple sclerosis but 'chic, smiling and gay in a pink dress', had assembled 200 disabled people in Whitehall, drawn from Penzance to the Outer Hebrides and including a woman with no legs from Blackpool and two men in iron lungs.[23] Harold Wilson was not at Number 10 to receive their petition, but the disabled were suddenly recognised as claimants on the benefit system in their own right.

Each of these campaigns, however, while generating a mix of optimism and outrage, only served to highlight apparent inadequacies in the welfare state at a time when strains on it seemed to be increasing in all directions. In 1969, Dick Crossman, not long arrived at the Department of Health and Social Security, found an 83,000-word report on cruelty and cover-up at the Ely mental hospital in Cardiff on his desk. Crossman, like Powell and Robinson before him, was horrified at the state of the long-stay mental hospitals. Tam Dalyell, his Parliamentary Private Secretary, recalled him returning stunned from a visit to Friern Barnet hospital. 'I never saw Crossman so subdued or shaken by the stench and the soaking walls and the consequent treatment of the helpless, incontinent and usually relationless patients,' Dalyell records. 'In his car on the way back to the

Elephant and Castle, he repeated: "I am responsible for the worst kind of Dickensian, Victorian loony bin." From that moment on, the issue of the mentally ill was at the top of his mental and ministerial in-tray.'[24]

Allegations of mistreatment in the isolated, introverted and understaffed environments of long-stay hospitals had been circulating for years, most powerfully in 1967 in *Sans Everything*, an undoubtedly true but ultimately unprovable account by nurses and social workers of mistreatment in geriatric hospitals. The Ely report, however, did contain proof. The inquiry had been headed by Geoffrey Howe, once again wearing his barrister's wig after entering Parliament in 1964 only to lose his seat in 1966. His report not only substantiated allegations first published in the *News of the World* but went beyond them. Howe had already had to out-manoeuvre an attempt by the Welsh health authorities to edit and prune the report and he was determined it should see the light of day.[25] So was Crossman. He told the department the NHS was facing 'a first-rate crisis' – noting, in tones markedly different from the ministerial view of the NHS in the 1990s, that 'we as a Ministry are responsible for our agents down there in the Health Service'.[26] Against strong departmental resistance,[27] he not only published the report in full but insisted that a Hospital Advisory Service be set up to visit the long-stay institutions, not just for the mentally ill but for the mentally handicapped and the elderly. In all but name, the HAS was an independent inspectorate: it was a measure of the influence of the medical profession that the word 'advisory' was used. Doctors, it was felt, could not be seen to be being 'inspected'. Crossman's determination both to publish in full and to create the HAS was 'perhaps the outstanding example of Dick's zeal for open government being carried forward to practical, reforming effect,' Anthony Howard, his biographer, has judged;[28] and although critics would argue that the HAS's impact over the years proved limited, the mentally ill were put on the political map in a way not even Powell's 'water-towers' speech had managed. Needless to say, however, Ely did little for the reputation of the NHS, and Crossman's fear at the time that further inquiries would reveal 'equally scandalous things'[29] proved depressingly correct. A decade-long catalogue of further horrors and inquiries was to follow on the long-stay wards of Farleigh, Whittingham, Napsbury, South Ockenden, St Augustine's and Normansfield, the last of which in 1978 'seemed to encapsulate all the failings' of the 1974 NHS reorganisation yet to come, with its introduction of consensus management.[30]

If Ely turned the spotlight on to the back wards of the NHS, the acute side was experiencing the paradox of what Rudolf Klein has dubbed 'growing scarcity in an era of growth'.[31] After the needless panics of the early 1950s, real terms spending on the NHS had begun to rise steadily from the late 1950s on – by almost 13 per cent between 1950 and 1958, but by double that in the following decade. Wages, however, make up around 70 per cent of NHS costs, and in the 1950s doctors, nurses, and other NHS staff did relatively badly compared to others in the economy; in a sense, therefore, the NHS was getting more for its money than the government deserved. From 1958 on this trend reversed: the greater increase in funding was in fact buying less than the figures seemed to indicate.

In addition, the service was facing both 'technological push' and 'demographic pull'.[32] The therapeutic revolution which had allowed the rundown of the mental hospitals to begin was being felt in almost all areas of medicine. By the later 1960s two health economists could estimate that 'ninety per cent of today's medicines were totally unknown in 1938, fifty per cent unknown only five or six years ago'.[33] These new drugs – from the Valium that became known as 'mother's little helper' and the contraceptive pill, to more powerful antibiotics and treatments for asthma – all achieved more, but also cost more than the linctuses and potions that they replaced. The pharmacological revolution was matched by a technological one. The first kidney transplant was performed in 1950. Kidney dialysis, heart-lung machines and other aspects of intensive care were developed. On 3 May 1968 the first liver transplant in Britain went by barely noticed because it coincided with one of those moments when science fiction became scientific fact and Frederick West, aged 45, received Britain's first heart transplant, surviving for forty-seven days. In the fevered atmosphere of post-devaluation Britain, Donald Ross and the rest of the surgical team were cajoled by the press into waving 'I'm backing Britain' union flags at the post-operation press conference.

Much of this pharmaceutical and technological advance was good news for patients, although some of it, such as the use of beating-heart donors, caused much ethical debate. All of it contributed to an emerging sense in Klein's phrase 'of the NHS at the mercy of the technological imperative'. Combined with this unease was, as ever, awareness of the ageing population. From just under seven million in 1951, the numbers past retirement had risen to 7.7 million by 1961. By 1971 they were to reach more than 9 million, with the proportion of very elderly, both those over 75 and over 85 who made the greatest demands on the service, also rising. The idea entered currency that the NHS was a bottomless pit into which any amount of money could be poured without satisfying the demand for health care. As much as anyone it was Enoch Powell who popularised this idea, when in 1966 he spoke of the 'infinity of demand' in his immensely influential book *Medicine and Politics*. The idea that there was a definable amount of care which was 'needed' and which, once met, would result in no more being demanded was, he said, 'absurd'.

> Every advance in medical science creates new needs that did not exist until the means of meeting them came into existence . . . For every heart-lung machine or artificial kidney in operation there must be many times that number of cases to which the treatment would be applicable . . . then again, there is virtually no limit to the amount of medical care an individual is capable of absorbing. The moment it was established that the cervical smear test enabled incipient or prospective cancer to be diagnosed, this check-up became a "need" . . . [Further] not only is the range of treatable conditions huge and rapidly growing. There is also a vast range of quality in the treatment of those conditions [with] hardly a type of condition from the most trivial to the gravest which is not susceptible of alternative treatments under conditions affording a wide range of skill, care, comfort, privacy, efficiency and so on . . . Finally there is the multiplier effect of successful medical treatment. Improvement in expectation of survival results in lives that demand further medical care. The lower, medically speaking, the quality of the lives preserved by advancing science, the more intense are the demands they continue to make. In short, the appetite for medical treatment *vient en mangeant*.[34]

This was the very antithesis of some early views of the National Health Service. Beveridge had believed an NHS would raise the general level of health and fitness of the nation and would therefore increase national prosperity through a reduction of sickness absence that would in turn raise productivity. A national health service could therefore broadly pay for itself – or at least not be subject to endlessly rising costs. In his 1942 report, he argued that 'there will actually be some development of the service, and as a consequence of this development a reduction in the number of cases requiring it' – a view which led him to assume that the NHS would cost the same £175m in 1965 as he tentatively assumed it would cost in 1945, the year he expected it to start.[35] Powell's argument that technological advance is going to bankrupt the health service is in fact contestable. Medical advance can save money as well as cost it, though that was perhaps less clear in the 1960s than today. The only well-documented examples then were poliomyelitis, virtually eliminated by the development of a vaccine, and tuberculosis, which had largely disappeared thanks to a combination of improved living conditions and new drugs. Huge sums which had been spent in the 1940s and 1950s on TB sanatoriums and fleets of mobile X-ray vans were now being saved. Equally, better anaesthesia was not only saving lives, it was reducing complications. The 1967 Abortion Act and the improved techniques which followed not only saved fifty lives a year from illegal abortions but avoided many more admissions for treatment of complications. In more recent times, new drugs for treating ulcers, epilepsy and hypertension have released hundreds of beds for other uses, producing savings far greater than the prescription costs. Calculations that new types of scanner, or some other new technique, drug or test, will bankrupt the NHS ignore a history of falling real terms costs for each and all of these as they become more widely used. It is true that as countries become wealthier they tend to spend a higher share of GNP on health, but that is not the same as arguing that health care costs will beggar the nation. Of course, theoretically a sufficiently hypochondriacal nation could spend its whole wealth on health care; it could equally do so on education, yet no one argues that education is a bottomless pit.

The sense that the NHS and other social services were under strain was enhanced by the repeated financial crises faced by the Wilson government. In the decade from 1959, state spending on housing, education, health, and social security rose by 137 per cent. The increase begun under the Tories after their third successive election victory and if anything accelerated once Labour was in power. But the measures which accompanied the 1964 balance of payments crisis, the sterling crises of 1965 and 1966, and most of all devaluation in late 1967 combined to provide an impression of cuts, or at the very least of grand plans repeatedly cut back, and consequently disappointed expectations. Roy Jenkins's 1968 Budget saw prescription charges reintroduced, the housing programme heavily cut and the postponement for four years of the raising of the school leaving age. These crises produced the first ministerial resignations over welfare state issues since Wilson himself had quit alongside Bevan in 1950 over NHS charges. The first came in July 1967, on the day BBC2 launched colour television in Britain with a transmisson from Wimbledon, as an emotional Peggy Herbison resigned as Minister of Social Security over deep divisions in Cabinet on how to tackle the family poverty which CPAG's campaign had publicised.[36] And in January 1968, Lord Longford, Labour's leader in the Lords, resigned over the failure to raise the school leaving age. A 'heartbreak' decision, it only got through Cabinet by one vote when Patrick

Gordon-Walker, the new Secretary of State for Education, accepted it to the contempt of Crosland, his immediate predecessor, who voted against[37] and the disdain of Crossman, who voted for while damning Gordon-Walker for 'pathetic weakness'.[38]

There were other disappointments for the left. In 1965, Crosland fulfilled a manifesto pledge by appointing a Public Schools Commission under Sir John Newsom to advise on the best way of integrating public schools into the state system in the light of the comprehensive policy. It worked long and hard but, in the words of Harry Judge, one of the commission's members, 'in the event . . . nothing was, or could be, done.'[39] The independent sector had shrunk from 9 per cent of the secondary school population in 1947 to 5.5 per cent twenty years later. But the public schools had adapted well and were, if anything more, not less, entrenched. They accounted for only 1.4 per cent of secondary school pupils, but their higher staying-on rates ensured that they had 12 per cent of seventeen-year-old boys – and thus of potential A-level candidates. Some commissioners, in Harry Judge's words, 'became unclear whether the public schools should be abolished because they were very good or very bad', and as work proceeded the 'very real' problem of the public schools proved 'insoluble'. 'It would have been wrong to propose that subsidized admission to such schools should be offered to very bright pupils, at the same time that comprehension was being commended (sometimes forcefully so) to grammar schools. It would have been wrong to propose abolition, and in any case no member of the Commission in fact believed it should be illegal for a parent to spend money on a child's education. History, in the shape of the tardiness of the public authorities in setting up a proper system of secondary schooling, was responsible for "the public schools problem".'[40] The commission's compromise of drawing a limited number of boarding schools into a partnership with the state won no friends and went nowhere.

Even when the government did act, there was a price. In answer to CPAG's campaign, Labour finally raised family allowances. That happened, however, only after a protracted and agonised battle involving the Treasury, the Inland Revenue and the Ministry of Social Security, which at one point produced 'one of the bitterest Cabinets I have ever attended' according to Crossman.[41]

The choice had been threefold: raising family allowances; introducing what in 1977 became child benefit by combining into a single payment family allowance and the money that could be saved by abolishing child tax allowances; or introducing a new means-tested benefit. Variations of the last (despite this being a Labour Government) were worked up in detail in both the Cabinet Office where Douglas Houghton was based[42] and in the Ministry of Social Security.[43] The leading candidate was a benefit for working families which Sir Keith Joseph finally introduced as Family Income Supplement but which in Labour's day was known within the ministry as 'Mr Abbot's Alternative' after the civil servant who was its staunchest advocate.[44] In Cabinet a range of ministers headed by James Callaghan, the Chancellor, firmly backed this means-tested approach rather than an increase in family allowances. At one crucial meeting in February 1968, the Cabinet reportedly divided 13:11 over whether to raise family allowances or to take the means-tested route.[45]

The option that became child benefit – abolishing child tax allowances and providing a single, enhanced cash payment for all children, in place of family allowances which went only to second and subsequent children – proved ten years ahead of its time. It would have helped poor families more than family allowances. Its net effect on government finances, as its advocates claimed, might have been broadly neutral.[46] But it would have appeared to raise taxes and increase public spending by around £600 million at a time when the government's standing with both bankers and taxpayers was already in jeopardy. In the end, Labour went for a highly ingenious but profoundly unsatisfactory compromise, deciding to raise family allowances. These were none too popular. Unlike other benefits, no party in twenty-five years had promised at election time to raise them and no government had increased them for a decade. The electorate, which was reported to believe that they went on nothing better than bingo and booze,[47] was beginning to prefer the thought of tax cuts to higher social security spending. None the less, family allowances did reach the most politically sensitive group that Abel-Smith and Townsend had identified – the working poor. Labour thus opted to increase them, but by too little to have a decisive impact on the problem. To reduce the cost it decided to 'claw back' the extra cash from middle income families by reducing their child tax allowance pro rata. The result proved an explosive cocktail: the husband's take-home pay went down while the wife's family allowance went up. Irate husbands failed to understand what was going on, not least because the change was made in four stages over eighteen months throughout which the tax and family allowance increases ran out of step. For that confusion Labour paid heavily in a string of by-elections in 1968, and as late as the general election in 1970, George Brown, the deputy Labour leader, found that 'the most unpopular thing the Labour government ever did was to arrange to "claw back" family allowances from the better off.'[48]

The claw-back was unpopular because it meant higher taxes at a time when the post-war growth in public spending, not just on the welfare state but on roads, defence, agriculture, nationalised industries and virtually everything else, had brought tax thresholds sharply downward, a trend Wilson's government had accentuated by favouring public expenditure over private in the earlier of its financial crises. As a result, while in 1949 a married man with two children had to earn three-quarters of average earnings to pay any income tax, by the late 1960s such a family was paying tax at just under half average earnings. For manual workers the picture was even bleaker. In the late 1940s an unskilled man with two children had to earn more than average pay in order to pay any direct tax at all. By the late 1960s the taxman was taking his share at little more than half the average manual wage. When the Beatles in 'Taxman' sang: 'Should 5 per cent appear too small (Taxman Mister Wilson) / Be thankful I don't take it all (Taxman Mister Heath)' they struck a chord with more than just the super-rich. As Crossman noted after a constituency meeting in January 1968: 'The trade unionists want to see us spending less on social services so there will be more for wage packets.'[49] The demand was for 'more half crowns jingling around in the pockets'. Opinion poll support for higher spending on social services plummeted from 77 per cent in 1964 to 43 per cent by 1969.[50]

With the less well off increasingly paying directly towards services, greater questioning of what was being delivered was inevitable. And as Deacon and Bradshaw have noted: 'In trying to dispel what they saw as the myths surrounding the welfare state, Titmuss and his colleagues also strengthened the hand of those who sought its abolition.' The proposition rehearsed by the One Nation group in the 1950s – that less money might be better spent if it was concentrated on those who really needed it – entered the political debate in a serious way for the first time since 1945.

It did so partly because on the Conservative side the rhetoric of a shift towards greater selectivity moved from papers like Howe's to conference platforms and on into the 1966 manifesto, with the issue widely discussed in the campaign. That promised 'an entirely new social security strategy designed to concentrate better care and biggest benefits on those most in need'. At Tory party conferences, Howe and others demanded 'radically new', if undefined, solutions for the social services and a willing acceptance of means-testing. Heath himself talked of the need for 'a new Beveridge' and in the foreword to the 1966 manifesto said: 'I want to see our social services recognise the overriding claims of those in most need.'

All this was seized on by Wilson and Crossman to accuse the Tories of planning to 'dismantle' the welfare state, a charge Heath dimissed as 'a pack of lies'.[51] He could do so with some conviction, for none of these calls for more selectivity was matched by much in the way of policies to take anything away from anyone, apart from opposition to Crossman's grand pension plan. Concrete proposals were chiefly limited to restoring prescription charges to fund hospital building (the choice Labour itself was shortly to make), and concentrating council house subsidies less on buildings and more on people. That would indeed mean higher rents for some, but there was a growing recognition that people earning good money were enjoying artificially low rents as a result of council house subsidies while the less well off could find themselves struggling to pay the same rent.[52] Heath's own view was clear that the purpose of greater selectivity was to allow modernisation of the welfare state, not its abolition.

But the case for selectivity also took root among some in Labour's ranks. In 1967, Douglas Houghton, having left his Cabinet post as social services overlord, wrote a pamphlet for the Institute of Economic Affairs in which he argued that there was 'a noticeable shift in public opinion towards bringing improved benefits to those most in need: away from "universalism" towards "selectivity".'[53] Universalism, he declared, was 'on the defensive', although he found himself as strapped as the One Nation group had been in the 1950s for detailed ideas about how the change might be achieved, let alone politically acceptable ones. The pamphlet pushed around the idea of using PAYE codes to levy charges for the NHS according to income – 'from each according to his ability', as Houghton put it, or, more brutally 'the more you earn the more you pay'. Even more tentatively he discussed vouchers. But the mere fact that this was a senior Labour politician writing for the Institute of Economic Affairs was significant. Houghton's interest in means-testing and selectivity dated back at least five years.[54] But his was no isolated aberration. As Banting has noted, 'the traditional battle-lines between means-tested and universal benefits were being broken down in the 1960s by the growing interest in solutions involving the tax system; as Crossman admitted, Labour's proposed Income Guarantee for pensioners was a means-tested benefit, albeit of a new variety.'[55] Patrick Gordon-Walker, Houghton's successor, said the integration of taxes and benefits would mean 'we can make our social services selective without any overt, or invidious income test.'[56] Callaghan as Chancellor said there need be 'no particular shame' about incomes testing if it was done without humiliation and without essential services being denied,[57] and both Ray Gunter, the Minister of Labour, and Brian Walden, the Labour back-bencher who later became a television interviewer, argued publicly for greater selectivity, Walden declaring that 'universalism in the social services must die'.[58] David Owen, somewhat nervously, canvassed hospital meal charges and earlier removal of benefit from long-term hospital patients as his contribution to the discussion.[59]

The debate, at least initially, was in the main unsophisticated. It took until the turn of the decade to get much beyond the most elementary labels of universality *v* selectivity.[60] Labour, however, was under sufficient pressure on the issue for the new Chancellor Roy Jenkins, introducing the claw-back on the family allowance, to describe it as 'civilised selectivity',[61] while Crossman dubbed it 'a new social service which is selective without the disadvantage of a means test'.[62] Stories about social security 'scroungers' began to receive a more regular airing, to the point where in 1968 the government introduced a 'four week' rule which constrained benefit for the single, fit unskilled man under forty-five. Rent and rate rebates, the first a function of cuts in council house subsidies which in practice made them more selective, the second necessitated by the remorseless rise in local government expenditure, both arrived under the Wilson government, although rent rebates were locally run, not yet a national scheme. Neither could have been a 'universal' benefit, specifically because both were aimed at helping the less well-off as alternatives to more generous overall subsidies for rent and rates. But the fact that both were means-tested marked a drift by Labour down the road to selection.[63] Equally, in 1967, Labour empowered local authorities to provide family planning but left it to their discretion whether they did so and whether supplies were free. Faced by local paper headlines of 'Sex on the Rates', many, at least initially, provided only a means-tested service 'for the sick and needy'.[64] Even measures frankly aimed at increasing equality of opportunity, such as option mortgages for the less well-off and extra cash for deprived inner city schools through the educational priority areas, could be seen from one end of the telescope as moves towards selectivity. Prescription charges returned, and pressure on NHS spending was such that even Crossman, a Labour Secretary of State, asked his department to work out how much a hospital boarding charge or a charge for visiting the GP would bring in before 'dismissing [them] out of hand'.[65]

In practice, the boundaries of what was done and how it was delivered barely shifted. That was not the impression of events, however, so that by the later 1960s arguments which have remained at the core of the debate about the welfare state – its affordability and its effects – had crystallised. The welfare state, in a sense, was enjoying the first of the great moral panics about its very existence. Few if any of the arguments were new, but a combination of disappointing economic growth, rising demographic and technological pressures, resistance to increasing personal taxation, and rapidly rising expenditure brought them sharply into focus.

The pressures are well reflected in the very dog days of the decade when Crossman in December 1969 delivered a Herbert Morrison lecture entitled *Paying for the Social Services*. In it he spelt out the rise in welfare state spending since the late 1950s. 'If you translate these figures into graphs and extrapolate the curve the prospects before us are truly terrifying,' he declared. He pointed to the growing numbers of elderly, a growth matched at the time by 'a youth explosion' that was stuffing primary schools with children and universities with undergraduates. 'With this increase in population . . . the cost of social services must rise automatically if we are not to see a reduction of standards. We have to run extremely fast in order to stand still.' In addition, there was the 'revolution of expectations' – in education, in housing and in living standards. In just the four years between 1964 and 1968, Crossman recorded, the percentage of households with washing machines had risen from 54 to 63 per cent, with refrigerators from 35 to 55 per cent, with cars from 38 to 49 per cent, with central heating from 13 to 23 per cent. In health, kidney dialysis had become possible, but a £1 million investment in dialysis machines had already produced a £1.5 million annual bill for running them.

None of this was new: Bevan had told the Labour Party conference in 1949 that 'it is the same story . . . in every social service. There is greater demand . . . because the standards of the working class population are higher than ever they were before.'[66] The Phillips Committee in 1954 had worried about the growing numbers of elderly and had recommended that women's pension age be raised to match men's at 65. Medical technology had been expanding since before the war. What was new was the sense of being on a treadmill, and that it was now undeniable that choices had to be made. Crossman declared that 'as many Conservatives as socialists' believed that if only the economy was growing fast enough, all could be afforded. There would then 'not be any need for the organised rationing of priorities which is now forced upon us': that, he said, was 'complete delusion'. The reality was that demography, technology and rising expectations 'will always together be sufficient to make the standard of social services regarded as essential to a civilised community far more expensive than that community can afford . . . there is no foreseeable limit on the social services which the nation can reasonably require except the limit that the Government imposes.'[67]

To prove that this was not just a politicians' debating point, a few months after Crossman's lecture the Department of Health appointed its first two economists, largely because of worries about the impact of technology on health care costs.[68]

Outside mainstream party politics, other arguments were causing unease as various arms of the welfare state reached their age of majority. If there were pressures from the right to roll the whole thing back, there were pressures from the left, too. The massive expansion in universities had seen a growth in Marxist analysis of the welfare state which saw its institutions and payments as being an extension of social control by capitalism, not a genuine liberation of the people, a theory that infected some parts of the Labour Party. Critics did not have to be Marxists, however, to question whether the welfare state in its broadest sense was failing. When poverty was found still to exist and Inland Revenue figures, somewhat misleadingly, showed relatively little redistribution of income and wealth since 1945,[69] those on the left started seeking a 'fundamental' redistribution of both, aided by a wealth tax. That, however, was on no Cabinet minister's agenda when falling tax thresholds and the introduction of the 'claw-back' were costing Labour votes.

Other forces were at play. Unemployment, the one giant undeniably slain since Beveridge's time, was crawling back to life. In January 1967 it passed the psychologically important 600,000 mark. Callaghan's 'steady as she goes' Budget in April, while it reduced the headline jobless total below 600,000, still left the rate running at well above 2 per cent. It mattered not that this was below Gaitskell's 3 per cent and a mere fifth of the figure that would be common in the 1980s: it was still a post-war record, and under a Labour Government. *The Times* declared Callaghan had broken with 'the full employment standard' in his Budget, which was prematurely judged to mark 'the end of the Keynesian era'.[70] By December 1969 unemployment had stood above half a million for twenty-nine continuous months against just eight months in total during the thirteen years of Tory 'misrule'.[71]

Meanwhile, in the summer of 1968 two friends had gone for a walk on Hampstead Heath. Both were English dons, editors of a small circulation but not uninfluential literary magazine called *Critical Survey*. They needed a price rise and were attempting to decide the subject for a bumper issue with which to accompany it. Brian Cox, who was to become the more famous and vilified of the two, had escaped life on the borders of the working class/lower middle class boundary of Grimsby via grammar school to Cambridge and the influence of F. R. Leavis. A first in English

Literature had led on to a university post at Hull and then at Manchester. Far more than most, C. B. Cox (as he then liked to be known) was someone whose views were shaped by his experience. In 1965 he had spent a year teaching at the University of California in Berkeley and had witnessed the great sit-in which proved the forerunner of the campus revolts which were to rock universities across the Western world in 1968. The Berkeley experience, its disruption and its slogans – including 'In Defence of Liberty, Extremism is no Vice' – deeply distressed a man whose painfully honest autobiography was later to reveal a complex, introspective and somewhat tortured soul.[72] In America, too, he had seen how neighbourhood schools could herd together the most disadvantaged and trap them in one location.

Cox was also influenced by a somewhat muscular Christianity brought on by a reading of C. S. Lewis's *Screwtape Letters*. He did not believe that children were naturally good. He had a distrust of IQ tests, the result of watching the 'blank despairing face of Audrey, a girl of some intelligence' who was condemned to secondary modern by the same eleven-plus examination which moved him on to grammar school, and by experience of IQ tests in the army during national service. In one, Cox was asked to define 'a heavenly place' beginning with the letters PAR. Too cleverly as it turned out, he thought of Parnassus rather than Paradise, the answer the examiner was looking for. Through *Critical Quarterly*, *Critical Survey* and summer school teaching he saw himself as pioneering new methods for teaching English to sixth formers. His own children had attended a new and 'progressive' primary school in Hull ('where', he explained, 'children wander around aimlessly all day choosing to do what ever takes their fancy')[73] and had been unhappy. The outcome was someone who at one and the same time was opposed to the eleven-plus, but in favour of selection; for experimental teaching methods, but against progressive primary schools; for equal opportunity for the working class, but doubtful that comprehensives delivered it; in all, a man profoundly suspicious of egalitarianism, yet who saw himself as coming from the liberal left.

To some extent, Cox merely represented some of the confusions of his times. The man who would shortly be dubbed 'the Enoch Powell of education', at a time when Powell was in his 'rivers of blood' phase, saw himself as a Gaitskellite. He not only voted Labour, in 1966 he had canvassed for Labour in Hull. His companion on the Hampstead Heath walk was A. E. Dyson, a close friend from Cambridge days whose background and career (Dyson was by then an English don at Bangor) closely matched Cox's. In the 1950s both had been Aldermaston-marching members of

CND, before they resigned when the Committee of 100 went in for civil disobedience. Tony Dyson too voted Labour and in the 1950s had founded the Homosexual Reform Committee, a group whose pressure had contributed to the 1966 legislation decriminalising homosexuality. Perhaps critically, both Cox and Dyson were forty, a whole decade past the cut-off point for the students of a generation chanting Jerry Rubin's 'yippie' slogan, 'Don't trust anybody over thirty' one first uttered at Berkeley in 1964 during Cox's stay there.[74]

At the time of their walk, student unrest was burgeoning at Essex, Sussex, Bristol and elsewhere. At the LSE a porter with a weak heart died barring the road to the student insurrectionists who managed for a time to close the school down. Cox and Dyson chose education as the subject of their magazine special issue. The first *Black Paper* – a joke of Dyson's against government White Papers – was conceived.

It started out chiefly as an assault on student revolt. It ended up detonating the debate over comprehensive schools and progressive teaching methods. Initially all the articles were on universities and the threat to academic standards and freedom: only late in the day was a circular sent out soliciting contributions on schools. The item which perhaps caused the biggest furore, by Miss C. M. Johnson, head of Prendergast Grammar School, was almost judged not worth printing. 'Her arguments seemed just pleasant, obvious common sense,' Cox recalled. 'We only decided to publish because the pamphlet was so obviously thin in its coverage of progressive education.'[75] Miss Johnson's complaint was that of the industrialist and of the *Daily Mail* leader page throughout history: educational standards were falling.

Reading the first *Black Paper* now (there were three by 1971, five in all), it is a little hard to conjure from it quite the smell of brimstone and the sense of the devil riding forth which its critics soon believed it to embody. It is a collection of disparate essays, not a single coherent piece. Much of its tone is élitist and profoundly anti-egalitarian. In places the language is alarming as it talks of 'the progressive collapse of education', of 'anarchy becoming fashionable' and of 'the grammar school concepts of discipline and work' being 'treated with contempt'. Elsewhere there are attempts at balance, welcoming the new but arguing it should not go too far. In yet other contributions reasoned argument is mixed with polemic, assertion and opinion, all amid a distinct lack of evidence. In the higher education section there was a powerful dose of 'I told you so' from Kingsley Amis, who recast his 1960 aphorism on university expansion that 'more will mean worse' into 'more has meant worse'. In some contributions there is the smell of fear as dons gaze uncomprehending at the sight of youth getting out of hand, something youth has managed from the dawn of time. In others there appears genuine alarm that the recently formed National Union of School Students might actually end up running the schools. And there is some heavy-handed, even sneering humour. 'Ask the young: they always know', a joke proverb declares. Another reads, 'At primary school children are taught nothing; at secondary school they discuss what they have been taught.'

In essence the *Black Papers* were a scream of pain against a growing anti-examination, pro-egalitarian culture in education, of dismay at the apparent destruction of authority in universities and secondary schools. This decline, in turn, was blamed on progressive education and comprehensives. In fact the Plowden report on primary schools was only eighteen months old when Cox and Dyson went for their walk, so those in universities could not possibly have been subjected in any numbers to the extremes of progressive education for which Plowden was blamed. The students who were revolting were overwhelmingly the products of the streamed and selective schooling of the late 1950s and early to mid-1960s which the *Black Paper* authors favoured. Equally relevant was the fact that the proportion of university students from comprehensives was as yet still tiny (in 1966 a mere 11 per cent). Something more than just the British education system was involved; the student protest movement was bigger, stronger and decidedly nastier elsewhere – in France in May 1968 it had for a moment appeared poised to bring down President De Gaulle.

None the less, the first *Black Paper* resonated among parents who were becoming unable to recognise the classrooms of their youth and at a time when phalanxes of not always well-prepared young teachers were pouring into primary schools from teacher training colleges into which 20 per cent more students had been squeezed to deal with the 1960s baby-boom. Worries about the standards of teacher training persisted to the point where the Tories promised an inquiry which they delivered once back in government.

This mélange was given, not entirely intentionally, a strongly political character by the opening essay. It was an assault on egalitarianism by Angus Maude, whom Heath had sacked from his shadow Cabinet in 1966 and who had become an increasingly strident critic of Heath's lack of a (right-wing) political philosophy. Somewhat naïvely, Cox and Dyson both insisted that they had 'considered their campaign as educational rather than political'[76] – a proposition rendered wholly untenable when Ted Short, now the Secretary of State for Education, joined the fray.

Initial reaction to the *The Fight for Education*, the first *Black Paper*, varied from mild interest and approval to a spread in *The Observer* headlined 'Education: The Backlash Starts'. The publication was ignored by the *Daily Mail* which was later to be an outspoken proponent of *Black Paper* views. It was Ted Short's hyperbole to the National Union of Teachers conference in Douglas on the Isle of Man a month after publication which really made its name: he condemned its arrival as 'one of the blackest days for education in the past 100 years'. Its 'backlash' was provoking 'the crisis of the century'. Cynics at the time suggested that Short's outburst (which won him a standing ovation) was motivated as much by the need for diversionary tactics to escape delegates' anger over pay as by genuine alarm at Cox and Dyson's work. Certainly his assault provided the *Black Paper* with a prominence it would otherwise never have enjoyed, propelling coverage from a single column buried on page ten of *The Times* when it first came out to a spread across the front.[77] His attack also prompted Rhodes Boyson, a mutton-chop-whiskered former Labour councillor in Lancashire and head of the new and highly rated Highbury Grove boys' comprehensive school in north London, to rush out and buy a copy. He wrote immediately to Cox in Manchester and was soon on a train to see him to ask 'what can I do?'[78] At the time Boyson was nearing the end of a journey from populist socialism to populist conservatism, the causes of which included Labour's determination to make comprehensives compulsory ahead of evidence that they produced better overall results than the tripartite system, and his view that the Labour-controlled Inner London Education Authority was denying his school its fair share of the top ability groups. The future Tory education minister was to edit later *Black Papers* and proved one of their greatest publicists both within and outside the Conservative Party. But if Boyson was elated, others shared Short's view, though in less extreme language. Timothy Raison, the future Tory MP and Home Office Minister who as editor of *New Society* had been a member of the Plowden committee, recorded that 'it was not only Short who thought it the worst thing to have hit education for a long time.'[79]

What the *Black Papers* did demonstrate, after the heady expansionism of the 1960s, was that Labour's determination to achieve entirely comprehensive education had broken a form of *laissez-faire* post-war educational consensus. Secondary organisation was the rock on which it foundered.[80] Many Conservatives under Boyle had been more than content to let comprehensives evolve: Labour, by pressing for them, brought the issue to a head. Before the *Black Papers* there had been repeated clashes between the platform and floor at Conservative Party conferences over Boyle's broad support for comprehensive schools. The demand that they should be halted and the grammar schools saved led in 1967 – the very year Heath had formally endorsed Boyle's approach – to the right-wing critics forcing the first conference ballot since 1950, in order to attack the leadership's 'even-handed' motion. The platform won, though by less than two to one. At Westminster the chairman of the back-bench education committee was ejected, to be replaced by a right-winger who believed in grammar schools. A whole string of right-wing and essentially Conservative educational bodies whose influence was to be felt by Kenneth Baker twenty years later were either revitalised or created in the wake of the *Black Papers'* publication.[81] And two weeks after the 1969 party conference, Boyle, according to John Campbell, 'sensing that he was not going to be Education Secretary in the next government . . . . decided to leave politics to become vice-chancellor of Leeds University'.[82] Heath replaced him with Margaret Thatcher, whose views were known to be distinctly less sympathetic towards comprehensives than Boyle's. The conflict only sharpened when Ted Short, under pressure from his own party conference to speed the process up, introduced a Bill just ahead of the 1970 election requiring local authorities to end selection. Labour's own incompetence in a Commons vote was all that prevented the Bill becoming law.

If the Conservative activists at the party conference wanted to retain selection in schools, and if more rhetoric about selectivity in general had crept into the 1966 manifesto – although little in the way of policies to implement that – there still remained clear electoral limits to this process. When the Conservative Research Department studied the issues again in 1967 and 1968, it concluded that while it was right to stress selectivity:

> A clear distinction must be drawn between the allocation of future resources and changes in existing services. There is a grave danger that we may lose many votes at the next Election if there were to be a suspicion that we were going to reduce present benefits. We should state loudly and categorically that we will not impose charges for hospital treatment or for primary and secondary education and that we will maintain the real value of the basic pension . . . While firmly maintaining the present structure of the social services we should concentrate on talking about how to distribute the extra resources that will flow from renewed prosperity under the next Conservative government, particularly towards the disabled, chronic sick, very old and very poor.[83]

"Jam tomorrow but never jam today—that is what the Government try to say to the people, but WE WANT JAM TODAY." Miss Barbara Betts supporting the demand for an immediate start on the Beveridge Report.

Above: The young Barbara Castle at the 1944 Labour Party conference showing the tenacity and fire that would mark her career.

Below: Dr Derek Stevenson, Secretary of the British Medical Association: Rex Harrison looks and a consultant's bedside manner with the public could not save the association from the most damaging dispute in its history.

Above: David Ennals in hospital on the thirtieth anniversary of the NHS in 1978. Soon he was to be declared a legitimate target for industrial action.

Left: 'Tormented by self-doubt, devoid of guile, with a passion to educate,' Sir Keith Joseph, nearing the end of his political career, at the 1985 Conservative Party conference.

Above: Numbers, numbers, numbers... Norman Fowler in 1986 insists that the NHS is getting better.

Right: Roy Griffiths, whose two modest reports transformed NHS management and community care.

Well nourished, or lean and hungry? Two possible Tory futures for the welfare state, as Kenneth Clarke and Michael Portillo share the Treasury steps.

It was advice Heath took. His introduction to the party's mid-term manifesto *Make Life Better* stressed: 'We will help to root out the poverty which remains in our society by concentrating *extra* help where it is most needed [my italics].'

The culmination of this process for the Conservatives in the 1960s came in fact on the last day of January 1970 at the Selsdon Park Hotel in Croydon. Heath had taken his shadow Cabinet away for a pre-election 'Chequers' weekend in an attempt to portray the Conservatives as the government in waiting. Needing to throw a bone or two to the press, he asked Iain Macleod what to mention. Law and order always went down well, Macleod suggested. Heath complied and by Monday *The Times* and others were reporting that Heath's priorities would be tax cuts, trade union reform, higher pensions for the over eighties, law and order and immigration control.[84]

It was Wilson, not Heath, who turned this programme into 'Selsdon Man', painting the Tories as planning to dismantle the welfare state and return to the capitalist jungle. 'Selsdon man is not just a lurch to the right,' Wilson declared, 'it is an atavistic desire to reverse the course of 25 years of social revolution. What they are planning is a wanton, calculated and deliberate return to greater inequality.'[85] Heath did little to dispel the impression that a decisive break was on the way with both the Butskellite past and the One Nation welfare state approach that he had himself helped devise as a young MP. When opinion polls showed tax cuts, not more spending on social services, to be the electorate's priorities, Selsdon Man, to Wilson's chagrin, proved to have a certain electoral appeal.

Given what followed, there has been a tendency to believe that whatever the case on the economic and industrial side, there was no proto-Thatcherism during the Selsdon Park weekend on social policy. That is almost true, but not quite. On housing the main debate was how to hand out more by providing rent rebates to private tenants. On social security the issue again was how quickly new benefits to the disabled could be brought in, not how to cut the system. On education, despite by then two *Black Papers* and nine months of debate about them, the most notable feature was the almost complete lack of discussion. The somewhat scrappy minutes record Heath refusing to back Margaret Thatcher's desire to give 'a fair wind' to the planned private and independent University of Buckingham. Thatcher wanted an approving paragraph in the manifesto. Heath said no. 'If people want to set it up they can do so,' he declared. 'But we do not want to be landed with subsidising it.'[86]

On health, however, there was a flavour of real radicalism. Maurice Macmillan, the shadow health spokesman, outlined a scheme whereby the NHS would provide 80 per cent of treatment, chiefly hospital care, while the remaining 20 per cent would be covered by a state-backed insurance plan. However, 'those who insured privately on as good terms or better could contract out.' The idea was as potentially Thatcherite an approach as any Selsdon Man could wish. But it was killed off in a few sentences by Macleod, now the shadow Chancellor. He pronounced himself 'flatly in favour of continuing broadly with the present system'. The 15s. 0d. (75p) a week charge that would be needed for each insured worker was 'quite unacceptable', he declared. Out with that went a draft manifesto paragraph: 'We will consider the financing of the health service with a view to finding ways of devoting more resources to the nation's health without increasing the burden on the taxpayer.' Out too went a paragraph stating that 'as in education, we warmly welcome the growth of private provision in health and welfare.' This interlude explains why the health section of the Conservative manifesto in 1970 is by far its weakest part. While full-blooded spending commitments in education, pensions, benefits for the disabled and housing are all spelt out and all founded on the assumption that 'tomorrow must be better than today', the section on health promises only reformed administration, a hint at more resources, and a rather tame declaration that it is 'right and proper' for people to have private health cover if they wish.

Thus while the 1970 manifesto undoubtedly offered a more free market approach to the economy, with no prices and incomes policy, no more nationalisation, a hint at some privatisation and a promise of tax cuts to be financed by unspecified spending savings, on the welfare state side there was anything but a promise to slash and burn. The odd phrase ('we will give priority to those most in need') could, if heaved sufficiently far out of context, be taken to threaten cuts in the welfare state. But on almost every specific, the promise was of more. Even the limited 1966 rhetoric of greater selectivity was toned down, the manifesto declaring that while 'immediately we can help by establishing more sensible priorities . . . the only true solution is to increase what we can afford.'[87] Before Heath was to reach Downing Street, however, two more events which may just have influenced the election result and certainly had some bearing on the future of the welfare state were to occur.

One concerned doctors' pay. Their review body reported in the spring of 1970 recommending no less than a 30 per cent pay rise. Crossman and Wilson sat on the report for seven weeks, and then on the Friday evening of a Bank Holiday weekend calmly told the doctors that it could not be published because an election had been called. The BMA was furious and after the resultant meetings between Stevenson, the BMA secretary, Crossman and Wilson, it got into the press that one reason for delaying the report was the state of the economy. This the Tories seized on. With the election looming, Crossman was aghast. He issued a statement denying that he had said in any talks, private or not, that the country was 'in a period of extreme economic peril' adding, to his own later consternation: 'Even if I did say it, I withdraw it.'[88]

Under mounting pressure, Wilson agreed to publish the report. Only the junior doctors, however, received the 30 per cent; the award for GPs and consultants was halved, the other 15 per cent being referred to the Prices and Incomes Board for consideration. In a blaze of front page news the review body resigned *en bloc* in protest at their recommendation being amended and GPs in droves breached their contracts by refusing to sign sick notes. Just to compound the government's problems, a national press strike then left doctors able to air their grievance in what was in 1970 a much more extensive local press while government spokesmen found themselves confined to radio and television. The scale of the row – and more importantly the suspicion it reinforced that something was wrong with the economy – may in a minor way have contributed to the government's defeat. Certainly senior figures in the BMA believed it had, and believed that senior Labour politicians took the same view.[89] As a result relations were already soured when Labour returned to power three and a half years later, helping fuel the nastiest confrontation between doctors and government that the NHS has seen.

The second influence on the election came from the Child Poverty Action Group. In the autumn of 1969, Frank Field had taken over from Tony Lynes at the CPAG. Field, intense, driven, imaginative, political, had read up on Crossman, the Secretary of State for Social Services, and seized on a belief of Crossman's that the most damaging thing you could do to a political party was to question its central myth in the run-up to a general election.[90] A central myth for Labour was that it was in the business of abolishing poverty and reducing inequality. Field took a memorandum Lynes had already prepared which examined what had happened to the poor under Labour, and rewrote it with a new and dramatic political edge. What started life as 'An Incomes Policy for Families' finished up covered by a press release which claimed 'The Poor Get Poorer Under Labour'. Before it saw the light of day, Field went to see Crossman.

We sat round one of those large polished tables which it would be possible to use as a shaving mirror. Crossman had with him his senior adviser, Brian Abel-Smith, together with a bevy of civil servants. Crossman began what can only be described as an extraordinary 'performance'. He banged the table, he shouted, and he mocked. There was endless machine-gunning of sarcastic jokes to which the civil servants responded as if part of a medieval court . . . for an hour . . . he played almost every trick in the book in order to keep attention to himself and away from the argument. The only action he didn't try was to swing from the chandelier.[91]

Peter Townsend, CPAG's chairman, was with Field, so the joint authors of The Poor and the Poorest were on opposite sides of the table. Field recalls Abel-Smith sitting silent, 'smiling like a Cheshire cat'[92] while 'Peter Townsend quietly argued back against this [Crossman's] torrent of abuse'.[93] At the end Crossman demanded to know what the group would do with the memorandum. 'I replied,' Field has recorded, 'that normal practice was to publish it. He said that nobody would believe what we were saying. My reply was that in that case he had nothing to worry about.'

In fact, Field was much later to admit, 'a careful reading of the memorandum showed that it did not contain the evidence'[94] to support the claim that the poor had become worse off under Labour. 'Looking back, the analysis was pretty poor – partly because the official statistics were so awful. If we had taken everything into account, I am not sure that even the claim that the poor had got relatively poorer would have stood up. We could have been fairer to the Labour Party. But I was shocked at how badly Labour appeared to be doing. We wanted to get the argument into the mainstream of political debate, and it certainly did that. But when I look back at that analysis I do think, "God, this is shaky".'[95]

Given its left wing roots, CPAG's assault on Labour gave it a new credibility as a body untainted by party allegiance. A meeting with Iain Macleod and correspondence with Ted Heath followed. Heath took up the theme. During the election he drove it home to the point where Alan Watkins, then the New Statesman's political correspondent, remarked that no rally was complete without Heath's reference to CPAG's finding that the poor had got poorer under Labour. If some believed the BMA's pay dispute affected the election outcome, more believed CPAG's campaign did; although as Field, now the MP for Birkenhead, points out, no political account of the election mentions it. 'It may have contributed marginally,' is his own judgement. 'For years afterwards, right up to the 1979 election campaign, when I stood up to speak on Labour platforms, people shouted Judas at me.'[96]

The claim divided the poverty lobby, both on how far it was true and on the tactics used. In March 1970, Abel-Smith and Titmuss refused to sign a letter of Townsend's to *The Times* supporting CPAG's position. The rift became public and the great triumvirate, Boyd-Carpenter's 'skiffle group of professors' that had done so much to drive Labour's conscience and thinking, was temporarily sundered. It was a fitting enough contribution to the paradox of the end of the 1960s – a welfare state which in many ways had never had it so good, with more spending, more programmes, more planning and more progress than ever before; but one which had never felt so bad about it, or so unsure of where it was going. A good time for the dawn of the Conservatives' last hurrah.

CHAPTER 14

The Tories' last hurrah: Conservatives 1970–74

> During Ted's premiership we were strongly committed to the post-war economic and social consensus in which the basic goal of economic policy was full employment. We recognised the need for an improved Welfare State. We believed in a society in which the social services should be expanded and more should be done about housing . . . Margaret [Thatcher] and Keith [Joseph were] the most voracious big spenders.
>
> *Jim Prior, Cabinet minister 1970–74, Leader of the Commons 1972–4, A Balance of Power, pp. 71, 132*

> There was a little Selsdon man phase at the beginning . . . I remember an entirely informal meeting with Geoffrey Howe and others to discuss refinancing the health service which came to nothing and wasn't heard of again . . . but so far as I can remember the Selsdon man phase lasted for three months, and certainly no longer than six months. For all practical purposes the Heath government was exactly like working for the Wilson government. So for people like me who thought we were in the civil service to do good, then once Keith Joseph had settled down he was exactly the same as Crossman – and in some ways more successful and effective because he actually did a lot of the things Crossman had only talked about doing.
>
> *Robin Wendt, Private Secretary to Crossman and Joseph, interview, 16 February 1994*

The Government was routinely attacked by Labour as the most reactionary for decades, intent on reversing all the advances in social provision and economic management since the war, dismantling the

welfare state, bashing the unions and deliberately creating
unemployment in order to grind the faces of the poor. This was
nonsense.

John Campbell, Edward Heath, p. 376

I time and again became a prisoner of the philosophy which the
civil service manifested: the good intentions of the Welfare
State.

Keith Joseph, Secretary of State for Social Services 1970–74; Ranelagh,
Thatcher's People, p. 107

FOR THOSE WHO wanted to believe that Selsdon man was real and
that the welfare state was about to be torn limb from limb it was,
fittingly enough, Keith Joseph and Margaret Thatcher who provided the
initial evidence.

Introducing his first White Paper as Chancellor in October 1970,
Anthony Barber declared:

> We intend to adopt a more selective approach to the social services. There
> will be increases in expenditure on basic structure – schools, hospitals,
> payments to those in need. But we aim to confine the scope of free or
> subsidized provision more closely to what is necessary on social grounds
> . . . Instead of the present indiscriminate subsidies, help will go where it
> is most needed.[1]

At the same time as Joseph was consigning Crossman's ambitious earnings-related pension scheme to the dustbin in favour of his own much more
modest plans, Barber's package included higher charges for prescriptions,
dentistry, spectacles and school meals. State sickness benefit was to be
paid only after the first three days. Cheap welfare milk was abolished,
and school milk disappeared for children aged eight to eleven. This last
was in Thatcher's new domain as Secretary of State for Education and was
the first action to make her famous as a national politician, bringing the
headline 'Milk Snatcher Thatcher'. It was a cut worth a mere £8m a year,
and 'an absurd issue on which to enter the national demonology' in Hugo
Young's words.[2] Labour in January 1968 had saved much more by ending
free school milk in all secondary schools – a measure that was little noticed
amid the postponement of the raising of the school leaving age, renewed
prescription charges and the other more dramatic cuts of the time.

Thatcher the Milk Snatcher, by contrast, appeared early proof of Selsdon man in action, not least because it followed on her apparent determination to block the change to comprehensive schools.

There were charges that she was destroying the health of underprivileged youngsters, while the whole issue was further curdled by some subconscious sense of the cruelty of a woman and mother taking milk from the mouths of, if not babes and sucklings, then at least schoolchildren. The *Sun*, not then the Tory tabloid it was to become, labelled her 'The Most Unpopular Woman in Britain' – and was probably right. Mrs Thatcher blamed her civil servants for not warning her of the likelihood of a row. There were said to be private tears, with Denis Thatcher even wondering whether she should not give up politics because of the strain. Her own later verdict was 'Iron entered my soul'.[3]

The dramatic part of Keith Joseph's share of the White Paper was not the higher health charges, which, for all the trouble they caused, left them as a proportion of NHS spending at only two-thirds the level they had reached in Powell's day. Instead it was what amounted to an instant breach of the election manifesto. As part of Macleod's and Heath's pre-election endorsement of the Child Poverty Action Group's line, both had signed up to CPAG's policy of raising family allowances and clawing the cash back from the better off by reducing tax allowances. It was, Heath had said, 'the only way of tackling family poverty in the short term'.[4] Macleod, however, had died in July 1970. The manifesto's wording was ambiguous. Barber was not signed up to claw-back. And Joseph on taking office had looked at the figures. In November he told the House of Commons that he had found three things.

First, about a third of the working families living below supplementary benefit had only one child. Raising family allowances would not help them because family allowance went only to the second and subsequent children. Second, any increase in family allowances which did not involve 'astronomic' figures 'could not provide the scale of help the very poorest of wage-earning households desperately need'. And third, tax thresholds had fallen so far that the claw-back would leave little cash in the hands of the poor. As Frank Field noted, this was an argument for raising the tax threshold rather than, as Barber had just done, cutting tax rates – but of course bigger issues had been at stake and bolder headlines were being sought than just helping the poor.[5]

Joseph's answer, therefore, was not to raise family allowances but to introduce a new means-tested benefit for poor families in work to be known as Family Income Supplement or FIS. That he could not only do so, but do so amazingly fast – the scheme was law by Christmas – was due to the fact that FIS was there to be plucked off the shelf. Civil servants in the Cabinet Office had drawn it up in Douglas Houghton's day, but had seen Labour narrowly reject it in favour of the family allowance and claw-back solution. When Joseph arrived and was told of the disadvantages of a further dose of claw-back, one of the civil servants involved recalls: 'I dug out my papers and handed them over. What was in them in effect became FIS.'[6] Crossman recognised the scheme, dubbing it 'an old friend of ours',[7] while hammering home its drawbacks.

To the outside world, not knowing this background, FIS came as 'something of a bombshell' given the manifesto commitment.[8] Townsend emerged, raging like a bear to damn it. 'He did what seemed like 5000 interviews that day, denouncing it from pillar to post on radio and television and in the press,' one of the civil servants involved recalled. 'It was a great performance.'[9]

The scheme plunged Joseph deep into controversy with lasting effects on both Labour and Tory attitudes. For a moment he found himself cast as the reincarnated villain of a late eighteenth-century piece of welfare state history: he was condemned for re-creating the notorious Speenhamland system. This was named after the Berkshire village in whose Pelican Inn on 6 May 1795 the local magistrates, with the most humane of intentions, decided to supplement the incomes of working family men who had been driven to destitution by bad harvests, the Napoleonic war, the effects of the industrial revolution and the enclosure of the countryside. Fairly or not, Speenhamland came to be seen as a means of allowing employers to use state subsidy to drive down wages – demoralising the workforce while at the same time destroying their incentives. It was Powell who reminded the Commons of this piece of history[10] and at first it was as good a charge as any to throw at an ex-director of a giant building company, even if it was one that Joseph could easily enough dismiss by pointing out that less than one per cent of households would gain from his new benefit while Speenhamland 'came to affect the majority of rural workers'.[11]

In that defence, however, lay a much tougher problem. For on Joseph's own figures the beneficiaries (who included single parents) would number only 160,000 families containing some 500,000 children at an estimated cost of £8 million. Even that figure, which Joseph admitted was only about half those classed as poor, would only be reached if it was assumed that 85 per cent of those eligible would take up the new benefit. Four months after the scheme's launch, however, and despite two costly and determined advertising campaigns, only 48 per cent of the 160,000 eligible families were claiming.[12]

The ever-anguished Joseph, who had been careful to canvass the case for FIS on practical not ideological grounds, went to the length of writing a personal letter to all social workers urging them to ensure that potential FIS families claimed. The take-up figures remained obstinately low, creeping up to barely 60 per cent even if they were claiming 75 per cent of the available money.[13] Apart from these difficulties, however, FIS brought a new and unwelcome concept into the social security language. The scheme worked by making up half the difference between a set amount and a worker's wage and then withdrawing the benefit at the rate of 50p for each extra £1 earned. However, earnings could easily be high enough to attract tax and national insurance contributions before FIS ran out. The net effect of tax being paid and benefit entitlement withdrawn was that 85 pence could be lost of every extra £1 earned. Given that higher earnings often also mean that rent and rate rebates were lost, along with free school meals, families could actually find themselves worse off by earning more. In a seminal article in the *New Statesman* Frank Field and David Piachaud dubbed the effect 'the poverty trap' – and thus a new social security phenomenon was born, one which proved highly charged for the Conservatives who were permanent advocates of the need to preserve work incentives. 'It is now a fact,' Field and Piachaud warned, 'that for millions of low paid workers very substantial pay increases have the absurd effect of increasing only marginally their family's net income and in some cases actually make the family worse off.'[14]

Family Income Supplement was to remain an established if, until the 1990s, a tiny part of the welfare scene under both Tory and Labour. But the psychological effects caused by its low take-up and its worsening of the poverty trap were profound. It injected fresh doubts about the merits of means-testing into Tory ranks to the point that no new means-tested benefit of any significance was introduced by the Conservatives for almost twenty years, even if the boundaries of existing ones were at times shifted. Far from being a jewel in the crown of Tory selectivism, the Conservatives became defensively apologetic about the benefit. 'I have never suggested that FIS was ideal,' Joseph was lamenting within a year of its introduction,[15] and the party's February 1974 *Campaign Guide* declared FIS to be 'only a temporary, first aid measure, pending more comprehensive arrangements for tackling poverty as a whole'.[16]

For Labour, FIS finally discredited means-testing to the point where opposition to the idea became a party shibboleth. In government, under

Wilson, Labour had introduced rate rebates and had actively encouraged local authorities to introduce rent rebates – both of which were means-tested. It had come within a few votes in Cabinet in February 1968 of adopting an FIS-like scheme itself.[17]. But to believe now in means-tests was to suffer eternal damnation in Labour's ranks – and this view was to persist right through the next Labour Government and on into the nineties. FIS was thus just one tiny item among many that helped shift Labour further to the left. It did so not least because, as the problems with FIS emerged, academic research was also starting to pile up the evidence that had been lacking or sketchy in the 1960s that means-tests produced low take-up wherever they were applied – whether to pensions or welfare milk, free prescriptions or rate rebates.[18] The sole exception appeared to be the 100 per cent willingness of the middle classes and everyone else to take up student grants.

The furious reaction FIS produced was partly due to Joseph's image. He had in Opposition already taken to preaching a milder version of the message of competition and free markets that was to emerge much more starkly and swathed in a monetarist straitjacket after Heath's defeat in February 1974. 'This country,' he used to tell his audiences, 'needs more millionaires and more bankrupts.' Responsible for industrial rather than social policy in Opposition, he had been dubbed 'Selsdon Man incarnate' by one commentator. 'Labour,' Morrison Halcrow, his biographer, recorded, 'seized on this image. Over the coming months Joseph was portrayed as the wild man who wanted to pull down all of society's safety nets, the ogre who would seize bread from the mouths of starving children.'[19]

Nothing could then have been further from the truth. A millionaire director of the construction company Bovis and a second baronet, Joseph had in fact been driven into politics by a deeply felt social conscience and his tortured sense of the need to search for solutions was from 1974 to make him one of the seminal figures of late twentieth-century British politics. The son of a Lord Mayor of London, Joseph as a short-trousered schoolboy had daily stolen food from the breakfast table to feed to a beggar in a Chelsea street. Harrow, Oxford, and a Quaker-linked holiday to an unemployed mining family in the late 1930s had been followed by an artillery captaincy in the Second World War – he fought at the battle of Monte Cassino and was mentioned in dispatches – a fellowship at All Souls, Oxford, and charity and social work in London's East End. Joseph belonged, Halcrow judged, 'to the honourable tradition of politicians whose starting point was improving the conditions of the poor'.[20] On his own admission, he was driven by a sense of guilt that he was well off.[21] He believed something could and should be done to improve the lot of the least fortunate. If the post of Secretary of State for Social Services had existed when he entered Parliament, he would tell reporters, that was the job he would have coveted. 'I've got it. And I'm very lucky.'[22]

The FIS episode over – and even that involved new money, not cuts – the scope of social security saw almost unremitting expansion during Joseph's tenure. New benefits that improved life for hundreds of thousands of people with disabilities which were due neither to industrial injury nor to war were introduced. Much of this was bipartisan, picking up word for word the disability elements in Crossman's failed pensions bill. As Pauline Thompson of the Disablement Income Group, whose pressure forced such benefits on to the political agenda, put it: 'We negotiated these with one lot and watched them be implemented by the other.'[23] The result was first a new and then later an improved attendance allowance for those needing care at home. There was a new invalidity benefit for the long-term sick, and a higher child allowance where invalidity allowance was paid. There was a promise further to review disability benefits in 1974, while for those aged between forty and fifty widow's benefits were introduced. Pensions for the over-eighties were increased. And in an odd quirk of 'charitabilis-ation' of the welfare state £3 million of public money was given to the Joseph Rowntree Memorial Trust to be spent entirely at its discretion to help families with severely congenitally disabled children. The Family Fund, as it became known, was a spin-off from the thalidomide scandal. As the battle for compensation for the victims of the morning sickness drug neared its climax, Joseph was brought up short when challenged over what he would do for other children who were equally if not worse off. His answer was a rapid raid on Treasury coffers and a scheme which still runs today and provided a model which helped Norman Fowler to solve his difficulties over the adult disabled twenty or so years later.

This expansion was not all plain sailing. It had to be achieved against steadily rising prices which produced double-digit inflation and repeated howls of pain from pensioners. Inflation forced annual benefit upratings rather than the biennial increases that Labour had been able to get away with, and in 1972 the falling value of old age pensions led to the 'tempor-ary' palliative of the £10 Christmas bonus – a real lump of cash when the weekly pension was only £6.75. Almost inevitably, the bonus became permanent, a standing lesson to social security ministers to avoid the temporary if at all possible. Never uprated, it survives, at the time of writing, with even such a self-proclaimed team of hard men as Peter Lilley and Michael Portillo, during a 'fundamental' review of expenditure, not prepared to take the political flak of killing it off. Had it been uprated in line with inflation it would in 1994 have been worth more than £70.

Joseph's time also saw changes of principle. First Beveridge's concept of a flat-rate minimum for all had the final hole blown in it by the discovery in the spending round for 1973 that there was not enough cash to do everything Joseph wanted to do. He therefore settled for giving a bigger increase to pensioners and those on invalidity benefit than to the unemployed and sick. This was done on the intuitive grounds that those on benefit long-term had the greatest need, while those sick or unemployed for short spells might have savings and could put off buying clothing, household items and similar expenses.[24] A much more limited move in this direction had been made in 1966. The result was a two-tier system of short- and long-term rates of benefit in place of Beveridge's single national minimum. A key proviso, however, was that the unemployed were excluded from the long-term rate no matter how long they had been out of work.

'There was an enormous argument in the department about that, with clear divisions among officials,' Robin Wendt recalled. 'Some of us thought that on grounds of morality and equity, and on Beveridge principles I suppose, the unemployed should be treated in exactly the same way as everybody else; others felt that to preserve work incentives you had to keep the rate down. Joseph took the latter view. Joseph, of course, won.'[25]

His view was not changed by the succeeding Labour Government, despite attempts to do so by David Ennals.[26] In part this reflected real anxieties about work incentives that were not purely a Conservative concern. Two years later, Joel Barnett, Labour's Chief Secretary to the Treasury, recorded similar worries that take-home pay could be little more and in some cases less than benefit.[27]

Joseph was also, however, under pressure to deal with what the Tory party manifesto had dubbed 'shirkers and scroungers'.[28] Indeed he appointed the Fisher committee which in 1973 came up with some fairly draconian recommendations for tackling what it described as the 'serious problem' of wrongful claims.[29] But once in government, as Johnathan Bradshaw noted at the time, ministers 'appear to have been more convinced than in opposition of how small a problem abuse really is, and how difficult it is to introduce further controls without making the process of claiming so unpleasant as to deter *bona fide* claims'.[30] And in tones very different from those heard from Peter Lilley in the 1990s, at the Tory party conference of 1973 Joseph faced down his critics over 'scroungers, lay-abouts and people who have never worked'. He told his audience it 'ought to face

the fact that there are a large number of people who are not employable
. . . [people] too inadequate to hold down jobs. And should their children
starve? Of course they should not.'[31]

None the less, Joseph's time in office did mark the start of harsher
treatment for the unemployed compared to other claimants, and particularly for the longer-term unemployed. For the first time since 1948 –
although Joseph did not phrase it like this – the benefit system appeared
to recognise the concept of the 'deserving' and the 'undeserving' poor.

His tenure also saw another departure from Beveridge's principles. The
new attendance allowance was non-means-tested, but it was also non-
contributory: it was paid to people many of whom had never worked and
who therefore by definition could not have contributed. Like the small
extra pensions suddenly paid out to the over-eighties, this was a clear
breach of the contributory principle of social insurance and there were
arguments in the department before it was adopted. But adopted it was:
it was plainly needed. These breaches, however, were to lead to other
non-contributory benefits, chiefly for the disabled, each of which further
blurred for the purists the clean lines of Beveridge's scheme.

If a relative bonanza of new benefits was not enough, Joseph joined
Barber in the Tories' version of the hunt for the philosopher's stone of
social security – a scheme that would combine tax and benefits in a single,
simple transaction which would pay out to those in need while taking
from those who could afford it, all without the traditional means-test. At
the same time it would cut both tax and public spending at a stroke.
Labour's version of the stone had been its failed income guarantee scheme.
The Conservative version was known as tax credits, which would exclude
those on supplementary benefit but include families with children, many
pensioners, and possibly single parents. A Green Paper was published, a
Commons select committee studied it, and Keith Joseph attempted to
explain it to the Conservative Party conference in October 1973. 'It is so
beautifully simple,' he told them.

> The essence is that tax allowances will be replaced by weekly credits for
> every wage-earner and for every child. Those weekly credits will be set off
> against tax on earnings or benefits. There will be a credit for every single
> wage-earner earning over £8 a week, every couple and every child. If the
> credit that is due every week exceeds the tax on the earnings or benefit,
> the difference will be paid along with the earnings or benefit, and the
> household or the individual will thus gain. The result will be automatic,
> not means-tested, weekly help to millions of those single or married with

children or without children, in work or retired who are now poor or hard-pressed.

Tax credits, he enthused, 'will improve incentives; tax credits will reduce the poverty trap. The scheme will be simple, understandable, automatic – but alas it is so big a change that it is going to take several years to introduce.'[32]

Alas, so big was it that Joseph's beautifully simple scheme proved no more simple, understandable and automatic than Labour's income guarantee had been. Nor would it have been any more affordable. To avoid the political unpopularity of losers it would in 1972 have cost £1.3 billion to implement, or around £4.4 billion in 1994 prices. The fact that Barber actually committed the government to making a start on it in 1974 should alone give the lie to charges that Heath's government was intent on dismantling the welfare state. None the less, the scheme, uncompleted and unloved, fell with the 1974 general election. Its one remnant, still with us like some piece of black radiation left over from the Big Bang, is child benefit – a change it was to fall to Labour to introduce.

With these grand schemes went grand ideas. On a trip up country Joseph ran into a social services director who told him that of the 20,000 households in his city 'nearly all our problems – delinquency, truancy, deprivation, poverty and the rest come from about 800 of them. And I think most of the families have been known to us for five generations.'[33]

The trip, coincidentally or not, helped set Joseph thinking at about the same time as he inherited the children's department from the Home Office as part of the Seebohm reorganisation of social services. Geoffrey Otton, who transferred across as the department's head, was somewhat horrified to find that Joseph regarded his new recruits 'as a set of sort of shock troops who had arrived from this rather classy place called the Home Office, with a certain éclat . . . he told us we were going to put the family right. Our jaws dropped somewhat. We thought of ourselves mainly as running approved schools.'[34] But Rolls Royce civil servants can produce a Roll Royce job and the outcome, after some prolonged hard work, a seminar at All Souls and umpteen drafts, was Joseph's 1973 'cycle of deprivation' speech to the Pre-School Playgroups Association. In it he postulated that poverty, poor parenting, poor education, personality disorder and emotional impoverishment could, for a section of the most vulnerable children, create a pattern which saw them in turn become the parents of deprived children. The speech brought forth profoundly different interpretations. To some on the left it looked like an appeal for community action. To others it appeared an attempt to blame the individuals and deny the state's responsibility. To the right it appeared to be a defence of the family. To many it seemed just common sense. The times being at least in some ways both gentler and saner, Joseph promptly commissioned a pile of research from the Social Science Research Council to see if the theory stood up. By and large it did not – or the social scientists involved failed to find that it did.

In hindsight, the speech was only a crucial step or two short of the Birmingham speech in 1975 that was to destroy Joseph's chances of the Tory party leadership. Equally in hindsight, the failure to provide neat answers to Joseph's questions may well have fuelled the contempt in which he came to hold the social sciences, producing his assault as Education Secretary on the Social Science Research Council. At the time, to many, the speech seemed to sum up much of the best of concerned progressivism, winning praise from both the *Guardian*'s more left-wing commentators and *The Times*'s more right-wing ones.

And this side of Joseph was more than just a public face. Alec Atkinson, a future permanent secretary in the department, judged Joseph 'a man who was genuinely out to do good as he saw it. I do not think he was doctrinaire when he was at social security – he was much more of an academic who looks at what ought to be done, sees what the possible solutions are, and does it.'[35] Robin Wendt, who served first Crossman and then Joseph as private secretary, recalls his concern about the homeless on the streets, 'even though the numbers then were nothing compared to the numbers now'.

> One night he arranged to go out with the St Mungo's charity team on the Embankment. He just went, anonymously, no press, no TV. He just put on his coat and scarf and went down there on his own. That said a lot about the man. Crossman – most ministers – would never have dreamt of doing that. And Joseph would not have found it easy because he was a shy and very fastidious person. But he did it because it came to him naturally.[36]

Public perceptions of Joseph had progressed from 'Selsdon Man incarnate' at the start of his term of office to 'almost single-handedly presenting the smile on the face of the tiger' as the *Guardian* put it in mid-term. By 1973 he was being dubbed 'The Tory Minister Who Really Cares' in an enthusiastic profile in the left-wing *Sunday Mirror*.[37] Despite FIS, Joseph was to become the first and probably the last social security minister to win a standing ovation from a CPAG conference. And as he went round, in his own phrase, 'filling gaps' in the system he became as Robin Wendt recalls, 'a sort of folk-hero within the DHSS both for his policies and his great ability to secure resources from the Treasury'.[38]

If social security took many of them, health and the personal social services also got their share.

Health

This is a very fine country to be acutely ill or injured in, but take my advice and do not be old or frail or mentally ill here.

Keith Joseph, 1971 onwards

In time of need for myself or my family I would now rather take my chance at random in the British National Health Service than in any other service I know.

Sir George Godber, Annual Report of the Chief Medical Officer, Department of Health, 1972

Before 1974, all the good stories came out of the local authority's health committee and the local medical officer of health – 'The Pill on the Rates' and that sort of thing. Hospital boards consisted of the odd Lord Lieutenant and ladies in big flowered hats who never seemed to have anything to decide. After 1974 the council no longer had any stories. They all came from the area health authority. But when you got there it consisted of dozens of administrators and appointees sitting round in great horseshoes so many rows deep that they scarcely fitted into the room – and they still weren't clear about who was deciding what about whom.

Celia Hall, Medical Editor, Independent, 1989–

We trained very hard, but it seemed that every time we were beginning to form up into teams, we would be reorganised. I was to learn later in life that we tend to meet any new situation by reorganising and a wonderful method it can be for creating the illusion of progress, while producing confusion, inefficiency and demoralisation.

Caius Petronius, d. AD 66

Administration is going to be the chief headache for years to come.

Aneurin Bevan, Webster, Aneurin Bevan on the National Health Service, p. 84

In the health service, Keith Joseph is remembered for just one thing – the 1974 reorganisation of the NHS which, like his policy on high-rise, was to be the cause of one of his great recantations. Reforming the NHS was something he had long thought about: in 1968 he had circulated to shadow Cabinet colleagues a paper advocating in the long term a switch to an insurance-based scheme and in the short term a £15-a-week bed charge to be covered by compulsory private insurance. Iain Macleod had dismissed the idea, but after the Selsdon Park conference, Joseph felt a renewed obligation to explore such approaches. Wendt recalls: 'He did have this entirely informal meeting with officials and one or two people he trusted including Geoffrey Howe who was solicitor general and nothing to do with health, but had written a pamphlet on the issue. We sat around for an afternoon in a sort of think-tank session exploring the feasibility and desirability of moving across to a wholly insurance-based, or largely insurance-based system. In the end, he decided nothing should be done. That the game wasn't worth the candle.'[39] Howe, in fact, had concluded from his days on the BMA's study of alternative finance for the NHS that whatever new system was adopted, the state would end up paying premiums or for the care of at least 60 per cent of the population. On that basis, the idea seemed not worth pursuing.[40] For the sake of form a review was set up, only to lead nowhere. None of this, of course, stopped the Treasury weighing in with its usual demands for a fee for each visit to the doctor, or a hospital boarding charge – items raised almost annually even under Labour governments. Yet again, the small sums that would be raised after necessary exemptions, and the political price of introducing them, precluded their adoption.

With the issues of principle over finance out of the way, Joseph set about spending, managing to achieve both a faster rate of growth and a bigger share of GDP than under Labour. His interests drove him into the less well endowed and loved areas of the NHS. It was under Joseph that the phrase 'the Cinderella services' became commonplace – services for the elderly, the mentally ill and the mentally and physically handicapped, none of whom had ever been to the NHS ball. Kenneth Robinson and Dick Crossman, his Labour predecessors, had started the shift of resources in their direction, but Joseph, in Sir George Godber's phrase, 'painted the picture in brighter colours'.[41] He also tried to enhance funds for 'the afflictions' – his label for conditions such as arthritis and deafness. Such non-life-threatening but incurable disabilities attracted more of his sentiment than the more spectacular demonstrations of acute medicine such as heart transplants, to which he effectively called a halt. It was Joseph, too, who obtained the funds to allow the new local authority social services departments to be set up in an expansionary frenzy that involved ten-year plans to be linked in to those of the reorganized NHS. Rates of growth between 1970 and 1973 of around 12 per cent a year were produced, with much more for some services.

Even advocates of the social services came to regard the expansion as 'uncontrolled'.[42] Intense professional rivalries developed as the old children's, health, and welfare sections were merged into unified social services departments. There were tensions between social workers and the remaining local authority medical officers of health, and between qualified and unqualified staff. The new tiers sucked the few qualified staff there were upwards into management, leaving their ranks thin on the ground. At the same time the new 'generic' social workers arrived. These last were not always a happy experience. Seebohm's desire for generic social work departments and less rigid divisions between the various practitioners became over-interpreted into generic social workers who acted as jacks of all trades and too often masters of none. Those used to dealing with the mentally ill were suddenly expected to handle the complex canon of child care law and procedures, and vice versa. The rapid expansion, not just of social work but of a whole range of caring services brought in a flood of young, raw recruits, trained in theory but lacking in experience. Too many were plunged into situations which they had neither the experience nor the back-up to cope with. Relations beween GPs and social workers in particular deteriorated: family doctors calling in the mental welfare officer to deal with a seriously disturbed patient, for example, would find that the old sweat from the armed forces with a good armlock had been replaced by a slip of a girl who did not in principle believe in sectioning patients and whom the doctor felt needed his protection rather than other way round. Money and unrealistic expectations were poured in equal measure into the social services, and a state of near-permanent revolution ruled as the old departments were reorganised into the new in 1971–2 only to be reorganised again along with the rest of local government and the NHS in 1973–4.

The contraceptive pill was finally made universally available on the NHS and free of all prescription charges, after a major parliamentary row over 'immorality at the taxpayer's expense'. And Joseph sensibly ignored the Bonham-Carter report which took to extremes the then fashionable search for economies of scale which was helping drive local government as well as health service reorganisation. Bonham-Carter suggested that for a really effective hospital service, and proper economy of scale, district general hospitals should be built with 1000–1500 beds rather than 600–800. When Aneurin Bevan had declared that he would 'rather be kept alive in the efficient if cold altruism of a large hospital than expire in a gush of warm sympathy in a small one',[43] he cannot have been thinking of the megaliths that Bonham-Carter proposed.

But it is for the 1974 reorganisation that Joseph will be remembered. Its origins lay in Bevan's split between hospital, general practitioner and local authority services and the inefficiencies and jealousies that had left behind. As early as 1962, the BMA-commissioned Porritt report had called for the three to be unified. By the time Joseph took office two Green Papers, one from Robinson and one from Crossman, had been published. The need for some greater unity was obvious, not least to make community care more than a well-meant slogan. While the hospital boards ran the hospitals, up to 1974 local authorities still ran district nursing, health visiting, midwifery, maternity and child welfare, ambulance services, home helps and vaccination and immunisation programmes. Ministers were becoming increasingly frustrated at their inability to make things happen. Almost every health minister from Bevan to Joseph had been alarmed at the level of care the mentally ill received, for example. Yet progress in improving their lot had been painfully slow despite departmental circulars and ministerial exhortations. Crossman, once safely out of office, was to damn the fourteen regional boards for behaving like 'semi-autonomous' satraps towards 'a weak Persian emperor'.[44] What was needed, it was believed, was an ability to plan, linked to a mechanism to deliver.

Joseph's answer was to set up a massive multi-disciplinary study group and bring in management consultants from McKinsey's and Brunel University. The search was on for managerial efficiency. Something fittingly known from its cover as the Grey Book eventually provided the broad outline. It looked beautiful on paper while proving something of a disaster on the ground. The whole was affected by the timetable of Peter Walker's great reorganisation of local government due to take effect in April 1974. Walker's reorganisation, in the interests of effiency, replaced 1400 local authorities with 420. Joseph's replaced 700 hospital boards, boards of governors, management committees and executive councils, with 14 regional health authorities, 90 area health authorities each with a linked family practitioner committee, and 200 district management teams each with a community health council to watch over it. Parallel and alongside this was an elaborate professional and advisory machinery, each with its own tier. The whole was so comprehensive that in time hospital porters were to demand (unsuccessfully) that there should be a district, area and regional porter to run their service, while civil servants became locked in theological debates about whether or not there should be a district remedial gymnast.[45]

Linked to the reorganisation was a desperate and ultimately unsuccessful search for something called co-terminosity – health service boundaries to match those of the (still changing) local authorities. The aim was to ease the work of the new statutory joint consultative committees set up between health and the newly Seebohmed social services departments. The whole massive structure was imbued with the latest outputs of fashionable management theory. 'Maximum delegation downwards' was to be accompanied by 'maximum accountability upwards' with the entire ship being run on 'consensus management' – an approach which worked well in some places but too often meant either that the lowest common denominator predominated, or no decision was taken at all. Everyone had a veto. No one alone could take a decision. Just as this organisational monstrosity was lurching into being, E. F. Schumacher published his epoch-making book *Small is Beautiful*.

The net result was pithily summed up by Patrick Nairne, the DHSS permanent secretary who inherited it, as 'tears about tiers'.[46] In theory, areas were to plan for their populations while the district management teams managed locally. In practice and despite all the tiers, the one issue which was almost totally neglected was the management of the hospitals in which patients were actually treated. They did not even appear on McKinsey and Brunel's beautiful organograms, and the hospitals' most able administrators, seeing the writing on the wall, bailed outward and upwards to the districts, areas and regions where power, prestige and money seemed to lie. It would be an exaggeration to say that there was no one left to run a hospital; but not much of one. Almost all decisions and disputes were referred upwards, and a system known as Cogwheel, which had begun to get doctors involved in management decisions about priorities at hospital level, beame largely redundant in the process. It was to be another decade before any serious further attempt to engage doctors in management was made.

Compounding all this disruption was speed. Despite the elephantine gestation since Kenneth Robinson's 1968 Green Paper, the exercise in the end was hopelessly rushed to tie in with the local government reorganisation. 'It was an absolute shambles,' Norman Warner recalled after he was moved on to the implementation team just after the Bill received Royal Assent in July 1973 – twenty-five years to the day from the start of the NHS and a mere eight months from vesting day.

My abiding memory is asking someone to get me the file on the allocation of functions to the new authorities – for region, area and district management teams. To my astonishment there wasn't one. There was a need for a circular, but no detailed work had been done. So I sat down for the afternoon and we concocted a draft circular in about 24 hours, shoved it round the department and that's what went out and became the basis for the secondary legislation on functions.[47]

By vesting day, vast armies of administrators still did not have their permanent jobs sorted out. When the dust finally settled ministers discovered that administrative and clerical staff had risen by 30 per cent in three years in an attempt to make it all work.[48]

It has become easy to pillory the reorganisation, but it was not all bad. For the first time there were health authorities responsible for planning all types of health services for their populations, not just dealing with their local hospitals and supporting them come hell or high water as the old hospital boards had done. A structure that eventually could plan more effectively did emerge. Improved if still imperfect relations with local government were established. Without that even the halting progress that was made in community care might well have been impossible. Teaching hospitals lost their boards of governors, their direct access to ministers and the respect Bevan had accorded them.[49] Guy's put up a 'melancholy' plaque in its boardroom recording the final meeting of its governors in their 248th year. A dozen years later it was to catch the eye of a Downing Street adviser, planting the idea of self-governing hospitals for the 1991 reform of the NHS.[50] In 1974, however, the change put the teaching hospitals under the new Area Health Authorities. This cost them some independence and freedoms; but it gave them a new and fruitful interest in their local communities.

Despite the effort that went into the reorganisation, the aim of unification was not achieved – not even between the hospital and GP services, let alone with all the local government services. GPs ensured that family practitioner committees kept only an arm's-length relationship with health authorities and a direct financial link to the department. It would be another twenty years, into the nineties, before serious mergers there would be achieved. And while the health services were moved across, transferring all welfare and social services from local authorities to the NHS to provide one seamless service proved politically no more possible than in Bevan's day.

With the reorganisation came the development of NHS complaints machinery, of independent patients' organisations and of Community Health Councils (CHCs) all of which helped ensure, in Rudolf Klein's phrase, that patients ceased to be 'the ghosts in the machine'.[51] The NHS also became much more politicised by the introduction of local authority members on to health authorities – an unintended side-effect of Walker's 1974 local government reorganisation. There had been local authority members on regional hospital boards and management committees since 1948, but they had been there as individuals, appointed after consultation, not as nominees from the local council. Their addition came from a mix of motives, with Barbara Castle increasing their numbers from a quarter to a third when Labour took power. They were there partly as elected consumer representatives, partly to try to make the local government links work, and partly, no doubt, as unconscious compensation to councils for the further loss of their health functions. The effect, however, was to ensure that the cacophony of complaint about the service's continuing inadequacies rose as councillors voted themselves the critics' role alongside that of the newly-created CHCs – who had at least been formally given that task. In addition, the quasi-representative role on authorities that the odd nurse, voluntary group, or trade union member now acquired, alongside the doctors who had always been there, provided a louder sounding-board than ever for professional and pressure group complaint. Enoch Powell's great dictum about the tax-funding of the NHS had been that it endowed 'everyone providing as well as using it with a vested interest in denigrating it'.[52] The 1974 reform – the first major reconstruction of the service since 1948 – handed them all a megaphone.

Education

Mrs Thatcher, appointed Secretary of State for Education and Science, was put in charge of one of the fastest-expanding budgets in the public sector and showed not the slightest inclination to curtail its growth.
Hugo Young, One of Us, p. 66

From Butler to Eccles to Boyle to Thatcher, the Conservative party could claim an expansionist record in education – certainly one as good as the Labour party. [The 1972 White Paper came to feel like] the Indian summer of British education.
Maurice Kogan, The Attack on Higher Education, p. 23

'Mrs Thatcher,' *The Times* observed mildly on the day she became Secretary of State for Education, 'is known to be less enthusiastic about comprehensive schools than Sir Edward' – her predecessor as Opposition education spokesman. She proved that in no uncertain manner. Within ten minutes of arriving in Curzon Street the new Secretary of State produced a page from an exercise book listing eighteen things she wanted done that day. 'Point one' was a new instruction to local authorities cancelling Crosland's circular and telling them they could keep their grammar schools if they wished and even open new ones. 'She had the draft of that circular on her desk that night,' Sir William Pile, her permanent secretary, recalled. 'She said "Action this day" and she got it.'[53]

Ten days later, out came circular 10/70 – its number (the tenth circular of 1970) providing a neat symmetry to Crosland's 10/65 and 10/66. It caused 'an absolute furore', her junior minister William van Straubenzee later recalled. It was 'a disastrous start'.[54] The educational establishment from the local authorities to the unions was outraged at the lack of consultation. Labour launched a censure debate. Grammar school defenders saw their chance and some authorities' comprehensive plans were withdrawn. But the move also split the Conservative Party. In places it set Conservative education committees against their own Conservative councils while an anonymous columnist in the Bow Group's journal declared Mrs Thatcher's decision bad for education and bad for the Conservative Party.[55]

The remarkable thing is, how little difference it made. The new circular did unleash three years of at times and in places vicious infighting over education both locally and nationally. Where she could, Mrs Thatcher rejected plans which she judged damaged grammar schools. But the move to comprehensive schools now had its own momentum and the tide was not stemmed. It may have been slowed. Certainly the chances of comprehensive schools succeeding were in places damaged by the Education Secretary's insistence that a selective grammar school be retained alongside them. But the fact remained that Margaret Thatcher was to go down as the Secretary of State who closed more grammar schools than any other, while the number of comprehensives rose more rapidly under her than at any time before or since.[56]

It was not what she wanted. Sir William Pile in later years told Hugo Young that her view of education was in favour of grammar schools, the better universities and the Science and Medical Research Councils.

To her they seemed to be the places where the best and most intelligent of minds would find themselves if the system worked. The top 25 per cent of the ability range would go to the grammar schools, the top 2 per cent of eighteen year olds would fetch up in the universities and all the best researchers in the hard elite sciences in those two research councils – though definitely not the Social Science Research Council or the Environmental Research Council which she regarded as 'pseudo-sciences'.[57]

She herself would say: 'There was a great battle on. It was part of this equalisation rage at the time, that you mustn't select by ability. After all, I had come up by selection by ability. I had to fight it. I had a terrible time.'[58] Terrible or not, it was a time that in the view of allies as well as enemies was to scar her view of the education department.

Stuart Sexton, who was to become Mark Carlisle's and Keith Joseph's special adviser when they were Secretaries of State for Education, and who was briefly a Thatcher speechwriter, believes she allowed departmental officials to impose their will on her over the grammar school issue.

I don't think she would ever admit this publicly, but I had the impression [from her] that she was not much more than a cypher as Secretary of State, and that the policy that had been going on in the sixties never really stopped. Why more grammar schools closed under her is that local education authorities had been persuaded and cajoled into putting schemes in and she approved them. The only one that she would proudly tell you about – umpteen times if you gave her the chance – was that she'd saved the four grammar schools in Sutton where they'd collected a petition of 24,000 signatures [against a Conservative education committee's plans to go comprehensive]. That was the only occasion I can remember where she actually put her foot down and said 'because of that petition I will refuse it'.[59]

The record, of course, shows that Mrs Thatcher saved more grammar schools than that, even if many of the reprieves proved to be temporary. But her perception of what happened was to be important for the future, fuelling her distrust of the department. And by the time she left, the 32 per cent of state school children attending comprehensives had almost doubled to 62 per cent.

If school milk, school meals and grammar schools were Mrs Thatcher's greatest controversies at education, much else happened. From day one she showed the same determination to hold her own with the Treasury that Keith Joseph displayed – a talent that was to produce the same result in education as in health: a faster increase in spending under the Tories than Labour had managed.

Her first victory was to fight off a determined Treasury attempt, which had back-bench and Tory party conference backing, to postpone yet again the raising of the school leaving age to sixteen.[60] Thus the move that had first been canvassed in the 1944 Education Act finally became reality from September 1972. Early on she also saved the Open University which was about to recruit its first students when she took office. The OU – originally the University of the Air – had been Harold Wilson's pet project, the achievement for which 'above almost anything else in his career' he wanted to be remembered, according to Ben Pimlott, his biographer. Conceived in tandem with the white heat of the technological revolution, Wilson had nursed the OU through nearly six years of Labour Government, initially putting it under the care of Jennie Lee, Aneurin Bevan's widow. Her task as Minister of Arts was to protect it from Crosland who had no love for the idea, while Wilson himself intervened with Callaghan as Chancellor to ensure the Treasury did not scupper it.[61] The association with Wilson, however, meant the OU was seen as a firmly socialist idea. Macleod had determined to kill it off as part of his tax-cutting plans. George Gardiner, Thatcher's hagiographic early biographer, claims she saved it because of her 'strong belief in giving educational opportunity to those prepared to work for it'.[62] Sir William Pile, her permanent secretary, recalled by contrast that she 'was all for killing the Open University, which I managed to argue her out of on the grounds that their degrees cost only half of Oxbridge's'.[63] Whatever the motivation, she fought the Treasury for it and won, allowing a socialist conception to be claimed in later years by herself and John Major as a Tory triumph.

There were also hints of future Thatcherite education themes. She told an education conference in 1971 that she would like in time to give parents more rights over choosing their schools.[64] And when the issue of education vouchers was again aired there was just a trace of the interest to come. Rhodes Boyson, who a year later was to become a Conservative MP and who was to go on to edit the fourth and fifth Black Papers and to become an education minister, had raised the issue again and put it nearer to the mainstream of the Tory party in a Conservative Political Centre pamphlet of 1973. At the party conference that year Mrs Thatcher did nothing formally to encourage the idea, but its supporters may have noted the 'before' in her sentence as she told the conference: 'We have too many schools which still need bringing up to standard, and we should do that in justice to the parents of the children who go there before we contemplate a voucher system.'[65] She also, in 1971, found more money for the (still selective) direct grant schools – but only roughly the sum Ted Short had stripped from them in 1969.[66] But when the Headmasters' Conference and Conservative backbenchers went on to press her to reopen the direct grant list so that more schools could join, she demurred. She had other things to spend the cash on. They included £48 million to make good a manifesto promise to improve and replace some of the thousands of decaying Victorian primary schools. In 1975, when talking to George Gardiner after becoming party leader, the flavour of Plowden and its policy of positive discrimination for educational priority areas still shone through Mrs Thatcher's explanation of the policy, reflecting her support for an idea that at least arguably was a lot more socialist than Thatcherite. 'A lot of these very old school buildings,' she told him,

> were in areas where the children tended to have a poor home background. Then you often found that these bad school buildings also had bad equipment, and that it was very difficult to get teachers to go there. So these children suffered a triple deprivation, lacking a decent home, proper school buildings and good enough teachers. If only you could give them a good school then this gave them some experience of a nice building and good conditions.[67]

All this, however, was as nothing compared to December 1972 when the White Paper *Education: A Framework for Expansion* was published just three months after the start of the school year which finally saw the leaving age raised to sixteen. It was to prove the last vision of a bigger and better future to emerge from the education department for at least fifteen years. More than that, it was in some ways the most ambitiously comprehensive view of its own world that the department had ever attempted – embracing as it did everything from the cheerful gregariousness of the nursery school to the loneliness of the long-distance postgraduate student. Mrs Thatcher, who four years later almost to the day would be bewailing the 'insatiable' appetite of the education service,[68] published plans for a rise in spending in real terms of 50 per cent over the following decade. The White Paper dealt in no number that was not enormous, and picked up the Plowden report's call for nursery education. The aim was a nursery place for half of three-year-olds and 90 per cent of four-year-olds within a decade. 'Areas of disadvantage' were to have early priority. Nursery schools, Mrs Thatcher later told George Gardiner, 'were especially needed in the deprived areas'.

> You found that by the time children came to school at the age of five, a lot of them were already behind because they came from homes where no interest was taken in the children, where the parents didn't talk to them . . . Of course, the State can never take the place of good parents – I mean ones who take an intense interest in their children. But it can help redress the balance for those born unlucky.[69]

This, in solidly Plowdenesque terms, was Margaret Thatcher's contribution to 'equality of opportunity' – an approach that in this limited area was indistinguishable from Crosland's, even if, according to Pile, Mrs Thatcher would have coloured it with an early test of success and failure. 'She thought all children should be given a chance at the beginning of their life to prosper. If they failed thereafter, then they had had their chance,' he told Hugo Young.[70]

The White Paper also outlined plans to expand the teaching force by 40 per cent over a decade in order to cut the pupil/teacher ratio, to allow for the nursery expansion and to introduce in-service training. In fact, with primary school rolls falling, this meant a contraction in the teacher training colleges; but despite that, higher education as a whole was expected to expand by 60 per cent by 1981, up from 463,000 students to 750,000. Such an expansion would have shifted the percentage of the age group in higher education from 15 to 22 per cent, with a third more students in higher education in 1981 than Robbins envisaged. To achieve such targets the polytechnics were expected to increase their numbers nearly three-fold from 90,000 to 265,000 over the decade. Four years later Mrs Thatcher would be arguing that 'industry and trade are the basic social service' because they created the nation's wealth.[71] But in the White Paper she approved a change in the justification of higher education from manpower planning to one of 'personal development'. In the light of experience, she also accepted that the arts would grow faster than the sciences, so that science students would make up only 47 per cent of the total by the decade's end.

There were contractionary edges to the White Paper. The universities were warned that the increase in unit costs needed to be arrested. A previous reduction in postgraduate numbers was confirmed. School building was reduced in real terms as rolls were expected to fall, but the programme remained substantial. Developments for the 16–19-year-old age group which might have threatened A-levels and grammar schools were excluded. The critics carped, but Mrs Thatcher was quite right when in a speech to the Schools Councils she retorted that when the White Paper talked about expansion 'it meant expansion, and not contraction'. In 1969, as Britain's role east of Suez shrank, education spending for the first time outstripped spending on defence. By the time Mrs Thatcher left office it had risen to 5.7 per cent of GDP, while defence spending had stayed put, a whole percentage point lower. Compared to 1945, there were almost nine million pupils in schools against five million thirty years previously. In higher education, there were close to half a million students against the 52,000 in universities in 1945, while the teaching workforce had risen almost two-and-a-half-fold to just under 422,000 – and yet more expansion was planned.

Housing

> The present system has led to a cossetted and privileged class in our society – the council house tenant. These people are jealous of their privileged position – because a council house is a prize hard to come by.
> *Richard Crossman in the People, 6 February 1966*

The third great expansionist of the Heath years was Peter Walker. A self-made millionaire, the Walker of Slater-Walker and the City, and at thirty-eight the youngest Cabinet member, he was put in charge of the newly-created monster Department of the Environment. From his arrival in Parliament in 1961 to his departure in 1990, Walker saw himself as the self-appointed inheritor and guardian of Macmillan's *Middle Way* brand of Conservatism. He did so with some flair – to the point where in 1977, removed from the shadow cabinet by Margaret Thatcher, he stubbornly quoted two whole pages of Egremont's famous 'One Nation' passage from Disraeli's *Sybil* in *The Ascent of Britain*, his account of his political beliefs. He too, however, was to contribute to the hard-faced image of the Heath government. The cause in his case was the 1972 Housing Finance Act, an attempt both to be more selective in awarding state aid and to bring help to people who had not received it before.

In essence, Walker redirected housing subsidies away from buildings and towards people, while for the first time providing help to private as well as public tenants. In place of a generalised housing subsidy, which local authorities variously used to keep all council house rents down, or to reduce the rates, or to run the locally-based rent rebate schemes which Labour had encouraged, he effectively nationalised the rent rebate schemes by making them mandatory. At the same time rebates for private tenants were introduced under the name of rent allowances. This was at a time when 1.3 million households still rented privately. The price, however, was that council house rents were to be progressively increased to 'fair rent' levels, with the rent rebates helping the less well off.

Walker presented this plan as a redistribution from the better off council house tenant to the less well off. There was some political mileage in this. The *People*, for example, had campaigned for years about 'the scandal of the wealthy tenant living in a council house at a subsidised rent' while those in greater need queued on the council houe waiting list. In 1966, Dick Crossman had been drawn into arguing that councils were not limited to charging an economic rent. 'Charge the rich man £1,000 a year rent – that'll sort the problem out,' he said.[72] Walker was to claim that Crossman, now editing the *New Statesman*, told him just before the Bill was published that the package was 'the most socialist housing measure this century'.[73] Its net effect, he was later to boast, was to make Britain 'the first capitalist country in the world where no-one could be evicted simply because they had not the money'.[74] The price, however, of switching subsidies from buildings and from all council rents was to put many more people on means-tested benefits in order to help them pay the higher rents being introduced.

Regardless of the fact that some of the least well off and least protected – the private tenants – now gained, Crosland damned the Bill as 'the most reactionary and socially divisive measure likely to be introduced in the lifetime of this Parliament' and pledged to repeal it. Come 1974, the rent increases indeed were repealed – only to be reintroduced two years later when the men from the IMF came knocking on Britain's door.

With Walker's measures came improved subsidies for slum clearance but an even more forceful switch towards home improvement and away from new building. This policy was driven partly on grounds of cost, but partly from a bipartisan realisation that wholesale redevelopment was ripping inner-city communities apart, and removing people from their jobs, friends, families pubs and clubs. Utilising the legislation that Anthony Greenwood had passed as Labour housing minister following *New Homes for Old*, Walker and Julian Amery, his number two, toured the country, ran exhibitions, sent out film vans and distributed millions of leaflets urging uptake of home improvement grants. The result was an increase from 170,000 housing improvements in 1970 to 453,000 in 1973, split roughly 60/40 between owner-occupied and council stock.[75] Walker was overdoing it when he claimed the result was 'an even greater impact on Britain's housing than the famous Harold Macmillan campaign to build 300,000 houses a year'.[76] But it did mark a decisive shift towards conservation and improvement at a time when a million households still had no indoor lavatory. It also marked a swing to government investment in the quality of the private as well as the public housing stock.

There were other shifts in favour of the private sector. Subsidies for slum clearance had previously been tied to council housing being built on the land: now anything from council to private housing to offices could be built. With all this went the first serious, if frustrated, drive to sell council houses, a renewed push towards a property-owning democracy. Julian Amery won a standing ovation at the Conservative Party conference of 1971 when he urged councils to sell, declaring he had 'a little list' of Conservative councils who were joining Labour ones in refusing to do so. 'We regard the selling of council houses as the best way of providing a healthy mix on council estates,' he said, adding that it would increasingly be the council's task to act not primarily as council house builders but to ensure that enough homes were for sale at prices people could afford. Relatively few – around 60,000 a year from 1972 – were in fact sold. And the tenor of the times is illustrated by Norman Tebbit, the future Chingford skinhead, telling the conference that: 'He did not ask that all council tenants should have a statutory right of purchase, but that no tenant should be gratuitously refused. Councils should make a case for saying no.'[77]

Despite this, new building did not cease nor was the private sector anything like the sole focus. The output of new houses did fall back towards 200,000 a year, but 40 per cent of these – a rather higher percentage than under Wilson – were in the public sector.

It was the imposition of higher rents that aroused the passions, however. So bitter was the opposition that several Labour councils refused to implement them, although only at Clay Cross, Derbyshire, did eleven councillors finally take their opposition to the extent of being surcharged. In so doing they turned themselves into working-class heroes whose role was seriously to embarrass the returning Labour Government in 1974 when the left demanded – to a refusal from Roy Jenkins – that their penalties be quashed. Their defiance was one more small contribution to the sense that the country was becoming ungovernable which came to dog the last days of Heath's government.

Walker's other great legacy to the welfare state, though an indirect one, was local government reorganisation. Labour had started the ball rolling with the Redcliffe-Maud inquiry. By the time Walker had revamped its recommendations, 1400 local councils outside London had been reduced to 420 in one of the more lasting, if least popular, of the Heath government's reforms. Its side-effect was to make local government more party political. Fewer, larger and therefore more powerful authorities were more worth controlling, and thus the political parties' interest in them grew. Independent councillors disappeared at a faster rate. Labour, Liberal and Conservative groups began to adopt more formal policy and tactics within councils, while the tendency of the parties to mount national campaigns around the annual local government elections increased. So, too, did the electorate's propensity in mid-term to vote in the opposing party to the government of the day. At the same time, reorganisation meant that education, once a proud fiefdom almost in its own right, now found that its chief officer sat alongside the new directors of social services, housing and other services. Each of these was answerable to a new breed of chief executive who was replacing the mild-mannered clerks and secretaries who had previously administered town and county halls. The chief executive was in turn answerable to a more politicised council. The stage was being set for the growing conflict between local and central government which was to mark the late 1970s and 1980s.

While Heath's three big spenders laboured away, reorganising all around them, the background against which they worked – the economy – was in turmoil. To an unprecedented extent, the bedrock on which Beveridge's welfare state had been founded was cracking.

Selsdon Man may have been a myth for the welfare state, but not for the economy. Economically Heath had set out to run a harsher, tighter ship by ending the feather-bedding of inefficient industry in the genuine belief that this was the way to long-term growth. The price, however, of 'no lame ducks' in a recession during which inflation was increasing, was steadily rising unemployment. Heath inherited a jobless total of just under 600,000 in June 1970. In the first four months of 1971 it began to rise dramatically, clearing the 700,000 mark in February, 800,000 in April, and 900,000 in August. In January 1972 unemployment reached a million, a level unprecedented since the Second World War.

As Heath's biographer John Campbell has reported: 'It was a moment of heavy symbolism no less devastating for being long predicted.' It was also a mark widely seen as unsupportable. 'It is morally, economically, socially and politically intolerable,' *The Times* under William Rees-Mogg had already thundered the previous November, 'that unemployment should remain at its present level.' When the figure was finally announced, Labour reacted with such fury that the Commons had to be suspended during Prime Minister's questions. Heath was faced with a choice: live with high unemployment in the hope it would mitigate both wage claims and inflation; or go for growth and attempt to control wages and inflation with a prices and incomes policy. Jim Prior has recorded: 'The high unemployment route was counter to everything Ted believed in and had hoped to achieve for Britain.' He 'utterly despised and detested the pre-war Conservative Governments, who had tolerated between two and three million unemployed. It was therefore no surprise in which direction Ted decided our economic policy should go.'[78]

There were pressures other than just the sheer total of jobless. It was a time when society seemed to be coming apart. The troubles in Northern Ireland had reached an unprecedented level of violence. The Angry Brigade, a few months earlier, had tried to blow up Robert Carr, the Employment Secretary. The government was locked in conflict with the trade unions, who had just put on the streets the biggest demonstration in their history against the Industrial Relations Act. Fear of the social consequences of unemployment was shortly to lead to the abandonment of the no-lame-ducks policy and the rescue of Upper Clyde Shipbuilders – a decision in part instigated by a warning from David MacNee, Chief Constable of Glasgow, that he would need an extra 5000 officers to keep the peace if the shipyards with their 4300 jobs went.[79] The first, and unexpected, miners' strike, following a power workers' go-slow the winter before that had blacked out hospitals as well as homes, was also just starting as unemployment passsed the million mark. 'Flying picket' was about to become part of the national vocabulary as the Saltley coke depot and Arthur Scargill, the Yorkshire president of the National Union of Mineworkers, were turned into household names. The fear was 'clearly present in the Cabinet room', according to John Campbell, that 'a million unemployed who felt that the Government was not doing all it could to help them might easily prove more than the police could handle.'[80]

The result was Heath's famous U-turn and the 'Barber boom' – a two-stage process that involved both the 1972 and 1973 budgets, the first of which alone pumped more than £2.5 billion into the economy in tax cuts and higher pensions and benefits. Whatever overall economic damage that did, the effect on unemployment was dramatic. By early 1974 it had fallen to the 550,000 mark – just below the level Heath inherited and back below Gaitskell's 3 per cent definition of full employment. The more prescient noted, however, that even as that low water mark was reached, unemployment had been left higher at the peak of each economic cycle than at the peak of the previous one. Very slowly, but very surely, one of the key conditions for an affordable and effective welfare state – full employment – was being eroded.

It was soon to receive a much more dire blow. In October 1973 the Yom Kippur War between Israel and the Arabs broke out. On 8 October, Sheikh Yamani, the Saudi Arabian oil minister who would soon be dubbed 'Yamani-or-your-life', met his counterparts from OPEC, the Organisation of Petroleum Exporting Countries, in Vienna. The outcome was a four-fold rise in the price of oil, the most dramatic and economically damaging global price rise in history. In Britain it produced the three-day week and the rash of industrial action which included the power workers, the railwaymen and the second miners' strike which finally brought Heath down. After the Barber boom, it produced the Barber cuts. The Chancellor told the Commons bluntly in December that those who said the situation was the 'gravest since the end of the war . . . do not exaggerate'.[81] More than £1.2 billion was to be lopped off public spending, he told MPs: 'by far the largest reduction in public expenditure for a succeeding year which has ever been made, both in absolute and relative terms'.[82] It turned a planned 2 per cent growth into a 2 per cent cut. Of this Joseph's share was £111 million, Thatcher's was £182 million, while housing in theory, though not in practice, was to be exempted. The grand plans for nursery education for all and a seemingly endless expansion of university and polytechnic places bit the dust, along with the ten-year plans for social services.

If there was one turning-point for the welfare state after 1945, this must be it. It took time and Labour's attempt to spend its way out of trouble for the full effects to be rammed home in 1976 with the visit of the IMF. There would in future be plenty of expansion, not just contraction, in the fields tackling Beveridge's five giants, and it would be far from all doom and gloom. But it would never again be quite such a glad, confident morning for the welfare state.

The ghosts at the feast that had been glimpsed with increasing clarity in the sixties – the difficulties of coping with adverse demography against poor economic performance, allied to technological advance and rising expectations – became permanent presences at the dining table. The Keynesian concepts of full employment and demand management were soon to be under fire as never before. And while in the past everything had always had to be fought for in the spending programmes that full employment and the taxes raised from it had made possible, in future the battles would be much fiercer.

As Kenneth Morgan has put it:

The turbulent events of the winter of 1973–74 . . . saw much more than the decline and fall of Edward Heath as premier, more even than the demise of 'one-nation Toryism'. They witnessed also the erosion of an ethical system. Conceived in an age of intellectual confidence, institutional strength and instinctive patriotism, it was now withering away in confusion and doubt.[83]

PART IV

THE TIME OF DISILLUSION

1974–79

CHAPTER 15

It was getting colder by the hour: Labour

1974–79

The party's over.
Anthony Crosland, addressing local government officers, 9 May 1975

The alternative to getting help from the IMF would be economic policies so savage, I think they would produce riots on the streets, an immediate fall in living standards and unemployment of three million.
Denis Healey, News at Ten, 29 September 1976

Looking back they were rather buoyant times. I felt I had come to a department where there were a lot of vigorous irons in the fire. Social services were growing fast. A lot of big hospitals were coming on stream despite the capital cuts. We were starting to make sense of NHS priorities – spending more on the deprived groups and starting to adjust geographic inequalities in health spending. There was the State Earnings Related Pension Scheme and child benefit and new disability benefits. We did in time, of course, begin to wake up to a much colder reality. But while we were aware, in Tony Crosland's phrase, that the party was over, we still had a hell of a lot of goodies that we were taking away from the party that we had been at.
Sir Patrick Nairne, Permanent Secretary at the DHSS 1975–81, interview

The decade as a whole was dominated by the struggle to contain inflation. This was true almost throughout, and it was true not just of the United Kingdom but of virtually all industrial countries. The most sensational economic events of the 1970s were the two

inflationary oil shocks in 1973 and 1979, price increases that helped
to bring the long secular boom of the post-war years to an end and
cut the rate of economic growth severely in nearly all advanced
industrial countries . . . The intellectual background was changing
too. There was more scepticism and distrust of the powers of
government. Some of those who had campaigned for more planning
at the beginning of the 1960s now campaigned for a more limited
agenda for the state. The use of the annual budget for the preservation
of continuous full employment was dismissed as 'fine tuning'. The
need to check inflation began to be given a hearing previously
reserved for those who claimed to have a cure for unemployment.
As fiscal policy came into disrepute, monetary policy was endowed
with almost magical properties . . . It was the heyday of
monetarism.

*Sir Alec Cairncross, Head of Government Economic Service 1964–9, The British
Economy since 1945, pp. 187–8*

L ABOUR'S RETURN as a minority government in February 1974 came
on the back of the miners' strike. Five years later it was to be swept
from power for a political generation by the 'winter of discontent'. Industrial action bracketed its birth and death. Incomes policy ran like a seam
of fool's gold throughout its agenda. More than a decade of intermittent
but increasingly persistent pay pause, pay freeze and pay norm had seen
the growth of white collar and public sector trade unionism. Nurses, ancil-
laries and local government staff had all increasingly become unionised,
while in 1970 the National Union of Teachers had joined the TUC. Belong-
ing to a union and taking industrial action came to be seen as the only
way for individuals to withstand rising inflation and repeated incomes
policies. The first year of the new government saw 30 per cent pay awards
for teachers (Houghton) and for nurses (Halsbury) before a further massive pay comparability exercise (Clegg) had to be launched to halt the
winter of discontent.

The defining moment of Labour's third post-war administration, however, came on the morning of Tuesday 28 September 1976. The pound,
which in March 1974 had been worth $2.30 was down below $1.70 and
falling fast. Denis Healey, at Heathrow to fly to international finance
ministers' meetings in Hong Kong and Manila, decided he could not risk
being cut off from London for the seventeen hours the flight would take.
He turned back. The markets reacted, in James Callaghan's words, with

ion

ation is a gigantic case study of how increased social and
idual activity and commitment – more expenditure, more
ings, more people, and more political support – do not
sarily lead to satisfaction and success . . . by the end of 1977,
the daring or the self-interested were able to call for more
tional growth as a certain way to economic and social salvation.
e Kogan, *The Politics of Educational Change*, pp. 25, 41

the major issues of social policy in the seventies, education
dered most controversy.
Marwick, *British Society Since 1945*, p. 236

n't need no education
n't need no thought control
k sarcasm in the classroom
IERS leave the kids alone . . .
ll you're just another brick in the wall.
Brick in the Wall'

s the conflict more firmly felt than in education. Urged on
ience of the left, Labour finally legislated first to do away
rant schools and then in effect to require local education
ho had not already done so to submit plans to go compre-
result was an equal and opposite reaction. Norman
s, the new Conservative education spokesman, moved shrilly
of both grammar and direct grant schools. In the case of
schools, he plotted with rebel Conservative local authorities
aw 'in a way not reckoned to be conventional in previous
St John-Stevas was an urbane, witty, liberal and irreverent
ic, who wondered at Thatcher's ability to see 'everything
ite, since the universe I inhabit is made up of many shades
was in almost all things what came to be known as a
was eventually sacked for it. On education, however, and
standards and selection, he was on the right. He entered
usto, noting that grammar schools were a 'uniting issue'
ht within the Tory party at a time when the two wings
art.[11]

the panic of 'screaming schoolgirls'.[1] The next day the Chancellor applied to the International Monetary Fund for a £2.3 billion loan to save sterling, producing a third round of cuts that had already lopped £2 billion from spending plans that year.

Just as Healey was returning to the Treasury, Callaghan was leaving his hotel in Blackpool to speak at his first Labour Party conference as Prime Minister. He produced, in his own words, a paragraph that really 'made the fur fly'. Unemployment stood at 1,588,000 – half a million more than the peak under Heath and a level which Cabinet ministers when they took office had believed would be utterly unsustainable.[2] Despite that, Callaghan announced the formal break with Keynesianism that Wilson and Healey had in fact instituted a year earlier when in 1975 they had cut spending in a recession. Callaghan told delegates:

> We used to think that you could spend your way out of recession and increase employment by cutting taxes and boosting Government spending. I tell you in all candour that option no longer exists, and that insofar as it ever did exist, it only worked on each occasion since the war by injecting a bigger dose of inflation into the economy, followed by a higher level of unemployment as the next step. High inflation followed by higher unemployment . . . that is the history of the past twenty years.

'For too long, perhaps ever since the war,' he told his audience, '. . . we have been living on borrowed time.' Money had been borrowed to maintain living standards, and the country had paid itself more than it could afford. 'The cosy world we were told would go on for ever, where full employment would be guaranteed by a stroke of the Chancellor's pen, cutting taxes, deficit spending – that cosy world is gone'.[3]

It was the moment which marked the first great fissure in Britain's welfare state: not the adoption of the full-blooded monetarism that Joseph, Howe and others were now advocating from the Opposition benches; not yet an acceptance by Labour that full employment was unachievable, or that Keynesian tools had no place – Callaghan was careful to add 'we reject unemployment as an economic instrument' – but it was an acknowledgement that in the changed world of floating exchange rates, of huge financial transactions in the markets and of rampant inflation which had hit 26.9 per cent in August a year earlier, then the old Keynesian economics as practised by post-war governments was, alone, no longer enough. The magic prescription of growth, public expenditure and full employment, paid for by higher taxation and perhaps slightly higher inflation, had ceased to work. Labour was discovering, as Heath had done, that you could have the inflation and the taxation, but without the growth and full employment. The money supply had acquired a new salience.

Labour had ended up in the arms of the IMF after Healey, a virgin Chancellor in economically uncharted waters, followed the Fund's advice and attempted to deal with the oil price rise by maintaining expenditure. He borrowed to meet the deficit. Most other Western countries cut spending hard, reinforcing a world-wide recession which itself helped restrict growth in Britain to virtually zero between 1974 and 1977. The result was that Labour put off for the better part of two years the action needed to deal with the oil shock. It did so partly because no one was to know until after the event how the price rise should be handled, but partly also because Labour was both a minority government which needed a rapid second general election, and one elected on a manifesto appreciably more left-wing than in 1964.

The manifesto had promised a 'fundamental and irreversible shift in the balance of power and wealth in favour of working people and their families'. Measures to achieve that included a wealth tax (not implemented), a substantial extension of public ownership (which saw takeovers of aerospace and ship-building industries and the rescue of British Leyland), and much else. Furthermore, in the wake of first Wilson's and then Heath's failed attempts to reform union law, Labour had also agreed the 'social contract' with the TUC. In theory this deal meant that unions would moderate their wage demands in return for the 'social wage' to which Labour was pledged – spending on pensions and the NHS, and on a new child benefit, along with food subsidies, price controls and restrictions on council house rents.

The result, in the words of Joel Barnett, Chief Secretary to the Treasury throughout the five-year term, was that 'the first months of the new Government were characterized by our spending money which in the event we did not have'.[4] Labour planned for levels of growth which simply never materialised, while the Chief Secretary's embittered summary of the social contract was that 'the only give and take in [it] was that the Government gave and the unions took.'[5]

As a consequence, in the three years to 1976 the economy grew hardly at all while public expenditure rose by 18 per cent. Borrowing and taxation both rose, and taxation not just of the rich, who saw their top rate rise from 75 to 83 per cent, but of those in the middle and at the bottom where the standard rate increased to 33 per cent. On top of that tax thresholds fell, so the less well off started paying tax earlier. The days had long gone

when massive sums could be raised merely by
which Denis Healey had first warned the pa
had underlined in 1973 when he told deleg
programme 'a lot of you will pay extra taxes

Thus in March 1974 an extra £2 billion
housing and food subsidies, including, in an
cent rise in pensions to £10 for single people
capital cuts, however, were largely left in
installed at the Elephant and Castle to run t
Social Security, was able to record that 'as
the government's side of the social contract
of my own way in Cabinet.'[7] It was not unt
announced to prevent spending drifting u
and 1976, when the first cuts began to bite
spending began. It did so just as Labour's
October 1974 election, started to be whittl
The government was soon again a mino
of 1977 on a pact with the Liberals.

In fact the 1974–9 government saw a
of marked progress as well as distinct set
into pre- and post- the IMF crisis. There
the welfare state as well as repeated ret
however, the period when the party
between the parties and within them.
that formed Labour and Conservative
under a new woman leader began to
into Thatcherism while the party's le
consensus in the centre. In Labour's
left had formulated over the Wilson ye
of another Labour Government respo
crises with yet another rounds of cu
Democracy, which was to provide th
1980s, was formed, while Roy Jenki
European Commission as a man wh
behind rather than the other way r

Educat

Educ
indiv
build
neces
only
educa
Mauri

Of all
engen
Arthur

We do
We do
No da
TEACH
All in
'Anothe

Nowhere wa
by the impa
with direct
authorities w
hensive. Th
St John-Steva
to the defenc
the grammar
to resist the
generations'.
Roman Catho
in black and w
of grey'.[10] He
Tory wet and
particularly on
the fray with
for left and rig
were pulling a

At his side was Stuart Sexton, a chemist made redundant by Shell, who combined a Tiggerish enthusiasm for overturning apple carts, a love of plots and a deep distrust of comprehensives. Sexton, then forty, had been a Croydon councillor and on its education committee. 'Normally the dries were interested in finance and went on to highways or whatever. My argument was that education, which affected everyone, was also the biggest item in the budget. I had a philosophical attraction to it.'[12] He also had experience. A governor of St Joseph's College on the borders of Croydon and Lambeth, where he had been a pupil and where his children now were, he had watched the school go comprehensive. 'I could see for myself how the standards were dropping even though I was a governor of the school. I could see it wasn't realistic to cater for such a wide range of ability, particularly if at the same time you were trying to keep up standards.'[13] This experience was mixed with ideology – an ideology transparent enough for Chris Patten, the new director of the Conservative Research Department, to turn him down for a job on its education desk. He told St John-Stevas that Sexton was 'far too right wing'.[14] Sexton however was sufficiently determined to effect change that he took a job direct with St John-Stevas on pay so tiny that for years his children were eligible for free school meals. He was to advise Tory education spokesmen and ministers in a rightward direction for a decade.

Between them St John-Stevas and Sexton arranged a half-million-strong petition against the abolition of grammar schools and filibustered as best they could the Bill to strengthen ministers' hands over comprehensive reorganisation. They also found Leon Brittan, a young Tory lawyer, to provide his services free in order to take Fred Mulley, the Secretary of State for Education, to court over the case of Tameside. In early 1976 the incoming Conservative council had overturned its predecessors' plan to go comprehensive that very year. Mulley ordered them to reverse the decision on the grounds that they were acting 'unreasonably'. The issue went to the Law Lords, who almost unprecedentedly sat on an August Saturday in 1976 to produce a decision before the beginning of term. They ruled in Tameside's favour. It was a spectacular if finally empty victory. The Education Act became law shortly afterwards and in 1983, back under local Labour control, Tameside eventually went comprehensive. The flavour of the times, however, is caught in St John-Stevas's comment on the ruling he had helped engineer: 'A further blow has been struck in the fight for parental influence and choice in education, for the independence of the local authorities and for the liberty of the subject. Never again will an education minister be able to behave with dictatorial arrogance to parents and councillors.'[15] The ruling seriously shook the confidence of the DES which had believed it would win. It was left feeling its limited powers over comprehensive reorganisation, and even more limited powers over the curriculum, were yet more limited than it had thought.[16]

The war did not stop there. Eight local authorities, including Essex, Sutton, Kingston and Trafford, remained determined to fight on after the Education Act. Sexton organised seven of them, the 'magnificent seven' as he dubbed them, to meet 'in total secrecy' at the Royal Air Force Club, Piccadilly, to co-ordinate their resistance. 'It was a game,' Sexton recalls, 'playing the department along. The authorities would get requests to go comprehensive and we would always reply by asking further questions. We didn't say we wouldn't go comprehensive. We just asked complicated questions – about how you were going to finance it and so on. We shared the replies amongst ourselves, we gummed up the whole works. The apparently unco-ordinated response from these authorities was not unco-ordinated at all. Norman wouldn't have anything to do with this.[17] He thought it was politically wrong for him to get associated with such overt opposition to what was Government policy and had been legislated for. So I just carried on and did it myself and left him in the dark.'[18]

St John-Stevas's own message to the grammar schools at the 1977 Tory party conference was 'hang on, because help is coming'. But the Conservatives knew that by and large the electorate no longer wanted the eleven-plus; at the same conference he emphasised that they would not bring it back and that the Tories' major effort must go into the comprehensives which 'are here to stay'.[19] A year later he reiterated the point. Parents did not want another 'educational earthquake'. The outcome was that a few grammar schools in a few places, about 150 in all, lasted long enough to be rescued by the Conservatives in 1979, providing not just a memory but a base on which to rebuild the idea of selection. By then more than 85 per cent of state pupils were in comprehensive schools and that figure continued to rise after 1979, suggesting that for most parents comprehensives retained an appeal.[20]

By then the direct grant schools had already gone – axed in a forty-five-minute late-night debate in October 1975. Of the 154 then existing, 51, chiefly Roman Catholic, became comprehensives. The remainder, and usually better known, opted for the perils of independence, producing the Tory jibe that Labour had successfully created more independent schools than any government since Edward VI. In one of those ironies which litter the tale of the welfare state, a move aimed at reducing divisions in the state sector in fact enlarged the private one for, against heady predictions from the left, the newly independent schools survived. Although they were only a minority – around 5 per cent – slightly more parents seemed prepared to buy their way out of a state system that they increasingly distrusted.

One reason for that may have been that if the structural battles over direct grant and grammars in the late seventies were noisy, even more turmoil now surrounded the very idea of education. The final collapse of the political consensus over comprehensives and direct grant schools coincided with falling primary school rolls, sharply rising secondary school numbers, ever tightening public expenditure, and growing controversy over educational methods. The post-war assumption that a steady expansion *of* education would produce an increasing satisfaction *with* education had fallen apart. A battle over standards, which not even twenty years and a national curriculum would begin to resolve, was about to be joined.

As unemployment rocketed, the familiar complaint of employers through the ages that they still could not get people who could read and write became louder. The Black Paperites, silent while the Tories were in power and remaining tactfully so about Mrs Thatcher's record as a grammar school destroyer, re-emerged with a vengeance. Standards were falling, they declared, demanding tests at seven, eleven and fourteen. Rhodes Boyson, now a Tory MP and a joint editor of the fourth and fifth *Black Papers*, was barely exaggerating when he declared he could fill any hall in the land. On neither side of the argument did there seem to be much desire nor ability to establish the facts. In 1974 the DES did set up an assessment of performance unit to attempt to provide evidence on standards, but it did little to help. Education, after all, is political. If Crosland and company believed education could change society for the better, the right was now equally convinced it was changing society for the worse.

Controversy was fuelled by some middle-class journalists in London who, finding their children in inner-city comprehensives rather than grammars, reacted with horror and in print at the size, scale and unruliness of some of the new schools. A famous, perhaps infamous, *Panorama* television programme in 1977 produced 'fly on the wall' footage of Faraday High in Ealing with scenes of indiscipline, chaos and incompetence which still stun today.[21] There was fierce controversy over how the programme was made and how fair it was. It seemed, however, only to reflect in a secondary school the horrors that a public inquiry had just established in a primary.

At the William Tyndale junior school in north London, teachers who, as Brian Simon puts it, 'seemed possessed of an apocalyptic vision as to

the role of education in achieving social change'[22] had been teaching in
such a highly permissive, child-centred and non-authoritarian way that
parents, horrified by the resulting mayhem, had over a fifteen-month
period increasingly voted with their feet and taken their children away.
Their protests to the local authority finally brought a school inspection.
The teachers, claiming as their professional right total autonomy to decide
what was taught and how, went on strike. The Inner London Education
Authority was forced to set up an inquiry.

This one tiny junior school in Islington successfully brought into focus
in one dramatic dispute and nine months of spectacular if not always
accurate press coverage ('why teach children to write when we have type-
writers?')[23] almost every educational issue other than comprehensives that
had been bubbling away under, and slowly up to, the surface since the
1944 Education Act. What should be taught in schools? How should it be
taught? And who was to decide: parents, teachers, the local authority, or
central government? In addition, who actually controlled a school? The
governors, the local authority, their inspectors, Her Majesty's inspectors,
or the Secretary of State? To whom were teachers, schools, even local
authorities accountable? The Auld report, as the Tyndale inquiry became
known, started to answer some of these, saying that the local authority
had failed in its duty to intervene. The Taylor report on the role of
governors, which had been commissioned in 1975 when the William Tyndale affair was merely brewing, was to tackle others. What was to be taught,
and who was to decide that, was, however, another matter.

In 1944 – as Butler had regretted in telling Churchill that attempts to
influence what was taught in schools were always 'frowned on'[24] – that
had been nothing to do with central government. George Tomlinson had
memorably pronounced: 'The Minister knows nowt about the curriculum.'[25] Central government's interest in such a key part of education had
not formally been acknowledged until 1960, when David Eccles in a debate
on the Crowther report referred to 'the secret garden of the curriculum'[26]
into which only teachers were allowed. 'We hardly ever discuss what is
taught to the seven million boys and girls in the maintained schools,' he
told the Commons. MPs treated the curriculum like 'the other place' (the
House of Lords) about which it was 'not done' for them to make remarks.
He would not attempt to dictate, he said. But in future he would 'try to
make the Ministry's own voice heard rather more often, more positively,
and no doubt, more controversially'. Just how controversially he was soon
to discover. The curriculum remained dynamite country. In 1954, Ronald
Gould, general secretary of the National Union of Teachers, had declared:

I have heard it said that the existence in this country of 146 strong vigorous local education authorities safeguards democracy and lessens the risk of dictatorship. No doubt this is true, but an even greater safeguard is the existence of a quarter of a million teachers who are free to decide what should be taught and how it should be taught.[27]

The curriculum had been left to teachers, and not just because it was thought teachers knew best. At a time when Nazi Germany was a decidedly fresh memory, there remained a real fear of government influence over what was instilled in children.

Eccles followed up his words with the establishment in 1962 of a Curriculum Study Group in the ministry, composed of administrators, a few of Her Majesty's Inspectors of schools, and educational experts. Its aim was to allow ministers at least a say in the debate. In the words of Maurice Kogan, one of its members, Eccles unwisely dubbed the group 'a commando type unit' though its aim was little broader than to identify and publicise good practice.[28] He was almost universally damned. Sir Ronald pronounced again, declaring that the group's mere existence posed a threat to English liberties.[29] Local education authorities joined the battle, insisting on an independent body. The furore was such that the group had to be wound up. Out of it in 1964 emerged the Schools Council, independent of ministers although with departmental representatives and embracing both the curriculum and examinations. But so sensitive was the issue of central control, and so much was the curriculum still seen as teachers' territory, that on every committee teachers had a majority. As a result, the Schools Council progressively came to be seen not as independent but as captive to teacher opinion, and in time to the teacher unions whose relationship with central government progressively soured, chiefly over pay, from the late 1960s on.

It was against this background that James Callaghan, speaking at Ruskin College, Oxford, in 1976, called for 'A Great Debate' on education. Callaghan could claim a lifelong interest in the subject, even telling Wilson when he resigned as Chancellor over devaluation in 1967 that his 'first choice' of alternative post was education, not the Home Office.[30] Until John Major, he was the only Prime Minister born this century not to go university, and he valued education highly for 'the doors it could unlock'.[31] He was only too well aware of the growing turmoil surrounding it. The head of the relatively new Downing Street Policy Unit was Bernard Donoughue, a former politics don at the LSE. State educated, he also had strong views on education linked to a suspicion of the vested interests of professions of which Margaret Thatcher would have been proud. He felt this particularly about the teaching unions whom he believed 'had become a major part of the problem. In all my many dealings with the NUT at that time I never once heard mention of education or children' – only money. Donoughue also believed that opinion surveys showed both parties to be out of touch: Labour with its belief in 'a liberal permissiveness in the classrooms' and the Conservatives with their dislike of comprehensives and their desire only to strengthen the élite sector.

'The majority of the public were actually content with the basic structure of education,' he believed. What they wanted was 'a more disciplined approach to reinforcing traditional standards in the hope of producing a literate, numerate and employable young generation.'[32] He therefore suggested education as a suitable topic for the new Prime Minister's interest. One of Callaghan's first acts was to call in Fred Mulley, the Secretary of State for Education, and demand a brief on what was happening.[33] The result was a sixty-page document which became known from its cover as *The Yellow Book*.

It reflected the anxious state of play in education. But it also explained it. Child-centred learning and informal teaching methods had in 'less able and experienced hands' gone too far in some primary schools. A 'corrective shift of emphasis' was needed. In the secondaries 'no one could deny that there are currently weaknesses'. Some of these were transitional, resulting from the switch to comprehensives and the raising of the school leaving age. Teachers, used to either grammar or secondary modern children, had found it difficult to adjust to teaching the whole ability range. Many new teachers had had to be recruited, first to cope with leaving at sixteen and then with the peak from the 1960s baby-boom. The result was a teaching force that was disproportionately young, inexperienced and short on qualifications.

Over time, some of these problems would improve, but for the present the DES admitted there were real difficulties. In addition, too much emphasis was being placed on preparing children for their role in society rather than their 'economic role'. This, the *Yellow Book* judged, was not solely the fault of the teachers, reflecting rather the mood of the country and the priority of successive governments. 'But here, as in the primary schools, the time may now be ripe for a change', the national mood having altered 'in the face of hard and irreducible economic facts'. The Schools Council, the only body with any oversight of the curriculum, was described as union dominated and 'mediocre'. And the Prime Minister was urged to refute what the teachers had sought to establish – 'that no one except teachers has any right to any say in what goes on in schools'. Finally, the time had now come to consider a 'core curriculum' to include vocational elements. The department should be allowed to give 'a firmer lead'.[34]

The *Yellow Book* marked in part the work of James Hamilton, the new Permanent Secretary. An engineer not an educationalist, he had been injected into the DES by Downing Street from the Cabinet Office a year earlier as a hard-nosed realist after Harold Wilson's complaints that the department acted as 'little more than a post box' between the local authorities and the teacher unions.[35] The *Yellow Book* was never published, but three days before Callaghan's speech at Ruskin College, it was comprehensively leaked in the *Times Educational Supplement*. The leak drew comments which angered Callaghan while defining for him part of the problem. He found himself accused of being a professional politician but an amateur educationalist, while 'the propriety of my raising questions on what should be taught and how it should be taught' was doubted. In Callaghan's view that was 'appalling educational snobbery'.[36] He had been told to 'keep off the grass' and that 'profane hands' should not touch education. In the speech he warned such stances could no longer hold.

> Public interest is strong and legitimate and will be satisfied. We spend £6bn a year on education, so there will be discussion. But let it be rational. If everything is reduced to such phrases as 'educational freedom *versus* state control' we will get nowhere. I repeat that parents, teachers, learned and professional bodies, representatives of higher education and both sides of industry, together with the Government, all have an important part to play in formulating and expressing the purpose of education and the standards that we need.

The speech in fact set large parts of the agenda for the next decade. Its echoes can be heard today, and a surprising amount of it could be repeated almost twenty years on as still unresolved business – a fact which does not say a great deal for either Britain's system of government or its culture.

At Ruskin, Callaghan made clear he favoured 'a core curriculum with universal standards', closer involvement of parents and industry in schools, and more technological teaching. This was combined with warnings that the pendulum must not swing too far in favour of creativity and against the three Rs, or for informal instruction against acquiring employable skills. Some method of monitoring performance against national standards was needed, he declared – an agenda likely to include more inspection and testing, although that was not spelt out. His remarks, he said, were firmly not 'a clarion call to Black Paper prejudices. We all know those who claim to defend standards but in reality are simply seeking to defend old privileges and inequalities.' The issues he had raised, however, were 'proper subjects for . . . rational debate based on facts'. The speech drew audible dissent from his audience.[37]

By the time Callaghan sat down, a new more centralising, more accountable era had dawned for education, even if it was to take well over a decade to come to maturity. Callaghan's speech, inevitably, was the product of its times as well as the creator of a climate. A month earlier, the Commons Expenditure Committee, cross-party but with a Labour majority, had criticised the DES for being too inactive, suggesting it should do more to shape the curriculum, and do more than just allocate resources. Hamilton had earlier given the committee that line himself, arguing that 'the key to the secret garden of the curriculum must be found and turned';[38] his predecessor Sir William Pile, too, had raised that idea and had begun to strengthen the inspectorate (HMI) into something rather tougher than just a source of friendly advice.[39] For more than a year HMI had privately been talking the language of the core curriculum.[40]

Reaction to Callaghan's speech was varied. With much of the public it struck a chord. In Donoughue's judgement it offended many Labour Party members, while leaving the NUT furious. Shirley Williams, who had just taken over as Secretary of State, was 'unhappy that the Prime Minister had trespassed into her ministerial territory, opened a can of worms, and left her to deal with the consequences'.[41] The department was split. The younger Turks and the very top of the office were delighted, believing in a core curriculum and greater central control, but significant sections of the department still believed in the partnership which gave local authorities the leading role.[42]

In practice, however, the next two and a half years went missing. Shirley Williams did remove the teachers' overall majority on the Schools Council and eight regional conferences of the Great Debate were held. A Green Paper emerged in July 1977: there are differing versions of its history. Callaghan records that he had to press to get in 'any references to the need for a core curriculum'.[43] Shirley Williams insists she wanted one, while admitting there were differences between her, Callaghan and Donoughue over how detailed and prescriptive it should be.[44] The Green Paper itself proposed little more than consultations about a review which would lead to consultations about the advice that the department might issue on the subject.[45]

It did, however, emphasise the productive goals required of education. 'Young people need to reach maturity with a basic understanding of the economy and its activities, especially manufacturing industry, which are necessary for the creation of Britain's economic wealth',[46] it stated, in words that Keith Joseph could have used. Government White Papers in 1985 would say precisely the same thing in remarkably similar phrases.[47] Meanwhile the Taylor report on the management of schools recommended that governing bodies should now include equal representation from parents and the local community, alongside local authority representatives and teachers, and that these governors be given more powers and limited oversight of the curriculum. The NUT general secretary dubbed the report 'a busybodies' charter'.[48] Shirley Williams attempted to create a General Teachers Council, both to turn teaching into a proper profession with educational standards – almost 40 per cent of non-graduate student teachers did not have a maths O-level in 1975[49] – but also so that teachers could be sacked, preferably by their peers, without producing strikes. The idea foundered when the general secretaries of the National Union of Teachers and the National Association of Schoolmasters 'had a shouting match and refused to sit down in the same room together'.[50]

Some, but not much, of the new thinking crept into the Education Bill of 1978. There was no mention of a core curriculum: no consensus for a statutory curriculum then existed and even if Labour MPs could have been persuaded to back one, there was no parliamentary majority to deliver it. When the Lib–Lab pact took effect in the spring of 1977, 'the Liberals, quite understandably, made it plain that as a party which cared passionately about the devolution of power to local government, they were not about to support us in passing legislation that would give powers to the DES over the curriculum,' according to Shirley Williams.[51] The Conservatives were still wary of the idea, and on Baroness Williams's calculations around 24 per cent of Labour MPs were ex-teachers, most of whose unions were firmly against any tampering with the curriculum. Robert Cook, general secretary of the National Association of Head Teachers, had declared bluntly on hearing Callaghan's 1976 speech: 'I was teaching in Nazi Germany in the thirties and saw what happened where the curriculum was nationally controlled. My history books were taken out and replaced.'[52]

The Bill did, however, provide that each school should normally have its own governing body rather than, as sometimes happened, being grouped with others under one set of governors or even run direct by the local education committee. Parent governors were to be appointed, community governors were to provide a tentative link to industry, parents were to have a right to more information about schools, and within certain limits parental choice was to be the key factor in allocating pupils – ending the zoning and in some cases bussing that local authorities had introduced to spread brighter pupils more evenly across comprehensives. The Bill went down with the March 1979 general election. But Labour and Callaghan had set a significant part of what was now also the Conservative education agenda – one bitterly contested by the Labour left and by the teaching unions, but one which to some degree could be said to reflect a new, less generous, more utilitarian consensus over what education should be trying to achieve and to whom it should be answerable. Educationalists, even in economic times that by late 1977 were beginning to improve, felt vilified and demoralised. The Conservatives, who saw massive political advantage in what even the Department of Education admitted was a controversy, used the advertising agency Saatchi and Saatchi to produce an election poster 'Educashun isnt wurking' while in 1979 any teacher who was not already shell-shocked must have winced at the brute nihilism of the chart-topping single 'Another brick in the wall'. It was not a good time to be a teacher.

It was not much better to be in higher education. The quinquennial settlements which had allowed universities to plan with complete confidence that the necessary cash would be available cracked under rampant inflation, never to be fully restored. The targets of three-quarters of a million students in the Thatcher White Paper were cut back to 640,000.[53] More students continued to be educated but at lower cost per head.[54] Later in the decade, colleges of education closed in droves as demand for teachers fell, mirroring the effects of falling birth rates. Capital spending was slashed to what was almost certainly its lowest since the war. The Houghton award for teachers increased pay in polytechnics, but university dons were caught by pay policy and were left, embittered, behind. In 1975, Malcolm Bradbury's excoriating and witty novel The History Man, portraying life in the new universities of the late sixties, burst upon the scene. Student unrest had died away. The first signs that there might no longer be easy jobs to go to produced students who cut their hair and worked harder rather than a generation dedicated to overturning the system. But the same nagging doubt which pervaded the schools over whether education was providing value for money also afflicted higher education. 'The new universities, the transformed colleges of advanced technology, the whole shining picture of 1964 had now, in the eyes of the Government, shrunk in the public mind back to a Gothic image of "Oxbridge" overlaid by [Bradbury's] University of Watermouth', or so it felt for John Carswell, secretary of University Grants Committee.[55] When the government finally peeked beyond the time horizon of the Robbins report and into the 1990s it produced not a printed HMSO document but a mimeographed 'Brown Paper' containing five options, and in Carswell's words 'no vibrant phraseology or policy decisions'. Its manner was 'tentative, even apologetic'.[56] Despite all this student numbers continued to rise, faster than either staff or higher education's real income. Arguably higher education was becoming more efficient. Unarguably, the gilded dawn of the Robbins era was well and truly over.

Housing

> Housing has had its successes, but . . . after 60 years of increasing
> State intervention in housing, we are reaching a situation where a
> large and growing proportion of the labour force, and possibly
> a majority of manual workers are treated as though they were unable
> to house themselves without State assistance. This seems economic
> absurdity.
>
> In the Conservative party we must have as our prime objective
> a big increase in home ownership. If some greater financial incentive
> is required, we shall have to be prepared to give it. It is better to
> help people towards self-reliance than State-reliance.
>
> Margaret Thatcher, shadow Environment Secretary, Daily Telegraph,
> 1 July 1974

Labour's first act in housing was to freeze council rents. It then repealed the more controversial aspects of Peter Walker's Housing Finance Act before setting up a review to sort out what Tony Crosland described as 'the dog's breakfast' that housing finance had become after seventy years of accretion, amendment and deletion. The review, however, became trapped between electoral reality, Labour's left-wing manifesto, the lack of a parliamentary majority and bitter clashes between officials and advisers.[57] The strong desire of the party's left – and of almost anyone who examined the issue rationally – to wind down mortgage tax relief foundered. It was now costing the Treasury £1.1 billion a year, only £250 million less than the total housing subsidy to local authorities. As ever, it helped the better-off most. But to have tampered with it when home ownership was continuing to rise, reaching 55 per cent by 1979, would have been electoral suicide. Instead, help was offered to first-time buyers. Rehabilitation was taken further with better improvement grants and the creation of Housing Action Areas, while public sector completions rose 40,000 from the 111,500 achieved in 1974 before falling back again to barely 95,000 by 1979. Council house renovations, however, fared badly, spending never reaching the level achieved in the last year of the Heath government.[58] Housing associations, through an expanded Housing Corporation, became bigger players in the game, accounting for a fifth of all public sector starts in 1978.[59] Furnished tenants finally acquired security of tenure, strengthening their rights but further discouraging private landlords who were worried that they might never get their houses or second homes back. A Liberal private member's Bill became the Homeless Persons Act of 1977, allowing Cathy, at least at one level, finally to find a home. In practice much of this represented a broad continuity of housing policy from the late sixties and early seventies as a 1977 Green Paper, widely perceived as insipid, finally produced a subsidy regime short of the one that Walker had introduced but still a system that the Conservatives said they could live with. Council house sales were allowed to continue, even if local authorities were told they were 'generally wrong' (they were banned in New Towns), and there was a move towards a charter for council tenants which had still not been fully delivered by the time of the election.

Health

We'll have to put people before buildings.
Barbara Castle to the TUC liaison committee, Daily Mail, 26 May 1974

I have had the sad duty of touring the country, inspecting large holes in the ground, and telling numerous people that their much-needed and much desired district general hospital cannot be built . . . large sums have now to be written off for designing hospitals that can never now leave the drawing board.
David Owen, In Sickness and in Health, p. 43

Morale has never been lower.
Dr Derek Stevenson, Secretary of the BMA, before the pay beds row

If there was a revolution of frustrated expectations [in the mid- to late 1970s], it was among the producers not the consumers.
Rudolf Klein, The Politics of the NHS, p. 125

Throughout its history, the NHS and its staff have been dogged by a sense of doing better and feeling worse.
Brian Edwards, Administrator, Leeds Area Health Authority 1974–6

The 1974 general election brought Barbara Castle to the DHSS for two of the most dramatic years in its history. Red-haired, vivacious, ferocious, intelligent, a fighter all the way, her standing had been damaged by *In Place of Strife* her attempt during the first Wilson government to reform trade union law – a defeat suffered at the hands of Cabinet colleagues as much as those of the unions. The politician who in other times might just have been Britain's first woman Prime Minister thus brought to her new post a determination to restore her reputation with all parties. She arrived to the briefest of lulls before the most outrageous of storms.

Her first decision was whether to let Keith Joseph's NHS reorganisation, due to come into operation on 1 April, go ahead. She had no choice. To unscramble an exercise already causing chaos was unthinkable. It was anyway a different NHS to the one Labour had left: the virus of industrial action had entered the service. Until the 1970s stoppages had been almost unknown. In the late 1960s there had been literally one or two tiny one-day strikes a year.[60] In 1972 the accidental breaking of traditional pay links with local government triggered an ancillary workers' strike that hit 750 hospitals nationwide. The emotional barrier to strike action in the health service had gone. The profound sense of shock which that caused was only worsened as a rash of disputes over pay differentials plagued the service through 1973 claiming 300,000 working days. After strikes by power workers and the miners in the early 1970s, the message had penetrated deep into white collar ranks and into the NHS that to join the big battalions and strike was about the only way to get what you wanted. And just as Kenneth Robinson inherited a GPs' dispute from Tony Barber, so Barbara Castle with even more explosive results inherited a hospital consultants' dispute from Keith Joseph.

Talks on a new contract for consultants had been under way since 1972 and the doctors' mood was already ugly. Even in 1973, some militant consultants had been talking of industrial action. The GPs' new contract had left them feeling that their income was being squeezed. As salaried employees of the government, they had been caught by repeated rounds of pay policy while lawyers and other comparable fee-charging professionals had escaped. High-tech medicine had increased their workload, as had the first tentative reductions in junior doctors' working hours. (In the immediate post-war period the most junior house officer at some hospitals was entitled only to Christmas Day off.)

Marked strains had developed within the consultants' ranks. The number of part-timers – those free to do private practice – stood at around 60 per cent of all consultants. The division between specialities, however, was sharp. Only 15 per cent of surgeons were whole-timers, against 90 per cent in geriatrics or mental handicap. Anthony Grabham, a Kettering surgeon who became the consultants' key negotiator, recalls 'a great divide that is forgotten now between gentlemen and players. The part-timers felt they were the gentlemen. They tended to look down on the full-timers ever so slightly, while from their point of view the full-timers often felt superior because they were not indulging in private practice. Around every lunch table in every hospital there was an almost discernible split between them and us. I wanted to get rid of that.'[61]

Alongside a full-time/part-time divide was an even more serious London/provincial split. Those outside the capital felt the BMA toffs in London, who had prime access to private practice, were doing a rotten job for the poor bloody infantry. A Regional Hospital Consultants and Specialists Association had been formed, transforming itself into a national body which took 4000 of the 11,000 consultants away from the BMA. 'I want my consultants back,' a furious Dr Derek Stevenson, the BMA secretary, used to intone as the HCSA took the BMA to court to demand a share of the sole negotiating rights that the BMA enjoyed with government. As in 1965, the BMA had a serious split on its hands and was once again having to look over its shoulder at a rival. To compound the situation, junior doctors were becoming alarmingly militant for similar reasons to their seniors but with the added complaint that they worked 102 hours a week before any extra duty allowance or overtime. Many were on call for even longer. There was simmering resentment that neither consultants nor government seemed prepared to do anything about it. The BMA's junior hospital doctors committee had itself come within a whisker of being taken over and taken out of the BMA by the yet more militant Junior Hospital Doctors Association.

The consultants' answer to their problem had been to demand, in effect, something close to a car-workers' contract – a 'closed' contract for all which would set a time limit on their NHS commitment and pay them extra for work over and above that. One of its effects would have been to free all to do private practice. At the same time, and because the consultants were as divided as the GPs had been, they wanted the option of an American-style contract giving them a fee for each item of service – a move open to all the objections Kenneth Robinson had raised when the GPs wanted it and with which neither Barbara Castle nor the Cabinet would have any truck. These 'pay and rations' complaints, combined with the Barber cuts, raging inflation, and the first serious industrial action by nurses, had left the service in a genuine sense of crisis. Not long after Labour took office the BMA demanded a £500 million cash injection to save the NHS – a massive sum when total NHS spending was only £3 billion – and a Royal Commission. Stevenson publicly trailed ideas for hotel charges, top-up insurance, charges for visiting the GP, an extra health stamp or even a sweepstake to raise more money. 'The fundamental thing is that it can't go on like this,' he declared,[62] adding the standing NHS refrain: 'morale has never been lower.' For once, it was almost certainly true. It was into this already heady brew that Labour stirred the final ingredient needed to make gunpowder. It had determined to phase pay beds out of the NHS.

Shortly after 1948 private health insurance had fallen sharply away. Private medicine had become largely the preserve of those who could pay out of their own pocket. The provident associations, of whom BUPA, the British United Provident Association, was by far the biggest, saw the numbers they covered fall. By 1950 barely 100,000 people had cover for private health care. The rising cost of increasingly sophisticated surgery soon meant, however, that fewer could afford to risk direct, out-of-pocket payment for private treatment, so the insurance market started to grow, encouraged by the new affluence among those who were becoming better off if by no means rich. By 1955 something over half a million people were covered; by 1960 it was just under a million. Pay restraint encouraged the use of company-paid schemes as an executive and even non-executive perk, so the numbers kept rising: they reached almost two million in 1970 and 2.3 million by 1974, two-thirds of whom were in company schemes. Thus while only just over 4 per cent of the population was covered, and while spending on private hospital care was comfortably less than 2 per cent of the total NHS budget, those numbers had almost quadrupled in twenty years.[63] When drawn as a graph, the growth in private practice appeared to the left to be rocketing away.

There were some 3700 beds in private hospitals. Many of these, however, were technically primitive, little more than grandiose nursing homes.

Outside London, and particularly for anything remotely high-tech, consultants remained heavily dependent on the NHS and its pay beds. To Labour's left, Bevan's peculiarly British compromise of private beds in health service hospitals remained an ideological blot on an otherwise pure NHS landscape. More importantly it allowed queue-jumping when the half-million-long NHS waiting list included patients who waited more than two years for non-urgent treatment; one memorable case discovered by Sir Alan Marre, the newly created health service ombudsman, had waited six years. The extent and scale of abuse which undoubtedly existed, and which included the trick of buying a private out-patient appointment to jump up the NHS in-patient queue, was never properly established. Enough concern was raised, however, for the Commons Expenditure Committee to look at the issue in 1971. The committee had a Conservative majority which the Labour members alleged was used to produce 'a massive whitewash job' when the report concluded that abuses were not 'widespread or of any magnitude'.[64]

Labour MPs preferred to believe the opposite. The committee had heard charges from junior doctors that consultants were skimping NHS work in favour of private practice and delegating too much to juniors; that NHS equipment was borrowed and not paid for; and that NHS queues were kept artificially long to encourage patients to go private. There were doubts whether health service charges for private treatment covered the actual cost. Mixed in with what were real issues was a fair dose of envy and an injured sense of equity – only consultants, not nurses, junior doctors or porters, benefited from the private practice gravy train, and the NHS was under pressure. The actual evidence the committee heard was thin, but in Labour's ranks the report resonated. By 1974 a manifesto commitment had been produced to 'phase out private practice from the hospital service'.[65] Such was the leftward shift of Labour in opposition, however, that even that had been a 'painfully achieved internal party compromise' reached to ward off an undertaking to abolish private medicine in its entirety, according to David Owen who was involved in the negotiations and was to become Minister of Health.[66]

Any chance that this might remain one of those quietly forgotten corners of the manifesto that most governments carry with them ended in the last week of June 1974. Members of the National Union of Public Employees blacked patients in the two twenty-bed private wards on the fifteenth floor of the brand new Charing Cross Hospital, known locally as the 'Fulham Hilton'. For the next ten days the rotund, archetypally Cockney figure of 'Ma' or 'Granny' Brookstone, a NUPE shop steward with tousled hair, a large black handbag and gold-rimmed glasses, became a national name as she regaled reporters with her views on private medicine – 'it should go outside the health service' – and her enjoyment of life. 'I've been married 38½ years. I've got four children, three grandchildren and my husband still chases me round the bedroom,' she told the nation.[67] The doctors were not amused. The unofficial NUPE action spread like wildfire. Inexorably, Castle, Owen, and the forces of the BMA were drawn into dispute. The Charing Cross crisis was only resolved temporarily after fraught late-night talks in which Castle renewed Labour's pledge to remove pay beds, promising action sooner rather than later.

At the time there were just 4500 NHS pay beds, barely one per cent of the total, treating fewer than 120,000 patients a year – less than half a per cent of the patients that the NHS treated annually. These beds, none the less, were to produce two years of the most bitter conflict the NHS had seen.

Castle had already referred their future to the consultants' contract working party which Owen was chairing. There the two issues, pay beds and a new contract, became inextricably enmeshed. Labour, partly because it wanted private practice out of the NHS, but also because it wanted to make the less glamorous specialities of the 'Cinderella' services more attractive, determined to offer an extra 18 per cent to those who took whole-time contracts with the NHS. In addition, Castle proposed that consultants' merit awards, which went disproportionately to those in glamorous specialities where most of the private practice lay, should in part become 'career supplements' or service bonuses. These would recognise dedication in unpopular specialities and unfashionable regions. They would also be available only to whole-timers. As the talks between Owen and the doctors, meant to be finished by November, dragged on an election intervened and negotiations were conducted against the background of sporadic guerrilla action by the unions against private patients, matched in places by retaliatory action by consultants, some of whom unofficially 'worked to contract' – limiting their hours to those for which they were formally contracted.

November became December, and just days before Christmas the talks broke down spectacularly. The consultants accused Castle of a 'take-it-or-leave it' offer. The incentives proposed for whole-time consultants were so large, they maintained, that, combined with the phasing out of pay beds, private practice would simply disappear in large parts of the country. That in turn, they argued (shades of 1946–8), would reduce them to employees of a state monopoly. 'We are fighting for the independence of the profession,' Walpole Lewin, the neurosurgeon who was the BMA's chairman of council trumpeted.[68]

For the first time in their history, consultants took industrial action. For sixteen weeks, to a greater or lesser extent and with enormous variations around the country, they 'worked to contract'. Out-patient sessions were cancelled, waiting lists grew, even the casualty department closed on alternate weekends in some places, while more than one patient found themselves anaesthetised and then not operated on because the doctor's time was up.[69]

As if a dispute with the seniors was not enough, Mrs Castle had then to head off one with the junior doctors, promising them a new forty-hour rather than eighty-hours-a-week contract which would start in October and would include at least some limited overtime payments. Just to compound the sense of crisis, GPs joined the act, collecting 16,000 unsigned, undated resignations in case Castle welshed on a pay award that was due in April 1975.

If Mrs Castle was beleaguered, the doctors became increasingly alarmed at the effects of their own action. Twice Stevenson and Lewin appealed to Harold Wilson to intervene. Twice he held firm, refusing to negotiate while the action continued. In the end the doctors sought what proved to be an all-night negotiating session with Castle in which the two sides effectively agreed to start all over again on the new contract. The worst, however, was yet to come. In August, Castle produced her consultative document on how pay beds were to be phased out. It included not just their removal, but strict licensing of new private sector beds to ensure that the total never exceeded the combined number of private hospital and NHS pay beds at March 1974. The aim was to prevent the private sector absorbing 'any undue proportion of scarce skills achieved by training at public expense'.[70] Its effect was to place a legal ceiling on the future expansion of private medicine.

The response not just of the BMA but of the medical Royal Colleges and the provident associations was apocalyptic. Castle's package was damned as 'sovietisation'. Unprecedentedly, some seventeen medical organisations united to declare that the proposals carried 'totalitarian' implications that could lead 'ultimately to the justification for the watch tower, the searchlight and the Berlin Wall'.[71] Not since Bevan's day had such language been used or the NHS been in such crisis. And any lingering doubts the doctors may have had that the ultimate objective was the entire elimination of private practice were removed a week later when the Labour Party conference, against Barbara Castle's entreaties, voted for just that – the complete abolition of private practice as a long-term aim.

Wilson flinched. In an attempt to appease the doctors he announced a

Royal Commission to investigate the NHS. He still, however, refused to refer the pay beds issue to it. In November 1975, on the eve of the Queen's Speech announcing the legislation, consultants' leaders called for emergencies-only cover and the collection of undated resignations from the NHS.

The wheel had come full circle. Doctors who eighteen months before had protested bitterly at the unconstitutionality of the unions attempting to remove pay beds before the government had legislated, were now taking action to prevent the elected government from legislating. To make matters even worse, their decision came shortly after the juniors had discovered that their new contract, which had just been introduced, produced losers as well as gainers – and that any attempt to negotiate more money to correct that was debarred by pay policy. At first unofficially, and then officially, they too started working to contract to devastating effect. Scores of casualty departments and whole hospital departments closed. The consultants joined them on 1 December. With increasing speed, the NHS was sliding into chaos.

The central issue, however, remained pay beds, and as Barbara Castle observed to her diary three days earlier after she had outlined her proposed Bill to colleagues, the Cabinet 'had no fire in its belly for this particular fight'.[72] Wilson's nerve cracked. 'When deadlock becomes total,' he observed drily in his memoirs, '. . . a telephone call is put through to Lord Goodman.'[73]

Goodman was already involved. Back in August he had been retained by Derek Damerell, the chief executive of BUPA, to advise on the pay beds dispute. Damerell was a complex man, whose views of the future of private medicine swung between a desire to keep it modest, compact and thus politically unprovocative, to an almost megalomaniac vision of how huge the private sector could become. Goodman soon found himself advising not just BUPA but the coalition of provident associations, the BMA and the Royal Colleges as they united to oppose the government. 'Some of the doctors,' Goodman recorded in his autobiography, 'were essentially reasonable men' – adding, however, 'alas, not many'. Most, he records 'had developed a positively insensate hatred for Mrs Castle'. Their reaction had become 'hysterical' while Castle in turn was showing 'total intransigence'.[74]

There was a real clash of personalities here. Castle's burning determination had come up against the iron will of Anthony Grabham who, although only forty-four, had become the consultants' chief negotiator and would be a key figure in medical politics for fifteen years. He came from a line of Conservative salaried public servants – police inspectors and fire chiefs – and had been 'absolutely torn' between being a doctor or a lawyer. He had been known to vote Labour as well as Conservative, having grown up in the wake of the Thirties depression and been influenced by treating the smashed bodies of miners as a young Tyneside doctor in the early 1950s.[75] But in his own phrase he 'instinctively loved the battle' and he brought to the previously gentlemenly conduct of government/doctor negotiations all the icy fire of a Tebbit-like Conservative shop steward, operating to a brief. He could be silkily rude. His instincts lay with the NHS, but he believed even more strongly in protecting what he saw as the interests of doctors, once memorably remarking, à la General Motors, that 'happy doctors make happy patients'. He was determined to preserve private practice. Assessments of his performance over the years vary enormously – from the best negotiator the BMA ever produced to 'the man who singlehandedly did more damage to British medicine than any other', in the anonymous words of one senior departmental doctor.

Goodman had already rung Wilson and offered to act not just as an adviser to the doctors but as an undeclared go-between, and a number of clandestine meetings had resulted between him and Mrs Castle at Goodman's 'gloomy' Portland Place flat, one wall dominated by an awesome Graham Sutherland portrait of its massive owner. Goodman was late, his housekeeper plying Barbara Castle with a silver teapot and the thinnest of cucumber sandwiches as she stamped her foot with impatience.[76] But when the consultants announced they were renewing their action, it was Wilson who called Goodman and asked him to move from being adviser to mediator. He agreed, and called in the doctors, led by Tony Grabham.

'The first thing to do is to resume discussions with the Secretary of State,' I told them. The howl of dissent that came from the entire room staggered me. 'Never,' they said, 'will we meet with that woman' . . . 'How [then] are we to make any progress? Who will you meet?' Rather grudgingly a voice said: 'The Prime Minister.'[77]

Goodman decided not to seek Castle's approval for such an approach to Wilson. 'My instinct, both of mercy and goodwill, was to seek Barbara's approval to a reference to the Prime Minister, but an even stronger instinct told me it was likely to be met by a flat refusal and the negotiating process would be stillborn.'[78] Despite earlier refusals to see the doctors while they were harming patients, Wilson this time agreed – and did so without consulting Mrs Castle. The rug, in effect, had been pulled out from under her and she was incandescent with anger, demanding a meeting with Wilson which the Prime Minister did his best to avoid.[79] At Downing Street on 3 December 1975 the very broad outlines of what was to be the settlement were agreed with the doctors, although almost a fortnight of daily, secretive and fraught negotiations followed including a meeting like 'a French farce' at Goodman's flat in which the doctors were closeted in the living room, Castle and company in the dining room, with Goodman shuttling between them.[80]

The deal when it came was that 1000 pay beds were to go within six months of the Bill becoming law. The remainder were to be phased out by an independent board but under no time limit. Just how tortuous the negotiations had been was revealed by the definition that this would happen only where there was 'reasonable availability of reasonable alternative facilities within a reasonable geographical distance and to which reasonable access is available . . .'[81]

So uncertain, even weak, were the consultants' leaders over the stand their own troops would take that, having called emergencies-only action without a ballot, they now, to almost everyone's fury, balloted on whether to accept the deal. As a result the industrial action continued for another two months. During that time the government's only consolation was that it managed to settle the juniors' dispute which had been pursued, with the acquiescence of consultants, with a ferocity which proved far more damaging to patients in terms of operations cancelled and casualty departments closed than the much longer-lasting consultants' action. In the end only 2048 consultants voted to reject the Castle package and resign from the NHS while 4438 voted to accept – a 54 per cent turnout that was paltry given the passion that had been aroused. Although serious skirmishes remained to be fought over the Bill, the major battle was over.

In the NHS the dispute changed things markedly. For a start it presaged the real take-off of the private sector. In 1975 and 1976 when the dispute was at its height and tales of patients being denied food and clean sheets filled the press, the numbers covered by private health insurance dipped by 80,000. But between 1977 and 1980 they rose by a spectacular 60 per cent to 3.5 million, heavily driven by company purchases in order to get around pay policy, but also by a perception that the NHS was no longer coping so well. By 1980, 6.4 per cent of the population was covered, against 4 per cent in 1976. At the same time, a dramatic expansion of private hospitals outside the NHS was launched to replace the beds to be phased out. By 1979 there were more than 6660 private beds – an 80 per cent increase – in 149 private hospitals that were becoming better equipped and less dependent on the NHS for sophisticated facilities. Consultants who traditionally had spent all their time in the NHS doing both NHS and private work now travelled down the road to the private hospital to operate. Castle had wanted to phase the pay beds out within a year, a measure that might have done irreparable damage to both the fabric and confidence of the still fledgling private sector. Wilson's intervention had produced a far slower timetable, and a board which by the time the Conservatives abolished it in 1980 had reduced the number of pay beds only from 3444 to 2533.[82] The private sector had been given time to react. Just as abolishing direct grant schools had expanded the private education sector, so phasing out pay beds in fact helped the private medical sector to grow. By an awful irony, Barbara Castle had become the patron saint of private medicine.

Yet the doctors had not really won. Far from it. Some 200,000 fewer patients were treated in 1975 than 1974, while waiting lists soared.[83] Dr Derek Stevenson, everyone's image of a senior consultant, limited the damage done by both the juniors' and seniors' action as best he could. In television appearances he conceded soothingly that 'yes, patients would suffer' but 'no, it was all the government's fault'. But the violence of the doctors' language, the misogyny with which Barbara Castle was attacked as 'the Red Queen', and most of all the sanctions they applied to patients all seriously undermined their standing with public and politicians alike while splitting a profession many of whose members took no part in the action. BMA membership dipped sharply. Sir George Godber, recently retired as Chief Medical Officer, wrote to The Times to declare that 'it must be axiomatic that a doctor cannot strike', and suggesting that he could no longer remain a member of a body 'which is prepared to pursue its objectives by methods harmful to patients'.[84]

Lord Goodman, having acted for them, similarly damned the doctors for failing to halt their action while they balloted. They were causing, he said, 'anxiety, pain and even the risk of death'. Doctors had a unique standing because of their tradition of service. 'If doctors of all people forsake this tradition and support the view that "everything goes" to achieve their ends, we are well on the road to anarchy and the abandonment of parliamentary procedures in favour of naked coercion.' Conservative politicians were as horrified privately as Labour ones were publicly. Norman Fowler, the Tory social services spokesman, stressed in the Commons that pay bed legislation was 'an issue to be decided in Parliament'[85] and he told the consultants privately that 'they could not justify industrial action'.[86]

The BMA may have confirmed its position as 'the shock troops of the middle classes' as its leaders sometimes liked to see themselves. But they had done so at the price of their secretary becoming known as 'Docker Stevenson' and the BMA as the 'British Money Association'.[87] Their moral authority to condemn industrial action by others in the NHS had gone, and the Tories, as much as Labour, marked the BMA down as a deeply troublesome and offensive trade union, a professional cabal which, like the teachers in education, seemed to have too much power and needed to be cut down to size. Within the BMA's own ranks a horrified sense of 'never again' developed. Dr Elston Grey-Turner, shortly to become BMA secretary, recorded that many doctors found the action 'deeply repugnant'.[88] It was to be the last war for at least twenty years at the end of which the BMA could in any real sense claim victory.

So intense was the battle over doctors' contracts and pay beds, it might be thought that Barbara Castle had no time for anything else. But in their two years at the Elephant and Castle she, David Owen and Brian O'Malley, the social security minister, introduced a vast volume of legislation – on pensions, child benefit, pay beds and the Children's Act – its scale being a measure of Castle's influence in the Cabinet. In addition, crucial decisions about the future of social security and health were taken.

Key among these was RAWP, the ugliest acronym in NHS history; the Resource Allocation Working Party had been convened when it became clear that, twenty-five years after the founding of the NHS on a principle of equal access for all, the variation in spending between one part of the country and another was as large as it had been in 1948. Crossman had tried to correct this, but money had still largely flowed to where buildings and staff already existed, so that the better provided parts of the NHS remained the better provided parts. If anything, things had got worse. Under something called Revenue Consequences of Capital Schemes (RCCS) new hospitals, which cost more to run, had their increased spending covered in full. This policy not only provided no incentive to design efficient buildings, it also tended to make the RAWP problem worse. Perhaps because they had easiest access to the Department of Health's headquarters, London and south-east England acquired much of the new hospital building that was approved in the 1960s. New teaching hospitals were built for the Charing Cross, the Royal Free, and St George's. Vast new blocks were added to Guy's, King's, and St Thomas's. Significant improvements were made at other London teaching hospitals and a string of new town hospitals were built, at Welwyn, Stevenage, Harlow and Slough, for example. RCCS ensured that these sucked southwards not just capital but also revenue, if anything widening the spending gap between the relatively well provided south and the historically poorer north.

Thus in the early 1970s it was found that spending per head was barely £15 in the Trent region, but two-thirds higher at £25 in North-East Thames. The variation between districts within each region was even greater. The working party adjusted these figures for 'need', allowing for age and sex because the elderly and children cost more to care for. They also adjusted them for death rates, these being the best proxy available for varying rates of illness which might in turn be due to social factors such as bad housing. Even after these allowances, there remained a 25 per cent variation in spending per head between regions. It needed to be balanced out.

Castle and Owen gave the go-ahead, at the same time continuing the wind-down of RCCS that had begun under Joseph in 1973. It was a brave decision. For the RAWP formula, as it remained known, was conceived in the days of rapid growth in NHS spending. The idea was that London and the south-east – the main losers – would advance more slowly while, year by year, the rest of the country caught up. RAWP, however, was launched into the vastly tighter financial regime of cash limits and little or no growth which faced David Ennals, Barbara Castle's successor. Thus the four Thames regions had broadly to stand still to let what growth money there was go to the deprived regions. And, given that the variations were bigger within regions than between them, that meant relative and sometimes actual cuts in the 'over-provided' big city centres as money and services were shifted to the suburbs and shires where more people now lived. It was the right thing to do; but it was the start of more than twenty years of pain and rationalisation in big city centres – and it was felt most acutely in London on whose doorstep the national media were camped and from whose state they tended to judge the state of the NHS.

Equally technical but just as far-reaching was the construction of a programme budget for the NHS. This, in many ways for the first time, provided some tools at national as opposed to local level to link money spent to the services provided, rather than simply measuring the inputs it bought such as extra staff. In considerable measure it was the work of Terri Banks, a formidable ex-Treasury civil servant in the Department of Health's finance division, who helped devise a formula that by the 1980s had become known as the 'magic 2 per cent'. By linking money to the services provided the department was able to show how much the NHS needed to cope with medical advance (0.5 per cent a year), to cover the rising numbers of elderly (which varied between 0.5 and 1 per cent a year) and to meet declared priorities such as the development of the 'Cinderella services' (usually around 0.5 per cent a year). This was, in a sense, the money the NHS needed just to stand still, without overall standards being reduced by the demographic and other pressures on it. In the straitened spending rounds to come it provided a crucial weapon, one which health still used in the 1990s to fight the Treasury, but Barbara Castle first put it in play to good effect in 1975.[89]

For the NHS it came just in time, providing a rational basis to defend the budget post-IMF. 'To a large extent it rescued that spending round for the health service,' Mrs Banks recalls, 'and it paid off throughout the eighties.'[90] It also allowed some choices to be made nationally between costed priorities. In *Priorities for Health and Personal Social Services in England* (1976), for example, it helped show that a falling birthrate had not been matched by reduced spending on maternity services. 'Nurses,' in the words of one senior civil servant, 'were kicking their heels doing two or three hours' work a day in maternity units while real costs per case were rocketing at 6 per cent a year.'[91] That money, the document said, could better be spent on geriatric care or mental illness. The programme budget thus enabled decisions to be taken to pull back on growth for acute services while transferring funds to primary care, children, the elderly, and the handicapped – targets which, at the margins and at a time of slow spending growth, were achieved.[92] This approach, combined with health authorities' new responsibilities for their populations, provided a sense that health services could be better and more efficiently planned. Equally the department discovered that more home helps and meals-on-wheels could help get people home, unblocking NHS beds to allow others to be treated. Joint finance was created – in effect health service money earmarked to be spent on such local authority services, and to help develop other forms of care in the community which would allow the long-stay hospitals to run down. Infuriatingly, some social services departments proved reluctant to take the money, not wishing to be told what to do, or to be held responsible, by the NHS. But despite this professional rivalry, some progress towards community care started to be made.[93]

Social Security

> This is the third major Bill on pensions in the last six years and
> many of us hope it will be third time lucky.
>
> *Paul Dean, Conservative social security minister 1970–74, speaking in the
> Commons debate on SERPS, 18 March 1975, Hansard col 1529*

> I have a major reservation on the question of who pays. As a
> generation, we have the collective effrontery to insist that our
> children make sacrifices on our behalf, on a scale we are not prepared
> to make on behalf of the elderly today.
>
> *Sir George Young in the same debate, col 1538*

> This Government recognises the importance workers attach to their
> occupational pensions . . . Instead of whittling down the standards
> of pension provision to a level that private schemes can afford, we
> have fixed the standards at the level necessary to remove poverty in
> old age, and then provided forms of State help to private schemes
> to enable them to meet the targets we have laid down. This unique
> form of partnership between the State and private schemes has been
> widely welcomed. This holds out the hope that the new scheme will
> endure.
>
> *Barbara Castle, presenting SERPS to the Commons, col 1489*

On the social security side, activity was equally furious. An early decision
in the face of continuing inflation and a manifesto commitment was to
make the annual uprating of benefits statutory. The big debate in the
DHSS was whether to link them to earnings or to prices. A link to earnings
would allow claimants to share in any growth in the wealth of the country,
but at a time when real living standards were being squeezed, a link to
prices might on occasion protect pensioners better. It was Tony Crocker,
a civil servant, who suddenly looked up in a meeting and said to Castle:
'Why not prices *or* earnings, whichever is the better, Secretary of State?'[94]
And so it became, although only for those on long-term benefits such as
pensioners and the long-term sick and disabled. The unemployed and the
short-term sick were guaranteed only a link to price rises, effectively
preserving the distinction between 'deserving' and 'less deserving' claimants that Joseph had drawn.

This decision had a consequence not foreseen at the time – and one certainly not foreseen by the Conservative Opposition, whose chief complaint was that benefits were to be raised only annually and not every six months as they had promised in their 1974 manifesto.[95] It created a 'ratchet effect': not only did it ensure that pensioners did not lose out, it ensured they would in the long run do better. In years when prices rose by less than earnings, they would do as well as those in work, but when prices rose by more than earnings they would do better. At least theoretically, therefore, they would take a rising share of national income. With pensioner numbers themselves rising, that had powerful implications over time for public spending;[96] and, while other factors contributed to the effect, that is what did happen on a small scale between 1974 and 1979, a fact spotted by Nigel Lawson, an aggressive member of the Tory shadow Treasury team who put in a private note to the shadow Chancellor, Geoffrey Howe, arguing that the link must be broken.[97]

With this price and earnings protection came a fresh batch of new and improved non-means-tested and essentially bipartisan disability benefits: mobility allowance, invalid care allowance, and a new non-contributory invalidity pension for those who had been unable to earn insurance benefits. The main stir they caused in the Commons was a tetchy squabble between Castle and Howe over which party should be take the credit for introducing them.[98] Equally bipartisan, though the subject of a great rumpus within the government, was the introduction of Child Benefit. First recognisably outlined in public as a scheme of 'child endowment' almost a decade earlier in *The Times* by Sir John Whalley, the former Deputy Secretary at the Ministry of Pensions, the idea had become cross-party policy. It involved scrapping both child tax allowances and family allowances and paying a single cash sum to the mother. Child benefit had become a key part of the Tory tax credits idea, a manifesto commitment for Labour and part of the social contract with the TUC.

There were, however, difficulties. Cash would disappear from pay packets as the tax allowance was withdrawn, producing a transfer 'from wallet to purse' as the mother claimed the new benefit for all children. It would therefore both cost more than the old family allowance (which went only to second and subsequent children) and produce a tax increase. That increase, however, would fall chiefly on men. There was a battle of the sexes in the making. Castle, who was all for a change that would shift resources from the better off to the less well off while giving women more of an income of their own, legislated. But in April 1976 she was sacked when Wilson resigned and Callaghan, whom Castle regarded as 'a bit of a male chauvinist',[99] became Prime Minister. She went before a cash sum for the benefit, due to take effect in April 1977, had been agreed. Seven weeks later David Ennals announced that the scheme was being postponed. As the *Daily Express* put it, the government had 'lost its nerve in the battle of the purse strings'.[100] Barely a fortnight later, however, an article in *New Society* revealed, in one of the more comprehensive leaks of Cabinet papers this century, just why and how that had happened.[101]

Headlined 'Killing a Commitment: The Cabinet v the Children', it was written by Frank Field, director of the Child Poverty Action Group, and it provided a detailed account of how the decision had been made. Denis Healey, many years later, recorded that it was Callaghan 'who first realised that Child Benefit . . . might cost us male votes' adding, 'I believe it had the effect Jim feared.'[102] What Field's account revealed was that Ennals and Healey had been unable to agree on a value for the new benefit. Ennals warned that if Healey's suggested £2.40 a week was accepted family support would be lower in real terms than under the Tories. Such a scheme 'would be condemned as a trick to give children less not more', Ennals told the Cabinet which began to move to the view that postponement might be safer if a full scheme could not be afforded.

On 6 May, Callaghan told the Cabinet he had received an 'excellent report' from the whips which had for him created fresh doubts about proceeding. Michael Cocks, the chief whip, reported that a 'survey of opinion' (which the *Sunday Times* later concluded was conducted 'entirely inside the Whips' office; backbench opinion was not sought at all') showed there would be 'grave political consequences' if child benefit went ahead. The issue, however, remained unsettled, not least because Ennals fought on, the essence of these Cabinet discussions trickling out through the columns of *The Times*. Sensing trouble, Barbara Castle, on the backbenches but still on the TUC/Labour Party liaison committee, used her position there in late May to persuade the committee to pass a resolution demanding child benefit be introduced the following year as planned. Later that day, however, Healey met the most senior of those same union leaders at a meeting of the National Economic Development Council, familiarly known as Neddy. According to the minutes, he told them that 'the majority view of the Cabinet' was in favour of deferment because 'in present circumstances the effect of the removal of the tax allowances on take-home pay would be catastrophic'. David Basnett, the general secretary of the general workers' union the GMBU, reported Healey as saying that it was Labour MPs who were opposing the transfer from wallet to purse. The next day, 25 May, the leaked minutes showed Healey reporting to Cabinet that: 'On being informed of the reduction in take-home pay which the child benefit scheme would involve, the TUC representatives had reacted immediately and violently against its implementation, irrespective of the level of benefits which would accompany the reduction in take-home pay.' That appeared unanswerable. Ennals was dispatched to announce the scheme's deferment that afternoon.

To the proponents of child benefit this looked like a classic stitch-up – Callaghan and Healey had opted for postponement, so Healey had told the unions that the Cabinet was against in order that he could then in turn tell Cabinet that the unions were opposed. In his memoirs Healey insisted that the union leaders did indeed recommend delay,[103] his opponents for ever believing that the unions only did so because that was what they thought the government wanted them to do.

The day Ennals's announcement was made, eighty-five Labour MPs signed an early day motion demanding that the decision to defer be reversed. The dramatic leaking of the Cabinet papers three weeks later only strengthened their arm. Frank Field, with a fine sense of theatre, dubbed his source for the Cabinet papers 'Deep Throat' after the source who had helped Woodward and Bernstein of the *Washington Post* bring down President Nixon over Watergate. As Field gave dramatic accounts of bundles of government documents being left regularly in brown paper shopping bags on the steps of CPAG's Macklin Street offices, Callaghan called in Commander Habershon from Scotland Yard. Everyone from permanent secretaries down found themselves fingerprinted and under suspicion. Field's phones were tapped, and he and others faced lengthy interviews with the police. The mole-hunt apparently revealed nothing, although the story claimed the front pages for days. The government was forced into retreat to the point where the Commons had to be adjourned for three hours when Mrs Thatcher tabled a motion on the issue – the government felt it could not risk a vote. In September retreat became rout and the phasing-in of child benefit, with payment to be made in full by 1979, was announced. What was to prove one of the more controversial of the welfare state's benefits, and its last new universal one, had finally arrived.

It had been narrowly preceded by the last great bipartisan social security development: the State Earnings Related Pension scheme, or SERPS. By 1974 it was approaching twenty years since Crossman had first drafted national superannuation, the earnings-related pension scheme which had stung Boyd-Carpenter into action. The intervening years had been ones of mounting uncertainty for a pensions industry which needed to plan in the long term. First, Crossman had intended to ditch Boyd-Carpenter's scheme, but had seen legislation for his own plan lost when the 1970 general election was called. Then Joseph had ditched Crossman's scheme to devise one of his own which had actually become law but had not been implemented when Castle took office in 1974. Her decision, in turn, was to scrap much of the Joseph scheme. With a dry smile Sir Lance Errington, the Permanent Secretary at Social Security remarked, 'We are going to design a new plane from the models that have crashed on the runway.' And so they did.

The Conservatives tabled a censure motion which Castle survived by just two votes as she, Brian O'Malley and the civil servants worked at speed to create a model that would be 'third time lucky'.[104] With a desperate need to have an alternative ready for the second election that year, work had to be rapid. 'Some of the key bits were done in a matter of a day or two,' one of the civil servants involved said. 'But they stuck'.[105]

There had been some nice paradoxes in the Crossman and Joseph plans which illustrate that in social security left/right divisions can fall in odd ways. Crossman's scheme had been fully earnings-related, with no flat rate basic pension, in an attempt to provide pensions that in all normal cases would end up above means-tested national assistance. Up to a ceiling, therefore, it had proposed more for the better off in return for higher contributions. Joseph's, by contrast, was a flat-rate basic pension, plus a 'reserve' earnings-related scheme to be run by the state for those whose employers did not provide even an occupational scheme on top. The aim behind that was to encourage private provision for the second pension. Under Joseph's scheme, however, the basic pension was to be paid for by graduated contributions – in other words, higher earners would pay more for the same basic pension. His scheme was thus more redistributive than Crossman's. It was also potentially more socialist.

Crossman's plan was 'pay-as-you-go': existing national insurance contributors would pay the pensions for existing pensioners. With growing numbers of elderly, that meant that as the scheme reached maturity over twenty years those still working would have to pay higher contributions to pay higher pensions to more pensioners. The Conservatives had criticised that and had therefore proposed that Joseph's reserve scheme should be fully funded; the contributions would be invested by the state in a fund from which the reserve scheme pensions would be paid. By the end of the century the scheme was expected to have taken in £7 billion to be invested by a management board in equities and property.[106] It was a huge sum, amounting to almost a third of the total investment by all occupational pension schemes at the time. This was potentially a dramatic, if arm's-length, form of back-door nationalisation, as a state-backed pension scheme would have taken significant shareholdings in significant numbers of publicly quoted companies, yet the political implications were scarcely addressed. Bryan Ellis, the Whitehall pensions historian who helped design SERPS, says the issue was mentioned in the committee stage of Joseph's Bill. There was 'some brief interest in the financial press'. But 'no sustained discussion followed on the financial and political consequences of placing investment capacity of this order in the hands of a single small group of trustees.'[107]

If Joseph's basic pension plan was more redistributive than Crossman's, however, his reserve scheme provided a poor deal for women. It also offered little chance for years of reducing the numbers dependent on means-tested pensions. The Castle/O'Malley scheme tackled both these issues. It mixed a flat-rate basic pension which would rise in line with earnings with an earnings-related pension on top which was to be inflation-proofed. To help three groups – those facing odd spells of unemployment, manual workers whose earnings often peak when they are younger, and women who spend time at home with their families – the scheme was based on 'the best twenty years' earnings. Contributions were to be earnings-related, and the whole would be phased in over twenty years. Occupational schemes with their eleven million members could contract out, claiming national insurance rebates, provided they offered a 'guaranteed minimum pension' to match the state one. And in some circumstances, the state would help them to achieve that.

The scheme combined the best of Crossman and Joseph, thus reconciling both Labour and Conservatives to the new plan. At the same time it produced clever innovations of its own which included the new contracting out rules. These involved an absolute acceptance in principle by Labour of the importance of occupational schemes, and thus of the private sector. Occupational schemes, the White Paper stated, 'make a valuable contribution to the economy through their encouragement of private saving'.[108] O'Malley, in particular, favoured this approach, wanting occupational pensions to be something that trades unions went in and negotiated for.

After all the controversies which had surrounded pensions for two decades, the Bill which was to affect the future pensions of millions was given an unopposed second reading with fewer than a dozen MPs in the chamber.[109] The opposition spokesman who waved it through was a fresh-faced Norman Fowler, just a few weeks into his new job. A decade later, he was to attempt to consign SERPS to history. But in 1975 the pensions industry was desperately concerned to have its future settled after the frustrations of the previous two decades. The new scheme did provide a clear role for the private as well as the public sector, a partnership that was crucial to the Conservatives' philosophy. And there was an element of exhaustion which helped produce a consensus. 'We didn't divide the house. I think the industry would have torn its hair out had that been done,' Fowler later recalled.[110]

Essentially unchanged, the Bill became an Act, its passage eased by Castle firing the big guns in Cabinet using the bullets and the technical grasp supplied by O'Malley who, his civil servants say, did 'a lot of oiling of wheels to ensure a pensions consensus'.[111] A former dance band leader and the only MP sponsored by the Musician's Union, he shared a passion for jazz, if not for suede shoes, with his opposite number, Kenneth Clarke. Deals, civil servants record, 'were stitched up between the two of them over supper – not to mention the odd trip to Ronnie Scott's'.[112] O'Malley died prematurely, aged forty-six, eight months after his Bill became law. His monument was, as Bryan Ellis put it, that 'for the first time in twenty years pensions and their future were off the political agenda.'[113] The hope that it would last was to prove in Sir Alec Atkinson's words 'a pipe dream'.[114]

Barbara Castle's other key decision had been her agreement in 1975 to breathe new life into the Supplementary Benefits Commission by appointing David Donnison as its chairman and accepting his demand that it publish an annual report – a tool Donnison was soon to use as a means of launching a wholesale review of supplementary benefit.

Nothing better illustrates the state the system had reached than Donnison's compelling memoir of his days there in *The Politics of Poverty*. Rising unemployment, more single parents, more disability, reductions in the real value of the student grant which led students to claim benefit in vacations – these and a host of other smaller factors had turned a safety net which Beveridge and then Bevan had both believed would need to be 'very small indeed'[115] into one on which five million people or nearly one in ten of the population now depended for at least part of their income. Since 1966 the number of pensioners relying on supplementary benefit had actually fallen, and the total numbers on the benefit had risen by only 12 per cent. The workload, however, had risen vastly more than that because pensioners' circumstances change little while the unemployed and single parents move on and off benefit, or see other changes in their circumstances, much more frequently. Staff numbers had doubled.[116]

On top of that, frontier problems had developed. Supplementary benefit and the rent and rate rebates introduced in the late sixties and early seventies each used different means tests. People might be better off on one than the other but had no easy way of knowing which. The 1966 switch to a rights-based system for the basic benefit had still left extra weekly and special one-off payments discretionary. But the judgements made by the commission's staff were appealable and the decade since 1966 had seen a mushrooming of welfare rights officers in charities, pressure groups and local authorities. As a result, by 1975 more than half of claimants were once again getting exceptional payments of one sort or another and, in a hopeless attempt to be fair across the country, each unique decision about a particular case meant a new rule for staff to follow in exercising their discretion. Donnison records that:

> As a result, the book of rules which in 1948 every National Assistance Board Officer had been able to carry around in his pocket had grown into several massive volumes, so often amended and so complicated that even the staff could not understand them. In the more hard pressed offices they were no longer using them: local rules of thumb took their place. All these trends were still flowing strongly – growing frontier problems, growing numbers on discretionary payments and growing complexity interacting to lead the system to chaos. Together they produced bewilderment, incomprehension, poor take-up of benefits, enormous [ten-fold] variations in practice from place to place, and a growing sense of injustice and hostility afflicting claimants, staff and the public at large.[117]

Or, in the more succinct words of Geoffrey Otton, the future second permanent secretary at DHSS and 'the tiger in the SBC's tank' according to Donnison who recruited him as the commission's chief mandarin: 'It was not a system, in the late 1970s, of which you could feel proud.'[118] In hard-pressed inner city offices, phones were taken off hooks, claimants were told that files had been lost, or giro cheques were 'in the post' just to deter claims and limit the workload. The system, in days when little of it was computerised, was at risk of collapse.

Donnison's answer was to launch a very public five-year campaign for a simpler system, based on legal entitlement that would remove most of the remaining discretion. He persuaded Ennals to back a review, which worked closely with the Commission. It had however to be nil cost and confined to supplementary benefit. The department's report, *Social Assistance*, starkly marked the changing – and increasingly defeated – climate of the times. For successive governments, it noted, the aspiration had been to reduce the numbers on means-tested benefits.

> But against the background of continuing restraint on public expenditure and public service staff, there is no prospect of finding the massive sums for national insurance benefits or the services that would be needed to reduce the number of supplementary benefit claimants . . . In our view the most realistic aim is to fit the scheme to its mass role of coping with millions of claimants in known and readily-defined categories for the foreseeable future.[119]

Beveridge's minimal safety net was now formally acknowledged as a permanent and 'mass' part of the scene. The review backed a simpler, rules-based system to be run by the department, with the rules published for claimants and their advisers to see. The Commission campaigned to set the changes in a broader context, arguing for improved child benefit, the higher benefit rate for the long-term unemployed, and the regular six-monthly lump sum that the review had said should replace most discretionary grants. It also developed plans for a unified housing benefit scheme to end the 'frontier' problems in housing aid. It was, however, to fall to the Conservatives to decide whether to legislate.

Meanwhile, in Donnison's phrase, it was 'getting colder by the hour'. High tax rates and higher unemployment brought out the worst in people and for a time the size of the 'black economy' became almost a national obsession, the chairman of the Board of Inland Revenue estimating it in March 1979 as £11 billion or 7.5 per cent of the whole gross domestic product. Moonlighting and tax dodges abounded. Company executives had their suits bought for them, or took payment in crates of wine, to avoid top rate tax. Lesser mortals negotiated fictitious allowances, to be paid as expenses to avoid lower rates of tax. The jobless at the bottom took small jobs on the side to make ends meet, while falling tax thresholds helped produce a shrinking gap between low-paid work and benefits which left growing numbers less certain that they were better off in work than out of it.

The result was envy and suspicion. The commission operated against a rising chorus of attacks on scroungers and tales of social security fraud, all exploited remorselessly by a Tory back-bencher called Iain Sproat. The Supplementary Benefits Commission was assailed by stories of claimants, usually 'a black man' who had been given large grants to buy a colour television with legs or with doors 'so it counted as furniture'. When the files were trawled, no such case could be found.[120] In 1977, Patrick Deevy was charged at Liverpoool Crown Court with claiming £57 by deception. During the hearing he cheerfully estimated that he had fraudulently claimed £36,000 in benefits, his spectacular accounts of by how much he had cheated the system producing headlines like 'King of the Dole Queue Scroungers', '£10,000-a-year life style for Dole Fiddler' and 'Six years for Dole Cheat who spent £25 a week on the Best Cigars'. It aided the SBC not at all to discover that half the identities and addresses that the con-man had told the court that he had used could not in fact be found.[121] The case unleashed a great surge of anti-welfare feeling that left the creaking social security system beleaguered and mistrusted. Similar cases had worried Wilson. 'We must not underestimate the effect of even a few of these press stories,' he said in note to Castle. 'Could you tell me what is being done to investigate cases of this kind?'[122]

Meanwhile, first millions and then billions were poured into employment measures of one sort or another – often through the Manpower Services Commission which Heath had created and which now oversaw the Industrial Training Boards – to relieve what Joel Barnett described as Labour's 'collective guilt complex' over the jobless.[123] There was the Temporary Employment Subsidy, the Job Release Scheme, the Youth Opportunities Programme, each constructed on the increasingly unsustainable assumption that there was a temporary blip in the labour market to be solved until the recession lifted. Such schemes were estimated to be keeping some 400,000 people off the unemployment total by 1978. 'We were also undoubtedly financing overmanning to the tune of hundreds of millions of pounds more in many parts of the public sector,' Barnett records.[124]

By 5 July 1978, the thirtieth anniversary of the welfare state, the Labour Government was plainly running out of steam. A celebratory booklet on the thirty years of the NHS was produced and a conference held at Lancaster House. But Callaghan's speech, as Donnison records, dwelt mainly on the NHS and personal social services, not on the great 'cradle to grave' social security measures which had equally dazzled Labour MPs at the time. 'History was being re-written,' Donnison records. 'Labour had lost its convictions about poverty and redistribution of incomes. Or perhaps the voters had lost those convictions and the Labour party was afraid to remind them.'[125] A small exhibition celebrating thirty years of social security was mounted, well out of the way, at the DHSS central office in

The poster that made Saatchi and Saatchi and helped eject Labour. 'We'd have been drummed out of office if we'd had this level of unemployment,' Mrs Thatcher said.

Newcastle upon Tyne. Not many of the public and even fewer journalists attended.[126]

In the NHS, after a couple of years of calm, the effects of the financial environment turning against it were being felt. A renewed sense that the service was in crisis erupted. In January 1979, David Ennals became the first minister responsible for the NHS, and a Labour one at that, to be sued by four hip replacement patients from Birmingham complaining they could not get treatment.[127] Backed by their orthopaedic surgeon, they alleged Ennals had 'failed in his duty to provide a comprehensive health service'. They lost because the NHS Acts are constructed to ensure they would lose. And their story in turn was soon lost in the explosion of the winter of discontent, with pickets turning cancer patients away from hospital, a hospital delivery entrance being blocked by a vehicle with slashed tyres,[128] food not delivered, rubbish piled high in the streets and even the dead not being buried in some parts of Manchester and Liverpool. In March, two days before he was due to meet the health unions for fresh talks, Ennals was taken to Westminster Hospital suffering from the leg thrombosis which plagued his time in office. His tea, mail and newspapers were promptly blacked by the ancillary workers. 'He is a legitimate target for action,' Jamie Morris, the NUPE shop steward declared, the *Daily Express* headlining the story 'No Mercy for the Minister'.[129]

Exactly three weeks later Callaghan lost the vote of confidence which followed the defeat of devolution in the Scottish referendum and called an election. Near the end of the campaign, Bernard Donoughue was driving round Parliament Square in Callaghan's official Rover:

I drew Mr Callaghan's attention to the recent improvement in the opinion polls, remarking that, with a little luck, and a few policy initiatives here and there, we might just squeak through. He turned to me and said quietly: 'I should not be too sure. You know there are times, perhaps once every thirty years, when there is a sea-change in politics. It then does not matter what you say or what you do. There is a shift in what the public wants and what it approves of. I suspect there is now such a sea-change – and it is for Mrs Thatcher.[130]

The post-war era was ending.

CHAPTER 16

'We were wrong all along': Conservatives
1974–79

A vital new debate is beginning, or perhaps an old debate is being renewed, about the proper role of government, the welfare state and the attitudes on which it rests.
Margaret Thatcher, in Let Our Children Grow Tall, 1975, p. 1

We were dominated by the fear of unemployment.
Keith Joseph, Reversing the Trend, p. 21

Why work, if you can get by without? Why save, if your savings are taxed away or inflated away, or both? Why do a good job, when you'll probably make out just as well if you do a bad one? Why bother to get extra qualifications, when differentials and earnings so often depend on political muscle, not personal merit? . . . We are a country profoundly ill-at-ease with ourselves.
Margaret Thatcher, Conservative Party conference 1978

'We are the music makers,
We are the dreamers of dreams . . .'
Keith Joseph quoting O'Shaughnessy

What lessons are to be learnt from the last thirty years? First, the pursuit of equality is a mirage. Far more desirable and more practicable than the pursuit of equality is the pursuit of equality of opportunity. Opportunity means nothing unless it includes the right to be unequal – and the freedom to be different . . . Let our children grow tall – and some grow taller than others, if they have it in them to do so.
Margaret Thatcher, op. cit., 1975, p. 12

People are hungry for ideas, hungrier than they have been for a
long time.

Keith Joseph, *Reversing the Trend*, p. 63

IT WAS JOSEPH who made the change. In Hugo Young's phrase, he
reached the 'shattering discovery' that, having joined the party twenty
years earlier, he had not really been a Conservative. 'It was only in April
1974 that I was converted to Conservatism,' he declared in 1975. 'I had
thought that I was a Conservative, but I now see I was not really one at
all.'[1]

By the time he said that, the mould-breaking speeches which provided
the earliest definitions of what was to become Thatcherism had been
delivered. They had been written after a period of study during which
Joseph repeatedly turned up on the doorstep of the cramped Georgian
town house that was now the Institute of Economic Affairs' Westminster
headquarters and had departed, armed with reading lists, books and contacts.[2] The reading included revisits to the monetarist economics of Milton
Friedman, the libertarian philosophy of Hayek, and two works of Adam
Smith: *Wealth of Nations* and *Theory of Moral Sentiments*. Of the
speeches, the most important was in Preston in September 1974, between
that year's two elections. It moved monetarism from an academic pursuit
into the centre stage of politics, and in doing so it made a clean break with
the post-war commitment to full employment as the overarching aim of
economic policy. Instead, inflation – then at 17 per cent and rising – was
defined as the number one enemy. With the opening line that 'Inflation
is threatening to destroy society', Joseph abandoned post-war Keynesianism two years ahead of Callaghan's Labour Party conference speech.

After declaring in his usual tortured tone that 'I begin by accepting my
full share of the collective responsibility', Joseph argued that governments
of all parties had been 'dominated by the fear of unemployment'. Sound
money had seemed out of date. At each downturn in the economic cycle
governments had tried to spend their way out of unemployment.

It is perhaps easy to understand: our post-war boom began under the
shadow of the 1930s. We were haunted by the fear of long-term mass
unemployment, the grim, hopeless dole queues and towns which died. So
we talked ourselves into believing that these gaunt, tight-lipped men in
caps and mufflers were around the corner, and tailored our policy to match
these imaginary conditions. For imaginary is what they were.[3]

They had not in fact existed since the war, he argued. There had never had been more than 100,000 to 300,000 people genuinely unemployed once allowance was made for frictional unemployment – those between jobs – and for the unemployable, the elderly, the fraudulent, and the voluntary unemployed. For almost all that period there had been several times more unfilled vacancies than genuinely jobless. 'We have had most of the time fuller than full employment.'

The price, however, had been desperate inflation which had debilitated the economy and left unemployment higher at the end of each economic cycle. Inflation 'is destroying not just the relative prosperity to which most of us have become accustomed, but the savings and plans of each person and family and the working capital of each business. The distress and unemployment that will follow unless the trend is stopped will be catastrophic.' Stopping it by controlling the money supply would mean unemployment for a time, he conceded. But once cured, 'a healthy economy in a world with normal trade conditions should sustain full employment . . .' The prescription 'will not be easy or enjoyable. But after a couple of years we should be on a sounder basis and able to move forward again.'

Much of this was to sound horribly hollow six years later when Joseph's theories were put into practice. Joseph, however, did not stop there. In October he was excoriating the 'permissive society' arguing that, 'Parents are being divested of their duty to provide for their family economically, of their responsibility for education, health, upbringing, morality, advice and guidance, of saving for old age, for housing.' Left-wing intellectuals, he argued, believed 'that the poor cannot be expected to help themselves, that they want the State to do more. That is why they believe in State ownership and control of economic life, education, health . . . I am not saying that we should not help the poor. Far from it. But the only real lasting help we can give the poor is helping them to help themelves; to do the opposite, to create more dependence is to destroy them morally, while throwing an unfair burden upon society.'[4] By 1976 he was spelling out that controlling the money supply meant retraction in the public sector if the private sector was not be to be crowded out. That would mean cuts, and: 'Cuts mean cuts . . . pseudo-cuts of programmes or future programmes will not be enough.'[5]

The Conservatives, he argued, had allowed themselves to become 'stranded on the middle ground', when what they should seek was 'the common ground'. The middle ground, he declared, was merely 'a slippery slope to socialism and state control'[6] because each Labour government, under pressure from its left wing, shifted leftward. The Conservatives, on each return to office, accepted many of those changes. 'We have replaced the pendulum in politics by the ratchet. The Socialists move it up a few notches during their term; at best we leave it still while we are in office.'[7] What was needed was to define a new common ground on which to stand.

Where Joseph led, Thatcher followed, though initially much more cautiously. In the summer of 1974 she had joined Joseph at the Centre for Policy Studies as a vice-chairman. Once she was party leader, it was used as a counter-think-tank to the Conservative Research Department whose new young head was Chris Patten, a 'wet' who once he became an MP was to form the 'Blue Chips' dining club and publish *The Tory Case*, a defiantly non-Thatcherite work, which he inscribed to his friends as containing 'a few ideas which may one day return to fashion'. It was in Patten's domain that Joseph's pained recasting of Conservatism earned him the sobriquet 'the mad monk'.[8]

At the end of 1975, Mrs Thatcher, in a speech which she chose to make in New York not England, attacked the 'progressive consensus' that 'the State should be active on many fronts in promoting equality, in the provision of social welfare, and in the redistribution of wealth and incomes.' The promotion of greater equality had gone 'hand in hand with the extension of the welfare state and State control over people's lives'. Far from helping society, however, this expansion had raised taxes, diminished incentives and crowded out the private sector, with public sector employment rising while the overall working population had contracted. The 'persistent expansion of the role of the state and the relentless pursuit of equality has caused and is causing damage to our economy in a variety of ways. It is not the sole cause of what some have termed the "British sickness", but it is a major one.'[9] A year later she shook Patrick Jenkin, her social services spokesman, who had laboured long and hard with her over a speech to the annual social services conference in Liverpool by throwing away the text he had helped her prepare and telling her audience that 'industry and trade are the basic social service because they provide a large number of jobs and without a job there is no way of looking after one's family'. Society, she declared, has 'concentrated too much attention on distributing the wealth we have and too little on adding to it'. Moreover 'the appetite of the education service, and of health and welfare, has proved insatiable . . . we must try to put responsibility back where it belongs with the family and with the people themselves.'[10] Her audience, Jenkin recalls, was 'mystified'.

Early that year she had first talked of Victorian values[11] – so that within two years of becoming leader many of the themes and leitmotifs of

Thatcherism, including 'rolling back the frontiers of the state', were well established. Yet while this message became increasingly clear in regard to taxation and the corporate and industrial state, for the welfare state as defined in this book it remained much more mixed. An assault on state subsidies to industry, on taxation, on the power of the unions, on public expenditure generally, were all clearly signalled. All these, plus the emphasis on individual enterprise and responsibility, had implications for social policy. But aside from clear signals that 'why work?' was seen as a problem and had to be tackled, on the core areas of welfare state provision – on education, health, even the rest of social security – the message was much more variable. Thus in a 1976 speech to the Institute of Directors (hardly members of the welfare state fan club) Mrs Thatcher in defining the boundaries of the mixed economy still listed Britain's 'long tradition of community provision for education and welfare'[12] as the second government priority after defence and internal security. In a party political broadcast in May 1977, when unemployment stood at 1.3 million, she declared: 'Sometimes I've heard it said that Conservatives have been associated with unemployment. That's absolutely wrong. We'd have been drummed out of office if we'd had this level of unemployment.'[13] And while she exalted the right of people to choose private medicine, she attacked Labour ferociously for its inability to fund the NHS fully.

There were myriad reasons for this. First and foremost, whatever her instincts she was as yet an insecure leader. She was patronised first by Wilson and then by Callaghan who by early 1978 had steadied the ship sufficiently to make it appear that it was Labour, the party that could deal with the unions, and not the Tories, who were 'the natural party of government'. This view held right up to the winter of discontent, particularly as living standards started to rise again. Joseph may have recanted the Heath years. Howe was soon on her side, able on some issues to offer evidence that he had been a Thatcherite before Thatcher. Whitelaw was to prove totally loyal. But the other key figures of Thatcherism like Ridley and Lawson and Tebbit were still junior. In the shadow cabinet she remained surrounded by Heathmen.

Furthermore, social policy – beyond a strong set of raw gut instincts – was not her forte. There was no evidence, to use the phrase of Timothy Raison, then a shadow cabinet member, that she had 'a strategic view of social policy in the way that Macleod and Powell had'.[14] She had been Secretary of State for Education, but in some ways that was now best forgotten. She had been in the Ministry of Pensions between 1961 and 1964, but had dealt only with a handful of insurance benefits in a social security system that had since proliferated dramatically. She had no experience of health and little of housing – she was environment spokesman and thus responsible for housing only between the February 1974 defeat and becoming leader a year later. The 'peasant's revolt'[15] that made her leader had been an anti-Heath vote, not a vote for Thatcherism, which had yet to be invented. In addition she had much else to learn: the whole sweep of foreign affairs, home and defence of which she also had little direct experience. And dominating all else, the thing that had got to be got right, was the economy. While it interlocked with the welfare state, it consisted of much more than that alone. 'Stepping Stones', a paper drawn up in this period which is perhaps *the* seminal document for the first Thatcher government, centred on the corporate state and how to unseat the power of the unions, not on how to roll back the welfare state.[16]

There were other difficulties in the face of anyone wanting to roll the welfare state back. A set of instincts is not a set of a policies. Even a conviction that the welfare state creates a culture of dependency does not provide a blueprint for changing it. And the welfare state had not, in the main, been an area for right-wing study. The IEA had argued long and hard for vouchers and various forms of privatisation. The Adam Smith Institute, founded in 1977, was soon to be firing such a grapeshot of radical and even rabid ideas that it could claim authorship of almost anything the Thatcher government subsequently did if only because, at one time or another, it had advocated almost everything. The Centre for Policy Studies was soon to provide the engine room for the rethink. But in the areas of the welfare state, these all shaped an intellectual climate far more than they provided anything remotely resembling a collection of policy blueprints. It was one thing for Rhodes Boyson in another of the *Black Papers* in 1975 to advocate tests for all at seven, eleven and fourteen, quite another to decide what should be in them and how they should be run. It was one thing for the IEA to say student loans or health vouchers were needed, quite another to devise them. Outside housing, which in large measure was about money, the right did not have the expertise. As Oliver Letwin, an adviser to Thatcher in the Downing Street policy unit, put it: 'There was plenty of intellect available. What there wasn't was knowledge.'[17]

For thirty years in the universities the democratic left had dominated the ideas and cornered the knowledge, in places like the LSE where Titmuss and his successors had the skills needed to work policies out to the point where politicians could adopt them knowing that the civil service would be able to refine and apply them. The right, in the late 1970s and beyond, was at the bottom of that learning curve. Those interested in welfare state issues tended to be philosophers and economists who dealt in theoretical constructs, not the practical understanding of how the system worked, information often needed in order to change it. They could hurl squibs, even great fire-bombs of ideas. But they lacked the competence to design anything very workable. In particular they lacked the expertise to work out how to get from here to there. To acquire these skills, they needed to be in government.

It is not much of a characterisation to say that up to the mid-1970s, the left had the ideas and drove the system while from the mid-1970s, as the system faltered, the right had all the ideas but didn't know how to apply them. That would take time, which Mrs Thatcher was in fact to gain by winning three elections. But as late as 1985, the IEA's founding guru, Lord Harris of High Cross, was recording his distress that Conservatives who had promised that the second term of Thatcherism would be radical were now saying 'look forward to the third'. 'It is,' he said, 'very much more difficult to unravel a lot of these programmes, particularly in taxation and welfare, than was ever contemplated back in the hopeful days of 1979.'[18]

Furthermore, politicians can in the end only go as far and as fast as they judge the electorate will allow. Whatever Mrs Thatcher's own views, there were votes to be won. And if stories about scroungers made good headlines and eased the case for social security cuts, education for all, along with the NHS, remained profoundly popular and popular not least with the middle classes, the Conservatives' natural constituency. In large measure that was because the welfare state, even the social security arm of it, had never been a mere safety net for the poor. It paid for everyone's education, for the student fees and grants from which the middle classes gained disproportionately, for the health care to which the private sector was only a minor augmentation, for the child benefit which middle-class mothers might use to buy a better bottle of wine, but which they none the less used, and for the basic state pension on which the middle classes could build their more comfortable retirements. And on top of that, the welfare state in its broadest definition employed millions of people, including a fair swathe of the middle classes from doctors and nurses to social workers and teachers, from managers and administrators to university dons, lawyers and accountants. That might, to the Thatcherites, be part of the problem. But it was a political reality.

Shadow cabinet policy-making took place under Keith Joseph's chairmanship. Each shadow minister set up his or her own working group. By October 1976 some ninety of them had reported – St John-Stevas alone set up seven on everything from tests and the curriculum to a possible voucher experiment. Patrick Jenkin's main two shadowed the Royal Commission's deliberations on reorganising the NHS and studied the possibility of alternative finance for it. In public he hinted heavily at possible new charges or a switch to an insurance base for the NHS, perhaps with the right to opt out.[19] But the study ran into the same problems of inexperience. 'We had a lot of meetings . . . but the work never got sufficiently detailed because the private sector people really didn't know enough about it,' Jenkin recalled. 'Some of them rather naïvely thought it could all be done on the BUPA principle without ever recognising what a very small proportion of health care was actually covered by BUPA-type protection.'[20] Jenkin was also hemmed in by the Royal Commission on the NHS, not due to report until 1979. It would be politically awkward if the Tories produced policy prescriptions which diverged too far from its recommendations, and they were not expected to include a switch to private health insurance. In fact, as Owen and Castle have made clear, the committee's membership had been 'rigged' to ensure it would not come out with a report opposing the basic principles of the NHS or having any truck with private financing.[21] And at the same time Jenkin matched heavy hints of new charges or of a new finance system with wholesale commitments to the NHS 'because it was enormously important not to give a peg to the Labour Party to say that the Conservatives were going to destroy the NHS'.[22] It was hardly surprising the public felt confused.

On social security, secret meetings at the Fentiman Road home of Geoffrey Howe, now shadow Chancellor, involved Joseph, Lawson, Peter Rees (a future Chief Secretary), Lord Cockfield and Jenkin. Primarily economic meetings, these pointedly did not involve Prior, despite his economic brief as employment spokesman, or anyone else who would later be classed as a wet. These 'Fentiman meetings' agreed the plans to switch from direct to indirect taxes by cutting income tax and raising VAT. It was agreed VAT would rise from 8 to 15 per cent (during the election campaign Howe was to deny Labour claims that he planned to double it).[23] After Lawson spotted the ratchet effect, it was also decided to break the link between pensions and earnings, and the similar link that the non-means-tested unemployment benefit enjoyed.[24] The group fretted long and hard over the 'why work' problem, and on whether they should index-link child benefit. Indeed, in the draft manifesto of 1978 there was a promise, later dropped, to raise child benefit, it being approved of as the first stage of the party's tax credit plans. These remained a policy goal despite doubts continuing to grow about their feasibility and affordability.

It was also decided to tax unemployment and sickness benefit, an objective which Labour ministers had reluctantly come to share. If they remained untaxed at a time when tax thresholds had fallen, people who moved in and out of low-paid work over a year could easily be better off than those who stayed in a job throughout. Some of these 'most difficult decisions' owed a good deal to the 'courage' with which Jenkin handled his brief, according to Howe.[25]

Despite secret agreement on these specific points, little else of detail on the welfare state was settled. In part again that was because the minority Labour Government lasted far longer than expected. From the spring of 1978 it was all waiting. And by then Mrs Thatcher, after a tentative beginning, had had less than three years to develop policy. As a result, the minutes show that throughout 1978 and 1979 the shadow cabinet had lengthy discussions about the economy, devolution, Rhodesia, immigration, and trade union law, all at the time deeply controversial. It even discussed, at inordinate length, Fowler's plan to privatise the National Freight Corporation. What was barely talked about at all, other than council house sales, was anything to do with the welfare state. Rolling it back was simply not put on the agenda.[26]

The idea of an experiment with education vouchers, for example, had been dropped by March 1978 when a draft manifesto was compiled.[27] St John-Stevas did propose a parents' charter requiring schools to take account of parental choice of school, with an appeals system, parent governors and the requirement to publish prospectuses and examination results. He also proposed a core curriculum up to age sixteen to include science, modern languages, and the arts as well as English and mathematics. National and local inspection was to be strengthened. Further there would be national standards for reading, writing and arithmetic, along with testing and remedial education 'especially in primary schools'.[28] At one level, none of this differed significantly from the agenda Callaghan had sketched out in his speech at Ruskin College. At another, much of it is recognisable as the skeleton of part of the 1988 Education Act, although the idea of opted-out schools is missing. That, like the concept of local management of schools, was still just the glimmer of an idea on the right. Stuart Sexton, for example, had arguably outlined it, unnoticed, in one sketchy paragraph of a 1977 Black Paper where he mused about returning not just admissions policy to the schools but 'a devolution of the rest of the administration . . . from the town hall . . . to the school itself. There is no reason why a maintained school should not be an independent unit just as in the private sector.'[29]

Yet just as Labour by the time it lost power in 1979 had failed to deliver on Callaghan's Ruskin speech, so by the time of the 1979 election, the idea of a core curriculum had gone from the Conservative manifesto. The testing of national standards in the three Rs had become something 'to be worked out with teachers and others, and applied locally by education authorities'.[30] In fact nothing was to happen for nine years until the 1988 Education Act. It was Chris Patten, the Conservative Research Department head when all this was being compiled, who was later to observe: 'She's the only party leader I can think of, certainly in the post-war period, who's been more radical in government than in opposition.'[31]

On housing the party was radical. Yet council house sales, the policy which was to do so much to change the political landscape and help lock Labour out of power, was anything but a uniquely Thatcherite proposition. The right to buy them had been in Edward Heath's October 1974 manifesto. Mrs Thatcher had announced the policy as shadow Environment Secretary, but only after arguing vigorously with Heath that it would not be fair on those who had saved to buy their homes. 'What will they say on my Wates estates?' she had demanded when Heath insisted that it went into the manifesto.[32] Since then a much more radical proposition had been advanced, though again not from the party's right. Peter Walker, whom Thatcher had sacked from the shadow cabinet, proposed in June 1975 that council houses should simply be given to those who had paid rent for twenty years and who had thus broadly paid for their construction cost. For others the remaining rent should be treated as a mortgage.[33] He produced elaborate sums showing that this would produce a large net gain to public finances because councils would no longer have to meet the cost of management and repairs,[34] but the idea proved too radical. Walker recorded that 'Margaret was against it because she felt it would upset "our" people who had struggled to pay their mortgages.'[35]

None the less, selling council houses on a less dramatic discount did come to appeal. Plans were worked out to provide a 33 per cent discount after three years' tenancy, rising by one per cent a year to 50 per cent after twenty years. Expanding home ownership, Michael Heseltine told the shadow cabinet, 'is one of the most important things we can do to spread wealth and ownership, and therefore independence from the State, among our citizens.'[36] With the sales went a swingeing reduction in housing subsidies which would push up rents (thus encouraging sales) while cutting public sector building. This was part of the 'real cuts' Joseph had argued would be needed. Not a mention was made of that part of the plan in the manifesto, however.

If the Conservatives saw sales as a way of spreading wealth, the nature of council housing had been worrying some Labour politicians for years. In 1971, Anthony Crosland had warned in the *Guardian* of the 'taint' attached to living in a council house – the 'whiff of welfare, of subsidization, of huge uniform estates, and generally of second-class citizenship'. Too many councils displayed the worst traits of 'landlordism', he complained. The council 'decides what repairs are to be done, what pets may be kept, what colour the doors will be painted, what play areas there should be, where a fence should be put up. The tenant is not consulted. He has no right of appeal. He has far less freedom than the owner-occupier to do what he likes in and around his home.'[37] Crosland's message was that too little had changed from the days when the LCC painted everything 'green, cream or battleship grey', arguing that economy of scale made supplying other colours uneconomic. Connie Reece, in new town Stevenage, remembered tangling with the corporation architect in the 1950s.

> I said: 'Look, I'm very sorry, we don't want black and grey any more, we want to have coloured street doors' and he said 'You can't have it, you've got to have what's on your docket'. More women came along and we said: 'We won't let them paint our doors. We just don't want battleship grey' and after three days of not letting the painters around or opening the windows, we won and we had nice white paint on our windows, and I had a blue door, the woman next door had a red door, and the woman next door had a yellow door.[38]

Crosland did not propose council house sales to solve this problem (though he did advocate that councils should build houses for sale), but he championed the need for a tenants' charter and for housing associations to be encouraged in order to end the council monopoly of rented social housing.

Then in July 1975, Frank Field, CPAG's director, a figure from the left, followed Walker in floating the idea of wholesale transfer of council houses to their tenants. The wealth it would distribute would promote both equality and freedom, Field argued, declaring it was time to 'free the council serfs'.[39] Labour-controlled Birmingham had already for some time been running a popular 'half and half' sales scheme. Meanwhile in Downing Street, Joe Haines, Harold Wilson's press secretary, reacted to Walker's proposal by producing his own plan for council house sales. It was 'enthusiastically' endorsed by Wilson according to both Haines and Donoughue, who pressed the scheme hard.[40] A long battle with advisers and ministers at the Department of Environment ensued before the initiative ran into the sand, Haines publishing an account of the tussle two years ahead of the 1979 general election. The Downing Street proposals, which involved a generation or two of 'lifetime enfranchisement', were a much less complete transfer than the Conservatives' plan for outright sale. None the less, the demand to own rather than to rent from the local authority was plainly there, to be heard on the doorsteps at the 1974 election by 'any Labour politician with ears to listen', according to Donoughue. Surveys showed 64 per cent, even 80 per cent of tenants approved of sales, even if only a third said they wanted to buy. And in 1976 the Building Societies Association told Labour's Housing Finance Review that '. . . the Association recognises that the sale of council houses must form an integral part of housing policy if the wishes of the public are to be transformed into reality.' The Tories did something about this, Labour didn't, and a flagship Thatcherite policy was born.

Thus the clutch of ideas that became Thatcherism had roots – and in places other than just on the right. So did some of its attitudes to the professionals and the bureaucracies which ran the welfare state. As early as 1960, Titmuss had attacked the 'pressure group state' in which professionals furthered their interests in the name of their clients.[41] In 1977, the title of Ivan Illych's book *Disabling Professions* encapsulated his argument in two words. And in 1976, Roger Bacon and Walter Eltis, a pair of Oxford economists, struck a chord with politicians well beyond those on the monetarist right when they published *Britain's Economic Problem: Too Few Producers*, a work which drew attention to a fifteen-year growth in central and local government employment at the apparent expense of the industry and commerce which generated the wealth to support the public sector. In the same year, for example David Owen, a Labour minister, was noting 'alarming' predictions that if the rate at which NHS manpower had grown for the past twenty years was continued, then the whole national workforce would be employed in the NHS by the year 2100.[42]

And indeed, when it came to the Conservative manifesto in 1979 there was precious little that could be dubbed a specifically Thatcherite approach to the welfare state, beyond the desire to cut taxes and generalised declarations that the share of national income taken by the State had to be reduced. In education and housing the initial policies were moving with the colour of the times, covering issues that at least some in Labour's ranks recognised had to be addressed. Over parts of social security, there was as much concern on the left as on the right about the 'better-off on benefit' problem. Poverty campaigners such as Frank Field, and Chris

Pond of the Low Pay Unit, were themselves complaining that 'many low wage-earners, especially those with families, would be better off unemployed and dependent on supplementary benefit', even if their solutions were very different to those the Thatcher government adopted.[43] In the NHS, the sense of crisis was only compounded by Ennals being sued during a winter of discontent which put 125,000 more people on the waiting list, taking it to a then record high.

Beyond that, however, there was on the democratic left, thirty-five years on from Beveridge, a sense of exhaustion of ideas. There seemed little to offer except more of the same – a recipe which lacked allure when what had been provided in terms of employment, the NHS, education, social security and social services, with their failure to prevent child abuse scandals, did not seem to be working too well. It would be some years before the figures became available to prove it, but income inequality, one very limited measure of the welfare state's success, had in fact narrowed appreciably if unevenly under both Labour and the Tories since 1957. Since 1976, however, the gap had started to widen again.[44] There was, to use Maurice Kogan's 1978 phrase, a 'dour and unreflecting pessimism' abroad which affected not just the educational world to which he applied it but much of the welfare state.[45] People's expectations of what it could and should provide appeared to have outrun their willingness to pay the necessary taxes. Blind faith in the idea was crumbling as the power centre in the Tory party shuffled rightward and Labour's constituency and union activists swung left. The traditional centre with its broad belief in the works of Beveridge and Butler and Bevan and Keynes was left dangling. Outside commentators were writing books about Britain with titles like *The Future that Doesn't Work* and *Is Britain Dying?*,[46] while in Wilson's and Callaghan's later days Labour ministers privately were saying that people no longer wrote to them complaining about unemployment.[47]

Margaret Thatcher's victory in June 1979 put Labour into opposition. The party, however, also went into oppositionalism and the internecine warfare which led to the formation of the Social Democratic Party. For more than a decade Labour simply stopped thinking constructively about the welfare state. It was, after all, their welfare state. It was soon to be clear that it was indeed under attack, and they were damn well going to defend it, warts and all – particularly against that woman.

PART V

THE WELFARE STATE UNDER FIRE

1979–92

CHAPTER 17

Cuts and catastrophes: Conservatives 1979–83

A wholesale counter-revolution would be rather unlikely. It is not, for one thing, in the nature of the British Conservative Party which . . . lacks the essential attribute of a counter-revolutionary party – a faith, a dogma, even a theory.
Anthony Crosland, The Future of Socialism, p. 60

'Where there is discord, may we bring harmony . . .'
Margaret Thatcher on the steps of Downing Street, 4 May 1979, quoting Saint Francis of Assisi

Margaret's choice of words [was] the most awful humbug . . . totally at odds with [her] belief in conviction politics and the need to abandon the consensus style of government.
Jim Prior, A Balance of Power, p. 113

Public expenditure is at the heart of Britain's present economic difficulties.
First sentence of Thatcher's first public spending White Paper, 1979

We were over-governed, over-taxed, over-borrowed, over-manned, under-defended, under-policed and rather badly educated. And those were as it were the first obvious targets. There were plenty of others.
Keith Joseph, The Downing Street Years, BBC Television, 1993

She isn't a One-Nation Conservative. She isn't really a believer in the 1944 White Paper on Employment.
Jim Prior, quoted in Young and Sloman, The Thatcher Phenomenon, p. 141

She was not so much a woman of ideas, as of beliefs.
Keith Joseph, Independent, 23 November 1990

THE NEXT DECADE of the welfare state's story was to depend crucially on the simple instincts but complex personality of Margaret Thatcher. Yet as she started her tenure in Downing Street, 'she didn't really look at the welfare state as a policy area – certainly in the early years.' That is the view of David Willetts, who was to become her key health and social security adviser in the Downing Street policy unit.

> She had a sense that it cost a lot. She asked why the budget rose all the time, and 'how the hell do we get a grip on it?' She suspected, or feared, that quite a lot of it was inefficient. And she did have a feeling that individual initiative and the drive for self-improvement could be undermined by too extensive a welfare state; that it could rot people's moral fibre. She did have a set of instincts. But she had no clear programme. In the early 1980s, social policy featured relatively little on the No 10 agenda. She was concerned with the economy, industrial relations, the unions and the nationalised industries – not with health, or social security or education.
>
> She was also, throughout, very political about it – acutely aware of the political costs of changing the welfare state. She was keen on radical thinking and didn't mind people debating all sorts of radical ideas in front of her; but she was reluctant then to go and implement, because she was aware of the political appeal of institutions like the NHS. People don't realise it. But she was very cautious.[1]

It is a view Nicholas Ridley, one of the chief guardians of the Thatcherite Grail, echoed. Soon after she became Prime Minister, he recorded, he talked over with her tackling parts of the welfare state. 'She was adamant she would not start down this sort of road at the beginning. There was enough to do sorting out industry, the economy, taxation and the trade unions. "The supply side must come first," she said.'[2]

Willetts argues: 'She also feared that the welfare state was Labour territory – that we weren't going to win on it. Certainly in the early years she was not wondering how we could have an exciting Thatcherite agenda for education, or health, or whatever. It was all about political containment. As time went on she got more radical in her rhetoric; but not a lot more radical in her actions. She remained wary, aware of the political costs.'[3]

Cautious in some things she may have been – and it can be argued that on the home front the poll tax was the exception that proved the rule. But the attitudes and instincts that informed Thatcher's view of welfare were strong. They could stun her ministers. Patrick Jenkin, Secretary of

State for Social Services, and a man who sees politics 'as a matter of reason' recalled: 'I will never forget the meeting where she said: "Well, we really have got to tackle this problem of people better off out of work. I think we will have to go back to soup kitchens." I said: "*Soup kitchens*, Prime Minister?" And she said: "Take that silly smile off your face, I mean it . . ." Of course, we never heard any more about it.'[4]

She was a marked supporter of the insurance principle, according to Norman Fowler, Jenkin's successor: 'so to that extent she was a Beveridge woman'. But she backed Fowler's desire to abolish SERPS. 'She did have this feeling about the insurance principle, that people who could afford to should insure for themselves,'[5] Fowler says – in other words, a preference for private and fully funded schemes rather than tax-funded and pay-as-you-go systems. She was generally, Fowler records, 'less at home'[6] on social policy than with the economy or foreign affairs. And outside insurance benefits, she had little interest in the rest of social security. A senior DHSS civil servant recalls: 'We had a lot of trouble educating her on how much the whole thing had grown since she had been there [in the early 1960s]. She had only been concerned with pensions and national insurance – not with the poor, because in her day that was still being run by the National Assistance Board. The benefits had proliferated madly between then and 1979 when she came in. So we had great problems getting her to take on board that there were now, I think, thirty-four social security benefits and she had probably been familiar with four or five. We did have to educate her.'[7]

On education, too, she had strong views, but, as Willetts says, also 'a problem'. 'She had been there and knew it. She was, for example, very nervous about saying anything good about grammar schools. She was very pro grammar schools, but very embarrassed about saying anything about them because she had pushed through more comprehensives [than anyone else] when she was Secretary of State for Education, and she knew she had. That made her very wary about big rallying cries in education. She was aware she would face the charge of inconsistency. She wanted neither to give a ringing endorsement to comprehensives, nor a rallying call for a return to grammar schools.'

Stuart Sexton, special adviser first to Mark Carlisle and then to Keith Joseph at the Department of Education and Science, recalls the profound suspicion she retained of the department she had run six years before.

She *hated* the Department of Education, because I think she realised they had taken her for a ride. She would say to me: 'Is old so-and-so still there?' 'Oh yes, Prime Minister, he's an assistant secretary now.' 'He's not, is he? – oh my goodness.' And she had this ingrained memory of name after name of officials who had been principals or assistant secretaries or whatever and she obviously hated them because they had imposed their view on her.

But whatever her desires, Sexton, too, recalls caution. He was an early advocate within government of vouchers so that self-managed schools could be made to compete for funding. But, he recalls, she was 'politically cautious. Much more than people give her credit for. She would agree entirely with the concept I had described. She would say: "Yes, let's have that." But then she would say: "But, of course, politically we will never get that through. We will have to persuade people of that, of where we are going."'[8]

On the NHS her instincts were if anything more powerful. The service was wonderful for car crashes, disasters, devastating illness, what she once called the 'great accidents' and 'terrible diseases'.[9] It had to be there for the poor. But otherwise people should pay their way. Kenneth Clarke, her Secretary of State for Health: 'She thought it was disgraceful that people who could afford it relied on the taxpayer to provide their health. She was positively proud of the fact that she looked after her own health and made no claims on it . . . she was quite happy that the vulnerable, the poor, should have the taxpayer do it for them. But people like you and me should take responsibility for our own lives and should insure for these things. And anyway it was all part of her great campaign to roll back the frontiers of the state.'[10]

That view is confirmed by Roy Griffiths, for four years her adviser on NHS management: 'She would have liked to have got away from it. If it hadn't been there she would never have invented it.' It was, he says, 'an easy dislike for someone like her. There was always the feeling that if anything went right with the health service it was because of this magnificent welfare state which the Labour Party had set up in the 1940s – and if anything went wrong it was all the fault of those damn Tories.' Had it been politically possible, Griffiths says, 'she would have got rid of it. But Maggie's great strength was that even if she didn't like something – and this may fly in the face of the popular perception – she was a realist. She knew she couldn't do it.'[11]

In fact the NHS was the one part of the welfare state protected from cuts for most of Thatcher's first term. Early in the election campaign, Jenkin had to appear on BBC TV's *Newsnight* with David Ennals, the pair of them dinner-jacketed after attending a Motability dinner. The Tory manifesto had carefully stated: 'it is not our intention to reduce spending on the Health Service'.[12] Labour, however, had written in significant increases for the next three years in its pre-election spending plans. Jenkin realised he would be asked whether the manifesto meant he would hold spending steady or honour Labour's plans. 'I had rung up Geoffrey Howe [the shadow Chancellor] earlier in the day and said: "Look Geoffrey, this is *the* election interview on the health service and I am going to be asked this . . . and I've got to be able to say that we will for those years maintain the planned expenditure figures." And he said, "Yes, I understand. You have my authority to say that."'[13]

Effectively, through the need to answer one question on television, Jenkin had bounced Howe into protecting the NHS for three years. In the first, ferocious spending rounds of the Thatcher years he was thus able to fight off the Treasury – raising prescription and dental charges, proposing, but then withdrawing in the face of furious opposition, a charge for eye tests, but none the less maintaining Labour's spending plans. He was to regard that protection for the NHS 'as one of the most valuable things I ever did in government',[14] at a time when the cuts were so fierce that in 1980 Howe and the Treasury proposed that pensions should not even rise in line with prices. That year, Jenkin recalled: 'I went to Cabinet armed with what Mrs Thatcher had said in a Sunday morning broadcast during the election: "We will maintain the purchasing power of the pension . . ." I read out the words, and Jim Prior [who had himself gone armed with Geoffrey Howe's and Keith Joseph's election addresses to the same effect] said: "Well that puts the end to that then, doesn't it?"'[15]

By then the link between pensions and earnings had already gone, a move announced in Howe's first 1979 Budget in which he talked of the need to 'roll back the boundaries of the public sector'.[16] Jenkin had agreed to the earnings link being broken. Never 'one of us' or categorisable as a 'wet' or 'dry', he acted in David Donnison's words as 'very much the head boy, loyal to his headmistress'.[17] While he was determined to protect the NHS, he was quite prepared to cut benefits. 'I still remember my officials' absolute astonishment when I got into the department and said "we are going to cut social security",' Jenkin recalled. 'They said: "But you have to defend the social security budget, Secretary of State, that's your job." I told them the whole government was committed to reducing the public sector borrowing requirement and this department would play its part – "now you go away and tell me how to do it".'[18]

The senior officials there at the time remember it slightly less dramatically. But the outcome, which got worse as the second oil shock struck in 1979, was that child benefit was frozen, the earnings link for pensions disappeared and a Social Security (No 2) Bill was introduced containing just six clauses. Every one of them was a cut: strikers had their benefits reduced; some sick pay costs were switched to employers; the earnings-related additions to unemployment and sickness benefit were abolished and the basic value of these and some other payments, including invalidity benefit, were cut by 5 per cent as a prelude to taxing them – a move that involved extremely 'rough and ready' justice as it hit many tens of thousands who would not have paid tax.[19]

There was uproar in the Commons. The committee handling the Bill had to be suspended twice. Changes of both principle and practice were involved. For a start, linking benefits only to prices effectively rejected the idea of relative poverty. Jenkin spurned pleas from the Supplementary Benefits Commission that, in breaking the 'better of earnings or prices' rule for pensions, he should at least link them to earnings so that pensioners and the long-term sick and disabled on insurance benefits would share in any rise in the country's prosperity.[20] He told the Commons that under the last Tory government, without a statutory link, they had in fact kept pace with earnings. Although now only linked to prices, he declared 'it remains the Government's firm intention that pensioners and other long term beneficiaries can confidently look forward to sharing in the increased standards of living of the country as a whole.'[21] That promise was not honoured for those who relied solely on the state pension. By the early 1990s its value was down from 20 to 15 per cent of male average earnings. Had the break not been made, an astronomic £43 billion more would have been paid over to pensioners between 1980 and 1992,[22] although what that would have done to the economy would be a matter for heated debate.

Equally, removing the earnings-related additions overturned a policy aimed at increasing job mobility which the Tories themselves had supported. The additions had been a regular Treasury target. Labour's Joel Barnett had proposed scrapping them during the IMF cuts in 1976.[23] In 1979, however, there was little discussion either in the department or in public over whether earnings-related benefits were right or wrong in principle. Such issues were too subtle for the times. Howe comforted himself with the view that removing them was 'getting back to Beveridge' and his flat-rate system.[24] But the real imperative was simply to save money – and Jenkin was prepared to believe that earnings-related benefits did contribute to the 'why work' problem.[25] The fact that these cuts were driven more by a desperate determination to reduce spending than by any ideologically coherent approach to means-testing or incentives was shown in the freezing of child benefit. Raising it would have helped with the 'better off on benefit' problem, a point Jenkin privately argued and acknowledged,[26] but raising it cost money. So it was frozen, making worse the 'why work' problem with which ministers remained obsessed and despite unemployment beginning its sharp, dramatic and apparently permanent rise.

As top rate tax was cut back sharply to 60p in the £ with bottom rate tax adjusted more marginally (reduced from 33p to 30p), it was clear that the main attack on 'why work' was to be through benefit cuts, not by raising tax thresholds. In the Commons, Thatcher defended the measures. 'It is right to have a larger difference between those in work and those out of work,' she declared.[27] Despite heavy civil service manpower cuts an exception was made for staff to tackle 'scrounging', but no similar exception was made to employ the extra tax inspectors whom Howe admitted would have made savings as large or larger by bringing in more revenue.[28] In well publicised 'raids' the DHSS arrested thirty people, had others jailed and trapped a council employee who had invented 115 people and was claiming benefit for all of them.[29] A clear message was being delivered in all this.

It was this early round of benefit cuts which was to contribute significantly, along with many other factors including the attack on trade union privileges and wages council powers and the inexorable rise of both unemployment and of benefit-dependent lone parents,[30] to the marked widening in the gap between rich and poor during the Thatcher years. It was one of the earliest acts of the Thatcher government. Yet, given ministers' endless and furious denials that the poor had got poorer, and repeated insistence until the late 1980s that wealth would 'trickle down' from the better-off to the less well-off, it is far from clear that the full long-term consequences of the cuts were thought through. For in many though far from all respects, the government continued to run on a broadly 1970s agenda for the welfare state during its first term. Through the most dramatic political change since 1945, great threads of continuity could still be seen.

Once the benefit cuts were over, Jenkin legislated to implement the more open and rules-based version of supplementary benefit which David Donnison and the SBC had recommended to the previous Labour Government. He did so working to the same nil-cost framework on which Labour had insisted, while ignoring, as Labour had looked set to do, the benefit improvements which the commission had sought. The legislation, none the less, was plainly that which Labour had planned, and the new benefit rates did provide more help for families with children – who had been shown to be the worst off – at the expense of the elderly.[31] The system, simplified a little, was able to stagger on while Jenkin took the decision to launch the Operational Strategy, the biggest civilian computer project in Europe, whose aim was to replace thousands of staff and the paper chase of lost files with desktop computers able to handle locally the one billion payments and the millions of claims made each year.[32]

In addition, Jenkin went ahead with the new housing benefit scheme that the Supplementary Benefits Commission had proposed to replace the existing mishmash of rent and rate rebates. Studies by the SBC had shown that about 270,000 households who were claiming would in fact have been better off on supplementary benefit rent payments. For at least another 90,000 the position was the other way round, while a further 400,000 were failing to claim either entitlement.[33] A unified benefit, run by town halls, would be fairer to claimants, cheaper to administer, and easier to understand, Donnison and his colleagues had calculated. The government legislated for it, though, in Donnison's words, in a slightly 'battered form'.[34] They were to pay the price for not doing it properly.

There was a continuing agenda, too, in the sense that social work had not delivered what was hoped of it. The great blush of optimism which followed Seebohm in 1968 had gone sour. As with so much else, the turning point was the visit from the IMF in 1976, according to Sir Peter Barclay, who was later to become a highly regarded chairman of the Social Security Advisory Committee but who for more than a decade was chairman of the National Institute of Social Work, and who was appointed by Jenkin in 1980 to review the role of social workers.

> From 1976 on it became a demoralising fight. Up to that time in social welfare it seemed that all we needed to do was identify problems, create an organisation to cope with them, and that would solve it. Social care, social work, social services – we all had unlimited resources, it then seemed. The national institute was a case in point. We needed a training school. So what did we do? We formed it, with money from Rowntree, money from Nuffield and a big injection from government. But from the mid-1970s social services and social care have really been in retreat, certainly beleaguered – much more so than social security.[35]

After the heady days of expansion in the early 1970s the manslaughter of Maria Colwell by her step-father in 1973 became the first of the string of horrific child abuse cases that were, however unfairly, to undermine social workers' standing. The Barclay committee's report, published almost unnoticed on the day British ships entered the Falklands waters, opened with the words: 'Too much is generally expected of social workers.'[36]

It was not, of course, all continuity. In 1977, David Ennals had commissioned from Sir Douglas Black, chief scientist at the DHSS, a report on health inequalities which was delivered in 1980. It showed, unmistakably, that the death rates for many given diseases were higher for the lower social and occupational classes than for the higher, and that while death rates for social classes I and II had improved over the twenty years up to the early 1970s, those for social classes IV and V had changed little or had even deteriorated.[37] Overall the standards of health of the population had risen, but despite the NHS and despite the welfare state, the health gap between rich and poor seemed to be growing. This was tolerably explosive stuff. The difficulty was that Black and his group – which included Peter Townsend, by now a figure who ranked high in the demonology of the right – concluded that the NHS had little to do with this state of affairs. More emphasis should go on prevention and primary and community care. But many of the key causes of the gap, in so far as they could be established, seemed to lie in issues such as 'income, work (or lack of it), environment, education, housing, transport and "life-styles"'.[38] The report's thirty-seven recommendations included a large increase in the value of child benefit, a quadrupling of the maternity grant to £100 to restore its 1948 value, a new infant care allowance, free school meals for all, a big increase in housing expenditure (and a distrust of council house sales), much more pre-school education and day care – and much else.

Jenkin panicked. He produced the briefest of forewords costing the recommendations at upwards of £2 billion a year (the total NHS budget was then only about £10 billion). Such a sum was 'quite unrealistic in present or any foreseeable economic circumstances, quite apart from any judgement that may be formed of the effectiveness of such expenditure in dealing with the problems identified,' he wrote.[39] Having rejected the report's recommendations, he then attempted to bury it, producing not a printed version but just 260 cyclostyled copies, a handful of which were put out to the press late on a Friday before the August Bank Holiday. There was no press release and Sir Douglas was told he could not hold a DHSS press conference. In defiance, and at journalists' insistence, he held one at the Royal College of Physicians, his report acquiring a notoriety for the way it was published that it would never otherwise have achieved.

The original blue-covered copies became collector's items. Labour, the unions and the medical profession took the report up, and Jenkin found himself heavily on the defensive.

The Black working group, while convinced that material deprivation lay behind its findings, had, in truth, little evidence that many of the specific measures it recommended would change the death rates it had identified. Its report, however, put health inequalities firmly on the map, not just in the UK but worldwide. It also launched the start of a decade of uncomfortable and ultimately unsustainable denials by government that health had anything to do with socio-economic conditions. For a government committed to praising inequality while believing the 'trickle-down' effect would benefit even those at the bottom, the Black report was an unwanted reminder of yesterday's agenda. In practice some small measures were taken to tackle health inequalities. And a decade later one of Black's key recommendations – that health goals should be set by government – did resurface in *Health of the Nation*, the 1991 document in which targets to reduce key diseases were set.

If many of the social security cuts had to be worked out once the Tories were in office, Michael Heseltine was able to announce broad details of council house sales within days of the election. It was to prove, though no one could know it then, the biggest single privatisation of the Thatcher era, raising £28 billion over thirteen years – more than the sale of gas, electricity and British Telecom put together.[40] It provided votes for the Tories in places they had never had votes before, hugely reinforcing the change in the political map of England and Wales which the 1979 election had already demonstrated. In conscious and provocative parody of Labour's 1974 manifesto promise to produce 'an irreversible shift in the balance of power and wealth in favour of working people and their families', Heseltine had promised that council house sales would mean 'an irreversible shift of wealth in favour of working people and away from the state'.

For a brief moment Labour, already lurching leftward towards the split that created the Social Democrats, held its breath – and then damned the policy to the skies. A Labour councillor who had already bought her council house found herself dropped.[41] Sales, with the better off in the better houses in the better areas likely to buy first, would diminish both the quality and quantity of the rented housing stock, the party argued, drowning out the lonely voices in Labour's ranks who argued that it should back sales but insist on a continued building programme. It was a building programme the Conservative Government was massacring. Spending on housing had been falling under Labour, but what Labour had done with reluctance the Conservatives did with relish in their drive to control public spending.

Across government, the cash limits for spending in the current year which Labour had introduced were reinforced by cash planning for later years. A general inflation assumption was built in for years two and three, but anything above that had to be argued out programme by programme with the Treasury, a far tougher discipline than the old volume planning system where a department could agree it would have so many teachers, or tanks or nurses or other services two or three years down the road, and then be given the cash whatever they then cost. In housing, expenditure was slashed from £5.5 billion in 1979 to £3.7 billion by 1984 – after inflation, an even bigger reduction than the raw figures suggested. Council house building was more than halved, reduced to 40,000 to 50,000 homes a year, while private house building suffered equally in the recession which Geoffrey Howe ratched up further in his 1981 Budget.

Overall, house building hit its lowest level since the war,[42] council house building having started a decline which would see it virtually disappear by the 1990s. In 1970, when the Tories first formally encouraged council house sales, one justification had been that the capital it raised would allow new build 'for the aged, the disabled and those on housing lists'.[43] Not so in the 1980s. Councils were debarred from spending most of the cash, told instead to use it to pay off their mountainous debts as part of the drive to reduce public spending.

The sales policy itself, however, proved such a success that 500,000 people had bought their council houses by 1983, and almost 1.5 million would do so by 1990. Meanwhile Wandsworth, the new jewel in the crown of Tory local government, pioneered the sale of entire high-rise blocks. These flats, once renovated, provided with gyms, six-foot fences, video security and lifts, became the home of the new breed of childless Yuppies – the Young Upwardly-Mobile Professionals who took the fast trains and tube to the City and whose existence became one of the most potent symbols of the Thatcher years. No one quite seemed to know where those who had lived there before had gone.

Renovations too slumped in the early eighties, although they were to rise again in the mid-1980s with the help of a 90 per cent grant. Rent restrictions were eased, and the right of private landlords to evict was strengthened somewhat, but neither measure brought back to life the private rented sector which in the decade from 1979 fell by another third to around 8 per cent.[44] Homelessness began an inexorable rise.

If housing provided both one of the sharper policy breaks as well as the biggest single instant cut in welfare state spending (the social security bill kept rising thanks to the growing armies of unemployed and elderly), education policy initially continued largely down the 1970s road. It did so, however, on a less lavishly provided highway.

'Cuts, Cuts, Cuts' was the headline on a survey by the *Times Educational Supplement* when it returned to the streets in November 1979 after a year-long fight with the print unions.[45] The man in charge of them was Mark Carlisle, a tall, florid-faced Heathite barrister who had been surprised to be brought into the shadow cabinet not long before the election to replace Norman St John-Stevas, now Leader of the Commons. Carlisle inherited a position where primary school numbers were falling fast and secondary school numbers were poised to decline. Only the total of 18–24-year-olds – the higher education sector – was still rising. With a manifesto pledge to boost defence, and with health and social services either protected or able to show demographic pressures rising, the Treasury wanted the money. Education started a six-year decline in its share of government spending, down from 5.5 per cent of GDP in 1980 to 4.8 by 1986.[46]

Carlisle was initially required to save £280 million and did so with an Education Bill which reduced local authorities' obligations under Butler's 1944 Act to provide school meals, milk and transport. Labour MPs accused him of gambling with children's health. Rab Butler in his last intervention in public life emerged in the Lords to team up with the Duke of Norfolk to defeat the proposal to let councils charge for school buses on the grounds that it would provide the death-knell for village schools. Peter Hennessy was later to record: 'It was as if Old England had risen for a last hurrah . . . He seemed like a benign and decent beached whale washed up on the harder shores of modern Conservatism.'[47]

Carlisle also abolished Labour's 1976 Act requiring councils to submit plans for comprehensives, though as with Thatcher's circular almost a decade earlier the momentum continued. Of the 315 grammars still extant in 1979, 130 had become comprehensive by early 1982.[48] Legislation also introduced parental choice of school and parent governors on lines broadly similar to the Labour Government's proposals and those of the Taylor report. This change is identified by Thatcherite educationists as the first legislated step towards opted-out schools and parental control in education, but it was a tiny step and it did not have to lead there. Local authorities had to pay more attention to parental choice, but those opposed to the idea could still be obstructive.

Much more controversially, with spending on education falling, Carlisle legislated for the Assisted Places Scheme under which the DES was to pay direct the fees of selected pupils at independent schools. This was largely Sexton's work, an outline of it having been tabled in 1976 as a failed Tory amendment to that year's Education Act. With direct grant schools abolished, the aim was replace the help they had provided to bright working-class children, but subject to a means-test. The scheme was meant to be better targeted on the less well-off than the old system of grants in return for a proportion of places, a method which had tended to benefit middle-class children at least as much as the less well-off. The idea, however, came close to being scuppered by the wets in the Cabinet where its scale was initially halved to 5300 places at a cost of £6 million. By 1994 it had grown to 34,000.[49] Neil Kinnock, Labour's education spokesman, pledged to abolish a programme which he attacked as élitist and divisive at a time when the squeeze on education spending was sufficiently tight for Carlisle himself to suggest that parents might like to help out by buying schoolbooks. Spending on these had started to fall under Shirley Williams but was tumbling under the Tories[50] as education authorities grappled with the cost of dispensing with teachers in the face of falling rolls, often by expensive early retirement packages.

Carlisle found himself facing mounting demonstrations and protests, and at the NUT's annual conference in 1980 he was heckled and jeered. His initially robust defence of the spending restrictions weakened as he himself became more worried about their impact.[51] He was most unhappy at their effect on the universities.[52] To begin with, Carlisle had promised them 'level funding', but that disappeared in the spending round of autumn 1980. Universities felt they had entered a new ice age. Because university spending was one of the few parts of the education budget the department controlled directly, it was easier to hit hard and fast than the schools budget, where the DES provided cash through the generalised rate support grant without being able to guarantee what councils spent it on. At the same time, the heavy skirmishes Labour had enjoyed with local government over spending were just turning nicely into what was to be a decade-long war between central and local government.

In 1981 universities were told that they were to suffer an 8.5 per cent cut which over three years meant they had seen a 13 per cent reduction.[53] Ten thousand academic and non-academic posts were set to go over two years in higher education, many of them by early retirements and redundancies, at a time when the numbers in the relevant student age group were still rising. The University Grants Committee, chaired by Dr Edward

Parkes, dug in, with unforeseen consequences for both the universities and government. In an attempt to maintain standards, the UGC insisted on preserving the 'unit of resource' – the funds for each student – thus ensuring that student numbers fell in line with funding. Even more controversially, the UGC decided not to spread the pain evenly, but to protect what it viewed as the 'best' academic universities. Some such as Bath and York, for example, faced minor reductions, while Aston and Salford, two of the more technological universities who were actually pursuing the government's wish that universities should work closely with industry, faced fearsome reductions of approaching 20 and 30 per cent.[54] The Vice-Chancellor of Salford reacted by marketing his university virtually as a business in its own right throughout the north-west, rewarding its academics for paying attention to the needs of industry and commerce rather than to the laurels of academe. Ministers and their advisers noted what a more entrepreneurial approach could do.

What ministers had failed to recognise was that while government could cut university monies, it could not control the polytechnics which, like the schools, had access to local authority funds. Students flooded across from universities to polys. Good courses closed in one sector, poor ones recruited in the other. Able university staff who could get jobs elsewhere took the 'golden suitcase', as the early retirement and redundancy packages became known, while some of the less able stayed on.[55] The 'overspend' in local government cancelled out or even exceeded the draconian cuts in the universities, and the result, in Stuart Maclure's words, was 'confusion. Ministers were frustrated, academics and university administrators were hopping mad, and the financial savings never materialised. It was a shambles.'[56]

Higher education, which valued itself, could not believe it was so undervalued by the government. The universities recoiled in horror. Their intelligentsia, for most of whom the words 'liberal' and 'radical' still had their sixties meanings, not the nineteenth-century connotations with which Thatcher and her think-tanks had started to imbue them, hardened their hearts against the Prime Minister and her works. The attitudes were formed that would see Oxford refuse her an honorary degree in 1985 on the grounds that she had done 'deep and systematic damage to the whole public education system in Britain'.[57] The impact, however, went beyond that. It became plain to the government that if it wanted change in the universities, it needed more control. The traditionally arms-length relationship became slightly less so as ministers began to send out letters of 'guidance' to the UGC establishing the government's priorities. The travelator which was to lead to a very differently constituted funding council replacing the UGC had started to move.

Meanwhile, although in broad terms the NHS was protected from cuts, perceptions were otherwise. As elsewhere in the public sector, the huge Clegg pay awards which the Tories had agreed to honour during the 1979 election campaign, came home to roost. Inevitably, they cost health authorities more than the extra cash that government provided. In addition, RAWP was starting to bite. London hospitals had begun to close, sometimes in a spectacular and unpleasant fashion: in late 1977, for example, administrators launched an evening raid to remove twenty-one elderly patients to the West Middlesex from Hounslow Hospital in order to end a nurses' sit-in and effect closure. Pictures of deliberately smashed beds, wrecked equipment and staff in tears painted a strange view of the NHS. Equally, because RAWP had moved more slowly than intended, new hospitals in gaining districts were sometimes completed before the cash to open them flowed. Thus as wards closed in London, ministers found themselves in 1980 and 1981 with the embarrassment of hundreds of unopened beds in hospitals mainly outside the capital.[58] In addition health authorities, often egged on by their local authority members, started resisting 'cuts' – most of which were in fact redistribution rather than any net loss of NHS money. Soon after Jenkin took office Lambeth, Southwark and Lewisham, the health authority which covered the three great teaching hospitals of Guy's, St Thomas's and King's, refused to lop £5 million off its £138 million budget. Jenkin suspended the authority and sent in commissioners, only to find he had acted illegally. Medical schools in the capital, which had bitterly resisted attempts to merge them in the 1960s,[59] found themselves shotgunned into marriage as the university spending cuts bit. The severe sense of crisis from the late seventies thus lingered on.

Into all this in July 1979 the report of the Royal Commission on the National Health Service intruded like the voice of sanity in a madhouse. Its 500 pages provided a far from uncritical but none the less overwhelming endorsement of the NHS. Too many tiers, too many administrators, a failure to take quick decisions and some money wasted, were its key criticisms. But 'the NHS is not suffering from a mortal disease susceptible only to heroic surgery'.[60] It recommended, in line with Jenkin's views and conventional wisdom, that the Area Health Authorities should go,[61] a process which threw the service into a second major reorganisation within a decade.[62] There was far more continuity here than change. The idea of a chief executive or general manager, one that would be enthusiastically adopted within five years, was rejected by ministers because it 'would not be compatible with the professional independence required by a wide range of staff employed in the service'.[63] Priorities for the Cinderella services remained the same. The concern, as in the 1970s, was with organisations and structure, Jenkin later boasting that with all the advisory machinery and sectors he had got rid of three tiers.[64]

None the less, having reacted against big is beautiful, Jenkin went to the other extreme. He tried to devolve and decentralise as much as possible (a muted, internal, NHS version of 'rolling back the frontiers of the state'). Partly to cut civil service numbers, he scrapped, by fiat, the programme budget and the planning system with its norms and targets which, because it took two years to get a planning cycle up and down the NHS tiers, had struggled to get going after the 1974 reorganisation. Jenkin's abolition of it meant that the NHS could no longer demonstrate clearly what it had done with its money, just at a time of mounting parliamentary (and Downing Street) concern over the inexorable increase in NHS manpower. This concern was taken to new heights when it was discovered that what had been expected to be 435 early retirements in the 1982 NHS reorganisation at a cost of £9 million had become 2830 at a cost of £54 million – and that some of those made redundant had then been re-employed. Overall administrator numbers had kept on rising.[65]

Fortunately for Jenkin, and for Fowler, who had later to defend both these figures and ministers' inability to demonstrate how efficiently NHS cash had been spent, the department's finance division, without telling Jenkin, quietly kept key parts of the system going in private.[66] As parliamentary pressure mounted, civil servants were able to dust them down and start to answer the critics, showing that the extra money was indeed buying extra services. *Health Care and Its Costs*, published on the eve of the 1983 election, demonstrated that between 1976 and 1981 productivity had in fact risen faster than resources.[67] In the words of Terri Banks, then head of health services finances at the DHSS, 'it was a very slow start to turning an appalling corner for the NHS.'[68]

There were other continuities. In these early days of Thatcherism, before the unions had been dealt with, it was still judged wise to buy off professional power blocks. Jenkin, to the GP negotiators' amazement, finally settled a long-standing bone of contention by allowing family doctors to employ their wives as secretaries and assistants, a practice previous ministers had felt was too open to abuse. Jenkin also settled the consultants' contract, on terms the BMA loved, eight years after talks had started under Joseph. Its wording had finally been agreed under Ennals, but when money was put on it by the review body, shortly after the election, the doctors did not like the deal. Tony Grabham, now chairman of the BMA council, was reading the report on a train down to London. 'It was a very poor deal. But there was a small sum of money the review body had identified for extra call-outs. It was just enough with which to do something.' Grabham proposed it should be used to move the part-time contract up from 9/11ths of a week to 10/11ths.

> We went to Jenkin, and I said: 'Look, we don't want this badly priced contract, but we know there is no more money around. Why don't we give this extra 10 per cent to the part-timers, but then compensate the whole-timers by letting them earn an extra 10 per cent as well? Here's a deal, Secretary of State which would get rid of the industrial-type contract which none of us ever wanted anyway. It would give the part-timers another 10 per cent for no extra work. It would let the whole-timers start dabbling in private practice if they want to. It will erode the gentleman and players distinction between consultants – and it won't cost you a penny.' It was an offer he couldn't resist.[69]

Indeed it was. Jenkin got two things at once: industrial peace with the consultants, who now had an earnings safety-valve when the government, as it did from time to time over the decade, squeezed their NHS income; and another signal of support for private practice through allowing even whole-time consultants to earn up to 10 per cent of their salary from private work. Growing numbers did so.

The first signal supporting private practice had been the abolition of the Health Services Board and its powers to phase out pay beds and license private hospitals. New pay beds were both encouraged and approved.[70] A couple of small, redundant NHS hospitals were sold off to the private sector and the minor tax concessions on company paid private health insurance which Labour had abolished were restored. But studies of alternative means of funding the NHS had been temporarily stymied by the Royal Commission, which declared itself unconvinced that the claimed advantages of insurance or charges would outweigh 'their undoubted disadvantages in terms of equity and administrative cost'.[71]

Yet it was around this issue of privatising the financing of the NHS that the profound suspicion of both NHS staff and the public over the Tories' intentions began to build. The messages, confused enough when Jenkin was in opposition, became even more so, chiefly because ministers themselves were unclear about where they were going.

Thus there were declarations of undying commitment to the NHS which were backed by evidence: relatively generous funding against other departments, a resumption of heart transplants, the saving of small hospitals from closure, the restoration of hospital building outside London, a plan to double the number of consultants, and a study of how to improve inner-city general practice. Yet at the same time health authorities were freed to fund-raise, bringing Labour charges of a return to the pre-1948 flag-days, although in practice health authorities raised little. And as the numbers covered by private health insurance suddenly rocketed by 26 per cent in 1980 (and by 13 per cent the year after), Gerard Vaughan, the Minister of Health, said he wanted to see one in five of the population having private medical cover by 1985 – which would have meant more than a four-fold increase in little more than four years.[72]

The sharp increase and Vaughan's prediction brought American health companies flooding to Britain in anticipation of rich pickings, producing an explosion in private hospital building that soon left the private sector with too many beds. Equally, Jenkin, and more particularly Vaughan, repeatedly hinted that new charges such as the first £10 of treatment, or a switch to private insurance, were under discussion.[73] The pair dined with private sector specialists at the Centre for Policy Studies, hosted by Alfred Sherman, the Thatcherite evangelist who was its director,[74] while the Adam Smith Institute demanded tax concessions for private insurance.[75] Faced with charges from Sherman and others of faintheartedness, and of being blocked by the civil service,[76] in July 1981 Jenkin announced a DHSS working party on alternative finance.[77] Unprecedentedly, two outside private sector advisers were put on it: Michael Lee, a sharp-tongued economist, and Hugh Elwell, a raffish character who was an adviser to BUPA and had a fondness for fine wine and fedoras. The suspicion grew that the Tories wanted to destroy the NHS.

Meanwhile unemployment had been rocketing. From 1,238,000 and falling as Mrs Thatcher took office, it cleared the two million barrier in November 1980 only to be given a further dramatic upward thrust in 1981 by Howe's most vigorously anti-Keynesian Budget yet. Budget day was the moment when Thatcher broke the Cabinet wets as they failed to combine to stop her. By June 1981, the jobless count was at 2,500,000. Seven months later it was to reach 3,000,000. In April 1981 and then even more dramatically in July the predictions of those who said you could not have three million unemployed without riots on the streets seemed right. First London's Brixton and then Toxteth in Liverpool erupted – the latter so violently that for the first time CS gas was used to quell a riot on the mainland of Britain. The rioting then spread to Manchester's Moss Side and was followed by a spate of smaller 'copy cat' incidents in thirty towns and cities up and down the country. Margaret Thatcher, her eyes glittering with strain, visited Liverpool unannounced to admit that the previous ten days had been the worst of her premiership.[78] Yet the predictions proved false. Harsh policing and racial prejudice as much as unemployment and economic disadvantage were the themes of the Scarman Report on the Brixton incidents when it came.[79] The riots soon died away. The unemployed fell silent again, even if a new thrust had been given to limited inner-city regeneration and youth training schemes.

Three months later, in September 1981, Mrs Thatcher produced her equivalent of Macmillan's 'night of the long knives', removing three 'wets' – Ian Gilmour, Christopher Soames and the increasingly unhappy Mark Carlisle –from the Cabinet, while Prior was shifted from Employment to internal exile in Northern Ireland. Joseph, at his own request, replaced Carlisle at Education.[80] Jenkin's reward was Joseph's job at Industry. And Jenkin was replaced by Norman Fowler, who at Transport had become one of the government's first privateers by disposing of the National Freight Corporation and insisting that local authorities put highways work out to tender.

Thus ended the first phase of Thatcherism and the welfare state. Everything and nothing had changed. The bedrock of the idea – full employment – had been abandoned, perhaps for ever, the belief in it disappearing alongside great chunks of the smokestack industries, metal bashing and, to a lesser extent as yet, coal mining. In parts of the north and even the midlands, for the first time since the war, teenagers were leaving school with no apparent prospect of ever finding a local job. Skilled men in their fifties were eyeing a lifetime on the dole. Norman Tebbit, the new Employment Secretary, rose at the party conference to say his father's generation had experienced worse unemployment in the 1930s. They had not rioted. 'My father got on his bike and looked for work.'[81]

Yet if a true Thatcherite had replaced Prior at employment, and education had seen the arrival of Thatcher's John the Baptist, health and social security did not gain a right-winger. Instead they got Norman Fowler who would soon have Kenneth Clarke as his Minister of Health. They proved a formidable team: Clarke, rumbustious, aggressive, entertaining, devil-may-care, and as yet unconvinced by almost any aspect of Thatcherism save for her profound distrust of professional self-interest. When challenged over whether he had private health insurance, his answer was a disarming declension: 'I don't have it, you don't need it, we have a National Health Service.'[82] Fowler wore his heart less on his sleeve. Like Clarke he was a post-war grammar-school boy and part of the 'Cambridge mafia' of the early 1960s which included Leon Brittan, Michael Howard, John Gummer and Norman Lamont, all of whom were now making their way up the Tory party. Nobody's wet, he remained in essence a One Nation Tory, who believed not just in equality of opportunity but that the country did not yet provide it.[83] He was a politician with 'a misleadingly low profile' according to Kenneth Stowe, his permanent secretary throughout Fowler's near six-year record tenure at DHSS.[84] As an ex-journalist, Fowler believed that information was power and he clung to it tightly. He used to operate by ignoring his in-tray – a way of ensuring it did not overwhelm him. 'He worked on the not unsound principle that anything really important would find its way to the top of it, and he would meanwhile set his own agenda,' one of his senior civil servants recalled. But in concentrating obsessively on one issue at a time, and crawling over every detail of it again and again, Fowler could drive his staff far beyond the call of duty and to distraction. Not many loved him. At the end of each parliamentary term, his private secretaries would trap him in the agonisingly slow ministerial lift which Keith Joseph had installed at the Elephant and Castle. It stopped only at the ground and ministerial level six floors up, giving them time during its snail's progress to insist that he pay attention to papers that he had to sign.[85] He was, moreover, deeply cautious, anxious to be sure where the political advantage lay for both himself and the government before he moved.

One of his earlier acts was to halt Jenkin's study of alternative health service finance. A first report in November 1981 had been thorough, but had come to no very particular conclusions. It was clear from it, in Fowler's words, that: 'There was no inherent cost advantage in moving over to an entirely new financing system and it was also clear that whatever system was chosen, taxation would still have to finance a giant share of the service. The unemployed, the poor, the chronically sick and of course children would need to be covered by public money . . . [and] the potential for a massive row was immense.'[86] To attempt to have privatised the NHS then 'would have been frankly political madness . . . in theory I can see the attraction of some other form of finance. But I think at that particular time it would have been several bridges too far.'[87]

Without consulting Mrs Thatcher, but after consultations with the Treasury, he killed the study off.[88] Fowler, however, in Rudolf Klein's phrase, was a sinuous politician. One of his favourite aphorisms was 'a politician never says never'. His written answer in July 1982 left just a chink open for a change of mind, should it ever be needed. 'The Government,' he announced, 'have no plans to change the present system of financing the National Health Service largely from taxation, and will continue to review the scope for introducing more cost consciousness and consumer choice and for increasing private provision which is already expanding.'[89] It was a masterpiece of unpunctuated civil service drafting.

It was barely noticed. For within months of his appointment – from just before, during and long beyond the period when a war in the South Atlantic was being converted into the Falklands Factor – Fowler had been locked into what became Britain's longest industrial dispute in fifty years. The issue was over the Cabinet's 4 per cent public sector pay norm. Nurses were differentially offered 6.4 per cent, but ancillary workers and most others were offered only the 4 per cent – just as top civil servants and judges were given a 14–18 per cent increase. The dispute lasted more than eight months, repeating in barely milder form the horrors of the winter of discontent. Three million working days were lost.[90] Tens of thousands of operations were cancelled. The waiting list, which had declined from 750,000 to 620,000, jumped 100,000.[91] Nurses in the main, though not entirely, kept working. When Fowler went to the National Association of Health Authorities annual conference in June, in a scene that would be utterly unthinkable by the mid-1990s, health authority chairmen and administrators kept him waiting while they passed a resolution condemning his offers as divisive.[92] Even the Whitley Council chairmen, who were negotiating on Fowler's behalf, publicly attacked his strategy. Such was the force of demonstrations that Fowler ended up with an armed police guard.[93] But in the end, in December 1982, the government won, rewarding the nurses for their 'no-strike' policy with the promise of a pay review body similar to that for doctors.

It was a watershed for both the government and the NHS. Having backed away from a showdown with the miners in 1981, this was the first big public sector strike that the government had undeniably won. It ended a decade of industrial unrest in the NHS, for not until the ambulance dispute of 1989 would the service again be seriously troubled by strikes. The outcome both exhausted and demoralised the unions, making possible the competitive tendering shortly to come for cleaning, catering and laundry services – moves which were to cut their members' jobs and pay as well as squeeze NHS costs.

It might have seemed Fowler was on a winning streak. But between January and July 1982,[94] Treasury ministers undertook some gloomy calculations which suggested that if growth was only 1 per cent a year then public spending was set to take at least a steady and possibly a rising share of national income. This was not what the electorate had been promised. Howe and Leon Brittan, the Chief Secretary to the Treasury, asked the Central Policy Review Staff, the Cabinet Office think-tank established by Heath, to suggest radical options which would prevent that happening.[95] Lord Hailsham, the seventy-three-year-old Lord Chancellor, was to record that when he read the outcome in September, 'my hair stood on end, and at my age that takes some doing'.[96]

The headline options included: ending even price protection for all social security benefits and ending state funding of higher education. Market fees (around £12,000 a year) could be charged for courses. State scholarships would be offered to some, but loans for both tuition and maintenance would be all that was available to others. Replacing the NHS with private health insurance might save 30–40 per cent of the £10 billion budget, the think-tank calculated, and in the meantime charges for visiting the doctor could be introduced. Vouchers for primary and secondary schooling were also canvassed, although the paper pointed out that costs would rise if those paying for private education also qualified. An alternative was simply to let the teacher/pupil ratio deteriorate.

This was dismantling the welfare state by anyone's standards. Howe and Brittan put the paper to Cabinet with proposals for a detailed six-month study. The wets for once combined, producing in the words of Nigel Lawson, then Energy Secretary, 'the nearest thing to a Cabinet riot in the history of the Thatcher administration'.[97] They forced the paper off the agenda of the Cabinet of 9 September 1982, and for good measure someone – Hugo Young suggests Peter Walker – leaked it to the Economist.[98]

The political reaction was dramatic, the proposal to abolish the NHS causing most opprobrium. Roy Hattersley, at a Labour Party rally, declared: 'Had such a staggering suggestion been made in the bar room of a public house, all those who heard it would have assumed that the story teller was drunk. The idea of replacing free medicine with health insurance is the most callous and brutal idea yet from this callous and brutal Government.'[99] According to Hugo Young, Mrs Thatcher clung to the CPRS paper until the majority of the Cabinet told her she had made a terrible blunder: 'When the voices were collected she said, in what one minister called a petulant huff, "All right then, shelve it."'[100] Certainly Leon Brittan fought on, declaring five days after the Economist leak that decisions had not been taken but that 'radical options have not been ruled out either'.[101] The belief that this really was the agenda was only fuelled by a speech Howe had made to the Conservative Political Centre a couple of months previously in which he had pointed to 'powerful reasons' why private provision should be considered to supplement 'or in some cases possibly replace' the role of government in health, social security and education.[102]

Fowler was furious. Abolition of the NHS had been proposed 'without any consultation with any health minister'.[103] He declared again there were no plans to change the financing, while yet again leaving for the suspicious a statement of fact which looked like a potential get-out clause. 'Taxation will remain, as now, the *predominant* way of financing [the NHS] . . .'[104] Less than a month after the Cabinet rows, on 8 October 1982, Mrs Thatcher had to tell the Tory party conference at Brighton: 'Let me make one thing absolutely clear. The National Health Service is safe with us.' Thus was born 'safe in our hands'.

The episode had been a catastrophe for the Conservatives. It dogged them down all the days of the eighties and into the nineties. Few did not now have at least a lingering suspicion that, in their heart of hearts, the Thatcherites would indeed like to unscramble the NHS. It was a suspicion only aided by the 1983 manifesto's declaration that: 'We welcome the growth in private health insurance . . .'[105]

Come the election, the CPRS report was leaked again in a fuller version by Peter Shore, but it made little difference. Health or education rarely win elections: the economy, and broader perceptions of the future, do. Living standards for those in jobs were once again rising. Labour had fissured over the Bennite revolution and produced a manifesto that Gerald Kaufman dubbed 'the longest suicide note in history'. Its less *dirigiste* pledges included nationalisation of private hospitals, abolition of private education, an end to the right to buy, and councils being empowered to buy back council houses on their first resale. In fact Labour's first task under Michael Foot in its worst organised campaign ever was to beat not the Tories but the SDP – something it managed by a mere 675,000 votes out of the 30 million cast. The Conservatives began and ended the campaign fifteen points ahead.

The first Thatcher government had given the nation a pop group which could call itself UB40 and everybody knew what it meant. It was shortly to produce the heartrending figure of Yosser Hughes in Alan Bleasdale's 1985 television drama *Boys from the Blackstuff*, pleading with anyone who would listen, 'Gissajob'. But with a divided opposition and with almost 90 per cent of the workforce still working, Mrs Thatcher achieved what four years earlier almost all politicians would have said was unthinkable

– re-election with a majority just two short of Labour's 1945 post-war record of 146, at a time when three million people were out of work. For the next decade and more the only opposition that was going to matter was the opposition on the government's own benches.

CHAPTER 18

Fighting Leviathans: Conservatives 1983–87

> Mr Lawson's move to the Treasury is clearly intended to set the tone of the new government . . . it will be abrasive, clever, argumentative and even more at loggerheads with spending departments than usual.
>
> *Economist, 18 June 1983*

> In narrow political terms, genuine educational reform is a particularly unattractive prospect for any government. Like all reform, it upsets all those with a vested interest [while the return] will not become apparent within the lifetime of even the longest-lived administration.
>
> *Nigel Lawson, The View from Number Eleven, p. 607*

> To be blunt the British social security system has lost its way.
>
> *First sentence, Green Paper Reform of Social Security, 1985*

> The £40 billion social security system has become a Leviathan almost with a life of its own.
>
> *Norman Fowler, June 1985*

> If Margaret Thatcher wins on Thursday – I warn you not to be ordinary; I warn you not to be young; I warn you not to fall ill; I warn you not to get old.
>
> *Neil Kinnock, speaking at Bridgend on the eve of the 1983 general election*

THE NEW PARLIAMENT brought a new Chancellor and a new round of spending cuts. Geoffrey Howe had delivered expansion before the election, but Nigel Lawson now found public spending mounting faster than planned. A month after taking office he launched a 'dawn raid' which lopped £500 million off the budgets of the biggest spenders including health and education while making it clear that he had in his sights social security, the biggest spender of all. As Norman Fowler observed, 'it needed no great powers of prophecy to realize that Nigel and I were on a collision course.'[1] Fowler's answer was to set up a review. It was the approach he used to almost every subject with which he ever dealt, aiming like Fabius Cunctator always to control the agenda before the Treasury or Downing Street controlled it for him. It was a trick which repeatedly worked. The great social security review had, however, small beginnings. Changes in Whitehall mattered as much as changes of ministers in getting it going.

For almost three years, Patrick Jenkin had ineffectually urged occupational pension schemes to do something about 'early leavers' – those who changed jobs and then found they had to leave their pensions, frozen in value, behind them. Fowler felt this personally. It had happened to him when he left *The Times* to become an MP. It had happened to his father, who died before pension age leaving Fowler's mother with returned contributions but no widow's pension.[2] He came to regard occupational pensions as 'golden handcuffs' which chained staff to their companies and reduced job mobility.[3] His own determination to do something about this was hardened by the Centre for Policy Studies which published papers on the issue in early 1983, while in Downing Street a new figure was taking a similar interest in the subject. The Central Policy Review Staff, whose welfare state report had caused such ructions, had been wound up – that report, indeed, being the immediate cause of its demise. As a result, the Number Ten Policy Unit which answered purely to the Prime Minister, not to the Cabinet, had been expanded and strengthened. Its new head was John Redwood, a slim, dark, razor-minded fellow of All Souls with cold eyes, who Matthew Parris, *The Times* sketch-writer, once memorably described as 'half-human, half-Vulcan, brother of the brilliant cold-blooded Spock'. Over the next five years, the unit was to provide the cutting edge of Thatcherism.

Redwood expanded the unit, bringing in new blood so that it now shadowed all the main Whitehall departments including health, education and social security, each of which had received only limited attention under Sir John Hoskyns and Ferdinand Mount, the unit's two previous directors. The possibility of creating a recognisably Thatcherite policy towards the welfare state began to emerge. Redwood's own immediate interest was pensions. He had been a fund manager and a director of Rothschilds and, having seen pension funds at work, 'I was not certain that they served people as well as they might.'[4] Redwood was also an early advocate of 'popular capitalism', wanting much wider ownership of stocks, shares, savings plans and other financial assets. In pensions, this meant the development of personal, portable pensions – the interest Fowler shared.

The third element that Redwood brought to the party was a desire that any review of pensions should be reasonably open. The CPRS leak was 'engraved on my mind'. He felt strongly that 'if we tried to have an internal exercise in Whitehall, a series of politically unacceptable options would be drafted by someone – probably not by a politician – and these would then be leaked, making the position almost untenable. Nothing good would then come of it, it would just be negative for government.'[5] He and Fowler therefore dreamed up the idea that was to form the basis of all four parts of the social security review: an 'open' review, chaired by a minister but with outside experts, inviting evidence and holding hearings, a sort of instant but ministerial Royal Commission which would report to itself. The technique was applied to early leavers and portable pensions. As it got under way however, the cost of SERPS intruded into the argument.

SERPS had already been looked at more than a year earlier when the CPRS had launched a study which concluded that it was going to cost too much in the twenty-first century. As the numbers of elderly rose, the number of contributors per pensioner was projected to decline from 2.3 to 1.8, pushing up national insurance contributions for those still in work. The think-tank had concluded that SERPS should be phased out and replaced by private pensions. Its report, however, had not only followed the famous leak of 1982 but had been handed to the Prime Minister in the spring of 1983 just as she was planning to go to the country. Thatcher was horrified. When John Sparrow, the head of the CPRS, was called in, thinking it was to discuss the findings with her, he found himself instead ordered to recover all departmental copies and destroy them.[6] By late 1983, however, the election was safely over and SERPS could be looked at afresh. Examination was eased by the arrival at the Treasury of Nigel Lawson, who regarded its ultimate cost as 'a doomsday machine'[7] even if the heaviest costs would not fall until the next century. Redwood, too, wanted rid of SERPS. When he again raised with the Prime Minister the idea of abolishing it, her immediate reaction when she realised that the savings would only come long term was, 'You want me to roll the pitch for someone else to bat on';[8] but she agreed to its inclusion in the review.

As the pensions review got under way, Fowler also found himself in deep trouble over the new housing benefit. Jenkin, in legislating for it, had ignored warnings from Donnison and others that extra cash would be required to make it work without unacceptable numbers of losers. Rather than find the money, ministers fiddled with the scheme. Instead of producing a unified benefit that combined supplementary benefit rent payments and the old town hall rent and rate rebates, ministers effectively ended up with the old systems running in parallel but with a third scheme, housing benefit supplement, imposed on top. To save the 2500 civil service jobs which the reform promised, the whole was introduced in such a rush that the computer programmes to run it were both desperately late and subject to endless amendment. The new benefit proved so complex that only about five people in the country seemed fully to understand it – none of whom proved to be the ministers responsible. And just as it was getting up and running, Fowler agreed in the 1983 spending round to lop another £230 million off its £4 billion cost.

The result, in the words of *The Times*, was 'the biggest administrative fiasco in the history of the welfare state'.[9] Across the country, dozens of council housing offices closed their doors early, took phones off the hook and locked long queues outside as they attempted to sort out backlogs which left claimants without rent and rates payments for weeks and in some cases for months. In places the police had to be called to quell disturbances. Evictions mounted. Private as well as public landlords were in despair. When Rhodes Boyson, the minister nominally in charge of the scheme, addressed a furious meeting of local authorities and housing pressure groups, his understanding of it was so poor that he refused to take questions and retreated from the hall to jeers.[10] Fowler was left with no choice but to review it.

Nor was that his only additional problem. The 1980 change to supplementary benefit, making it a more rules-based system and thus in theory more open, understandable and controllable, had largely failed. In January 1984 a report the department had commissioned two years earlier from the Policy Studies Institute landed on Fowler's desk. It made sobering reading. The mass of old supplementary benefit guidance had now been turned into 16,000 paragraphs of enforceable and appealable rules. The PSI study showed that claimants and staff alike were bamboozled by them. Families with children were suffering real hardship. Three out of five adults on the benefit lacked basic items such as a warm coat or change of shoes, both for themselves and their children. More than half were in debt, usually over fuel bills. More than half ran out of money most weeks facing problems caused 'by the routine expenses of normal living, not by unusual events'.

In theory, the system was no longer a matter of discretionary state charity. The extra weekly payments for heating, diet, laundry and the like were now an entitlement if the qualifying conditions were met. The same was true for one-off payments such as cookers, floor coverings (not carpet) and beds. Yet three-quarters of claimants had 'no idea at all' how the payments worked and half did not even know they existed. This picture of 'utter bewilderment' the report said, may not surprise, 'but it should cause shock'.[11]

Fowler recognised that families with children were doing badly, but he was equally alarmed by the spiralling bill for the one-off and weekly 'extras'. Half of the seven million people now dependent on social security might not know they existed, but the other half did and so did welfare rights advisers and Labour councils who had long ceased to feel any affinity for the Thatcher government. They used the open, published rules to ensure that claimants claimed. Some, like Strathclyde, started running take-up campaigns, placing advertisements in the papers and inviting people to tick boxes for items they felt they needed and send the forms to the DHSS. It was an approach which deeply irritated Fowler,[12] while further burdening an already overloaded system. Many of the claims, however, proved valid. This should not have been surprising: the PSI study had already shown, for example, that two-thirds of claimants were entitled to some extra payment once a welfare rights adviser looked at their case and had equally demonstrated that much of the money was needed. The result from Fowler's and the Treasury's point of view, however, was that for the third time in twenty years the bill for special payments, while still less than 5 per cent of the supplementary benefit budget, was again rocketing upwards and out of control. With the PSI report on the table and Lawson closing in, Fowler made a virtue of necessity. Two more reviews were added to the pensions and housing benefit studies: one into supplementary benefit and another into benefits for children and young people. As he proudly told the Commons in April 1984, the biggest review of social security since Beveridge was now under way. Only disability benefits were not being tackled, although a survey of the disabled was commissioned from the Office of Population Censuses and Surveys.

It was no coincidence that of the three main arms of the welfare state – health, social security and education – it should be social security which underwent the major review first. It was, after all, the biggest spender. It was also the one where spending was least under control because it could not be cash-limited. Still rising unemployment, the increase in council rents which was dramatically inflating the housing benefit bill, and rising numbers of elderly people and single parents were all ratcheting spending upwards, despite the cuts in entitlement already made. Social security, Mrs Thatcher told the *New York Times* not long before the reviews began, was 'a time bomb' whose consequences needed to be addressed 'before it is too late'.

But if it was the biggest worry financially, it was also the one area where ministers could pull levers and make things happen. Much of the story of education, health and social services during the 1980s is of a search by ministers for levers which, when pulled, produced measurable results. Education remained a decentralised and increasingly unhappy partnership between central and local government, where ministers had only the most limited powers to ensure that what they said happened. In social services the position was even worse, the Department of Health and Social Security having an even more tenuous ability to influence what local authorities did: 'like wading through treacle,' was Fowler's verdict.[13] Health – the NHS – was midway between education and social security, with a largely policy-oriented department slowly building up more direct management skills, a trend strengthened under Fowler after being put into reverse by Jenkin. Only in social security in the early 1980s was the minister's word law. It was a department the head of which was linked directly to a delivery mechanism through 500 local offices and a couple of central computers. It also had a tradition of doing its own thinking and dreaming up its own schemes, relatively independent of ministers, a legacy from the days of the semi-independent National Assistance Board and Supplementary Benefits Commission. Legislation might be needed to change benefits. But once done, as Fowler himself said, 'the great thing was that what you said should happen, happened.'[14]

None the less, Fowler's review when it got going was not as wide-ranging as he wished. Many Conservatives still hankered after tax credits. Fowler had wanted to include both taxation and national insurance contributions in his study, for both had profound effects on those on low income and in the poverty trap. The large sums forgone through the married man's tax allowance (paid whether or not there were children), mortgage interest tax relief and other 'tax benefits' might have been used to allow a saner overall system to be devised. Lawson would have none of it. He stuck by the 'hallowed Treasury doctrine' that taxation is for Chancellors only. The benefits to be gained from tax credits, basic income guarantees or similar schemes were in any case illusory, he argued.[15] Fowler believed it was a missed opportunity.[16]

Even with tax excluded, the review involved shifting a mountain of paperwork and ideas. The final outcome, however, for all its billing as the most comprehensive review since Beveridge, proved – with two important exceptions and one symbolic one – to be a set of relative molehills, even if some of them were cleverly designed molehills. The review turned supplementary benefit into income support, providing a basic benefit for adults to which premiums were added for groups such as families, children, pensioners and the disabled. The scheme became less sensitive to individual needs, but easier to understand and administer. It also became much easier to computerise – a vital requirement given the collapsing state of the system's administration.

Housing benefit was also simplified and Family Income Supplement for those in work became the more generous Family Credit. For the first time the same means-tests were used for all three benefits, a marked simplification, and the means-test for Family Credit was applied to post-tax income. That meant virtually no one would now lose more than 100 per cent of each extra £1 they earned from the combined effects of taxes being paid and benefits being withdrawn as their income rose. The very worst effects of the poverty trap had thus been eased, though at the expense of doubling the numbers of people in work who lost between 50p and 80p in the pound as housing benefit was made less generous by withdrawing it more quickly. The poverty trap, in effect, had been made wider, but shallower.

Overall, families with children and the elderly gained marginally from the changes at the expense of the unemployed, those without children and particularly those under twenty-five, whose benefit was cut markedly in an attempt to cajole them to either stay in the parental home or get into work.[17] This attack on the 'why work' problem was one of the two notably ideological aspects of the review, throughout which unemployment ran at well above three million. Despite this previously inconceivable total of jobless, significant sections of the Cabinet still believed that too many people were better off out of work. 'David [Lord] Young, the Employment Secretary, came in with the most incredible figures about the numbers of long-term claimants in London and the south-east when there were masses of vacancies and London Transport was cancelling trains because it couldn't get staff,' David Willetts, then Thatcher's social security adviser in the policy unit recalled.[18] Cutting benefits for single people, and making family credit more generous for those with children, aimed to make the gap between work and benefit greater, while protecting children.

The other ideological element, and the single most important change, was SERPS. The assertion about its final costs was in fact debatable. The growing numbers of elderly were a certainty; but the numbers who would be in work to support them were a matter of guesses about the birth-rate, future economic performance, and the number of women likely to be employed. On top of the costs argument, however, Fowler maintained there was another case for getting rid of it. The state was right to be in the business of providing a basic pension, but not a second pension on top – particularly not when the second pension, because it was earnings-related, was more generous to the better off. This fitted not at all with a Tory ideology of targeting help on those who most needed it. Second pensions, Fowler argued, should be supplied privately. Lawson and Thatcher took the same view, although there was to be an important division between them. Thatcher and Fowler wanted to abolish SERPS and replace it with *compulsory* private pensions. Without the compulsion to guarantee that people would save for their old age, Thatcher feared the abolition of SERPS would not be politically acceptable.[19] It would also risk the state having to support those who failed to provide for themselves.

Initially Lawson concurred. As the social security reviews were being completed, his eye was on the 1985 Budget. He failed until the last minute to work out what the costs of compulsory occupational pensions would be in terms of extra tax reliefs and the contributions private industry and the public sector would have to make. When he did so, he found the figures 'alarming' and told MISC 111, the Cabinet committee which Thatcher was chairing on the review reports, that he could not accept a compulsory replacement for SERPS.

'I had never seen Norman so cross,' Lawson recorded in his memoirs.[20] Fowler halted the Cabinet committee dead in its tracks. He refused to proceed and, with Thatcher still firm for a compulsory replacement, a less costly modified version was worked out and finally published in a Green Paper in July 1985. It provoked, however, such opposition from employers over the potential costs that Fowler and Thatcher were forced into retreat. The fall-back position was that SERPS would be retained but cut back sharply with generous incentives offered for people to opt out of it. The scheme would now pay only 20 per cent of lifetime earnings, not 25 per cent of the best twenty years. Only half the pension, not the whole, would pass to widows. The effect was to halve the estimated cost in the year 2033 from £25 billion a year to £13 billion. Meanwhile a stack of rebates and incentives was introduced to encourage people to quit the second state pension for their own personal scheme. These proved successful beyond the government's wildest dreams. By 1993, not the 500,000 originally planned for, but more than five million people had opted out of SERPS. The government had forgone £9.3 billion in national insurance rebates and 'incentives', and a further £2.8 billion bill was incurred in 1993–4, the year in which it emerged that half a million people had succumbed to high pressure salesmanship and had been talked into leaving good occupational pensions schemes in which they should have stayed.[21]

In this way, at considerable current cost, though at a much greater long-term saving, pensions became the one large part of the welfare state where the Thatcher government did succeed in rolling back the frontiers, though even here a large, if much less generous, State Earnings-Related Pension Scheme remained. For those who quit the scheme, one uncertainty replaced another. In place of doubts about whether the next generation would pay the taxes needed to provide this generation's pensions came the doubt about what their money purchase pensions would prove to be worth one, two or more decades hence; and whether future shareholders would allow the scale of dividends needed to fund the pensions that people now expected. For Fowler, his failure to get rid of SERPS completely in return for providing every worker in the country with an occupational pension, remained 'the worst decision I have ever had to take in government'.[22]

The second significant change that the review brought was the Social Fund. This was the final – and as it proved the harshest – attempt to settle the extra payments problem in supplementary benefit. Regular weekly additions were abolished and the one-off payments for cookers, beds and the like were transformed into loans. They were awarded on a discretionary basis, not by right – a reversal both of the 1980 change and the trend towards greater rights that had been evident since 1948. In addition, the fund was cash limited, so local offices could and did run out of money. It was to prove the most controversial and painful part of the reform, remaining right into the nineties the one that the ministers and civil servants involved were least happy to defend. The loans were interest free – a significant improvement on the rates of interest that loan sharks charged to those who had to borrow – and the fund put an end to tribunal cases over whether someone was entitled to a grant for a hot water bottle or not.[23] But the Social Fund's primary aim was to cap a budget which had ballooned from £44 million in 1981 to £220 million by 1984 as the system sprung leaks at the hands of claimants and welfare rights groups. As fast as one source of claims had been halted – clothing grants in 1980, for example – others would emerge – household goods and floor covering. To the Treasury, and to Fowler in his sourer moods, this was evidence of abuse. To his critics it was evidence that benefit rates were too low, particularly as two-thirds of the payments went to families with children, the group whom the PSI study had shown to be the worst off.

For the more seriously disabled, ministers did recognise that the social fund's effects would be over-harsh. Their answer was to 'charitablise' one small corner of the welfare state. They agreed to grants rather than loans for the most seriously disabled but provided them at arms-length and on a discretionary basis by giving cash to the Independent Living Fund, a charity set up on the lines of the Rowntree Family Fund. After much soul-searching, the Disablement Income Group agreed to run it after the Family Fund, which had been offered the job, turned it down, judging the budget on offer to be 'totally inadequate'.[24] Some years later, in a masterpiece of understatement, the National Audit Office observed drily that the Social Fund had succeeded entirely in its primary aim: it had capped the single payments budget. But by making those who took loans live on less than the basic income support rate, without the occasional lump-sum top-up, it also made life for those on benefit for any length of time measurably harder.

If SERPS and the Social Fund were the significant changes, the symbolic one was that, technically at least, Fowler's review ended the 'cradle to grave' span of the social security system. Beveridge's £25 maternity grant and his £30 death grant, two of the genuinely 'universal' benefits paid to all, were abolished. No government had uprated them for years. The maternity grant by 1985 bought less than half the cost of a baby's cot; the death grant less than 10 per cent of a cheap funeral. In future, the remaining, more generous help for funerals and baby equipment would be heavily means-tested. These had once been two of the more popular benefits. Their disappearance caused barely a stir, the lesson being that if politicians want to get rid of a universal benefit, their first aim should be to freeze it, letting it 'wither on the vine'. It was an approach John Moore was soon to try with child benefit. It does not always work, however. The £10 Christmas bonus to pensioners, worth around a fifth of its value when it was introduced, survived Fowler's axe; the political cost of getting rid of it was judged too great.

As Richard Berthoud, the author of the PSI study, concluded, claims that the outcome of the review represented fundamental reform were 'grossly exaggerated'.[25] But in its own way, it remained an achievement. Fowler emerged with his £40 billion budget largely intact. He did so despite Lawson's insistence as the reviews neared completion that they produce £2 billion a year in savings – a second occasion when Fowler refused to proceed until that demand was withdrawn[26] – and despite the *Economist* noting that other ministers had come to see the review as 'the new North Sea: a source of dream money for all'.[27] All Fowler agreed to was a £450 million cut in housing benefit, barely 1 per cent of the total social security budget. Even that proved, to use Nigel Lawson's phrase, to be something of a 'boomerang offer'[28] – the sort that comes back on the Treasury because the political cost proves too high and Cabinet either refuses to agree it or has to revise it on implementation. John Moore was to find that the housing benefit cut fell into the latter category. As one senior DHSS civil servant put it: 'Fowler was much more successful in defending the social security system. Under Jenkin it felt like a loss leader to keep health going.'[29] Of course, to the more radical members of his party Fowler's success represented failure, but the right had proved to have no coherent alternative to offer in place of Fowler's combination of managerial pragmatism and the defence of some old-fashioned Conservative values.

The reviews swallowed significant amounts of Fowler's time, leaving Clarke as Minister for Health with a freer hand than most Ministers of State enjoy. Much of the first year of their joint tenure at the Elephant and Castle had been swallowed by the NHS pay dispute. That coincided with expiry of the pledge that Labour's three-year NHS spending plans from 1979 would be honoured. Moreover the NHS, like other departments, was now facing cash rather than volume planning for future years. Life for the health service was suddenly financially much tougher. Between 1982 and 1987 when Fowler departed, these changes resulted in volume spending on the hospital and community health services – what health authorities could buy after pay and price rises – remaining largely static.[30] Virtually all improvements had now to come from greater efficiency. Faced with such a squeeze, not to mention the £140 million or 1 per cent cut in planned spending from Lawson's 1983 'dawn raid', the reaction of many health authorities was to close beds and wards, often as loudly and publicly as possible in the hope that would avert further cuts next year. 'When Norman and I arrived,' Clarke recalled,

suddenly we and the NHS were in the real world, just coming out of recession, with an icy chill in the financial climate, cash limits counting for the first time, and the politics dominated by cuts in services. So we had somehow to get hold of this Leviathan and seek to deliver the service properly.

The problem was that there wasn't a management system worth the name. There was next to no management information of any kind, no one knew what the devil we were spending the money on, and the whole thing was dominated by political campaigning. If we were going to get growth in the actual service delivered out of the money we had available we had to constrain cost in some way that didn't itself damage the service.[31]

The result was a maelstrom of initiatives, a dose of centralisation and an attempt to make the NHS more accountable for its performance. The initiatives included assumptions that health authorities would generate savings of 0.5 to 1 per cent of their cash limits each year; the introduction of annual reviews by ministers of each region's performance against agreed targets (this was in fact a secret return to a form of the centralised planning that the 1970s had made possible and which Jenkin had scrapped); the setting up, in turn, of similar reviews by each region of its districts; a dozen Rayner scrutinies on everything from selling off nurses' homes to advertising vacancies; strong pressure on authorities to sell surplus land to raise capital, a move which helped restore a significant hospital building programme; and the introduction of 'performance indicators' which at least allowed questions to be asked about the relative efficiency of the 191 districts. (They rapidly showed there were 191 different health services in operation, not one national one.)

Where it was cheaper, health authorities were encouraged to buy operations from the private sector, and Clarke demonstrated a remarkable even-handedness by requiring private hospitals to pay a handling charge for supplies from the NHS blood bank. In addition there were, what Clarke was later to admit were some 'rather arbitrary', manpower targets, combined with the rigorous enforcement by ministerial bullying of a requirement that health authorities put their cleaning, catering and laundry services out to competitive tender.

Coming shortly after the think-tank report, this last was inevitably seen by opponents as the first step towards privatising the NHS. It was initially resisted by those health authorities who did not believe Mrs Thatcher would last for ever. The chairmen of such authorities, however, soon learned that their reward for such gestures was to be stamped on by Clarke who insisted that they take the lowest tender at the same time as he debarred authorities from stipulating that private companies must match NHS pay rates. Chairmen who failed to deliver found they were not reappointed: 'the only lever I had and the one I continued to pull all the way,' according to Clarke.[32]

The great majority of contracts in fact were awarded in-house, but at the cost of cuts in jobs and pay which released millions of pounds for patient care while slashing the directly-employed ancillary workforce by more than 30 per cent by 1989. A decade on, the cumulative savings from such measures – though equally the lost pay for an already low paid section of the workforce – was put at £1 billion.[33] Much of the cleaning went private, but much of the catering and laundry, where NHS costs were already low, did not. Clarke recalled: 'I think I provoked the biggest provision of new kitchens and laundries ever seen in the NHS, because the reaction of half the authorities was to cancel their capital projects on anything to do with patients and rush out and invest in new equipment to win the contracts. So we had lots of cook-chill kitchens installed with staff who weren't trained to use them and were still boiling things up on top of them.'[34]

The manpower targets produced an even bigger row. Under fire from the Public Accounts Committee and with some authorities literally unable to state how many staff they employed, Fowler and Clarke insisted they not only control numbers but cut them by some 5000 or about half a per cent. They were to hit the administrative tail, not front-line doctors and nurses. It took months of wrangling, scores of damaging headlines and bitter protests from health authorities to get the cuts through. In Brent, Nina Talmage, the chairwoman of the local health authority, fled through the french windows as demonstrators disrupted a health authority meeting where a Methodist minister joined local councillors in leading resistance to 110 job losses and other cuts needed to halt a £250,000 overspend. Only the threat of dismissal finally brought them into line.[35] In Downing Street, the recalcitrance of health authorities when they contained locally-elected members was noted.[36] Their days were to be numbered.

'We spent all this time under tremendous attack for cutting the health service when the one thing I was determined to do was not cut the health service,' Clarke recalls.[37] Tight as things were, it was difficult for the government to prove that the service overall was not reducing. Fowler, with Thatcher, as his echo, resorted to the only weapon he had: a numbers game in which he endlessly recited the litany of more money spent, more patients treated, more doctors and nurses employed, more hips, hearts and cataracts repaired; figures which showed that output was rising even if others could demonstrate that real terms cash inputs were not, once the magic 2 per cent formula was allowed for. It was a subtle argument to sustain. Added to that, health service administrators and members, faced by this whirlwind of centrally-dictated efficiency drives, were becoming increasingly resentful.

So for a time was Clarke. Thatcher was worried not only by the noise about the NHS, but about the fact that NHS manpower genuinely appeared to be out of control. Shouldn't someone from industry be brought in to sort it out? In January 1983, Kenneth Stowe, Fowler's permanent secretary, was given from the list of the great and the good the name of Roy Griffiths, the managing director of the supermarket giant Sainsbury's and an old acquaintance from their days at Exeter College, Oxford. Clarke bristled. 'There I was clattering about, contracting out this and manpowering that in an attempt to get some management into the service, and here's this bloke they want to bring in to spend twelve months doing a study . . . in fact Roy produced a very good report. My reluctance about it turned out to be a terrible mistake.'[38]

Initially, Griffiths was asked to 'take a look at manpower in the NHS' and promptly refused. 'I think he [Stowe] was a bit taken aback when I said it didn't make any sense just to look at manpower,' Griffiths said. 'Quite clearly, if the manpower is out of control, you have got management problems . . . so [after a meeting with Fowler and Clarke] the remit was changed to look at the management of the health service.'[39]

With three other businessmen[40] and the help of Cliff Graham, an ebullient and iconoclastic civil servant, Griffiths set out on his inquiry. Almost instantly, he recalled, 'all hell broke loose'.[41] Four businessmen wandering about the NHS less than six months after the think-tank report only set off fresh charges that the secret agenda was privatisation. The sneers were loud and frequent over what on earth supermarkets had to do with running the National Health Service, while doubts about the government's commitment were only underlined when in August 1983, Margaret Thatcher pointedly chose a private rather than an NHS hospital for a minor eye operation.

In fact Griffiths was deeply committed to the health service. The son of a colliery overman in North Staffordshire, he had childhood memories of the thirties depression, of 'five bob to go to see the doctor' because the miners were covered but their wives and children weren't, and of the 'great and glorious days'[42] when the Beveridge report came out. He had been a Bevin Boy down the mines, before an Oxford scholarship, a brief spell with the National Coal Board, and a career with Monsanto that eventually led him to Sainsbury's in the days when it still ran shops with counters, not out-of-town supermarkets.

For his management inquiry, Griffiths took no formal evidence, planned no formal report, and intended merely to deliver a little healthy advice. In the end he was talked into an interim paper which went to Downing Street. Mrs Thatcher demanded a full version, and Griffiths, protesting that he was still the full-time managing director of Sainsbury's, agreed to take a week off and write Fowler 'a letter'.[43] It proved the most unconventional NHS report of all time. For a start it was written backwards. It began with seven pages of recommendations. These were followed by thirteen of diagnosis, while the evidence, so beloved of most formal inquiries, was simply omitted. It warned that speed was 'essential': the NHS could not afford 'any lengthy self-imposed Hamlet-like soliloquy as a precursor or alternative to the required action'. The twenty-four pages of typescript demanded not a paragraph of legislation, yet its recommendations proved the most important single change to the NHS since 1948, allowing a service which was cracking under the strain to survive into the twenty-first century. Its central message was graphic and simple. 'If Florence Nightingale were carrying her lamp through the corridors of the NHS today,' Griffiths wrote, 'she would almost certainly be searching for the people in charge.'

Those people, who had disappeared as a result of Joseph's 1974 reorganisation, should, he said, be appointed. Managers, of whatever discipline, should replace administrators. Consensus management should go. Doctors should become involved in running budgets. Cost improvement programmes should be better established. Treatments should be evaluated to see if they were effective in both clinical and cost terms. And while responsibility and budgets should be discharged to as low a level in the NHS as possible, those having them should be given targets and held to account. At the centre, a supervisory board chaired by ministers to set strategy should be created, while for management 'a small, strong general management body is necessary (and that is almost all that is necessary at the centre for the management of the NHS).'[44]

It really was almost that simple, though it took Fowler eight months of consultation and fourteen drafts of the implementing circular to finally bite the bullet.[45] The chief difficulty was the centre. The department liked the report's recommendations for local management, but it strongly disliked the threat to its empire posed by a small, strong and separate central management board. Anxious questions (still unresolved in the mid-1990s over Next Steps agencies and the NHS itself) were raised about how far the department and ministers could remain accountable if management of the service was separated in this way. In the end the boards were set up. But they functioned with marked difficulty for five years until a prime ministerial edict at the time of the 1989 NHS review, and Clarke's belief in the idea, demanded of the civil service that it allow the recast version of them, created in 1989, to work better.[46]

When the Griffiths report was published – on the day Neil Kinnock made his Commons debut as leader of the Opposition – nurses exploded, seeing their painfully created and jealously guarded position in the administrative hierarchy being removed. They responded with a £250,000 advertising campaign asking why Britain's nursing was being run by people 'who don't know their coccyx from their humerus'. Doctors were wary. Administrators saw their chance. As implementation went ahead, it was chiefly they who became the managers, despite Clarke and Fowler ruffling feathers by insisting come hell or high water that at least some of the new appointments would be doctors and nurses and that some would come from outside the NHS.

After some stumbles on the way, what was finally created with the help of individual performance review and performance pay, was a line management system which ran from the newly-created management board at the top of the NHS to the hospitals at the bottom. It was something the service had never had before and remained more than a little fuzzy in places. It was confused by the existence of a parallel political system of regional and district chairmen who were themselves increasingly held to account by ministers. The management board at the centre was distrusted by the senior civil service who not infrequently tried to cramp its style. True delegation was hampered by ministers' inability to let go of any decision they thought might rebound in Parliament; Bevan's great dictum that 'every time a maid kicks over a bucket of slops in a ward an agonized wail will go through Whitehall'[47] still, at this stage, held true. In addition, the system remained complicated by the continued existence of health authorities which retained both statutory responsibilities and an unchanged membership. The new management system, none the less, had the makings of a lever, which when pulled at the centre would produce results on the ground. Without it, the much more dramatic reforms to come in 1991 would simply not have happened. There would have been no one to deliver them.

As the NHS set off on its third reorganisation in a decade and the most significant since 1948, the report itself was already a sign of the way the power structures within the NHS were changing. A good health services reporter in the mid-1970s needed a detailed knowledge of the committee structure of the BMA and lots of home numbers for its committee members. The newspaper stories were all about doctors' terms and conditions of service, and doctors' views on the NHS. By the mid-1980s, the BMA's view seemed barely to matter. The only phone numbers really needed were those of health authority treasurers in order to understand the awesome complexities of NHS finance, and those of the few managers who were in touch with ministers' latest policy proposal and who could predict its effects. The NHS story had become all about money and numbers. Was there enough of it? Would it last the year? Was the system really treating more patients? Much less was it about 'what did the doctors think?'

In some of this the BMA connived. Dr John Havard had become its secretary in 1981 determined to end the jibe about the British Money Association. 'By the early 1980s the BMA had begun to realise that it had a terrible image. We were losing members hand over fist. We were getting a terrible press as just money-grubbers. People wanted to know what we were doing about health and to influence legislation that involved health.'[48] As far as possible, Havard stopped the BMA talking about pay and contracts in public. Instead he promoted the work of the BMA's Board of Science under Dr John Dawson, a young, radical and charismatic assistant secretary. This may have helped endear the BMA to the public. It did little, however, to endear it to government.

The BMA began producing reports in areas where doctors clearly had a voice: on boxing, seat belts, drink-driving, the ethics of test-tube babies, for example. But it also campaigned vigorously for the right of girls under sixteen to have confidential contraceptive advice and supplies; for a tobacco advertising ban; against significant parts of the government's criminal justice legislation; for confidentiality of patients' records; and for improved nutrition for the elderly in ways that raised themes from the Black report. Most controversially, it published a report on the medical effects of nuclear war which demonstrated how meaningless civil defence plans would be. The report was delivered just when it was not inconceivable that the hugely revived Campaign for Nuclear Disarmament would be a real threat to the government ahead of the 1983 general election. The more impressionable ministers who had already been taught by Thatcher's Adam Smith acolytes that 'all professions are a conspiracy against the laity' began to suspect that the BMA might also be a conspiracy against the government.

This change in public face coincided with a fundamental change within the BMA. From the mid-1970s on, a new generation of leaders had begun to emerge: John Marks, Tony Grabham, Paddy Ross, Michael Wilson, GPs and surgeons who went on variously to be chairmen of council, of the key craft committees and of the Joint Consultants Committee. All of them were strong supporters of the NHS. There was genuine commitment in this but also generational change, for by then all junior doctors and most GPs and consultants had known nothing except the NHS. Doctors are as conservative as anyone in defending what they know, and as the

leaders from the early 1980s onwards became increasingly passionate advocates of the NHS, they were doing no more than reflect their members'
views as well as their personal commitment. The effect was to turn the
BMA from an organisation still sufficiently sceptical about the NHS in
the late 1970s to have submitted evidence to the Royal Commission arguing for charges, into the service's biggest defender. It was no longer interested in schemes for refinancing or privatising it. The irony – and a source
of future conflict – was that the BMA finally came to reject such ideas
just as the country for the first time in forty years had elected a government which was seriously interested in them.

The change in the BMA's stance was signalled while Jenkin's working
party on alternative financing was sitting. A paper put to the association's
annual conference in 1981 rejected the idea of any new charges for the
NHS and blew colder than ever before on any scheme for financing it other
than from general taxation.[49] The net effect was that if the government was
developing less trust for the doctors over their campaigning activities –
which seemed to demonstrate along with dons, teachers, scientists and
lawyers, a certain scepticism over the Thatcherite project – the doctors
were equally becoming less trusting of government and its intentions for
the NHS, particularly after the think-tank leak on NHS refinancing.

Events soon reinforced this view. In December 1983, just weeks after the
Griffiths report was published, there was a row over the deputising services
which family doctors used for night and weekend cover. These had been the
subject of some fairly meaty scandals. Clarke, with none of the usual prior
consultation with the BMA, simply announced unilaterally that he was
changing the rules for using the services. An over-enthusiastic piece of drafting by a civil servant led him to overstep the mark, and he had partially,
though only partially, to retreat. But in contrast to Jenkin, who had tickled
the doctors' tummies at the start of the Thatcher era, this was the first sign
that here was a minister who believed the BMA was just another trade union
which should be dealt with in the same way that the government was dealing
with other trades unions – by, as far as possible, ignoring it.

That message was rapidly confirmed. Less than a year later Fowler and
Clarke announced the limited list: in effect a list of brand-name drugs
considered largely ineffective or ludicrously over-priced for which the
ministry would no longer pay. The list included tranquillisers and sedatives
but was mainly composed of remedies for coughs, colds, minor pain relief
and indigestion. Again the BMA was given no prior warning. Clarke
merely wrote to the doctors underlining that the government was committed to the principle of the change, aimed at saving £100 million a year,

and that he would consult only on the details of implementation.[50] When they protested, Clarke echoed Aneurin Bevan forty years earlier, telling the BMA that 'private formal consultation' in advance of proposals is 'no way to run a system of parliamentary government'.

The BMA reacted with a fury only outstripped by that of the pharmaceutical industry which took out alarmist newspaper advertisements and so browbeat backbench Conservative MPs that its campaign both embarrassed the BMA and proved counter-productive.[51] The BMA attempted to bar doctors from talking to Clarke about the changes,[52] and so angry were the BMA's leaders that Sir Donald Acheson, the government's chief medical officer, found himself cold-shouldered and virtually sent to Coventry by BMA leaders at a reception they all attended.[53] Meanwhile family doctors leafleted their patients in their surgeries against the changes.

Clarke and Fowler, however, had chosen well. There were more than 6000 drugs of varying efficacy on the market, a volume so vast that no doctor could know all of them, along with their interactions and their side-effects. At least 150 hospitals had drawn up their own limited lists, producing savings per hospital of up to £500,000 a year and allowing hospital doctors to provide not only cheaper but better treatment. Only drugs known to be effective were used, and detailed knowledge of them reduced the risks of side-effects and interactions.[54] The result, for all the GPs' fury, was a divided profession. Clarke and Fowler discovered they had what at first sight appeared somewhat unlikely allies: doctors who would normally be seen to be well to the left of Conservative health ministers but who had long been critical of the excesses of the drug industry. Public backing for the government's stance came from Dr Andrew Herxheimer and Dr Joe Collier, the editors of the influential *Drugs and Therapeutics Bulletin*. A quietly furious Donald Acheson used his own networks, so that despite the BMA's attempted ban distinguished physicians did agree to advise Clarke on how to improve the distinctly uneven initial list which the department had drawn up in four days flat once Fowler had agreed the saving as part of that year's spending round.

In April 1985, the limited list, suitably modified and with the expected savings down to £75 million, was introduced. It settled down rapidly, with none of the dire consequences for patients that had been predicted, and has since been extended. It marked, however, a watershed in relations between the government and the BMA, demonstrating once and for all that ministers could defeat the association. In dealing with the doctors, it was as important psychologically for the government as the 1982 victory over the other health service unions. It also, however, convinced Dr John

Marks, now chairman of the BMA's council, and who was to remain in the post for an unprecedented six years, that the Conservative Government could not be trusted with the NHS.

Since 1982 the BMA had been discussing with the health department ways of limiting the drugs bill, including allowing pharmacists to substitute cheaper generic drugs for branded ones where the GP agreed. The association had, of course, been aware that hospital limited lists existed and in 1983, almost a year to the day before Fowler's announcement, Roger Thomas, a GP who was Labour MP for Carmarthen, had asked Clarke in the Commons whether he had any plans to introduce 'a list of drugs prescribable by doctors?' Clarke's written reply had stated: 'No. We are not convinced that such a list, confining the judgement of doctors, would be in the best interests of patients.'[55] Yet a year later that is precisely what was introduced. 'We had been quite certain there was going to be no limited list,' Marks recalled. 'Then it came, out of the bloody blue . . . as far as I was concerned, 8 November 1984 was the moment when I became convinced that the government intended to undermine the NHS.'[56] At the time he saw the proposals as the thin end of a wedge. If the government could get away with a limited list for painkillers and sedatives, he told the public it could have one for antibiotics. 'There will be one health service for the rich and one for the poor . . . in my view that is the end of the NHS as I know it.'[57]

It was not just the drugs issue which convinced Marks and others that, whatever the government said, the NHS was not safe in their hands. For those who paid, charges for dentistry and NHS spectacles were soaring along with prescription charges as Fowler and Clarke attempted to protect core NHS services from a ravenous Treasury.[58] Opticians found first their monopoly to sell glasses removed, then the ban on advertising spectacles ended, and then, as the limited list of drugs came in, an announcement that NHS frames would disappear to be replaced by vouchers for those previously eligible for free frames and lenses. The less well-off, who would no longer be confined to NHS frames, gained greater choice; but that was offset by the fact that the full cost of the new glasses of their choice might not be met. As for the better-off, only the free sight test remained from an NHS optical service over which Aneurin Bevan and Harold Wilson had resigned when charges for it were first mooted. In November 1987, the end of even the free eye test was announced along with the abolition of free dental check-ups. Yet Marks and the BMA had on file a letter written by Mrs Thatcher in 1980 to one of her constituents saying the government had dropped a previous attempt to introduce charges for eye tests. They had done so, she said, after strong representations 'that such a charge would be wrong in principle and could deter patients from seeking professional advice.' In Marks's view 'a pattern was being set'. The government could deny it was going to do something – abolish free sight tests, bring in the limited list – and then still do it. 'All governments speak with forked tongue and I don't give a bugger what they do about other things, but I did happen to believe very strongly in the principle of the NHS,' Marks recalled.[59] Many others in the medical profession shared his view. The stage was being set for the great confrontation over the NHS reforms.

Against this background of mounting suspicion, GPs and the government had also been looking at updating the family doctors' contract. As long ago as 1979, family doctors' leaders had produced a new 'charter' for general practice. In the early 1980s, the non-cash-limited family practitioner budget had repeatedly overrun and in 1981 ministers had launched a study group on primary care. In 1982 at the behest of the Treasury they had commissioned Binder Hamlyn to look at ways both of improving forecasting but also of cash-limiting family doctor services. The report, which was never published, recommended greater payment by capitation fees and less by item-of-service as a way of improving forecasting. Finally, after endless debate, Fowler and Clarke in April 1986 eventually came up with a decidedly green Green Paper, canvassing a string of changes to primary care.[60] Taken on their own, none of the paper's firmer proposals was desperately radical. The package included a 'good practice allowance' for GPs who were personally available to patients (awakening echoes of the deputising row) and who provided a wide range of services while using drugs and hospital services economically. There were moves to make it easier to change doctor. There was a shift to provide more of GPs' income in capitation fees, reflecting the number of patients on their list, and less from other allowances and fees, for example for immunisations.

Taken as a whole, however, and set in their political context, the Green Paper proposals were much more explosive. The aim was plainly to stimulate competition for patients among GPs, getting them to enter something more like a market in which patients would have more choice and GPs would have to be more responsive. Tensions between Downing Street and health ministers were evident in the paper's 'hope' that private general practice would develop. Discussion on whether GPs should be able to charge for medical check-ups was invited. There were strong hints that the government wanted GPs to advertise, and the idea of for-profit businesses running 'health care shops' employing GPs, pharmacists and dentists all under one roof, was canvassed. A package which included many proposals that would have improved general practice was consequently greeted with profound suspicion by the BMA and its GPs' chairman Dr Michael Wilson who, like Marks, was a survivor of the limited list and deputising débâcles.

The Green Paper not only raised tensions between the BMA and government, it produced overt hostility between the BMA and the Royal College of General Practitioners. The college's leaders believed general practice needed improving and that the existing system of payments penalised those GPs who provided the best service. They had been happy to talk about this to ministers, the department and to David Willetts, the health and social security specialist in the Downing Street policy unit. But these contacts with the RCGP came at a time when the BMA felt itself increasingly shut out of the corridors of power. It could talk to the DHSS, but the department no longer seemed to listen. So when the Green Paper rightly attributed the idea of the good practice allowance to the college, the BMA told the college bluntly to take its tanks off the BMA's lawn. Terms and conditions of service, it declared, were BMA territory not college terrain; some in the BMA accused the college leaders of behaving like Quislings in telling the government the things it wanted to hear, a view only reinforced when the college's own membership voted down the good practice allowance. By the time of the BMA's GP conference on the package in November, Wilson was saying that it showed government had a 'faltering commitment to the NHS. It contains proposals which if implemented could undermine the basic principles.'[61]

Quite rapidly, however, the momentum behind the Green Paper dissipated. Clarke was moved, given a Cabinet job as Paymaster General to be 'Lord Young's representative on earth' as the Employment Secretary's Minister of State in the Commons. The Green Paper remained green in the face of other problems piling on to Fowler's desk. The latest was community care.

After the IMF crisis, capital for new places in local authority homes for the elderly and disabled had dried up. Voluntary organisations, too, provided such homes, but social services departments, their budgets under pressure, became increasingly unwilling or unable to buy places from them. From around 1979, the voluntary homes, faced with a cash crisis, began to persuade social security offices to meet the fees for their residents. What started as strictly local agreements spread so fast that in 1983 these arrangements were formalised into a national policy covering the private as well as the voluntary sector. The full consequences of this decision in the face of a rapidly ageing population were simply not realised at the time. Private and voluntary homes were soon to prove the single fastest growth area in public spending. Numbers and costs virtually doubled each year, the bill rising from £10 million in 1979 to £500 million by early 1986. In 1979, just 11,000 people were financed in such homes. By 1992, more than a quarter of a million were, and the bill had reached £2.5 billion.[62] Unwittingly, the Conservatives had created a new state-financed, if privately run, industry. Yet as this corner of the social security bill rose almost exponentially, the local authorities, locked into an ever more vicious battle with central government over spending, found they had too little cash to provide much cheaper, and in some cases much better, care for people still living at home. In addition, the shift of resources to social services from the NHS had simply not kept pace with the run-down of the long-stay hospitals, the first of which finally closed in Devon in 1986, more than twenty years after Powell's 'water towers' speech.

The human problems, particularly with the mentally ill, were becoming ever more evident on the streets of London and other big cities. This developing disaster was clinically exposed in December 1986 by the Audit Commission in the hardest-hitting report it had so far produced. Much of the £6 billion a year that services for the elderly, mentally ill and handicapped cost was being misspent, it said. The finance, organisation and staffing of the transfer from NHS to community care was such that it was 'little short of amazing' that any successful schemes had been introduced. Relatively independent people were getting residential care at £200 a week on social security when cheaper care in their own homes could have been provided, and while yet others were getting no support at all. Councils who built up good services were being penalised by the grant system to the point where £1 of extra care could cost their ratepayers £2; and the lack of any bridging cash meant that 'two inadequate systems', one in the hospitals and one in the community, were 'struggling along in parallel indefinitely'. At worst, the commission said, many vunerable and disabled people were being left 'without care and at serious personal risk'. 'The one option that is not tenable,' it declared, 'is to do nothing.' The government must launch a review.[63]

For Fowler, whose response to any difficulty was to do just that, the recommendation came like manna from heaven. Roy Griffiths, now promoted to be the Prime Minister's personal adviser on health care management, was whistled up and set forth once more to produce what became known as Griffiths Two. It was virtually Fowler's last act before the general election that finally provided his release from the longest period of service any Secretary of State for Social Services had seen. It had proved a remarkable exercise in holding the fort. Given what followed, it came also to look like a great escape.

Education

What [Joseph] contributed to the radical reforms which followed
his departure from office was of central importance: a heightened
public anxiety.

Stuart Maclure, Education Re-formed, p. 167

[Teachers and local authority advisers in the 1960s] became hooked
on some perfectly respectable philosophies, such as child-centred
education and learning by doing . . . teaching by projects rather
than the more formal subject-based lessons of the past. There is
nothing inherently wrong in any of these methods . . . [but] they
have to be used as part of a balanced curriculum and must not become
an end in themelves as they did in some schools through the 1970s
and 1980s . . . [by the 1980s] most teachers were caught between
the new methods and old in a feeling of uncertainty. The problem,
however, did not rest with them but with a small number of their
more extreme colleagues who were grabbing headlines with their
over-enthusiastic support of the new methods. As a result, the public
perception was that children spent no time on the three Rs but were
all playing in sand trays . . . the ultimate effect was that whatever
the reality, many parents thought that nobody was doing any
grammar, nobody was doing any tables, nobody was being extended,
expectations were too low: the familiar litany that has spawned the
battle slogans of the right wing.

*Duncan Graham, chairman of the National Curriculum Council, A Lesson for
Us All, pp. 1–2.*

Joseph appeared to be visibly torn between the constraints of
monetarism and the need to invest in education.

Ibid., p. 6

There has been the odd report recently that Thatcherism has run
its course, and is on its way out. As an informed source close to
Downing Street, I have to report that these reports are eyewash.
We're only just beginning. We've barely got past the stage of
excavation.

Margaret Thatcher, March 1986

Housing: Not all Bevan's council housing matched these relative palaces in Hainault *(right)*.

Rising expectations: a newly modernized bathroom and un-modernized washing facilities in flats on the LCC's Millbank Estate, 1964 *(left)*.

Death of a dream: Ronan Point collapses in 1968 *(right)*.

And the rise of one: council houses from the 1940s are transformed by their owners for the 1990s in St Paul's Cray *(below)*.

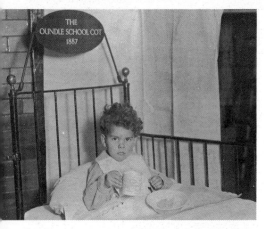

Health: The changing face of care – from a child in hospital in the 1930s *(left)*, to 'babies under glass' in 1944 *(below)*, to the modern intensive care of the 1990s, where the baby weighs less than a bag of sugar *(bottom)*. By the late 1980s, some managers were again seeking 'sponsors' for NHS beds.

Opposite page: Education: Onward and upward? Classes at Snowsfield Primary School, Bermondsey, in 1944 *(top)*, 1954 *(middle)* and 1994 *(bottom)*.

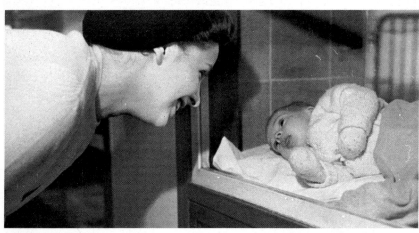

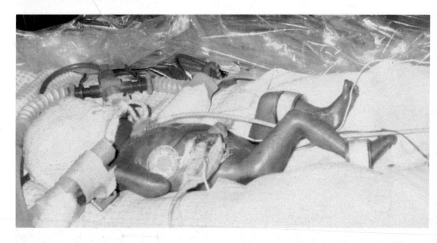

Social Security: From the hope of the first family allowance day in Stratford, East London, 6 August 1946 *(left)* to the blank despair of a London social security office in the 1980s *(below)* to a 'new look' office of the 1990s *(bottom)*.

If Fowler's tenure was a record, Sir Keith Joseph's four-and-a-half years at education was not far off one. It proved, however, a vastly more pain-ridden period for education than Fowler's skilled if penny-pinching time at the DHSS. Joseph arrived in 1981 at his own request. He became the first Thatcherite to move into a spending department, one prepared to preach the message that education was as much about wealth creation as anything else. 'Keith will be happier there'[64] was the Westminster verdict after his unhappy spell at the Department of Trade and Industry where political reality had forced him to continue supporting British Leyland and other 'lame duck' nationalised industries. Joseph being Joseph, the prediction proved unfounded. In Nigel Lawson's words, 'tormented by self-doubt, devoid of guile, and with a passion to educate', his spell at education successfully exposed all his best and worst features. He found education in the doldrums and left it in a crisis. On the way he provided much diagnosis and some important initiatives on teacher training, exam-inations, the curriculum, parental rights and school governance and man-agement. His record is better than it is usually rated. Yet, against the background of a bitter pay dispute, he failed to convince the outside world that he was producing progress.

He inherited the university and school spending cuts that had so dis-tressed Mark Carlisle who, according to Stuart Sexton his political adviser, used to 'come back bleeding' from his encounters with the Treasury. Carlisle had hated in particular 'the damage that he saw was being done to higher education'.[65] Joseph was made of different stuff. He was soon admitting there would be fewer university places while arguing that was all the country could presently afford. Fewer students might mean higher quality, he suggested. When teachers complained about spending cuts, Joseph pointed out that there was precious little correlation between the quality of education and the amount each school spent. 'More money does not necessarily mean higher standards,' he declared.[66] His pronouncement was greeted with cries of 'codswallop' at the education conference where he delivered it, but it was to become one of the harder lessons of Thatcherism in health, education and elsewhere. The Audit Commission was soon independently demonstrating the same thing throughout local government. The idea that simply spending more was not necessarily the answer to all evils took root, even if by the time of Joseph's departure it was clear that the financial hair-shirt he had made his department wear was doing enormous damage to education.

Joseph retained all his fascination with ideas. The first and most radical was vouchers. Ferdinand Mount, now head of the Downing Street Policy

Unit, was interested in them. The Institute of Economic Affairs peddled them endlessly. Margaret Thatcher, who variously called them 'education cheques' or 'education credits', wanted them.[67] Twenty-five years after they were conceived, Joseph finally put them centre stage. Within weeks of taking office, at the 1981 Tory party conference, he declared himself 'intellectually attracted' to the concept.[68]

The idea was beguilingly simple. Parents would get a voucher with which to 'buy' education at the school of their choice. Schools, forced to compete, would become more responsive. Good schools would expand, bad ones would improve or close. Parents – not teachers, the educational establishment or local and national politicians – would thus determine the nature of schools and would more than likely reopen the door to selection. Education would become consumer- not producer-run and local authority control of it would be broken. It was the first attempt at a thoroughly Thatcherite change to the welfare state: the introduction of markets within a state system.

The idea stayed firmly on the ground. It did so partly because the voucher proved not to be one clear, well-articulated idea, but many. Endless variations were possible, some producing much more radical change than others. Would the voucher cover the full cost of a state education or would parents have to supplement it? Would it be a fixed sum, but means-tested? Could parents top it up if they wanted to? Could it be spent in private and independent schools, or only in state schools? If only in state schools, was it any more than the open enrolment – parents' freedom to chose their child's school and the school's freedom to fill all its available places – which the 1980 Act theoretically provided? If it could be spent in independent schools was it worth the dead-weight cost of subsidising the 5 per cent of parents who already opted for the private sector, a sum sufficiently large to cause the Treasury permanent concern? Would the voucher be a flat sum or a relative one, given that education costs varied by 50 per cent between schools? The list went on and on.

What followed was a two-year stately quadrille as the Department of Education, led by its deputy secretary Walter Ulrich, whom Kenneth Baker was later to describe as 'a formidable intellectual bully',[69] outlined every objection to vouchers that could be found while Joseph and his advisers failed to overcome them.[70] To argue the case alongside Stuart Sexton, whom the department made a determined if unsuccessful attempt to get rid of on Carlisle's departure,[71] Joseph recruited Oliver Letwin, a young Thatcherite double first from Darwin College, Cambridge, whose parents

Joseph knew through the IEA and the Centre for Policy Studies. His intellectual distinction was matched on his arrival only by his complete ignorance of the state schooling system, a defect senior members of Her Majesty's Inspectorate of Schools attempted to put right. Letwin recalled:

> Keith Joseph's conception of government has always been to conduct it as a kind of seminar or Socratic dialogue. So he set it up so that the senior officials, led by Walter Ulrich, the deputy secretary, were at one side of the table in that awful building by Waterloo station and Stuart and I were at the other and we were meant to battle it out. With these unequal forces we needless to say repeatedly lost the argument due to insufficient technical knowledge. It was a vast learning process.[72]

Sexton remembered: 'They would raise all the practical questions. We answered, thinking we'd answered every one. They would produce a paper, we would produce a paper, there was a lot of paper flying about – and Keith simply presided over it, although he wasn't always present.'[73] At least one scheme got as far as a Cabinet committee,[74] but the outcome still remained defeat. At the Conservative Party conference in 1983, Joseph announced: 'The voucher, at least in the foreseeable future, is dead'.

What finally killed it, according to its proponents within the DES was that schools were simply not equipped to cope with the implications of receiving a set sum per pupil and running their own budgets. 'You couldn't have a voucher unless the school was accustomed to handling its budget,' Sexton said. Local management of schools, the scheme pioneered in Cambridgeshire in 1985 in which budgets were partially devolved to schools, was still 'still some years off' when the voucher was being batted about in the department, while the idea of independent state schools (grant maintained schools as they became) was as yet just a gleam in the eye of Sexton and the wilder think-tanks. 'The position in state schools in 1983 was not such that you could introduce a voucher scheme,' Sexton later accepted. 'I have to concede that although the officials were against it philosophically . . . they also had right on their side in the sense that until you put in place all the necessary steps, you could not get there. Hence Keith's famous statement at the party conference that he was "philosophically persuaded" but that the idea was "technically flawed".'[75] Or as Letwin put it: 'The ultimate knock-down argument was that if faced with a situation in which they basically became small businesses . . .

schools would not know how to handle the situation.' Some might have gone bankrupt, leaving children without education when government plainly had 'a duty of supply'. In the end, Letwin says, 'the crunch was that he [Keith Joseph] didn't have the confidence it would work.'[76]

Thatcher never gave up the idea. In July 1985 she said on television: 'I think I must have another go.'[77] In her final party conference speech, just weeks before her downfall, she brandished the idea again. It may yet come. In many respects, the 1988 Education Act reforms of local management of schools, formula funding and open enrolment provide many of the features of a voucher system. But it does not provide the psychologically important piece of paper to spend, nor can it be used at any school. 'Paradoxically,' Letwin believes, 'it may be a Labour Government which introduces it. It seems to me that turning the state funding of schools into something which nevertheless promotes the ability of the less well off to exert pressure is something that by accident was invented by the right, but it might well have been invented by the left. It all depends on the colours in which you paint it.'[78]

The defeat of the voucher did not mean any lack of other initiatives. On the contrary, during Joseph's tenure teacher training was revamped, HMI reports on individual schools were published and schools were required to give parents an annual report. After several postponements and endless debate between the Department of Education and Downing Street it was finally agreed that the GCSE, first outlined in a White Paper in 1978, would replace the old O-level and the Certificate of Secondary Education, the two examinations having preserved the old secondary modern/grammar school distinction within secondary schools.

With the new examination, in what can be seen both as one of the last victories of the education professionals and also as a reflection of Joseph's interest in vocational education, came more course work and less emphasis on traditional exams. The Schools Council was finally abolished, replaced not by an organisation on which teachers and local authorities were represented, but by two ministerially appointed bodies, one to oversee examinations, the other to advise on the curriculum. Attempts to gain greater influence, if not yet total control, over the curriculum grew. Under Carlisle the DES, HMI and the Schools Council all published curriculum documents in the wake of Callaghan's great debate – more in three years, as one observer noted, than had been published in the whole of the preceeding century.

Despite talk of a core curriculum, however, government was still offering, in Harry Judge's phrase 'no more than an agenda',[79] a view confirmed as late as 1985 in Joseph's White Paper *Better Schools*, in which he stated it would be wrong to legislate. Government would set out policy statements for a number of specific areas such as English, maths and science, the White Paper said; but, 'It would not in the view of the Government be right for the Secretary of State's policy for the range and pattern of the 5–16 curriculum to amount to the determination of national syllabuses.'[80] As ever, Joseph could see the arguments for a national curriculum, but also the arguments against.

Much of this was what Stuart Maclure has called 'the Callaghan consensus' in action[81] – a drive for more accountability, which turned out in practice to mean more centralisation. It reflected ministers' mounting distrust of local government, not to mention Downing Street's profound distrust of the Department of Education. That last was demonstrated most dramatically in the wake of the 1981 riots and the alarming rise in youth unemployment which saw the Youth Opportunities Programme hugely expanded and then transformed into the Youth Training Scheme. An initial £1 billion and later much more was provided in an attempt to guarantee either further education or a training place to jobless sixteen-year-old school leavers. The cash, however, went through the Manpower Services Commission (MSC), not the DES. On a smaller scale, the Technical and Vocational Educational Initiative (TVEI) was also run by the MSC, this time operating not as an alternative to schools but directly inside them. Here two people with a shared concern came together. Joseph, with his unerring ability to put his finger on the sorest point, had early on discovered what he dubbed 'the bottom 40 per cent' – the children who were 'bored, bored, bored' by school, who left with 'nothing like their potential . . . developed', with either no qualifications or none worth mentioning.[82] What was to be done about them, he demanded?

At the same time David, later Lord, Young, the new chairman of the MSC, had become equally alarmed about what this meant for industry. The endless issue of Britain's failure to take technical and scientific education seriously was surfacing yet again. Young's initial idea, a relation of the City Technology Colleges to come, was for a string of technical schools aimed at firing the less academically able with enthusiasm for a practical education. Young had been Joseph's special adviser at the Department of Trade and Indstry. In August 1982 he invited the Education Secretary to stay at his country home in Graffham, Sussex. Sitting in glorious sunshine in the garden, he spelled the idea out.

'We must find a way to motivate the majority of young people who simply don't benefit out of the existing comprehensives with their watered down academic system,' he told Joseph. The schools, however, would need to be run through the MSC. 'Keith Joseph sat and thought about it for a moment, and then just said "yes". I do not think any other colleague as Education Secretary would have agreed . . . he knew full well that he would be subjected to a shower of abuse by the whole of the educational establishment for selling his birthright to the MSC.'[83]

Fourteen demonstration projects were launched, despite a boycott by some Labour authorities and charges from Neil Kinnock that the scheme was designed to produce 'factory fodder'. It went ahead in existing schools rather than specially created ones after a successful intervention by senior DES officials to protect their patch,[84] and it generated much initial enthusiasm before going national and becoming much less generously funded the more widespread it became. The MSC also moved heavily into non-advanced further education, in time financing a quarter of the colleges' work.

One reason for using the MSC was that it did at least guarantee that the cash went on what was intended. It would not be lost through the local authorities' block grant to other parts of education or even simply to other parts of local government. The DES had no power to earmark cash in that way. When Shirley Williams had attempted to boost in-service training for teachers through the rate support grant, the result according to Ted Wragg, Professor of Education at Exeter, had been 'like pouring champagne into the Thames'.[85] On a small scale, Joseph rectified that. He took powers for DES to provide Education Support Grants amounting to not more than 1 per cent of the budget. These went initially on teacher training and micro-technology for schools. But the cumulative effect was, as George Cooke, general secretary of the Society of Education Officers, put it: 'a clear rejection of the former "partnership" and a massive vote of no confidence in the ability of local government (and equally the DES) to tackle the problems of youth unemployment and training swiftly and decisively.'[86]

The problem was not just in local government. Confidence in education and in the government's handling of it was collapsing all round. 'It's a disaster,' one of Mrs Thatcher's advisers was heard to mutter as early as 1983 when she was asked about education at a press conference.[87] The impression that nothing was going right was not helped by Joseph's endless concentration on the system's failures: the bottom 40 per cent, the bad teachers, the perennial question of whether standards were falling. That issue appeared finally settled in 1983, when Professor Sig Prais of the National Institute of Economic and Social Research published findings showing that in mathematics, German pupils in the bottom half of the ability range did as well as the average for the whole ability range in England and Wales. Sterile controversy about whether standards were higher or lower than they had been suddenly ceased to matter if they were plainly inferior to those of a key competitor – a finding subsequently reinforced by studies of other countries.

Joseph won few more friends in universities than in the schools. He did find some 'new blood' money to restore a small part of the cuts Carlisle had had to agree to. This allowed a limited number of young lecturers to be recruited, preventing the complete sclerosis of the academic profession which the huge wave of redundancies would otherwise have produced.[88] For a time an uneasy, stagnant calm overtook higher education. Numerically the polytechnics flourished, their student numbers accelerating to the point where in 1987 they would have more full-time equivalents than the universities.[89] Their unit costs fell by 20 per cent. But the government, despite a clear ideology, lacked any strategic vision for higher education. Odd rows festered. The Social Science Research Council was set up for abolition by Joseph, finally escaping with a change of name and emphasis – it became the Economic and Social Research Council. In late 1984, Joseph was forced into a humiliating retreat by Tory MPs 'baying for blood' over a deal to increase science spending which he had made with the Treasury. To pay for this he had agreed both to squeeze student grants further and, much more dramatically, to pick up a cut-down version of the 1982 Central Policy Review Staff's suggestion that tuition fees should be charged for higher education. He proposed making middle-income parents contribute to tuition fees on a means-test.

This was a Conservative constituency under fire, and on the government back-benches, as Lawson recorded, 'all hell broke loose'. Within twenty-four hours the plan was withdrawn. When in 1985 Joseph did finally produce his view of the future of higher education, his Green Paper[90] took a distinctly utilitarian stance. Higher education should serve the economy 'more effectively', the paper declared, but it should do so on resources that were expected to fall by 2 per cent a year. Joseph faced charges of 'short-sighted philistinism'[91] and Oxford refused Mrs Thatcher her honorary degree.

In the schools, the sense that the system was unloved and failing was tipped over into crisis by the dispute over teachers' pay. This ran as a counterpoint to Joseph's period of office from late 1984 on, before rising to a crescendo at its end. Byzantine in its complexity it was fuelled by Joseph's reluctance to spend public money and Lawson's refusal to give it.[92] The dispute took place against the background of the government excluding unions from GCHQ, the intelligence monitoring centre in Cheltenham, in 1984, defeating 'the enemy within' in the shape of the miners in 1985, and entering the deepest period of its trench warfare with local government as the Greater London Council was abolished and rate-capping bit at its hardest. At the same time Neil Kinnock was fighting his own battles with Militant and the 'loony left'. The Prime Minister appeared as determined not to surrender to the teachers as she was to the miners. On one occasion when Joseph attempted to take the dispute to arbitration he reportedly returned from Cabinet to declare that the outcome had been 'Fifteen "ayes" and one "no" – and the "no" had it.'[93]

The dispute was initially conducted by the unions in what one of their senior officials later called a 'post-imperial glow'.[94] 'Teachers did not at first realise just how far power had shifted from them since the 1970s.' It was to be the last great public sector dispute of the Thatcher era. The union's mix of strike and non-strike action initially attracted considerable parental support. Teachers were better loved than the government. But as the dispute dragged on, damaging children's education and disrupting the work and lives of parents, public support turned into exasperation and the calling down of a plague on both houses. Splits emerged, both between the unions and within them, and by the time it was all over they were exhausted, parents were confused and the government was wounded for the run-up to the 1987 general election. Ministers finished up with a teaching force that felt rejected and reviled and whose loyalty to and enthusiasm for the job remained unrepaired years afterwards. Yet in the end, the dispute's chief effect was to prepare the ground for the radical changes to come, heightening the sense that something had to be done about education while leaving the unions too weakened to oppose.

Amid this gathering storm, as 1985 became 1986, Joseph turned himself from a wounded politician into a lame duck by announcing in January that he planned to leave the Commons at the next election. The disclosure merely unleashed all the pent-up fury within and outside government over its education record. Joseph was not replaced by Kenneth Baker until May. But throughout 1986 great bolts of lightning illuminated the blackening sky as the think-tanks, the endless groupings of 'Tory educationalists', individual ministers and cliques of backbenchers such as the right-wing 92 Group and the newly formed 'No Turning Back' Group which had been created to fight the consolidators within government, propounded and re-propounded their schemes to rescue and reinvent education.

There was much more at stake here than just education. A government weakened by the Westland helicopter crisis of 1985 and widely perceived to have wasted much of its second term was under fire from its own supporters on the right and from a Tory press which appeared to have become more Thatcherite than Mrs Thatcher. *The Times*, having been acquired by Rupert Murdoch, now believed its job was to keep the government up to the mark from the right: 'we support the Government, but we attack it for not being radical enough,' the editor Charles Douglas-Home confided on the paper's 200th anniversary in 1985.[95] For Margaret Thatcher, all this put a renewed premium on radicalism, and the resulting government rethink, culminating in that year's party conference under the slogan 'The Next Moves Forward', was to stretch well beyond education into housing, into a new view of local government that went much further than mere attempts to restrain its expenditure, into the final fatal commitment to the poll tax, and into the more dramatic and controversial privatisations such as water and electricity. It was to be the move that finally brought markets into the welfare state.

Over education, a fierce battle was being fought between the traditional paternalistic centralisers and the pure free marketeers. The former believed government itself should wrest control of education from local councils, find a way to fund schools from the centre and enforce a national curriculum – in effect producing a national education service. The latter wanted nothing except vouchers and parent-power, with schools operating independently in a market, the curriculum decided by parents' wishes. The eventual outcome was to be a dose of both to the complete satisfaction of neither.

Within the government, Joseph himself in 1985, Norman Tebbit as party chairman in March 1986, and, in July that year, Nigel Lawson as Chancellor (who had just been fired up by reading Correlli Barnett's *The Audit of War* which blamed Britain's economic failure on her educational one)[96] were all submitting papers to the Prime Minister. Of these, Lawson's was judged to be the most influential by the policy unit which had not long before acquired a new head, Professor Brian Griffiths, who brought his own interest in education to the scene.

The connections that were to provide a recognisably Thatcherite approach to the welfare state were beginning to fall into place. In health, an American academic in 1985 produced a paper suggesting an internal market in the NHS as a mean of increasing its efficiency. In housing, Ridley determined to revive the private rented market. Within education, the moves needed to achieve a quasi-market had already received a thorough airing through the vouchers debate. An idea for grant-maintained schools had been canvassed within the policy unit as early as 1984 when John Redwood and Oliver Letwin had been looking for ways to rescue under-subscribed rural primary schools.[97] In the summer of 1985, Stuart Sexton, frustrated by Joseph's lack of progress, had secretly bypassed his boss and sent direct to Thatcher proposals to 'privatise' schools by letting them opt for direct-grant or independent status.[98] Lawson's paper of July 1986, written by John Anson, 'a shy, dry Wykehamist Under Secretary' at the Treasury, had proposed taking the funding of education off the rates, laying down a core curriculum and attainment standards, and funding self-managed schools from the centre based largely on the number of pupils they attracted. For Lawson the scheme had an added appeal. Because local authority education expenditure almost exactly matched the rate support grant, councils would be left raising all the money for the other services they ran. Two-tier local government (education was run by counties) could be removed, rate-payers would know precisely whom to blame for which service, and the poll tax would not be needed, Lawson argued.[99]

By late 1986, Caroline Cox and John Marks, veteran proponents since the late seventies through the Centre for Policy Studies of vouchers, student loans, and an end to academic tenure[100] had helped to form the Hillgate Group (so named after the street in which Jessica Douglas-Home, the widow of the editor of *The Times*, lived and in whose home they met). Its members, who included the heads of Eton and of Highbury Grove, Rhodes Boyson's old school, had close links to Bob Dunn and Angela Rumbold, right-wing education ministers under Baker. Their December paper *Whose Schools?* trailed most of the ingredients of the Baker reform plan. The right-wing educationalists at times argued fiercely among themselves: Sexton, for example, was bitterly opposed to a national curriculum. But they had captured the high ground of policy ideas. As Baker was later overheard to state: 'These are the people who are setting the educational agenda.'[101] It was a field of battle from which the educational establishment was notable entirely by its absence, a voice no longer heard or heeded.

Into this seething sea of ideas Baker had been recruited to replace Joseph in May 1986. The contrast could not have been greater. The anguished, principled, unworldly high priest of monetarism was replaced by a man 'whose instinctive answer to any problem', in Nigel Lawson's words, 'is to throw glossy PR and large quantities of money at it'.[102] Baker was cultured and clever. His political beliefs had travelled a long way with his ambition from his wilderness days after being a junior minister and PPS to Ted Heath, to becoming Minister for Information Technology before being promoted into the Cabinet as Secretary of State for the Environment. There he had designed the poll tax and abolished the GLC. He was fast becoming what he eventually became – one of Mrs Thatcher's most dedicated servants. Education, however, he cared for.

He opened by telling Thatcher that money would have to be spent,[103] and duly extracted it – £20 million to ease the introduction of the GCSE, £54 million to stop local authorities closing almost 10,000 polytechnic places, and more than £2.4 billion over four years (twice the sum Joseph had put on the table) to solve the teachers' pay dispute. It was finally ended by the brute expedient of rushing through an Act of Parliament abolishing the Burnham committee that negotiated teachers' pay and scrapping the unions' negotiating rights. The imposed settlement, however, contained enough cash to produce a 25 per cent pay rise over eighteen months, some of it linked to incentive payments for 'good' teachers. Eventually, in 1992, the teachers were given an independent review body to recommend their pay rates on the lines of those for doctors and nurses.

These, however, were only part of the business needed to rescue the Conservatives from the wreckage that their seven-year stewardship of education had wrought. Baker resolved the problem, Houdini-like, by blaming both the system ('maverick, eccentric and muddled')[104] and everyone in it while absolving the government. 'Many people have no idea how decentralised the education system is,' he told the party conference in 1986. 'I get just as frustrated as parents when I read that this or that school is short of textbooks or needs a coat of paint. I think it is important to realise that I am not responsible for that . . . my privilege is largely restricted to picking up the bills which other people run up.'

A fraught Cabinet committee, chaired by Thatcher, was created to reform education.[105] According to both Lawson and Ridley, Baker and his proposals were regularly shredded by the Downing Street machine, a beaming Secretary of State for Education being repeatedly dispatched back to his department to redraw them.[106] Initially, Baker had appeared to believe in the old central government/local education authority partnership. He told the Commons in his first set-piece speech as Education Secretary: 'We operate through a decentralised school system and I believe in such diffusion of power. It is right to devolve responsibility even in a national service like education. I have been asked frequently whether I favour adopting the Fench centralised system. I want to make clear I do not.'

Once he had seen the way the wind was blowing, however, four key issues drove Baker. He believed profoundly that technical education in Britain had to be improved, a belief partly fuelled by his time as information technology minister when he had run the 'micros in schools' project. He was determined to get a broad national curriculum, complete with testing to measure children's progress. He wanted more 'half-way houses' between the 'island' of private education which catered for 7 per cent of the children and the 'continent' of state education in which the other 93 per cent were taught. And, despite advocating 'diversity' – which was usually Conservative code for grammar schools and selection – Baker, certainly at that time, was against reopening the grammar school debate or charging fees for schooling. The Prime Minister, by contrast, wanted only a core curriculum of English, maths and science. She hankered after a return to selection – she was to tell the Young Conservatives in February 1987 that abolishing grammar schools was 'one of the biggest mistakes ever made'.[107] And she favoured the return of partial fees, allowing parents to 'top-up' state funding of schools.[108]

Their common ground became the desire, without formally having vouchers, to achieve some of their claimed benefits – notably competition between schools, with more information and power for parents as the consumers of education and less power for the producers. It was that which finally produced local management of schools, open enrolment, formula funding under which schools were to receive so much for each pupil, and finally grant-maintained status, the credit for the creation of which Thatcher gives to Brian Griffiths,[109] though many others have claimed it.

As the June 1987 general election drew closer, Baker began to trickle out the ideas that were to form the manifesto platform. At the party conference in October, he made it clear that radical change really was in the air by announcing the creation of up to twenty City Technology Colleges, state-funded but business-sponsored, intended for inner cities. These marked the first break with the comprehensive system in twenty years. Cheers greeted his announcement that they would be 'government-funded independent schools run by educational trusts and not part of the local education authority'.[110] Business sponsorship and their technological bias aside, CTCs contained several of the ingredients of the main reform to come: they were to be directly funded by the DES on a per capita basis, running on their own budgets to a centrally decided curriculum. Baker had had to fight off an attempt by Thatcher for them to be left free to charge fees.[111]

Then in December, on the television programme *Weekend World*, he announced he intended to establish a national curriculum enforceable by law;[112] in January he told an education conference there would be attainment targets;[113] and in February he told the Young Conservatives that there would be external tests at seven, eleven and fourteen.[114] While promising consultation, he told educationalists: 'We cannot continue with a system under which teachers decide what pupils should learn without reference to clear nationally agreed objectives'.[115] In April he said he wanted to see 'all secondary schools and the bigger primaries' running their own budgets within four years and 'able to determine how many staff and what kind they should have'. He added: 'Everything that can be delegated . . . will be delegated.'[116] And at the end of that month he dropped the heaviest hint yet of what had already been leaked to the press as the potential centrepiece for the election manifesto: the right of schools to opt out of local authority control. CTCs, he told the Commons, 'point the way ahead for many other types of school after the election.'[117]

It was this package, noted by dedicated educationalists but scarcely registered by the outside world, which burst upon the electorate as the eight-page centrepiece of the Conservatives' 1987 election manifesto. If the bare bones of the reforms were clear they remained decidedly short of flesh – and the purpose to which they were to be put was plainly not agreed. Three days into the campaign, quizzed about the freedoms that 'opt-out' schools would enjoy, Thatcher said she would not wish to 'preclude' the possibility of the schools raising extra sums, and she added that 'if schools go independent it will be up to them to pursue their own admissions policy.'[118] The spectres of a return to fee paying, selection and even the eleven-plus had been raised. Baker was furious at Thatcher's 'gaffe', the result, he calculated, of her 'speaking from the heart rather than from her brief'.[119] Frantic 'clarifications' had to be issued first by Thatcher from her campaign bus, then by Baker in a weekend speech. The row took a week to die away as both fees and a return to the eleven-plus were ruled out. Thatcher, however, did not give in, repeating on a radio phone-in that it would be no bad thing if the opted-out schools asked for 'a few written tests' before selecting their pupils.

The rumpus made no difference to the general election result. Labour during the campaign fell apart on tax and spending, was caught on its non-nuclear defence stance, and won few new friends with its desire to crack down on private health and education. Health played a bigger part than usual in the campaign. After years of headlines about cuts the opposition painted the bleakest possible picture of the state of the NHS, with waiting lists beginning to rise again as five years of financial squeeze finally took their toll. Thatcher produced complex reverberations when challenged on why she went for private treatment – 'to enable me to go into hospital on the day I want, at the time I want and with the surgeon I want – for me that's absolutely vital.'[120] And the government's cause, with its endless battery of statistics as its chief defence, was not helped by Sir Bryan Thwaites, chairman of the Wessex regional health authority, announcing during the campaign that rationing was inevitable.[121] Prosperity was still increasing for those in work, however, and with unemployment finally turning down from its January 1986 peak of 3.4 million to dip below 3 million in the final week of the campaign, the outcome on 11 June was another 100-seat majority. Thatcher was into what proved to be the radical, but for her fatal, third term.

CHAPTER 19

Forming the future: Conservatives 1987–92

Housing was the area where Margaret Thatcher thought it was easiest to start to dismantle the dependency culture.
Nicholas Ridley, My Style of Government, pp. 86–7

There is no such thing as society. There are individual men and women, and there are families. And no government can do anything except through people, and people must look after themselves first. It is our duty to look after ourselves and then to look after our neighbour.
Margaret Thatcher, Woman's Own, 31 October 1987

Up to 1987 we had proved that we could run the economy, and because of that we had been able to spend more than Labour spent. We could batter anybody and everybody with statistics to show that things had got better – and the argument may well have been true. But it didn't seem the right argument for a Thatcherite government. The question became – and we got into it first in 1985 and 1986 with education and the GPs' contract – 'is there a Thatcherite way we can improve the quality of the welfare state services without the public having to pay for them?' The answer was internal competition. Once you say 'we want the good features of competition, with independent bodies competing, in a service that remains publicly funded', then the internal market just falls out as the conclusion . . . for us 1988, with the Education Reform Act, the NHS review, the Griffiths report and the Housing Act, was the annus mirabilis of social policy.
David Willetts, interview

T HE SIGNS THAT this time Thatcherism would be radical on the welfare state were all around. John Moore, a fair-haired, blue-eyed, forty-nine-year-old with a Kennedy smile, was appointed to health and social

434 THE WELFARE STATE UNDER FIRE

security, the first right-winger to be let loose on the most sacred of the welfare state's turf. Before the election, the Institute of Economic Affairs had set up a health unit in January 1987 with the declared aim of developing ways of privatising the NHS.[1] On 11 June, election night, on the staircase of Tory Central Office, Mrs Thatcher celebrated her third victory by targeting education, housing and the inner cities as the next areas for action. In addition, the poll tax, the flagship that finally helped sink her, was on its way, designed to bring under control the 'profligate' spending of local authorities, and particularly of Labour-controlled inner-city authorities, much of whose budget was concentrated on education and social services now that their spending on housing had been shrunk.

The signs that this time it would be radicalism all round were, however, misleading.

In education and housing, third-term Thatcherism did see a real chance to roll back the welfare state – if not in financial terms, now that schooling was pledged to remain free, at least in managerial ones. On health and social security, however, profound caution still ruled. The legislation for Fowler's social security review had been put in place, but the changes had still to be implemented. No grand new agenda was yet possible there. Equally health had been by far the blandest part of what was otherwise a genuinely radical manifesto, one that included the privatisation of water and electricity in the wake of gas and British Telecom. Moore, on his appointment, was given no brief by Mrs Thatcher to be radical on the NHS.[2] Indeed, when soon afterwards in July he raised the possibility of an NHS review with her, she firmly warned him off.[3] 'All my attempts to argue for one were rebuffed,' he recalled.[4] The omission of health from Mrs Thatcher's priorities on the Central Office staircase had therefore been significant: the third term might be ripe for some radical thinking about the NHS, but there was no plan for action. Any change, if change there was to be, would be a fourth-term project.

Thus it was to education and housing that third-term Thatcherism first turned. In the 1983 government, housing had not featured large. Discounts on council house sales had been improved. Purchase of council flats had been made easier. Home improvement grants were made more generous before being cut back by means-testing. House building recovered from the depths of the 1981 recession, but never matched the numbers achieved in the 1970s. Of the 200,000 starts in 1986, just 30,000 were in the public sector and most of those were undertaken by housing associations through the Housing Corporation. The one significant change had been that housing associations were allowed for the first time to find private sector cash to augment their public sector grants. This was to be the first beginnings of private finance for public, or semi-public, projects.

By 1987, however, housing had been caught in the same revival of radicalism that had made education the centrepiece of the manifesto, the intent being, in Thatcher's words, for the state to withdraw 'just as far and as fast as possible' from the building, ownership, management and regulation of housing.[5] 'The next big push after right to buy,' said William Waldegrave, the new housing minister, 'should be to get rid of the state as a big landlord.' If schools could opt out of local authority control, why not allow council tenants to do the same, opting to run the housing themselves or adopting any one of a range of approved new landlords? Equally, under Tenants Choice, as this policy was dubbed, landlords would be allowed to bid to take over council housing. For the very worst run-down estates, Housing Action Trusts (HATs) were planned to take them over, do them up, and transfer their ownership to almost anyone so long as it was not the local council. In addition, the most dramatic attempt since 1957 was promised to revive the still declining private rented sector, not least to get back into the market the 550,000 private homes which were standing empty at a time when homelessness was rising.

All this was put into effect by the fiercely free market Nicholas Ridley as Secretary of State for Environment. The results, however, were nothing like as dramatic, or as clear-cut, as he or the Prime Minister desired. The HAT scheme proved in Ridley's words 'most unpopular and [it] didn't achieve its objective'.[6] Such had become the suspicion, irrational fear even, of Thatcher and all her schemes, that tenants on the most appalling estates would not vote for the millions in improvement monies on offer. They preferred to stick with councils which had hardly done well by them, and to whom the government would not give the cash direct. By 1994 only five HATs were in operation and even these retained council involvement – decidedly not what the government had originally envisaged.

Transfers of council housing to new owners did take off, though painfully slowly and again not in the way the government planned. Neither tenants nor private landlords showed much interest in Tenants' Choice. Some councils, however, did begin to see advantages for themselves in disposing of their stock to a housing association or a management buy-out. The capital could be used to cut debt, reduce council tax bills and even build non-housing facilities such as swimming pools. Thus it was councils themselves, who were meant to be the victim of the government's policy, who developed what became known as large-scale voluntary transfers. By mid-1994, thirty local authorities – nearly all small, nearly all

Conservative and nearly all in the south – had transferred half a million tenants in 150,000 homes to housing associations, raising £1.2 billion in the process. In the cities, however, the great bulk of municipal housing was still council owned, 3.7 million council houses remaining in England in 1994 compared to 5.1 million in 1979 and 4.2 million in 1988.

In addition to the effort to 'demunicipalise' council housing, sweeping changes were made to housing finance in an attempt to reverse the continuing decline of a private rented sector which now accounted for a mere 8 per cent of all housing against around 12 per cent in 1979. Rent controls were removed from all new lettings (with some new protections for tenants), and tax breaks were offered to encourage institutions and private investors to build homes for rent. Ridley's attempt to create a proper market in rented housing included phasing out the subsidy of council and housing association rents. These were to be progressively raised to match those charged by private landlords who had been unable to compete with subsidised public sector rents.

It was a long-term policy which only began to bite in 1989 and 1990 and which ministers themselves said would take a decade to work through. It represented by far the largest stride yet down the road of subsidising people rather than buildings – targeting help on those judged to need it, rather than subsidising rents regardless of a tenant's income. The change meant that housing subsidies would fall, but that the housing benefit bill would rise – and, as it proved, rise so sharply that, fuelled by another dose of increasing unemployment, it virtually doubled in five years. Indeed, cutting it was to become a priority for Peter Lilley when he became Secretary of State for Social Security in 1992. The higher rents meant not just bigger payments to those already on housing benefit, but more claimants. A paradox was evident. In the name of ending a generalised 'culture of dependency' on low rents, more individuals were made dependent on social security through having to claim housing benefit. As even Mrs Thatcher came to acknowledge, 'more people on housing benefit means more welfare dependency.'[7] The government found itself caught between conflicting objectives: reviving the private rented market and reducing benefit dependency.

Council house building, meanwhile, was wound down to the point where it virtually ceased to exist. In 1993 councils built just 2300 homes against more than quarter of a million in their peak years in the 1950s.[8] By contrast, council house renovations did rise sharply if briefly in the late 1980s only to fall again in the early 1990s. Housing associations, seen as more flexible, more friendly, and above all not part of the state, became the official providers of virtually all new 'social' or subsidised housing, although even in 1993 their new build across Great Britain totalled only 34,000 units.[9]

Even this proved not without its problems. In line with keeping public borrowing down and the developing policy of getting private finance in, housing associations from 1988 were required, not merely permitted, to raise an increasing proportion of private funds to augment public grants towards their new build. To pay the interest on such loans, rents went up further in housing that was intended for the less well-off. Progressively fewer housing association tenants were able to afford to work and pay such rents. By 1993 studies were showing that where associations were taking advantage of their new financial power and a decimated building industry to build or buy new estates rather than individual houses, new 'welfare ghettos' were being created. Two factors drove this development. Increasingly, only those on income support, whose housing benefit was paid in full, could afford to live there; and secondly, councils had increasingly to use housing associations to house their statutory homeless. The mistakes of the 1960s, leading to the creation of new 'sink' estates in which seriously disadvantaged and vulnerable people were grouped together, were being repeated. 'This is clearly a result which nobody wanted, and apparently no one foresaw,' David Page, the housing association specialist who diagnosed this fresh disaster in the making, concluded.[10]

Education

Five years ago this proposal [to let schools opt out] would have been dismissed as one of the hare-brained schemes of right-wing Turks.
Jack Straw, Labour education spokesman, committee stage of the Education Bill

We have strangled the middle way. Direct grant schools and grammar schools provided the means for people like me to get on equal terms with those who came from well-off backgrounds. I would have liked grant-maintained schools . . . perhaps supplemented by a [perhaps means-tested] voucher applying in public and private sectors alike . . . to move us back to that 'middle way'.
Margaret Thatcher, The Downing Street Years, p. 578

When I first became an education correspondent more than twenty years ago, outside of the comprehensive reorganisation, we hardly bothered with what the ministers or the civil servants were thinking. That wasn't where the power lay. All the interesting stories were down in the schools – what new forms of assessment, or ways of teaching, or of curriculum were being developed in particular schools or local education authorities. Now we have ministers deciding what is history and how the apostrophe should be used.
Peter Wilby, Education Editor, Independent, 1986–9

Amidst all the bombast claiming that this was the biggest ever education reform, he [Baker] genuinely believed it could change British education for the better and that he had rescued it from the worst.
Duncan Graham, A Lesson for Us All, p. 7

The ultimate triumph of the comprehensive socialist philosophy, part of the command economy.
Rhodes Boyson on the national curriculum, Sunday Times, 12 July 1990

If the housing changes were heavily technical, and difficult for the opposition to turn into a drama, there was no such problem with education. Given that it would take up to seven years to get a national curriculum in place, Baker saw speed to be of the essence. The one thing the government would not do over the next two years was pause for serious thought. By the end of July, six weeks after the election, four consultation papers were issued. Even though schools were on holiday, 20,000 replies running to 25 million words flooded in from an educational world stunned at the scale of what was contemplated.

There was by now, a decade on from Ruskin, a longstanding if loose consensus that some form of national curriculum was needed, along with some means of assessing progress against it. None the less, criticism of the Baker package was overwhelming. On opted-out schools, the opposition was almost unanimous.[11] Baker found himself under fire not just from teachers but from Tory local education authorities, some of whom were as horrified as their Labour counterparts at the thought of their schools going freelance. At the Conservative Party conference, David Muffett, chairman of the Hereford and Worcester education committee, said the plans would do 'immense and lasting damage' to the millions receiving

Kenneth Baker introduces GERBIL.

an excellent education from Tory authorities. 'Don't demolish the house just to get even with the Philistines,' he pleaded. 'It didn't do Samson any good.'[12]

The biblical reference would have pleased the churches. Led by the Roman Catholics, they too opposed opting out. Baker found himself treading the great oak staircase of the Cardinal's palace in Westminster to treat with prelates just as Butler had climbed the massive palace stair at Southwark for the same purpose forty-five years earlier. The man who was unstitching Butler's 1944 settlement between the churches, central government and local authorities found himself faced with the 'scarlet and purple apparition' of Cardinal Basil Hume, telling him there was a 'fundamental doctrinal objection' to opting out. Catholic parents and teachers should not be put in the position of arguing against the authority of their bishops. The Pope had confirmed this, he told the Education Secretary. Baker 'amazed that the Holy Father had taken such a close interest in my education Bill'[13] refused to give ground. It was the Reformation argument of Henry VIII all over again; Church versus State. As politely as he could, Baker told the Cardinal that Parliament was supreme. Catholic schools could not be left out of the proposals. He was less polite to the Church of England, and when it came to the educational establishment, the brilliantine smile turned brutal. 'We will not tolerate a moment longer,' he told the party conference in October, 'the smug complacency of too many educationists, which has left our educational performance limping along behind that of our industrial competitors.' Eight years into Conservative rule – a whole generation and more of secondary schoolchildren – fault still lay everywhere but with the government.

If Baker was beleaguered from the outside, he was also embattled within. He was determined, despite the manifesto's reference to a 'core' curriculum, to have a ten-subject national curriculum, one that included technology to age sixteen as well as science, and one that corrected Britain's 'abysmal' record on foreign languages. He wanted history taught in a way that ensured children could distinguish between Charles I and Cromwell as well as between a brontosaurus and a tyrannosaurus. He wanted art, music, sport and geography included.[14] Mrs Thatcher wanted only a core curriculum of English, maths and science.[15] Later, when Baker's elaborate and highly prescriptive curriculum appeared set to collapse under its own weight, her right-wing supporters heard her plaintively complain: 'But all I wanted was the three Rs.'[16]

To allow that, Baker believed, would be to provide 'a curriculum more suited to the nineteenth century than the 21st'.[17] The Conservatives would have stood accused of being 'narrow, utilitarian, Gradgrind'.[18] In 1987, on Baker's figures, just one in eight fifth-year pupils (fifteen-year-olds) studied a modern language and technology. Only one in 100 studied all ten of the subjects that Baker believed made a rounded education.[19] Without a full curriculum, poor schools would simply continue as before, he argued. Outside the core subjects, standards would not rise.[20]

Thatcher would not let the issue drop, returning endlessly to fight battles she had lost.[21] In October 1987, three weeks before the Bill was published, the minutes of a Cabinet committee recorded that the curriculum would take up only 70 per cent of school time, that attainment targets would be set only for the core subjects, and that art and music would no longer be compulsory. Baker took the unusual step of challenging the Cabinet record, saying that was not what had been agreed. He told Mrs Thatcher: 'If you want me to continue as Education Secretary then we will have to stick to the curriculum I have set out in the White Paper.'[22]

There were other rifts, not least over the pace and objectives of change. Baker believed initially that few schools would opt out, his advisers even suggesting that a mere half-dozen would do so by the end of the decade.[23] Instead he painted grant-maintained schools as a threat to local authorities in order to make them perform, rather than as the model to which all schools should aspire. Existing grammars and schools run by left-wing inner-city authorities would want to opt out, he told the *Daily Mail* in May 1987, but 'a vast number won't want to'.[24] 'There isn't going to be a massive movement of children around the system. All we are doing is putting sufficiently more on the edge to stimulate local authorities.'[25] By September, however, Mrs Thatcher was telling the *Independent*, 'I think most schools will opt out'[26] and at one point she argued for budgets to be devolved to schools at a pace and in a way that would have 'spelt the end of LEAs in a matter of months', according to Baker.[27]

There were further clashes over testing. A leaked letter showed the Prime Minister wanting simple tests of children's achievement against the more complex assessment involving teachers' judgements which Baker had endorsed.[28] As each of these battles became public – Thatcher wanting the changes to be simpler, faster and more radical; Baker wanting them to be comprehensive, slower and more cautious – the impression grew that education was being redrawn, in the phrase of Jack Straw, Labour's education spokesman, 'on old fag packets and the backs of envelopes'.[29] That impression was only reinforced by the fact that when the Bill was tabled it ran to 137 clauses yet when it emerged from Parliament, in essence unscathed, it totalled 238, mostly additions laid by government. In the Commons, Heath rose, a giant wraith from another age, to condemn its measures for parental choice as 'largely a confidence trick'. Opting-out, he said, would inevitably lead to selection and fee-paying. The package was contrary to the One Nation Tory tradition. It would 'undermine and destroy the educational system'.[30] He was, however, the only Conservative to abstain as the Bill received its second reading and right-wing back-benchers bayed at him as he did so.

The final outcome, 'a Gothic monstrosity' of legislation in Peter Wilby's phrase, amounted to five Acts in one. Aside from the sweeping changes to schools and the introduction of a national curriculum and testing, it also tackled universities and polytechnics, ended academic tenure and abol-ished the Inner London Education Authority. No legislation since Bevan's NHS Bill had aroused so much professional opposition. No measure had taken so much parliamentary time.[31]

Throughout the debates ran fears over greater central government con-trol. On some counts, Baker took 415 new powers to the centre in the Great Education Reform Bill, or GERBIL, as it ironically became known.[32] Yet while the curriculum was plainly being nationalised, and grant main-tained schools would be centrally funded, other measures were decentralis-ing, handing more powers to governors and parents in something that was a long way short of a real market, but was recognisably more market-like than the set-up it replaced. Baker acknowledged some of the fears, in particular the dangers that a centralised national curriculum could hold in the hands of unscrupulous ministers. Not only that, he wanted the edu-cation world to 'own' the curriculum it would have to deliver. Thus, against the advice of his civil servants who wanted the job done in-house, he created a National Curriculum Council along with a School Examin-ations and Assessment Council to oversee testing.[33]

This proved to be the moment, as far as the right wing of the Tory party was concerned, when the empire struck back. Ministers alone cannot devise a curriculum. Professionals have to. And as the much reviled edu-cation professionals set to work, the building site became, in a well-turned phrase of the time, one on which ten ambitious quantity surveyors began operating without benefit of an architect.[34]

The writing had been on the wall from day one. Even before the election, Baker had appointed a working group on mathematics which rapidly disin-tegrated into factions, irreconcilably divided on such apparently simple issues as whether children should be taught to use calculators or should learn all their tables and the details of long division. If the politically neutral subject of mathematics could produce such ructions, what would happen when it came to English, Geography or History? And so it proved. Duncan Graham, a member of the maths group who was appointed chairman to rescue its report and then became chairman and chief executive of the National Curriculum Council, bravely took on the thankless task of delivering to an almost impossibly tight timetable a national curriculum which turned Britain from being one of the few industrialised countries without some form of national curriculum into the country that for a time arguably had the most detailed and prescriptive curriculum of them all.

'The appointment of individual subject working groups guaranteed that zealots outnumbered cynics . . . and that no subject would be knowingly undersold,' Graham recorded. 'When the full enormity of the consequences became clear, complexity and over-prescription became the cry of those [the ministers] who had caused it.'[35]

Passionate arguments erupted over what should or should not be on the English reading list and the precise role of grammar, 'standard' English and dialects. Physicists annexed Earth Sciences from geographers. Art teachers fought desperately to retain Design, as Technology claimed Design for itself. All subjects and sub-subjects fought for inclusion, fearful that failure would mean they would not be taught at all given that the compulsory curriculum was already threatening to fill more than the school day. Graham despairingly recorded that, when asked to produce half-courses to allow subjects to be combined, most working groups produced something nearer nine-tenths.[36] The outcome proved vast, and ultimately unmanageable, while too much of the reform, with its key stages, attainment targets and profile components, remained cast in language that required parents to become education experts to understand it.

Baker had originally announced the national curriculum before taking it to Cabinet for fear that ministers would use their own 'individual memory and prejudice' to shape its contents.[37] He soon well illustrated that fear himself by insisting that primary school children should learn poetry by heart. 'Harmless as it was,' Graham later said, 'Baker's intervention was the first indication that ministerial whim could be enshrined in law.'[38]

Far greater controversy was to follow. C. B. Cox, seen as a right-wing educationalist acceptable to Downing Street, was asked to chair the working group on English. In a fairy-tale transformation, the villain of the *Black Papers* became the white knight of English teachers: Brian Cox, as he now called himself, produced a broadly-based curriculum and stood up to Baker and Thatcher over the role of grammar and use of dialect.[39] Over history, bitter disputes swayed back and forth between Downing Street, the National Curriculum Council and the DES over how far pupils should be taught skills or facts and over how British and propagandist history teaching should be.[40] Just when all seemed settled, Kenneth Clarke, Baker's successor but one at education, arbitrarily ruled that anything more modern than twenty years ago was not history at all but current affairs and therefore should not be taught as history to 14–16-year-olds. The decision to create an artificial end to history that would include the start of the post-1945 Cold War was taken little more than a year after the fall of the Berlin Wall marked its end, and just months after the fall of the 'iron lady' – Margaret Thatcher – in November 1990. Schoolchildren would not be able to be taught about either event as history until around 2010. To many in education and outside, it looked as though Clarke, whose heart never quite seemed in the education job, was doing no more than play to the Tory right which simply did not trust teachers to impart its view of more recent events. It was 'the first major and quite political intrusion into what was taught in the country's schools,' Graham noted.[41]

By the time that row was boiling, Baker was long gone, moved to the chairmanship of the Conservative Party and leaving a legacy his successors would struggle with well into the nineties. Baker's other contributions included a real improvement in the level of education spending, in universities and colleges as well as in schools, and the introduction of student loans.

Joseph, after the bitter rebuff in 1984 of his plans for parents to contribute to tuition fees, had attempted to introduce student loans in 1985. The idea was knocked back by Mrs Thatcher and by Cecil Parkinson, then Tory party chairman. The Prime Minister, to the surprise of many of her colleagues, was 'implacably opposed to it, seeing any flirtation with student loans as political dynamite,' Nigel Lawson recorded.[42] Parkinson argued fiercely that without a grant people like him from modest backgrounds would never have gone to university.[43] The seed of the idea had been planted, however. By the time Baker arrived, student numbers in higher education, chiefly through the largely unplanned expansion of polytechnics, had risen while the student grant, repeatedly raised by less than inflation, had fallen in value by 20 per cent. In growing numbers students were claiming social security – an early and unwelcome induction course, ministers felt, into 'the culture of dependency'.

On top of £120 million in social security, the maintenance grant was costing £500 million a year, and with a further expansion in student numbers now intended, Britain's position as the only Western country without some form of student loan was repeatedly driven home by ministers who pointed out that when the mandatory maintenance grant was introduced in 1962 just 175,000 students were expected to benefit against the 400,000 receiving them by 1988.[44] A reluctant Mrs Thatcher was persuaded to rethink; in 1990 the maintenance grant was frozen and the first 'top-up' loans were introduced, their arrival coinciding with a dramatic expansion in student numbers.

For a time, Baker's giant Bill and his undoubted expansionism regained the initiative for the Conservatives in education. But as the mighty task of implementing his massive Act got under way, as rows erupted over curriculum content, and as schools, despite generous capital grants, proved reluctant to rush to grant-maintained status, the sense that education remained in crisis grew. It was a perception not eased by the fact that after the unusual, if not notably successful, stability of two Secretaries of State in seven years, the DES from the time of Baker's arrival was to have four in six years, and five in eight – a rate of musical chairs which makes the story of education from the late 1980s no easier to tell.

In Baker's time, Labour local authorities in the inner cities bitterly resisted City Technology Colleges, believing they would cream off many of their better motivated pupils, leaving their own schools open to further ministerial attacks over their resulting poorer performance. They refused to provide even redundant buildings for them, while mainstream industry proved deeply reluctant to stump up cash for what proved a very controversial idea. Initial estimates of capital costs of £2 million apiece turned into a bill of more than £120 million to get only fifteen, not twenty, pilot schools up and running. Rash talk before the election by Bob Dunn, a junior education minister, of 200 or more such schools was quietly abandoned.[45]

Grant maintained status proved initially just as disappointing. In the first year, from September 1988, parents at only eighteen schools, led by Skegness Grammar and Audenshaw High in Tameside, voted to opt out. A year on, by September 1990, the numbers had risen to fifty out of the 7500 eligible. For those who wanted to see grant maintained schools destroy local authority control of education, this was next to no progress at all. John MacGregor, Baker's successor, responded by offering larger financial inducements and by removing size limits so that 24,000 schools became eligible to opt out. Yet eighteen months on in April 1991 there were still only seventy grant maintained schools. Clarke, by now MacGregor's successor, scrapped Baker's assurance that opted-out schools would not be able to change their character for five years, saying they were now free to apply to do so. The possibility of schools going selective – even of joining the remaining 150 grammar schools – still did little to accelerate the pace. Fervently, Clarke argued that only the fear of a Labour Government pledged to bring grant maintained schools back under local authority control was preventing 'a flood' of applications.[46] But by the 1992 general election, only just over 200 schools had opted out, and while the numbers did rise after the election the deluge still failed to materialise. Five years from the start, in August 1994, the number of grant maintained schools had only reached 1000 or less than 5 per cent of all schools. Among secondary schools, however, roughly 16 per cent or one in six of both schools and pupils were grant maintained.

Meanwhile, as MacGregor and then Clarke talked up the advantages of grant maintained status, both went to work to cut back the multi-headed hydra that Baker had created. MacGregor dropped plans for formal tests for seven- and eleven-year-olds other than in English, maths and science[47] and then simplified those that remained. Despite these moves taking education more in the direction Mrs Thatcher had wanted, MacGregor, ironically, was perceived to be listening too much to the teachers – and not pushing grant-maintained schools hard enough. In the reshuffle forced by Geoffrey Howe's resignation, he was replaced in November 1990 by Kenneth Clarke, who simplified tests further and reduced the compulsory curriculum after age fourteen to English, maths, science, technology and a foreign language.[48] Clarke also took MacGregor's fate to heart. He ensured he would gain no reputation for being soft on teachers by launching a furious controversy over teaching methods in primary schools. A government which had begun in 1987 by wanting to decide what children should be taught was now engaged in a debate about how they should be taught it. The distance travelled from Butler was almost immeasurable.

Social Security

> John Moore went out there to demonstrate what a real man could do if he had right-wing credentials. He was carried off into the wide blue yonder.
> *Cabinet colleague*

> It is a happy feature of a progressive society that the luxuries of one age become the necessities of the next.
> *Harold Macmillan, Tides of Fortune, p. 455*

It can hardly be denied that, as we grow richer, that minimum of sustenance which the community has always provided for those not able to look after themselves, and which can be provided outside the market, will gradually rise.

F. A. Hayek, *The Constitution of Liberty*, pp. 257–8

By necessities I understand not only commodities which are indispensably necessary for the support for life but whatever the custom of the country renders it indecent for creditable people, even of the lowest order, to be without.

Adam Smith, *The Wealth of Nations*, Bk.V, ch.15, pt.ii, art.iv

John Moore's arrival at the DHSS briefly brought one of the quietest periods in its history. It was to be the lull before the storm. For three months he went into a strange form of purdah, remaining silent on policy. But over the summer months he did rashly co-operate in a string of embarrassingly favourable media profiles, including a star-struck edition of *Panorama*, each of which painted him as the leader in waiting, Mrs Thatcher's heir apparent.[49] A former junior Treasury minister and Secretary of State for Transport, Moore was the self-made son of a publican and a waitress. He was an LSE graduate, and had been a Kennedy Democrat during a spell in the United States as a financial analyst. He plainly considered himself a member of the Prime Minister's praetorian guard.

None of the profiles, however, could quite decide whether he had been sent to the DHSS to present the caring face of Thatcherism, to look after those who had been left out in the Thatcherite economic 'miracle', or to rethink in its entirety the world of welfare. Moore himself at first seemed no clearer. He read voraciously, everything back to Beveridge and the founding debates over the NHS. But his lengthy silence baffled both the media and the health service. He scarcely ventured out to see the NHS on the ground. When he did so, to Cheltenham, in early September he was greeted with a press release from the health authority headed 'Health Cash Crisis' – it was one of the early but fast growing signs that the NHS was about to enter a form of financial meltdown.

Throughout the summer, operations were being cancelled because of a shortage of theatre and intensive care nurses, not from lack of cash but because their pay had got so out of kilter that too few nurses had felt it worth while to train to be specialists. Moore said nothing. A sense began

to develop that he was fiddling while Rome was starting to burn. When
he did finally emerge on to a public platform his chosen subject was not
health – where he had been warned off any instant radical review – but
social security.

It was a speech which provided by far the starkest statement yet from
a spending minister of the right's belief that the welfare state had created
a culture of dependency. The text here was not William Beveridge but
Losing Ground,[50] a book by the American welfare guru Charles Murray,
newly popular with the British right. His view, crudely characterised,
stated that the United States 'Great Society' programmes of the 1960s,
far from helping the poor, had created a welfare underclass and a culture
of dependency. This, he argued, was best dealt with by withdrawing
benefits and making people stand on their own two feet.

Moore's tone could not have been more different from Fowler's cautious
pragmatism. For more than quarter of a century, he declared, 'public
opinion in Britain travelled down the aberrant path toward ever more
dependence on an ever more powerful state. Under the guise of compassion, people were encouraged to see themselves as victims of circum-
stance, mere putty in the grip of giant forces beyond their control.' Welfare
recipients, he declared, needed to be moved 'away from dependence and
towards independence'. The moves already in hand towards personal pensions and more targeted social security injected 'some long overdue mod-
esty' into the government's attitude to welfare spending. By targeting
resources, he declared, 'we will be able to provide more real help where
need is greatest.'

The words, in truth, were just words – heavily trailed beforehand to
ensure maximum coverage for the man apparently prepared to rethink
from scratch the British welfare state. He used language that Fowler would
never have used. What was lacking was one concrete illustration of what
all this meant for policy. The rhetoric was grand; the reality was missing.
It was, however, soon to arrive, and in two ways. To prove his credentials,
Moore's contribution in the 1987 spending round was to freeze child
benefit and pump some of the saving into the means-tested family credit.
If this hardly amounted to a massive rolling back of the frontiers of the
welfare state, it was for Moore at least a move in the right direction. But
it caused a sizeable row, given that the manifesto had declared that 'Child
benefit will continue to be paid as now, and direct to the mother.' In a
Commons vote the government found its 100-seat majority halved to 47.
Moore followed this up in the next spending round with an offer to taper
the benefit away to nothing for the better off, or to tax it. He found,

however, that even if he did not believe himself bound by the manifesto wording, the Prime Minister did.[51] Moore's case was not helped by John Major being the newly appointed Chief Secretary to the Treasury. Just before the election, as Minister for Social Security, Major had told *Poverty*, the journal of the Child Poverty Action Group, that child benefit 'will continue as a non-means-tested universal payment, paid to the mother and tax-free. There ought to be no question about that.'[52] So for all the radicalism of his rhetoric, Moore found himself unable in any serious way to tackle child benefit, the payment that for a true believer in selectivity was at one and the same time the softest and yet most controversial target in the social security budget. The best he could do was freeze it for a second year in 1988 – a process which over time would destroy it, but only slowly. And again a paradox was apparent. By freezing child benefit, the minister who deplored welfare dependency was in fact making more people reliant on means-tested family credit.

By then, however, the reality of cutting benefits had already dawned for Moore in a harsher way. Fowler's agreed housing benefit changes in 1985 had lopped some £450 million off the housing benefit bill, a figure that by implementation day in April 1988 had risen to £650 million. In the autumn of 1987 the scale of what that meant became clear: close to six million losers from housing benefit alone, one million of whom would be losing the benefit entirely. Come April, MPs found themselves deluged with letters from those affected. People on incomes of as little as £100 a week found themselves £10 worse off. Two weeks after implementation, Moore, his touch rapidly deserting him, was forced humiliatingly to the Commons with a package which restored some £100 million of the cuts. A few months later, his reputation battered and the NHS review in disarray, he found his job split in half, the health side going to Kenneth Clarke while he retained social security.

The one lasting change from Moore's day, which contributed to the overall cut of 6 per cent in spending on means-tested benefits as the reforms came in,[53] was that from September 1988 the right to income support for 16- and 17-year-olds was withdrawn as part of the government's guarantee of a Youth Training Scheme place to all those not in work or education. The idea fitted with Moore's theories and Thatcher's instincts. Its origins, however, lay with Lord Young. In 1984, during Fowler's social security review and as he became Secretary of State for Employment, Young had been persuaded by a Tory back-bencher to read a rather ragged copy of the Beveridge report which the Cabinet Office managed to turn up for him – warning Young that it was 'the only one left' and to treat it with care.[54] Deeply worried by the soaring youth unemployment of the time, Young noted Beveridge's stricture that for young people 'there should ideally be no unconditional benefit at all; their enforced abstention from work should be made an occasion for further training.'[55] Young pressed for such a scheme, which was trailed in the 1987 manifesto.[56] As it came in, Moore argued that it removed the 'demoralising option' of a school leaver going straight on to the dole and 'into the benefit culture'.[57] Young maintained that 'the only option which is being taken away from young people is the option to spurn the offer of a training place and live on benefit.'

It sounded fine in theory. It turned out not to be fine in practice. Such neat constructs ignored children who ran away from abuse at home, some who were discharged from care, those for whom the government in fact failed to find a YTS place, and those sacked, for good or bad reasons, from the job or the course they held. Some of them would soon be literally on the streets.

Attempting still to show, in Nigel Lawson's phrase, that he was 'a new Thatcherite broom', Moore continued with speeches aimed at changing the nature of the debate about the welfare state. His message that a vital rethink of the dependency culture was necessary was made no easier to deliver by Nigel Lawson's spectacular 1988 Budget which slashed top-rate tax from 60p in the £ to 40p. Champagne flowed in the City as never before, as top executives on £70,000 a year suddenly found themselves £150 a week better off. They did so, however, in the same week as some young couples with children on a total income of only £150 a week found themselves worse off as the social security changes came in.[58]

The denouement came on 11 May 1989, in a speech that Moore rashly titled 'The End of the Line for Poverty' – a weak joke aimed at Townsend's adoption of income support and its multiples as an unofficial 'poverty line'. Poverty, Moore protested, had not appeared in the index of *Hansard* between 1948 and 1965, the year Townsend and his colleagues had 'rediscovered' it. He pointed out forcefully that if income support was used as the poverty line, then making benefits more generous simply increased the numbers claimed to be living in poverty because more people were brought within their scope. Claims that one-third of the population was now living in poverty or on its margins were 'bizarre'. When among the poorest fifth of families 70 per cent had a colour television, 85 per cent had a washing machine and nearly 50 per cent had a car, it was 'utterly absurd to speak as if one in three people in Britain today is in dire need'. Such claims were 'false and dangerous'. What was being measured, he said, was not absolute poverty, or even, in any real sense, relative poverty, but a set of statistics.

> What the new definition of relative poverty amounts to in the end is simply inequality. It means that however rich a society gets it will drag the incubus of relative poverty with it up the income scale. The poverty lobby would, on their definition, find poverty in paradise.[59]

Moore's technical arguments had some validity. His politics, however, were awful. The speech included language which came close to painting the poverty lobby, who on his definition might fairly be said to include such thoroughly reputable bodies as the National Association of Citizens' Advice Bureaux, as a neo-Marxist grouping out to discredit capitalism. By attacking the big numbers that were assembled when 140 per cent of supplementary benefit was taken as the poverty line, he appeared to deny that anyone in Britain was in any sort of need. The Child Poverty Action Group's reaction was that Moore was 'trying to define the poor out of existence'.[60] Worst of all, the speech was out of tune with times in which the rich were plainly getting richer while homelessness around the country was rising, the cardboard cities were growing on London's South Bank and the teenagers barred from benefit the previous September in the YTS changes were beginning to appear begging on the London Underground. As Paul Dunn, a news editor on the *Independent* put it when he read Moore's words: 'This is the speech of a man who no longer travels by tube.'

Moore found himself under fire from Labour, the churches and a proportion of his own back-benchers; Robert McCrindle, a Tory MP, accused him of trying 'to use an academic proposition to disprove a physical fact'.[61] Independent analysts proved no more sympathetic. The first official figures had already started to emerge showing that Britain was indeed becoming a more unequal society under Mrs Thatcher, reversing a trend towards greater income equality, which, however haltingly, had persisted for a century.[62] Moreover, a week before Moore's speech, the independent Institute of Fiscal Studies had produced figures showing that the single unemployed had become the first group to be worse off in real terms than in 1979. Andrew Dilnot, the institute's future director, said: 'Mr Moore is right to say that compared to 100 years ago all those on benefit are not in the sort of grinding poverty seen then. But within that there is a subset of benefit recipients, including the homeless, who are poor to the point where it's affecting their health, and another group who are better off but nonetheless seriously excluded from things they should not be excluded from. Whether you want to call that poverty, most people would call it unacceptable.'[63]

Two and a half months later Moore was sacked. He was replaced by Tony Newton, the epitome of careful, caring, cautious Conservatism, a man guaranteed not to attract a headline, and a social security expert dedicated to doing good where he could by stealth. A string of minor but far from insignificant improvements to benefits followed, including a reform of means-tested disability benefits in 1990 which, with the Disabled Working Allowance as a sort of parallel to Family Credit, brought the first new disability benefits since the mid-1970s. The package inevitably caused controversy but was undeniably more generous, if not spectacularly so, than what went before.[64] Talk of a radical reshaping of social security would have to await the arrival of another right-winger. For now, it disappeared from the agenda.

Yet Moore may have achieved more than he is given credit for. For it is from around this time that the words 'welfare state' began to lose some of their traditional feeling of being a positive good. More of the American connotations of the word 'welfare' began to attach to them. In the United States, social security, meaning insurance-based pensions, remains a valued good; but welfare is for the poor, provided to those at the bottom of the heap, something with which no right-thinking person wants to be associated. Moore encouraged this perception, deliberately talking about 'welfare' rather than social security, about the 'benefit culture' rather than about poverty and unemployment traps, about 'our health service' rather than 'the National Health Service'. If language shapes an agenda, Moore played his part.

The one headline-grabbing creation during Newton's reign was the Child Support Agency, a project in which Mrs Thatcher took a deep personal interest.[65] It had been a long time in gestation. Willetts's final act as he left the policy unit in December 1986 had been to write a paper drawing attention to the continuing rise in single parents and commending the child support enforcement programmes he had seen in the United States that autumn. The agency's aim, as the Prime Minister herself spelt out, was that 'no father should be able to escape from his responsibility'. The measure came on the back of an explosion in the numbers of lone parents, whose numbers had more than doubled between 1974 and 1989 to 1,150,000 or one in five of all families with children. Two-thirds of these relied on income support, while considerably less than a third received any regular maintenance payments.

The aim of the agency, which was given uniquely draconian powers of pursuit, was to ensure that maintenance was paid, thus increasing the incentive for lone parents to work while cutting both dependence on income support and public spending.[66] There was a protracted battle between Tony Newton and the Treasury over Newton's desire to let those on income support keep a share of the maintenance paid, as in Australia, as an incentive both for the mothers to co-operate and the absent parent to pay. The Treasury refused on principle, arguing that no one else on income support was allowed to keep any outside payment without their benefit being reduced. As a result, from the public launch of the idea, the agency's rules were fiercely criticised for ensuring that the Treasury, not lone parents, gained for as long as they remained on income support. The idea contained many obvious Thatcherite themes. By giving priority to the first partner and offspring, the measure implicitly discouraged illegitimacy, separation, divorce and the creation of subsequent children. But, perhaps in a measure of the changed times, its claim in 1990 to be a uniquely Thatcherite project was heavily diluted by the unanimous cross-party support for its aim of ensuring that men contributed to the support of children they had fathered – even if its methods and performance when it began work in 1993 were to arouse as much, if not more, controversy as any social security change in the previous forty-five years.

Health and Social Services

> The National Health Service is the closest thing the English have to a religion, with those who practice in it regarding themselves as a priesthood. This made it quite extraordinarily difficult to reform.
> Nigel Lawson, The View from Number Eleven, p. 613

> After 40 years that had brought a regular procession of Americans [who run the most profligate health system in the world] to Britain to find out the secrets of the NHS's success, the process was being reversed: the anorexic were seeking a cure from experts on obesity.
> Rudolf Klein, The Politics of the NHS, p. 236

Moore's worst troubles had come not from social security, but from health. Since 1982, NHS spending had been tightly squeezed. Expansion beyond that needed to match demographic and other demands had come almost entirely from greater efficiency. Year after year, Fowler had displayed the art of getting just enough cash to survive. In the autumn of 1986 he took his case to Star Chamber, the final court of appeal for spending ministers before risking taking the issue to Cabinet. That year his former comrade in arms, Kenneth Clarke, now a Cabinet minister in his own right at Employment, was one of those sitting in judgement. There was still no certainty that 1987 would be election year. 'Fowler got something extra out of Star Chamber,' one of his senior civil servants recalled, 'but not enough. He got the very bottom of our bottom line.'[67] It was a decision, ironically, that in little more than eighteen months would help propel Clarke into his former boss's job and in many ways make his name.

Over five years of financial squeeze, health authorities had become appreciably more efficient. But they had also increasingly adopted two stratagems to balance their books whenever the money ran out, as it tended to, towards the end of the financial year. The first was to close beds and wards from January onwards. The second was to put off paying bills until the new financial year arrived in April. Year by year, the amounts the NHS was carrying forward in terms of debt to its suppliers was rising. By the time February 1987 arrived, an election was looking likelier. Bed closures, never welcomed by ministers, were even less welcome than usual. The word went out to managers to 'keep the lid on'.[68] They did. But many did so by simply ceasing to pay bills at all until the new financial year. By the end of March, the NHS owed its suppliers almost £400 million – as much as a quarter of the total non-pay budget in some districts.[69] On top of that, the government failed to fully fund pre-election pay rises, landing health authorities with a further £150 million bill.[70] By the time John Moore arrived in June the health service knew it had a full-scale financial crisis on its hands. According to civil servants, Moore was warned in July.[71] In the same month Ian Mills, the director of financial management, told the management board chaired by Tony Newton, the Minister of State for Health, that the NHS was now 'technically bankrupt'.[72] In later years, Moore was to accuse Fowler of leaving him 'blank cheques'.[73] But he made no formal approach to the Treasury for extra cash.[74]

Outside Whitehall, the storm signals were already flying. On the day of the general election, too late to be accused of affecting the polls, Barbara Young, president of the Institute of Health Services Management, had called for 'a radical review of all the options possible for financing health care'. Money was so tight, she warned, that rationing was now 'inevitable'.[75] By July, the cancellation of operations because of specialist nurse shortages was compounded by St Bartholomew's in London announcing that it was so strapped for income that it was offering to sell its services to whoever would buy them: other health authorities, overseas governments or the City.[76]

Moore maintained his silence. In August, Barbara Young announced that in the absence of a government review of NHS finance, the institute would run its own. 'It is clear that we are not going to have a lot more taxpayers' money put into the health service because we don't have that political climate for at least five years, if not for longer,' she said. 'There may be ways in which funding can be enhanced without it coming directly from government.'[77] Two weeks later it emerged that a similar study was being launched by the independent and highly respected health think-tank the King's Fund Institute. Demand was rising 'at a rate far exceeding the realistic capacity of the public sector to finance it', Ken Judge, the institute's director, said. 'Is there greater scope for supplementing NHS provision by private finance?'[78] It began to look as if the government might not need an NHS review; the health service would do the job for it.

Amid despair in the service over whether the government would ever fund it properly, beds started to close in ominous numbers as health authorities, the election over, moved to balance their books. Bed closures in February and March had become routine; but beds closing in September and October was not. Still Moore behaved as if nothing was happening. His speech to the Conservative Party conference in October called for myths to be swept away and sacred cows dispensed with, but there was no promise of a review nor any acknowledgement of the storm about to break. Instead, legislation was trailed which would allow health authorities to run business ventures, take advertising and make profits from private patients instead of merely recovering their costs. As a cure for the NHS's ills, this appeared as a mere bottle of coloured water to be thrown at the financial hurricane about to strike. NHS morale was not raised by the barely disguised message in Moore's speech that private was good and public was bad, the Secretary of State raising hackles by persistently referring to 'our health care industry' rather than to the National Health Service by name.

As the party conference ended, so did the spending round. Any illusions Moore fostered that, in the first year after an election, he could set the books straight with a generous settlement were dashed. His civil servants heard that Lawson had congratulated him in Cabinet for settling so reasonably. 'That was the death sentence,' one recalled. 'I had seen this with Patrick Gordon-Walker in the Labour Government when as education minister he thought it his duty to help out his old friend Roy Jenkins over the spending cuts. Roy Jenkins got the credit and Patrick Gordon-Walker was finished. Moore did the same. He thought it was his duty to help. He had been a Treasury man. But he didn't help the government, he didn't help the Treasury, he didn't help himself and he certainly didn't help the NHS.'[79]

In mid-November, as the pressure mounted, Moore suddenly collapsed with pneumonia. He was taken not to an NHS hospital but to the private £195-a-day Parkside Hospital in Wimbledon for treatment, the first serving Secretary of State for Health ever to use the private sector. For some the signal could not have been clearer. Days later it was left to his deputy, Tony Newton, to announce that £170 million was to be saved by withdrawing free eye and dental check-ups as part of what was now a White Paper on Primary Care, involving both a new contract for GPs and the promised legislation to free hospitals to make profits out of private patients and business deals. Such ventures, it was estimated, might raise £70 million a year within three years.[80]

Dame Jill Knight, chairman of the Conservative back-bench health committee, erupted, leading a back-bench revolt in which she damned the charges for eye tests and declared of the income generation plans: 'You can't buy billions by selling buns. We don't need a modest increase. We need hundreds of millions of pounds.'[81] Edwina Currie, the junior health minister, swept into fresh prominence by Moore's illness, acknowledged that the NHS was under pressure but urged the nation to use its growing wealth to take out private health insurance or buy an operation rather than have a second holiday. 'If people have got the money – and many people have done rather well out of this Government – I would encourage them to seek their health care elsewhere [other than in the NHS],' she said.[82]

As she spoke health authorities, aware that the spending round would now not save them, were closing beds by the score. Regional general managers warned the department privately that the NHS was entering a 'spiral of despair'.[83] As November turned to December, regional chairmen delivered an equally blunt message to Newton at a meeting in Cambridge. With no extra cash to come for next year 'there was no light at the end of the tunnel,' according to Ian Mills, the director of financial management on the NHS management board. 'The will to fight had gone.'[84]

By early December 4000 beds had shut.[85] To compound matters, the shortage of intensive care nurses hit Birmingham and David Barber, a hole-in-the-heart baby, had his operation cancelled five times in six weeks amid legal action by his parents and a growing blaze of publicity ahead of his death.[86] In Manchester intensive care cots closed, while in London 'nightingales', St Thomas's nurses, spent a week in their uniforms picketing Parliament in defiance of the law but with the compliance of the police. Downing Street phoned the hospital to demand what on earth was going on. Any doubts that this was the worst crisis the NHS had seen in forty years were dispelled by the presidents of the three senior Royal Colleges. In their most dramatic initiative since they helped Bevan establish the health service they issued a statement warning that the government must act to save the NHS. 'Additional and alternative funding must be found. We call on the Government now to do something to save our National Health Service, once the envy of the world.'[87]

In normal times such a call might have been the cue for a wily minister to turn the college presidents from being the midwives of the NHS forty years before into its executioners forty years later. The call for 'alternative' finance might have provided cover for a really radical change. But with Moore ill, ministers locked into the Great Education Reform Bill, and the Prime Minister ever cautious about reforming the NHS, the government appeared to be trapped rabbit-like in the headlights as the great NHS crisis ran it down. Downing Street sources attempted, blatantly but unattributably, to blame the 'restrictive practices and deeply entrenched attitudes' of doctors for the chaos.[88] Such casuistry collapsed in the face of a petition handed in to Downing Street by Nigel Harris, a London surgeon who only in June had shared an election press conference with Fowler and Newton in order to defend the government's NHS record. 'If I had known then what I know now I would never have appeared on that platform,' he declared.[89]

In mid-December, Newton rose to announce an extra £101 million to bail out the NHS, a chunk of it for 'storm damage' to pay for roofs ripped off hospitals by the great hurricane of October 1987 which seemed to symbolise all that was happening to the health service. The money, too little to solve the underlying problems, brought the briefest of relief. In January night nurses in Manchester went on strike. Their action triggered a spate of similar strikes over plans to scrap special duty payments in return for a new grading structure intended to end the shortage of specialist nurses which had created the Baby Barber problem. Blood transfusion staff became embroiled in a separate and equally unintended dispute, while GPs took out newspaper advertisements to tell their patients that despite the extra money, they still could not get them treated for lack of cash.

On 19 January, John Moore, back at work but with his voice weakened by a quite separate illness, found himself mauled in a Commons debate in which he was able to offer no promise of a review and only a statement that extra NHS resources would have to come from co-operation with the private sector.[90] Six days later, Mrs Thatcher in an interview on *Panorama* stunned everyone, ministers and civil servants included, by announcing that an NHS review was under way – although in fact it was not formally established until three days later, on 28 January 1988.[91] It was the review that nobody wanted: NHS professionals for fear of what it would bring, the government because it had no clear idea about what it wanted to do to the NHS, and the public who still did not trust the government with the service. It had all been the most awful mistake.

The review, however, did not quite start with a blank sheet of paper. In 1984, Professor Alain Enthoven, a one-time Assistant US Secretary of State for Defence in the Johnson era and now a health management specialist from Stanford University, had been invited by the Nuffield Provincial Hospitals Trust to take a 'sympathetic' look at the NHS. After a quick tramp round the service, his recommendation had been to create an 'internal market' to increase efficiency within the system. Health authorities should be freed to buy and sell services among themselves and from the private sector. They would no longer attempt to become self-sufficient in everything. Instead, they would purchase services for their resident populations from the hospital offering 'the best combination of cost, quality and convenience' even if that was outside their district. Money, in other words, at least at the margins, would follow the patient. As he was drawing them up, Enthoven discussed these ideas with Redwood and Willetts of the Downing Street policy unit.[92] It was one more contribution to the development of what became one of the core ideas of the Thatcher era, applied not just not to the welfare state but to large parts of government – a split between purchasers and providers.

The *Economist* noted presciently when Enthoven's proposal was published in 1985 that it 'could be very important'.[93] Elsewhere in the media, however, his uninspiringly titled *Reflections on the Management of the National Health Service* was barely noticed. It made 'almost no splash at all', according to Gordon McLachlan, director of the trust which had invited Enthoven to the UK.[94] Downing Street, however, had noted it, and McLachlan made sure those who mattered in the NHS read it. By late 1986 and early 1987, teaching hospitals in London and elsewhere had begun unilaterally to put into practice Enthoven's suggestion that charging other districts for treating their patients might avoid their being 'ground down' by RAWP.[95] They started doing so only on a small scale, and chiefly for highly specialist services. 'We are just nibbling away at an internal market at the moment,' Ken Grant, the doctor who managed Barts, declared in April 1987. 'But I believe it has got to come.'[96]

David Owen, joint leader of the SDP/Liberal Alliance took up the idea, forcing it into the Alliance's manifesto for June 1987 against the wishes of his Liberal partners. But health ministers, when questioned about it during the election campaign, pretended never to have heard of the idea.[97] In fact, Mrs Thatcher had become increasingly attracted to the notion of money following the patient and had explored both Enthoven's ideas, and variations on them, with Willetts and Fowler well ahead of the election. In January 1987, Fowler at Thatcher's request had prepared a paper examining a possible switch of NHS funding to a national insurance 'health stamp'.[98]

These discussions in turn followed yet earlier work in which the policy unit, health ministers and DHSS civil servants had all studied Health Maintenance Organisations (HMOs) – comprehensive pre-payment health insurance plans developed in America which seemed to provide incentives for doctors to treat patients cost-effectively. A couple of senior Department of Health civil servants had managed to get to America to look at them,[99] and as early as June 1984 at a conference in Windsor Great Park, Alan Maynard, a health economist at the University of York, and Nicholas Bosanquet, an economist from City University, had theorised on the possibility of family doctors being given a budget to buy hospital services, an idea which linked across to HMOs and to which Willetts was exposed at a follow-up meeting in October 1985.[100]

These ideas had all been injected into the Whitehall discussions of the new contract for GPs, but no one could quite see how to make them work in a British context and they had come nowhere near being adopted. They got no nearer when Fowler and Thatcher discussed them again in early 1987. Even according to Thatcher, these pre-election meetings were 'long range discussions' and 'very theoretical debates'.[101] 'The NHS was seen by many as a touchstone of our commitment to the welfare state,' she said, 'and there were obvious dangers in coming forward with new proposals out of the blue.'[102] As a result there was nothing remotely resembling an agenda for action, either before the general election or immediately after it.

In December 1986, Willetts had left the policy unit to head Mrs Thatcher's old stamping-ground, the Centre for Policy Studies. As the NHS crisis worsened the following autumn, Thatcher called him in and suggested that the think-tank might take a look at the NHS. 'We need a radical review of the health service, and it is not for government to do it,' she told him. 'It can't have any official status. Why don't you do it at the CPS?'[103] Events soon overtook any such approach. It did mean, however, that as the storm broke, Willetts was ready in January with a paper by John Redwood, newly an MP, and Oliver Letwin, who had left the policy unit, arguing for a cascade of changes which would eventually turn the NHS into an insurance-based system from which people would be able to opt out, claiming a rebate if they made their own private provision.[104] Other papers were also on the stocks.[105]

All this provided some grist to the mill for one of the strangest and most secretive reviews ever of a major British institution. The group undertaking the task – it was not even formally a Cabinet committee – consisted of just five ministers, John Moore and Tony Newton from health, Nigel Lawson and John Major from the Treasury, and the Prime Minister herself. Roy Griffiths, as her personal adviser, was involved, but the review's immediate support was limited to an extremely tightly drawn group of three deputy secretaries and the policy unit advisers.

A financial crisis had created the NHS review, and it was on finance that it first focused. Moore was convinced that the answer was to get more private money into health care. He had become obsessed with a set of OECD figures which showed that while Britain did indeed spend less on health care than other countries, a fair part of the gap was due to less private spending.[106] He also wanted a health stamp or a hypothecated health tax, so that people would see the cost of the service in their pay-packets and would no longer, at least in theory, treat it as a free good. Once that was done, people could also choose to opt out, as with SERPS, taking a rebate in return for providing their own private health insurance. Several variants of such schemes were assembled. But according to Willetts, who saw the Cabinet papers throughout, 'none of these ideas really got past first base'.[107]

The difficulty with opting out was what is known as the 'healthy-wealthy' effect. Younger, healthy, employed people who rarely use the NHS would be able to take their NHS rebates and buy private cover relatively cheaply. The elderly, children and the chronic sick on whom the bulk of NHS spending goes, would by contrast not be able to afford the cost of private cover. They would stay with the service. The NHS would lose a lot of income from the healthy and wealthy, but not a lot of business. Or, as Willetts put it, 'every employed adult male would leave the NHS taking his rebate with him, but NHS spending would hardly be affected at all. The sums just didn't add up.'[108]

Nigel Lawson's answer to the need for more money was to discover that the proportion of total NHS finance which came from charges was now little more than half what it had been in the 1960s. He proposed a 'considerable' extension of charging. Mrs Thatcher, who in the past had wondered out loud about hotel charges,[109] would not touch the idea, fearing the political unpopularity.[110] Within the review team, Lawson says, 'I was isolated.'[111] A big increase in charging, Mrs Thatcher believed, 'would have ditched the review'.[112]

Her answer was tax concessions across the board on private health insurance in order to encourage growth of the private sector.[113] John Moore, if he could not have a health stamp and opt-outs, wanted the same. On this proposition, however, the pair faced an implacable foe in Lawson who had devoted much of his Chancellorship to simplifying the tax system and getting rid of tax reliefs (on life assurance and home improvement loans, for example), while progressively taxing benefits in kind. He also had no wish, ideologically, to subsidise the private sector. Tax concessions, he argued, would be likely to produce 'not so much a growth in private health care, but higher prices'.[114] Furthermore, Lawson decided that international comparisons showed that other health care systems all had their own acute problems and that on the measures available the NHS was shown to be both effective and a good buy. Any change to another system would be 'out of the frying pan (and not such a bad frying pan at all) and into the fire,' he argued.[115] For a government dedicated to containing public expenditure, the NHS remained the best cost-control device available.

While these arguments about finance raged on, the review also examined how the NHS was delivered. Mrs Thatcher wanted the money to follow the patient.[116] But how could that happen when she had been told that the NHS could not cost its treatments and thus could neither buy and sell services internally nor recognise a good buy from a private hospital when one was offered?[117] What, she asked Roy Griffiths, was being done about that? He explained that six pilot hospitals were already being computerised. If that worked, the system would be rolled out to the rest of the NHS. 'By when?' Mrs Thatcher demanded. 'By 1992,' he replied on a February day in 1988. 'But that's longer than it took to win the Second World War,' the Prime Minister exploded.[118] Anyway, she went on, why could the NHS not cost its treatments when BUPA could? Patiently, the Sainsbury grocer explained to the grocer's daughter the difference between price and cost. 'BUPA don't know their costs, Prime Minister. They know their charges. There is a big difference.'[119]

In March and April, Mrs Thatcher held two meetings at Chequers with NHS 'trusties' – doctors and managers whom Willetts and John O'Sullivan, now the health adviser in the policy unit, felt would be at least partially on the government's side. At these meetings every possible prejudice and pat solution was aired. Many of these Mrs Thatcher would then throw into the next meeting of the review. 'These were,' one of those present recalls, 'just awful. Margaret at her worst. We would have two- or three-hour meetings and she would end up screaming like a fishwife and complaining about the bloody consultants and the hospitals, and her doctor friends had told her this, or told her that, or we would end up with unbelievably rambling conversations in which we failed to get to grips with anything.'[120] Slowly but surely, however, it became plain that in terms of big ideas for reforming the delivery side of the NHS there was only one idea in town: some version of Enthoven's internal market with its purchaser/provider split. The review gravitated toward it.

Yet if the internal market was the obvious answer, it was far less clear who the purchaser should be – health authorities, GPs, patients with a voucher, family practitioner committees, or some new organisation? Other elements entered. Moore put up a paper seeking ways of making hospitals independent, or even private, through charities, straight privatisation or management buy-outs.[121] No one could quite see how to do that. Then Ian McColl, Professor of Surgery at Guy's, who in 1994 was to become John Major's Parliamentary Private Secretary in the Lords, appeared. He hankered for the days before 1974 when his teaching hospital had been independent of the health authority with its own Board of Governors. Was there not some way that independence could be restored? Willetts, who remembered the Guy's boardroom plaque mourning the passing of the hospital's governors, arranged for him to talk to the Downing Street policy unit. The idea of self-governing hospitals took shape. If schools could opt out of local authority control, and if council tenants could do the same, why not have hospitals opt out from under their local health authority?

None of this, however, was as well focused. In May, Moore emerged to announce there would be no 'big bang' in the NHS, although when the rest of his words were examined the pronouncement proved more Delphic than enlightening.[122] A sense grew that the review was drifting, even though many of the elements finally to emerge – self-governing hospitals, and health authorities doing the purchasing – were present. In July, beset on health and beleaguered on social security, his performance never having quite recovered from his winter illness, Moore found his job split and himself consigned to its less glamorous half. Almost to the day of the fortieth anniversary of the NHS, a date no one felt like celebrating as they were still unsure what it would be like by its forty-first, Kenneth Clarke was made Secretary of State for Health.

It was Clarke's arrival that finally killed off any plans to refinance the NHS by something other than general taxation. Moore had never quite given up such ideas, but by June they had become in Willetts's phrase, 'a poor bedraggled beast'. Clarke 'finally put them out of their misery'.[123] The one element that did survive was a measure of tax relief on private health premiums. Determined to boost the private sector, Moore and Mrs Thatcher had refused to give up on that. 'In the end the pressure was such that, mistakenly, I offered Margaret a compromise,' Lawson recalled.[124] He accepted that tax relief could be 'just about justified' for the over sixties, many of whom as they left their company-paid schemes found they could not themselves meet premiums which rose ever more sharply as they aged. 'Had I known within weeks that John Moore would be replaced,' Lawson recorded, 'I would not have made even this concession.'[125]

Clarke no more wanted tax relief than Lawson and one of his first actions with Lawson's backing was to attempt to reverse the Chancellor's concession. Mrs Thatcher countered by reopening the whole issue, pushing once more for tax breaks across the range of individuals and companies.[126] 'Nigel and I got rid of all that,' Clarke recalled, 'but Margaret was still sticking out for pensioners. In the end, after another of these bloody great rows, Nigel was walking back to No 11 and I was walking across the front of No 10 and we agreed we'd settle for pensioners, because in my view nobody would ever sell private health insurance to elderly people anyway.' This prediction proved largely true, the tax relief doing little to boost the business. Lawson introduced the measure in the 1989 Budget, 'trying to conceal my embarrassment'.[127] Clarke, at the press conference which launched the reforms, came as close to disowning it as a serving minister decently could.

Clarke's arrival, in the view of many of those involved, rescued the review. With him there, the reforms at last began to take shape. What worried Clarke about the internal market was that all the purchasing of health care would be done by managers. GPs, the gate-keepers to the service, simply did not feature. The past examination of American HMOs, and Maynard's and Bosanquet's work, had led to an examination of the idea of GPs' buying hospital care, but still no one could see how to make it work; the review had judged that family doctors lacked the financial expertise and motivation to handle budgets and had given up the idea.

Clarke, however, was acutely aware that while the government would claim that money would follow the patient under the internal market, in many cases patients would in practice follow the contracts – certainly in the early days when block rather than individual contracts would have to be used. For a government that was increasingly trumpeting the supremacy of the consumer, some way to get purchasing nearer the patient was needed.

With typical insouciance, Clarke disappeared on holiday shortly after getting his new job. But he carried on thinking. And so it was (while half Fleet Street scoured the Continent looking for him after a row over the new nurses' grading structure had blown up in his absence) that, in his own words, 'on holiday on a headland near Pontevedra in Galicia, I came up with GP fund-holders.'[128] Family doctors would be offered budgets with which to buy a range of operations and out-patient treatment as well as pay for the drugs they prescribed. But to reduce the risks and difficulties, there would be a cap on how much each case could cost them, and a limit on the types of operation and service they could buy. Emergencies and very costly cases would be excluded. The health authority would remain responsible for these. But anything fund-holders saved on any part of their budget could be spent on any other part of it or on improving their practice.

The review was still months from completion and furious arguments remained about the practicality and acceptability of the various proposals. Both Clarke and Thatcher made up their minds by argument. Both revelled in it. Both knew the stakes were high. The result, Clarke recalls, was that 'there really were some blasting rows. The Cabinet Office would ring up back to the department and mark them on the Richter scale as I used to go back and debrief on what we had or had not agreed.'[129] Even ideas that became central to the review – self-governing hospitals, for example, and how they would survive in the market – were subject to doubt. Clarke remembers having Ian McColl of Guy's in to talk the ideas through with David Mellor, the Minister for Health.

> How would a hospital manage itself? How would it cope? Even Ian thought there were pretty dotty parts to the idea, and we all sat there, McColl, Mellor and Clarke, and agreed this bit was a bit off the wall, and no, we didn't think that part would work. In the end all three of us became great protagonists of the idea, but it took a lot of discussion to put flesh on the bones . . . we were still piecing together the market and how it would work.[130]

They were in fact still piecing it together many months after the NHS review was finally given the most lavish launch ever seen for a government initiative on 31 January 1989. A million pounds was spent on a staff video and a laser-lit, closed-circuit telecast from Limehouse to 2500 managers, doctors, chairmen and nurses who had been assembled in television studios and hotels in six cities. Clarke was transported to Limehouse by riverboat from the Commons. The White Paper *Working for Patients*[131] presented only the bare bones of the scheme. Eight working papers were still to come, and Duncan Nichol, the new NHS chief executive appointed too late to have much influence on the contents, hovered anxiously asking reporters what they thought of it.

There were essentially three ideas: the internal market with its purchaser/provider split, with health authorities doing the purchasing and hospitals, both public and private, doing the providing. But on to this was grafted self-governing hospitals (later to be known as NHS Trusts as part of the massaging of language that was to occur), and a second set of purchasers in the form of GP budget-holders (later to become fund-holders in an attempt to avoid connotations of budgets running out). Both the latter, however, were to be voluntary. As the correspondents of *The Times*, the *Independent* and the *Guardian* left the press conference they tried to open a book on the minimum Clarke would need by the launch date of 1991 to make these apparently wilder elements of the NHS review credible. They were unable to do so, agreeing that Clarke would need and would probably get ten self-governing hospitals and perhaps twenty practices involving around 100 GPs from among the 28,000 then practising. It was a massive misjudgment.

The Opposition was convinced that Thatcherism had finally gone a step too far. Robin Cook, Labour's health spokesman, declared 'by God the government is going to get it in the neck'.[132] Clarke had taken the precaution of signing Mrs Thatcher up in a foreword in which she stated: 'The National Health Service will continue to be available to all, regardless of income, and to be financed mainly out of general taxation.' But the BMA and others noted that the cover of the White Paper spoke of 'The Health Service' omitting the word 'national'. And while an embarrassed Clarke did his best tacitly to disown the tax relief on health insurance for the elderly, Mrs Thatcher at Prime Minister's questions rose to the bait and declared: 'Those who can afford to pay for themselves should not take up beds from others.'[133]

The BMA, which had read the leaks of the review and had already set aside a war chest to fight them,[134] held its fire. As with deputising, the limited list, and the Griffiths report, it had been excluded from any consultation at all, and this time on a change that was the most profound the NHS had seen. On publication day, however, Dr John Marks, the BMA's chairman of council, was careful to state only that the association would consult its members. Clarke did the opposite: he assaulted the BMA for attacking the plans before they had even done so. 'The BMA, in my unbiased opinion, has never been in favour of any change of any kind on any subject whatsoever for as long as anyone can remember,' he told his television audience.[135]

This attack, according to Clarke, was deliberate. 'Margaret was very annoyed with me when I presented the White Paper to Cabinet, for I told colleagues there was going to be one hell of a political row. I told we were going into Tavistock House [BMA headquarters], lifting most of the tablets of stone and smashing them on the pavement in front of their eyes. These guys are going to mount one hell of a campaign.' The decision to get his retaliation in first was based on Clarke's experience of the BMA as

a very powerful, Imperial Guard-type organisation in politics . . . the one thing we had to do was knock the BMA off its pedestal . . . so long as the BMA emerged as the spokesman for the savers of lives and the healers of the sick, and the people whose only concern was for the welfare of the poor and the elderly, we were in a no-win situation . . . we had to pull them into the mud with us and make it clear that this was just another trade union, actually one of the nastiest I had ever dealt with, and battle it out.[136]

Without that, he believes, the reforms would not have happened.

The BMA for its part argued that the reforms not only fragmented the service but 'lay the groundwork for the future dismantlement of the NHS'.[137] There were, as Clarke believed, good trade union issues here. The BMA knew that the review had looked long and hard at rewriting consultants' contracts, a move it finally backed away from when it realised that the existing contract, if actually enforced, was not so bad. Furthermore, Clarke had decided that with the government already at loggerheads with GPs over their terms and conditions, a similar battle with the consultants might actually, even for him, be one battle too many. He had insisted, however, that self-governing hospitals would be free to set their own terms and conditions of service for doctors, a move which could crucially undermine the BMA's role and would in time produce new and varying consultant contracts.

The BMA did indeed want to stop that. But their self-interest was married to a genuine attachment to an NHS which they believed the reforms would break up. Their fears were not assuaged by cheerful admissions from Clarke a good six months into the process that he was still effectively 'making it up as he went along'[138] nor by suggestions from Willetts that the reforms were intended to 'destabilise' the existing NHS in order to produce change.[139] In all the furore about what the reforms would mean, it was barely noticed that a review triggered by a financial crisis had in fact done nothing about refinancing the NHS. Rather, it had become almost a celebration of the service's success, with the 1948 settlement reaffirmed by Mrs Thatcher in the foreword where she had promised to preserve a tax-funded system largely free at the point of use. Money had, however, been a chief cause of the problem, and Clarke's formidable skills as a spending minister, along with Lawson's conviction that this time the money would buy real benefits, soon saw the NHS in 1988 enjoying the first of a series of relatively generous settlements after the years of financial drought.

As Clarke and the BMA slugged it out, the atmosphere was further poisoned by the GPs' contract remaining unresolved. The new contract had only indirect links to the other changes, but family doctors saw it would increase their workload, make them compete with each other, and subject them to central direction about what types of screening and other procedures they would have to carry out. There was enough overlap for the contract negotiations and the NHS reforms to become hopelessly entangled. Clarke threatened to impose a new contract in an attempt to get it out of the way while meetings of GPs up and down the country were attended on a scale not seen since the 1960s charter negotiations. Repeated threats of resignation from the NHS were uttered, though whether over the NHS reforms or the new GP contract, or both, was often as confused as was the concept that doctors would somehow protect the NHS by leaving it.[140] Clarke successfully inflamed the situation by saying at a dinner of the Royal College of General Practitioners: 'I do wish the more suspicious of our GPs would stop feeling nervously for their wallets every time I mention the word reform.' In the next breath he equally upset the consultants by pointing out, entirely correctly, that fund-holding would profoundly change GPs' relations with them to the family doctor's advantage. Fund-holding would ensure, he said, that 'some consultants pay more attention to GPs than they do now.'[141] As Clarke delivered his speech, Professor Sir Dillwyn Williams, chairman of the conference of medical Royal Colleges, was seen to go white with anger.[142] 'Feeling for their wallets' became a phrase that would haunt Clarke. As the temperature rose, the BMA launched the start of what was finally to be a £3 million advertising campaign. The message on its posters was that the NHS was 'underfunded, undermined and under threat'.

By now, the informal channels between the BMA and the Department of Health which had so eased negotiations in the past had virtually gone. Almost all talks, now, had to be formal talks. The one attempt at an informal resolution was a secret dinner for four in a private room in the Carlton Club organised by Sir Arnold Elton of the Conservative Medical Society. Marks and Dr John Havard, the BMA secretary, urged Clarke to introduce the reforms as a trial in one region. 'If I do that,' Clarke replied with a grin, 'you buggers will sabotage it.'[143] For by far the biggest row over the NHS since its inception, the Conservatives had found themselves their own Nye Bevan, but one who on the major NHS reforms found no need this time to compromise at all.

Marks's great fear was that the GPs would indeed resign over their contracts. 'The government,' he says, 'would have yodelled from the rooftops. The NHS would have been finished and whose fault would it have been? The grasping doctors reaching for their wallets.'[144] Negotiations were in the hands of Dr Michael Wilson, a quiet, Boycott-like Yorkshireman, and the antithesis of Clarke's ebullient brashness. In hindsight, colleagues judged of the GPs' chairman that 'he tended to negotiate by repeating himself. He didn't finally know when to give and take.'[145] In early May, however, a deal was finally struck over ten hours of sandwiches, low-alcohol beer and Kenneth Clarke's cigar smoke during which Wilson and his colleagues won some significant concessions and agreed to commend the package to their members. Clarke that night was at his most hectoring, behaving, on his own account 'extremely badly' as he missed the Prime Minister's tenth anniversary dinner in order to achieve a settlement.

Five weeks later, a special GPs' conference called to ratify the deal threw it out on the narrowest of margins, 160 votes to 155, and a subsequent ballot in which 82 per cent of GPs rejected it by three to one.[146] For the first time in the history of the NHS, the troops had proved more militant than the BMA's leaders. The vote, however, proved merely to be a defiant gesture. Clarke's exasperated response was finally to impose the contract, this government having ceased to be one that allowed professional opposition to stand in its way. A few isolated further calls for resignation from the NHS gained no momentum. Wilson had spoken no less than the truth when he had warned his members at their special conference that the Secretary of State for Health 'holds all the aces'.[147]

That proved to be as true over the wider reforms as it was over the contract, although it would take at least another year for it to become plain. At the beginning, Clarke did not expect to get large numbers of self-governing hospitals or GP budget-holders. As Baker first expected a limited role for opted-schools, so Clarke recalled: 'We didn't think we'd get very many. The object was to get them going and then make them the envy of the service . . . I saw a slower pace of spread.'[148] What he and others had not allowed for was the change wrought to the NHS by Griffiths's introduction of general management. Fearful that any public sign of compromise would stall the whole process, Clarke and Duncan Nichol repeatedly declared that the changes were 'non-negotiable': advice was welcome on how to implement them, but not on whether to. The still relatively new breed of managers soon came to believe this. They were instinctively more sympathetic to the planned change than the doctors. They also saw it would bring them power, while delivery of what the government wanted appeared also the surest route to promotion.

Added to that, their current employers, the health authorities, were to be disbanded. The events at health authorities in Brent, Lambeth and elsewhere had come home to roost. Councillors, along with all other forms of quasi-professional representation on health authorities, were to go. In future the boards of authorities and trusts would all be appointees, placed there by people, from ministers downwards, who wanted the changes delivered. For managers, therefore, the future lay in delivering the future, not in fighting it. In addition, there were no awkward quasi-democratic procedures in the health service opt-outs – unlike the parental ballots for grant-maintained schools which Clarke, when he moved on to education, would happily have got rid of.[149] As a result, by May, Clarke had not ten or a dozen expressions of interest in self-governing hospitals but 140, almost all of them promoted by managers and some actively opposed by their hospital's doctors.

But it was also becoming clear that, however vocal the opposition, the profession was split. Some hospital doctors, long interested in the internal market, did back the essence of the changes and growing numbers of GPs, even when they did not approve, came to understand the power that fund-holding could give them. Before 1948, consultants in the voluntary hospitals had depended on GPs for the private practice referrals from which they earned their living. Once consultants became salaried and private practice less important, GPs had become supplicants, dependent on consult-

MRS. THATCHER'S PLANS FOR THE NHS.

DON'T LET HER STEAMROLLER THE WHITE PAPER THROUGH. WRITE TO YOUR MP TODAY.

ants for their patient's place on the waiting list. Fund-holding would put the boot back on the other foot, with consultants needing the money that the GPs' patients would bring in order to keep their units and themselves in business. By December 1991, it would be consultants sending GPs Christmas cards, and not the other way around. Added to that was both the flexibility fund-holding offered and the initially generous incentives in terms of extra equipment and staff. Emotions ran as high as they had in 1948; again doctors who co-operated with the government's programme found themselves dubbed 'Quislings'. There was talk of threats, and intimidation. Progressively, however, the BMA's call on doctors not to co-operate[150] rang hollow. In hospitals it became irrelevant as it became evident that most of the changes were managerial, not medical. Certainly at the national level, and frequently locally outside fund-holding, the changes did not require the doctors' assent. The BMA was effectively being marginalised.

Politically, it did not feel like that. Opinion polls showed almost three-quarters of voters, and more than half of Conservatives, opposed to the reforms and believing the changes were the first step in privatising the NHS[151] – the charge the Labour Opposition repeatedly made, and with which it was to have a field day just before the 1992 election. It was a difficult accusation to deny when Clarke was honest enough to admit that almost everything in the reforms, if not intended to lead to privatisation of the service, would unquestionably make any subsequent privatisation simpler.[152]

Dr Chris Tiarks, a GP, stood in the Vale of Glamorgan by-election in May 1989, and although he lost his deposit he was widely credited with making the NHS changes the centre of a campaign in which the government was humiliated and Labour claimed its first by-election victory of the 1987 Parliament. The BMA stepped up its advertising with posters of memorable brilliance, one depicting merely a steamroller and the caption 'Mrs Thatcher's plans for the NHS' (*see left*). Another, black letters on a bright yellow background, asked simply 'What do you call a man who ignores medical advice? Mr Clarke.'

But while the BMA and the other serried ranks of opposition were winning the propaganda battle, implementation was slowly but surely taking place. A government with a 100-seat majority could not be shifted on the Bill, and by December 1990 the first 57 NHS Trusts had been named. In April 1991, on D-day, the first 306 fund-holding practices, containing 1700 GPs, joined them in the brave new world of the new NHS. The numbers were far greater than anything anyone had expected on a cold January day two years earlier, and the trusts now included community and ambulance services as well as hospitals. Some of the language had changed. The service was being urged to achieve a 'smooth take-off' and a 'steady state', avoiding too much disruption and change in a first year that happened also to be the run-up to the general election. The NHS market was to be much less red in tooth and claw than it could have been within the framework of the original White Paper.[153] But no one – not the BMA, the political opposition, nor anyone else – had managed in any way to derail the scheme. The person who had come nearest to doing that was the Prime Minister.

April 1990 had seen the community charge, or poll tax, arrive accompanied by a riot in Trafalgar Square and bills vastly higher than the government had originally predicted. It was to prove one of the principal causes of Mrs Thatcher's downfall as well as one of the inspirations of the Conservatives' massive by-election defeat in Mid-Staffordshire in late March 1990. By early summer Mrs Thatcher was worrying that there might be other potential time bombs in the government's locker. In June, a mere nine months from the NHS changes taking effect, Sir David Wolfson, the businessman who had been head of her political office from 1979 to 1985, was dispatched around the NHS along with Lord Rayner, the Marks and Spencer chairman who had been Mrs Thatcher's efficiency adviser, and his successor Sir Robin Ibbs, by then deputy chairman of Lloyds Bank.

Their task was to make an assessment of whether the reforms would work. Their conclusion was that they would not. Clarke was summoned to Downing Street along with the top three NHS executives – Nichol, his deputy Peter Griffiths, and Sheila Masters, the private sector finance wizard who was overseeing the transition – to face what turned out to be a Spanish inquisition. Mrs Thatcher, in Clarke's words, 'wanted to scrap the health reforms – put them off, postpone them until after the election – taking much longer over it and spending much more time on costing systems and management techniques.' Details of her cold feet had been leaked ahead of the meeting to the *Economist*, which went as far as to say the decision had been taken, headlining the story 'NHS Retreat' and 'Treatment Suspended'.[154] It was, Clarke says, 'a tee-up; a deliberate attempt to make sure that was what happened.'

Nichol and his colleagues, on their own admission, did not perform well.[155] Clarke says it was not surprising. 'They were good people . . . but if you sit them down in Downing Street in front of Margaret Thatcher in full and glorious flight, doing her handbagging and surrounded by Captains of Industry saying you are talking rubbish and that what you are planning won't work, people do get nervous. They didn't do well.' Peter Griffiths recalls:

> We really felt we'd let Clarke down. She delivered this great tirade with Ken sitting there and refusing to give ground as we failed to provide adequate answers to her questions. Finally she had to leave to go to another meeting. As she left she spat out at him: 'It is *you* I'm holding responsible if *my* NHS reforms don't work.'[156]

In the end they went ahead because of Clarke's adamantine refusal to postpone them. 'It would have been a political disaster to stop them so close to the election. We just couldn't do that.' The casualty, instead, was community care.

Roy Griffiths's second major commission from government, following the Audit Commission's condemnation of community care in late 1986, had proved a tougher assignment than his management inquiry. There his business background and instincts had led almost straight to the answer. Community care, by contrast, was scattered around health, social security and the Department of the Environment. It took in hospitals and GPs, local authority social services, voluntary organisations, housing and the private sector. It involved many institutions and many more individuals, some of whom were providing enormous amounts of care with precious little support. It was, in the words of Griffiths's eventual report, 'a poor relation; everybody's distant relative but nobody's baby'.[157] The question, as in the NHS inquiry, was: who should be in charge? There were, according to Griffiths, 'eight or nine alternatives' including handing the job of running community care to GPs. But in essence the choice boiled down to three: giving the job to health authorities, local authorities, or some new organisation.[158]

Griffiths, no lover of organisational change for its own sake, soon ruled out creating a new body. That would entail too much time and turmoil for too uncertain a gain when the problem was plainly urgent. He also judged that much of what was needed was social rather than medical care – it involved housing, meals-on-wheels, home helps and nurses, rather than the attention of doctors. The divide was far from clear cut. But Griffiths did not want a medical, even institutional, model dominating a service which was meant to support people in their own homes as far as possible. In addition, he believed, 'any government has got to differentiate between the free health service and the means-tested social services. If you start putting them both under the health service you are blurring a crucial line.'[159] On top of that, the NHS was in disarray and under review by the time his report was completed in February 1988. A service about to undergo its own revolution was in no fit state to take on fresh responsibilities. The answer was local authorities, for whom Griffiths in fact had a high regard. The problem, he knew, was that the government did not.

Before he wrote the report, Griffiths went to see John Moore to check that local authorities would be an acceptable recommendation. Accounts of the conversation differ. Moore was not sure he was really asked that question.[160] Griffiths was equally clear that he was. There would be no point in producing a solution that would be ruled out of court, he argued.[161] But as one of the senior civil servants who finally delivered the policy put it: 'Roy can be very allusive. If he did say "are local authorities acceptable?", he may not have said it clearly enough. If he did say it clearly enough, John Moore didn't understand him. Whatever happened, when the report came in Moore was beside himself. He knew she [Mrs Thatcher] wouldn't want it.'[162]

The report landed right at the start of the NHS review. Government moved to bury it. To Griffiths's anger, it was not only published the day after Lawson's spectacular 1988 budget, an attempt he believed to distract attention from it, but it was offered up merely 'for consultation' with the government specifically stating it would bring its own proposals forward later.[163] By the time Clarke arrived to replace Moore, nothing had happened to it, but Clarke's arrival provided it with no warmer a friend. He held his own abiding distrust of local government, one whose origins are not clear even to his biographers,[164] but one which his recent spell as inner cities minister had only reinforced as he tangled with some of the more extreme left-wing Labour councils.

An inter-departmental committee of civil servants had been set up to crawl all over the issue again only to conclude that Griffiths was broadly right. No one, however, believed Mrs Thatcher would accept that conclusion. Clarke toyed with giving the job to the health service before he and John Major, now Chancellor of the Exchequer, attempted what Clarke later admitted to be a 'ding-bat' solution.[165] According to Griffiths, this amounted to little more than submitting those seeking social security payments for residential and nursing homes to a medical and social work test in an attempt to contain the explosive growth of that budget.[166] On its own, that would do nothing to improve services to people in their own homes, or shift mental illness and other money out of hospitals into social care.

Griffiths Two, as it became known, in fact had its friends, among them David Mellor, the Minister of Health, who argued the case with his boss, and Nicholas Ridley, the Secretary of State for the Environment. Ridley, at first sight, seemed the least likely ally. He was well known to be no friend of local authorities. He saw them as expansive, expensive and inefficient, pulling an ever larger share of national wealth into the public sector. His favourite council was said to be one in mid-west America which employed almost no one and met just once a year to award all its contracts to the private sector. In the same month as the Griffiths report landed, Ridley was taking a small step in that direction for Britain, piloting through Parliament a Bill making compulsory competitive tendering for refuse collection, street cleaning and for four other local authority services, a practice which councils such as Southend and Wandsworth had already pioneered voluntarily.

Ridley, however, had also that month published what proved to be a profoundly influential pamphlet for the Centre for Policy Studies called *The Local Right* and subtitled 'enabling not providing'. Its argument was that local authorities should be stimulators, facilitators, enablers and monitors – but that they did not necessarily need to provide services themselves. They could buy in much of what was needed from the private and voluntary sector, gaining the benefits of competition and flexibility. With this prescription from the radical right, the Griffiths report chimed, winning it Ridley's support. While local authorities should have the key role in running community care, Griffiths said, they should by no means attempt to provide it all. They should buy it in from whoever offered the best value, deliberately stimulating the private and voluntary sectors to provide a 'mixed economy' of care. 'This is a key statement,' Griffiths said. 'The role of the public sector is essentially to ensure that care is provided. How it is provided is an important, but secondary consideration and local authorities must show that they are getting and providing real value.' In other words, on 12 February 1988, a mere fortnight after the launch of the NHS review which a year later was finally to recommend its own purchaser/provider split, Griffiths was proposing the same idea for community care. Social services departments should organise it, Griffiths said, but as enablers. 'It is vital that social services authorities should see themselves as the arrangers and purchasers of care services – not as monopolistic providers.'[167]

Griffiths thus provided the makings of a full house for what, in the space of little more than two years, had become a coherent Thatcherite agenda for the welfare state in health, social services and education – one where, at least for now, services would remain publicly funded, but where market forces would be applied, creating, in the academic jargon, 'quasi-markets'. This was to be done by using tools from a kit which included the purchaser/provider split, making state-owned providers as independent as possible, and ensuring that all providers, whether state-owned or not, had to compete for business. The precise means of achieving that varied with the service, from competitive tendering, contracting out, and some direct privatisation, to ensuring that extra students brought extra funding, to attempting to make money follow the patient in the NHS. Because real customers could often not be created, proxies were sought: GP fund-holders for the patient in the health service, or a 'care manager' buying in services for social service clients. Many more services would be defined by contract, much more would be subject to competition. New types of organisation were created: NHS Trusts and grant maintained schools, for example. These were neither private sector nor old-fashioned state managed but a new form of non-profit making, state-regulated, half-way house. It was an approach that was soon to stretch across great swathes of both local and central government, affecting to varying degrees much else beside the core services of the welfare state as chunks of civil service departments found themselves turned into agencies operating on contract to their former headquarters.

Griffiths Two contained much more than just a purchaser/provider split. It retained strong planning elements, with a minister in charge at the top and annual plans to be drawn up by councils in consultation with health authorities and voluntary bodies. Central government was then to provide cash for the plans once they had been approved. That money would be 'ring-fenced' to ensure it was spent on community care, not highways or libraries. Councils' performance would also be reviewed annually, while social security payments for people in residential and nursing homes would be transferred to local authorities who could then use the money either to buy places in such homes or to support people in their own homes. The perverse incentive to use residential care, which had seen the social security bill continue to balloon from £500 million when the Audit Commission reported in 1986 to £1 billion by 1989 and finally to £2.5 billion by 1992,[168] would be removed.

Despite what might be seen as the essentially Thatcherite nature of the change, and despite Ridley's support for it, local authorities, Labour as well as Conservative, queued up to back it. With their historic role in housing and education being stripped away, running community care provided the chance to live to fight another day. Besides, some on the left soon came to see that the task of defining what needed to be bought and then buying it was not necessarily a policy of either right or left. It was just a tool, one which could be used to spend more as well as spend less, which could force clearer thinking about precisely what services should be bought, and might allow the shape and type of services to be changed more clearly and quickly than under directly managed systems. Thus while Labour nationally was bitterly attacking the purchaser/provider split for the National Health Service, Labour locally – and nationally through the various local authority associations – was arguing for the idea in community care.

Support from the Labour-controlled Association of Metropolitan Authorities only served, however, to increase Clarke's suspicion of the plan. Ministers remained obsessed with Liverpool, Brent, Lambeth and the others among the half-dozen authorities out of the 120 involved who might reasonably be expected to make a hash of running the new system. Clarke got close enough to getting his 'ding-bat' solution accepted by the summer of 1989 for him to persuade the Prime Minister that she really ought to see Griffiths, her personal adviser on health care management, to tell him his solution was being rejected. At virtually the same moment, Griffiths, on his own initiative, had put in a paper arguing that the Clarke/ Major plan would not work. It did not address a problem that went far wider than the social security budget, he argued, and it underestimated the seriousness of the crisis affecting the mentally ill, the elderly and the handicapped. Griffiths was invited in. His half-hour with the Prime Minister became an hour and a quarter as he went through the arguments all over again. 'I didn't think I had persuaded her, although I had answered all her questions.'[169]

The following Wednesday, however, there was a Cabinet committee at the end of which Griffiths received a call asking if he wanted to know the result. 'Not particularly' he said, having seen the depressing minutes of previous meetings. 'Oh don't be like that,' the official replied. 'She came back from Luxembourg last night about ten o'clock and said: "Get me the papers on community care." She spent three hours going through them, read your report again, walked into the committee this morning, waved your report and said: "Give me one good reason why we can't implement this?" And they all just stared back at her – they thought she was the one good reason.'[170]

Thus it was that in July 1989, eighteen months after Griffiths reported, the government finally backed a scheme that by the mid-1990s would make social services, not education, the most powerful and sought-after committee chair in local government. Even then, however, key elements of the package were not adopted. There was no separate minister, no cash attached to plans, and while many hundreds of millions of pounds were transferred from the social security to local government budgets, the full 'ring-fencing' of community care money, and the full formalised planning system which Griffiths sought were not adopted. It was those decisions which contributed to community care's postponement. By June 1990, doubts did exist about whether all local authorities would be ready by the April 1991 launch date, and about whether it was wise to transform two huge undertakings, the NHS and community care, on the same day. Much more important politically was that without the full 'ring-fencing' of cash, the new system would have marginally pushed up poll tax bills – then the most sensitive political issue in town. So the NHS changes survived, while the full community care reforms were pushed back to 1993, more than six years after the Audit Commission's report first burst upon the scene. If the charge was that things were changing too fast in education and the NHS, they were changing too slowly in community care.

The decision to postpone was one of the last that Mrs Thatcher made about the welfare state. By November 1990, Nigel Lawson, her 'unassailable' Chancellor had been gone a year. The boom unleashed by his 1988 Budget had started to go bust. Mortgage rates had hit 15 per cent, punishing home owners in a housing market where prices had started to fall. Unemployment, which in June 1990 had finally dipped below 1.6 million, its lowest level for a decade, was once again rising sharply. Labour enjoyed a massive lead in the opinion polls, a string of by-election defeats for the government reflecting both these problems and the unpopularity, either in contemplation or execution, of the poll tax and both the health and education reforms. Just ahead of the Conservative Party conference John Major, the new Chancellor, and Douglas Hurd, the Foreign Secretary, coerced Mrs Thatcher into the European exchange rate mechanism, but when she returned from a subsequent European summit to declare that she would never accept a single currency, Geoffrey Howe, for some time a simmering figure of resentment after his demotion from Foreign Secretary to Leader of the House, finally turned. His dramatic resignation statement, with its barely coded appeal to colleagues in its final sentence to revolt, saw Michael Heseltine enter the lists and the process begin from which John Major, to his own surprise as much as anyone else's, emerged blinking into the premiership.

At the end of the Thatcher era a remarkable paradox was apparent. A woman whose instincts were to unscramble the NHS and to increase charges, to roll back social security and social services, and to return schools to selection and fee paying, had instead headed a government which found itself promoting reforms that, however controversial, were plainly intended to improve existing health, education and social services. Each of them through the structures they introduced might make future privatisation easier, but none of them need automatically produce that result. Furthermore, some of the aims espoused, such as shortening NHS waiting lists or making schools more responsive to parents, were in the very areas which traditionally made the private sector more attractive to the better-off.[171] Thus the middle classes, instead of being encouraged to abandon these key services, actually found their concerns being addressed. If anything they were being tied in to these parts of the welfare state rather than pushed out. Only in pensions, where the better-off in large numbers had taken the incentive to bail out of SERPS, and in housing, where council house sales had heavily redrawn the map, had the state really been rolled back. In the mid-1970s, at least a quarter of every section of the population outside the top fifth, lived in a council home. By 1990, such social housing had become predominantly the safety net provision for the least well-off – it had become marginalised.[172]

It remained true that a powerful case could be constructed by the Opposition, and was, that many of the changes in health, education and social services made future privatisation easier. That held true both for privatisation of supply, by for example hiving off NHS Trusts or grant maintained schools into the private sector, and for privatisation of demand. Schools and hospitals used to coping with budgets would be undeniably better equipped to cope with vouchers, charges, fees or other methods of direct or top-up payment by their 'customers', if that was the way government chose to go. For the Conservative ideologues this plainly remained the longer-term agenda. But the political requirement to deny such intentions and to insist that the reforms had merit in their own right ironically made the public finance of such services safer for the five years after 1987 than they had been, at least theoretically, for the previous five years when vouchers, opt-out insurance, co-payments and other methods of increasing private provision had all been seriously studied within government.

This of course did not represent a change of mind by the free-market Conservative right. Rather it was a response both to some pragmatic considerations and two political realities. The first was that despite a decade of Thatcherism, the British Social Attitudes Surveys showed not diminishing, but strongly growing support for a centralised, tax-financed welfare state.[173] The idea remained deeply embedded in the British political psyche. Indeed the longer Mrs Thatcher was in power, the more the British public said it would prefer increased spending on health and education to tax cuts, however it then voted when it came to general elections. The disillusion of the seventies, when people's expectations had outrun their willingness to pay the necessary taxes, had to a degree dissolved. As the British Social Attitudes Survey concluded in 1991 (and again in 1994), 'there is still no evidence that a rolling back of the welfare state would be in accord with popular opinion.'[174] The other reality was that whatever the dominant ideology in the Conservative Party – if Thatcherism can be delineated as an ideology – the bulk of MPs, the Cabinet and party members in the country still in the late 1980s believed in public finance and provision of health, education and social security.

None the less, the arrival as Prime Minister of a man about whom remarkably little was known appeared to herald a kinder, gentler time for the welfare state. It was widely known that Major was the only member of the Cabinet who had been unemployed. He had been there and understood, it was said. As Minister of State for Social Security he had undergone a baptism of fire over cold weather payments, but had emerged with some credit. He was known to be a supporter of the NHS to the point where in an early interview in his premiership he even claimed to have been born under it – five years before it was founded. The Thatcherites had adopted him as Mrs Thatcher's heir, mainly, it seemed because Thatcher herself had done so without inquiring too closely into what it was that she was investing. The party's left, by contrast, was convinced they had acquired a solid One Nation Conservative. The welfare state, Major instantly declared, was 'an integral part of the British instinct',[175] adding, in unspoken but clear-cut contrast to his predecessor, that 'I unfailingly use the NHS.'[176] For a brief and heady period, the new Prime Minister appeared genuinely to be all things to all men, speaking with apparent sincerity of wanting to create a nation 'at ease with itself' and 'a classless society'.[177]

His early actions appeared to confirm that. Haemophiliacs infected with Aids through transfusions of blood products were suddenly awarded compensation after three years of resistance from government. A bitterly cold spell showed the cold weather payment system still had its problems: Major cut through the bureaucracy, ordering automatic and higher payments in advance on predictions of cold weather, rather than payment in arrears. One of his last acts as Chancellor, when Mrs Thatcher appeared to be panicking in the wake of the 1990 Eastbourne by-election defeat, had been to unfreeze child benefit, which had not been uprated for three years, restoring some of its lost value by paying a higher rate for the eldest child. This in part shot a Labour fox – restoring the value of child benefit was one of Labour's two main spending pledges. But the decision seemed to signal more than that. Spending on the NHS received an unexpected in-year boost,[178] while spending for 1991–2, agreed by Major as Chancellor, rose by 6.6 per cent in real terms. Some of that cash was essential to get the NHS market up and running, but it remained a settlement generous beyond that. Education, too, gained as Major put it 'top of my personal agenda'.[179] With the Prime Minister's approval, Chris Patten, the new party chairman, started trying to carve out a post-Thatcherite programme around a Conservative version of the social market economy which had been defined and developed by the German Christian Democrats.

It was, Patten declared, a 'proper target' to create standards in schools, hospitals and other public services so high 'that no one will seriously believe that the private sector should be an automatic choice for those who have the resources to opt for it'.[180] It was the approach which was to lead to the Citizen's Charter with its attempts to guarantee public service standards – and it produced some of the earliest storm signals for the new Prime Minister. For even as Peter Walker in his autobiography was hailing the party's return under Major to its One Nation roots, Nicholas Ridley in his was protesting that talk of public services so good that no one would use the private sector was not at all what Mrs Thatcher had in mind. 'This,' he growled ominously, 'is a very large change of emphasis.' Her view, he stressed, had been that 'welfare was for those in true need'; for those 'who could not afford private health, education or housing . . . a free service for those who could not afford higher standards.' It was not meant to be some socialist collective provision for all.[181]

And indeed Major was soon to prove a prisoner of a much more recent past than the One Nation tradition. The economy stopped turning into recession and started plunging into it. In February 1991 unemployment once again cleared two million. In May, Norman Lamont, the Chancellor, declared it to be 'a price well worth paying' to get inflation down.[182] Ten months later the price seemed somewhat more dubious for both people and party as the jobless total topped 2.5 million and kept on climbing.

The recession, which was to become the longest and deepest since the 1930s, proved very different in character to that of the early 1980s. It struck first in the south and then deep into the middle classes. This time it was not just employees in smokestack industries and overmanned factories who were hit, but the estate agents, computer programmers, lawyers, merchant bankers and middle managers of Tory England, along with hundreds of small businesses, whose owners, sometimes by mortgaging a house whose value was now falling, had joined the enterprise culture. The first Tory recession of the early eighties had, at least to some extent, included an inevitable shakeout to pay for the sins of the seventies; but that was not felt about this new plunge into what the economists euphemistically called 'negative growth'.

Home repossessions, at 40,000 in 1990, hit a post-war record before rising further to 75,000 in 1991. The same year 48,000 businesses failed and more than 250,000 people were at least six months behind on their mortgage repayments. Government spending, already rising in prospect of a general election, was forced up further by the recession. The social security bill in particular started to soar at a time when government revenues were falling. In his March 1992 Budget, just ahead of the general election, Norman Lamont forecast a budget deficit of £28 billion. It was a figure which was to prove a cruel deceit.

As the recession deepened, Major negotiated the Gulf War where the Star Wars efficiency and miraculously low casualty rates on the Allied side were somewhat marred by the failure to unseat Saddam Hussein. In April 1991, the NHS reforms finally took effect. Despite the softer language and gentler approach of William Waldegrave at the Department of Health, anything and everything that happened in the NHS was either blamed on, or put down to the credit of, the new-style system – including some spectacular job cuts to balance the budget at Guy's Hospital, the flagship NHS Trust.

In its first year the new market was heavily managed, and as it became clear that it would rapidly and chaotically force the reorganisation of London hospitals, something that had been consistently ducked from the mid-1950s on, Waldegrave kicked for touch. He pumped extra cash into the capital and set up the Tomlinson inquiry to report after the election on how London should be rationalised. 'What the new system will do is force some decisions out of us cowardly politicians who for twenty years have put them off', Waldegrave said. It was to fall to his successor, Virginia Bottomley, to reap that whirlwind. Labour meanwhile insisted that the government's agenda remained 'creeping privatisation' producing from John Major at the 1991 party conference the statement: 'No privatisation of health care, neither piecemeal, nor in part, nor in whole, not today, not tomorrow, not after the next election, not ever while I am Prime Minister.'

A decade on, elements of the Black Report finally surfaced when the government committed itself to *Health of the Nation* – a brave and ambitious initiative to set targets to cut smoking and heart disease by a third by the year 2000, along with premature deaths from breast cancer and suicides, while reducing teenage pregnancies and sexually transmitted disease. The programme required action across government, not just from the NHS, but it also provided some purchasing priorities for the new-style health authorities, the first integrated attempt in nearly fifty years to improve health as well as health care. A government which had come to wear as a badge of pride its frequent ability to be out of step internationally suddenly found the European director of the World Health Organisation declaring: 'This is exactly what we would like every country to do.'[183] As with the league tables which began to be proposed for schools and local authorities, as with much of the Citizen's Charter initiative, this was a further effort to concentrate on the output and outcomes of public services, rather than argue merely about the financial inputs. The unlikely but welcome sight of a government creating a stick with which others would beat it if the health targets were not met was matched only by an admission from William Waldegrave that Mrs Thatcher's ministers had long denied: that there was indeed a link between poverty and ill-health. Reducing health inequalities was 'a perfectly legitimate target', Waldegrave said, even if it was too tough a one for government to lay down.[184]

Meanwhile, across at education the decibel count remained high. Clarke had wanted to see the NHS reforms through and had come within an ace

of the risky step of refusing Mrs Thatcher's insistence that he give way
to Waldegrave in the reshuffle that followed Geoffrey Howe's 1990 resignation.[185] He rapidly gave education correspondents the impression that
he had little real interest in the subject other than an eloquent barrister's
grasp of the brief, a desire to keep in with the Tory right who had increasingly made education their own, and a wish to apply the market-like
solutions he had learnt at health.[186] Clarke's tenure thus saw legislation
for league tables of school exam results to be published and for a hugely
extended and partially privatised system of school inspections. More significantly, it saw the culmination of measures which were producing a
wholly unexpected metamorphosis in higher education.

This had begun under Baker. In a speech at Lancaster University in
January 1989, he had hinted at a radical switch in British higher education
from what was still an essentially élitist system to one that would involve
'mass higher education'. Student numbers had more than doubled in the
quarter-century since Robbins, Baker noted. That still, however, left only
15 per cent of eighteen-year-olds going on to higher education, a figure
well below that of our industrial competitors. Over the next twenty-five
years, he suggested, there was 'scope for even greater advance', speculating
that the participation rate would again double.[187]

The speech, together with measures already enacted in the 1988 Education Act, set higher education off on a dizzying merry-go-round of
change. By the time Clarke rose in the Commons in May 1991 to launch
the government's second higher education White Paper in four years,[188]
Baker's speculation had hardened into a target. The aim was to have one in
three eighteen-year-olds enter higher education by the end of the century,
against one in five in 1990, and the one in eight who had gone to university
or polytechnic in 1979.[189] Aided by a recession which encouraged teenagers
to stay in education rather than try to find work, Baker and Clarke were
to discover that they had unwittingly launched a rate of expansion which
made the Robbins era look like an afternoon stroll. The government's
target was all but hit not in 1999 but in 1993,[190] when 31 per cent of
eighteen-year-olds became students, encouraged by a more market-like
funding system which meant that the more students a university took,
the more income it received. Full-time equivalent student numbers
rocketed from 700,000 in 1988 to more than a million by 1993 – a rate
of increase almost three times faster than in the first five years after
Robbins.[191]

What was nothing short of a revolution had started from the disaster
of the early 1980s university cuts, progressed through attempts by both

government and the UGC to manoeuvre universities into a more responsive, accountable and, in the government's view, economically relevant
role, and had moved on to Baker's 1988 Education Act. It disbanded the
old non-statutory Universities Grants Committee and replaced it with a
Universities Funding Council with powers to impose contracts on universities in return for their grants – a formalisation, but a powerful one, of
the 'advice', specific earmarking of grants, and ranking of universities
according to their research outputs that the UGC had already started.

This was the means to give effect to the utilitarian thrust of Joseph's
Green Paper and Baker's white one,[192] each seeking a performance from
higher education much more closely linked to the needs of the economy,
with less dalliance in the groves of academe. Higher education, Baker's
paper had said, should 'serve the country more effectively . . . and have
closer links with industry and commerce and promote enterprise.' The
government and its funding agencies 'will do all they can to encourage
and reward approaches by higher education institutions which bring them
close to the world of business.'[193]

In the same measure polytechnics were removed from local authority
control and placed under a Polytechnics and Colleges Funding Council, a
move many of them welcomed and which proved to be the crucial step
towards ending the binary divide in higher education. The change had
been on its way for years. Attempts had been made in the 1970s to
strengthen the national framework in which polytechnics and colleges
operated and a national advisory board for polytechnics had been created
in 1982. The growing overlap in courses, content and even, in places,
research had blurred the differences between the two types of institution.
While Oxford University was plainly a different animal to Portsmouth
Polytechnic, the distinctions between some of the better polys and the
less favoured universities were by no means so clear-cut. Without the
government quite planning it, and because they had taken up the slack
from the UGC's initial refusal to lower costs per student, the polytechnics
had become, in Peter Scott's phrase, 'the Government's favourite higher
education institution',[194] their lower unit costs, greater efficiency and
apparently greater sympathy for the enterprise culture all suiting the
government's book. Given the scale of their operations and the fact that
their students had long been drawn from a national and not just a local
pool, their extraction from under the wing of local authorities had a logic
all of its own, quite apart from the government's almost ideological
removal, piece by piece, of local government functions. Their reward,
paradoxically, was independence through a form of nationalisation.

With the two higher education funding councils operating on similar principles, it became only a matter of time before the formal distinction between polytechnics and universities was abolished. Clarke announced that in his 1991 White Paper. From 1993 the polytechnics could adopt the title of university, while they would compete against their longer established rivals for student numbers and for funds that would be channelled through a single Higher Education Funding Council. All of higher education was thus subjected to 'market' pressures. But at the same time, through the funding council's planning and accountability requirements, it was also made subject to the 'greater social control' that Crosland had used to justify the original binary divide. Some of the universities felt they had got the worst of both worlds. Similar arrangements were also announced for the 480-plus further education colleges. From 1993 they too were made independent of local authorities, their expansion encouraged by a funding system which augmented their core budgets with payments matched to the number of students they recruited and retained.

These changes produced, in Malcolm Bradbury's words, 'a transformation in British higher education more profound and fundamental than any since the postwar years'.[195] It was a revolution which happened so fast and so silently, however, that it was almost invisible, barely debated in public at all. Universities found themselves made accountable in new and sometimes painful ways, their dons rated for research, with some under pressure to become 'teaching only' institutions.[196] Almost all were desperately searching for ways to enhance their income. The spectacular expansion in numbers was not matched by a physical expansion in facilities or libraries, particularly in the former polytechnics. Higher education was left operating as a leaner, meaner, more crowded and more impersonal machine. Student to staff ratios leapt by 30 per cent, reaching 13.3:1 by 1991 in the original universities and more than 17:1 in the former polytechnics.[197] Experiments began with 'fast-track' two-year courses, and two-term years,[198] while newly entrepreneurial vice-chancellors began to tout the idea of top-up fees, a graduate tax, or loans for tuition as well as for student maintenance.[199]

The pressure on universities and their teachers had never been so intense. Their traditional privacy and independence, which had lasted well into the seventies, was breached by external inspection, formal assessment and ranking of their academic and teaching quality. Unit costs tumbled by 25 per cent in five years and staff workloads rose. This great expansion proved no return to the brief academic Eden of the mid-1960s. It was indeed a time of opportunities, but it was also one of angst, particularly for those with memories of a gentler *ancien régime*. The Mekon-like figure of Lord Annan, the distinguished former vice-chancellor of London University, rose in the Lords to rail at the government's 'ideology of consumerism and accountability', saying the government had shown 'they do no trust universities to teach or to research'. 'Let me not mince words,' he said. 'The government treats universities like so many piles of dung.'[200]

Behind this transformation in their fortunes and way of life, however, lay a renewed faith in the value of further and higher education that had crept up almost as unnoticed as the university revolution itself. Gone was the pessimism of the late 1970s over higher education's worth; gone, too, were the cuts of the 1980s. Instead from the later 1980s on, everyone from government ministers to the Confederation of British Industry[201] and Her Majesty's Opposition became suddenly transfixed by international comparisons showing Britain's low participation rate in higher and further education.[202] A renewed conviction that economic success in a world of spectacular technological change depended on a skilled and educated work-force combined with reports that South Korea planned to have 80 per cent of its youth qualified for university entrance by the year 2000. This was the late 1980s equivalent of the Soviet Union launching the Sputnik. Overnight a new conventional wisdom emerged to be claimed as its own by all political parties: Britain needed a skills revolution. Education, since the mid-1970s one of the sourer parts of British public life, again became an unchallengeable economic good, though often as part of a new if not always closely defined construct called 'education'n'training'. The old themes that had haunted Butler, Eccles, Robbins, Callaghan, Joseph and Young about the need for more high-grade technical and technological education played again with renewed force.

Outside higher education, and particularly in the training sphere, the government failed effectively to act.[203] Twenty-six years to the day from the announcement of their creation, the demise of the remaining Industrial Training Boards was promulgated. They were replaced by Training and Enterprise Councils to be run by employers. Union representation was excluded. Ministers argued that the voluntary commitment of private sector employers would work better than the statutory levy system. Shortly after their creation, the government funds they received for Employment Training and YTS were cut back and Michael Howard, the Secretary of State for Employment, withdrew formal targets for training which the government wished to see achieved. An irked TEC chairman complained, 'You cannot have world-class targets for training with a Third World budget.'[204] Within higher education, expansion occurred so fast that in 1993 the Treasury called a halt; now universities suddenly found themselves facing fines if they recruited too many students.

As the guillotine fell for the 1992 general election, Clarke's last act as Education Secretary was to get through his Schools Bill covering league tables and inspection. The Conservatives turned to face a Labour Party nearly fourteen years out of office which had itself put education high on the agenda. It was, however, a party which had applied precious little fresh thinking to the welfare state during its vast stretch in the wilderness years. Instead, a profound conservatism reigned. During the first Thatcher administration, Labour had stayed on the old 1970s tramlines, producing an odd mix of opposition to every cut combined with continued disillusion with the whole project.

In 1982, Julian Le Grand's *The Strategy of Equality* had shaken Labour's egalitarians by concluding bluntly that 'the strategy of equality through public provision has failed.'[205] Examining health care, social services, education, and transport, Le Grand used a snowstorm of statistics to demonstrate that 'almost all public expenditure on the social services in Britain benefits the better off to a greater extent than the poor'[206] – a conclusion since modified but not discarded.[207] The finding that the middle classes exploited the welfare state more effectively than the less well-off won plaudits from both ends of the political spectrum. To the militant left it was proof that Labour had let down the poor, and backing for their desire to see a much more revolutionary redistribution of income and wealth. But to the right it equally provided ammunition for their view of how the welfare state had failed; and that much money could be saved and more achieved if only the middle classes could be weaned off the thing, allowing clearer targeting on the 'genuinely' needy. Those who believed in the project were left struggling in the middle.

The early eighties also saw the zenith of what had been a growing left-wing concern with the 'other' states of welfare, a classification first drawn up by Richard Titmuss in 1958 in an essay entitled *The Social Division of Welfare*.[208] In it he had drawn attention to tax reliefs for children and dependants, and to occupational benefits in cash and kind ranging from employers' pension schemes to their contributions to private health cover and luncheon vouchers. Each of these operated as a form of welfare state just as much as the benefit system, he argued. These fiscal and occupational welfare states, however, reinforced inequalities rather than reduced them.

By 1981, these three 'welfare states' had been developed into five in Frank Field's *Freedom and Wealth in a Socialist Future*. There, on top of benefit payments, tax allowances and company benefits, he identified 'the welfare state resulting from unearned income and inheritance'[209] and the 'private welfare state' of private medicine and education. All needed to be reformed – in essence cut back – to allow more generous and more redistributive social security payments, he argued.

It was an analysis which seemed wildly out of step with the times. First, what had been a key part of Labour's constituency – skilled trade union workers such as the electricians and others – were themselves opting for company-paid benefits, such as private health cover, in their drive, in Sid Weighell's memorable phrase, to 'get their snouts in the trough'.[210] The politics of envy of the late 1970s and early 1980s consisted less of 'take it off the rich and give it to the poor', and more of 'I'll have a piece of the action if I can get it'. But it was also an agenda which the Conservative Government managed to make less relevant, first by the scale of top-rate tax cuts and then by the reduction in tax allowances and finally by the taxation of benefits in kind which Lawson launched and his successors continued. Tax reliefs and company-paid benefits, while they far from disappeared, became less valuable.

If Labour remained locked on an old agenda, it was perhaps hardly surprising. When Neil Kinnock, then education spokesman, insisted in 1980 that it would be 'hopelessly dishonest' to promise to restore all the Tory education cuts, he found himself in boiling water with the party's left and his own constituency.[211] Further, whenever Labour's front bench was brave enough to attempt new thinking out loud, it tended to walk into a minefield. In 1985, Michael Meacher, the party's social security spokesman, in his own phrase 'got my leg blown off'[212] when in a parallel exercise to Norman Fowler's social security review he suggested phasing out mortgage tax relief. Despite this being a proposition that every serious commentator favoured, and a course the Conservatives themselves started to adopt in the 1990s, it was not practical politics at the time. Meacher found himself disowned by his front bench, ridiculed by the Tories and in the embarrassing position of letting Norman Fowler off the hook in a debate originally called to highlight an awkward leak of Fowler's own social security plans. On the Labour benches in the 1980s it remained far easier, and much safer, to oppose than to think. Labour remained too much a party, to adapt Tom Sawyer's phrase after the 1987 election, in which 'the only true test of radicalism is a deep conservatism in thought and ideas.'[213]

As a result Labour went into the 1987 election with a welfare state shopping list that can be summed up by the one word 'more' – a programme whose priority jobs and welfare element was alone costed by the party at £6 billion[214] and by the Tories at several times more. Beyond that, the manifesto included more spending on the NHS, on social services and on education. When the Conservatives unleashed their storm of new thinking on welfare state structures in education, social services and health after 1987, Labour was neither remotely prepared nor intellectually equipped. The election over, the party's approach to the welfare state went, like everything else, into its policy review. It emerged largely shorn of spending commitments but otherwise unchanged in substance. There were reasons for this. Just as welfare state issues had been second order questions for the Conservatives between 1975 and 1979, Labour similarly had much more pressing items to settle – its non-nuclear stance, its policies on trade union law, renationalisation and the economy generally; a recognition of the need to earn wealth before it could spend it; and deeper questions about precisely whose interests the party thought it was representing.

As the Conservative reforms in education, health and social services developed, they provoked on the left a turmoil of new thinking around the Tory propositions, one reflected in the rise and eventual demise of the journals *Marxism Today* and *Samizdat*. Labour, however, proved unable to take advantage of this ferment. For a start, the party had lost the key ability, which had given it the cutting edge on social policy after 1945, of tapping into academic thinking. As early as 1981, after the Conservatives had dropped their first flirtation with student loans, academics from Sussex and Brunel urged Labour to adopt the idea as a more egalitarian and effective route into mass higher education than grants.[215] The plea fell on deaf ears. After 1987, analysts sympathetic to the left developed a string of proposals for a graduate tax,[216] child care vouchers in place of nursery education,[217] positively discriminating vouchers for education which would pay more to the less well off,[218] and even a form of health voucher to make GPs more responsive,[219] in each case arguing that these could be used to achieve left wing ends every bit as much as right wing ones.

Labour failed to react. Much of this thinking, it is true, came to fruition as its policy review was being completed, and by then the review had set much of the party's traditional approach to the welfare state in stone. Only in local government services, where Labour's own experience of the 'loony left' had led it to recognise the need to treat citizens more as customers, did new thinking produce Citizens' Charter-type proposals for guaranteed levels of service well ahead of John Major's advocacy of the idea. In most other areas, when academics with ideas came knocking on the doors of Labour's front bench, no one seemed to want to listen. The only spending commitments to survive the policy review (at the hands of John Smith who chaired the economic equality working party) were a promise to restore the value of child benefit, to raise pensions by £5 for a single person and by £8 for a couple, to restore the link between pensions and earnings, and to introduce a national minimum wage. These proved a millstone.

As the Conservatives' education and health reforms materialised, Labour adapted on parts of education while remaining bitterly opposed to grant maintained schools. On health, the party gave no ground, opposing anything and everything that the government proposed, outside essentially non-contentious items such as the development of medical audit. Robin Cook, Labour's health spokesman, proved a fine flayer of Conservative health ministers. He was widely seen to have one of Labour's best brains. He did indeed consult a group of Labour-supporting NHS managers and academics who in private discussions believed they had persuaded him of the merits of the purchaser/provider split.[220] But politically Cook believed Labour's advantage lay in a policy of no surrender – that the NHS was Labour's issue and any concession to the government line would weaken the perception of Labour as the service's great defender. The result was a brace of policy documents on health which, while saying Labour would abolish NHS Trusts and fund-holding, were elsewhere so ambiguous about the internal market that they could be read by proponents of either side to favour their view.[221]

Neil Kinnock is clear that had he become Prime Minister in 1992, the purchaser/provider split would have remained. 'We would have had to accept and work within it – we couldn't have unscrambled it without wasting time and creating chaos.' The key insistence would have been that both purchasers and providers remained in the public sector.[222] The one risk Labour did consider in the winter of 1990 was to cut the standard rate of income tax from 25p in the pound to 12p, turning the other 13p into a hypothecated tax for the NHS. Given the public spending pressures Labour knew it would face, it was, Kinnock considered, 'the only way in which to ensure that we could guarantee in the lifetime of a Labour government, really tangible progress in this vital sphere.' People, he believed, would if necessary pay more for the NHS because, as he later argued, 'it is by any amount the most popular and required service – nothing compares with it; not housing, not benefits, not pensions, nothing.'[223] He canvassed Robin Cook and John Smith, Labour's shadow Chancellor, on the idea. Cook, Kinnock judged, was wholly in favour. Smith, however, was not, fearing among other things, that pressures would be generated to allow people to opt out of such an earmarked tax.[224] The idea died, unaired.

Labour thus went into the election committed chiefly to its child benefit and pensions pledges, with John Smith having to construct his shadow Budget in March 1992 around them in order to raise their £3.3 billion cost. By then they seemed the wrong priorities. The sense of national crisis was far greater over health and education, but the benefit commitments meant that Labour could offer only £1 billion and £600 million as early extra spending in those areas. Even the pension promise, which would have had to be £7 for single people and £11 for couples to have kept pace with inflation since 1987, seemed unexciting, so long had it been around. None of the package struck a chord to match the Liberal Democrat offer to put a penny on income tax, if necessary, to improve education.

Worse, raising the cash meant lifting the ceiling on employees' national insurance contributions, an arguably logical approach given the distortion it brings to the tax system. But it proved profoundly unappealing as the Conservatives hammered home the message that everyone earning more than about £21,000 would pay more tax – a sum that was £5000 above average earnings, but within too many people's aspirations to be politically popular. Equally, Labour's post-election analysis showed the low-paid were as worried about losing their jobs if a minimum wage was introduced as they were excited at the prospect of earning more.

Labour, Kinnock later argued, had to retain the child benefit and pension pledges after 1987 because so much else in Labour's policy was being reshaped:

> We had to back up our complaints about what the Tories were doing [to social security] with some commitments that were tangible, specific and costed. It was necessary to do that for reasons of principle, morality and credibility. But there were also straightforward political reasons for doing it. Challenged with 'what is still socialist about the Labour Party?' here was hard evidence that we were willing to make commitments for redistribution that nobody else was willing to make.[225]

When, against expectations and the polls, the Conservatives with John Major's soapbox and their 'tax bombshell' posters won again by 21 seats on 9 April 1994, the effect on Labour was traumatic. Despite Kinnock's red rose transformation of the party; despite a recession in the Tory heartlands; despite John Smith's bank managerial probity over his fiscal and economic plans – despite all this it appeared the electorate would not back what, by Labour's past standards, was an extremely mild version of 'tax, spend and redistribute'. All the painful transformation Kinnock had taken Labour through had resulted in just a 2 per cent increase since 1987 in Labour's share of the popular vote with the Tories left seven points ahead.

Instantly, John Kenneth Galbraith's latest book *The Culture of Contentment* was much cited, its thesis being that American society was dividing into the two-thirds that had, who no longer cared for the one-third who did not. The intellectual foundations which had underpinned key parts of Labour's mainstream for thirty-five years since Anthony Crosland's *The Future of Socialism* were shaken. If Labour could not deliver at least some redistribution, what could it deliver? Suddenly, all taboos went. Something close to panic set in. Bryan Gould, the party's leadership challenger, hinted that universalism needed to be reassessed when he argued that support for child care which enabled women to earn should be given priority over child benefit and 'the palliative of redistributive taxation'.[226] Labour, he said, had alienated one set of voters by appearing 'to cap their aspirations' while failing to impress another by the offer of higher benefits. Labour should instead give the less well-off routes to wealth creation rather than 'pauperising' them by treating them as welfare dependents. 'You can,' one policy adviser muttered during the shell-shock of election defeat 'even utter the dread word "targeting" around here without being denounced.'[227]

Smith's response, while stressing his personal belief in 'universal' child benefit and pensions, was to promise a Commission on Social Justice – a sort of 'new Beveridge' but one which would think the unthinkable for Labour about tax and welfare. Among the 'painful' issues it would address was the balance between universal and selective benefits, he said.[228] 'No policy must be regarded as out of bounds for the searching review the Labour party must now mount.'[229]

If Labour's response was a loss of nerve over its commitment to welfare and redistribution, the Conservative reaction to the election was soon no less dramatic. For the fourth victory proved to be a bitter one. The recession may technically have ended in July 1992, but unemployment, which lags behind both downturn and recovery, kept on rising, reaching a fraction under three million in December. Government finances proved to be in far worse a state than anything predicted before 9 April. The £28 billion deficit Norman Lamont had prophesied turned into almost £37 billion for 1992 and a projected £50 billion for 1993. In September 1992, five months after the election, the pound crashed out of the Exchange Rate Mechanism, effectively destroying a Chancellor who had sworn he would never devalue, while deeply wounding John Major. 'Black Wednesday' coincided with Major discovering that he had acquired a problem similar to that which plagued his predecessor in her early days. He had inherited a new intake of MPs cast much more in Margaret Thatcher's mould than the older and often broadly Heathite generation of politicians that they replaced. As his party came close to splitting over ratification of the Maastricht Treaty, Major soon found himself blown about in the wind of party opinion to a greater degree than any post-war Prime Minister.

Apart from the Citizen's Charter, which itself tended to reinforce the impact of the market approach to public services, Major proved to be a man of no new ideas. And so it came about that it was under Major rather than under his predecessor that the Thatcherite revolution in public services began to run its full course: the tool-kit of contractorisation, privatisation, market testing and private finance turning from a means to an end into something close to a dogma. The sense that now it was the Conservatives who had nothing new to offer except more of the same, and that in the process some valuable institutions might be destroyed, began to match the similar mood about Labour in the late 1970s.[230]

Moreover, the £50 billion deficit was rapidly seized on by the neo-Thatcherite right as the chance to do what Thatcher herself had largely failed to do – roll back the welfare state financially as well as managerially. With such a huge deficit, action to control spending was inevitable. But on 8 February 1993, Michael Portillo, chief secretary to the Treasury, rose to announce long-term reviews of government spending which would include a search for areas from which the state could quite simply withdraw. The first government departments targeted were health, social security, education and the Home Office – the core of the welfare state. Every spending programme would have to be re-justified, Portillo said. He was looking for areas 'where better targeting can be achieved, or from which the public sector can withdraw altogether'.[231]

In a way previously unparalleled, the welfare state was now formally under review and when Labour MPs demanded to know just what might go, Portillo's retort was that Labour had set up its own commission 'to think the unthinkable'. With pointed relish, he threw back at the Opposition benches John Smith's own words: 'We should be prepared to re-examine everything. I've not ruled anything out of court.' What was sauce for the goose, Portillo told the Commons 'is sauce for the gander'.[232]

Fifty years almost to the month from Beveridge, and as it celebrated what might otherwise have been the arrival of a mature middle age, the welfare state and its purposes were in question on both sides of the political divide in a way they had never been before.

PART VI

FIFTY YEARS ON

CHAPTER 20

Retreat or renewal?

The 1990s show opened just as the 1980s show had opened, with the gloomy recession act taking up most of the time before the first interval; seat prices had doubled, and everyone was 25 per cent better off, but fearful of finding they had no job when they came out.
Christopher Johnson, The Economy Under Mrs Thatcher 1979–90, p. 255

When I hear teachers grumble now I could smack their behinds at what they grumble about.
Sybil Marshall, former schoolmistress at Kingston Village School in East Anglia where for eighteen years from 1948 she taught thirty pupils aged 3½ to 11; Guardian, 9 February 1993

I came to office with one deliberate intent. To change Britain from a dependent to a self-reliant society – from a give-it-to-me to a do-it-yourself nation; to a get-up-and-go instead of a sit-back-and-wait-for-it Britain.
Margaret Thatcher, The Times, 9 February 1984

Hell hath no fury like the middle class when its subsidies are at issue.
George Will, London correspondent International Herald Tribune, commenting on Keith Joseph's plan to reduce student grants and charge tuition fees

Thatcherism is not for a decade. It is for centuries.
Margaret Thatcher, Newsweek, 15 October 1990, six weeks before being ousted as Prime Minister

Look after unemployment and the budget will look after itself.
John Maynard Keynes, quoted by Robert Skidelsky, Independent, 28 June 1993

Freedom from want cannot be forced on a democracy or given to a democracy. It must be won by them.
Sir William Beveridge, Social Insurance and Allied Services (The Beveridge Report), p. 172

THE STATE OF WELFARE that John Major had inherited, Labour was rethinking and Michael Portillo was attacking could be viewed through many different lenses.

In the long view, there had been a simple rhythm to the previous fifty years: the majestic period of construction in the forties and fifties; the accelerating swing of expansion through the fifties and sixties and on well into the seventies – an expansion, however, progressively offset by bouts of self-doubt and by a less certain consensus. By the end of the seventies an ideological battle had developed, though one fought as much within Conservative ranks as between Labour, the Conservatives and the other parties. Then came the eighties, with their attempt first at retrenchment and then at radical reform of the delivery systems, to be followed by the angst and uncertainty which soured the early to mid-1990s. For the individual services their moments in the sun and shade varied. But all, if individually out of step, marched broadly to that beat.

The state of welfare could also be examined purely by numbers. These came big. To take but a few: Britain's housing stock had almost doubled from just over twelve million dwellings in 1945 to around twenty-four million by 1992. During that time the UK population had risen by only a little over a fifth, from 47.3 million to just under 58 million. Of the thirteen million new houses constructed since 1945, approaching half had been built in the public sector[1] and could thus be attributed directly to the welfare state. The decline of private renting, however, combined with council house sales, meant that more than two-thirds of UK homes were owner-occupied against a quarter in 1947. By 1991, barely one per cent lacked a basic amenity such as a wash-basin, a bath, a shower, or a WC. Forty years earlier almost four in ten had no bath, while 22 per cent still lacked one as late as 1961. That same year more than one household in eight still had either no indoor WC or had to share one.[2]

The scale of educational change had been equally awesome. In 1950 only 30 per cent of fifteen-year-olds were still at school. By 1992 virtually all were. In 1945 barely 50,000 students went to university. In 1993 the full-time equivalent of more than a million were on degree courses with all that implied for more schools, more teachers and more and higher examination passes. During the war years just 14 per cent of pupils achieved any passes in the School Certificate. In 1991, 65 per cent had gained at least one GCSE at the equivalent grade, and fewer than one in ten boys and one in fifteen girls left with no graded results.[3]

In social security, greater longevity meant that the number of pensioners had risen from fewer than seven million in 1951 to more than ten million

Plus ça change . . . Low on Churchill's dilemma in 1950.

in 1992. Well over two million people received disability benefits which had simply not existed in 1945.

Life expectancy had climbed for men from around sixty at birth in the 1930s to seventy-three by 1991, with women at each stage expecting to live about five years longer. Perinatal deaths, those around the time of birth, had fallen from 56 per 1000 in 1940 to just over 8 in 1993. The welfare state could not claim all the credit for these changes, the figures being affected by life-style and living standards as well as by health care; but it could claim some. Equally, counting the courses of treatment may not be the best measure of either the health of the nation or the performance of the NHS. None the less a hospital service which treated barely 4 million in-patients in 1954 treated a record 9.6 million in-patients and day cases in 1993.

If these figures point to many of Beveridge's giants having been, if not slain – they are probably in absolute terms unslayable – then at least cut down to size, there were plenty of less proud numbers available. This in part was because the welfare state was having to cope with a very different world from 1945: one with more unemployment, more one-parent families, and markedly different employment patterns where people were in work.

From barely one million people on national assistance in 1948, of whom just 53,000 were unemployed, the numbers by 1993 had risen more than five-fold to 5.6 million on income support.[4] Add in dependants, and 20 per cent of the population was living on means-tested benefits, against perhaps 4 per cent in 1948. Unemployment, even on a count repeatedly massaged downwards during the 1980s, was almost ten times its 1948 level. More than a million of the almost three million unemployed had been out of work for more than a year. And 30 per cent now lived in households in receipt of one or more of the major income-related benefits.

Lone parents contributed to the high numbers on income support. From 8 per cent of all families with children in 1971, by 1992 they made up 19 per cent, or almost one in five. Partly because work was harder to find, 70 per cent now lived on benefit against 37 per cent in 1971.[5]

In place of the world that Beveridge had assumed, with men working full time and most women staying at home, by 1992 women made up nearly half the workforce and full-time male employment was in decline. Many more jobs, however, were part-time.

There were other negatives, from the numbers of homeless people on the streets to the number of murders committed by discharged mental patients. And despite a fifteen-fold increase since 1945 in the proportion of eighteen-year-olds in higher education, one in five 21-year-olds still had trouble with basic maths, and one in seven with basic reading and writing.

Yet even on the downside, gains could be recorded. The means-tests and tests of availability for work, while harsher than in the fifties and sixties, were still less humiliating than those from the thirties. Tuberculosis had reappeared among the homeless, but the rickets, stunted growth and scurvy in the children of the 1930s had not resurfaced, despite doctors looking for them anxiously amid the greater unemployment and harsher benefit regimes of the 1980s and 1990s. The country as a whole was some three times richer than in 1950. There were, however, worrying signs that in the very poorest areas, death rates for men aged 15–44 were actually rising.[6]

Over the years, the modern welfare state had meant many different things to different people. Its half-century had affected, broadly, four generations, but even within them had had different effects. To take my own family and friends, my grandparents' generation – the one that had fought the First World War and who were on their way to retirement in the later 1940s and 1950s – had been the first to gain. For them, the welfare state brought NHS care and a pension they might not otherwise have had.

The generation of my mother and father had grown up in the twenties and thirties and had voted in 1945 in order to ensure that a Labour Government turned the architects' plans into a welfare state building. For them, the welfare state meant much more. My mother, born in 1921, was the middle child of a middle-class family of five – four girls with a boy as the youngest, but spread over sixteen years. The two eldest left school at fourteen in the late twenties and early thirties for two years at a fee-paying commercial college which taught them secretarial skills and French, leading them to decent middle-income jobs before marriage. There was no thought that they would go to university. Nor was there at first for the younger girls. There was, after all, only so much money. That was earmarked to ensure that John, the youngest, the only boy and thus some future family's breadwinner, could get a fee-paying place at grammar school if he proved not bright enough to win one. But when he won a grammar school scholarship, the money was there to ensure that his sisters, three and six years ahead of him, could stay on at the schools at which they had won places. In 1944, Eileen, the youngest, became the first to go to university, via two grants, one from the Carnegie Trust which sponsored places at the London School of Economics and the other from Bristol city council. John who won a place at Manchester before the war, returned from it to college as one of the welfare state's first beneficiaries from the army's late entrance scheme.

For my in-laws, there were no such university pretensions. Just a few years older, and therefore that few more years pre-war, this generation all left school at fourteen becoming variously bricklayers, environmental health officers and, in the case of my father-in-law, the son of a lower middle-class quantity surveyor, an accountant who was trained on the job. For my parents-in-law the welfare state, after a wait, meant transfer from private lodgings to a council flat, to a council house as the children arrived, and then on to owner-occupation. As they paid their taxes, the welfare state educated their children, free of school fees, sending one to teacher training college, one to Liverpool University and the other to Oxford – like Neil Kinnock, the first in a thousand generations of the family to reach university, or be able to afford to do so.

As this generation aged, the NHS operated on them instantly for emergencies and, sometimes after a wait, for other conditions; and the state paid the pensions which they started to draw in the 1980s. These pensions no longer went up alongside earnings, but they did at least rise in line with prices unlike their occupational pensions. Their greater longevity carried a price. When they died cleanly and acutely after a brief illness, the NHS looked after them and well. But if they died slowly and forgetfully, as one grandmother did, first capital and then some of the next generation's income vanished in the longer-term care which, during the 1980s, the NHS no longer provided on a sufficient scale to match the growth in the numbers of elderly.

Another half-generation down, the welfare state meant something different again to the family of a friend. There is endless argument about the education system's failure to equalise class-based chances of higher education; but there is no argument that it expanded such opportunity. For Eva, a docker's daughter from Plaistow, where in the 1960s local families still used the public baths because the rows of Rachman-style privately rented terraces, now long demolished, had no bath in the home, the welfare state meant cod liver oil, free orange juice, free school milk and the school health checks which the NHS slowly took over. It also, however, meant university, this time followed by a higher qualification. Her parents and their brothers and sisters had all won scholarships for secondary school, but their parents had been unable to afford to let them go. They had all left school at fourteen.

Eva is a 1950s child, one of the true children of the welfare state and perhaps of its most favoured generation. In my case, born the year after the NHS was founded, it helped see me from cradle through school to university to emerge in 1971 into Heath's one million unemployed, the first generation of graduates to face even the slightest difficulty finding a job. There were greater doubts by the early 1990s about how comfortably it would see me to my grave. The state pension was withering away, still providing a platform to build on but a smaller one in a stormier sea. The certainty of a final-salary, possibly even inflation-proofed occupational pension, on offer for many when I started work, was available to increasingly few. The promise of a SERPS pension totalling half average earnings had been replaced by the gamble of a money-purchase scheme. For the first time in fifty years, no one could assume they would get through to retirement without experiencing unemployment.

For my children's generation, the early years brought all the welfare benefits their parents had seen, except for the cod liver oil and free orange juice that a richer and better fed nation no longer felt it necessary to force down its children's throats. The NHS saw them born, through the minor childhood ills and into school. But as the older ones head for higher education, the full grant my generation had enjoyed, together with the easy casual jobs and the chance to sign on in the vacations if need be, had all shrunk or disappeared, replaced by the promise of debt to pay off. By the time the younger ones get there, the taxpayer may well be less generous again, offering loans for fees as well as maintenance.

Such stories illustrate the welfare state's collective smoothing of income across the life-cycle, with people paying in through tax and national insurance during good times to receive in bad, or at times of heavy burden – when children are educated or pensions are needed. But they also point to shrinkage. By 1992, much of the operation felt appreciably less generous. This is hardly surprising. From the mid-1970s on, the welfare state had been hit, in Julian Le Grand's memorable phrase, first by 'an economic hurricane' and then by 'an ideological blizzard'.[7] By the early 1990s, however, what was remarkable was how much, not how little of it remained.

The sums are too complex to rehearse here, but the best academic analysis of the time showed that, contrary to all popular perception, from 1976 on the welfare state had not declined in scale at all.[8] Indeed, from Michael Portillo's point of view as he addressed the Commons in 1993, that was precisely the problem. Reports of the death of the welfare state under Margaret Thatcher had been greatly exaggerated. For as Portillo spoke, spending on the 'five giant' services – health, education, social security, housing and personal social services – totalled almost £160 billion, virtually two-thirds of all government spending and more than a quarter of national income. Not only that, these services were taking the largest share ever of the national cake as recession shrank the domestic product and pushed up the costs of unemployment.

It was true that since 1976, the welfare state had become less expansionary. Expansion, however, had not ceased. In 1946 the big three – social security, health and education – had taken just 6 per cent of a much smaller national income, a figure that rose to 11 per cent by 1951 and reached 20 per cent by 1976.[9] There, broadly, it stuck. With ups and downs reflecting the economic cycle, welfare state spending oscillated around a figure of just under a quarter of GDP. That constant share of a larger income, however, still allowed more to be done. In John Hills's phrase, since 1974 there had been 'neither inexorable growth nor decline in the relative scale of the welfare state'.[10]

There had, however, been marked changes in the composition of the spending. Since 1979 housing had seen its share decline sharply with the effective halt in council house building. But the switch away from subsidising homes towards subsidising people produced a soaring housing benefit bill which meant that what looked like a real halving of expenditure on housing was in fact a cut of about a third. Once allowance was made for the extra tax forgone by the Treasury in mortgage relief as home ownership rose, the overall subsidy to housing was little changed. Education's share of overall welfare state spending also fell, recovering somewhat after 1987 – more being spent per head on schoolchildren but much less per head on students as the combination of loans and increased student/lecturer ratios took effect. The gainers were health and social security, where the demographic pressures of an ageing population had been greatest. Their share of the cake had risen.

But if the welfare state had not reduced in scale since the mid-1970s, it had reduced in scope; and it was these changes, and not least their impact on middle income groups, which produced the perception that it was on its way out. In schools, for example, parents were being asked to contribute more to 'extras'. In universities there had never been more chance of being a student, but individual students had never had it so tough. Legal aid, which once covered nearly 80 per cent of the population, had been pegged back, turned much more into a safety net for the least well-off. In social security, the 1981 breach of the earnings link for long-term benefits meant that the basic state pension was withering away. By 1992 it had become worth only 15 per cent of male average earnings compared with around 20 per cent in the late 1970s. It was actually worth less than the amount paid to pensioners on the means-tested income support. Projections showed that by 2030 it was likely to be worth only 8 per cent of average earnings.[11] The fall in its value, however, came as pensioners overall had become wealthier: the great growth in occupational pensions in the fifties and sixties having ensured that by 1994, 55 per cent retired with an occupational pension against a third in 1979. In turn, those pensions were in general worth more, and younger pensioners were starting to gain from SERPS maturing. The two nations in old age that Titmuss had noted developing in 1955[12] had become many, pensioner incomes increasingly reflecting the diversity of income in work. The losers were those who had relied only on the state.

In housing, the picture was equally complex. England's housing stock in 1991 had overall never been in better condition, even if one in twelve homes was still deemed unfit.[13] But in 1992 the Audit Commission, hardly a hotbed of revolution, calculated that on 'even the most optimistic' assessment 12,000 more homes a year needed to be built, while producing figures which suggested the gap might be nearer 50,000 or 70,000 a year. On existing policies it warned, 'little progress can be expected in improving either the public or the private sector housing stock.'[14] It was a document which the commission hoped would have the same impact on government as its assault on community care six years earlier,[15] but it left ministers unmoved. Meanwhile, official homelessness had never been higher. In

1978, when local councils' statutory duty to house the homeless was expanded, 51,000 households in England were accepted. In 1992, the figure was 143,000.[16] This near three-fold rise did not include those who were outside the legislation because they were single, literally roofless and on the streets – 'the people you step on when you leave the opera', Sir George Young, the Housing Minister, noted with an irony that was lost on Her Majesty's Opposition.[17]

In the NHS, bits had fallen off the edges. Outside hospital, the optical service was now both means-tested and privatised. To the middle class, it had become invisible, save for free eye tests for their children. Yet for the less well-off, three million vouchers for spectacles and eye tests were issued in 1992 and the taxpayer was still spending £172 million, or 80 per cent in real terms, of the amount the service had cost in 1979.[18] Equally, NHS dentistry had virtually disappeared for those on middle incomes. Patients paid 80 per cent of the cost of treatment where they could find a dentist willing to provide it. Even so, those charges covered only 40 per cent of the £1.4 billion spent by the government on dentistry and more than £840 million in 1992 was still being provided for free dental care for children and the least well-off. These arms of the NHS therefore still existed; but they had been means-tested, residualised, and made invisible to the middle class.

Equally, NHS prescription charges, which had not been raised at all between 1971 and 1979, had gone up virtually annually from 20p in 1979 to reach £4.75 an item in 1994 – an increase 40 times the rate of inflation – and £5.25 in 1995. Yet the combination of an ageing population and higher unemployment meant that more than 80 per cent of prescriptions were dispensed free in 1992 against a mere 60 per cent in 1979.[19] In other words, those who paid, paid more, their contribution to the drugs bill having doubled; but at the same time, more people were receiving more prescriptions free. Overall, despite this greater targeting, NHS charges in all their forms still accounted for only 3.7 per cent of NHS spending in 1993 against 5.6 per cent at their peak in Enoch Powell's day.

By far the most dramatic reduction in the scope of the NHS, however, had been in long-term care, particularly of the elderly. Here the boundaries between means-tested social care and free health care had shifted significantly, though less as a deliberate act of government policy than as a by-product of the incentive systems created. Once the trend was established, however, government did little to reverse it.

The shift followed the dramatic growth in the early 1980s of independent residential and nursing homes funded through social security. From the mid-1980s on, some health authorities realised they could use social security money to release themselves from long-term care. They began closing their long-stay beds so that by 1993 perhaps a quarter had gone.[20] Some replaced a proportion of these by buying places in independently run nursing and residential homes; others made no provision at all. They simply allowed social security to pick up the bill for nursing those patients poor enough to qualify. For the less well-off that could be fine. But it left anyone slightly better-off paying their own way until their savings and the proceeds of selling their homes, if they were single, were used up. Families that had hoped to bequeath houses and wealth to the next generation saw assets which had taken a lifetime to accumulate being consumed at a rate of around £20,000 a year for long-term care.

The impact around the country varied widely. Not all health authorities withdrew from long-term care, or did so entirely. In 1993 the NHS still spent almost £1.5 billion on its own long-stay beds, and another £170 million in nursing homes.[21] None the less, in 1994 the trend was hurled into the headlines when the NHS ombudsman took the unprecedented step of issuing a special report to condemn Leeds General Infirmary for discharging to a private home a fifty-five-year-old man whose stroke had left him doubly incontinent, immobile and brain-damaged, unable to communicate, or to feed or clothe himself. That he needed full-time nursing care was not in dispute. The hospital argued, however, that because his condition could not be improved medically, he was no longer an NHS patient. His wife, despite the couple being on income support, was left to find £6000 a year to top up the private home fees. As the ombudsman ruled that Leeds should pay up, health authorities nationally warned that 'a financial time bomb' was being placed under the NHS if they were expected to cover all such cases.[22]

The ombudsman's action led to a redrawing of NHS guidance. Ministers issued a draft insisting at one and the same time that health authorities had to buy or provide some long-term care, but that for most less spectacular cases the shift towards means-testing would continue, the patients being classified as needing nursing, not medical, care. The government found itself accused of ending the 'cradle to grave' NHS.[23] Even here, however, the reduction in scope was not the result of any overall cut in provision: £2.5 billion was being poured into nursing and residential homes through income support. Rather it was a failure to match rising demand from an ageing population, allied to structural changes which encouraged more means-testing.

Despite these difficulties, the NHS overall had increased its performance dramatically since the mid-1970s. Activity was up by 35 per cent on 1979 and treatments barely dreamed of fifteen years earlier were available. The NHS had improved its efficiency by more than 20 per cent[24] – while managing daily, as it had since 1948, to give the impression of being in crisis.

Private health care and private education had both grown. From negligible levels after 1948, the proportion of the UK population with private medical insurance had reached 5 per cent by 1979 and had then more than doubled to just over 11 per cent in 1990. The numbers then stagnated in the recession.[25] The figures, however, exaggerated the degree of growth. To increase the market, insurers repeatedly cut the cost of their products by restricting the conditions covered or the hospitals that could be used, by setting ceilings on the sums paid out, and by producing low-cost plans which, for example, only triggered if the wait for NHS treatment was more than six weeks. The result, very broadly, was that more and more people were covered for less and less compared to the relatively Rolls-Royce policies of the 1970s. In addition, by 1992 only 12 per cent of patients in private hospitals paid for themselves against 28 per cent in 1981.[26] To some extent, insurance was substituting for direct payment.

However, private provision of health services, as opposed to private purchase of them, had exploded. By 1993 independent hospitals and nursing homes accounted for nearly 19 per cent of all expenditure on hospitals and nursing homes, against just under 10 per cent in 1986. This was startling growth by anyone's standards. But most of this growth was in long-stay rather than acute care, and most of it (chiefly income support payments for nursing home places) was publicly funded. Private spending on acute care as a percentage of all NHS, pay bed, independent hospital and nursing home provision rose only from 6.2 to 7.6 per cent between 1986 and 1994.[27]

Private education too had expanded, although much less dramatically. The proportion of children in independent schools rose from just under 6 per cent in 1979 to 7.5 per cent in 1990, before falling back to nearer 7 per cent in the recession. The two sectors, however, were qualitatively different. Movement from the NHS to private care is episodic: the decision to buy a particular operation privately or on insurance does not take people out of the NHS for good. Leaving state education tends to mean exit: once children go to private or public schools they usually stay there.

Overall, therefore – outside council house sales and the beginnings of progress on tenant transfer, and aside from the large-scale substitution of private pensions for a scaled-down SERPS – the welfare state in terms of the services it provided, remained remarkably unrolled-back thirteen years years after Margaret Thatcher took power and as the country elected its fourth successive Conservative Government. The stark change there had been was the growth in economic inequality.

On one level this had been deliberate. 'Opportunity means nothing unless it includes the right to be unequal,' Mrs Thatcher had declared in 1975. 'Let our children grow tall, and some grow taller than others if they have it in them to do so.'[28] The intellectual underpinning for this philosophy came from Milton Friedman and from Friedrich von Hayek, who had argued to an unlistening world in the 1960s that the wealthy were merely 'ahead of the rest' in material advantages. Their ownership of the first cars, or refrigerators, or radios had been followed by mass production of these goods, he said. But they had only become available to the less well-off because 'in the past others with larger incomes were able to spend on what was then a luxury.' The rich acted as 'scouts', finding the path that could then be built for 'the less lucky or less energetic' to follow. 'If we all had to wait for better things until they could be provided for all, that day would in many instances never come,' Hayek maintained. 'Even the poorest today owe their relative material well-being to the results of past inequality.'[29]

On this argument inequality was a necessity, but wealth would still, in the phrase that Ronald Reagan popularised, 'trickle down' over time towards the less well-off. Society as a whole would become richer. 'If allowed to,' Keith Joseph had argued when he picked up Hayek's arguments in the 1970s, 'the market will provide a constantly rising set of minimum standards – including rising minimum income standards.'[30] Put another way, a rising tide would lift all the boats.

So early signs that tax cuts and other economic changes were making the rich richer were not a problem for the Thatcher governments. Such inequality was to be applauded. What was a problem was evidence which began to mount in the mid-1980s that the poor were also getting poorer. It was furiously denied by ministers. In 1988, Mrs Thatcher angrily told the Commons that 'everyone in the nation has benefited from the increasing prosperity – everyone.'[31] In fact official statistics were later to show that by then the bottom 10 per cent of households had become 6 per cent worse off in real terms compared to 1979. By 1990 that disparity had risen to 14 per cent and by 1992 to 17 per cent. Suggestions that the figures were distorted by self-employed people with sharp accountants declaring no income at all led to a recalculation which excluded the self-employed. Even then, income had still fallen by 9 per cent for the bottom range of households and had not risen at all for the next 10 per cent.[32] These were not, of course, the same people as in 1979. The composition of the group had changed. There were many fewer pensioners – 9 per cent of the grouping against 31 per cent – and the unemployed made up 34 per cent of the total, not 17 per cent. It appeared unarguable, however, that the bottom 10 per cent of households were worse off in real terms than the bottom 10 per cent in 1979.

While their share of income had fallen, the income for the population as a whole had risen by 36 per cent, but only the top three-tenths had seen an increase as good as or better than that. While the income of the bottom tenth had fallen, that of the top tenth had risen by 62 per cent. The overall result was that by 1992 a quarter of the population had an income below half the average, against only 10 per cent in 1979. Almost one child in three lived in such a household, against one in ten in 1979.

The causes of this widening income inequality went well beyond the 'five giants' alone to the whole thrust of economic and social policy and to technological and social changes including an increasingly global market which went far beyond the control of any single government. It reflected not just higher unemployment, but changed tax regimes and benefits rising with prices, not earnings, and in the case of some allowances not even rising in line with prices. It reflected the fact that while salaries at the top end of the earnings range had exploded, those at the bottom end had fallen. That, in turn, was the outcome of reduced trade union rights, the contracting-out of services which often deunionised workforces and reduced their bargaining power, the abolition of wages councils and a sharp increase in part-time working. Such lower wages in turn enforced the need for the 1988 benefit cuts for the childless unemployed and the young in order to preserve work incentives.

Yet for all the tighter rules drawn around benefits for the jobless, one of the welfare state's greater successes over the period from 1979 was, however uncomfortably, to look after the unemployed, thus preserving the peace. They and their children remained fed, educated, and cared for by the NHS. Even if there was a sharp rise in crime, there were not on any lasting scale riots on the streets – despite three million unemployed for much of the period. If under Mrs Thatcher unemployment was made to seem electorally irrelevant, and even perhaps acceptable, it may para-doxically have been the underpinning provided by a welfare state which she deeply distrusted which made that possible. It was under John Major, as the second great recession bit deep into the middle income groups, and as the Thatcher revolution was seen to have failed to deliver a lasting economic transformation, that the perception altered and permanently high levels of unemployment, with the consequent social divisions, came to seem less acceptable.

By 1992, some things had changed perhaps for ever. The idolisation of management and measurement which the Thatcher years brought, topped up by endless league tables of performance under Major, had brought a profounder realisation that outputs from services mattered at least as much as inputs: that the amounts of money, staff and other resources poured in, while important and the subject of fierce political interchange, were not the only things worth measuring. Outputs – what was acquired with the money and how well it was spent – mattered too. More money had ceased to be seen as the only answer to every ill.

In health and education the radical reforms of the 1987 Parliament were beginning to work through. Both services felt trapped into permanent, almost Maoist revolutions, their internal landscapes changing at a bewildering pace. In contrast to the 1974 reorganisation, in the NHS many of the best managers headed downwards to run Trust hospitals at high salaries, rather than staying in health authorities to do the purchasing. A climate developed which led Sir Duncan Nichol, the chief executive, to call for a halt to 'macho management' as the new hands-on NHS Trust chairmen and their senior managers (who overnight had restyled themselves wholesale as chief executives) began to tell managers to 'clear your desk by tomorrow'.[33]

The reforms seemed to bring out bits of both the best and the worst that had been promised. As in 1974, bureaucracy rocketed as staff were recruited to run the internal market. Manager numbers rose by 36,000 in three years.[34] A now marginalised BMA complained bitterly though impotently that GP fund-holding was producing a two-tier service, with fund-holders' patients fast-tracked over those paid for by district health authorities. That put in question the NHS's ancient, if not always achieved, aim of equal treatment for equal need. Yet fund-holding rapidly also brought more flexible and responsive services from hospitals, and the BMA soon found itself having to represent fund-holding doctors or risk losing members.

Aided by large transfusions of cash to get the new system running, the numbers of patients treated rose sharply by 16 per cent in three years. So, however, did waiting lists, hitting one million in England alone for the first time. The longest waits, however, disappeared, the result of a Patient's Charter promise that no one would wait more than two years and then, for some key conditions, eighteen months. The health departments claimed this was all due to rising efficiency from the new system. Critics suspected it was extra cash, more focussed management at the expense of other priorities, and a little manipulation of the figures that had done the trick.

Health and family health authorities began to merge into new commissioning agencies in an attempt, in places successful, to break down forty-year-old barriers between hospital and primary care. Then NHS Trusts and hospitals began to merge, sometimes voluntarily, sometimes under compulsion, most notably in London. Guy's, the flagship of the NHS Trusts, suddenly lost out to St Thomas's as the new market put health care in the big cities through the mill. Plans were laid to abolish regional health authorities, and ministers worried about how to bring the benefits of fund-holding to all while still retaining enough planning to hit *Health of the Nation* and other targets. A sense began to grow that a beast had been created which could no longer entirely be controlled. Alan Langlands, the new NHS chief executive, when asked in January 1994 whether in three years' time health authorities might not be a thing of the past, replaced by GPs controlling the whole of the NHS budget, replied disarmingly: 'I honestly don't know the answer to that question.'[35]

Virginia Bottomley, now Secretary of State for Health, travestied the past by describing it as Soviet-style 'command and control' – the two things health ministers had never felt they had. The new one, she declared, was 'light touch', a euphemism for attempting to push responsibility for what services were provided away from government and down to individual arguments between local health authorities, hospitals, GP fund-holders and their patients, staff at the same time being increasingly subject to 'gagging clauses' in contracts. As far as possible a deaf ear was turned to Bevan's dropped bedpans. When government-determined targets were on the line, however, or the political heat over a particular issue rose high enough, the ministerially appointed chairs of trusts and health authorities provided a line management system Stalin himself might have envied. What was lacking was a sense of where all this was meant to be leading, and whether the core NHS values of equity and priority according to need could remain. Ironically, hospital doctors appeared to adapt better to the new environment than GPs, despite their new-found power. From more than 50 per cent of medical students wanting to be family doctors in the 1980s, some GP training schemes by 1994 were having trouble finding any recruits.[36] Doctors as a whole, however, became so unnerved by the new power of managers and so alarmed at the new market's erosion of their ethical values and status that medical organisations from the Royal

Colleges down held an unprecedented two-day seminar in late 1994 in an attempt to chart a new course for medics in the brave new world.

The drive to get private finance and operators into the NHS continued, but with limited initial success. The NHS remained so sensitive politically that in the summer of 1994, Mrs Bottomley found herself denying the ultimate logic of the NHS reforms: that the service could one day end up publicly funded but almost entirely privately provided.[37] Her denial came as her department insisted that when it came to community care, councils had to spend in the independent sector 85 per cent of the 'care' element of ear-marked cash which they received – in order, over time, to achieve precisely that outcome: a publicly funded service independently provided, with the council reduced to an 'enabler'.

In education the continued pace of change was if anything more frenetic as Baker's Act proved to have reopened old controversies, even if in new forms. Religion re-entered the fray, with Muslim groups wishing to use the grant-maintained mechanism to create their own schools.[38] In 1993 the Queen Elizabeth School in Penrith, Cumbria, became the first grant maintained comprehensive to go fully selective, joining the 150 surviving grammars. A string of other schools around the country moved to select between 30 and 100 per cent of their pupils, fearful that if they did not, they would lose brighter pupils to rivals. This was not yet a return to the eleven-plus, but it was the beginnings of a return to selection. Where it happened it generated as much controversy and heat at packed parents' meetings as the abolition of the grammar schools had twenty and thirty years earlier.[39]

John Patten, in the least happy reign of any Secretary of State for Education, completely misjudged the mood of teachers who, after six years cowed by the lash of the government's education reforms, suddenly redis-covered a moment from the seventies and boycotted in spectacular style what was meant to be the first round of testing for fourteen-year-olds in 1993. It was arguably the biggest trade union victory since 1979. In an attempt to appease them, Patten appointed Sir Ron Dearing, a former Post Office chairman, to run a new School Curriculum and Assessment Authority and to review the whole curriculum and testing regime. Dearing diagnosed over-complexity and overload and acted accordingly. The con-tent of the ten-subject curriculum below age fourteen was reduced; for 14–16-year-olds it would in future take only 60 per cent of school time. This allowed vocational courses for the less academic back into schools. The testing regime received similar surgery, and teachers were promised no further big changes to the curriculum for five years from 1995. It remained a long way short of Mrs Thatcher's minimalist core curriculum: elements of technology and a foreign language remained for all 14–16-year-olds, for example, and science and technology, subjects which had tended to go by the board in some schools, remained locked into the curriculum for younger pupils. This was all ground Baker had fought for in an attempt to produce a better-equipped country. It was, however, a dramatically reduced edifice from the one that he had ordered up. In training, thirty-five years after they had first been advocated, vouchers were taken a stage further in 1993 when a pilot group of school-leavers were given credits nominally worth £1000 which could be spent with employers for training. Vouchers were chosen too as the way to enhance nursery provision after John Major at the 1994 Tory party conference revived once again a promise to make a start on Margaret Thatcher's twenty-year-old pledge of pre-school education for all parents who wanted it. Right wing hopes that this would prove the Trojan horse which would allow vouchers to be introduced for all schooling were, however, promptly quashed by the Prime Minister. For nursery schooling, yes; for all schooling, not this side of an election.

These changes in the organisation and delivery of services, however, took place against the turmoil of the government's 'fundamental' spending review, one which the right saw as the chance finally to shift the boundaries between public and private funding.

Portillo's announcement and Labour's Social Justice Commission between them launched a burst of pamphleteering not seen for half a decade. Into the breach Portillo had opened, Peter Lilley, the Secretary of State for Social Security, soon rode. The first right-winger in the post since John Moore published projections showing that the underlying growth in social security 'has exceeded and will continue to exceed, growth in the economy'. The message, he said, was 'uncomfortable' but had to be faced.[40] 'There is no escaping the need for structural reform.' And that, he said, 'must' involve 'either better targeting or more self-provision, or both'.[41]

In fact the projections equally showed that a halving of unemployment and 2 per cent a year growth – admittedly a less than likely scenario on immediate past performance – would in fact result in social security taking a smaller share of GDP by the turn of the century. Such possibilities held little attraction for the Thatcherite right, however. Five MPs from the new intake to the No Turning Back Group published proposals to abolish SERPS and allow people irreversibly to opt out of the basic state pension. They should also be allowed to opt out of unemployment and invalidity benefit by substituting private insurance for the state-run scheme, the MPs suggested, while employers should insure their own employees against industrial injuries. Child benefit, mortgage interest tax relief and maternity allowance should all go, to be replaced by a combination of a single integrated, means-tested benefit and child tax allowances.[42] Many of these ideas, and others including requiring those taking out a mortgage to insure themselves against unemployment, had first been canvassed within days of Michael Portillo's announcement.[43] Michael Howard, the Home Secretary, joined the fray by attacking benefits for single mothers. John Redwood, the Secretary of State for Wales, did the same, while in a little-noticed speech, he put down a marker for the future by declaring that the boundary between what was publicly provided for in health care and what was privately provided, was a matter for debate, but one he had no desire to reopen 'today'.[44] Cuts in the level of benefits for future lone mothers began to look increasingly likely.

Suddenly any and every welfare state chestnut was emerging from the fire, from NHS 'hotel' charges, to a fee for visiting the GP, to an end to free prescriptions for pensioners, a fresh examination of charging students tuition fees, and a questioning of whether benefits should even rise in line with prices – options most of which Portillo appeared to confirm were under scrutiny.[45] Norman Lamont, who after 'Black Wednesday' increasingly aligned himself with the right, did nothing to discourage such speculation. In late May 1993, however, he finally fell, to be replaced by his 'good friend' Kenneth Clarke. In his first speech as Chancellor, Clarke declared 'anybody who thinks I came into office in order to dismantle the welfare state has not the slightest idea where I come from nor my record . . . I am not remotely interested in dismantling the welfare state. I have spent my entire lifetime seeking to modernise it, seeking to give it a chance of survival.'[46] Hotel charges in hospital, he declared the same day, were 'corny old rubbish'.[47]

Michael Portillo, Clarke's number two, however, continued the attack, suggesting it was 'reasonable and responsible' to warn under-40s to make their own private arrangements for pensions, and that it was 'unsustainable' for government spending to continue at 45 per cent of the national income.[48] But when Peter Lilley told Young Conservatives in December that in the 'welfare society' of the future 'an increasing share of provision will be made by individuals, families and companies', Clarke intervened to say the basic state pension was a key part of the welfare state. 'I do not see that as being opted-out of – or left as a vestigial remain for those who cannot provide for themselves.' He added: 'This government will never take part in any attempt to dismantle the welfare state.'[49] A battle was under way for the soul of the Conservative Party over the future of the welfare state. Which side the Prime Minister would finally be on, as he nodded one day to the right on the issue, and the next to the left, no one now could be very sure. Meanwhile Labour, while trumpeting the fact that the tax burden was now higher than it had been in the dying days of the 1974–9 Labour Government, was left with the problem of how it would improve services without raising taxes still further.

In December 1993, the first fruits of Portillo's 'fundamental' review emerged. Unemployment benefit was to be removed from 100,000 people by renaming it the 'Jobseeker's Allowance', to be paid in future for six months instead of twelve and linked to signing a 'jobseeker's agreement'. It was the first time entitlement to a weekly national insurance benefit to which people had contributed had been cut back. Invalidity benefit – the costs and numbers had soared to the point where 1.5 million people were claiming – was reined in by a tougher medical test which was expected to remove 200,000 claimants and prevent 55,000 new cases a year from claiming. The savings from the two measures were put at £2.5 billion over three years. These were significant sums and a significant change. Pensions aside, the cuts were amongst the biggest to individual benefits that the Conservatives had introduced in fifteen years, and were the first attacks on contributory benefits below pension age. Nonetheless, the £3.75 billion saving over a period when the total social security budget was expected to cost around £260 billion amounted to barely a 1.5 per cent reduction. Pension age for women was also equalised upwards to sixty-five over a ten-year period starting in the year 2010, a long anticipated move which would eventually save £3.5 billion a year. The Act which implemented that also introduced what were initially described as 'technical' changes to SERPS which on closer examination proved likely to once again halve its final cost in the mid-21st century. On maturity, it was to be worth only somewhere between a quarter and a third of its value when originally set up in 1975. In addition, from October 1995 those taking out new mortgages were effectively told they would need private insurance to cover their interest payments for the first nine months of unemployment. If this reflected Peter Lilley's stated aim of a 'sector by sector' review of social security, rather than a 'big bang' approach[50] it also plainly amounted to incremental rather than fundamental change to the welfare state, at least in the short term. In the longer term, and on his own figures, Lilley had lopped £14 billion a year off the cost of social security by the middle of the next century, chiefly by raising women's pensionable age and introducing the second big cut to SERPS. In the shorter term, however, his calculations also showed that by 1995 the measures he had taken were projected to have saved only £4 billion annually a year by the year 2000. The same December 1993 Budget which heralded most of these changes saved almost as much in the short term by continuing the progressive erosion of mortgage tax relief, part of the fiscal welfare state. From April 1995 it would be paid at only 15 per cent – less than the basic rate tax – with the likelihood that it would disappear by the year 2000.[51]

As the NHS and education appeared to emerge from the fundamental review unscathed, it was clear that rolling back the frontiers of the welfare state was no easier a task in the 1990s than it had been in the 1980s. Too many people had too much of a stake in it. The same old mixture of self-interest and altruism which had preserved the idea for fifty years was in play.[52] If it was to be rolled back, it would have to be by a process of erosion. That was by no means impossible. The review, as Portillo had pointed out, was a programme for a Parliament and beyond, a period over which incremental change could indeed produce a profound transformation of the welfare state's borders. But as the review continued the sense of national unease grew. Unemployment, while falling, remained high, fuelled by the large-scale disappearance of middle management and administrative jobs, the result of information technology and the government's own drive to market test as much of central and local government activity as possible. From talk a mere eighteen months before of the 'comfortable' but uncaring majority, the talk by 1994 was of the 'insecure' majority, fearful for their jobs and future.

Full employment suddenly soared back up the political agenda, not least because its costs were seen as a key factor in the perceived crisis of the welfare state. With at least £13.5 billion of the £50 billion deficit due to the jobless,[53] it seemed hardly surprising if the welfare state had cracked under the press of mass unemployment. For the first time in fifteen years, in politicians' rhetoric if not yet in their actions, full employment was again respectable. From 1987 on, Labour had dropped any overt commitment to the idea, Neil Kinnock in May 1990 having come close to dimissing it as 'a slogan'.[54] But first John Smith then other leading Labour figures restored it as a goal, at least in terms of the 1944 White Paper definition of 'high and stable' levels of employment. John Major, in words Margaret Thatcher could never have uttered, acknowledged that 'every Prime Minister wishes to achieve full employment'.[55] Clarke went further. Tackling it had to be 'the main pre-occupation of economic policy makers in the 1990s',[56] he declared, while the need to at least aim for full employment dominated the Labour leadership contest in the wake of John Smith's death in 1994. 'No one pretends [the goal] will be easy or could be accomplished overnight. But we should start now,' Tony Blair said shortly before becoming Labour leader.

In the speeches of both Conservative and Labour politicians a new emphasis emerged, if as yet only the most limited of new policies, in which the welfare state's task, not least through the benefit system, was seen as retraining people and helping them back into work, not merely supporting them out of it. Health and education remained core to the public's concept of the welfare state.[57] But on benefits, Tony Blair turned Labour thinking on its head by arguing that a big social security bill was 'a sign of failure, not a sign of success'. He wanted, he said, a system which provided 'a springboard to success and not a road to dependency'. It could almost have been Macmillan talking about the 'opportunity state'. Blair stole more Tory-sounding language, declaring the state should offer 'a hand up' not 'a hand out' and that Labour was 'not about bigger benefits but moving people from benefit to work'. Gordon Brown, the shadow Chancellor, began to explore new 'welfare-to-work benefits', ways of using the benefit system to subsidise wages, or to allow people more low-paid, part-time work, or to ease transitions into work, rather than merely insisting that people remain idle in order to be entitled to benefits. Much of this looked likely to require a minimum wage, but it was all a far cry from Labour's bitter opposition to Family Income Supplement in Keith Joseph's day.

Clarke moved in a similar direction. 'Workstart', a pilot scheme to help 1000 long-term unemployed back into jobs by offering employers a £60 subsidy to hire them, was announced in the December 1993 Budget, as were means-tested child-care allowances for families and the disabled. He was to go further in his 1994 Budget, announcing a baker's dozen of measures to help people back into work, including a pilot study which would pay a Family Credit-style benefit to people in low-paid work who did not have children. Portillo, now Secretary of State for Employment, accepted some of these with ill-disguised bad grace. He continued to warn rigorously against subsidised workers replacing unsubsidised jobs. The need was to 'build bridges out of dependency'[58] and help people into low-paid jobs, Clarke argued. Family Credit, once a laughing stock for its low take-up, rapidly came to support well over half a million workers, creating a new independence for those it helped into work but also a new form of dependency on benefits for those in work.[59]

While Labour, awaiting its Social Justice Commission, pondered how radical it could or should be on welfare provision, the Conservative splits over the future of the welfare state became almost as deep as its divide over Europe. Portillo emerged again to complain that over the past thirty years (twenty of them, though he did not mention the fact, years of Tory government) the safety net had become 'thicker, higher and wider',[60] a characterisation most would have had difficulty recognising as a description of the previous two decades. What was needed, Portillo said, was more self-reliance and personal responsibility, and greater penalties for 'feck-lessness'. Clarke, by contrast, acknowledged that the pace of change caused by technology, free trade and markets, 'has created fears and uncertainties in every walk of life'. His prescription was 'not only adequate state welfare provision but a whole range of other social policies'.[61] The manager in 'middle England' whose organisation was being 'de-layered' or 'down-sized', he later declared, '. . . will want to feel there is a high quality health and education system on which his family can depend. He will want to know that there is a modernised, affordable welfare system which will assist him to retrain and to find new employment.'[62]

When Labour's Social Justice Commission emerged, it proved to be no new Beveridge.[63] Its plethora of proposals included raising child benefit while taxing it for higher rate tax payers. It argued for subsuming the basic state pension into a new, earnings-linked income guarantee for the elderly. And it wanted a new form of graduate tax to cover a portion of tuition, as well as maintenance, costs. Where Beveridge had been entirely expansive, the commission had to mix retrenchment on past policies with its proposals for a welfare state relaunch. Its package effectively means-tested all pensioners, abandoned Labour's pledge to uprate the basic state pension in line with earnings, and canvassed ideas on funding higher education for which Jeff Rooker, the party's front bench spokesman on the subject, had been sacked a year before for airing.[64] Yet despite attacking these and other Labour shibboleths, the report failed to cause instant outrage in the party. Rather, there were signs that its recommendations, which included a call for an end to the 'plague' of long-term unemploy-ment and a set of 'benefit-into-work' proposals, might break up the ice-pack of Labour's thinking over the welfare state.

A new debate was beginning, or perhaps an old one was being renewed, as to whether Britain was really an individualist's society, in which the collective provision of the post-Beveridge era was something of an aberra-tion, or whether Thatcherism, with its desire, but its failure, fundamen-tally to shift the boundaries, was the exception. It was a debate about whether Britain and the Conservatives did still believe in more than a minimalist provision for the poor, with everyone else required or encour-aged to provide for themselves privately; one in which it looked as though

Labour would have to modify some old certainties if it was to have policies to match the needs of the twenty-first century.

It was a debate about whether the tide of elderly which had been rising steadily since the welfare state's foundation would finally overwhelm it, despite Britain being better placed in that regard than most of its competitors; and about whether in an increasingly global market something close to full employment could be restored, thus transforming the welfare state's finances. There was also the question of whether the electorate, deeply shaken by a tax increase equivalent to 7p in the £ to pay for the recession and by the Government's spending promises ahead of the 1992 election, would remain willing to pay the taxes needed to support the system, even though British taxation levels remained low by European standards.

Outside the immediate clash of party politics, interesting new alliances were forming. On both the British right and left there was fascination with the ideas of Amitai Etzioni, a Professor of Sociology at George Washington University and the guru of the American communitarian movement, who rejected the purely market driven approach to solving social issues advocated by Charles Murray for one, but still emphasised responsibilities every bit as much as rights. The Joseph Rowntree Foundation completed a massive inquiry into the income and wealth divide in Britain with a report calling for new 'benefit-at-work' and active labour market measures which was remarkable for being signed both by John Monks, the general secretary of the TUC and Howard Davies, director general of the Confederation of British Industry – two bodies barely able to talk to each other during the Thatcher years. Both were interested in a welfare state which invested in success, rather than paid for failure.

In the speeches of Clarke and Blair, the outlines were visible of a potential new settlement over the welfare state – its role modified, its boundaries and mechanisms fought over as furiously as they had been over the previous fifty years, but its purpose essentially the same. In the stance of Michael Portillo and his post-Thatcherite colleagues, a very different future was on offer.

TABLES

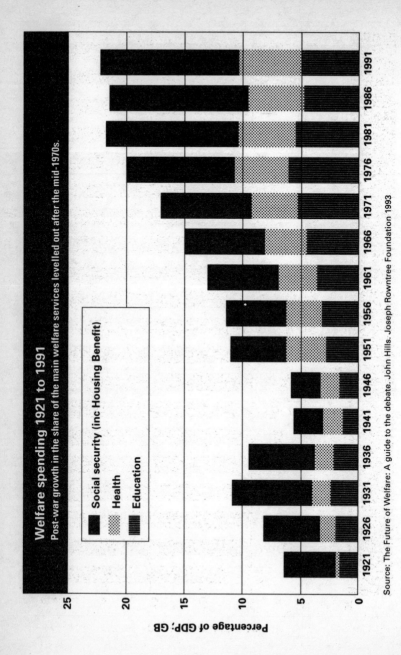

Welfare spending 1921 to 1991

Post-war growth in the share of the main welfare services levelled out after the mid-1970s.

Social security (inc Housing Benefit)

Health

Education

Percentage of GDP; GB

25

20

15

10

5

0

1921 1926 1931 1936 1941 1946 1951 1956 1961 1966 1971 1976 1981 1986 1991

Source: The Future of Welfare: A guide to the debate. John Hills. Joseph Rowntree Foundation 1993

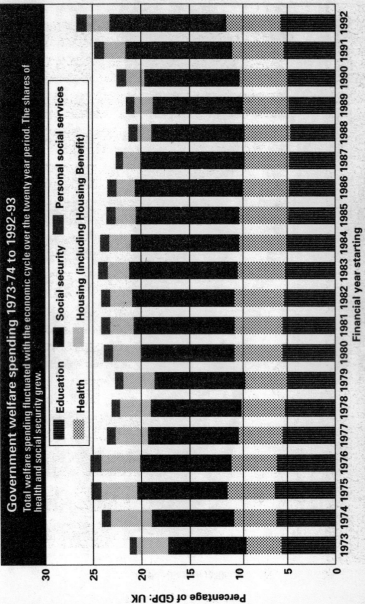

Government welfare spending 1973-74 to 1992-93

Total welfare spending fluctuated with the economic cycle over the twenty year period. The shares of health and social security grew.

Legend:
- Education
- Social security
- Personal social services
- Health
- Housing (including Housing Benefit)

Y-axis: Percentage of GDP: UK (0, 5, 10, 15, 20, 25, 30)

X-axis: Financial year starting
1973 1974 1975 1976 1977 1978 1979 1980 1981 1982 1983 1984 1985 1986 1987 1988 1989 1990 1991 1992

Source: The Future of Welfare: A guide to the debate. John Hills. Joseph Rowntree Foundation 1993

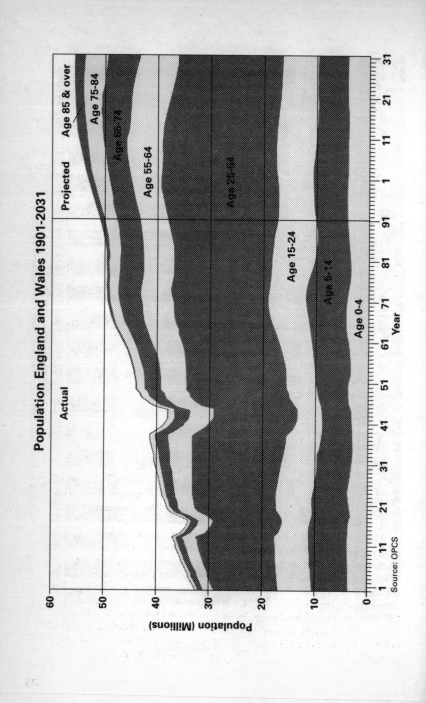

Population England and Wales 1901-2031

Actual

Projected

Age 85 & over

Age 75-84

Age 65-74

Age 55-64

Age 25-64

Age 15-24

Age 5-14

Age 0-4

Population (Millions)

Source: OPCS

Year

Notes

Introduction

1. Simon, *Education and the Social Order*, pp. 162–9; Charles Webster in Anne Oakley and Susan Williams, ed., *The Politics of the Welfare State*, UCL Press, 1994, pp. 54–75; Rodney Lowe, 'Resignation at the Treasury; The Social Services Committee and Failure to Reform the Welfare State, 1955–57', in *Journal of Social Policy*, vol.18, no.4, pp. 505–26. On student loans, *Hansard*, 8 May 1968, col.430.
2. José Harris, 'Enterprise and Welfare States', *Transactions of the Royal Historical Society*, 1990, vol.40, pp. 175–95.
3. Cairncross, *The British Economy since 1945*, p. 5.
4. Norman Chester, *The Nationalisation of British Industry 1945–51*, HMSO, 1975.
5. See Rodney Lowe, *The Welfare State in Britain Since 1945*, pp. 9–10; Hennessy, *Never Again*, p. 121: Gregg, *The Welfare State*, pp. 3–4.
6. Gregg, loc. cit. The 1955 definition was 'a polity so organised that every member of the community is assured of his due maintenance, with the most advantageous conditions possible for all'. By 1964 it was defined by its attributes: 'one having national health, insurance and other social services'.

7. Harris, *William Beveridge*, p. 448.
8. Interview with Sir Geoffrey Otton, 1 September 1993.

1 'Thank you, Sir William'

1. Harris, *William Beveridge*, p. 376. This whole chapter, and particularly the account of his early life, draws heavily on her subtle and lucid account of Beveridge's life and times.
2. Tom Wilson, *Beveridge and the Reform of Social Security – Then and Now* in *Government and Opposition*, LSE, vol.28, pp. 353–71.
3. Beveridge, *Power and Influence*, p. 9.
4. *Ibid.*, titles of Chapters I to III.
5. Quoted in Addison, *Churchill on the Home Front 1900–1955*, p. 51.
6. Derek Fraser, *The Evolution of the British Welfare State*, pp. 145–6. This is the single definitive text on the welfare state up to Beveridge.
7. Addison, op. cit., p. 62.
8. Harris, op. cit., pp. 1–2.
9. Calder, *The People's War* (all citations from Pimlico edn, 1992), p. 526. An outstanding account of life and politics between 1939 and 1945.
10. Quoted in Addison, *The Road to 1945*, p. 212. The matching book to Angus Calder's and every bit as good.
11. Harris, op. cit., p. 363.

12. *Ibid.*, p. 2.

13. Quoted *ibid.*, p. 1.

14. This and succeeding paragraphs are drawn from *ibid.*, p. 368f.

15. Morgan, *Labour People*, p. 150.

16. Harris, op. cit., p. 376.

17. *Ibid.*

18. *Ibid.*

19. Brian Abel-Smith, 'The Beveridge Report; Its origins and outcomes'. Proceedings of *50 Years After Beveridge*, University of York conference, September 1992, p. 9.

20. Beveridge, op. cit., p. 297.

21. Addison, op. cit., p. 169.

22. Quoted by Howard Glennerster and Martin Evans, 'Beveridge and his Assumptive worlds: The Incompatibilities of a Flawed Design', York Conference papers, vol.I, p. 17.

23. Unattributable interview.

24. Cmnd 6404, *Social Insurance and Allied Services; Report by Sir Wiliam Beveridge*, HMSO, 1942.

25. A considerable part of the paper is reproduced as an appendix in Fraser, op. cit., p. 265.

26. Beveridge, op. cit., p. 298.

27. Cmnd 6404, p. 2.

28. Harris, op. cit., p. 362.

29. Peter Baldwin, 'Beveridge in the Longue Durée', York Papers, vol. A, p. 37.

30. Harris, op. cit., p. 387.

31. Information from HMSO.

32. Addison, op. cit., p. 217.

33. Cmnd 6404, pp. 6-7.

34. *Ibid.*, p. 170.

35. *Ibid.*, p. 14.

36. R. J. Cootes. *The Making of the Welfare State*, p. 79.

37. Fritz Grunder, 'Beveridge meets Bismarck', York Papers, vol. I, p. 69.

38. Chapter title in *The Road to 1945*.

39. *Ibid.*, p. 17.

40. Christopher Wright, *The Welfare State*, Batsford, 1981, p. 52.

41. Fraser, op. cit., p. 166.

42. Calder, op. cit., p. 29.

43. Quoted in Fraser, op. cit., p. 166.

44. *Report of the Poor Law Commissioners* (1834), quoted *ibid.*, p. 237.

45. Fraser, op. cit., p. 169.

46. Priestley, *English Journey*, p. 294.

47. Fraser, op. cit., p. 180.

48. *Ibid.*, p. 183.

49. Correspondence, Sir George Godber, July 1994.

50. Cootes, op. cit., p. 54.

51. Fraser, op. cit., pp. 180, 262.

52. Priestley, op. cit., p. 390.

53. Calder, op. cit., p. 28.

54. Priestley, op. cit., pp. 372-3.

55. *Ibid.*, p. 296.

56. *Ibid.*, p. 384.

57. *Ibid.*, p. 375.

58. *Ibid.*, p. 378.

59. In that first September alone, one quarter to one third of the population moved; Calder, op. cit., p. 38.

60. Addison, op. cit., p. 130.

61. Titmuss, *Problems of Social Policy*, p. 182, quoted in Calder, op. cit., p. 35.

62. Wicks, *No Time to Wave Goodbye*, p. 87.

63. *Ibid.*, p. 90.

64. *Ibid.*, p. 89.

65. *Ibid.*, p. 91.

66. *Ibid.*, p. 88.

67. Butler, *The Art of the Possible*, p. 92.

68. Calder, op. cit., p. 223.

69. Nicholas Davenport, *Vested Interests or Common Pool*, Gollancz, 1942, quoted in Addison, op. cit., p. 130.

70. Titmuss, *Problems of Social Policy*, pp. 506-38, quoted in Hennessy, *Never Again, Britain 1945-51*, p. 50.

71. Hennessy, op. cit., p. 48.

72. Ibid., p. 52.

73. Calder, op. cit., p. 322.

74. Ibid., p. 292.

75. Ibid., p. 293.

76. Barnett, The Audit of War, p. 29.

77. William Temple, Citizen and Churchman, Eyre & Spottiswoode, 1941.

78. Picture Post, 29 October 1942.

79. Calder, op. cit., p. 292.

80. Quoted in Addison, op. cit., p. 126.

81. Calder, op. cit., p. 264.

82. Ibid., p. 260.

83. Addison, op. cit, p. 137.

84. Harris, op. cit., p. 414.

85. Quoted in Addison, op. cit., p. 214.

86. Ibid., p. 214.

87. This paragraph draws heavily on Harris's chapter 'The Making of the Beveredge Report' in op. cit., pp. 378–418.

88. Calder, op. cit., p. 527.

89. Addison, op. cit., pp. 215–16.

90. Harris, op. cit., p. 421.

91. Addison, op. cit., p. 216.

92. Ibid., p. 217.

93. Ibid.

94. Cmnd 6404, p. 171.

95. Calder, op. cit., p. 304.

96. Ibid., pp. 304–5.

97. Cmnd 6404, p. 172.

98. Harris, op. cit., p. 421.

2 From cradle to grave

1. Addison, The Road to 1945, p. 217.

2. The Times, 2 December 1942.

3. Addison, op. cit., pp. 217–18.

4. Ibid., p. 218.

5. Quoted in Hennessy, Never Again, p. 74.

6. Addison, op. cit., p. 220.

7. Harris, William Beveridge, p. 412.

8. Ibid., p. 423.

9. José Harris, 'Enterprise and Welfare States', Transactions of the Royal Historical Society, 1990, vol.40, p. 187.

10. Addison, Churchill on the Home Front, p. 366.

11. Harris, William Beveridge, p. 422.

12. The Times, 2 December 1941.

13. Addison, op. cit., p. 367.

14. Harris, op. cit., p. 425.

15. Donoughue and Jones, Herbert Morrison, pp. 314–15.

16. Ibid., p. 314.

17. Addison, op. cit., p. 365.

18. Hennessy, op. cit., p. 76.

19. Ibid., p. 76.

20. Calder, The People's War, p. 531.

21. Ibid., p. 533.

22. Hailsham, A Sparrow's Flight, p. 211.

23. Ibid., p. 216.

24. Ibid., p. 210.

25. Donoughue and Jones, op. cit., p. 314.

26. Calder, op. cit., p. 531; Hennessy, op. cit., pp. 76–7.

27. Addison, The Road to 1945, p. 225.

28. Ibid., p. 227.

29. Quoted in Barnett, The Audit of War, p. 31.

30. Addison, op. cit., p. 228.

31. Calder, op. cit., p. 532.

32. Abel-Smith, York Papers, vol.A, p. 15.

33. Harris, op. cit., p. 428.

34. Barnett, op. cit., p. 33.

35. Harris, op. cit., p. 435.

3 A very British revolution

1. Wilson, Beveridge and the Reform of Social Security in Government

and Opposition, LSE, vol.28, pp. 353-71.

2. Cmnd 6404, p. 15.

3. See e.g. Cmnd 6404, pp. 15, 170.

4. *Ibid.*, p. 7.

5. *Ibid.*, p. 14.

6. *Ibid.*, p. 77.

7. *Ibid.*, p. 85.

8. *Ibid.*, p. 87.

9. *Ibid.*

10. *Ibid.*

11. *Ibid.*, p. 86.

12. Donnison, *The Government of Housing*, p. 186.

13. Cmnd 6404, p. 84.

14. Glennerster and Evans (see ch.1, n.22), p. 27.

15. Cmnd 6404, p. 49.

16. Quoted in Glennerster and Evans, op. cit., p. 24.

17. Calder, *The People's War*, p. 312.

18. Cmnd 6404, p. 53.

19. *Ibid.*, p. 154.

20. *Ibid.*, p. 52.

21. Glennerster and Evans, op. cit., p. 25.

22. Cmnd 6404, p. 50.

23. *Ibid.*, p. 49.

24. *Ibid.*

25. Ruth Lister, 'She has other duties – women, citizenship and social security', York Papers, vol.5, pp. 15-25.

26. *Ibid.*, p. 16.

27. Calder, op. cit., p. 314.

28. Cmnd 6404, p. 7.

29. *Ibid.*, pp. 11-12.

30. Inland Revenue Statistics, 1992.

31. Cmnd 6404, p. 167.

32. *Ibid.*, p. 108.

33. *Ibid.*, p. 7.

34. *Ibid.*, p. 118.

35. Harris, op. cit., p. 2.

36. Cmnd 6404, p. 154.

37. *Ibid.*, p. 57.

38. *Ibid.*, p. 58.

39. Excellent accounts can be found in Hennessy, *Never Again*, Addison, *The Road to 1945*, Calder, *The People's War*.

40. Hailsham, *A Sparrow's Flight*, p. 209.

41. Quoted in Calder, op. cit., p. 569.

42. Horne, *Macmillan*, vol.I, p. 286.

43. Hailsham, op. cit., p. 216.

4 Butler – Education

1. Compiled from Butler, *The Art of the Possible*, p. 90 and Howard, *RAB*, pp. 109-10.

2. Howard, op. cit., pp. 113-14.

3. Barnard, *A History of English Education from 1760*, pp. 55-6, 69.

4. Cootes, *The Making of the Welfare State*, p. 20.

5. Fraser, *The Evolution of the British Welfare State.*, p. 76.

6. Maclure, *Educational Documents*, p. 4; Cootes, op. cit., p. 20.

7. W. E. Forster in the House of Commons, 18 February 1870, quoted in Maclure, op. cit., p. 99.

8. Fraser, op. cit., p. 72.

9. Maclure, op. cit., p. 100.

10. *Ibid.*, p. 103.

11. Judge, *Founders of the Welfare State*, p. 62.

12. Barnett, *The Audit of War*, p. 214.

13. Maclure, op. cit., pp. 85-6.

14. Quoted in Barnett, op. cit., p. 217.

15. *Ibid.*, p. 215.

16. Hennessy, *Never Again*, p. 149.

17. Quoted in *ibid.*, p. 151.

18. Barnard, op. cit., p. 199.

19. Judge, 'R. J. Morant' in Paul Barker, ed., *Founders of the Welfare State*, p. 61.

20. Quoted in Hennessy, op. cit., p. 153.

21. Maclure, op. cit., pp. 10-11,

from which much of this section is drawn.

22. Butler, op. cit., p. 91.

23. Simon, *Education and the Social Order*, p. 26.

24. Quoted *ibid.*, p. 24.

25. Hennessy, op. cit., p. 147.

26. Barnett, op. cit., p. 201.

27. *Ibid.*, p. 202.

28. *Ibid.*, p. 203.

29. Simon, op. cit., p. 30.

30. *Ibid.*, p. 30.

31. *Ibid.*, pp. 204–5.

32. Barnett, op. cit., p. 201.

33. Butler, op. cit., p. 92.

34. Hennessy, op. cit., p. 154.

35. Summarised in Maclure, op. cit., pp. 179–87.

36. Graves, *Goodbye to All That*, p. 37.

37. Quoted in Simon, op. cit., p. 39.

38. From Chuter Ede's diaries quoted in Howard, op. cit., p. 120.

39. *Ibid.*

40. *Ibid.*, p. 41.

41. *Ibid.*

42. *Ibid.*, pp. 119–20.

43. See Simon, op. cit., pp. 38–45.

44. Patricia Rowan, in 75th anniversary supplement to the *Times Educational Supplement*, 5 September 1985.

45. Simon, op. cit., p. 55.

46. *Ibid.*, p. 37.

47. *Ibid.*, p. 57.

48. Addison, *The Road to 1945*, p. 172.

49. Butler, op. cit., p 93.

50. Addison, op. cit., p. 172.

51. Howard, op. cit., p. 112.

52. Butler, op. cit., p. 98.

53. *Ibid.*

54. *Ibid.*, pp. 98–9; Howard, op. cit., p. 114.

55. Kevin Jeffereys, 'R. A. Butler, The Board of Education and the 1944 Education Act', in *History*, vol.69, 1984, pp. 415–31.

56. Quoted in Howard, op. cit., p. 115.

57. Butler, op. cit., p. 94.

58. *Ibid.*

59. *Ibid.*, pp. 94–5.

60. *Ibid.*, p. 95.

61. Barnett, op. cit., p. 280.

62. Butler, op. cit., p. 99.

63. *Ibid.*

64. *Ibid.*

65. *Ibid.*, p. 102.

66. Calder, op. cit., p. 485.

67. Howard, op. cit., p. 118.

68. Butler, op. cit., p. 102.

69. Jeffereys, op. cit., pp. 415–31.

70. Butler, op. cit., p. 103.

71. Howard, op. cit., p. 118.

72. Butler, op. cit., p. 101.

73. Howard, op. cit., p. 130.

74. Butler, op. cit., pp. 105–6.

75. *Ibid.*, p. 107.

76. Butler quoted in Hennessy, op. cit., p. 154.

77. Howard, op. cit., p. 129.

78. Butler, op. cit., p. 108.

79. Howard, op. cit., pp. 128–9.

80. *Ibid.*, p. 133.

81. Butler, op. cit., p. 120.

82. Howard, op. cit., p. 121.

83. Simon, op. cit., p. 64.

84. Butler, op. cit., p. 119.

85. Howard, op. cit., p. 121.

86. Butler, op. cit., p. 120.

87. Howard, op. cit., p. 122.

88. Roy Lowe, *Education in the Post-War Years*, p. 51.

89. Howard, op. cit., p. 122.

90. Norwood report quotations taken from Maclure, op. cit., pp. 201–4.

91. Quoted in Addison, *Now the War is Over*, pp. 146–7.

92. Maclure, op. cit., pp. 198–9.

93. Quoted in Simon, op. cit., p. 56.

94. *Ibid.*, p. 47n.

95. Butler, op. cit., p. 11; Addison, *The Road to 1945*, p. 238.
96. *Educational Reconstruction*, Cmnd 6458, HMSO, 1943.
97. Butler, op. cit., p. 117.
98. *Ibid.*, p. 116.
99. *Ibid.*, p. 122.
100. Howard, op. cit., p. 138.
101. Butler, op. cit., p. 120.
102. Hailsham, op. cit., pp. 217–21.
103. Howard, op. cit., p. 139.
104. Butler, op. cit., p. 122.

5 Butler's legacy

1. Butler, *The Art of the Possible*, p. 118. For a good summary, see Maclure, *Educational Documents*, pp. 222–5.
2. Howard, *RAB*, p. 127.
3. Education Act 1944, Section 1.
4. Butler, op. cit., p. 109.
5. Speech to North of England Conference, Rotherham, 9 January 1987.
6. Jefferys (see ch.4, n.55), p. 427; Howard, op. cit., p. 117.
7. Jefferys, op. cit., p. 422.
8. *Ibid.*, p. 427.
9. Butler, op. cit., p. 124.
10. I am grateful to Stuart Maclure for the following argument.
11. Maclure, op. cit., p. 223.
12. *Ibid.*, p. 283.
13. Barnett, *The Audit of War*, p. 285.
14. José Harris, 'Enterprise and Welfare States', *Transactions of the Royal Historical Society*, 1990, vol.40, p. 192.
15. Barnett, op.cit., p. 282.
16. *Ibid.*, pp. 201–2.
17. *Ibid.*, p. 291.
18. Simon, *Education and the Social Order*, p. 76.
19. Drawn from Maclure, op. cit., pp. 206–9.
20. Simon, op. cit., p. 145, n.44.
21. Jefferys, op. cit., p. 422.
22. *Ibid*, p. 428.
23. Barnett, op. cit., p. 302.
24. Jefferys, op. cit., p. 430.

6 Bevan – Health

1. Morgan, *Labour People*, pp. 204–5.
2. Quoted in Macmillan, *Tides of Fortune*, p. 65.
3. *Ibid.*, p. 49.
4. Grey-Turner and Sutherland, *History of the British Medical Association 1932–1981*, p. 3.
5. Foot, *Aneurin Bevan*, p. 102.
6. Calder, *The People's War*, pp. 538–9; Addison, *The Road to 1945*, p. 179.
7. Webster, *The Health Services Since the War*, pp. 3–4.
8. Whitehead, *National Health Success*, p. 19.
9. Klein, *The Politics of the NHS*, p. 4. There is a large and high-quality literature on the founding of the National Health Service, including Klein's examination of health service politics up to the 1980s, Charles Webster's lucid and weighty official history, *The Health Services since the War* (HMSO, 1988) which runs up to 1957 with Volume II still in preparation, John Pater's *The Making of the National Health Service* (King Edward's Hospital Fund for London, 1981), a study drawn from the official papers by a Department of Health civil servant closely involved in the founding period, Michael Foot's brilliantly partisan biography of Bevan, Harry Eckstein's *The English Health Service* (Harvard University

Press, 1958), and Frank Honigsbaum's *Health, Happiness and Security. The Creation of the National Health Service* (Routledge, 1989).

10. Whitehead, op. cit., p. 20.

11. Rivett, *Development of the London Hospital System*, p. 214.

12. *Ibid.*

13. *Ibid.*, pp. 223–5.

14. *Ibid.*, p. 341.

15. Tudor Hart, *A New Kind of Doctor*, pp. 2–3.

16. Webster, op. cit., p. 6.

17. Whitehead, op. cit., p. 20

18. Abel-Smith, *The National Health Service: The First Thirty Years*, p. 4.

19. Whitehead, op. cit., p. 8.

20. Webster, op. cit., p. 11.

21. Whitehead, op. cit., p. 10.

22. *Ibid.*, p. 12.

23. Foot, op. cit., p. 106.

24. Quoted in Klein, op. cit., p. 5.

25. Grey-Turner and Sutherland, op. cit., p. 32.

26. Quoted in Klein, op. cit., p. 8.

27. Grey-Turner and Sutherland, op. cit., pp. 36–8; Foot, op. cit., pp. 108–9.

28. Grey-Turner and Sutherland, op. cit., p. 40; Beveridge, Cmnd 6404, p. 160, para.431.

29. Calder, op. cit., p. 539.

30. Cmnd 6502, HMSO, 1944.

31. Klein, op. cit., p. 14.

32. *Ibid.*, p. 15.

33. Grey-Turner and Sutherland, op. cit., p. 42.

34. Quoted in Foot, op. cit., p. 111.

35. Pater, op. cit., p. 104.

36. Webster, ed., *Aneurin Bevan on the National Health Service*, p. 4.

37. *British Medical Journal*, ii, Supplement, 15 September 1945, p. 64.

38. Foot, op. cit., pp. 40, 119–20, 127.

39. *Ibid.*, p. 131.

40. *Ibid.*

41. Morgan, *Labour in Power 1945–51*, OUP Paperback, p. 153.

42. Foot, op. cit., p. 124.

43. Foot, op. cit., p. 132.

44. Webster, op. cit., p. 73.

45. All the credit for the detective work on what is probably Bevan's most famous aside goes to Charles Webster, who relates it in *Aneurin Bevan on the National Health Service*, pp. 219–22.

46. Abel-Smith, *The Hospitals 1800–1948*, pp. 486–7.

47. Foot, op. cit., p. 137.

48. Hennessy, *Never Again*, p. 139.

49. *Memorandum by the Minister of Health*, 'The Future of the Hospital Services', CP (45)205, 5 October 1945, PRO CAB 129/3, reproduced in Webster, op. cit., pp. 31–9.

50. *National Health Service: The Future of the Hospital Services. Memorandum by the Lord President of the Council*, CP (45) 227, 12 October 1945, CAB 129/3.

51. *National Health Service. The Hospital Services. Memorandum by the Minister of Health*, CP (45) 231, 16 October 1945, CAB 129/3.

52. Morgan, op. cit., p. 155; Pater, op. cit., p. 109.

53. Hennessy, op. cit., p. 140.

54. Foot, op. cit., p. 134.

55. Cmnd 6761, 1946.

56. Grey-Turner and Sutherland, op. cit., p. 51.

57. *Ibid.*, p. 56.

58. Foot, op. cit., p. 181.

59. *Ibid.*, p. 143.

60. *Ibid.*, p. 121; Pater, op. cit., p. 173.

61. Hill, 'Aneurin Bevan among the

doctors', *British Medical Journal*, 24 November 1973, pp. 468–9.

62. Morgan, op. cit., p. 157.

63. Pater, op. cit., p. 140.

64. Grey-Turner and Sutherland, op. cit., p. 50; Pater, op. cit., p. 106.

65. Foot, op. cit., p. 135.

66. Grey-Turner and Sutherland, op. cit., p. 56.

67. *Ibid.*, p. 60.

68. *Ibid.*, p. 75.

69. Foot, op. cit., p. 156.

70. *Ibid.*, p. 144.

71. *Ibid.*, p. 158.

72. See note 9, above.

73. Grey-Turner and Sutherland, op. cit., p. 62.

74. Foot, op. cit., p. 168.

75. *Ibid.*, p. 172.

76. Grey-Turner and Sutherland, op. cit., p. 63.

77. *Ibid.*, p. 64.

78. Foot, op. cit., p. 193.

79. Correspondence with Sir George Godber, July 1994.

80. Webster, op. cit., p. 116.

81. Foot, op. cit., p. 201; Grey-Turner and Sutherland, op. cit., p. 69.

82. Webster, op. cit., pp. 119–20.

83. Grey-Turner and Sutherland, op. cit., p. 66.

84. *Ibid.*, p. 70.

85. *Ibid.*, p. 65.

86. Foot, op. cit., p. 208.

87. Grey-Turner and Sutherland, op. cit., p. 72.

88. *Ibid.*, p. 73.

89. Webster, op. cit., p. 127.

7 'With a song in my heart' – Health and Social Security

1. Raison, *Tories and the Welfare State*, p. 18.

2. Foot, *Aneurin Bevan*, pp. 60ff.

3. CP (45) 227, CAB 129/3, Morrison's 12 October 1945 memorandum; Pater, *The Making of the National Health Service*, p. 184.

4. Correspondence with Sir George Godber, July 1994.

5. Pater, op. cit., p. 184.

6. Quoted in Foot, op. cit., p. 157.

7. The amendment read: 'That this house, while welcoming a comprehensive health service, declines to give a Third Reading to a Bill which discourages voluntary effort and association; mutilates the structure of local government; dangerously increases ministerial power and patronage; appropriates trust funds and benefactions in contempt of the wishes of donors and subscribers; and undermines the freedom and independence of the medical profession to the detriment of the nation.'

8. Raison, op. cit., p. 18.

9. *Independent*, 5 July 1988.

10. Cootes, *The Making of the Welfare State*, p. 106.

11. Interview, June 1993.

12. 'Celebrating the Birth of Health Care for All', *Independent*, 5 July 1988.

13. Webster, *Health Services Since the War*, p. 145.

14. Foot, op. cit., p. 211.

15. Webster, *Aneurin Bevan on the National Health Service*, op. cit., p. 21.

16. Beveridge, *Full Employment in a Free Society*., pp. 259–74.

17. *Hansard*, 22 March 1951; *Problems of Unemployment and Inflation*, UN Department of Economic Affairs, 1951, p. 80.

18. Hennessy, *Never Again*, p. 277.

19. Jay, *Change Fortune*, p. 249.

20. Morgan, *Labour in Power*, p. 170.

21. Griffiths, *Pages from Memory*, pp. 70, 79, 80.

22. *Ibid.*, p. 81.

23. Foot, op. cit., p. 138.

24. Morgan, op. cit., pp. 142–51.

25. Griffiths, op. cit., p. 81.

26. *Ibid.*, p. 83.

27. *Ibid.*, p. 84.

28. *Ibid.*, p. 86.

29. Brian Abel-Smith, 'The Beveridge Report: Its origins and outcomes', York Papers, vol.A, p. 15.

30. Griffiths, op. cit., p. 87.

31. Abel-Smith, op. cit., p. 14.

32. *Hansard*, 6 February 1946, col.1742.

33. Griffiths, op. cit., p. 85.

34. Abel-Smith, op. cit., p. 16.

35. Griffiths, op. cit., p. 86.

36. Abel-Smith, loc. cit.

37. Deacon and Bradshaw, *Reserved for the Poor: The Means Test in British Social Policy*, pp. 30, 49.

38. Rhodes, *Setting up a New Government Department*, from which much of these paragraphs is drawn.

8 'The Tremendous Tory' – Housing

1. Donnison and Ungerson, *Housing Policy*, p. 141.

2. Nuttgens, *The Home Front*, p. 67.

3. Calder, *The People's War*, p. 563.

4. *Ibid.*, p. 563.

5. Foot, *Aneurin Bevan*, p. 62.

6. Donnison and Ungerson, loc. cit.

7. Ministry of Reconstruction, *Housing*, Cmnd 6609, HMSO, 1945.

8. Donnison and Ungerson, loc. cit.

9. Donnison, *Housing Policy since the War*, p. 11.

10. Calder, op. cit., p. 314.

11. Hennessy, *Never Again*, p. 169; Calder, op. cit., p. 579.

12. Foot, op, cit., p. 63.

13. Morgan, *Labour in Power*, p. 163; Hennessy, op. cit., pp. 169–70.

14. *Picture Post*, 28 September 1946.

15. Morgan, op. cit., p. 163.

16. Foot, op. cit., pp. 127–8.

17. Hennessy, op. cit., p. 171; Foot, op. cit., p. 67; Nuttgens, op. cit., p. 67.

18. Donnison, op. cit., p. 10.

19. Nuttgens, op. cit., p. 58; and figures from Donnison, *The Government of Housing*, p. 186, table.

20. Morgan, op. cit., pp. 165–6.

21. Foot, op. cit., p. 76.

22. *Ibid.*, p. 63.

23. Jenkins, *The Forties*, p. 63.

24. Foot, op. cit., p. 84.

25. Hennessy, op. cit., p. 170.

26. Figures for Britain, drawn from official housing returns, Morgan, op. cit., p. 167; Foot, op. cit., p. 86.

27. Foot, op. cit., p. 82.

28. *Ibid.*, p. 78.

29. *Ibid.*, pp. 82, 78.

30. *Ibid.*, p. 80.

31. Nuttgens, op. cit., p. 38.

32. Peter Hall, 'Urban Development and Urban Policy; Where Have We Come From?', *Proceedings of the Royal Society of Art*, July 1993, pp. 511–12.

33. Hennessy, op. cit., p. 172.

34. Harris, *William Beveridge*, pp. 453–4.

35. Hennessy, op. cit., p. 173.

36. *Ibid.*, p. 305.

37. Foot, op. cit., p. 95.

38. Morgan, op. cit., p. 167.

39. Foot, op. cit., p. 96.

40. *Report of the Annual Conference of the Labour Party, Blackpool, 1949*, pp. 217–8.

9 *The Final Foundations*

1. Vernon, *Ellen Wilkinson*, pp. 2, 156.
2. Simon, *Education and the Social Order*, p. 89.
3. *Ibid.*
4. *Ibid.*, p. 97; Roy Lowe, *Education in the Post-War Years*, p. 9.
5. Hennessy, *Never Again*, p. 160; Simon, op. cit., p. 100.
6. Lowe, op. cit., p. 28.
7. Simon, op. cit., pp. 98-9.
8. *Ibid.*, p. 100.
9. Hennessy, op. cit., pp. 161-2; Simon, op. cit., pp. 99-100.
10. Simon, op. cit., p. 144, n.30.
11. Vernon, op. cit., p. 233.
12. See Simon, op. cit., pp. 88-143; Caroline Benn, 'Comprehensive School Reform and the 1945 Labour Government', *History Workshop Journal* 10, Autumn 1980, pp. 197-204.
13. Vernon, op. cit., p. 1.
14. *Ibid.*, pp. 6-7.
15. *Ibid.*, pp. 217-22.
16. Quoted in Simon, op. cit., p. 105.
17. Lowe, op. cit., p. 39.
18. Vernon, op. cit., pp. 222-3.
19. Simon, op. cit., p. 112.
20. Quoted in Vernon, op. cit., p. 219.
21. Dent, *Growth in English Education*, 1946-52, p. 79, quoted in Hennessy, op. cit., p. 158.
22. Simon, op. cit., pp. 110, 130; Hennessy, op. cit., p. 158.
23. Simon, op. cit., p. 103.
24. *Ibid.*, p. 139.
25. *Ibid.*, pp. 126-7.
26. Morgan, *Labour in Power*, p. 174.
27. Quoted in Lowe, op. cit., p. 48.
28. *Ibid.*, p. 22.
29. *Ibid.*, p. 40.
30. Maclure, *Educational Documents*, pp. 230-2.
31. Lowe, op.cit., p. 67.
32. Simon, op. cit., p. 92.
33. Maclure, op. cit., p. 232.
34. Simon, op. cit., p. 93.
35. Carswell, *Government and the Universities in Britain*, pp. 14, 18; Lowe, op. cit., p. 60.
36. Hennessy, op. cit., p. 161; Maclure, op. cit., p. 231; Simon, op. cit., p. 597, table.
37. Lowe, op. cit., p. 61.
38. Morgan, op. cit., pp. 177, 179.
39. Simon, op. cit., p. 143.
40. Lowe, op. cit., p. 34.
41. *Ibid.*, p. 33.
42. Webster, op. cit., p. 135.
43. Foot, op. cit., pp. 293-6. And Lord Morrison of Lambeth, *Herbert Morrison: An Autobiography*, Odhams, 1960, p. 267.
44. Morgan, op. cit., p. 442.
45. Resignation letter to Attlee quoted in Foot, op. cit., p. 332.
46. Macmillan, *Tides of Fortune*, p. 378.
47. Webster, *The Health Services Since the War*, p. 173.
48. Quoted in Morgan, op. cit., p. 454.
49. Hennessy, op. cit., p. 417.

10 *Conservatives, Consensus and the New Jerusalem*

1. Rodney Lowe, *The Welfare State in Britain since 1945*, p. 10.
2. Webster, *The Health Services Since the War*, pp. 71-5.
3. Minutes of the Special Representative Meeting of 3 and 4 May 1945.
4. Quoted in Foot, *Aneurin Bevan*, p. 218.
5. *Ibid.*, p. 191.

6. Quoted by Attlee; see *Report of the 59th Annual Conference of the Labour Party 1951*, p. 87.

7. Butler, *The Art of the Possible*, p. 126.

8. James, *Anthony Eden*, p. 326; Macmillan, *Tides of Fortune*, pp. 287–8.

9. Butler, op. cit., p. 129.

10. *Ibid.*, p. 130.

11. *Ibid.*, p. 132.

12. *Ibid.*, p. 133.

13. Howard, *RAB.*, p. 155.

14. Butler, op. cit., p. 134.

15. Macmillan, op. cit., p. 306.

16. Butler, op. cit., pp. 146–7.

17. Quoted in *ibid.*, p. 146.

18. *Ibid.*, pp. 146–7.

19. Howard, op. cit., p. 156.

20. *Ibid.*; Butler, op. cit., p. 148; Macmillan, op. cit., p. 303.

21. James, op. cit., p. 328.

22. *The Right Road for Britain*, 1949, Conservative Party Archive, Bodleian Library, Oxford.

23. *Ibid.*

24. Butler, op. cit., p. 155; Howard, op. cit., p. 172.

25. Butler, loc. cit.

26. Morgan, *The People's Peace*, pp. 120–1.

27. Butler, op. cit., pp. 158–60.

28. For a good analysis of competing political theories of the welfare state, see Rodney Lowe, op. cit., pp. 9–38.

29. See Peter Hennessy and Arthur Seldon, eds., *Ruling Performance*, Blackwell, Oxford, 1987, pp. 310–11.

30. A. H. Halsey, 'A Sociologist's View of Thatcherism', in Skidelsky, ed., *Thatcherism*, p. 186.

31. Marwick, *British Society Since 1945*, p. 75.

32. Extrapolated from *Social Trends 10*, HMSO, 1980.

11 'You've never had it so good' – Conservatives 1951–64

1. *Economist*, 13 February 1954.

2. Butler, *The Art of the Possible*, p. 160.

3. Morgan, *The People's Peace*, p. 175.

4. Macmillan, *Tides of Fortune*, p. 376.

5. Horne, *Macmillan*, p. 332.

6. Macmillan, op. cit., p. 399.

7. *Ibid.*, p. 383; Butler, op. cit., p. 157.

8. Macmillan, op. cit., p. 406.

9. *Ibid.*, p. 375.

10. *Ibid.*

11. *Ibid.*, pp. 396–400.

12. Diary entry quoted in Horne, op. cit., p. 336.

13. Macmillan, op. cit., p. 412.

14. *Ibid.*, p. 404.

15. Horne, op. cit., p. 338.

16. Macmillan, op. cit., p. 406.

17. *Ibid.*, pp. 401, 430.

18. *Ibid.*, pp. 374–8.

19. *Ibid.*, p. 403.

20. Donnison and Ungerson, *Housing Policy*, p. 151.

21. Macmillan, op. cit., p. 418.

22. Horne, op. cit., p. 337.

23. *Ibid.*

24. Donnison and Ungerson, op. cit., pp. 147–8.

25. Macmillan, op. cit., p. 417.

26. *Ibid.*, p. 444.

27. *Ibid.*

28. Department of Environment, *Departmental Report 1994*, HMSO, 1994, p. 85.

29. Macmillan, op. cit., p. 452.

30. *Ibid.*, p. 457.

31. *Report of the 55th Labour Party Conference*, Blackpool, 1956, p. 98.

32. *Ibid.*, pp. 98–100.

33. *Hansard*, 17 November 1955,

quoted in Raison, *Tories and the Welfare State*, pp. 40–1.

34. Nuttgens, *The Home Front*, p. 67.

35. *Ibid.*, p. 68.

36. Glendinning and Muthesius, *Tower Block*, p. 251.

37. Hackney, *The Good, the Bad and the Ugly*, pp. 7–8.

38. Interview with Terry Coleman, *Guardian*, 12 November 1973.

39. Halcrow, *Keith Joseph*, p. 31.

40. Quoted in Nuttgens, op. cit., p. 82.

41. Hackney, op. cit., p. 17.

42. Nuttgens, op. cit., p. 93.

43. Glendinning and Muthesius, op. cit., p. 321; *Guardian*, 24 September 1977, 7 January 1978.

44. Hackney, op. cit., p. 42.

45. Nuttgens, op. cit.,, p. 69.

46. *Ibid.*, p. 86.

47. Interview, 2 August 1993.

48. Banting, *Poverty, Politics and Policy*, p. 14.

49. Figures from National Income White Papers quoted in Conservative Campaign Guide 1959, p. 219.

50. Macmillan, op. cit., p. 445.

51. Banting, op. cit., p. 18; G. R. Mitchison, Labour MP for Kettering, *Hansard*, Standing Committee A, 19 February 1957; Marcus Lipton, MP for Brixton, *Hansard*, 6 November 1957.

52. Banting, op. cit., p. 17.

53. *Manchester Guardian*, 1 December 1958.

54. Banting, op. cit., pp. 19–22.

55. *Sunday Times*, 7 July 1963.

56. *Ibid.*; *Observer*, 21 July 1963.

57. *Report of the Committee on Housing in Greater London* (the Milner Holland report), Cmnd 2605, HMSO, 1965, p. 252.

58. *The Times*, 29 August 1963, quoted in Banting, op. cit., p. 23.

59. *Independent*, 10 May 1988.

60. Banting, op. cit., p 27.

61. Macmillan, op. cit., p. 460.

62. Crossman, *Diaries*, vol.I, p. 24.

63. Quoted in Banting, op. cit., p. 36.

64. *Hansard*, 28 November 1963.

65. Deacon and Bradshaw, *Reserved for the Poor*, p. 99.

66. *Ibid.*, pp. 98, 100.

67. Lynes, *Social Security and Poverty in the United Kingdom*, pp. 98, 101.

68. Deacon and Bradshaw, op. cit., p. 100.

69. Titmuss, 'Pensions and Population Change', 1955 lecture in *Essays on the Welfare State*, p. 73.

70. Jay, *Change Fortune*, pp. 250–1.

71. Crossman, *Backbench Diaries*, p. 584.

72. Fabian Tract 303, p. 4, quoted in Ellis, *Pensions in Britain 1955–75*.

73. Ellis, op. cit., p. 10.

74. *Ibid.*, p. 11.

75. Cmnd 538, HMSO, 1958.

76. Interview, 28 November 1993. See also John Boyd-Carpenter, *Way of Life*, Sidgwick & Jackson, pp. 134–6.

77. Rodney Lowe, 'Resignation at the Treasury', *Journal of Social Policy*, 18, 4, pp. 505–26.

78. Simon, *Education and the Social Order*, pp. 163–4.

79. *Ibid.*, p. 165.

80. Fred Blackburn, *George Tomlinson*, 1954, p. 202.

81. *Economist*, 21 March 1953.

82. Simon, op, cit., p. 581, table.

83. *Ibid.*, p. 597, table.

84. Quoted in *ibid.*, p. 180.

85. Kogan, *The Politics of Education*, p. 20; Gordon, Aldrich and Dean, *Education and Policy in the Twentieth Century*, p. 71.

86. Chapter title in Simon, op. cit.

87. Rodney Lowe, *The Welfare State*

Since 1945, p. 206; Simon, op. cit., p. 214.

88. Speech in Bradford in January 1956, quoted in introduction to the White Paper *Technical Education*, Cmnd 9703, HMSO, 1956.

89. Roy Lowe, *Education in the Post-War Years*, p. 75.

90. *Ibid.*, p. 152.

91. *Ibid.*

92. *Ibid.*, p. 161.

93. Carswell, *Government and the Universities in Britain*, p. 14.

94. *Ibid.*, p. 34.

95. *Ibid.*, p. 12.

96. Including the first report from the National Advisory Council on Education for Industry and Commerce (NACEIC), 1950; the White Paper on *Higher Technological Education 1951*; the 1952 NACEIC report, a *Memorandum on Higher Education* from a Parliamentary and Scientific Committee in 1954 which calculated there was a 15,000 a year shortfall in qualified engineers, to another NACEIC report in 1955.

97. Aston, Battersea, Bradford, Bristol, Brunel, Cardiff, Chelsea, Loughborough, Northampton, Salford. Bristol and Battersea later became the Universities of Bath and Surrey; Northampton College became City University; Cardiff became UWIST.

98. Carswell, op. cit., pp. 20–2.

99. Senker, *Industrial Training in a Cold Climate*, p.vii.

100. *Ibid.*, pp. 27–8.

101. Report of the Labour Party Annual Conference, Scarborough 1963, Harold Wilson, pp. 132–40, 141.

102. Cmnd 2154, p. 8.

103. *Grants to Students*, Cmnd 1051, HMSO, 1960.

104. Carswell, op. cit., pp. 23–4.

105. *Ibid.*, p. 41; Robbins, op. cit., pp. 209–12.

106. Eckstein, *Pressure Group Politics*, p. 55.

107. Fisher, *Iain Macleod*, p. 86.

108. Webster, *Health Services since the War*, p. 189.

109. Interview, 21 June 1993.

110. Royal Commission on the National Health Service, Cmnd 7615, 1979, p. 436.

111. Grey-Turner and Sutherland, *History of the British Medical Association*, pp. 108–9; Webster, op. cit., pp. 197–9.

112. Ronald Bedford, profile of Derek Stevenson, *General Practitioner*, 9 July 1976.

113. Webster, op. cit., p. 198.

114. Grey-Turner and Sutherland, op. cit., p. 109.

115. Webster, op. cit., p. 204.

116. Shepherd, *Iain Macleod*, p. 85.

117. Cmnd 9663, *Report of the Committee of Enquiry into the Cost of the National Health Service*, p. 1.

118. Webster, op. cit., p. 207.

119. Abel-Smith and Titmuss, *The Cost of the National Health Service in England and Wales*, p. 60. The key findings of the study are in the Guillebaud report, op. cit., and are summarised in Webster, op. cit., pp. 204–11.

120. Cmnd 9663, op. cit., para.721.

121. Webster, op. cit., p. 210.

122. Correspondence, 15 June 1994.

123. Cmnd 9663, para.98.

124. Webster, op. cit., pp. 213, 215.

125. Roth, *Enoch Powell*, p. 233.

126. *Ibid.*, p. 234.

127. Report on the Control of Public Expenditure (The Plowden Report), Cmnd 1432, HMSO, 1961.

128. Klein, op. cit., p. 66. Bevan's phrase was 'generalise the best', *Hansard*, 30 April 1946, col.45.

129. Cmnd 1604, HMSO, 1962.
130. Webster, *Conservatives and Consensus*, p. 67.
131. Cmnd 7615, p. 436.
132. *Daily Herald*, 2 February 1961, quoted in Webster op. cit., p. 72.
133. *A Hospital Plan for England and Wales*, Cmnd 1604, 1962, pp. 1–2, 13.
134. *Daily Telegraph*, 9 February 1955.
135. Interview, August 1993.
136. *Ibid.*
137. *Hansard*, 19 February 1954, col. 2293.
138. Webster, *Health Services Since the War*, pp. 329–30.
139. Quoted in Murphy, *After the Asylums*, pp. 52–3.
140. Jones, *Asylums and After*, p. 149.
141. Cmnd 169, HMSO, 1957.
142. Quoted in Jones, op. cit., p. 155.
143. See Ministry of Health Circular HM (59) 46 and Jones, op. cit., pp. 154–8.
144. Murphy, op. cit., pp. 58–9.
145. Jones, op. cit., pp. 162–4.
146. Titmuss, *Commitment to Welfare*, pp. 104–9.

12 *Hope springs eternal: Labour 1964–70*

1. Craig, *British General Election Manifestos 1959–87*, p. 43.
2. Morgan, *The People's Peace*, OUP Paperback, 1992, p. 156.
3. Carswell, *Government and the Universities in Britain*, p. 66.
4. Dalyell, *Dick Crossman*, p. 82.
5. Quoted in Howard, *Crossman*, p. 266.
6. Interview, September 1993.
7. 'I was deputy shadow on health to Edith Summerskill. I think it was at Nye Bevan's instigation, I think he suggested it to Gaitskell, saying to me: "For the moment it will be deputy, but don't worry about Edith, she'll be kicked upstairs soon" – and she was.' Interview, 21 September 1993.
8. *British Medical Journal*, Supplement, 1958, 1, p. 27.
9. Ann Cartwright, *Patients and their Doctors; A Study of General Practice*, Routledge & Kegan Paul, 1967, p. 58, quoted in Tudor Hart, *A New Kind of Doctor*, p. 85.
10. Cartwright, op. cit., pp. 41–2.
11. J. S. Collings, 'General Practice in England Today', *The Lancet*, 1950, i, pp. 555–85.
12. Interview, 21 June 1993.
13. Interview, 21 July 1993.
14. Quoted in Gordon Macpherson, 'Reviving the fortunes of general practice: James Cameron and Kenneth Robinson', *British Medical Journal*, 5 July 1982, pp. 26–9.
15. Tudor Hart, op. cit., p. 91.
16. Interview, Marks.
17. Macpherson, *BMJ*, loc. cit., p. 26.
18. Interview with Kenneth Robinson.
19. Macpherson, *BMJ*, loc. cit.
20. Interview, 21 September 1993.
21. Ronald Butt, *The Times*, 6 May 1971.
22. Interview.
23. Macpherson, *BMJ*, loc. cit.
24. Robinson, interview.
25. Interview.
26. Interview, 23 July 1993.
27. Grey-Turner and Sutherland, *History of the British Medical Association*, p. 154.
28. Macpherson, *BMJ*, loc. cit., p. 27.
29. *Ibid.*
30. Tudor Hart, op. cit., p. 85.
31. Interview.
32. Interview.

33. British Medical Association, *Health Services Financing*, p.xvi.

34. Interview.

35. Interview. Expectant and nursing mothers were also exempted. Total exemptions halved the £50m that would otherwise have been raised from the 2s. 6d. (12.5p) charge; Wilson, *The Labour Government 1964–70*, p. 614.

36. *Daily Telegraph*, 25 January 1968.

37. Wilson, op. cit., p. 56

38. Deacon and Bradshaw, *Reserved for the Poor*, pp. 103–4.

39. *Ibid.*, p. 105.

40. Lapping, *The Labour Government 1964–70*, p. 146.

41. Houghton, *Paying for Social Services*, p. 12.

42. *Ibid.*

43. Wilson, op. cit., p. 281.

44. Crossman, *Diaries*, 14 December 1965.

45. Wilson, op. cit., p. 282.

46. Lapping, op. cit., p. 152.

47. Lynes, *Social Security and Poverty in the United Kingdom*, p. 12.

48. Labour Manifesto, quoted in Craig, op. cit., p. 53.

49. Craig, op. cit., p. 32.

50. Lapping, loc. cit.

51. Watkin, *Documents on Health and Social Services*, p. 448.

52. Cmnd 3703, *Report of the Committee on Personal and Allied Social Services*, HMSO, 1968.

53. Howard, op. cit., p. 267.

54. *Listener*, 15 March 1973, pp. 335–8.

55. Correspondence from David Donnison, 10 October 1994.

56. Banting, *Poverty, Politics and Policy*, p. 27.

57. Howard, op. cit., p 274

58. Craig, op. cit., p. 87.

59. *Ibid.*, pp. 274–5.

60. *Ibid.*, p. 76.

61. *The Housing Programme 1965–70*, Cmnd 2838, HMSO, 1965.

62. Quoted in Maxwell Hutchinson, *The Prince of Wales: Right or Wrong?*, Faber, 1989, p. 69.

63. Nuttgens, *The Home Front*, p. 85.

64. Hutchinson, op. cit., p. 93.

65. Nuttgens, op. cit., p. 85; *Guardian*, 16 August 1979.

66. John Burnett, *A Social History of Housing, 1815–1985*, p. 302.

67. Quoted in Burnett, op. cit., p. 302.

68. Lapping, op. cit., p. 170.

69. *Homes for Today and Tomorrow* (The Parker Morris Report), HMSO, 1961, p. 7.

70. Malpass and Murie, *Housing Policy and Practice*, p. 81.

71. Hutchinson, op. cit., p. 68.

72. Skelmersdale (1961), Telford (1963), Redditch, Runcorn and Washington (1964), Milton Keynes and Peterborough (1967), Northampton and Warrington (1968), and Central Lancashire (1970).

73. Donnison and Ungerson, *Housing Policy*, pp. 155–6.

74. Simon, *Education and the Social Order*, p. 176.

75. *Early Leaving: Report of the Central Advisory Council for Education (England)*, HMSO, 1954; report of the same, entitled *15 to 18* (The Crowther Report), HMSO, 1959; report of the Minister of Education's Central Advisory Council entitled *Half our Future* (The Newsom Report), HMSO, 1963.

76. Data from *Early Leaving* quoted in Judge, *A Generation of Schooling*, p. 41.

77. Simon, *Education and the Social Order*, p. 177.

78. Alfred Yates and D. A. Pidgeon,

Admission to Grammar Schools,
Newnes, for National Foundation for
Educational Research, 1957.
79. Pedley, *The Comprehensive
School,* p. 15.
80. Simon, op. cit., p 185.
81. See Denis Marsden, *Education
for Democracy,* Penguin, 1970,
pp. 140–2.
82. Kogan, *The Politics of Education,*
pp. 19–20.
83. *Ibid.,* p. 56.
84. *Ibid.,* p. 57.
85. Quoted in Simon, op. cit., p. 273.
86. *Ibid.,* p. 78.
87. Kogan, op. cit., p. 67.
88. Maclure, *Educational
Documents,* p. 279
89. Kogan, op. cit., p. 18.
90. *Ibid.*
91. *Ibid.,* p. 91.
92. Susan Crosland, *Tony Crosland,*
p. 144.
93. *Ibid.*
94. Kogan, op. cit., p. 191.
95. Simon, op. cit., p. 281.
96. Conservative Party Campaign
Guide Supplement, 1964, p. 129;
Ben Pimlott, *Harold Wilson,*
p. 512.
97. 'Tony was never certain that
Wilson had a great interest in
equality,' Susan Crosland, op. cit.,
p. 169; 'Every really radical solution
makes Harold shiver, especially in the
educational field,' Crossman, *Diaries,*
28 November 1968.
98. Judge, op. cit., p. 68.
99. Susan Crosland, op. cit., p. 146.
100. Circular 10/65 is reproduced in
Maclure, op. cit., p. 301.
101. *Children and their Primary
Schools, A report of the Central
Advisory Council for Education
(England),* HMSO, 1967.
102. Carswell, *Government and the
Universities in Britain,* p. 67.

103. Kogan, op. cit., p. 193.
104. *Ibid.*
105. Quoted in Simon, op. cit.,
p. 251.
106. Quoted in Gordon, Aldrich and
Dean, *Education and Policy in
England in the Twentieth Century,*
p. 240.
107. Carswell, op. cit., p. 74.
108. Susan Crosland, op. cit., p. 159.
109. Lapping, op. cit., p. 179.

13 *The dawn of doubt: Labour and
Conservatives 1949–70*

1. Conservative Political Centre, *The
Right Road for Britain,* p. 10.
2. Conservative Political Centre, *One
Nation,* p. 9.
3. Powell, 'Conservatives and the
Social Services', *Political Quarterly,*
1953, vol.24, p. 157.
4. Conservative Political Centre,
Social Services: Needs and Means.
5. For a history of vouchers see
Harris and Seldon, *Over-ruled on
Welfare.*
6. *Ibid.,* p. 61.
7. *Ibid.,* and R. G. West, *Education
and the State.*
8. Conservative Political Centre, *The
Future of the Welfare State,* p. 8.
9. *Ibid.,* p. 14.
10. Howe, 'Reform of the Social
Services: Conservatism in the
post-Welfare State', in *Principles in
Practice,* p. 61.
11. *Report of the 58th Annual
Conference of the Labour Party,
Blackpool, 1959,* p. 84.
12. Banting, *Poverty, Politics and
Policy,* pp. 69–70.
13. Abel-Smith, 'Whose Welfare
State?', in N. Mackenzie, ed.,
Conviction, McGibbon & Kee, 1958,
p. 69.

14. Abel-Smith and Townsend, *The Poor and the Poorest*.

15. Banting, op. cit., p. 68.

16. Peter Marris, *Widows and their Families*, Routledge & Kegan Paul, 1958; Virginia Wimperis, *The Unmarried Mother and her Child*, Allen & Unwin, 1960; Harriett Wilson, *Delinquency and Child Neglect*, Allen & Unwin, 1962; Dorothy Cole and J. Utting, *The Economic Circumstances of Old People*, Codicote Press, Welwyn, 1962. I am grateful to Dr Harriett Wilson for this list of references.

17. Personal communication.

18. Interview with Frank Field, 31 March 1993.

19. Field, *Poverty and Politics*, p. 24.

20. Banting, op. cit., p. 72.

21. SHELTER's first press release, quoted in Des Wilson, *I Know It Was the Place's Fault*, p. 147.

22. *Ibid.*, p. 150.

23. *The Times*, 31 July 1967.

24. Dalyell, *Dick Crossman*, p. 177.

25. Howe, *Conflict of Loyalty*, p. 42.

26. Crossman, *Diaries*, 12 March 1969.

27. *Ibid.*, 10–27 March 1969; Howard, *Crossman*, pp. 194–5; Dalyell, op. cit., pp. 178–83.

28. Howard, loc. cit.

29. Crossman, op. cit., 12 March.

30. Edwards, *The National Health Service: A Manager's Tale: 1946–92*, pp. 58–9; Diary of Key Events, 1978.

31. Klein, *The Politics of the NHS*, p. 67.

32. *Ibid.*, p. 68.

33. M. H. Cooper and A. J. Culyer, *Health Services Financing*, BMA, 1968, p. 199.

34. Powell, *Medicine and Politics*, 1975 edn, pp. 26–7.

35. Cmnd 6404, p. 105; S.P. W. Care in *Oxford Textbook of Public Health Vol I*, 1984, pp. 13–14.

36. *The Times*, 26 July 1967; for a full account of Labour's struggle with CPAG's early campaign see Banting, op. cit., pp. 66–108.

37. Susan Crosland, *Tony Crosland*, p. 194.

38. Crossman, op. cit., 5 January 1968.

39. Judge, *A Generation of Schooling*, p. 90.

40. *Ibid.*, p. 95.

41. Crossman, op. cit., 19 July 1967.

42. Unattributable interview.

43. Banting, op. cit., pp. 89–91.

44. *Ibid.*, p. 89.

45. *Ibid.*, p. 103.

46. Sir John Walley, 'A New Approach to Abolishing Child Poverty', *The Times*, 11 December 1967.

47. Banting, op. cit., p. 91.

48. Brown, *In My Way*, p. 270.

49. Crossman, op. cit., 5 January 1968.

50. Banting, op. cit., p. 80.

51. Campbell, *Edward Heath*, p. 207.

52. See, e.g., Richard Crossman, *People*, 6 February 1966.

53. Houghton, op. cit., p. 10.

54. *Hansard*, 1 November 1962, col.444.

55. Banting, op. cit., p. 90.

56. *The Times*, 19 June 1967.

57. *Hansard*, 24 July 1967, cols.98–9.

58. *Sunday Times*, 19 August 1967 (Gunter), 25 June 1967 (Walden).

59. David Owen in *Social Services For All?*, Fabian Tract 385, 1968.

60. Compare, for example, the sophistication of the arguments in Houghton, *Paying for Social Services*, and Townsend *et al.*, in *Social Services For All*, with the essays in Bull, ed., *Family Poverty*.

61. Deacon and Bradshaw, *Reserved for the Poor*, p. 69.

62. Crossman, *Paying for the Social Services*, p. 17.

63. Brian Abel-Smith in *Social Services for All?*, Fabian Tract 385, p. 113

64. Leathard, *The Fight for Family Planning*, pp. 109, 158–62.

65. Crossman, *A Politician's View of Health Service Planners*, Univ. of Glasgow, 1972, p. 18.

66. *Report of the 48th Annual Conference of the Labour Party*, Blackpool, 1949, p. 217.

67. Crossman, op. cit., pp. 9–10.

68. Bryan Jennett, *High Technology Medicine: Benefits and Burdens*, Oxford University Press, 1986, p. 150.

70. Morgan, *Labour People*, p. 273.

71. Conservative Campaign Guide, 1970, p. 6.

72. Cox, *The Great Betrayal*.

73. *Ibid.*, p. 148.

74. Popularised by Rubin, first attributed to Jack Weinberg during a free speech demonstration at Berkeley in 1964.

75. Cox, op. cit., p. 151.

76. Cox and Dyson, *The Black Papers on Education*, p. 10.

77. *The Times*, 5 March, 9 April 1967.

78. Interview with Sir Rhodes Boyson, 19 October 1994.

79. Raison, *Tories and the Welfare State*, p. 64.

80. The phrase is Stuart Maclure's in *Educational Developments and School Building*, p. 240.

81. An indigestible account of these is given in Knight, *The Making of Tory Education Policy*.

82. Campbell, op. cit., p. 237.

83. Raison, op. cit., p. 67.

84. Campbell, op. cit., p. 264

85. *Ibid.*

86. Conservative Research Department Archive, Bodleian Library, CCO 500/56/1.

87. Craig, *British General Election Manifestos*, p. 124.

88. Ronald Bedford, *General Practitioner*, 9 July 1976; Crossman, *Diaries*, 28 May, 2, 4, 5 and 8 June 1970.

89. Interview with Dr John Marks.

90. Field, op. cit., p 30. Much of what follows is drawn from the chapter called 'Three Major Campaigns', pp. 29–50. See also Crossman, *Diaries*, 27 January 1970.

91. *Ibid.*, p. 33.

92. Interview, 31 March 1993.

93. Field, loc. cit.

94. *Ibid.*, p. 34.

95. Interview.

96. Interview.

14 The Tories' last hurrah: Conservatives 1970–74

1. *Hansard*, 27 October 1970, col.37.

2. Young, *One of Us*, p. 73.

3. *Ibid.*, p. 74.

4. Field, *Poverty and Politics*, p. 40.

5. *Ibid.*

6. Unattributable interview.

7. *Hansard*, 10 November 1970, col.253.

8. Deacon and Bradshaw, *Reserved for the Poor*, p. 79.

9. Unattributable interview.

10. *Hansard*, 10 November 1970, col.262.

11. David Barker in Bull, ed., *Family Poverty*, p. 81.

12. Deacon and Bradshaw, op. cit., p. 81.

13. Keith Joseph, *Guardian*, 3 January 1972.

14. *New Statesman*, 3 December 1971, pp. 772–3.

15. *Guardian*, 3 January 1972.

16. *Campaign Guide*, Conservative Central Office, 1974, p. 337.

17. Banting, *Poverty, Politics and Policy*, pp. 102–4.

18. Tony Lynes, 'The Failure of Selectivity', in Bull, ed., *Family Poverty*, pp. 19–28; Deacon and Bradshaw, op. cit., *passim*, but especially pp. 93–4.

19. Halcrow, *Keith Joseph*, p. 43.

20. *Ibid.*, p. 7.

21. *Sunday Mirror*, 25 March 1973.

22. *Guardian*, 12 November 1973.

23. Interview, 20 December 1993.

24. Lynes, *Maintaining the Value of Benefits*, 1985.

25. Interview.

26. Donnison, *The Politics of Poverty*, pp. 73, 155.

27. Barnett, *Inside the Treasury*, p. 124.

28. Craig, *British General Election Manifestos*, p. 126.

29. *Report of the Committee on the Abuse of Social Security Benefits*, Cmnd 5228, HMSO, 1973.

30. Johnathan Bradshaw, *Social Security Under the Tories*, Yearbook of Social Policy 1971, Routledge & an Paul, p. 167.

    Conservative Party Conference Record, 1973, p. 98.

32. *Ibid.*, p. 96.

33. *Guardian*, 4 June 1973.

34. Interview, September 1993.

35. Interview.

36. Interview.

37. *Sunday Mirror*, 25 March 1973.

38. Interview.

39. Interview.

40. Interview with Lord Howe, 6 September 1994.

41. Correspondence with Sir George Godber, 29 July 1994.

42. Adrian Webb, in Townsend and Bosanquet, eds., *Labour and Equality*, pp. 285–6.

43. *Hansard*, 30 April 1946, col.44.

44. Crossman, *A Politician's View of Health Service Planning*, p. 10.

45. Interview with Norman Warner.

46. Interview, 14 October 1993.

47. Interview.

48. Klein, *The Politics of the NHS*, p. 125.

49. See Chapter 6.

50. Interview with David Willetts; and David Willetts, *Reforming the Health Service*, Conservative Political Centre, 1989, p. 39.

51. Klein, op. cit., p. 77.

52. Powell, *Medicine and Politics*, p. 16.

53. Young and Sloman, *The Thatcher Phenomenon*, p. 24.

54. *Times Educational Supplement*, 12 June 1987.

55. Simon, *Education and the Social Order*, p. 411.

56. Young, op. cit., p. 68; Simon, op. cit., p. 415.

57. Young, op. cit., p. 70.

58. Wapshott and Brock, *Thatcher*, quoted Young, op. cit., p. 68.

59. Interview, 18 August 1993.

60. Gardiner, *Margaret Thatcher*, pp. 106–7.

61. Pimlott, *Harold Wilson*, pp. 513–5.

62. Gardiner, op. cit., p. 102.

63. *Independent*, 29 April 1989.

64. Gardiner, op. cit., p. 132.

65. *Ibid.*, p. 131.

66. Simon, op. cit., p. 423.

67. Gardiner, op. cit., p. 103.

68. Thatcher, *Let Our Children Grow Tall: Selected Speeches, 1975–77*, p. 82.

69. Gardiner, op. cit., p. 111.

70. Young, op. cit., p. 70.
71. Thatcher, op. cit., p. 82.
72. *People*, 6 February 1966.
73. Walker, *The Ascent of Britain*, p. 189.
74. Walker, *Staying Power*, p. 88.
75. Walker, *The Ascent of Britain*, p. 173.
76. *Ibid.*
77. *Guardian*, 16 October 1971.
78. Prior, *A Balance of Power*, p. 74.
79. Campbell, op. cit., p. 443.
80. *Ibid.*, p. 411.
81. *Hansard*, 17 December 1973, col.952.
82. *Ibid.*, col.965.
83. Morgan, *Labour People*, p. 357.

15 'It was getting colder by the hour': Labour 1974-79

1. Callaghan, *Time and Chance*, p. 428.
2. Barnett, *Inside the Treasury*, p. 192.
3. Labour Party Conference Annual Report 1976, p. 188.
4. Barnett, op. cit., p. 23.
5. *Ibid.*, p. 49.
6. Healey, *The Time of My Life*, pp. 150, 367.
7. Castle, *Fighting All the Way*, p. 459.
8. Barnett, op. cit., p. 34.
9. Kogan, *The Politics of Educational Change*, p. 150.
10. St John-Stevas, *The Two Cities*, p. 16.
11. *Ibid.*, p. 49.
12. Interview, 18 August 1993.
13. *Ibid.*
14. *Ibid.* 'Chris Patten interviewed me. I didn't get on with him at all. And he reported back to Norman St John-Stevas that in no way was he going to accept Stuart Sexton because Stuart Sexton was far too right wing.'
15. St John-Stevas, op. cit., p. 51.
16. Interview with Shirley Williams, 18 September 1994.
17. St John-Stevas in fact told the Commons, 'We have not counselled delaying tactics.' *Hansard*, 4 November 1977, col.186.
18. Interview.
19. Conservative Party Conference Report, Blackpool, 11 October 1977.
20. Simon, *The Politics of Educational Change*, p. 590.
21. *Ibid.*, p. 442; extracts shown in *From Butler to Baker*, BBC2, Education Unit, 1994.
22. Simon, op. cit., p. 446.
23. Morris and Griggs, *Thirteen Wasted Years*, pp. 5-6.
24. See Chapter 4.
25. Barber, *Education and the Teacher Unions*, p. 39.
26. *Hansard*, 21 March 1960, cols.51-2.
27. Quoted in Barber, op. cit., p. 135.
28. Kogan, op. cit., pp. 63-4.
29. Barber, op. cit., p. 40.
30. Callaghan, op. cit., p. 222.
31. *Ibid.*, p. 411.
32. Donoughue, *Prime Minister*, pp. 109-10.
33. Callaghan, op. cit., p. 409.
34. Extracts from the *Yellow Book*, in *Times Educational Supplement*, 15 October 1976, pp. 1-3.
35. Donoughue, op. cit., p. 110.
36. Callaghan, op. cit., p. 410.
37. Baker, *Who Rules Our Schools*, p. 30.
38. Quoted in Simon, op. cit., p. 448, from Keith Fenwick and Peter McBride, *The Government of Education*, London, 1981, p. 220.
39. Maclure, *Education Re-formed*, p. 164.

40. Judge, *A Generation of Schooling*, p. 173; *Times Educational Supplement*, 15 October 1976, leading article p. 1.

41. Donoughue, op. cit., p. 112.

42. Interview with Shirley Williams, 18 September 1994.

43. Callaghan, op. cit., p. 411.

44. Interview.

45. *Education in Schools: A Consultative Document*, Cmnd 6869, HMSO, 1977, pp. 10–11.

46. *Ibid.*

47. *Better Schools*, Cmnd 9469, HMSO, 1985; *The Development of Higher Education into the 1990s*, HMSO, 1985.

48. Maclure, *Educational Documents*, p. 385.

49. *Times Educational Supplement*, 22 October 1976, p. 2.

50. Interview with Shirley Williams.

51. Interview.

52. *Times Educational Supplement*, 15 October 1976, p. 3.

53. Carswell, *Government and the Universities in Britain*, p. 147.

54. *Ibid.*, p. 148.

55. *Ibid.*, p. 150.

56. *Ibid.*, p. 156.

57. Donoughue, op. cit., p. 105.

58. David Webster in Townsend and Bosanquet, eds., *Labour and Equality*, p. 257.

59. *Ibid.*, p. 259.

60. *Royal Commission on the National Health Service*, Cmnd 7615, HMSO, 1979, p. 163.

61. Interview, 5 August 1993.

62. *Daily Express*, 1 July 1974.

63. Figures on private insurance market from any edition of *Laing's Review of Private Healthcare*. Calculation that private care amounted to 2 per cent of NHS spending based on calculation of provident association's payouts, plus one-third

to allow for self-payers, divided into NHS expenditure for given year.

64. *Fourth Report from the Expenditure Committee, NHS Facilities for Private Patients*, HMSO, 1972; *The Times*, 30 March 1972.

65. Craig, *British General Election Manifestos 1959–87*, p. 192.

66. Owen, *Time to Declare*, p. 232.

67. *Daily Express, Guardian*, 3 July 1974.

68. *The Times*, 31 December 1974.

69. *The Times*, 17 January 1975; *Sunday Times*, 16 March 1975; interview with Dr John Marks, who had a patient anaesthetised but not operated on.

70. *The Separation of Private Practice from NHS Hospitals*, HMSO, 1975.

71. National newspapers, 26 September 1976.

72. Castle, *The Castle Diaries 1974–76*, entry for 27 November 1975. Castle's diaries contain an accurate and stirring account of the whole dispute. Most of the references cited here can be found in the shortened version, Macmillan Papermac, 1990.

73. Wilson, *Final Term*, p. 191.

74. Goodman, *Tell them I'm on my Way*, p. 233.

75. Interview with Sir Anthony Grabham, 5 August 1993.

76. Castle, op. cit., 24 November 1975 *et seq.*

77. Goodman, op. cit., p. 236.

78. *Ibid.*

79. Castle, op. cit., 2 and 3 December 1975

80. *Ibid.*, 14 December 1975.

81. *Ibid.*, Appendix VI, 'The Goodman Proposals'; *The Times*, 16 December 1975.

82. *Health Services Board Annual*

Report, HMSO, 1979, quoted in Klein, op. cit., p. 123.

83. *NHS Hospital Activity Statistics for England 1974-85*, Bulletin 2/86.

84. *The Times*, 31 December 1975.

85. *The Times*, 15 December 1975.

86. Fowler, *Ministers Decide*, p. 78.

87. Interviews with Dr Gordon Macpherson, Dr John Havard.

88. Grey-Turner and Sutherland, *History of the British Medical Association*, p. 304.

89. Castle, op. cit., 24 November 1975.

90. Interview, 12 July 1993.

91. Private information.

92. Nicholas Bosanquet in Townsend and Bosanquet, op. cit., pp. 216-7.

93. *Ibid.*, pp. 217-18.

94. Interview with Sir Geoffrey Otton, 1 September 1993.

95. Lynes, *Maintaining the Value of Benefits*, pp. 12-13.

96. *Ibid.*, pp. 13-16.

97. Conservative Research Department Archive, Bodleian Library, CRD 4/7/14.

98. *Hansard*, 21 November 1974, cols. 1565-7.

99. Hilary Land, 'The Child Benefit Fiasco', in *The Year Book of Social Policy in Britain 1976*, Routledge & Kegan Paul, p. 124.

100. *Ibid.*, p. 125.

101. Subsequent account drawn from Hilary Land's excellent summary and her cited sources, plus Frank Field, *Poverty and Politics*, pp. 43-50 and pp. 108-13 which contain the *New Society* article.

102. Healey, *The Time of My Life*, pp. 448-9.

103. *Ibid.*, p. 449.

104. Ellis, *Pensions in Britain 1955-75*, p. 46. This is an excellent and extremely readable account of the development of SERPS.

105. Unattributable interview.

106. Ellis, op. cit., p. 41.

107. *Ibid.*

108. *Better Pensions*, Cmnd 5713, HMSO, 1974, quoted in Ellis, op. cit., p. 48.

109. Fowler, op. cit., p. 73.

110. Interview with Norman Fowler, 6 July 1993.

111. Unattributable interview.

112. Unattributable interview.

113. Ellis, op. cit., p. 56.

114. Atkinson, *Pensions World*, October 1992, p. 37.

115. Donnison, *The Politics of Poverty*, p 14.

116. Deacon and Bradshaw, *Reserved for the Poor*, pp. 107-8.

117. Donnison, op. cit., pp. 42-3.

118. Interview.

119. *Social Assistance: A Review of the Supplementary Benefits Scheme in Great Britain*, HMSO, 1978, p. 5.

120. Donnison, op. cit., p. 43.

121. *Ibid.*, p. 66.

122. Zeigler, *Wilson*, p. 436.

123. Barnett, op. cit., p. 50.

124. *Ibid.*, p. 49.

125. Donnison, op. cit., p. 156.

126. Interview with Sir Alec Atkinson.

127. *Daily Telegraph*, 16 and 25 January 1979.

128. *Daily Telegraph*, 2 February 1979.

129. *Daily Express*, 7 March 1979.

130. Donoughue, op. cit., p. 191.

16 'We were wrong all along': Conservatives 1974-79

1. Joseph, *Reversing the Trend*, Foreword.

2. Halcrow, *Keith Joseph*, p. 64.

3. Joseph, *Stranded on the Middle Ground*, pp. 21-2.

4. Speech at Birmingham, reprinted *Sunday Times*, 20 October 1979.

5. Stockton lecture, 1976, quoted in Halcrow, op. cit., pp. 113–14.

6. Joseph, op. cit., p. 20.

7. Joseph, *Reversing the Trend*, p. 60.

8. Halcrow, op. cit., p. 101.

9. Thatcher, *Let Our Children Grow Tall*, pp. 1–13.

10. *Ibid.*, pp. 81–6; interview with Patrick Jenkin, 1 July 1993.

11. To the Greater London Young Conservatives; see Raison, *Tories and the Welfare State*, p. 93.

12. Thatcher, op. cit., p. 74.

13. Young, *One of Us*, p. 140.

14. Raison, op. cit., p. 95.

15. The phrase is Julian Critchley's.

16. Conservative Research Department Archive, Bodleian Library, CRD 4/4/81, 4/4/82.

17. Interview, 1 October 1993.

18. Young and Sloman, *The Thatcher Phenomenon*, p. 137.

19. *Sunday Times, Sunday Mirror*, 30 October 1977.

20. Interview.

21. Hennessy, *Whitehall*, pp. 549–60; Owen, *Time to Declare*, p. 237; Castle, *Diaries*, 5 November 1975.

22. Interview.

23. Conservative Research Department Papers, CRD 4/7/74, Paper for 7 March 1979 meeting, Bodleian Library.

24. *Ibid.*, and interview with Patrick Jenkin, 1 July 1993.

25. Howe, *Conflict of Loyalty*, p. 99.

26. Leaders Consultative Committee minutes 1978–9, Conservative Research Department Archive, Bodleian Library.

27. *Ibid.*

28. *Ibid.*

29. *Black Paper*, Temple Smith, 1977, p. 88.

30. Craig, *British General Election Manifestos 1959–87*, p. 279.

31. Young and Sloman, op. cit., p. 135.

32. Young, op. cit., p. 83.

33. *The Times*, 23 June 1975.

34. Walker, *The Ascent of Britain*, pp. 163–76.

35. Walker, *Staying Power*, p. 141.

36. Conservative Party Papers, LCC (78) 182, *The Sales of Council Houses, A Paper by Michael Heseltine*, Bodleian Library.

37. *Guardian*, 16 June 1971; see also Crosland, *Socialism Now*, pp. 129–33.

38. Sally MacDonald and Julia Porter, *Putting on the Style: Setting up Home in the 1950s*, Geffrye Museum, London, 1990, p. 16.

39. Field, *Do We Need Council Houses*, Catholic Housing Aid Society, Occasional Paper No 2, 1976; *Roof*, Vol.1, No 3, May 1976, p. 1.

40. Haines, *The Politics of Power*, pp. 94–111; Donoughue, *Prime Minister*, pp. 106–9.

41. Richard Titmuss, *The Irresponsible Society*, Fabian Society, 1960.

42. Owen, *In Sickness and in Health*, p. 31.

43. Field, Meacher and Pond, *To Him Who Hath*, p. 231.

44. Joseph Rowntree Foundation, *Income and Wealth*, 1995, p. 13.

45. Kogan, *The Politics of Educational Change*, p. 158.

46. R. Emmett Tyrrell Jr, *The Future that Doesn't Work: Social Democracy's Failure in Britain*, New York, 1977; Isaac Kramnick, *Is Britain Dying? Perspectives on the Current Crisis*, London, 1979.

47. Anthony Bevins, 'The Thatcher Years', *Independent*, 1 May 1989.

17 *Cuts and catastrophes: 1979–83*

1. Interview, 3 May 1993.
2. Ridley, *My Style of Government*, p. 83.
3. Interview.
4. Interview, 1 July 1993.
5. Interview, 6 July 1993.
6. Fowler, *Ministers Decide*, p. 357.
7. Unattributable interview.
8. Interview, 18 August 1993.
9. *Independent*, 8 June 1987.
10. Interview, 14 June 1993.
11. Interview, 13 July 1993.
12. Craig, *British General Election Manifestos 1959–87*, p. 280.
13. Interview.
14. Interview.
15. Interview; see also Prior, *A Balance of Power*, p. 130; Howe, *Conflict of Loyalty*, pp. 189–90.
16. *Hansard*, 12 June 1979, col.246.
17. Donnison, *The Politics of Poverty*, p. 166.
18. Interview.
19. Lynes, *Maintaining the Value of Benefits*, pp. 18–24.
20. Donnison, op. cit., p. 168.
21. *Hansard*, 13 June 1979, col.439.
22. *Hansard*, 2 June 1992, col.490W.
23. Benn, diary entry for 7 December 1976, *Against the Tide*, p. 683.
24. Interview with Lord Howe, 6 September 1994.
25. Interview.
26. Private information.
27. *Hansard*, 1 May 1980, col.1616.
28. Interview with Patrick Jenkin.
29. There are 24 references to Social Security scroungers and fraud in *The Times* index for 1980.
30. Numbers had risen from 125,000 in 1966 to 260,000 (24,000 of them on FIS) in 1971. By 1981 they had almost doubled again to 455,000 (392,000 on income support, 63,000 on FIS), only to more than double to

1,030,000 by 1991 (135,000 on Family Credit, rest on income support, a 126 per cent rise). By 1994 a further 200,000 had been added: 1,013.000 on income support; 228,000 on Family Credit.
31. Deacon and Bradshaw, *Reserved for the Poor*, p. 115; Donnison, op. cit., pp. 178–83.
32. Ivan Fallon, *The Paper Chase*, HarperCollins, 1993.
33. Donnison, op. cit., p. 185.
34. *Ibid.*, p. 191.
35. Interview, 8 July 1993.
36. *Social Workers: Their Role and Tasks*, National Institute for Social Work, Bedford Square Press, 1982.
37. *Inequalities in Health: The Black Report and the Health Divide*, Penguin, 1988, p. 2.
38. *Ibid.*
39. *Ibid.*, p. 4.
40. Steve Wilcox, 'Making the Most of Council Housing', in *Fiscal Studies*, vol.15, no 1, Institute of Fiscal Studies, February 1994, p. 44.
41. *Daily Telegraph*, 2 January, 16 February, 24 May, 1979.
42. John Burnett, *A Social History of Housing 1815–1985*, Methuen, 1986, p. 290.
43. Craig, op. cit., p. 125.
44. Peter Kemp, 'Housing', in *Implementing Thatcherite Policies*, OUP, 1992, p. 71.
45. *TES*, 16 November 1979; see also Simon, *The Politics of Educational Change*, p. 479.
46. Hills, ed., *The State of Welfare*, p. 38.
47. Hennessy, *Never Again*, p. 146.
48. Simon, op. cit., p. 483.
49. Interview with Sexton; figures from Department for Education Departmental Report, Cmnd 2510, 1994.
50. *The Times*, 28 May 1980; and

Maureen O'Connor in 'Education Guardian', *Guardian*, 2 February 1982.

51. *Guardian*, 5 July 1981.
52. Interview with Stuart Sexton.
53. Kogan, *The Attack on Higher Education*, p. 12.
54. *Ibid.*, pp. 61–4. A spirited account of the whole episode.
55. Martin Holmes, *The First Thatcher Government 1979–83*, Wheatsheaf, Brighton, 1985, pp. 115–16.
56. Correspondence, 18 September 1994.
57. Young, *One of Us*, p. 402.
58. Seventeenth Report from the Committee of Public Accounts, Session 1980–81 and Session 1981–82, HMSO, 1981, 1982.
59. Correspondence, Sir George Godber, July 1994.
60. *Royal Commission on the National Health Service*, Cmnd 7615, HMSO, 1979, p. 355.
61. Interviews with Patrick Jenkin and with Sir Patrick Nairne.
62. The government's proposals were spelt out in *Patients First*, HMSO, 1979.
63. *Ibid.*, p. 7.
64. Interview.
65. Edwards, *The National Health Service, A Manager's Tale*, p. 62.
66. Private information.
67. *Health Care and Its Costs*, HMSO, 1983.
68. Interview, 12 July 1993.
69. Interview, 5 August 1993.
70. *The Times*, 12 June 1981.
71. Cmnd 7615, p. 377.
72. *The Times*, 23 June 1980; correspondence with Dr Vaughan, 1993; interview with Michael Lee, 2 November 1993.
73. *Guardian*, 19 July 1979; *Daily Telegraph*, 15 August 1979.

74. Interview with Michael Lee.
75. *Guardian*, 27 July 1981.
76. Interview with Patrick Jenkin.
77. The report was never published. Its main findings are summarised in the *Independent*, 8 February 1988.
78. *The Times*, 14 July 1981.
79. *Brixton Disturbances Enquiry* (The Scarman Report), Cmnd 8427, HMSO, 1981.
80. Halcrow, *Keith Joseph*, p. 164.
81. Tebbit, *Upwardly Mobile*, p. 236.
82. Clarke to author, 1983.
83. Fowler, op. cit., p. 43.
84. Kenneth Stowe to author.
85. Unattributable interview.
86. Fowler, loc. cit.
87. Interview with Norman Fowler.
88. Interview. An account of the report's findings can be found in the *Independent*, 8 February 1988.
89. Fowler, op. cit., p. 185; *Hansard*, 30 July 1982, col.860.
90. Kember and Macpherson, *The NHS – A Kaleidoscope of Care*, p. 241.
91. Department of Health Statistical Bulletins, Elective Admissions.
92. Fowler, op. cit., p. 177.
93. *Ibid.*, p. 172.
94. Howe, op. cit., pp. 257–9.
95. Blackstone and Plowden, *Inside the Think-Tank*, pp. 95–6; see also Leon Brittan's speech in Conservative Central Office press release, 591/82, 22 September 1982.
96. Fowler, op. cit., p. 186.
97. Lawson, *The View from Number Eleven*, p. 303.
98. *Economist*, 18–24 September 1982, pp. 25–6; Young, op. cit., p. 301.
99. Labour Party press release, 17 September 1982.
100. Young, loc. cit.
101. Conservative Central Office

press release, 591/82, 22 September 1982.

102. Howe, op. cit., p. 258.

103. Fowler, op. cit., p. 186.

104. *Ibid.*, p. 187. Speech to Conservative Party conference 1982.

105. Craig, op. cit., p. 334.

18 Fighting Leviathans: 1983–87

1. Fowler, *Ministers Decide*, p. 202.

2. *Ibid.*, p. 203.

3. *Ibid.*, p. 204.

4. Interview, 11 May 1993.

5. Interview.

6. Blackstone and Plowden, *Inside the Think-Tank*, p. 128.

7. Lawson, *The View from Number Eleven*, p. 588.

8. Interview with John Redwood.

9. *The Times*, 20 January 1984.

10. *The Times*, 21 January 1984. Rhodes Boyson has a slightly different version (and date) in Boyson, *Speaking My Mind*, Peter Owen, 1995, p. 190. The author, who was there, prefers his.

11. *The Reform of Supplementary Benefit*, Policy Studies Institute, 1984.

12. Interview, 28 July 1993.

13. Interview.

14. Interview.

15. Fowler, op. cit., p. 209; Lawson, op. cit., pp. 596–7.

16. Fowler, op. cit., p. 224.

17. For a detailed assessment of the impact, see *The Effect of the 1986 Social Security Act on Family Incomes*, Joseph Rowntree Foundation, York, 1994.

18. Interview.

19. Lawson, op. cit., p. 590.

20. *Ibid.*, p. 589.

21. Figures from Report by the Government Actuary, Cmnd 2445, HMSO, 1994.

22. Fowler, op. cit., p. 222.

23. *The Times*, 21 June 1985.

24. Interview with Sir Peter Barclay, 8 July 1993. At the time £3m was offered. Within a few years the Independent Living Fund was spending £90m.

25. *The Times*, 28 January 1986.

26. Fowler, op. cit., p. 216.

27. *Economist*, 24 November 1984.

28. Lawson, op. cit.,, p. 89.

29. Unattributable interview.

30. Figures from BMA in Nicholas Timmins, *Cash, Crisis and Cure, The Independent Guide to the NHS Debate*, Newspaper Publishing plc, 1988, p. 7.

31. Interview, 24 June 1993.

32. Interview.

33. Virginia Bottomley, Speech to the Chartered Institute of Public Finance, 10 May 1994.

34. Interview.

35. *The Times*, 10 October, 4 November 1983. A fuller account is in the *Guardian* around these dates.

36. Interview with David Willetts.

37. Interview.

38. Interview.

39. Interview with Sir Roy Griffiths, 13 July 1993.

40. Michael Bett, Jim Blyth, Sir Brian Bailey.

41. Interview.

42. Interview.

43. Interview.

44. *NHS Management Inquiry* (The Griffiths Report), HMSO, 1983.

45. Kember and Macpherson, *The NHS – A Kaleidoscope of Care*, p. 35.

46. Unattributable interviews.

47. Foot, *Aneurin Bevan*, p. 195.

48. Interview, 26 July 1993.

49. *The Times* and the *Guardian*, 29 June 1981; *The Times*, 14 April 1982.

50. *The Times*, 9 November 1984.

51. Fowler, op. cit., p. 194; interview with Dr John Marks.

52. *The Times*, 13 December 1984.

53. Unattributable interview.

54. *The Times*, 1 February 1985.

55. *Hansard*, 22 November 1983, col.114.

56. Interview, 21 June 1993.

57. *General Practitioner*, 16 November 1984.

58. *The Times*, 6 March, 1 April 1985.

59. Interview.

60. *Primary Health Care; An Agenda for Discussion*, Cmnd 9771, HMSO, 1986.

61. *British Medical Journal*, 1986, vol.293, p. 1384.

62. Laing, *Financing Long-Term Care*, pp. 25–7.

63. *Making a Reality of Community Care*, Audit Commission, HMSO, 1986.

64. Halcrow, *Keith Joseph*, p. 167.

65. Interview with Stuart Sexton, 18 August 1993.

66. Simon, *The Politics of Educational Change*, p. 490; *The Times*, 27 October 1981; *Guardian*, 12 November 1981.

67. Interview with Stuart Sexton; interview with Oliver Letwin, 1 October 1993.

68. Keith Joseph to Conservative Party conference 1981; see also letter to Friends of the Education Voucher (FEVER), reproduced in Seldon, *Riddle of the Education Voucher*, p. 36.

69. Kenneth Baker, *The Turbulent Years*, p. 167.

70. The nature of the DES opposition is evident from even a cursory reading of their 1981 memorandum on the issue, reproduced in Seldon, op. cit., pp. 37–42.

71. Interview with Sexton; Halcrow, op. cit., p. 172.

72. Interview, 1 October 1993.

73. Interview.

74. *The Times*, 7 February 1983.

75. Interview.

76. Interview.

77. Seldon, op. cit., p.xii.

78. Interview.

79. Judge, *A Generation of Schooling*, p. 192.

80. *Better Schools*, Cmnd 9469, HMSO, 1985.

81. Maclure, *Education Re-formed*, p. 167.

82. *Sunday Times*, 22 April 1984.

83. Young, *The Enterprise Years*, p. 90.

84. *Ibid.*, p. 94.

85. Quoted by Peter Wilby, *Sunday Times*, 22 April 1984.

86. Quoted in Simon, op. cit., p. 506.

87. *Guardian*, 23 February 1983.

88. Peter Scott, 'Higher Education', in Kavanagh, D. and Seldon, A., eds, *The Thatcher Effect*, OUP, 1989, p. 202.

89. *Ibid.90. Higher Education into the 1990s*, Cmnd 9524, HMSO, 1985.

91. Scott, op. cit., p. 203.

92. Lawson, op. cit., p. 604.

93. Unattributable interview.

94. Unattributable interview.

95. *The Times: Past, Present and Future*, Supplement to 200th anniversary edition, p. 19.

96. Baker, op. cit., pp. 162–3; Lawson, op. cit., pp. 606–9.

97. Interview with John Redwood.

98. Interview. His paper, largely unchanged, was published in 1987 as *Our Schools – A Radical Policy*, by the Institute of Economic Affairs Education Unit.

99. Lawson, op. cit., pp. 608–9.

100. Interview with John Redwood.

101. Peter Wilby and Simon

Midgley, *Independent*, 23 July 1987.
102. Lawson, op. cit., p. 606.
103. Baker, op. cit., p. 169.
104. Speech to the North of England Conference, Rotherham, 9 January 1987.
105. For accounts of its traumas see Lawson, op. cit., pp. 609–10; Baker, op. cit., pp. 160–232 *passim*.
106. Lawson, op. cit., pp. 609–10; Ridley, op. cit., p. 94.
107. *Independent*, 9 February 1987.
108. Baker, op. cit., pp. 182–97; Thatcher, *The Downing Street Years*, pp. 578–9, 593.
109. Thatcher, op. cit., p. 592.
110. *Independent*, 8 October 1986.
111. Baker, op. cit., pp. 182–3.
112. *Independent*, *Guardian*, 8 December 1986.
113. *The Times*, 10 January 1987.
114. *Independent*, 9 February 1987.
115. *Independent*, 10 January 1987.
116. *Independent*, 11 April 1987.
117. *Independent*, 3 March, 29 April 1987.
118. *Independent*, 23 May 1987; Baker, op. cit., p. 194.
119. Baker, loc. cit.
120. *Independent*, 5 June 1987.
121. *Independent*, 28 May 1987.

19 Forming the future: Conservatives 1987–92

1. *Independent*, 11 June 1987.
2. Interview with John Moore, 17 June 1993.
3. Lawson, *The View from Number Eleven*, p. 614.
4. Interview; Thatcher, *The Downing Street Years*, p. 608.
5. Thatcher, op. cit., p. 600.
6. Ridley, *My Style of Government*, p. 89.
7. Thatcher, loc. cit.
8. *Social Trends*, HMSO, 1994, p. 111.
9. Department of the Environment, *Housebuilding Information Bulletin*, August 1994.
10. David Page, *Building for Communities: A Study of New Housing Association Estates*, Joseph Rowntree Foundation, York, 1994, p. 49.
11. Haviland, *Take Care Mr Baker!* expertly summarises the response.
12. *Independent*, 8 October 1987.
13. Baker, *The Turbulent Years*, pp. 217–8.
14. *Ibid.*, pp. 193, 196.
15. *Independent*, 14 September 1987.
16. Interview with Stuart Sexton, recalling a meeting Thatcher attended at the Centre for Policy Studies.
17. Baker, op. cit., p. 196.
18. *Guardian*, 24 November 1992.
19. *Daily Telegraph*, 20 November 1987.
20. Baker, op. cit., p. 196.
21. *Ibid.*, p. 195.
22. *Ibid.*, p. 197.
23. *Independent*, 21 September 1987.
24. *Daily Mail*, 28 May 1987.
25. *Independent*, 21 July 1987.
26. *Independent*, 14 September 1987.
27. Baker, op. cit., p. 221.
28. *Independent*, 10 March 1988.
29. *Independent*, 27 January 1988.
30. *Hansard*, 1 December 1987, col.771ff.
31. Peter Wilby and Ngaio Crequer, *Independent*, 28 July 1988.
32. *Ibid.*
33. A riveting account of National Curriculum Council's creation and unhappy early years is contained in Duncan Graham's *A Lesson for Us All*.

34. Alas, I have been unable to trace the author of this quip.

35. Graham, op. cit., p. 118.

36. Ibid., p. 74.

37. Baker, op. cit., p. 191.

38. Graham, op. cit., p. 51.

39. A fascinating account of the development of the English curriculum is in Cox, The Great Betrayal, pp. 242–59.

40. Thatcher, op. cit., pp. 593–7; Baker, op. cit., pp. 205–7; Graham, op. cit., pp. 66–70.

41. Graham, op. cit., p. 70.

42. Lawson, op. cit., p. 601.

43. Ibid., p. 601; Baker, op. cit., p. 238

44. Baker, op. cit., p. 238; figures from Conservative Campaign Guide 1991, p. 213.

45. Simon, Education and the Social Order, pp. 533, 552–3.

46. Independent, 2 May 1991.

47. Independent, 28 June 1990.

48. Independent, 5 January 1991.

49. The Times, 18 June 1987; Daily Mail, 20 July 1987.

50. Charles Murray, Losing Ground: American Social Policy 1950–80, Basic Books, New York, 1984.

51. Independent, 1 July, 24 October 1988.

52. Poverty, Spring 1987, p. 8.

53. See The Effects of the 1986 Social Security Act, Joseph Rowntree Foundation, York, 1994.

54. Young, The Enterprise Years, pp. 127–9.

55. Cmnd 6404, p. 58.

56. Craig, British General Election Manifestos 1959–87, p. 432.

57. Moore, Institute of Directors Annual Lecture, 8 June 1988.

58. Independent, 6 April 1988.

59. Moore, Speech to the Greater London Areas Conservative Political Centre, St Stephen's Club, 11 May 1989.

60. Independent, 12 and 13 May 1989.

61. Observer, 14 May 1989.

62. Social Trends 17, HMSO, 1987. Article by A. H. Halsey, p. 17.

63. Independent, 13 May 1989.

64. The Way Ahead, HMSO, 1990.

65. Thatcher, op. cit., p. 630.

66. Children Come First, HMSO, 1990.

67. Unattributable interview.

68. Unattributable interview.

69. Independent, 3 March 1988.

70. Independent, 12 December 1987.

71. Unattributable interview.

72. Interview with Ian Mills, 12 October 1993.

73. Interview with John Moore, 17 June 1993.

74. Unattributable interview.

75. Independent, 12 June 1987.

76. Independent, 28 June 1987.

77. Independent, 3 August 1987.

78. Independent, 18 August 1987.

79. Unattributable interview.

80. Independent, 26 November 1987.

81. Quoted in Edwards, The NHS – A Manager's Tale, p. 130.

82. Independent, 7 December 1987.

83. Edwards, op. cit., p. 129.

84. Interview, 12 October 1993.

85. Independent, 9 December 1987.

86. Independent, 26 November 1987

87. Independent, 7 December 1987.

88. Sunday Times, 13 December 1987.

89. Independent, 14 December 1987.

90. Independent, 20 January 1988.

91. Lawson, op. cit., p. 614.

92. Interviews with Redwood and Willetts.

93. Economist, 22 June 1985.

94. Interview with Gordon McLachlan, 27 July 1993.

95. Enthoven, Reflections on the

Management of the National Health Service.

96. *Independent*, 30 April 1987.

97. Personal experience.

98. Thatcher, op. cit., p. 607.

99. Unattributable interview.

100. *A New NHS Act for 1996? Papers for a Discussion Meeting at Cumberland Lodge, 7 and 8 June 1984*, Office of Health Economics, pp. 22, 35; and Alan Maynard in *Health Education and General Practice, Papers for Discussion Meeting 30 October 1985*, OHE, p. 46.

101. Thatcher, op. cit., p. 607.

102. *Ibid.*, p. 571.

103. Interview with David Willetts.

104. Redwood and Letwin, *Britain's Biggest Enterprise; ideas for radical reform of the NHS*, Centre for Policy Studies, 1988.

105. Michael Goldsmith and David Willetts, *Health Review* series, Centre for Policy Studies, 1988.

106. *Financing and Delivering Health Care*, OECD, Paris, 1987. In 1985 the UK spent 5.9 per cent of GDP on health care, 5.2 per cent public, 0.7 per cent private. The OECD average was 7.4 per cent, 5.7 per cent of it public, 1.7 per cent private.

107. Interview.

108. Interview.

109. *The Times*, 25 February 1986. The story came from a Downing Street lunch.

110. Lawson, op. cit., p. 616.

111. Interview with Nigel Lawson, 15 September 1993.

112. Thatcher, op. cit., p. 608.

113. Interviews with Griffiths, Moore, Lawson; also Lawson, op. cit., p. 616.

114. Lawson, loc. cit.

115. Interview and loc. cit.

116. Peter Jenkins, interview with Margaret Thatcher, *Independent*, 14 September 1987.

117. Enthoven, op. cit., p. 2.

118. Interviews with Griffiths and Moore; slightly different version in Thatcher, op. cit., p. 611.

119. Interview with Griffiths.

120. Unattributable interview.

121. Interview; Thatcher, loc. cit.

122. *Independent*, 18 May 1988.

123. Interview with Willetts.

124. Lawson, op. cit., p. 617.

125. *Ibid.*

126. Interview with Nigel Lawson.

127. Lawson, op. cit., p. 617.

128. Interview.

129. Interview.

130. Interview.

131. *Working for Patients*, Cmnd 555, HMSO, 1989.

132. *Independent*, 30 January 1989.

133. *Independent*, 1 February 1989.

134. *Independent*, 28 January 1989.

135. *Independent*, 2 February 1989.

136. Interview.

137. *British Medical Journal*, 1989, vol. 298, pp. 340–1.

138. *Independent*, 28 July 1989.

139. *Independent*, 9 February 1989.

140. *Independent*, 9 March, 11 March, 19 April 1989.

141. Speech to Royal College of General Practitioners, 9 March 1989; *Guardian*, 10 March 1989.

142. Interview with John Marks.

143. Interview with John Marks.

144. Interview.

145. Unattributable interview.

146. *Independent*, 21 July 1989.

147. *Independent*, 22 June 1989.

148. Interview.

149. Unattributable interview.

150. *Independent*, 18 May 1989.

151. *Independent*, 5 July 1989.

152. Alan Pike, interview with

Kenneth Clarke, *Financial Times*, 11 April 1989.

153. For a good account of this see Butler, *Patients, Policies and Politics*, particularly pp. 99–116.

154. *Economist*, 16 June 1990, p. 33.

155. Interviews, Duncan Nichol, Peter Griffiths.

156. Interview with Peter Griffiths.

157. *Community Care: Agenda for Action*, HMSO, 1988.

158. Interview, 13 July 1993.

159. Interview.

160. Interview with John Moore, 17 June 1993.

161. Interview with Griffiths.

162. Unattributable interview.

163. *Independent*, 17 and 18 March 1988.

164. See, e.g., Balen, *Kenneth Clarke*.

165. Interview.

166. Interviews, Clarke and Griffiths.

167. *Community Care: Agenda for Action*, HMSO, 1988.

168. Laing, *Financing Long-Term Care*, p. 27.

169. Interview.

170. Interview.

171. Julian Le Grand, in Hills, ed., *The State of Welfare*, pp. 355–6.

172. Paper by John Perry of the Institute of Housing for the Social Security Advisory Committee, reported in the *Independent*, 19 August 1994.

173. Peter Taylor-Gooby, in *British Social Attitudes, 8th Report*, Dartmouth Publishing, Aldershot, Hampshire, 1991, pp. 23–41.

174. *Ibid.*, p. 25.

175. *Independent*

176. *Ibid*, 5 December 1990.

177. *Independent*, 29 November 1990.

178. *Independent*, 19 December 1991.

179. *Independent on Sunday*, 10 February 1991.

180. Speech to Policy Studies Institute, *Independent*, 6 February 1991.

181. Ridley, op. cit., pp. 78–81.

182. *Hansard*, 16 May 1991, col.413.

183. *Independent*, loc. cit.

184. *Health of the Nation*, HMSO, 1991; *Independent*, 5 June 1991.

185. Interview.

186. Interview with Colin Hughes, Education Editor, *Independent*; David Tytler, *Guardian*, 4 February 1992.

187. Baker, *Higher Education: The Next 25 Years*, Address at Lancaster University, 5 January 1989.

188. *Higher Education: A New Framework*, HMSO, 1991.

189. *Hansard*, 20 May 1991, cols.639–41.

190. *Guardian*, 27 November 1993.

191. Department for Education *Departmental Report*, Cmnd 2510, 1994, p. 39; Robbins Report, Cmnd 2514, 1963, p. 67.

192. *Higher Education: Meeting the Challenge*, Cmnd 114, 1987.

193. *Ibid*.

194. Peter Scott, in *The Thatcher Effect*, p. 210.

195. *Guardian*, 17 August 1994.

196. *Independent*, 5 March 1992.

197. Department for Education, *Departmental Report* 1994.

198. *Daily Telegraph*, 7 April 1993.

199. *Independent*, 17 July, 20 August 1993; *Daily Telegraph*, 24 September 1993.

200. *Lords Hansard*, 16 December 1993, cols.790–1.

201. Confederation of British Industry, *Towards a Skills Revolution*, 1989.

202. *Independent*, 9 December 1993.

203. The case for transforming further education is well argued in Maclure, *Missing Links*.

204. Seker, *Industrial Training in a Cold Climate*, pp. 152–60; Lisa Wood and John Gapper, 'An Urgent Need to Turn the Tide of History', *Financial Times*, 26 November 1990.

205. Le Grand, *The Strategy of Equality*, p. 151.

206. *Ibid.*, p. 3.

207. See for example Owen O'Donnell and Carol Propper, *Equity and the Distribution of National Health Service Resources*, STICERD Welfare State Programme, LSE, 1989.

208. Titmuss, *Essays on the Welfare State*, pp. 34–55.

209. Field, *Freedom and Wealth in a Socialist Future*, p. 17.

210. This is not an entirely fair attribution. For its origin see David Butler and Gareth Butler, *British Political Facts 1900–1985*, p. 255. In July 1979, the electricians union the EPTU negotiated a pay deal which gave 40,000 of its members private health cover.

211. Robert Harris, *The Making of Neil Kinnock*, Faber, 1984, p. 134.

212. *Independent*, 18 May 1992. Meacher's package consisted of much else. See Meacher, 'The Good Society', in *New Socialist*, June 1985.

213. Quoted in Colin Hughes and Patrick Wintour, *Labour Rebuilt*, Fourth Estate, 1990, p. 43.

214. Craig, op. cit., p. 460.

215. Mary Farmer and Ray Barrell, 'Joint Interest Compounded', *Guardian*, 27 October 1981.

216. Nicholas Barr, *Student Loans: The Next Steps*, Aberdeen University Press, 1989.

217. Patricia Hewitt, 'A Way to Cope with the World As It Is', in *Samizdat* No 6, 1989.

218. Julian Le Grand, in J. Le Grand and S. Estrim, eds., *Market Socialism*, Oxford University Press, 1989, pp. 193–211.

219. Michael Young, 'A Place for Vouchers in the NHS', in *Samizdat* No 6, 1989.

220. Private information.

221. *A Fresh Start for Health*, Labour Party, 1990, and *Your Good Health*, Labour Party, 1992; see coverage in daily papers for 21 February 1992 for varying interpretations of the plans.

222. Interview, 15 July 1993.

223. Interview

224. Private information.

225. Interview.

226. *New Statesman*, 15 May 1992.

227. Alan Travis, *Guardian*, 13 May 1992.

228. *Independent*, 1 May 1992.

229. Press statement by John Smith at launch of *New Paths to Victory*, his leadership address, 30 April 1994; *Independent*, 1 May 1994.

230. John Gray, *The Undoing of Conservatism*, Paper No 21, Social Market Foundation, 1994.

231. *Hansard*, 8 February 1993, col.683.

232. *Ibid.*, cols.684–7.

20 Retreat or renewal?

1. Calculated from *Social Trends No 4* (1973), table 118, p. 156, and *Social Trends No 24* (1994), table 8.3, p. 110; plus figures for 1945–50 from Malpass and Murie, *Housing Policy and Practice*, p. 72.

2. *Social Trends No 5*, HMSO, 1974, table 138.

3. *Social Trends 24*, HMSO, 1994, p. 51.

4. *Social Trends No 5*, HMSO, 1974, table 74; *Department of Social Security Annual Report 1994: Expenditure Plans 1994–95*, HMSO, 1994.

5. Louie Burghes, *One-parent Families; Policy Options for the 1990s*, Joseph Rowntree Foundation, York, 1993.

6. Interview with Sir Donald Acheson, 8 June 1993. Rising death rates in *British Medical Journal*, 1994, vol. 308, pp. 1125–8.

7. Le Grand in Hills, ed., *The State of Welfare*, p. 350.

8. See Hills, op. cit.; and John Hills, *The Future of Welfare*. The following paragraphs are almost entirely indebted to these works.

9. Hills, *The Future of Welfare*, p. 9.

10. *Ibid.*, p. 10.

11. Paul Johnson, *The Pensions Dilemma*, Commission on Social Justice, Institute of Public Policy Research, 1994, p. 5.

12. See Chapter 11.

13. *English House Condition Survey 1991*, HMSO, 1993.

14. *Developing Local Authority Housing Strategies*, Audit Commission, HMSO, 1992.

15. *Independent*, 28 May 1992.

16. Department of Environment, *Annual Report*, HMSO, 1994, p. 99.

17. Quoted in *Today*, 29 June 1991.

18. Department of Health and Social Security, *Departmental Report*, HMSO, 1994, p. 16.

19. *Ibid.*, p. 15.

20. This is a subject fraught with statistical difficulty; the best available are in Laing, *Financing Long-Term Care* and *Laing's Review of Private Health Care*.

21. *Laing's Review*, p. 185.

22. *Independent*, 3 February 1994.

23. *Independent*, 13 and 15 August 1994, 24 and 25 February 1995.

24. Department of Health, 1994, ibid, pp 41–2.

25. *Laing's Review*, pp. 140, 152–3.

26. *Ibid.*, p. 101.

27. William Laing, private communication, and *Laing's Review 1995*, p. A92.

28. Thatcher, *Let Our Children Grow Tall*, p. 12.

29. F. A. Hayek, *The Constitution of Liberty*, Routledge & Kegan Paul, 1960, p. 44.

30. Joseph, *Stranded on the Middle Ground*, p. 61.

31. *Hansard*, 17 May 1988, col.801.

32. *Households Below Average Income*, HMSO, 1988, 1992, 1994. All figures quoted are after housing costs.

33. Speech to the Institute of Health Services Management, June 1992.

34. *Guardian*, 9 December 1993.

35. *Independent*, 25 January 1994.

36. *Independent*, 30 August 1994.

37. *Independent* and *The Times*, 24 August 1994.

38. *Daily Mail*, 30 December 1993.

39. 'Guardian Education', *Guardian*, March 1994.

40. Foreword to *The Growth of Social Security*, Department of Social Security, HMSO, 1994.

41. Lilley, Mais Lecture to City University, 23 June 1993.

42. *Who Benefits? Reinventing Social Security*, No Turning Back Group, Conservative Political Centre, 1993.

43. *Ibid.*; *Guardian*, 3 August 1993; *Independent*, 10 February 1993.

44. Speech, 16 November 1993; Welsh Office press release, 15 November.

45. *Guardian*, 22 May 1993; *The Times*, 14 May, 27 July 1993; *Independent*, 21 May 1993.

46. *Guardian*, 10 June 1993.

47. Interview, *Today* programme, BBC Radio 4, 9 June 1993.

48. *Daily Mail*, 8 November 1993.

49. *The Times*, 2 December 1993.

50. Lilley, Mais Lecture.

51. *Financial Times*, 1 December 1993.

52. Roger Jowell *et al.* ed., *British Social Attitudes, the 11th Report, 1994–95 edition*, Dartmouth Publishing, Aldershot, 1994.

53. Department of Social Security, Departmental Report, Cmnd 2513, HMSO, 1994, p. 4.

54. *Independent*, 25 May 1990.

55. *Independent*, 10 March 1993.

56. Clarke, Mais Lecture, City University, 4 May 1994; *Independent*, 5 May 1994.

57. *British Social Attitudes*, 11th report, op. cit.

58. Clarke, Social Market Foundation lecture, London School of Economics, 12 July 1994.

59. In 1994, 570,000 families, 42 per cent lone parents, were on Family Credit, DSS, *Quarterly Tables*, July 1994.

60. *Guardian*, 23 April 1994.

61. Clarke, Mais Lecture.

62. Clarke, Social Market Foundation Lecture, London School of Economics, 12 July 1994; *Independent*, 5 May 1994.

63. *Strategies for National Renewal; The Report of the Commission on Social Justice*, Vintage, 1994.

64. *The Times*, 8 November 1993.

Select Bibliography

With some exceptions, the bibliography is restricted to the main books, pamphlets and government publications, chiefly Green and White Papers, cited. Articles, Public Record Office papers, Conservative Party archives, interviews, newspaper and Hansard references are detailed in the endnotes.

Abel-Smith, Brian, *The Hospitals 1800–1948: A Study in Social Administration in England and Wales*, Heinemann, 1964

Abel-Smith, Brian, *The National Health Service: The First Thirty Years*, HMSO, 1978

Abel-Smith, Brian, and Titmuss, Richard, *The Cost of the National Health Service in England and Wales*, Cambridge University Press, 1959

Abel-Smith, Brian, and Townsend, Peter, *The Poor and The Poorest*, LSE Occasional Papers on Social Administration, No 17, 1965

Addison, Paul, *Churchill on the Home Front 1900–1955*, Jonathan Cape, 1992

Addison, Paul, *The Road to 1945*, Jonathan Cape, 1975

Addison, Paul, *Now the War Is Over*, Cape/BBC, 1985

Audit Commission, *Making a Reality of Community Care*, HMSO, 1986

Baker, Kenneth, *The Turbulent Years*, Faber & Faber, 1993

Baker, Mike, *Who Rules Our Schools*, Hodder & Stoughton, 1994

Balen, Malcolm, *Kenneth Clarke*, Fourth Estate, 1984

Banting, Keith, *Poverty, Politics and Policy, Britain in the 1960s*, Macmillan, 1979

Barber, Michael, *Education and the Teacher Unions*, Cassell, 1992

Barnard, H. C., *A History of English Education from 1760*, University of London Press, 1947

Barnett, Correlli, *The Audit of War*, Macmillan, 1986

Barnett, Joel, *Inside the Treasury*, André Deutsch, 1982

Benn, Tony, *Against the Tide: Diaries 1973–76*, Arrow Books, 1989

Beveridge, Sir William, *Full Employment in a Free Society*, George Allen & Unwin, 1944

Beveridge, Lord, *Power and Influence*, Hodder & Stoughton, 1968

Black, Sir Douglas, *The Black Report* in *Inequalities in Health*, Penguin, 1992

Blackstone, Tessa, and Plowden, William, *Inside the Think-Tank: Advising the Cabinet 1971–83*, Heinemann, 1988

Blake, Robert, *The Conservative Party from Peel to Thatcher*, Fontana, 1985

Boyd-Carpenter, John, *Way of Life*, Sidgwick Jackson, 1980

British Medical Association, *Health Services Financing*, 1967

British Social Attitudes Surveys, *8th and 11th reports*, Dartmouth Publishing, Aldershot, 1991, 1994

Brown, George, *In My Way*, Penguin, 1971

Bull, David, ed., *Family Poverty*, Duckworth, 1972

Burnett, John, *A Social History of Housing, 1815–1985*, Methuen, 1986

Butler, David, and Butler, Gareth, *British Political Facts, 1900–85*, Macmillan, 1986

Butler, John, *Patients, Policies and Politics*, Open University Press, 1992

Butler, R. A., *The Art of the Possible*, Hamish Hamilton, 1971

Cairncross, Alec, *The British Economy Since 1945*, Blackwell, Oxford, 1992

Calder, Angus, *The People's War*, Jonathan Cape, 1969; Pimlico, 1992

Callaghan, James, *Time and Chance*, Collins, 1987

Campbell, John, *Edward Heath*, Jonathan Cape, 1993

Carswell, John, *Government and the Universities in Britain*, Cambridge University Press, 1985

Castle, Barbara, *The Castle Diaries 1974–76*, Weidenfeld & Nicolson, 1980

Castle, Barbara, *Fighting All the Way*, Macmillan, 1993

Cmnd 555, *Working for Patients*, HMSO, 1989

Cmnd 1051, *Grants to Students*, HMSO, 1960

Cmnd 1604, *A Hospital Plan for England and Wales*, HMSO, 1962

Cmnd 2154, *Higher Education* (The Robbins Report), HMSO, 1963

Cmnd 3703, *Report of the Committee on Personal and Allied Social Services* (The Seebohm Report), HMSO, 1968

Cmnd 5228, *Report of the Committee on the Abuse of Social Security Benefits*, HMSO, 1973

Cmnd 5713, *Better Pensions*, HMSO, 1974

Cmnd 6404, *Social Insurance and Allied Services; Report by Sir Wiliam Beveridge*, HMSO, 1942

Cmnd 6458, *Educational Reconstruction*, HMSO, 1944

Cmnd 6502, *Statement on a National Health Service*, HMSO, 1943

Cmnd 6502, *A National Health Service*, HMSO, 1944

Cmnd 6527, *Employment Policy*, HMSO, 1944

Cmnd 6609, Ministry of Reconstruction, *Housing*, HMSO, 1945

Cmnd 6869, *Education in Schools: A Consultative Document*, HMSO, 1977

Cmnd 7615, *Royal Commission on the National Health Service*, HMSO, 1979

Cmnd 7746, *The Government's Expenditure Plans 1980–81*, HMSO, 1979

Cmnd 8427, *Brixton Disturbances Enquiry* (Scarman Report), HMSO, 1981

Cmnd 9469, *Better Schools*, HMSO, 1985

Cmnd 9517, *Reform of Social Security*, HMSO, 1985

Cmnd 9663, *Report of the Committee of Enquiry into the National Health Service*, HMSO, 1956

Cmnd 9771, *Primary Health Care: An Agenda for Discussion*, HMSO, 1986

Cmnd 9524, *The Development of Higher Education into the 1990s*, HMSO, 1985

Cmnd –, *Community Care: Agenda for Action*, HMSO, 1988

Commission on Social Justice, *Strategies for National Renewal*, Vintage, 1994

Conservative Political Centre, *The Future of the Welfare State*, 1958

Conservative Political Centre, *One Nation*, 1950

Conservative Political Centre, *The Responsible Society*, 1959

Conservative Political Centre, *The Right Road for Britain*, 1949

Conservative Political Centre, *Social Services: Needs and Means*, 1952

Cootes, R. J., *The Making of the Welfare State*, Longman, 1984

Cox, Brian, *The Great Betrayal*, Chapman, 1992

Cox, C.B. (Brian), and Dyson, A. E., *The Black Papers on Education*, Davis-Poynter, 1971

Craig, F. W. S., *British General Election Manifestos 1959–87*, Dartmouth Publishing, Aldershot, 1990

Crosland, Anthony, *The Future of Socialism*, Cape, 1956

Crosland, Anthony, *Socialism Now*, Cape, 1974

Crosland, Susan, *Tony Crosland*, Jonathan Cape, 1982

Crossman, Richard, *The Backbench Diaries of Richard Crossman*, Hamish Hamilton, 1981

Crossman, Richard, *Diaries of a Cabinet Minister*, Hamish Hamilton/Jonathan Cape, 1975

Crossman, Richard, *Paying for the Social Services*, Fabian Tract 399, 1969

Crossman, Richard, *A Politician's View of Health Service Planning*, University of Glasgow, 1972

Dalyell, Tam, *Dick Crossman, A Portrait*, Weidenfeld & Nicolson, 1982

Deacon, Alan, and Bradshaw, Jonathan, *Reserved for the Poor: The Means Test in British Social Policy*, Basil Blackwell/Martin Robertson, 1983

Deakin, Nicholas, *The Politics of Welfare*, Methuen, 1987

Deakin, Nicholas, *The Politics of Welfare: Continuities and Change*, Harvester Wheatsheaf, 1994

Donnison, David, *The Government of Housing*, Penguin, 1967

Donnison, David, *Housing Policy Since the War*, Codicote Press, 1960

Donnison, David, *The Politics of Poverty*, Martin Robertson, 1982

Donnison, David, and Ungerson, Clare, *Housing Policy*, Penguin, 1982

Donoughue, Bernard, *Prime Minister: The Conduct of Policy Under Harold Wilson and James Callaghan*, Jonathan Cape, 1987

Donoughue, Bernard, and Jones, G. W., *Herbert Morrison, Portrait of a Politician*, Weidenfeld & Nicolson, 1973

Eckstein, Harry, *The English Health Service*, Harvard University Press, Cambridge, Mass, 1958

Eckstein, Harry, *Pressure Group Politics*, George Allen & Unwin, 1960

Edwards, Brian, *The National Health Service: A Manager's Tale: 1946–92*, Nuffield Provincial Hospitals Trust, 1993

Ellis, Brian, *Pensions in Britain 1955–75*, HMSO, 1989

Ellis, Terry, *et al.*, *William Tyndale, The Teacher's Story*, 1976

Enthoven, Alain, *Reflections on the Management of the National Health Service*, Nuffield Provinical Hospitals Trust, Occasional Paper 5, 1985

Field, Frank, *Freedom and Wealth in a Socialist Future*, Constable, 1987

Field, Frank, *Poverty and Politics*, Heinemann, 1982

Field, Frank, Molly Meacher and Chris Pond, *To Him who Hath: A Study of Poverty and Taxation*, Penguin, 1977

Fisher, Nigel, *Iain Macleod*, André Deutsch, 1973

Foot, Michael, *Aneurin Bevan. A Biography. Vol. One: 1879–1945, Vol. Two 1945–60*, Four Square, 1966, 1973

Fowler, Norman, *Ministers Decide*, Chapman, 1991

Fraser, Derek, *The Evolution of the British Welfare State*, Macmillan, 1973

Friedman, Milton, *Capitalism and Freedom*, Chicago University Press, 1962

Gardiner, George, *Margaret Thatcher: From Childhood to Leadership*, Kimber, 1975

Glendinning, Miles, and Muthesius, Stefan, *Tower Block: Modern Public Housing in England, Scotland, Wales and Northern Ireland*, Yale University Press, 1994

Goodman, Arnold, *Tell Them I'm On My Way*, Chapman, 1993,

Gordon, Peter, Richard Aldrich and Dennis Dean, *Education and Policy in England in the Twentieth Century*, Woburn Press, 1991

Graham, Duncan, with David Tytler, *A Lesson for Us All: The Making of the National Curriculum*, Routledge, 1992

Graves, Robert, *Goodbye to All That*, Penguin, 1960

Gregg, Pauline, *The Welfare State*, Harrap, 1967

Grey-Turner, Elston, and Sutherland, F. M., *History of the British Medical Association 1932–1981*, BMA, 1982

Griffiths, James, *Pages from Memory*, Dent, 1969

Griffiths, Sir Roy, *NHS Management Inquiry* (The Griffiths Report), DHSS, 1983

Hackney, Rod, *The Good, the Bad and the Ugly; Cities in Crisis*, Muller, 1990

Hailsham, Lord, *The Door Wherein I Went*, Collins, 1975

Hailsham, Lord, *A Sparrow's Flight*, Collins, 1990

Haines, Joe, *The Politics of Power*, Coronet, 1977

Halcrow, Morrison, *Keith Joseph: A Single Mind*, Macmillan, 1989

Harris, José, *William Beveridge, A Biography*, OUP, 1977

Harris, Ralph, and Seldon, Arthur, *Over-ruled on Welfare*, Institute of Economic Affairs, 1979

Haviland, Julian, *Take Care Mr Baker!*, Routledge, 1988

Hayek, Friedrich von, *The Road to Serfdom*, Routledge, 1945

Hayek, Friedrich von, *The Constitution of Liberty*, Routledge and Kegan Paul, 1960

Healey, Denis, *The Time of My Life*, Michael Joseph, 1989

Hennessy, Peter, *Never Again, Britain 1945–51*, Jonathan Cape, 1992

Hennessy, Peter, *Whitehall*, Fontana, 1989

Hills, John, *The Future of Welfare: A Guide to the Debate*, Joseph Rowntree Foundation, York, 1994

Hills, John, ed., *The State of Welfare*, Clarendon Paperbacks, Oxford, 1991

Honigsbaum, Frank, *Health, Happiness and Security. The Creation of the National Health Service*, Routledge, 1989

Horne, Alistair, *Macmillan, The Official Biography, Volume One*, Macmillan, 1988

Houghton, Douglas, *Paying for Social Services*, Occasional Paper 16, Institute of Economic Affairs, 1967

Howard, Anthony, *Crossman: The Pursuit of Power*, Pimlico, 1990

Howard, Anthony, *RAB: The Life of R. A. Butler*, Jonathan Cape, 1987

Howe, Geoffrey, *Conflict of Loyalty*, Macmillan, 1994

Howe, Geoffrey, *Reform of the Social Services*, in *Principles in Practice*, Conservative Political Centre, 1961

James, Robert Rhodes, *Anthony Eden*, Weidenfeld & Nicolson, 1986

Jay, Douglas, *Change Fortune*, Hutchinson, 1980

Jenkins, Alan, *The Forties*, Heinemann, 1977

Jones, Kathleen, *Asylums and After*, Athlone, 1993

Joseph, Keith, *Reversing The Trend: A Critical Re-Appraisal of Conservative Economic and Social Policies*, Barry Rose, 1975

Joseph, Keith, *Stranded on the Middle Ground: Reflections on Circumstances and Policies*, Centre for Policy Studies, 1976

Joseph, Keith and Sumption, Jonathan, *Equality*, John Murray, 1979

Joseph Rowntree Foundation, *Income and Wealth*, York, 1995

Judge, Harry, *A Generation of Schooling*, Oxford, 1984

Judge, Harry, 'R. J. Morant' in Paul Barker ed., *Founders of the Welfare State*, Methuen, 1968

Kavanagh, Denis and Seldon, Anthony, eds, *The Thatcher Effect*, OUP, 1989

Kellner, Peter, *Thorns and Roses: Neil Kinnock's Speeches 1981–91*, Hutchinson, 1992

Kember, Tony, and Macpherson, Gordon, *The NHS – A Kaleidoscope of Care – Conflicts of Service and Business Values*, Nuffield Provincial Hospitals Trust, 1994

Klein, Rudolf, *The Politics of the NHS*, Longman, 1989

Knight, Christopher, *The Making of Tory Education Policy in Post-War Britain, 1950–1986*, Falmer Press, 1990

Kogan, Maurice, *The Attack on Higher Education*, Kogan Page, 1983

Kogan, Maurice, *The Politics of Education*, Penguin, 1971

Kogan, Maurice, *The Politics of Educational Change*, Fontana, 1978

Laing, William, *Financing Long-Term Care*, Age Concern, 1994

Laing, William, *Laing's Review of Private Health Care, 1994*, Laing and Buisson

Lapping, Brian, *The Labour Government 1964–70*, Penguin, 1970

Lawson, Nigel, *The View From Number Eleven*, Bantam, 1992

Leathard, Audrey, *The Fight for Family Planning: The Development of Family Planning Services in Britain 1921–1974*, Macmillan, 1980

Le Grand, Julian, *The Strategy of Equality: Redistribution and the Social Services*, George Allen & Unwin, 1982

Lowe, Rodney, *The Welfare State in Britain since 1945*, Macmillan, 1993

Lowe, Roy, *Education in the Post-War Years; A Social History*, Routledge, 1988

Lynes, Tony, *Maintaining the Value of Benefits; Studies of the Social Security System No 9*, Policy Studies Institute, 1985

Lynes, Tony, *Social Security and Poverty in the United Kingdom: A Background Paper*, Policy Studies Institute, 1981

Maclure, J. Stuart, *Educational Documents, England and Wales 1816–1968*, Methuen, 4th edn, 1979

Maclure, Stuart, *Educational Developments and School Building: Aspects of Public Policy, 1945–73*, Longman, 1984

Maclure, Stuart, *Education Re-formed*, Hodder & Stoughton, 1989

Maclure, Stuart, *Missing Links*, Policy Studies Institute, 1991

Macmillan, Harold, *Tides of Fortune*, Macmillan, 1969

Malpass, Pete, and Murie, Alan, *Housing Policy and Practice*, Macmillan, 1987

Marwick, Arthur, *British Society since 1945*, Penguin, 1982

Morgan, Kenneth O., *Labour in Power, 1945–51*, OUP, 1984

Morgan, Kenneth O., *Labour People – Hardie to Kinnock*, Oxford Paperbacks, Oxford University Press, 1992

Morgan, Kenneth O., *The People's Peace, British History 1945–90*, OUP, 1990

Morris, Max, and Griggs, Clive, *Thirteen Wasted Years*, Falmer Press, 1988

Morrison of Lambeth, Lord, *Herbert Morrison: An Autobiography*, Odhams, 1960

Murphy, Elaine, *After the Asylums*, Faber, 1991

Nuttgens, Patrick, *The Home Front*, BBC Books, 1989

Orwell, George, *The Road to Wigan Pier*, Penguin, new edn, 1989

Owen, David, *In Sickness and In Health; The Politics of Medicine*, Quartet Books, 1976,

Owen, David, *Time to Declare*, Michael Joseph, 1991

Pater, John, *The Making of the National Health Service*, King Edward's Hospital Fund for London, 1981

Pedley, Robin, *The Comprehensive School*, Pelican, 1963

Pimlott, Ben, *Harold Wilson*, HarperCollins, 1993

Powell, J. Enoch, *Medicine and Politics: 1975 and After*, Pitman Medical, 1976

Priestley, J. B., *English Journey*, Penguin, 1977

Prior, Jim, *A Balance of Power*, Hamish Hamilton, 1986

Raison, Timothy, *Tories and the Welfare State*, Macmillan, 1990

Ranelagh, John, *Thatcher's People*, HarperCollins, 1991

Rhodes, H. V., *Setting up a New Government Department*, British Institute of Management, 1949

Ridley, Nicholas, *The Local Right*, Centre for Policy Studies, 1988

Ridley, Nicholas, *My Style of Government*, Hutchinson, 1991

Rivett, Geoffrey, *Development of the London Hospital System 1823–1982*, King Edward's Hospital Fund for London, 1986

Roth, Andrew, *Enoch Powell: Tory Tribune*, Macdonald, 1970

Royal Commission on the National Health Service, HMSO, 1979

Seldon, Arthur, *Riddle of the Education Voucher*, Hobart Paperback 21, Institute of Economic Affairs, 1986

Senker, Peter J., *Industrial Training in a Cold Climate*, Avebury, Aldershot, 1992

Shepherd, Robert, *Iain Macleod: A Biography*, Hutchinson, 1994

Simon, Brian, *Education and the Social Order*, Lawrence & Wishart, 1991

Skidelsky, Robert, ed., *Thatcherism*, Chatto & Windus, 1988.

St John-Stevas, Norman, *The Two Cities*, Faber & Faber, 1984

Tebbit, Norman, *Upwardly Mobile*, Futura, 1989

Thatcher, Margaret, *The Downing Street Years*, HarperCollins, 1993

Thatcher, Margaret, *Let Our Children Grow Tall: Selected Speeches, 1975–77*, Centre for Policy Studies, 1972

Thompson, E. P., *The Poverty of Theory*, Merlin, 1978

Titmuss, Richard, *Commitment to Welfare*, Allen & Unwin, 1968

Titmuss, Richard, *Essays on the Welfare State*, Allen & Unwin, 1958

Titmuss, Richard, *Problems of Social Policy*, HMSO, 1950

Townsend, Peter, and Bosanquet, Nicholas, ed., *Labour and Equality, A Fabian Study of Labour in Power 1974–79*, Heinemann, 1980

Tudor Hart, Julian, *A New Kind of Doctor*, Merlin Press, 1988

Vaizey, John, *The Costs of Education*, Allen & Unwin, 1958

Vernon, Betty D., *Ellen Wilkinson*, Croom Helm, 1982

Walker, Peter, *The Ascent of Britain*, Sidgwick & Jackson, 1977

Walker, Peter, *Staying Power*, Bloomsbury, 1991

Wapshott, Nicholas, and Brock, George, *Thatcher*, London, 1979

Watkin, Brian, *Documents on Health and Social Services: 1834 to the Present Day*, Methuen, 1975

Webster, Charles, *Aneurin Bevan on the National Health Service*, Wellcome Unit for the History of Medicine, Oxford, 1991

Webster, Charles, 'Conservatives and Consensus: The Politics of the National Health Service 1951–64' in A. Oakley and A. Williams, ed., *The Politics of Welfare*, UCL Press, 1994

Webster, Charles, *The Health Services Since the War, Volume 1: Problems of Health Care. The National Health Service Before 1957*, HMSO, 1988

West, R. G., *Education and the State*, Institute of Economic Affairs, 1965

Whitehead, Margaret, *National Health Success*, Association of Community Health Councils, 1988

Wicks, Ben, *No Time to Wave Goodbye*, Bloomsbury, 1988

Wicks, Malcolm, *A Future for All*, Pelican, 1987

Willetts, David, *Modern Conservatism*, Penguin, 1992

Wilson, Des, *I Know It Was the Place's Fault*, Oliphant, 1970

Wilson, Harold, *Final Term: The Labour Government 1974–76*, Weidenfeld & Nicolson/Michael Joseph, 1979

Wilson, Harold, *The Labour Government 1964–70*, Pelican, 1971

Wilson, Harold, *Memoirs: The Making of a Prime Minister 1916–64*, Weidenfeld & Nicolson/Michael Joseph, 1986

Young, Hugo, *One of Us*, Macmillan/Pan, 1990

Young, Hugo, and Sloman, Anne, *The Thatcher Phenomenon*, BBC, 1986

Young, Lord, *The Enterprise Years*, Headline, 1990

Zeigler, Philip, *Wilson – The Authorised Life*, Weidenfeld & Nicolson, 1993

Index

family
Joseph and 289–90, 358; Thatcher on 359
family allowance 40
and Beveridge Report 20, 21, 24, 39, 45, 55;
Child Poverty Action Group and 257;
clawed back 264, 266, 269, 282–3; Howe
on 253; introduced 133–4, 137–8; Joseph
and 282; and means-test 263; middle
class and 163; raising of 263–4; replaced
by child benefit 345; Thorneycroft's
proposed cuts 178; universalism of 253
Family Allowances Act (1945) 49, 133, 161
Family Budget Survey 52
Family Credit 401, 516
Moore and 448, 449
Family Fund 286
Family Income Supplement
based on 'Mr Abbot's Alternative' 263, 283;
introduced by Joseph 263, 282–5;
opposition to 284–5, 516; replaced by
Family Credit 401; take-up figures
283–4
family planning 7, 267, 293, 411
Festival of Britain 172
Fidler, Sheppard
on high-rise housing 185
Field, Frank
on 'better-off on benefit' problem 367;
coins phrase 'poverty trap' 284; director
of CPAG 257, 277–8; on five welfare
states 487–8; Freedom and Wealth in a
Socialist Future 487–8; leak of Cabinet
papers 346, 347; on tax threshold 282;
transfer of council houses proposal 366
The Fight for Education (Black Paper) 271–4
First World War 14, 25–6, 31
Fisher, Dr Geoffrey
and public schools 85, 86
Fisher, H.A.L. 72, 91
Fisher committee on benefit fraud 287
Fleming, Lord
public school inquiry 85, 86, 95–6
food
effects of war 34; subsidies 6, 7, 317;
welfare 7
Food, Ministry of Food
Beveridge in 14; and war-time black market
34
Foot, Michael
on Bevan 113, 114, 115, 122, 142; on
Dalton 134; on housing shortage 140; as
Labour leader 393

Forster, W.E.
and Elementary Education Act 68, 69
Fowler, Norman
and adult disabled scheme 286; community
care review 417; at DHSS 386, 389–91,
417; on 'golden handcuffs' 396; Green
Paper on primary care 415; and Griffiths
report 409; housing benefit review
397–8, 449; and Lawsom 396; and
limited list 412–14; on never saying
never 390; and NHS abolition proposal
393; and NHS funding 454, 459; and
NHS internal market 459; and NHS
manpower cuts 407; and NHS numbers
game 407; and NHS pay dispute 391; on
NHS privatisation 390–1; as One Nation
Tory 390; on pay bed row 340; and
personal pensions 397; and SERPS
349–50, 373, 402–3; on social security
18; on social security as Leviathan 395;
social security review 227, 396–405, 434,
488; as social services spokesman 340;
and supplementary benefit 398, 399; on
Thatcher as 'Beveridge woman' 373; as
Transport Minister 364, 389; on wading
through treacle 400
Fraser, Sir Bruce 207–8, 210
Fraser, Derek
on education 68; on unemployment benefit
28–9
Fraser, Michael (Lord Fraser of Kilmorack)
170
on welfare state consensus 171
Freeman, John 158
Friedman, Milton
and education vouchers 251; and
monetarism 357; and inequality 508
Friendly Societies
and social insurance 20, 45
full employment
abandonment of 357, 389; and Beveridge
Report 16, 20, 24, 39; Beveridge's
follow-up report on 49–50; Callaghan's
break with 269; consensus on 169; effect
on education 200; erosion of 177, 308;
Full Employment in a Free Society 23,
50, 132; Gaitskell's definition of 133;
Keynes on 133; Labour and 315, 515–16;
post-war 53, 133, 280, 358; and
redistribution 249; return to agenda
515–16
further education

The English
A Social History 1066–1945

Christopher Hibbert

'Christopher Hibbert writes so well, and presents a huge amount of material with such skill, that this 900 page volume can be read more quickly and enjoyably than many novels . . . an admirable evocation of the past and a lasting analysis of the English character'

JOHN MORTIMER *Sunday Times*

'From tournaments, pilgrims and kings through to bus conductors and summer holidays, he isolates the changing habits of successive generations. His greatest – and extraordinary – success is to have extracted from this mass of material the exact character of each century he touches'   *The Independent*

'Enthralling . . . Barons and peasants, contemporaries of Pepys and Boswell, a people revolutionised by technology – all leap from his pages like figures on a canvas by Lowry . . . How anyone can write as much and as well as Hibbert is a mystery. His big, rich book deserves a place on the shelves of anyone remotely interested in our history'

Mail on Sunday

'A glorious cavalcade of 900 years of life and death, work and play, sex and sensibility amongst the English . . . Christopher Hibbert blends erudition, energy and elegance to perfection . . . Get beyond the myths of history; treat yourself to this feast of a book'

ROY PORTER *The Standard*

'Compiled with flair and skill and with that flair for particularity and even oddity which no historian, "popular" or otherwise, can afford to dispense with'   *Times Literary Supplement*

0 586 08471 1

FontanaPress
An Imprint of HarperCollins*Publishers*

Demanding the Impossible

A History of Anarchism

Peter Marshall

'To be governed means that at every move, operation or transaction one is noted, registered, entered in a census, taxed, stamped, priced, assessed, patented, licensed, authorized, recommended, admonished, reformed . . . exploited, monopolized, extorted, pressured, mystified, robbed; all in the name of public utility and the general good.'

So said Proudhon in 1851, and from the Ancient Chinese to today's rebel youth many have agreed – among their number Godwin and Kropotkin, Bakunin and Malatesta, Tolstoy and Gandhi, the Ranters and the Situationists, de Sade and Thoreau, Wilde and Chomsky, anarcho-syndicalists and anarcha-feminists. Peter Marshall, in his inclusive, inspirational survey, gives back to the anarchistic, undiluted and undistorted, their secret history.

'Reading about anarchism is stimulating and funny and sad. What more can you ask of a book?'   Isabel Colegate, *The Times*

'Massive, scholarly, genuinely internationalist and highly enjoyable . . . this is the book Johnny Rotten ought to have read.'
David Widgery, *Observer*

'Large, labyrinthine, tentative: for me these are all adjectives of praise when applied to works of history, and *Demanding the Impossible* meets all of them. I now have a book – Marshall's solid 700 pages and more – to which I can direct readers when they ask me how soon I intend to bring my *Anarchism* up to date.'   George Woodcock, *Independent*

'This is the most comprehensive account of anarchist thought ever written. Marshall's knowledge is formidable and his enthusiasm engaging . . . he organizes a mass of diverse material with great subtlety and skill, presenting a good-tempered critique of each position with straightforward lucidity.'   J. B. Pick, *Scotsman*

ISBN 0 00 686245 4

Fontana Press